THE LEGACY OF HOMER

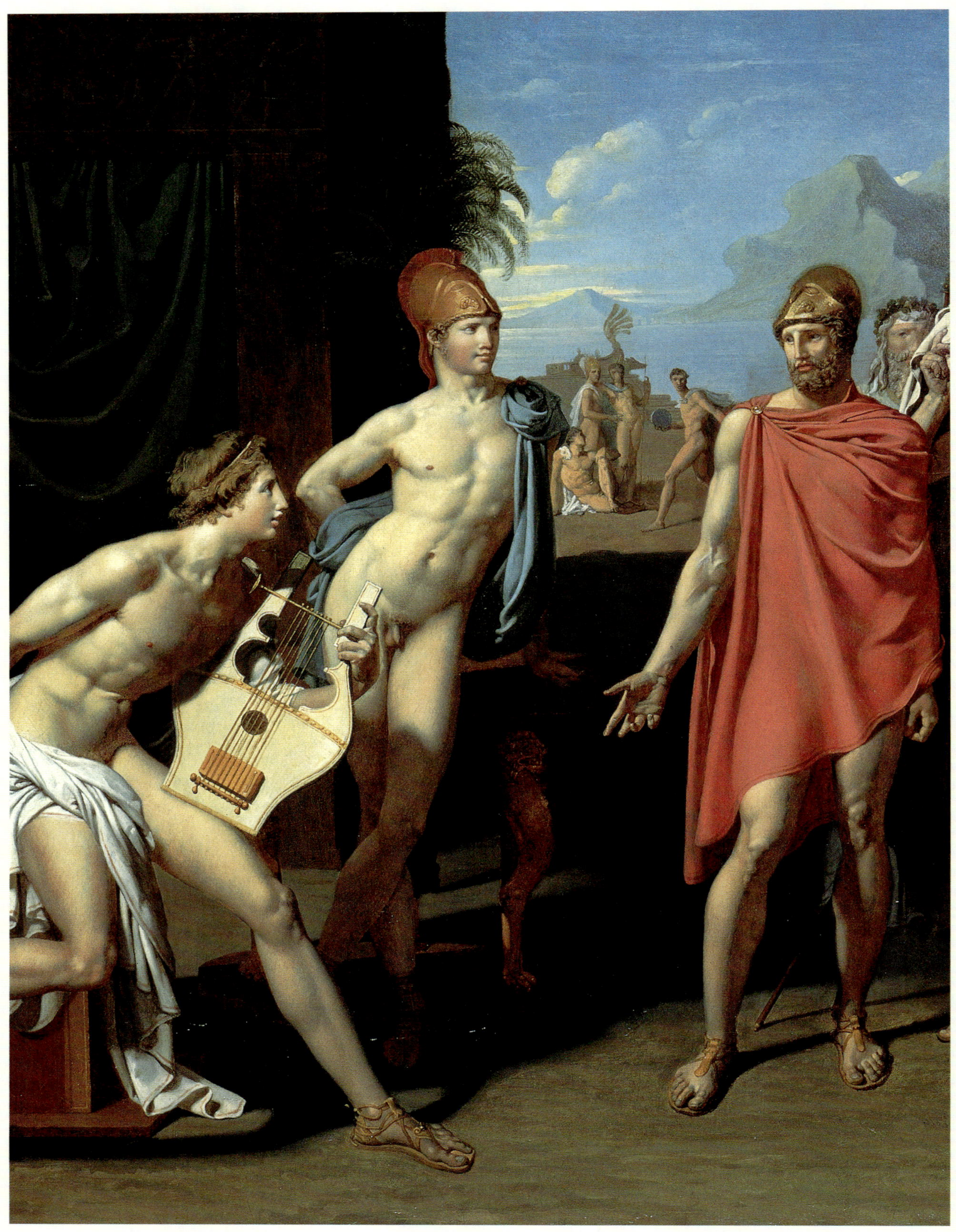

THE LEGACY OF HOMER

Four Centuries of Art from the École Nationale Supérieure des Beaux-Arts, Paris

Emmanuel Schwartz

WITH CONTRIBUTIONS BY

George Steiner and Philippe Sénéchal

DAHESH MUSEUM OF ART | *New York*

PRINCETON UNIVERSITY ART MUSEUM | *Princeton*

YALE UNIVERSITY PRESS | *New Haven and London*

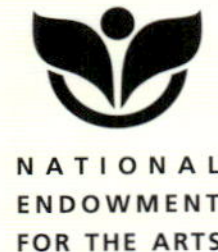

NATIONAL ENDOWMENT FOR THE ARTS

This project is supported in part by an award from the National Endowment for the Arts.

The presentation at the Dahesh Museum of Art is supported also by the Grand Marnier Foundation and the Stavros S. Niarchos Foundation.

Published in conjunction with the exhibition *The Legacy of Homer: Four Centuries of Art from the École Nationale Supérieure des Beaux-Arts, Paris*

ÉCOLE NATIONALE SUPÉRIEURE DES BEAUX-ARTS, PARIS
September 21–November 28, 2004

PRINCETON UNIVERSITY ART MUSEUM
October 8, 2005–January 15, 2006

DAHESH MUSEUM OF ART, NEW YORK
October 11, 2005–January 22, 2006

Originally published as *Dieux et Mortels: Les thèmes homériques dans les collections de l'École nationale supérieure des beaux-arts de Paris*

MANAGING EDITOR: Jill Guthrie, Princeton University Art Museum
EDITORS: Betsy Rosasco, Princeton University Art Museum, and Roger Diederen, Dahesh Museum of Art
COPYEDITOR: Henry Krawitz
PROOFREADER: June Cuffner
INDEXER: Kathleen Friello

Yale University Press
PUBLISHER, ART & ARCHITECTURE: Patricia Fidler
ASSISTANT EDITOR, ART & ARCHITECTURE: Michelle Komie
SENIOR PRODUCTION EDITOR: Kate Zanzucchi
PRODUCTION MANAGER: Mary Mayer
PHOTO EDITOR & ASSISTANT PRODUCTION COORDINATOR: John Long

Designed by Leslie Fitch
Set in Adobe Minion and FF Meta type by Leslie Fitch
Printed in Singapore by CS Graphics

LIBRARY OF CONGRESS CATALOGING-IN-PUBLICATION DATA
Schwartz, Emmanuel.
[Dieux et Mortels. English]
The legacy of Homer: four centuries of art from the École Nationale Supérieure des Beaux-Arts, Paris / Emmanuel Schwartz; with contributions by George Steiner and Philippe Sénéchal; [translation from the French by Christopher Miller].
p. cm.
Translation of: Dieux et Mortels: les thèmes homériques dans les collections de l'École nationale supérieure des beaux-arts de Paris.
Catalog of an exhibition that appeared at the École in Paris in fall 2004, and will be on view simultaneously at the Dahesh Museum of Art, New York, and the Princeton University Art Museum in fall 2005.
Includes bibliographical references and index.
ISBN 0-300-10918-0
1. Mythology, Greek, in art—Exhibitions. 2. Homer—Illustrations—Exhibitions. 3. Art—France—Paris—Exhibitions. I. Title: Four centuries of art from the École Nationale Supérieure des Beaux-Arts, Paris. II. Schwartz, Emmanuel. III. Steiner, George. IV. Sénéchal, Philippe. V. École nationale supérieure des beaux-arts (France). VI. Dahesh Museum of Art. VII. Princeton University Art Museum. VIII. Title.

N7760.S3515 2005
704.9'47'0744361—dc22 2005042602

The paper in this book meets the guidelines for permanence and durability of the Committee on Production Guidelines for Book Longevity of the Council on Library Resources.
10 9 8 7 6 5 4 3 2 1

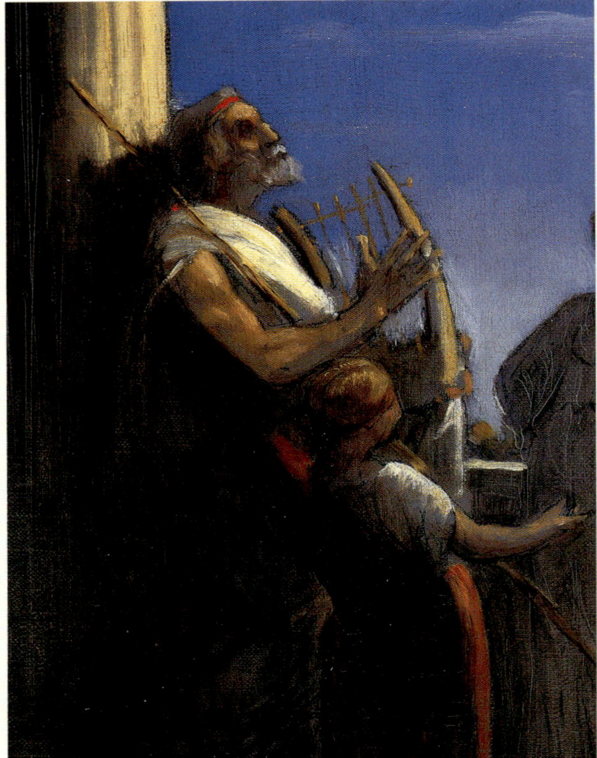

Frontispiece: Jean-Auguste-Dominique Ingres, *Achilles Receives the Ambassadors of Agamemnon* (detail of cat. no. 24)

Page iv: Clément-Amédée Bidot, *Homer Requesting Hospitality* (detail of cat. no. 4)

Page xxii: Jean-Charles Frontier, *Vulcan Enchaining Prometheus* (detail of cat. no. 106)

Page 76: Jacques-Louis David, *Andromache Mourning Hector* (detail of cat. no. 42)

Page 296: Diogène-Ulysse-Napoléon Maillard, *Homer on the Island of Scyros* (detail of cat. no. 2)

Jacket illustrations: (front): Michel-Martin Drölling, *The Wrath of Achilles* (detail of cat. no. 23); (back): Pierre-Amédée Durand, *Ulysses Recognized by His Dog* (cat. no. 79A)

All works illustrated are in the collection of the École nationale supérieure des beaux-arts, Paris, unless noted.

Contents

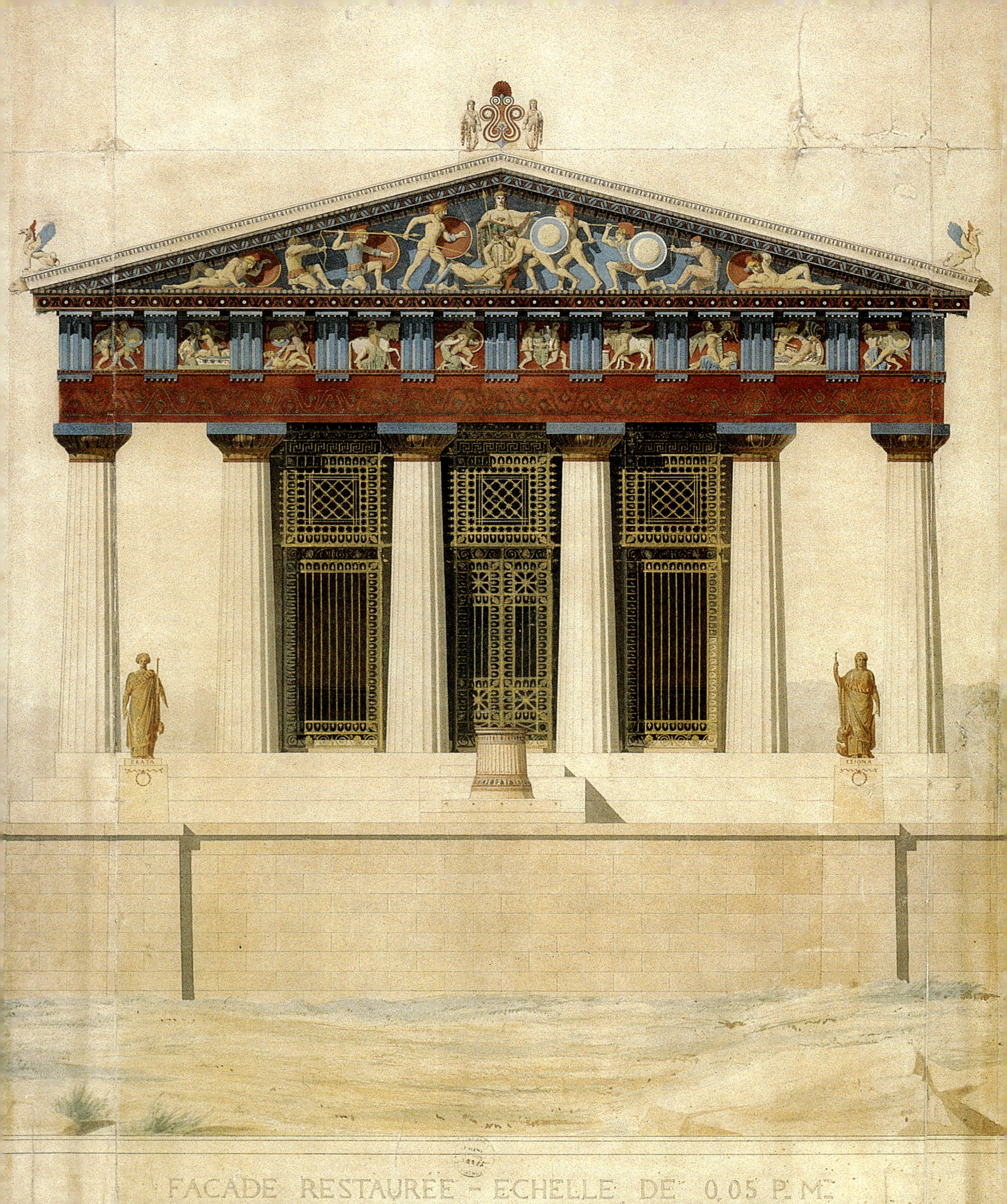
FACADE RESTAURÉE – ECHELLE DE 0,05 P. M.

Foreword

THAT THE TEACHING OF A SCHOOL HISTORICALLY AS FAMOUS AS OURS CONTINUALLY intersected with the fortunes of the most ancient of all poets, and that the models, the works we take as our most venerated examples, were nourished by the poet's fabulous accounts and unforgettable images is, in itself, an astonishing subject of study. But that these models—in a country that George Steiner rightly emphasizes was initially attuned to Virgilian culture before paying tribute to the blind poet, much later than happened elsewhere—were better understood than the official translations, and became Homer's most faithful interpreters, especially in the nineteenth century, through the artists trained under the aesthetic imperatives of the Prix de Rome: this is quite another subject for study!

Upon close inspection, one can note a certain correspondence between the story of the diffusion of Homer's oeuvre in France and that of the history of the institution, founded in 1648 as the Académie royale de peinture et de sculpture, and its successor, the École nationale supérieure des beaux-arts, which still flourishes today. While the sixteenth century was the quintessential epoch of Homer's rediscovery, it was the mid-seventeenth century that finally recognized Homeric subjects as a repertory of references for artists, as much for their Grand Prix works as for their reception pieces for the Royal Academy. From the *Andromache Mourning Hector* (1783) of Jacques-Louis David (who would later find the means to brutally suppress the Academy in 1793, only to see it reborn four years later as an École) to the last pompous and emphatic dramaturgies of later Prix de Rome works, the inspiration of Homer can be followed throughout the nineteenth century. It forms an avenue that leads to what today can only be considered a surprising renewal, particularly in the field of the humanities (*les Sciences Humaines*). Did the artists long ago prepare the conditions for this new recognition of the first poet, and, despite themselves, spin the thread that would allow for continuity, a thread

DETAIL OF CATALOGUE NO. 8

though now broken that has been passed to other disciplines?

This inspiration accounts for a large part of the École's holdings, including paintings, sculptures, and prints, many of which are published here, delivering to the public record this portion of its neglected, not to say unknown, collections. These works, once considered of modest interest as documents of study and pedagogy, may well upset many preconceived notions about the nature of "academicism"—and one would like to add and its "phantasm," to quote Michel Thévoz, who was among the first to question this concept. Should we, then, seek to chart the history of a time long past, even if there is still so much to be learned? Or should we study how our own period interacts with this historical era—a new episode in the desperate quest, like that of Ulysses, to fathom the inexhaustible story of the relations between gods and mortals?

I leave to the authors of this catalogue, a tremendous compilation, the task of defining the contours of the inviolate yet meticulously surveyed continent of these two tales—the *Iliad* and the *Odyssey*—where myth is inextricably linked to poetry. Myth and creation have always been complementary; and poetry, from its legendary beginnings to its present forms, is certainly relevant to modern artistic creation.

With his customary verve, Emmanuel Schwartz brilliantly and wittily surveys the complex Homeric world, like a latter-day Ulysses. I wish to acknowledge the architect of this ambitious project, and express my gratitude for the explorations he directs, conscientiously and with minute attention. The director of the École and all those for whom this world still has meaning—and there are many—have watched this project attentively and welcomed it with high expectations.

My thanks also go to my American colleagues at the Princeton University Art Museum and the Dahesh Museum of Art, who have carried this inquiry beyond the Atlantic by showing in the United States the greater part of the exhibition, which was originally shown in Paris. Finally, I want to thank George Steiner, one of the great figures in the Homeric revival in our time, who gives the ancient poet and his world a voice that reanimates them, and shows they are still essential. He honors us, in the preface of this catalogue, with a dazzling survey recalling and illuminating that which, since the Renaissance, has united Homer and French culture.

Henry-Claude Cousseau
Director of the École nationale supérieure des beaux-arts, Paris

Author's Acknowledgments

I would like to acknowledge Madame Jacqueline de Romilly of the Académie française and all those people—professors, artists, authors—who have dedicated their lives to the transmission of their faith in ancient Greece. This publication has particularly benefited from the teaching and writings of Noémi Hepp, professor emerita at the University Marc-Bloch in Strasbourg. Thanks are due also to Philippe Sénéchal for having given a rigorous art historical point of view on a subject that has more often led to literary considerations than to indispensable artistic analysis. The organization of this exhibition was facilitated by the support of the Direction of the Musées de France, particularly for the restoration of the sculptures from the École des beaux-arts. The Musée du Louvre generously authorized the presentation of its works on deposit at the École and financed their restoration.
I thank all those who worked to translate into English the remarks written in a Franco-centric perspective: Roger Diederen, Jill Guthrie, Henry Kravitz, Chris Miller, and Betsy Rosasco.

Emmanuel Schwartz

Foreword

THE LEGACY OF HOMER: FOUR CENTURIES OF ART FROM THE ÉCOLE NATIONALE Supérieure des Beaux-Arts, Paris addresses issues central to the interests of the Dahesh Museum of Art and the Princeton University Art Museum. The exhibition considers how the visual arts have transmitted, preserved, and renewed the vision of Greek antiquity, and examines how young artists, studying the art of the ancient world and reading ancient texts, imagined the world of Homer. The exhibition also demonstrates how the reading of Homer's texts, the foundation of Western literature, affected the art of the four centuries that preceded our own and witnessed the birth of the modern age. We are privileged to offer to our American audiences an exhibition and book that examine these issues in French art of the seventeenth to early twentieth centuries through the presentation of selected works from the rich collections of the prestigious École nationale supérieure des beaux-arts in Paris.

We thank Henry-Claude Cousseau, director of the École, for proposing the exhibition and, having ascertained the strong interest of both institutions, for allowing us to divide the exhibition between Princeton and New York in order to show the two parts simultaneously. All aspects of the project have been an exemplar of collaboration.

The Dahesh Museum of Art, founded to encourage the study of nineteenth-century academic art, has often collaborated on exhibitions with the École, the heir of the ancien régime's Académie royale de peinture et de sculpture, and the leading center of the academic teaching of art. Attended in the nineteenth century—as it still is now—by students from France and also from other nations who wish to pursue the study of art, the École lent its name to the term "Beaux-Arts style." Princeton University's School of Architecture is a descendant of the nineteenth-century École des beaux-arts, since it was closely allied with the École's traditions and methods through the teaching of Professor Jean Labatut, among others. Donald Drew Egbert, architectural historian in Princeton's Department of Art and Archaeology, studied the architectural tradition of the École and the influence of the Beaux-Arts style in the United States. In presenting *The Legacy of Homer*, therefore, both museums celebrate ties to the École, and to the traditions that have informed our respective institutions.

The subject of this exhibition was the inspired idea of Emmanuel Schwartz, curator in chief of the patrimony at the École. He brings to the project the erudition and sensibility of the classicist he is by formation, and also his intimate familiarity with both the Homeric texts and the artists and traditions of the École. We thank him for the presentation of the works in a way that will serve those viewers and readers interested in the literary themes as much as the artists, both famous and less well-known, represented in the exhibition. His examination of the École's history and pedagogic methods will be of particular interest to all who seek to place these works in the context of the students' lives, the *Gradus ad Parnassum* of their training, and subsequent careers. We are grateful to George Steiner, who contributed a magisterial essay on Homer's critical fortunes in France from the perspective of an intellectual equally versed in French and English literature and able to draw fine distinctions between the two approaches. Finally, we thank Philippe Sénéchal for his illuminating insights into the neglected subject of the theory of drapery, a quintessential classical theme.

We appreciate the contributions of Véronique Rabin Le Gall, director of international affairs for the École, who was responsible for the registrarial details, but also so much more for the organization of the exhibition and preparation of the catalogue. The staff members at the École who made it possible for the project to move forward include exhibition officer Sophie Kaplan and Pascale Le Thorel-Daviot, director of publications, who coordinated the original French-language catalogue from which the English edition has been developed.

The exhibition at the Dahesh Museum of Art was coordinated by Stephen R. Edidin, chief curator; Roger Diederen, curator; and Frank Verpoorten, assistant curator; and at the Princeton University Art Museum by Betsy Rosasco, research curator of Later Western art. Their advocacy for and dedication to this project have indeed made this exhibition and publication possible. The efforts of Alexia Hughes, assistant registrar at Princeton, were indispensable in bringing the works of art from France.

The production of the catalogue was taken on by Yale University Press, and we thank Patricia Fidler, publisher, art and architecture, and Kate Zanzucchi, senior production editor, at Yale, and Jill Guthrie, managing editor at Princeton, for their remarkable efforts in shepherding the book to completion. Christopher Miller, translator, and Henry Krawitz, copyeditor, worked meticulously and under considerable time pressures to produce the manuscript. Design and installation of the exhibition were overseen at the Dahesh by Dan Kershaw and Jeremy Benjamin, and at Princeton by Calvin Brown and Michael Jacobs: we are delighted with their success in maximizing the visual impact of these important works of art.

The project, as envisioned and presented at the École in the fall of 2004, was of such a scope and scale that neither institution could have presented it alone. We are grateful to the National Endowment for the Arts for recognizing the merit of our alliance and enhancing the presentation through an Access to Artistic Excellence grant. We owe particular thanks to Robert Frankel and David Bancroft in the museum program of the NEA for their encouragement. The Dahesh Museum of Art is grateful also for the generous support from the Grand Marnier Foundation and the Stavros S. Niarchos Foundation for the presentation in New York.

Finally, we would like to acknowledge the leadership of both institutions for their support in bringing the exhibition to the United States. At the Dahesh, we thank the members of the Board of Trustees, in particular, Amira Zahid, who visited the École with us during our preliminary conversations. At Princeton, we gratefully acknowledge President Shirley Tilghman and Provost Christopher Eisgruber for their continuing commitment to the museum's programs and exhibitions.

We are delighted to share with our respective audiences this unprecedented exhibition of art inspired by the Homeric ideal from the rich holdings of the École nationale supérieure des beaux-arts.

SUSAN M. TAYLOR
Director, Princeton University Art Museum

PETER TRIPPI
Director, Dahesh Museum of Art

Preface

George Steiner

AN ALMOST METAPHYSICAL BOND WITH THE SEA. ENGLISH TEACHING METHODS: the solidarity of boarding school, regiment, and Oxbridge college. But also the solidarity of sports and politics. Not homosexuality plain and simple (though there's plenty of that) but rather the solidarity of a homoeroticism tinged with nostalgia and uncomfortable around women. Consequently a cult of the male friend, of the warrior, athlete, and explorer. The English self-image, the icons in which the English perceive themselves, as manifested in their literature — all have contributed. The English could hardly do otherwise than identify with the Homeric epic. Only think of their attitude to defeat: the mythology of catastrophes, like Dunkirk, has its own very specific nobility. The fall of Troy and the death of Hector have moved the English since the Middle Ages. The funeral oration for Hector in Shakespeare's *Troilus and Cressida* rivals that of the *Iliad.* How like Patroclus were the young heroes cut down at Gallipoli — so close to the fatal plain of Troy — and how many of them were, like Homer's warriors, lovers, aristocrats, and sportsmen.

Hence the proliferation of English and subsequently American translations, many of them built to last. Hence the multiple variants of the *Iliad* and the *Odyssey,* the echoes, pastiches, and parodies which punctuate English literature, art, and music from Chaucer and Shakespeare to Joyce, Pound, and Walcott; and from the eighteenth-century caricaturists to Turner, Blake, and Caro. Almost every generation has made its own translation or partial translation of the two epics and the "Homeric" hymns. Bibliography is overwhelmed. There are hundreds of versions. You are an Anglican vicar in the late eighteenth/nineteenth century, a schoolmaster, or a prime minister (like Gladstone) in love with the classics: What do you do? You translate Homer. Hence the dissemination of innumerable and often anonymous fragmentary versions of Homer through gazettes, periodicals, scholarly journals, and newspapers. Some are in dialect, some in Gaelic or Scottish, and some in

Latin (a strangely instructive exercise for the unfortunate pupil). "We are all Greeks," announced Shelley, translator of the *Hymns*.[1]

The first book printed in English was a *Recuyell of the Historyes of Troye*, which appeared in Bruges in 1475. The first attempt at translating Homer, made by Arthur Hall, was preceded by Chaucer's peerless *Troilus and Criseyde* (1382–86), which in turn inspired Shakespeare. We do not know whether Shakespeare had even indirect access to Homer. He may have seen the translation made by his contemporary George Chapman. Often approximate in meaning, Chapman's tumultuous version is worthy of the original in its powerful evocation of combat and ocean. How different is Thomas Hobbes's translation! Launched into the resounding silence that greeted his philosophical works, it is unbearably stilted but of the utmost political interest. Next came the fragmentary translations of Dryden and the complete version by Pope (1713–20). Drawing on Houdar de la Motte and Madame Dacier, Pope's *Iliad* and *Odyssey* are—despite their Neoclassical constraints—the most important epics in English after Milton: they placed the Homeric world at the center of English poetry. Pope's "Preface" and "Observations" afford a rare example of the theoretical and critical authority of a very great poet.

The Romantic and Victorian epoch abounded in translations, evocations, and echoes of Homer (Keats, Shelley, Tennyson, Gladstone, and Matthew Arnold). Scholars made interlinear translations for schoolchildren. Imitations of ancient Greek elicited many attempts to domesticate hexameters and syllabic meter. On the threshold of modernism, Samuel Butler argued that the author of the *Odyssey* was a woman (Nausicaa?). Is Lawrence of Arabia replying to this when he prefaces his *Odyssey* with the remark that only one who has fought hand to hand can comprehend and re-create the power of Homer's inspiration? Joyce's *Ulysses* operates a transformation of the Circe episode; it and Pound's *Cantos* make Homer the godfather of twentieth-century Anglo-American poetics and thus of twentieth-century poetics in general.

Translations have poured out of England and America since 1945, many of them complete. No publisher can do without one. We have the scholarly version by Richmond Lattimore, the *Iliad* as Robert Graves's "first novel," the superlatively poetic translations of Robert Fitzgerald, the astounding pastiche-fragments by Christopher Logue, the worldwide success (even on CD) of Robert Fagles's Homer. As the culmination of such efforts, the Nobel Prize was awarded to Derek Walcott for his *Omeros*, which sets the endurance and discoveries of Ulysses in the Caribbean with an "innovative fidelity" bordering on the miraculous. The endlessly renascent elective affinities between Homer and English (now world English) have lasted more than ten centuries.[2]

The French have shown no such affinity. Let me venture a gross simplification: two impulses inherent in French civilization stand between Homer and an analogous cultural predominance. French remains profoundly Latin. Its roots are in Latin. The generative grammar of French is that of Latin. Since the Renaissance, in particular since the domination exercised by French Enlightenment culture over Europe as a whole, this Latin origin and its linguistic embodiment have found expression through Cartesian logic, through the essentially *rhetorical* stamp of French political, religious, and educational discourse. There would have been no Montesquieu, no Bossuet—and no Baudelaire either—were it not for this organic Latinity. Catholic Christianity—Roman Christianity—has molded not merely the history of France but its landscape: its cities in the shadow of its cathedrals, its villages huddled around their bell towers. It is intimately linked to the Latin structuring of France's public and psychic being. The "genius of Christianity" is inseparable from the destiny of Gallicanism: hence De Gaulle's choice of Chateaubriand as the most illustrious French writer.[3] The point of reference for French *civilitas*—for the spirit of its laws, for the ideal of clarity (which has had almost juridical consequences in French philosophical thought), an ideal as powerful in Descartes as it is in

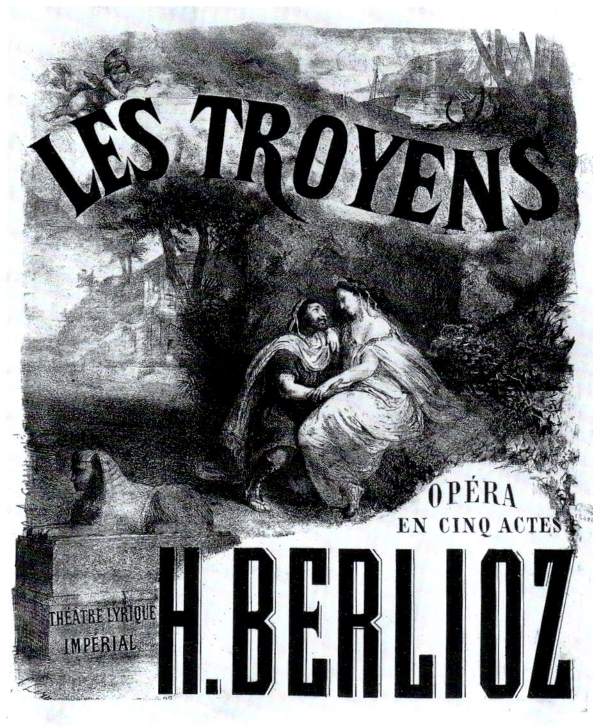

FIGURE 1 | Poster for the world premiere of the second part of *Les Troyens*, by Hector Berlioz (1803–1869), at the Théâtre Lyrique Impérial, 1863. Bibliothèque Nationale de France, Bibliothèque-Musée de l'Opéra.

Auguste Comte—is Rome: the Rome of the tribunes, consuls, and emperors but also that of the poets.

Hence the constant and fertilizing presence of Horace, Catullus, and Ovid in French poetry; that of Cicero at the very center of eloquence but also in informal prose; and that of Seneca at the root of French moralism. The poetics of *litotes* is borrowed from Tacitus. The history of comic theater in France is the imitation of Plautus and Terence. Juvenal underpins Boileau's achievement.

But the principal role in the evolution of French letters has been played by Virgil. Since Ronsard, the dream of a national epic has been founded in overt *imitatio* of the *Aeneid.* The bucolic line in French lyricism is profoundly Virgilian, as is the ideal of a public poetics, celebrating the destiny of the nation and imparting a civic moral. This Virgilian melancholy inspires the Pléiade, Chénier, Lamartine, and Bonnefoy. In Proust, Charlus seeks "a shepherd out of Virgil."[4] To all of which must be added the capture of Virgil—in the form of the Fourth Eclogue—by the church and by medieval and Renaissance hermeneutics. In this perspective Virgil announced the advent of the Savior and the miracle of His birth. He is therefore, as Dante implies, a Christian prophet. In a culture that tends simultaneously toward the classical and the Christian, toward the Rome of Augustus and that of Saint Peter, Virgil occupies a talismanic role. The "Homeric" masterpiece of French culture, Berlioz's *Trojans*, is wholly Virgilian (fig. 1). Berlioz's conception of the fall of Troy derives from the *Aeneid.* Not Helen but Dido obsesses him. Valéry, who translated Virgil, asked Gide: "Was there ever a more wearisome text than the *Iliad*?"[5]

Homer, then, goes against the grain of the French. The history of French-language Homer translations is nonetheless of considerable interest.[6] It begins in the sixteenth century with the *Illustrations of Gaul and Singularities of Troy* (1510–13) by Jean Lemaire de Belges, which is based on a prose version of Homer in Latin by the eminent Lorenzo Valla. There follow the *Iliad* of Jehan Samxon, who used the same source; two books of the *Odyssey* (1577) by Jacques Peletier du Mans; and a version of both epics (1589) by Henri Estienne II. Homer is mightily (if tacitly) present as the father of all wisdom in the letter from Gargantua to Pantagruel. Commentary on his work was on the syllabus of the Jesuit schools and the new Collège de France. Much philological work and scholarly interpretation was incorporated into Jean de Sponde's 1583 edition. Virgil remained the tutelary deity, but Ronsard (in his *Franciade*) and Du Bellay longed for a French Homer. Distrust of the *Iliad* and the *Odyssey* burgeoned under the influence of Julius Caesar Scaliger. Virgil was, as ever, the beneficiary, but with Salomon Certon's translation of the *Odyssey* (1604) and the occasional partial translation, efforts were made to restore Homer's honor. Alas, after Paul Pellisson and his attempts at translation (1650), knowledge of ancient Greek all but vanished. Homer was merely an absence. His return was, as it were, oblique.

In 1662, the young Racine, bored to death at Uzès, composed his *Remarks on the "Odyssey" of Homer*—which was only first printed in 1825! When he placed Homeric characters and situations on the stage in *Andromache* (1667) and *Iphigenia* (1674), he made no reference to Homer since Euripides was his source and his model. Yet there is a short passage in which—perhaps for the first time in French literature—the spirit of the *Iliad* can be clearly heard. These are the words Ulysses speaks in *Iphigenia*:

> The Hellespont churned up beneath our oars,
> See, and perfid Ilium weltering in flames,
> Its warriors in chains, old Priam on his knees,
> And Helen to her husband's arms restored;
> Your ships again cast anchor here unharmed,
> Returning to Aulis, bows garlanded with crowns,
> And your triumphant exploit shall become
> The eternal topic of the centuries to come.

Bossuet's love of Homer left little trace. By contrast, it would be difficult to overstate the European-wide impact of the *Adventures of Telemachus,* published in 1699 by Bossuet's adversary Fénelon. The characters are Homeric, but Fénelon's suave and chaste pedagogy barely impinges on the world of the *Odyssey.* The primary point of reference is Virgil and a bucolic ideal in which innocence is the enemy of sin, a theme that inspired Voltaire's remark that "happiness resembles the island of Ithaca, which remained always one step ahead of Ulysses." Fénelon's tones can still be heard in *Émile.* Homer educated the senses, in Rousseau's view. The courage of Achilles is a divine gift and not a virtue acquired by human effort. Diderot transforms the suffering of Priam into mere bourgeois bereavement. And the young Marivaux produced his ephemeral *Homer Burlesqued.*

It was through a notorious scholarly polemic that Homeric epic finally attained a modicum of interest in France. Houdar de La Motte's translation of 1714 reproached Homer for his lack of taste, morality, and reason, eliciting a reply in the form of the translations and essays of Madame Dacier, which appeared between 1711 and 1716. A war of pamphlets and academic commentaries resulted. Pope was inspired and enriched by Madame Dacier, who in turn drew on Pope for her second edition. In March 1854, two of Sainte-Beuve's *Causeries du lundi* offered a lucid summary of the debate. Madame Dacier had, he said, played "an unexpected and rather important role in the history of French literature."[7] Her translation was "generous and noble" and "gives the clearest image of her Homer."[8] It was Madame Dacier's Homer that inspired the young Madame Roland with her vision of a heroic destiny.[9] In spite of the disdain of Voltaire and Louis-Sébastien Mercier ("your divine Homer is a bore")[10] Sainte-Beuve was happy to concur with père Buffier's judgment: "Homer is one of the great minds of the world. He first fashioned a poem to which no other has, *all things considered*, either been preferred or indeed preferable."[11] Only Chénier and Chateaubriand, said Sainte-Beuve, had come close to the power of the *Iliad* and the *Odyssey.*

Chénier did indeed perceive himself as the last of the *Homeridae* and a direct descendant of Homer. He pays a moving homage to the blind bard in "The Beggar": "For every wandering mortal long desires / Again to see the land where he was born." He returns to this motif in his *Bucolics* (1819) in "The Blind Bard": "But the omnipotent gods reserved for my decline / Darkness, exile, penury, starvation and repine." Reading this poem, Heredia felt "dazzled as if by lightning."[12] It is this same unfortunate Homer who, in Hugo's *All of the Lyre,* "beneath the weight of somber destiny expires."[13] But how much more Hugo feels the influence of Virgil and Shakespeare! Romantic French literature pays Homer only the most fleeting and conventional lip service.

By contrast, Homer obsessed Leconte de Lisle: "Eros! Carry me over the ocean wave!" exclaims Helen in *Antique Poems.*[14] He began translating Homer in 1845; his *Iliad* appeared in 1867, and the *Odyssey* and the *Hymns* a year later. He set out, he said, to correct the "wretched travesties" of his predecessors by closely imitating the sounds of the original.[15] The result was an unconvincing tribute to the past, although its archaizing style sometimes cast a scholarly light on epic forms and formulae; and Taine vaunted its merits to the students of the École des Beaux-Arts. In the verdict of Paul Mazon, most nineteenth-century translations "belong to the history of philology rather than the history of literature."[16] His judgment could only be reinforced by Littré's bizarre attempt to "recompose" Homer in medieval French. Hugo pays his respects to the greatness of the *Iliad* in his *Shakespeare* (1864) but seems not to have known the *Odyssey.* For Hugo and many of his contemporaries the voyages and memoirs of Chateaubriand were its sole French counterpart. Chateaubriand alone could "revive the extinguished dust" of Troy.[17] A Greek-Latin edition of Homer accompanied him in all his peregrinations.

It is something of a paradox that Homer was restored to his rightful place by Péguy. "Three thousand years of reading" came before Péguy's in 1910.[18] The infinite, he said, is sometimes revealed in a single verse, like "a distant glimmer on the unploughed ocean."[19] "The gods would be nothing, and not just the gods but men, had he not sung of them."[20] As if anticipating Simone Weil's absurd interpretation of the *Iliad,* Péguy knew that for Homer the greatest destiny a man could enjoy was "to die young in military combat."[21] The mysterious purity of the Homeric spirit struck Péguy as an "ever-flowing river: the more one takes, the more remains."[22] To translate the two epics was, he said, "at once so easy and so impossible."[23]

In 1914 Péguy again immersed himself in Homer. It was, he said, "fresh as the morning, whereas nothing is more ancient than the newspaper of the day."[24] The power of Homer was unique, giving us "the maximum of clarity with the maximum of depth."[25] And in his "Conjoint Note on Monsieur Descartes" we find the striking observation that Ulysses undoes the entire system of hand-to-hand combat. He "replaces the system of battle by a system of victory. . . . In this sense . . . from the outset Ulysses is already a Roman among the Greeks. He has already ceased to be a braggart and a battler. He is already the man who says nothing—and wins."[26] Péguy's very Homeric death moved many of his contemporaries and readers. Péguy embodied the conviction that the *Iliad* was, in the words of Montaigne, the "seedbed of every kind of knowledge,"[27] the manual of the man facing death.

Proust's contemplation of "the Homer phenomenon" was intermittent but unceasing. He translated Homer from the Greek in class. In the *Recherche* the ineffable Bloch pastiches the version by "papa Leconte."[28] For the duchesse de Guermantes, Zola is "the Homer of night soil."[29] Proust several times tried to convince Reynaldo Hahn that the unity of the *Iliad* and the *Odyssey* bore witness to supreme literary genius,[30] that they were the work of a master whose blindness made of him a clairvoyant, a *voyant* in Rimbaud's term. Seven cities competed for the status of Homer's birthplace, but, said Proust, "Auteuil-Paris alone can call me hers."[31] More seriously, the narrator of *Le Temps Retrouvé* claims that, like the Homeric bards and Ulysses in the Underworld, he too can waken the dead to eternal life.[32]

The philosopher Alain read and reread Homer, in which he found "the just measure of men and gods." He devoted a chapter of *The Gods* (1934) to Homer: "The Gods are moments of mankind. This thought is not abstract; it is written into the skirmishes of the *Iliad* and the navigations of the *Odyssey.*"[33] In combat scenes "the supernatural is what the physiological would be."[34] In Homer, he said, "the hero is the only enemy worthy of man."[35] Curious observation: "Eternal text and true mirror of humanity. But Achilles neither takes time to read nor leaves anyone time to read."[36] The human being alone, claims Alain, "is god. Homer implies this."[37] Even before Christianity, Alain argues, Homer knew that god had become man—a notion registered

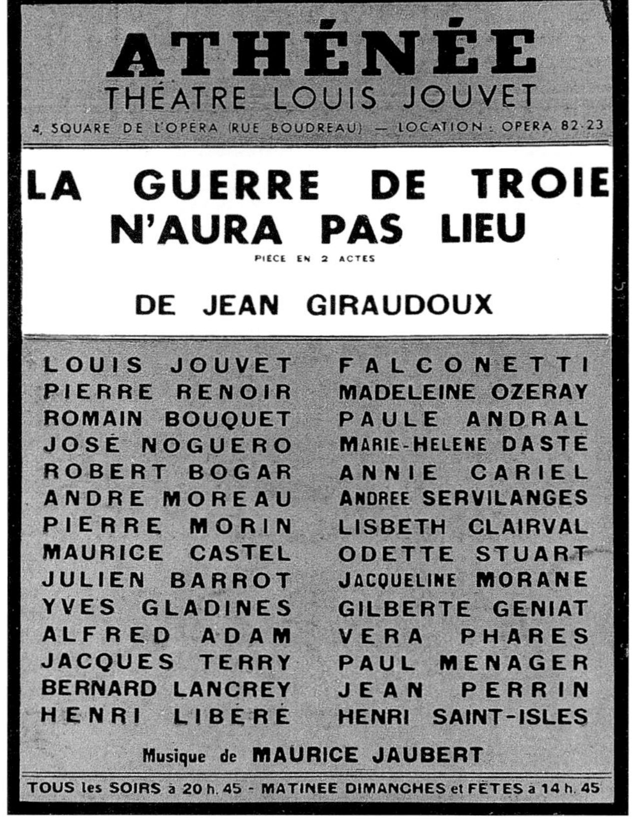

FIGURE 2 | Poster for *La Guerre de Troie n'aura pas lieu*, by Jean Giraudoux (1882–1944), at the Théâtre de l'Athénée, 1935.

by Alain's pupil, Simone Weil. No doubt unaware of his continuity with Proust, in 1937 Gide read the last two books of the *Iliad* and concluded that "no intransigent heterosexual could truly appreciate Greece."[38] This judgment was preceded by his *Philoctetes* (1892–98).

If the nineteenth century has been described as "silent about Homer," the twentieth century saw a multifarious revival of Homeric motifs. It gained much from the worldwide prestige of Joyce's *Ulysses* (1922), which was first published in France. That same year saw Aragon's *Adventures of Telemachus.* From Giraudoux came a great welling up of things Homeric: *Elpenor* appeared in 1920, the first versions of *The Cyclops* and *The Sirens* in 1926, followed in 1935 by the incandescent political intelligence of *The War of Troy Shall Not Take Place* (fig. 2). Giono's novel *Birth of the Odyssey,* written between 1923 and 1928, offered a realist deconstruction of Ulysses. To these should be added Claudel's *Proteus* (1913) and Sartre's updating of Euripides' tragedy about the fall of Troy and the abominable fate of Hecuba.

Translations followed one after another. Bérard's thesis of a "Phoenician Odyssey" influenced Joyce. Paul Mazon deemed Bérard's translation of the *Odyssey* into six-syllable blank verse "a lasting achievement."[39] Mazon's own somber and scholarly version of the *Iliad* (1937; reprinted in 1998) remains a point of reference. Émile Lasserre's *Iliad* came out in 1932. As of 2004, an *Iliad* by Philippe Brunet was in progress: "In the abrasion of the two languages," Brunet has said, "the translation of Homer works like a musical game."[40] Amid this abundance, Philippe Jaccottet's *Odyssey* (1982) stands out. Like the "statues and columns resplendent in the crystalline air of Greece," Jaccottet's articulation of the gap between Homer and French is also "a radiant connection."[41] Is this not, at last, a French version to rival the highest achievements of the Anglo-Saxon Homeric lineage?

Three moments in the history of French music. Between 1855 and 1858 Berlioz composed *The Trojans,* probably the culmination of the lyric art in French culture. This is a work of genius, as I have said, and essentially Virgilian. "What a great composer Virgil is! What a melodist, what a harmonist!"[42] It was the *Trojan Women* by Euripides and Seneca that inspired Berlioz. But it is the promise of Rome in the *Aeneid* toward which music and libretto so magnificently tend. In Berlioz's view Shakespeare "made Hector greater even than Homer made him."[43] Nevertheless, the suffering and violence with which the first part of *The Trojans* ("the capture of Troy") is imbued is entirely Homeric. (Berlioz himself bore the name Hector and called his son Achilles.) Cassandra makes only three appearances in Homer, but the figure created by Berlioz is one of the most authentic descendants of the *Iliad.* How scandalous that the first complete performance of this

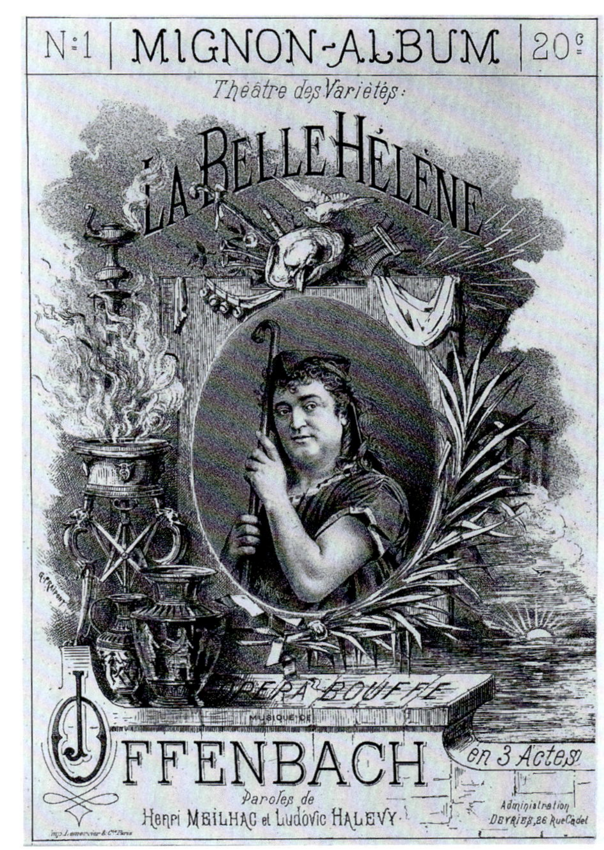

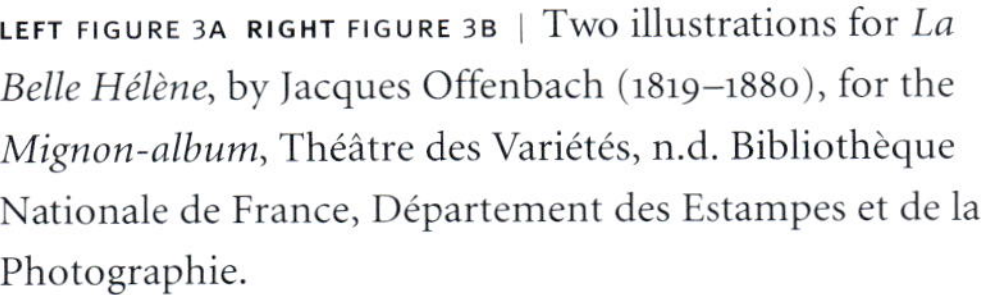

LEFT FIGURE 3A RIGHT FIGURE 3B | Two illustrations for *La Belle Hélène*, by Jacques Offenbach (1819–1880), for the *Mignon-album*, Théâtre des Variétés, n.d. Bibliothèque Nationale de France, Département des Estampes et de la Photographie.

masterpiece in Paris was only given in 2003—and even then under a British conductor!

Offenbach's *La Belle Hélène* opened in Paris in December 1864 (fig. 3). In this ironic pastoral, Meilhac and Halévy offered a disabused view of Second Empire morality, while Offenbach's sparkling score placed the dazzling Hortense Schneider center stage. "Masterpieces profaned!," lamented Jules Janin.[44] "To attempt to ridicule Homer's heroes is blasphemy!,"[45] bellowed Théophile Gautier. "Ah, how tedious they are with their old Homer . . . that immortal vagrant!,"[46] retorted Jules Vallès. The operetta was a huge success. Does it distantly anticipate Giraudoux's ironies? It certainly predicts the devastating war that broke out six years later.

Gabriel Fauré spent five years on his *Pénélope*, which opened at the Opéra de Monte-Carlo on March 4, 1913. Despite the use of leitmotifs, the chastity and inwardness of the work are remote from Wagner. Monteverdi seems the proper comparison. Fauré bestows on his heroine a profound vocal authority. He expertly suggests both the ambiguities attending Ulysses' return and the eventual blossoming of love. The opera is rarely staged and ripe for rediscovery. Like *La Belle Hélène*, it is a work composed in the shadow of a war more murderous than that of Troy.

The iconography of Homer in France extends from medieval illuminations to Picasso. It has never, I believe, been studied in its totality. The Middle Ages were acquainted with the "matière de Troie" and Odysseus's peregrinations through the *De excidio Trojae* (attributed to Dares Phrygius) and a fourth-century Latin historical novel associated with the legendary figure Dictys Cretensis, but the principal source was once again Virgil. It was a vision marked by the allegories of the virtues and vices in the pseudo-Homeric narration and by the ambition of the great royal and aristocratic houses of Europe to claim Trojan descent through Aeneas, Brutus, and other lofty figures of ancient Rome. The wealth of illuminations and paintings of the fifteenth and sixteenth centuries illustrating Homeric episodes is prodigious. Greek ships; the towers of Troy; the duels and jousts of Ajax, Achilles, and Hector; the dazzling fate of Helen and the wooden horse—all fill the condensed space of the miniature with a paradoxical grandeur, a background often mysteriously expanded. One example among many: the sumptuous Munich Boccaccio illustrated by Jean Fouquet and his son (?) around 1459–60. When Latin versions of the *Iliad* and the *Odyssey* were printed alongside the Greek text, Homeric iconography proliferated. Costume, landscape, combats, and shipwrecks remained medieval, but reference to the original intensified—as did the identification between Troy destroyed by fire and the European cities razed by war, an identification theatrically reprised in 1945 amid the ashes of Berlin. Idealization of the Trojans became a moral and political convention. Hector and Priam, worsted by Greek cunning and treachery, were singled out for this treatment. A preference as marked in Dante and Shakespeare as in Berlioz, it characterizes the entire Homeric lineage in European fine arts. The farewell of Hector and Andromache, the lucid despair of Cassandra, the death of Priam in the blazing citadel, and the heroic flight of Aeneas toward a new imperial dawn—all these inspired painters and sculptors alike. For a long time neither Achilles nor Ulysses had a very good press.

In Italian painting Homeric moments are featured in works by Botticelli, Guido Reni, Giulio Romano, Polidoro da Caravaggio, Tiepolo, and in the ironic twilight of Giorgio de Chirico. I have already pointed to the work of Blake and Turner in England. In France art turned toward Homer in the seventeenth century but drew principally on Homeric themes reworked by Ovid. It also imitated the Italian masters, notably in the many versions of the amours of Mars and Venus. Particularly influential were the fifty-eight compositions in the Galerie d'Ulysse at Fontainebleau; attributed to Primaticcio, they were destroyed in 1736. Claude Lorrain painted some Odyssean subjects as commissions in Rome. However, contact with the text remained tangential. Ulysses appears in a series of pictures by Simon Vouet, delivered to Claude de Bullion, the superintendant of finances, around 1634–35; they were subsequently reproduced on Gobelins tapestries. No further notable illustrations of the *Iliad* emerged until Antoine Coypel's three paintings inspired by Madame Dacier. It was the legend of Paris that gained a certain currency. The *Judgment of Paris* was painted by Claude in 1663, by Poussin around 1660, by Watteau in 1718–20, and by Boucher on many different occasions. There are two versions by Fragonard dating from 1773–76 and two by Cézanne from 1860–61. Renoir returned to this theme several times between 1908 and 1915, Maillol evoked it in 1940, and Picasso drew it in 1951. David's *Courtship of Paris and Helen* dates from 1788. Around 1852 Moreau painted a *Rape of Helen.*

Finally, Homeric inspiration in French art is inseparable from the history and aesthetics of the Prix de Rome.[47] The vast sequence of such works begins with the large Homeric canvases produced between 1775 and 1789 by Joseph-Marie Vien, director of the French Academy in Rome and subsequently First Painter to the King. His pupil David was a prisoner in the

Luxembourg jail when he composed his magnificent wash drawings representing every social class crowding forward to hear Homer perform. In the Salon of 1800, a *Consternation of Priam* swept all before it. Thereafter a flood of Homeric painting was released upon the nation. Outstanding among these is Ingres's *Achilles Receiving the Ambassadors of Agamemnon*, which won the Prix de Rome in 1801. The touching encounter of Ulysses and Nausicaa was the subject of the Prix de Rome in 1833 and 1845. In 1812, the examiners set the subject of the return of Ulysses. The obscure Gumery won the Prix de Rome in 1850 with his *Death of Achilles*, defeating Carpeaux in the process. Achilles' return to combat was the subject of Henri-Frédéric Schopin's work, which won the prize in 1831, while Jules Lefebvre triumphed in 1861 with *The Death of Priam*.

Homages to Homer combine with visions of the blind and penniless bard to form a group apart. They include Ingres's *Apotheosis of Homer* (1827). Delacroix twice returned to the theme of *Alexander and the Poems of Homer* (1846–47). Around 1800, Clodion sculpted the pathetic spectacle of Homer attacked by dogs, as if in antithesis to the Odyssean motif of the dog Argos greeting his tattered master. In quite another tradition one notes the superb lithograph of *The Fall of Troy* by Fantin-Latour, offered in homage to Berlioz around 1860; six etchings by Matisse for a deluxe edition of Joyce's *Ulysses* (1935); a drawing by Rodin illustrating the education of Achilles (1917); and Picasso's vision of the Sirens dating from 1947, a subject in which Moreau had preceded him. In the very first rank comes David's *Andromache Mourning Hector*, which dates from 1783.

Perhaps the outstanding masterpiece of this tradition is a series of caricatures. Daumier, says Baudelaire, draws his Homeric characters with "the logic of the scholar transposed into a light and ephemeral art, which has against it the very mobility of life."[48] The fifty plates comprising Daumier's *Ancient History* appeared in *Le Charivari* between December 1841 and January 1843, thirteen of them directly illustrating Homer. This "anti-apotheosis" is Daumier's revolt against the "Pagan School" and the very *official* classicism of the 1840s and 1850s. Nightcaps for Nestor and Ulysses, inebriated gods and heroes, heroines like Penelope portrayed as vulgar scolds—this is a fancy-dress ball commented upon by irreverent quatrains:

> Seeing our hero all muddy and sordid,
> Others fled. Only Nausicaa applauded.
> She looks up from her soaping to say:
> "Noble stranger, what brings you this way?"

Is the derision of Daumier and Offenbach the most authentic manifestation of the reception accorded in France to the *Iliad* and the *Odyssey*? Two jewels that properly belong in this concise anthology might be cited to counter that view. Too often quoted, Du Bellay's "Heureux qui comme Ulysse" has lost none of its elegance. Let me conclude with Bonnefoy's *A Helen of Smoke and Air* (1990):

> There: the semblance of Helen was merely a fire
> To cry beauty: the protest of mind against death.
>
> Helen fades and disappears, she was
> Merely the intuition that made Homer dwell
> On sounds lower again than his strings in our
> Clumsy lyre of terrestrial words.
>
> Word by word I restored the text,
> But mine can be no more than a shade,
> One might think
> The source is a burning Troy,
> Beauty a regret, and the work will accept
> Fully alone a water that water withholds.[49]

"Burning Troy" is indeed a source and has never stopped casting its somber light over the destiny of the West—thus defining my theme.

NOTES

1 Percy Bysshe Shelley, preface to "Hellas. A Lyrical Drama," in *Shelley: Poetical Works*, ed. Thomas Hutchinson (1950; rpt. Oxford, 1978), 447.

2 See *Homer in English*, ed. George Steiner, with the assistance of Aminadav Dykman (London, 1996).

3 Chateaubriand's *Génie du christianisme* first appeared in 1802. [Trans.]

4 See Marcel Proust, *À la Recherche du temps perdu*, ed. Jean-Yves Tadié (Paris, 1987–89), 3:710.

5 André Gide, *Journal, 1889–1939* (Paris, 1939), 1:1325; letter dated October 25, 1938.

6 See the following: Noémi Hepp, *Homère en France au XVIIe siècle* (Paris, 1968); Didier Pralon, "Traductions françaises de l'*Iliade* (1519–1989)," in *La Traduction: Problèmes théoriques et pratiques* (Aix-en-Provence, 1993), 135–77; and Françoise Létoublon and Catherine Volphilhac-Auger, eds., *Homère en France après la Querelle (1715–1900)*, Actes du colloque de Grenoble, 1995 (Paris, 1999).

7 Charles-Augustin Sainte-Beuve, "Madame Dacier," *Les Causeries du lundi*, March 6 and 13, 1854, 7:488.

8 Ibid., 7:490, 491.

9 Ibid., 7:490.

10 See Louis-Sébastien Mercier, "Contre l'Homère traduit en Français," in his *Mon Bonnet de nuit*, 4 vols. (Neuchâtel, 1784), 1:290.

11 Sainte-Beuve, "Madame Dacier," *Les Causeries du lundi*, 7:507; citing Claude Buffier's *Homère en arbitrage* (1715).

12 André Chénier, *Les Bucoliques, publiées d'après le manuscrit original par José-Marie de Heredia* (Paris, 1907), xviii.

13 Victor Hugo, *Toute la lyre* (sec. 4, poem 5), in *Oeuvres complètes. Poésie*, vol. 4, ed. Bernard Leuilliot (Paris, 1986), 315.

14 Charles-Marie-René Leconte de Lisle, "Hélène" (sec. 7), in *Oeuvres poétiques, Poèmes Antiques*, vol. 1, ed. Edgard Pich (Paris, 1977), 115.

15 Leconte de Lisle, introduction to *Poèmes Antiques*, ed. Claudine Gothot-Mersch (Paris, 1994), 313.

16 Paul Mazon, *Madame Dacier et les traductions d'Homère en France*, The Zaharoff Lecture for 1935 (Oxford, 1936), 21.

17 François-René de Chateaubriand, *Mémoires d'Outre-Tombe*, 1849–50 (Paris, 1951), 1:665.

18 Charles Péguy, "Clio: Dialogue de l'histoire et l'âme païenne," in *Oeuvres en prose complètes*, 3 vols., ed. Robert Burac (Paris, 1992), 3:1015.

19 Ibid., 1152.

20 Ibid., 1155.

21 Ibid., 1167.

22 Ibid., 1168.

23 Ibid., 1185.

24 Charles Péguy, "Note sur M. Bergson and la philosophie bergsonienne," in *Oeuvres*, 3:1255.

25 Ibid., 1251.

26 Charles Péguy, "Note conjointe sur M. Descartes," in *Oeuvres*, 3:1344.

27 Michel de Montaigne, "On the Most Excellent of Men" (2.36), in *Complete Essays*, trans. M. A. Screech (London, 1991), 851.

28 See Proust, *À la Recherche*, vol. 3, notes to pp. 15, 88, 102, 234, 293, and 488.
29 Ibid., 2:789.
30 See, in particular, Marcel Proust, *Correspondance*, 21 vols., ed. Marcel Kolb (Paris, 1970–93), 5:327–28.
31 This remark was called forth by a pun on blindness (*cécité*) and the seven cities (*sept cités*) that claimed the honor of Homer's birthplace. See Proust, *Correspondance*, 15:199.
32 Ibid., 3:196.
33 Alain (pseud. Émile-Auguste Chartier), *Les Dieux* (Paris, 1947), 171.
34 Ibid., 172.
35 Ibid., 173.
36 Ibid. [According to Alain, the shield of Achilles shows that "works are everything and accomplish everything." This is the "eternal text" Achilles does not read and his opponents do not live long enough to decipher. Trans.]
37 Ibid., 174.
38 André Gide, *Journal, 1889–1939* (Paris, 1939), 1:1271; entry dated September 1, 1937.
39 Mazon, *Madame Dacier*, 27.
40 Philippe Brunet, "Le Rêve d'une langue mesurée," *Le Magazine littéraire*, no. 427 (January 2004): 39.
41 For both quotes, see Homer, *Odyssée*, 2nd ed., trans. Philippe Jaccottet (Paris, 2004), 9.
42 See Hector Berlioz, *Correspondance générale*, 8 vols., ed. Pierre Citron, Hugh Macdonald, and Yves Gérard (Paris, 1972–2003), 4:574.
43 Ibid., 5:362–63.
44 Jules Janin, "La Semaine dramatique," *Le Journal des Débats*, January 9, 1865.
45 Théophile Gautier, "Revue des théâtres," *Le Moniteur Universel*, December 26, 1864.
46 Jules Vallès, "Paris," *L'Événement*, no. 105, February 17, 1866.
47 See Philippe Grunchec, *Le Grand Prix de Peinture: Les Concours de Prix de Rome de 1797 à 1863*, exh. cat. (Paris, 1993).
48 See Charles Baudelaire, "Quelques caricaturistes français," in *Oeuvres complètes*, 2 vols., ed. Claude Pichois (Paris, 1976), 2:556.
49 Yves Bonnefoy, *Une Hélène de vent et de fumée* (Paris, 1990); reworked as "De vent et de fumée" in *La Vie errante* (Paris, 1993), 91–99.

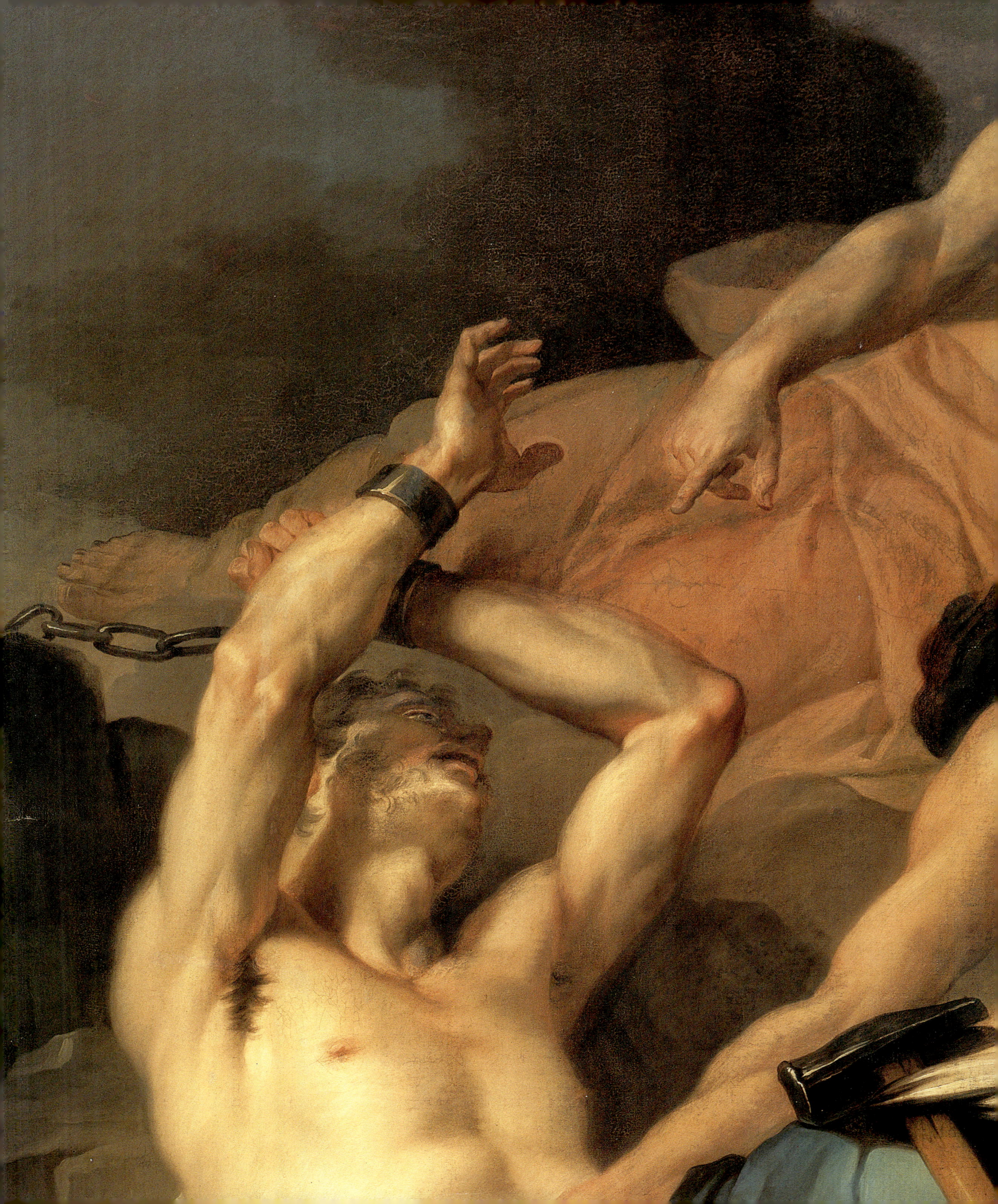

THE GREEK PARADIGM

Homer, Costume, and the Academy

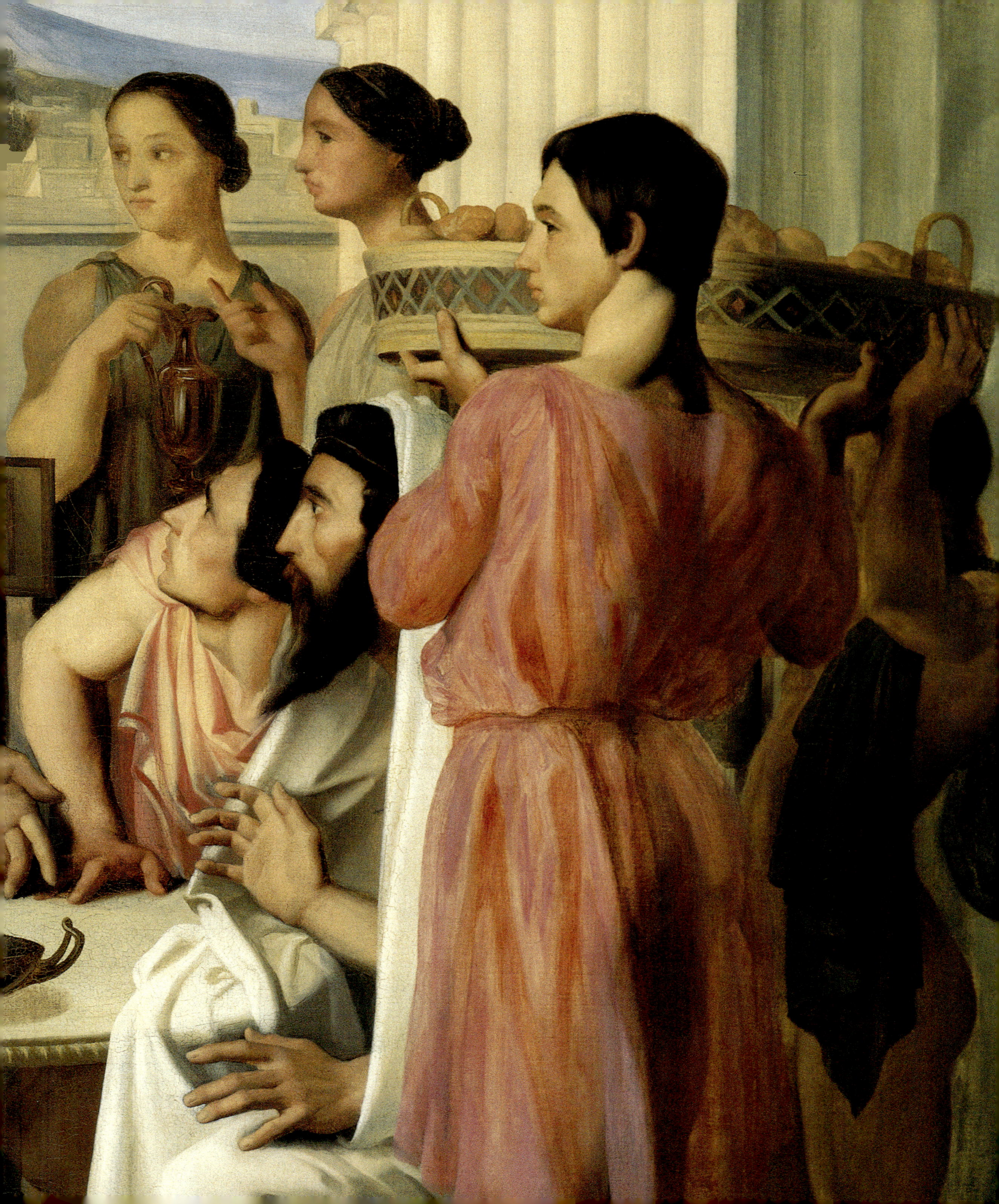

Reading Homer in France | From Text to Image

Emmanuel Schwartz

FROM PREHISTORY WE INHERIT EPICS, SONGS, AND STORIES. THEY COME DOWN TO us from before the birth of our own history, surviving in oral tradition until at last recorded in writing. Nations have founded their prestige and religions their sacred status on the primordial material thus transmitted. The *Iliad* and the *Odyssey* are works of this kind, but they are also unique, for they did not teach the Greeks that they must believe in nothing but themselves and their destiny, nor did they create an explanatory myth valid only for speakers of Greek. Homer taught the Greeks to speak to humanity as a whole. When the Albanian author Ismail Kadare tells the story of a local incident such as might have given rise to the Homeric legend, he places it in his own land, a small country with an archaic language on the borders of ancient Illyria and Epirus, whose coastline looks out on Ulysses' island.[1] In thus adapting Homer to his own locality, Kadare is typical. European civilization in its entirety was nourished on Greek epic. Homer's biographers tell us that when Homer sang, his audience was overwhelmed. His listeners are represented looking out onto the garden of the universe, while the light of the world's dawn plays on their faces. For their pleasure and ours, Homer invented characters who, like Athena, were born directly into adulthood. He offered his contemporaries not merely delightful stories—these already existed—but the freedom to assess mortals and immortals by their own lights, recognizing their lies and half-truths, their tragic beauty and inevitable blemishes. He taught them how to unravel this skein of illusions, simulacra, and mirages. Although originality is not the forte of Ingres's Homer illustrations, his view is representative. "Homer," he observed "was the first to disentangle by his poetry the beauties of nature, just as God organized life by extracting it from chaos. His teachings are eternal and universal; he codified beauty in immortal precepts and examples. All the great men of Greece—poets, tragedians, historians, artists of every kind, painters, sculptors, architects—owe their paternity to Homer"[2] (fig. 4).

DETAIL OF CATALOGUE NO. 104

Alas, all too soon one began to seek examples in Homer. Yet it is precisely the merit of Homer's art to show that ideal models—like certainty—do not exist. True, the world of Homer brings together all the qualities that define literature and art. It entertains, it reveals the grandeur and fragility of the human condition, and it offers a vision of things that subsequent intellectual revolutions have renewed, destroyed, enriched, and re-created. Later periods, however, convinced that they had reached a zenith of social and moral perfection, found it hard to explain their attraction to Homer. How could one be entertained by these cruel, immoral stories? A work that threatens the reader's selfish and complacent beliefs could hardly be described as amusing. From Plato's time onward, readers of the *Iliad* and the *Odyssey* have taken refuge in self-contradictory interpretations justifying or denouncing their shameful pleasure. Particularly in France, the history of ideas, letters, and the arts was long driven by absurd or ingenious retranslations and rewritings of Homer—hence the famous *querelles d'Homère*—until at last it was acknowledged that such "improvements" constituted yet another form of homage. Comparing these successive readings, one contemplates the fragility of absolute convictions and of the morals and hierarchies that underpin social organization. Such comparisons help to define Homer's personality; he was the first poet in history to make others aware of their naïveté, errors, and disorientation—without which they would, of course, be the merest shadows, devoid of all substance and color. Painters and sculptors conjuring figures from the imagination often looked to Homer's verses to supply the inner life of their creations. Was inspiration always forthcoming? The works in the collection of the École des beaux-arts, distinctive in their scholastic and academic origins, provide the most varied and surprising answers to this question. They provide a similarly varied response to all those doctrines that affirm, in art and in life, the primacy of individual liberty and dignity.

Definitions of Epic

Homer came to France in an unexpectedly roundabout fashion. Using a set of legends that offered him anecdote rather than rounded characters, he fashioned two works whose influence would extend as far afield as India and that became the model for many subsequent epics. But he drastically curtailed the heroic narratives upon which he drew, reducing the ten years of the Trojan War to the wrath of Achilles, and the restoration of peace to the voyages of Ulysses. The heroes of the Trojan War lived on nonetheless, their glory unabated by omission from the two Homeric epics. Centuries after the *Iliad* and the *Odyssey*, long sequels were written, restoring the broader epic context that Homer had shorn from his characters. Two late texts transmitted the Trojan War to the medieval West. The first of these was *Ephemeris belli Troiani* (fourth century A.D.), allegedly composed by Dictys Cretensis, a Greek warrior; the second, *De Excidio Troiae Historia* (sixth century A.D.), was the supposed work of Dares Phrygius, a Trojan.

THE COURTLY TRADITION

In these evidently apocryphal narratives the mortals eclipse the gods. In the process they voice a gallantry toward women that was quickly taken up by the French courtly tradition. The most widely read poem to emerge from this tradition was *Le Roman de Troie* (ca. 1160) by Benoît de Sainte-Maure (or Sainte-More), in which the defeated Hector is portrayed as the great hero of the Trojan War, worsted only by treachery and a literal stab in the back. Hector consequently entered popular imagery as a model hero, making appearances, for example, on playing cards. All Sainte-Maure's Trojan women are completely infatuated with Hector—the only warrior in the saga to remain devoted to his own wife. In this tradition women have their own wars to wage, and they relate only incidentally to the war described by Homer. A newcomer, Briséide, who inherits the combined roles of Briseis and Chryseis,

OPPOSITE FIGURE 4 | JEAN-AUGUSTE-DOMINIQUE INGRES (1780–1867), *The Apotheosis of Homer*, 1827–33. Oil on canvas, 386 × 512 cm. Musée du Louvre, Paris.

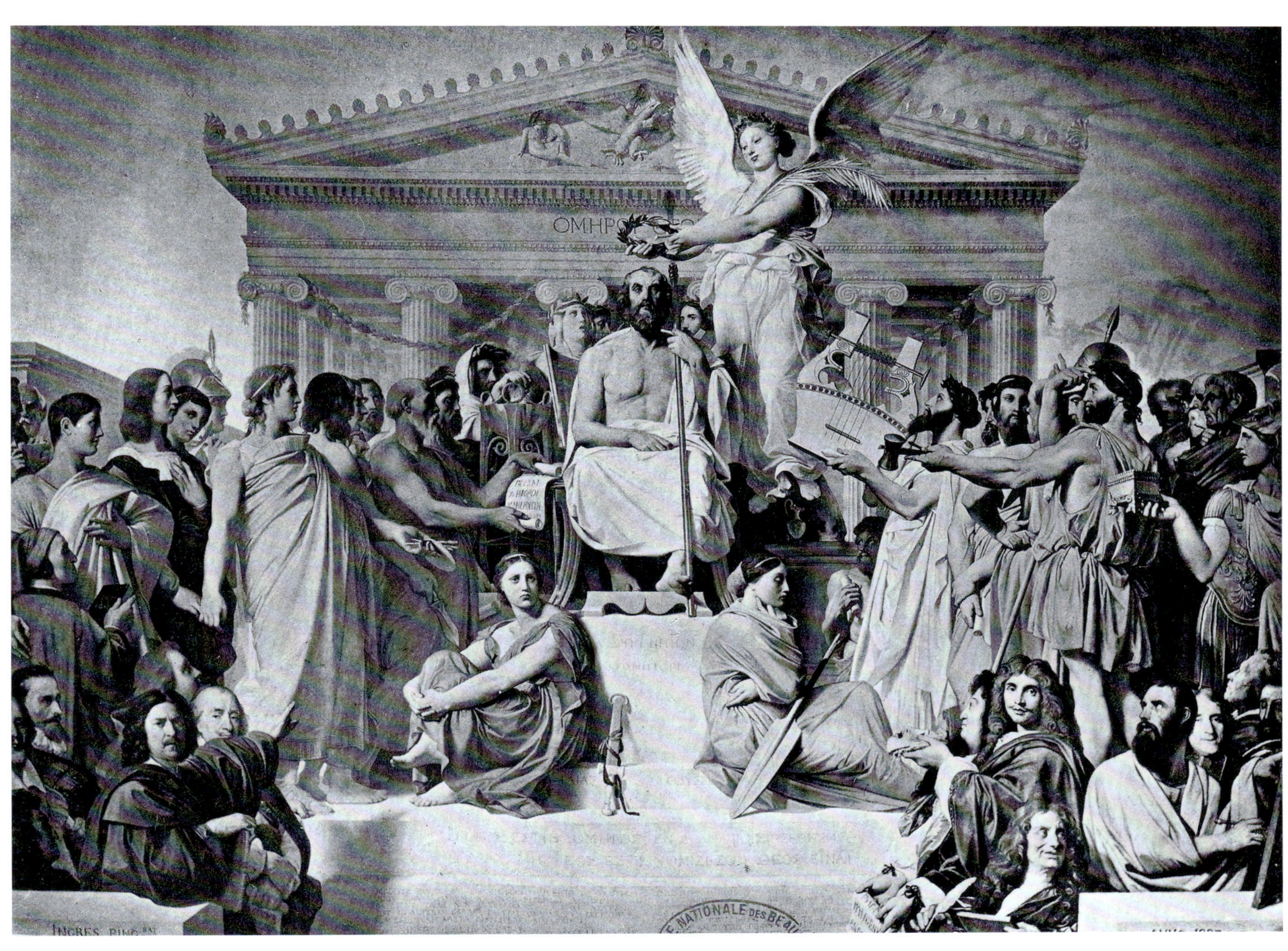
ΟΜΗΡΟΣ

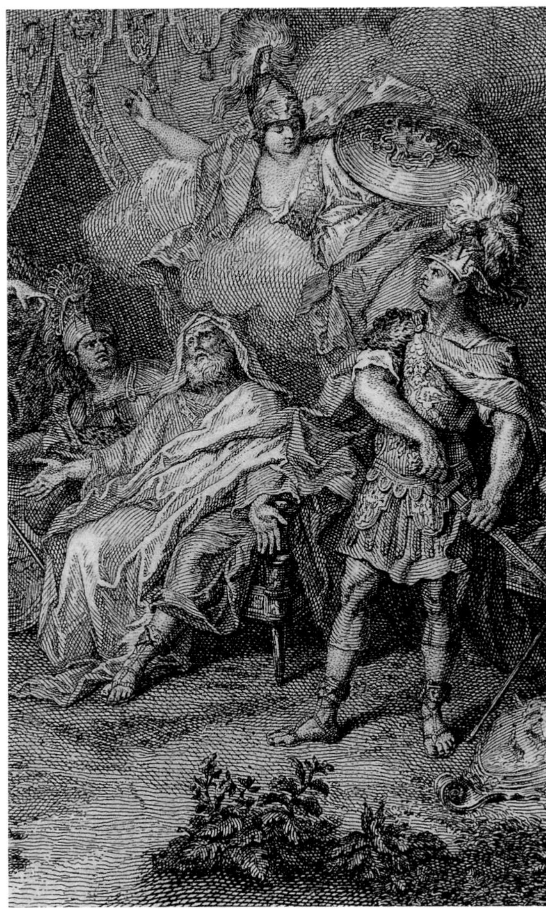

ABOVE AND OPPOSITE FIGURE 5 | ANTOINE COYPEL (1661–1722), *The Wrath of Achilles*, 1717–22. Details of engravings by Tardieu, Tardieu the Younger, and Simonneau after a tapestry cartoon.

breaks the heart of Troilus and many another after him. She is better known in the history of poetry and theater as Cressida. Achilles meanwhile casts aside the memory of Patroclus in favor of Polyxena. The *Roman de Troie* enjoyed enormous popularity. In 1450 a certain Jacques Millet drew on it to create a narrative in dialogue form bearing the magnificent if misleading title *The Destruction of Troy the Great, and the Rape of Helen by Paris Alexander, Composed in French Rhythm by Maître Jehan de Mehun,*[3] *First Inventor of French Rhetoric: With the Noble Gestures, Warlike Feats and Virtues of the Doughty Hector, the Hateful Treachery Committed by the Greeks, and the Description of Unstable, Mutable Fortune: In All Truth Newly Revised and Corrected and Very Assiduously Wrought into the True French Language, Historiated with New Stories Containing the Entire Deeds of the Trojans and Greeks.* We are nowadays somewhat suspicious of the notion that the Homeric poems were conceived as a *précieux* novel or work of chivalry. But the tradition of a war fought for the fair eyes of Helen long persisted. In the seventeenth century the *précieuses* were happy to rediscover in the plain of Troy Mlle de Scudéry's *Carte du Tendre* (an allegorical map of the tender sentiments).[4] The gentlemen, never falling below courtly elegance, strode upon it wearing comely expressions and were painted by Antoine Coypel (fig. 5) as they had been described by the poet Malherbe:

> Achilles, he was broad of beam,
> His locks were sown with gold
> His face was all a lady's dream
> They lavished sighs untold;
> At song might none excel him,
> Nor dance, nor leaping high,
> No man could better draw the bow,
> No wrestler came him nigh.[5]

Readers were long divided into two or three camps: admirers of the Greeks; partisans of the Trojans; and lovers of womankind, who for the most part identified with the Trojans. The women of the Homeric stories are indeed more independent than their lords, fathers, or husbands: they change sides; abandon, betray, and deceive their men; and sometimes find it necessary to stab their husbands. Courtly love forgives them this. As to the human condition—the contention between individual and destiny—no reader of the *Roman de Troie* cared about it. When the artists of the modern world came to illustrate Homer, they did not attempt to learn theoretical lessons from the dialogue of epic and philosophy or from the mysterious affinities between poetry and painting. Instead, joyful courtly

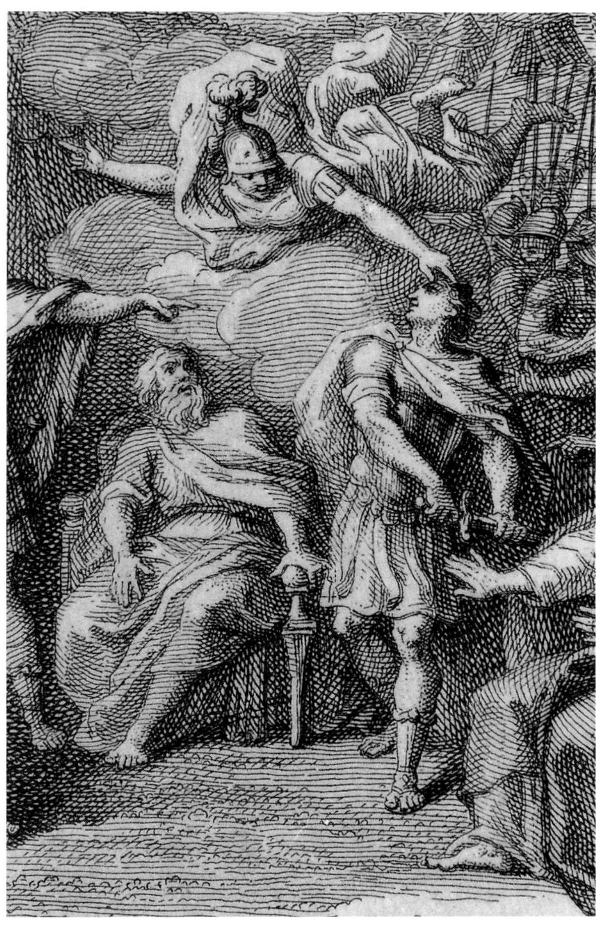

adventures unfolded in miniatures, on *cassoni* (marriage chests), and on the tapestries decorating the walls of lordly residences. In everyday life such interpretations of Homer found a curious echo in the *plaquettes* worn on belt or hat as an emblem of fidelity to one's mistress. The handsome, lovelorn gentlemen who wore them were famous for their facility with tears—weeping, it was said, like so many Magdalenes. The Three Graces did not then bear the features of the jealous goddesses but were simply three views of a single perfect beauty. From Flanders to Italy—not to mention seventeenth-century France—the Trojan War was portrayed as a parade led by a handsome wooden horse (fig. 6).

We come now to the time of the Humanists, when Homer is restored to center stage in the Trojan War. In 1488 Demetrios Chalcondylas, a scholar of Greek origin working in the court of the Medici, published the first modern edition of Homer in Florence. Homer's Greek was thus restored to a primacy long wrested from it by the vernacular poets. Chalcondylas published not only the *Iliad* and the *Odyssey* but also the *Homeric Hymns* and the strange *Batrachomyomachia*, or *Epic of Frogs and Rats*. The last of these is certainly not the work of Homer, although the fifteenth century saw no inconsistency between it and the two epics. Even in sixteenth-century France, Homer could be read only in Greek or French, and many humanists chose the Greek. The first Latin translation by Henri Estienne appeared in 1566 and was published not in France but in Geneva. The disciplined hexameters of Virgil had not yet come between Greek and French, between the language that invented irony and one whose genius was just emerging.[6] The French translations of Homer in the sixteenth century had a natural elegance and lack of pretension that were soon lost to archaeological pedantry. The image of Helen was that afforded by the third book of the *Iliad*, where she stands at the Scaean gates—a name that will often recur in this essay—surrounded by the ribald, comfort-loving Trojan elders and by "many a Trojan woman and high-born damsel," as Salel and Jamyn's translation has it. Ronsard, smitten with a more recent Helen, wrote (*Sonnets for Helen*, II, lxviii): "What more fertile theme can I indite/ Than that which made great Homer write:/ The all-divine, the virtuous Hélène?"[7]

For a time, then, court life in France took its rhythm from the supple music of Homer's hexameters. Poets and painters alike read him. Primaticcio's Gallery of Ulysses at Fontainebleau[8] celebrated the vitality of the ancient heroes: their womanizing, fortunes, and

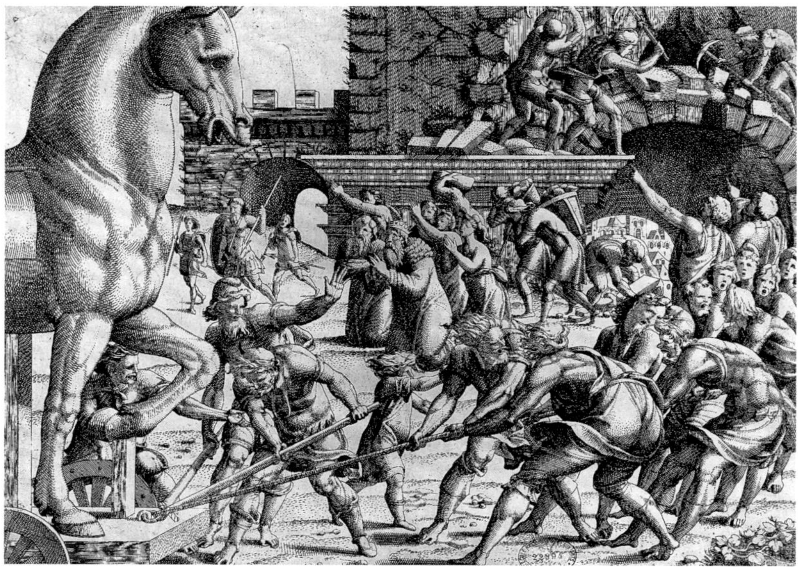

FIGURE 6 | JEAN MIGNON (active 1537–ca. 1555) after Luca Penni (1500–1556), *The Trojans Pulling the Trojan Horse Into Their City*, ca. 1545. Etching, 31.7 × 44 cm.

disasters; their voyages and combats. Ronsard did likewise:

> Or leaf through something better still,
> Read out to us in gravest style,
> How Venus once from Menelaus stole
> Her Paris in a sudden misty veil.
> The lesser Atrides gained but the sallet,
> No head within. Then Hector at the gallop
> Slew Patroclus unknown in borrowed garb,
> And now the Greeks' Achilles at his harp
> And sighing for the girl they stole,
> Beseeched he should relent and hear
> How Trojan flames their ships came near.
> He heard, and with his god-forged blade
> Felled bold Hector in the Trojan glade,
> As lightning fells the pine. For such a song
> The oaks grow ears and forward throng.[9]

THE NATIONAL EPICS

Now that the poets knew Homer, it was the turn of the nations to play at Trojan Wars.[10] The *Iliad* expertly alternates perspectives, passing from the tents of the Greeks to the citadel of the Trojans and looking from one camp into the other. The scene at the Scaean gates is among the most audacious and provides the most vertiginous view. It takes place high on the ramparts of Troy, looking out over the entire plain. There Helen the Greek describes the combatants to a group of Trojans made up of old men and women incapable of bearing arms. She does not favor one side over the other and there is no trace of patriotic fervor in her words. Homer, in short, had no notion of founding a literature of national propaganda, especially since nations can hardly be said to have existed in his time. But we have seen that the Middle Ages systematically took the part of Troy and its women against the Greeks, who show a brutality and cunning incompatible with chivalry. All the women in the *Iliad* are Trojans either by birth or amorous election. All, moreover, are captives or destined to endure captivity. Thus, the men of the Middle Ages followed in the women's wake, as men have done since Homeric times, and medieval virility claimed its descent from Troy.

Nations, like their inhabitants, love to flatter themselves by inventing a prestigious past or birth. Julius Caesar let flatterers argue that his *gens Iulia* descended from Iulus/Ascanius and thus directly from Aeneas, the hero of the *Aeneid*. The dukes of Burgundy followed Caesar's example. Lemaire des Belges, author of *Illustrations of Gaul and Singularities of Troy* (1509–12), traced the origins of France to Troy. Ronsard's *Franciade*, modeled on the *Iliad* and the *Aeneid*, tells how Francus (a supposed son of Hector) escapes the sack of Troy to found the future France. Ronsard's idea was not new since Francus had already emerged in the work of Fredegarius (seventh century A.D.), a chronicle supposedly imitated from Eusebius, and was taken up by Vincent de Beauvais in his *Speculum historiale*.[11] The *Franciade* sought to make France into a distant cousin of Greece and its history into a fearsome nationalistic chant. It was an immediate and lasting failure. Montaigne was, as always, the most skeptical reader of Homer: "Nothing lives like his fame and his works on the lips of men: nothing is so known or accepted as Troy, Helen and Homer's wars, *which may never have existed*" (*Essays*, bk. 2, chap. 36).[12] Founding his argument on this "*may never have existed*," Montaigne drew up a catalogue of lands that claimed to have their roots in the plain of Ilium—among them the Muslim Turkey of Mehmet II, which, like the entire Christian world, claimed descent from the pagan and polytheistic warriors of Homer. The Turkish claim at least had the merit of geographic proximity. Future readers of Homer, alas, disregarded Montaigne's warning. Every army in France—indeed, in all of Europe—felt obliged to adopt a Homeric hero as its mascot. More and more often they chose the camp of the winners. The two founding epics of the Greco-Roman world—the inspiration of Alexander, Caesar, and Augustus—thus served to guarantee the pedigree of Western armies if not of the Western nations. But as the nation-states were constituted during the seventeenth century, they grew too proud to trace their ancestry to the vanquished Hector. He was gradually effaced from their warmongering imagery, to be replaced by Achilles, Aeneas, and even Ulysses. For all that, Homer's Ulysses infrequently distinguishes himself in the melee, preferring the camp of the winning side.

The quest now began for still earlier warriors, for genuinely unscrupulous heroes. On epics are nations founded, and heroism has the virtue of limiting doubts. Before Ulysses and Achilles came the heroes of the first Trojan War, the expedition of the Heraclidae (companions of Hercules, discussed elsewhere), and Homer's heroes knew that others before them had struggled and died in a similar cause. Hercules, symbol of pure physical strength, wrestled with Antaeus, son of the Earth, combating the powers of nature that preceded humankind, such as the formless Hydra. He thus became an emblematic figure for the Renaissance humanists, who

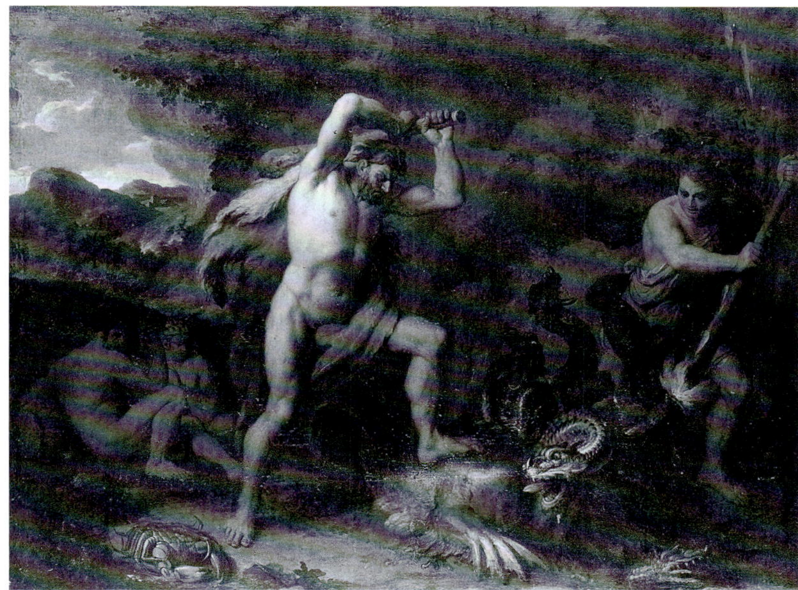

FIGURE 7 | RENÉ-ANTOINE HOUASSE (1645–1710), *Hercules Crushing the Hydra with the Aid of Iolas*, 1673. Oil on canvas, 149 × 195 cm. Royal Academy reception piece.

burdened his shoulders with the history of nascent civilization. Move forward to the reign of Louis XIV and the Académie royale de peinture. Academicians remembered the worthy Hercules and raised him to the role of a primitive hero loyally serving his master, and therefore the better fitted for courtly allegory. The artists of the king and courtiers of the princes imposed on the labors of Hercules interpretations intended to please their patron, which formed part of the syllabus of their École de peinture for almost a century. Henceforth Hercules killing the Lernean Hydra, as painted by Houasse in 1673 (fig. 7), represented Louis XIV pillaging the Netherlands the previous year.[13] *The Conquest of the Golden Fleece* (1664, the earliest surviving Academy prizewinner; cat. no. 100) portrayed the king as Hercules, pilot of the Argo, in order to commemorate the capture of Dunkirk a few months earlier.

These courtly works were explicated in a series of lectures—the text has been lost—given in 1684 by

Guillet de Saint-Georges, secretary and *historiographe* (or hagiographer) of the Academy. We know their tenor from summaries in the *Mercure galant.*[14] Pursued from birth by Juno's hatred, Hercules incurred a further humiliation. The prestigious *Farnese Hercules* sculpture, a work whose plaster cast looms large in the history of the École royale de Paris and, indeed, in that of all the schools related to academies, gave the son of Alcmene an exaggerated corpulence. Many such reception pieces portraying Hercules survive in the collection of the École des beaux-arts (e.g., Michel Corneille, *Hercules Killing Busiris,* 1675).[15]

FABLE VERSUS EPIC

The repertory of legend and epic included many stories that Homer judged too well known or too flimsy to figure in his narrative. The episodes he omitted—the first Trojan War, the death of Achilles, the fall of Troy, and the cycles about gods and demigods—were sung in Rome by writers far superior to Dictys and Dares. Virgil wrote his *Aeneid* entirely in the interests of Rome and Augustus, representing the emperor as a new Achilles or Aeneas building a new Troy that would triumph over the now Hellenized Orient. Ovid in his *Metamorphoses* and *Heroides* gave a sensual body and erotic words to the heroes and heroines of myth. Virgil therefore shoulders responsibility for bellicose interpretations of epic, while the refined imagery of Ovid—and of Apuleius in his wake—provided both a foil for moralists and a model for artists and writers enamored of handsome women and divine pleasure.

In his beautiful, celebrated, and misleading "Isolated Thought on Painting," Diderot made a distinction between the narratives of Ovid and Homer: "Ovid, in his *Metamorphoses*, will supply the painter with bizarre subjects; Homer will furnish great ones." Diderot's worst enemy—or at least one of his worst enemies—was the comte de Caylus (1692–1765), academician, archaeologist, and artist. As is so often the case with the Academy, however, the more radical styles of thought found some echo within it. Caylus shared many of Diderot's views, transcribing them in his less vigorous but nonetheless charming style. Diderot's literary verdicts found in Caylus their application to pictorial composition; Caylus studied Raphael and Giulio Romano rather as Diderot read Ovid and Homer. Raphael's reading of classical antiquity was, Caylus thought, superficial and even frivolous. Worse, its influence had been widely diffused through engravings. "Raphael found charming images in poetry and made them the subject of multitudes of paintings; to these he added new grace and charm inspired by his own delicate and refined genius." (Caylus refers to the Villa Farnesina frescoes, copied by Ingres in one of his dispatches from Rome.) Neither Diderot nor Caylus could admit Homer provided material for the sensual pleasures of art. Caylus cited Raphael's attitude toward Homer as proof of this:

> In Raphael were all the talents required to make a great poet, and we cannot without injustice suppose that, when he read Homer and Virgil, he was indifferent to the number and grandeur of events that these marvelous poets place at the painter's disposition; we must presume he found them too austere. He ceded them to Giulio Romano, his much-loved disciple, whose fiery genius avidly explored the great poets of antiquity, enriching itself with the picturesque ideas that lie everywhere underfoot in their works.[16]

Less heroic than brutal and sarcastic, Giulio Romano's engravings give a very vivid and amusing notion of the Trojan War; his frescoes in Mantua also illustrate Homeric themes. Caylus's judgments are perceptive, therefore, even if they are deficient as art history. He correctly noted that the vision of Homer transmitted by Raphael, Giulio Romano, and Primaticcio had shifted from the courtly to the "fiery," becoming a vision full of color and grandeur. When, in the eighteenth century, the attempt was made to separate heroism and sensuality, Diderot was quick to perceive the danger: heroism that takes no pleasure in killing and dying induces not virtue but tedium. As late as the nineteenth century, many of the paintings made in the École des beaux-arts were still steeped in the blood of Homer's Troy (see "Achilles" and "The Fall of Troy"). By contrast, the glacial eroticism that we first find in early Poussin—for example, in the indoor scene *Mercury, Herse and Aglauros* (cat. no. 17)—comes from Ovid. The academicians of the following century transposed this eroticism into the wooded grasslands of mythology, where immobile nymphs are courted by frigid youths (for an early example of such a setting, see François de Troy, cat. no. 14). The "grandeur" that Diderot saw in Homer is not easily defined. But the "bizarre" subjects that he perceived in Ovid came to be called Poesy or Fable and were defined as "picturesque"[17] and "*galant*." They are nonetheless very close to the spirit of Homer since Ovid himself paraphrased the Trojan War in the *Metamorphoses*. Ovid's gods also reside on earth and, like mankind, are attentive to the beauty of landscape and the attractions of women both mortal and immortal. True, they don't respect the world's military order in the human world, but in the eighteenth century Ovid's work was subsumed under the rubric "fable" and was considered a treasury of childish and picturesque narratives. Manuals of fable were written, the most popular of which was Chompré's *Dictionnaire de la fable* (1727). Homer and Virgil, meanwhile, were considered masters of the adult genre of epic. The Academies imposed this hierarchy of literary genre on the visual arts.

THE HIERARCHY OF FABLE

The Savonarolas of epic—more epic than the epic poets—elaborated a poetic history of humanity. The chevalier de Jaucourt wrote the entry for "fable" in Diderot's *Encyclopédie*. In it he placed the world of the warrior above, or at least prior to, either art or literature (including Homer), and defined that world as giving rise to *historical fable*. As we have seen, in the litany of wars and warriors Hercules came well before Achilles: "It must be admitted that the century most fertile in fables and heroism was that of the Trojan War. We know that this famous city was twice captured, the first time by Hercules, in the year 1760; the second, some forty years later, by the army of the Greeks led by Agamemnon." Next in order of gravity come philosophical, allegorical, and moral fables. Lowest in rank are the fables "invented merely for pleasure" and, he continued, "such is the *fable* of Psyche." (Our understanding that the tale of Psyche in *The Golden Ass* by Apuleius is not only a fable but also a Neoplatonic allegory—illustrating the agreeably erotic adventures of the soul in its search for the Good—postdates the *Encyclopédie*.) What Homer himself thought of war and warriors is the subject of a later section of this essay. One thing is certain: when faced with illustrations of Homer from the period when his works were read as if they were a military report, we can match them only with the most swashbuckling accounts of our author:

> Since the renewal of the arts, painters have chosen subjects from the *Metamorphoses* [of Ovid] . . . most of which require a commentary. What is lacking in the tableaux of Homer? They afford pleasure, power, exactitude, grand motivations and nobility; in short, everything that conduces to the most perfectly heroic subject, which is the principal object of an Art such as Painting. . . . The subjects of the *Metamorphoses* . . . often express nothing whatsoever.[18]

Caylus's admonitions were accepted by the schools.[19] Ovid rarely was among the subjects set for the École's prizes in the eighteenth century. If, however, a subject had first been featured in Homer and then received Ovidian treatment in the twelfth and thirteenth books of the *Metamorphoses*, it might be acceptable. In that case the key to success was a strongly pictorial treatment combined with the influence of ancient sculptures, then at the height of their fame—for example, the Florence *Niobe*. In such pictures the dominant theme was death. In the École royale, the children of Niobe, slaughtered by the caprice of the young gods, were considered no less essential to the subject than the tears of their rebellious mother (cat. no. 99).

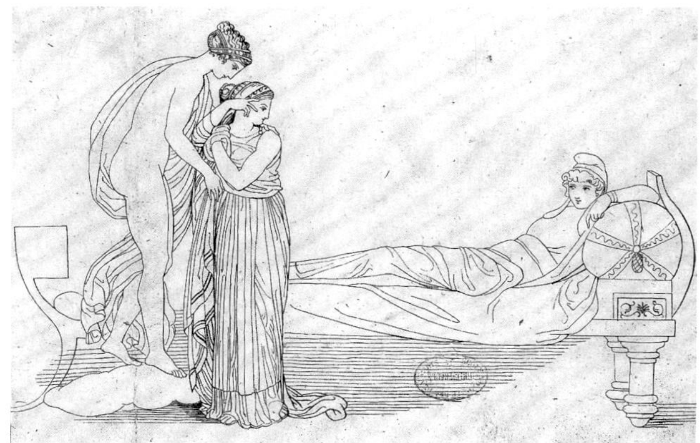

FIGURE 8 | JOHN FLAXMAN (1755–1826), "Venus Leading Helen to Paris" (1793), in *Iliade d'Homère / gravée par Thomas Piroli*, book 3, engraving 5.

Toward the end of the century the originality of a few great interpreters of Homer brought new insights to the dichotomy observed in the fine arts between a heroic and serious—in short, a Virgilian—reading of Homer, and a sensual, skeptical, and therefore Ovidian treatment. The English draftsman and sculptor John Flaxman was familiar with both Greek vase paintings and the humanist interpretations of the Quattrocento. He made engravings of Homeric subjects in which processions (*theoriai*) of protagonists unfold, each with his own individual silhouette and pose (fig. 8). Flaxman lacked the humor of Primaticcio, but he possessed a meditative sense of tragedy quite outside the range of the Paris Academy. The young Ingres learned the most from Flaxman, incorporating his lessons into the painting that won him the Prix de Rome in 1801 (cat. no. 24). The master of this newfound taste for classical antiquity was David, and in his studio two groups conducted a refined but passionate debate. One side earned the more attractive names: the "Thinkers," "Primitives," "Greeks," or "Beards," led by one Maurice Quaï,[20] who had himself dubbed "the Agamemnon"! Quaï left nothing to posterity but the ambition of a Homeric masterpiece, *Patroclus Sending Briseis Back to Agamemnon*, painted "on a thirty-foot canvas"[21] of which nothing remains, not even a sketch. It was never finished. These "Greeks" were devotees of line, like Flaxman; their opponents were the "Romans," who cultivated sculptural volume. The art students' debate between Greeks and Romans produced brilliant contrasts of style and contributed to the renewal of history painting, which was then stuck somewhere between the vulgar facility of Rococo and patriotic/revolutionary pomp. For a while the paintings of Ingres—for example his *Wounded Venus* (1803; Kunstmuseum, Basel)—combined the Greece of vase painting with the Rome of the Augustan bust. That astonishing fusion of cold, nervous, ironic, erotic draftsmanship and powerful, heroic volumes is perfectly illustrated in his Prix de Rome work *Achilles Receives the Ambassadors of Agamemnon* (cat. no. 24). In their later careers Ingres and his master David did not always contrive so satisfying a synthesis. While visiting Paris in 1801, Flaxman singled out Ingres's handsome if rather scholastic achievement.[22] Ingres, he perceived, spoke both Latin (the statuesque envoys) and Greek (the group sensually arranged around the lyre). The piece with which James Pradier won the sculpture prize in 1813 similarly reconciled these antagonistic styles (cat. no. 49). Artists such as Anne-Louis Girodet-Trioson, technically adept but lacking in vigor, returned to this synthetic style in works like *Aeneas Meets the Shade of Dido* (an illustration in his *Énéide, suite de compositions,* engraved by Lancrenon), but it gradually fell out of use in the academic art of the nineteenth century.

Young artists were perhaps particularly sensitive to this style. The pupils of both David (e.g., Langlois, cat. no. 35) and Ingres (e.g., Flandrin, cat. no. 104) imparted spirituality and vigor to their volumes, as did dozens of sculptors whose reputations I hope this book will restore. In 1859 Alexandre Falguière contrived a combat of heroes and horses (cat. no. 94) that is something more than a mere play of musculature. In both sculpture and painting this balance was long maintained in the art of the sketch. Individuals or groups were set down in rough outline using thick impasto, volumes were defined by their contrasts, while speed of execution imparted urgent life to the draftsmanship. The considered lines of the definitive composition often dissipated this urgency. The spirit of Homer is better adapted to the vivacity of the sketch than the frozen immobility of the completed work.

HORROR AND PASSION

The loyalties of history painting are necessarily owed to war. But to what war? A precise illustration of Homer's combat narratives might, it was feared, reveal nothing so much as the poet's underlying pacifism. This was the period when soldiers went to war wearing lace, and there was a certain reluctance to display "heroic butchery" in all its gory detail. On this point Lessing and Caylus are at one: no blood should fall on the painted battlefield.[23] When reality was imitated without the purifying effects of tragedy or aesthetics, mere horror resulted. But in relation to classical subjects, Diderot was less certain. He was more than a little tempted by the language of violence, which he termed passion. For him Boucher was a "stranger to veritable taste, truth, right notions, and to the severity of art"[24]—in short, to all the criteria by which Diderot condemned the "overt libertinism, the glitter, the pom-poms, the breasts and buttocks, the epigram of Boucher." Diderot therefore proposed one or two exemplary brutes—for example, Diomedes. Repainting in his own words a work of François Doyen, in 1761 he reproached the painter for his omission of spurting blood and splintering bones: "I should have raised Diomedes on a heap of corpses. Blood would have run at his feet. Terrifying in appearance and attitude, he would have menaced the goddess with his javelin."[25]

The ambiguous fascination of bestiality was guaranteed to alarm French rationalism. Depictions of the lumbering Cyclops Polyphemus by artists ranging from Tempesta to Goya, however, have forced art lovers to contemplate that very theme; among the most famous examples are Annibale Carracci's frescoes in the Palazzo Fava in Bologna. Diderot deemed this monster a fit subject for painting: "Virgil's Polyphemus is horrific, but he is beautiful."[26] Or perhaps not. Among the "Additions to the Letter on the Deaf and the Dumb" we find a letter written to a sensitive young lady that includes the following words: "Poetry makes us love images that would be unbearable in painting: our imagination is less scrupulous than our eyes."[27] Diderot would, he said, find intolerable a painting of "Polyphemus cracking in his teeth the bones of one of Ulysses' companions. Who could feel anything but horror at the spectacle of a giant holding a man crossways in his enormous mouth, with blood running down his beard and onto his chest?"[28] Here is a further Ovidian scene representing the repulsive Argus decapitated by Mercury: "This sleeping Argus is very lean, very dry, as a guardian should be, but he's stiff and hideous in a way that no painted figure should be. And this cow lying down between him and Mercury, it's just a cow, no pain, no *passion*, no boredom, nothing that indicates the metamorphosis."[29] One can thus make an informed guess as to whether Diderot would have liked what the École's painters made of Mercury and Argus (cat. nos. 14–16).

Diderot was asking these questions of himself. The grandeur and violence that he desired in painted figures, which he termed *passion*, was something venerated in greater or lesser measure by all the theoreticians and critics of the time, from Lessing to Shaftesbury and Caylus. But what, exactly, it is, they seem unable to say. Clearly it is no longer heroic patriotism. The eighteenth century wanted no new *Franciade*. Yet passion for passion's sake was the prevailing aesthetic in the Academy, where a competition for the study of an expressive head (*tête d'expression*) had been instituted by Caylus himself. It involved painting or sculpting from life a specific expression or passion, which was often modeled by an actor or actress. There was something schematic about this passion. So often in the work of the history painters it rages in the void. By conscious reference to Homeric characters, David d'Angers, Ramus, and Rude (cat nos. 55, 48, 43), managed to avoid this schematization. In the gaze of their Andromaches, Laocoöns, and Philoctetes we perceive the revolt of reason and, indeed, of humanity as a whole against the malice and injustice of the gods.

In his *Laocoön* (III) Lessing vehemently rejected Caylus's arguments on this subject. The example he chose was one of the most intelligent mise-en-scènes in all of Greek epic, although the scene itself is far from epic. For Caylus expressive passion was the key. The painter representing Helen at the Scaean gates should therefore paint not Helen herself (a white veil should mask her body) but "the avid gaze and other marks of admiration displayed on the faces of men whom age had frozen";[30] not female beauty but senile lubricity; not an imaginative staging of the scene but unbridled passions registered in facial expressions. Lessing demanded a sight of Helen's nudity and cared little about the salacious grimaces of old men. The solution preferred by all the theoreticians was, as we know, to avoid outbursts of lascivious violence or physical ugliness, to avoid the moment when the serpents crush Laocoön's cry and instead choose the fertile or suggestive moment. This was the moment when passion assumed a stable, dense, intelligent form. Neither Lessing nor Caylus, however, could identify the fecund moment in Helen's walk along the battlements by the Scaean gates. There they were faced with a typically Homeric composition made to bring a smile to the lips rather than a tear to the eye. And this was a problem in itself, for what was such a smile doing in an epic of grandeur and passion? Ronsard catches exactly the smile of Priam and his companions in his *Sonnets for Helen* (II, lxvii):

> It should be no surprise, said the good old men
> On the Trojan wall, watching *la belle Hélène*,
> If for so much beauty we suffer so much pain.

In Ronsard's century, epic was not required to give lessons in either grandeur or passion, and Helen's transparent robes could display her beauty among women nearly as beautiful as herself in front of admiring old men, as they all looked down on the combats of moderately ferocious warriors.

By Diderot's time, however, passion had become obligatory. He therefore detects it in Homer: "Do you want to hear the words that pain inspires in a father who has just lost his son? Listen to Priam speaking to Achilles . . . : 'I am at your feet, and I kiss your hands, stained as they are with the blood of my son.'"[31] A single word in this translation betrays the weakness of Homeric interpretation in the eighteenth century. Homer does not speak of Achilles as the killer of Hector but rather as *paiodophonos*, a child killer or son killer in general: the killer of all Priam's sons and of all sons of all fathers. Priam hates all wars and all warriors, not only the murderer of his child. Passion reduced to the instant loses both power and universality. It becomes bourgeois drama. To avoid Boucher it succumbs to Greuze.

THE WORLD'S TEACHER

The stifling effect of heroic enthusiasm on the reading of Homer and on readers of Homer was more than matched by another influence—that of scholarship. Alexander was able to conquer the world, it was said, because Aristotle had made him learn his Homer by heart. Aristotle's "lesson" was constantly depicted with conviction (e.g., by Eugène Delacroix at the Assemblée Nationale). Alexander took the copy of the *Iliad* given him by Aristotle on his campaigns and treated it as his greatest treasure, locking it up in a casket captured from Darius.[32] He who read Homer, it seemed, found knowledge and wisdom enough to enable him to dominate the universe. The actions described in the *Iliad* and the *Odyssey* unfold on earth and on sea, among the living and among the dead. It was therefore concluded not that Homer had a vivid imagination but that he knew everything about all things and had the answer to every question. Historians and geographers—especially Herodotus, the first historian—constructed their weltanschauung on the basis of what could be seen from the plain of Troy, which afforded a rather shallow prospect.

Over the centuries, adoring compilers have created a vast literature detailing Homer's scientific, historical, and philosophical achievements. These scholars—who include Heinrich Schliemann and the distinguished twentieth-century classicist Victor Bérard—entrusted themselves confidently to Homer's winds, currents, and islands like that poor sailor Ulysses, who experienced a series of fatal shipwrecks.[33] Homer's astronomy was taken for the real thing[34] when, in truth, it was like the dead reckoning of Ulysses, who got lost in every ocean he sailed. Troy was sought, nay, discovered where Homer, in his poetic fantasy, had placed it. Jean-Baptiste Le Chevalier made his *Voyage de la Troade* in the years 1785 and 1786. He heroically asserts that "without regard for the Ancients and Moderns, who had declared the theater of the *Iliad* to have been destroyed, I was convinced I would rediscover it just as the greatest of Poets and the most exact of geographers had depicted it."[35] Comte Choiseul-Gouffier created an impeccable "Picture of the plain of the Troad, with a map geometrically made in 1785–86" (fig. 15). Many others similarly discovered and mapped their "historic" Troad.

The more lucid were merely amused to see how easily a justification for any belief could be plucked from Homer's hexameters. Seneca noted that all schools of thought claimed to derive from Homer.[36] But the Greek bard could not persuade Montaigne to believe in anything at all:

> Is it possible that Homer really wanted to say all that people have made him say, and that he really did provide us with so many and so varied figurative meanings that theologians, legislators, military leaders, philosophers, and all sorts of scientific authors (no matter how differently they treat him) can refer to him and cite his authority as the Master General of all duties, works, and craftsmen, the Counselor General of all enterprises? Anyone on the lookout for oracles and predictions has found plenty of material there."[37]

A still more skeptical and subtle literary critic, Rabelais makes extravagant fun of all those who take Homer for the gospel truth. He does this first in the prologue to *Gargantua*, then allows his hero to take up his pen in the *Letter to Pantagruel*, where Gargantua's program of scholarship omits Homer altogether. Rabelais suspects that "Homer, paragon of all philologers" wrote prompted by alcohol, "eating and drinking."[38] A shared pleasure in words brought the humanists closer to the Greeks than any that came after them; they drank Homeric gaiety at its source.

Most other readers, earlier or later, treated Homer with religious veneration, although what they worshiped was not so much the Homeric text as the commentaries based on it. They allowed themselves to perceive neither irony nor fantasy in these ancient verses. We must therefore attempt to do the same, if only in order to respect history and understand the past. A pontificating gravity marks the features of Homer and his protagonists in the innumerable variations on the classical and academic style produced by the École royale (later the École des beaux-arts). But a debate arose among Homer's interpreters concerning the person of Homer himself, which enriched even the most modest works. Perhaps Homer himself had, in his genius, foreseen it. The debate left its most visible traces in the lineaments of the poet's face. The ancient accounts, which many painters chose to illustrate (see "The Historical Background and the Homeric World"), attributed to Homer the features of an old sage, like Nestor. The Academies relished this cliché. The poet, blind and endowed with a long beard, is seen teaching music and beauty to young shepherds or craftsmen in city squares or amid the market stalls (cat. nos. 1, 3, 4). The ancient pseudo-historians accorded the poet a divine lineage. Consequently, in 1894, during the Symbolist years, Marcel Béronneau, a pupil of Gustave Moreau, painted Apollo in the guise of Homer: "dark, dark, dark, amid the blaze of noon" stood the god of light[39] (cat. no. 9). Homer, the *poète maudit* wandering through the land in search of popular recognition, was bitterly described by the sculptor Étienne Falconet in his tempestuous correspondence with Diderot.[40] Falconet believed that Homer had died of hunger and was celebrated only posthumously. But why stop there? From the

Revolution through the nineteenth century, André Chenier's poem "The Blind Bard" set the tone, with Homer acquiring not merely the mask of heroism awarded to his heroes but the halo of a martyr to boot. A sightless soothsayer like Tiresias, Homer now became an omniscient beggar, an immortal genius in an ailing mortal body, fighting in academic representations the same solitary battle as those other literary invalids, Cervantes and Leopardi. The romantic cliché that bestowed on the blind Homer the prestige of a martyr flourished in examination pieces for the École des beaux-arts. Homer's thought, however, has nothing in common with that of an anchorite or a mendicant monk.

Homer between Vice and Virtue

Under the heading "Heroes" in his *Dictionary of the Arts of Painting, Sculpture, and Engraving* (1792), Watelet requires that the artist bestow on each character in an epic a moral function, the aspect of a specific virtue:

> Homer is no less master to artists than to poets, and the artist should express the idea he gives of *heroes.* Their nature should be superior to that of humanity. . . . Although in their youth they are not wholly Apollos, they at least resemble Antinous; in the flower of adulthood, although they are not the *Olympian Jupiter,* it should be recognized that they are inferior to Jupiter alone. . . . Their majestic old age displays no hint of decrepitude. . . . [I]t has the authority of wisdom.[41]

These pious clichés inspired by the statues then in vogue are wholly at odds with Homer's detachment if, that is, one is willing to read Homer as he wrote. Pierre de Lancre, the great Inquisitor of witchcraft, no doubt read Homer merely in order to convict him. In 1607, he demanded that Homer be placed on the index: "He makes of this same Achilles a lunatic transported with rage, spiteful and cruel. . . . Of Agamemnon a great mastiff. Of Patroclus a slut. . . . Of Hector a raving madman. . . . Of Nestor, a charlatan."[42] Here, at least, are less exemplary faces. And what of the immortals, who behave with a modicum of decency in the *Odyssey* only because Odysseus asks them to! Left to their own devices they swap partners, drink to excess, shamelessly tell lies, and happily set upon each other on the battlefield. Between the vicious author read by his enemies and the virtuous author identified by his well-meaning partisans, Homer inspired images as ambiguous as they were false.

Not all is virtue in the private lives of Homer's gods and heroes. And not all the bizarreries—strange acts of warriors and immortals—were invented by Ovid. Ulysses undoubtedly lies a great deal—to women, to his adversaries, and, indeed, to his friends and family. No less certain is the disrespect shown for the sacred laws of marital fidelity by Agamemnon, Achilles, Neoptolemus, Paris, and Helen. The medieval versions of the Trojan War therefore rewrote the narrative, clearly distinguishing the "good" Hector and Aeneas from the "bad" Greeks. True, Virgil was somewhat embarrassed by Aeneas's boorishness in abandoning Dido and offering pathetic excuses to her ghost. The artists who depicted this scene had trouble salvaging even a modicum of honor for Aeneas (cat. no. 91) but in the long run this domestic tragedy could be overlooked in the name of a higher interest—history. Had Aeneas remained, Rome would never have been founded. In the sixteenth century, when scholars gave up these medieval rewritings in favor of Homer himself, they were somewhat reluctant to face the reality of his mendacious, cowardly, malicious gods and heroes. Consequently the author and his creations, mortals and immortals alike, were all condemned under the same head, as though the sins of his wayward protagonists had been committed by the author. At this point, literary criticism rediscovered the words of Plato, Homer's earliest and greatest enemy, the philosopher of idealism and founder of the original Academy.

In the *Republic,* Plato drew up a list of the misdeeds of Zeus and Hera.[43] He was reluctant to admit that Zeus, the creator of all things, was also the creator of evil, and scandalized to see the king of the gods distribute fortune and misfortune from his jars of good and evil in such arbitrary fashion. Misleading dreams sent to Agamemnon; arrows perfidiously launched from the heavens to exacerbate the bloody confusion of mortal combat; the passions and weaknesses of the heroes: in the Homeric narrative every crime and every vice has a divine origin.[44] Plato was most afraid of the charm exerted by poetic license, the poetic lie that becomes a divine principle in the *Iliad* and a literary methodology in Homeric storytelling. Walking by the banks of the Ilissos, Socrates warns his interlocutor, the naïve Phaedrus, against both the poet who recounts the crimes of Helen and the simplistic explanations that destroy the poetry of storytelling and lead to atheistic materialism.[45] How difficult it is to interpret a beautiful lie! But this is what I now attempt.

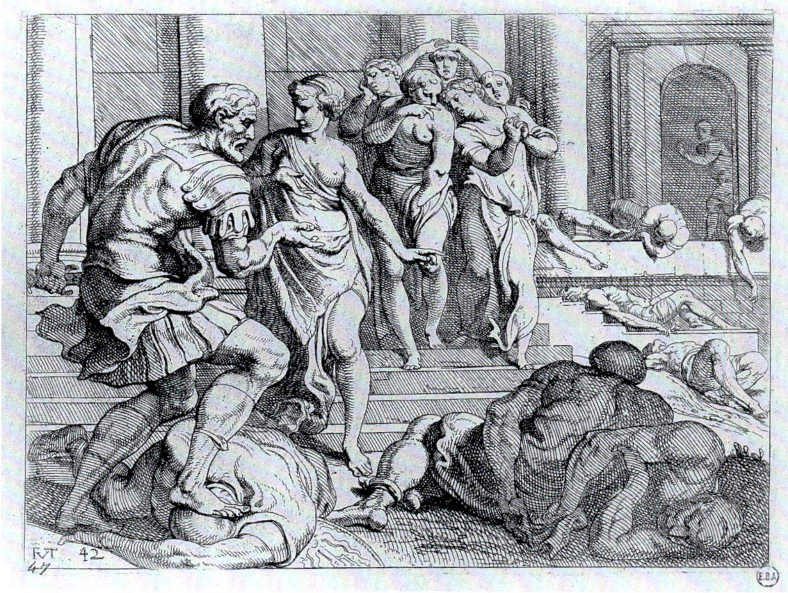

FIGURE 9 | THEODOR VAN THULDEN (1606–1676) after Primaticcio (1504–1570), "Ulysses Condemns the Guilty Serving-Women" (1633), in *Les Travavx d'Vlysse, desseignez par le sievr de Sainct Martin, de la façon qv'ils se voyent dans la maison royalle de Fontainebleav.*

HOMER MORALIZED

The prevailing tone in Homer is the rivalry between gods and men, at the root of which is a sense of divine injustice; between the *Iliad* and the *Odyssey*, the interpreter observes, Zeus somewhat belatedly begins to teach the Olympians the notion of justice.[46] It is a notion entirely at variance with their habits, and Zeus cannot count himself very successful. The *Odyssey* is slightly more moral than the *Iliad*, opening with Zeus deploring the unjust fate suffered by Ulysses, who is held captive on her island by the goddess Calypso, there to serve her immortal pleasures. The poem ends with those carousers the suitors dispatched for their debauchery; they have earned an ignoble death and are refused burial. The gods, however, invariably persist in their criminal intents and acts and their relentless persecution of defenseless mortals. Achilles himself cites the worst offenders, the two childishly malicious gods who persecute Niobe and her innocent children (*Il.* 24.602–17). Laocoön, Iphigenia, and Ulysses are among the many martyrs of divine sadism.

What is the reader in quest of moral instruction to make of these imperfect heroes, these gods wedded to their petty resentments? Some deny the evidence and decree that Ulysses and Agamemnon are men with great and beautiful souls. The seventeenth century abounds in such demonstrations of morality. Melchior Tavernier invented splendid ones for the prints of the Gallery of Ulysses illustrated by Theodor Van Thulden.[47] When Ulysses spends a year in the arms of Circe, Tavernier notes that "pleasures, charming though they be, eventually lead to a tragic and fatal event." When Ulysses massacres his serving women (fig. 9), this handsome deed teaches us that "a Prince who wishes to impose justice in his land must begin by wreaking justice on his servants when they are disloyal to him." Throughout the seventeenth century, Ulysses wore the features of Bluebeard under the mask of Tartuffe, and it is no surprise that this paradoxical manifestation garnered little sympathy.

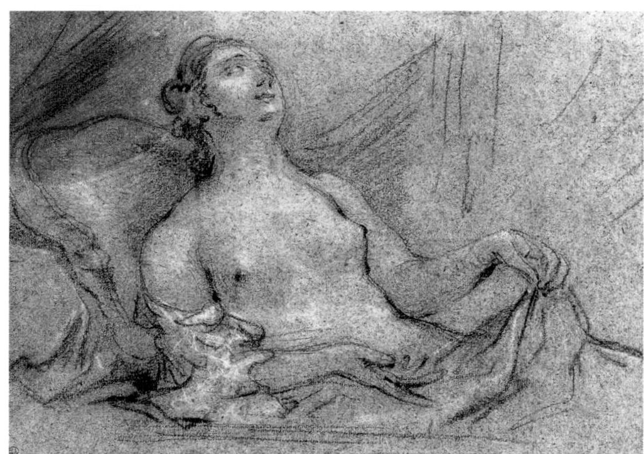

FIGURE 10 | MICHEL-FRANÇOIS DANDRÉ-BARDON (1700–1783), *Danaë Receiving the Golden Rain* (n.d.) Charcoal with white highlights on paper, 23.7 x 32.4 cm.

Others exaggerated still further and tried to dissolve the sulfur in holy water. Certain examples may appeal to the reader's taste for the picturesque. Pierre Lescalopier, a Jesuit priest, observed with satisfaction in his *Theologia Homeri* (1660) that Homer speaks of Zeus as eternal, thus indicating or prefiguring his successor, the god of the Christians. True, Lescalopier is at a loss to explain the finitude of the Greek gods, who, like Thetis, take time to move from one place to another. Zeus is perhaps neither omniscient nor omnipotent. No matter; our Jesuit is happy to discover in Homer a monotheist,[48] with one god, Zeus. It is in this guise that he reigns in many eighteenth-century academic pictures (cat. no. 18): a serious, full-bearded god imbued with his own immensity; an eternal father perched in the upper regions of the sky; generally surrounded by pretty young women, who lead him by the nose.

Translator of the *Iliad* and the *Odyssey*, Madame Dacier—despite having read Homer in Greek—devised a Christian theology on his behalf, and perceived in the enforced fall of Vulcan the fall of Satan. The all-powerful Zeus is divided into a Trinity: "As a theological poet, he [Homer] shared a single idea of the simple and unique essence of God in several persons, as if in so many attributes, under the different names of Jupiter, Juno, Neptune, etc." Thereafter the torrent of Christian sentiments excavated their own channels in Homer. In Madame Dacier's adaptation, the libertine Zeus weeps tears of contrition: Don Juan in danger acts the prude. In the scene on Mount Ida, he is excited by the perfumes and attractions of his lawful wedded wife and is suddenly transformed into a faithful husband—or at least a gallant one: "Juno smiled: 'Well, my husband! Do I now seem / As beautiful as Calisto? As pretty as Alcmene? / Am I the equal of Europa and Semele?'/ 'Let these names,' he said, 'from your lips depart. / You are avenged, and they effaced from my heart.'" Danae, who merits a mention in Homer for her intercourse with the divine light—Zeus as sky god—is taken to prefigure the Immaculate Conception. Compare her depiction by Dandré-Bardon (fig. 10) with Bernini's *Saint Teresa*, caught in mystical ecstasy.[49] In a short and moving book, Simone Weil much more sincerely compares Prometheus, Jupiter's victim, with Christ; both sacrificed themselves for the sake of humanity.[50] For a long time the Prometheus of the painters did indeed resemble Christ (cat. no. 106).

Jesuit education encouraged the study of mythology. Given the distancing effects of time and improbability, mythology seemed less dangerous than the eroticism of certain exponents of northern realism or the divine boudoir scenes of Boucher. The church was, in a sense, a victim of its own sincere admiration of antiquity. It thought of Latin and Greek as holy languages when they were merely beautiful.[51] In the name of the humanities and of Beauty—born Greek but necessarily Christian and Catholic—it wanted to conserve and put to use the ancient myths and their evocation of a pre-Christian world. A moral justification was required and assumed. According to Christian readings, the monsters of the pagan world had perished at the hands of heroes such as Telemachus and Mentor, who prefigured the upright Christian hero. The quarrels and dalliances described by Homer and Ovid provided sinners with a delicious opportunity to contemplate the mortal dangers they had escaped by having been born after the Revelation. Baroque Rome was therefore covered with "the filth of the gods," as La Bruyère described the works of the Carracci brothers.[52] The church used amoral ancient narratives to attract the sinner toward a sweet redemption.

FÉNELON AND HOMERIC FELONS

The goals of bishop and author François de Salignac de la Motte Fénelon (1651–1715) were not unlike those of the Jesuits, although his methods were somewhat different. He distrusted Homer and felt obliged to rewrite the Homeric narrative *ad usum delphini*—the future *dauphin*, the duc de Bourgogne, grandson of Louis XIV, for whom Fénelon was the tutor. This retelling became *The Adventures of Telemachus*. Appointed archbishop of Cambrai, Fénelon denounced the Greek original from the height of his pulpit:

> Homer's heroes do not resemble honest people, and his gods are quite beneath the heroes themselves, so unworthy are they of the idea of the gentleman. No one would want a father as vicious as Jupiter, nor a wife as insupportable as Venus. And who would want a friend as brutal as Mars or a servant as thieving as Mercury? The enemy of mankind seems to have invented these gods expressly to authorize crimes and ridicule divinity.[53]

Thus the "swan of Cambrai." His sermons accurately stigmatize Mars—a mere armed brute even in the arms of Vulcan's wife; Zeus and Hera's hellish marriage; and Mercury's lighthearted killing and pilfering.

When he came to compose fairy tales for his royal pupil, this same Fénelon read his own love of virtue into Homer.[54] Thus, in *Telemachus* the bawdy mendacious gods are consigned to oblivion, replaced by Mentor, whose wise old features disguise none other than the chaste goddess Athena, now converted to a form of Christianity whose blandness pervades the moralizing paintings of the École (see "The Adventures of Telemachus"). For the protagonists of *Telemachus*, temptation wears a woman's face, and they only succumb to it in order to feel contrition, an obligatory stop on the road to redemption. Fénelon's Catholicism was of a more serene and quietist temper than that of the Baroque, borrowing from antiquity a charming panorama replete with springs, grasslands, nymphs, and noble sentiments. In his way he, too, restored the Homeric world, finding for it a place in Christian history before Revelation and almost before sin. If the world could be Christian before Christ, if Telemachus could encounter beauty, harmony, and wisdom in a desert peopled with anchorites (having put aside the temptation of a few seductive dryads), it was clear that God had loved humankind for all eternity. Fénelon, in turn, detected certain "Christian" figures in Homer, some of them a little more plausible than Zeus: Was Nausicaa not an example of the virtuous virgin shaming the court gossips?[55] Fénelon first attempted a simple translation of the *Odyssey* shortly before writing *Telemachus* (perhaps in 1693). His *Précis of the Odyssey* steered the poem toward good taste, good governance, and Christianity. It is easy to understand why his choice then fell on the Telemachy, a young man's happy discovery of the beauty of the world and its inhabitants. By isolating it from its context, he could depict a world in which sin had germinated but was not yet rankly flourishing. Telemachus and Calypso are thus made to appreciate the glamour of the forbidden but also to delight in the taste of repentance. The mature Ulysses, the roving husband (in every way), could not—since he lacked all sense of remorse—serve to illustrate Fénelon's theses. Ulysses lives in the world of choice and self-will, Fénelon in the narrow circle of sin, shame, and submission. His Telemachus submits to the superior wisdom of Hasaël. The perils of pleasure or curiosity hold no fears for Ulysses, who doesn't fret about morals before taking the plunge. He is neither obsessed with modesty nor afraid of lechery and luxury. He broods on neither prejudice nor remorse. Fénelon, by contrast, perpetually expects, dreads, and desires exciting ordeals of the soul. He is tempted by evil, knowing that goodness exists only for those who believe in evil.

One De Périsse, prefacing an edition of Fénelon's *Telemachus*, established an impeccable literary hierarchy founded on the moral value of the works assessed:

> The purpose of the *Iliad* is to show the fatal consequences of disunion among the heads of an army; the *Odyssey* shows what can be done by a king who combines courage and foresight; in the *Aeneid* the actions of a courageous and dutiful hero are depicted. But such individual virtues are not those on which the happiness of the human race depends. *Télémaque* goes well beyond all these levels in the grandeur, number, and extent of its moral views.[56]

Moral value or moral conformity? The reader may judge by some of the illustrations it inspired (see "The Adventures of Telemachus"). This overrefined story, in which the pleasures of humility rank high, centers on the character of Telemachus. Today's reader of the *Odyssey* tends to overlook the episodes of the Telemachy, but the young Telemachus should perhaps be compared to the subtle Nausicaa, who shares his age and has the same function as he on the distaff side. Legend consequently marries them off a few years after the end of the *Odyssey.* In the nineteenth century the École tended to turn Telemachus's intervention into a Christian parable. Thus, as late as 1880 Henri-Lucien Doucet depicted Telemachus as the prodigal son at his father's knees (cat. no. 77), whereas Homer had based his entire poem on the escapades of the unworthy father!

This moralizing platitude too closely resembles the image of a king counseled by the goddess of wisdom and therefore disinclined to intellectual or political independence. Like the Academicians, Fénelon read Homer as a manual of good governance. Now might be the moment to consider the civic side of Homer. The Ulysses of Homer and Sophocles is indeed princely, if only in the Machiavellian sense. But the virtue ascribed to him is quite different: a love of his subjects. The *Encyclopédie* is categorical on this point: "The perfect hero combines the abilities and courage of a great military leader with a sincere love and desire to promote his people's happiness."[57] In the eighteenth century the critic La Font de Saint-Yenne vaunted the merits of the *Iliad* and the *Odyssey* as a source of edifying historical subjects.[58] Among the subjects he himself suggests, however, few come from Homer. Like everyone else, he repeatedly turned to Aeneas, the docile pupil, son, and soldier. The politicians and gods of the *Iliad* and the *Odyssey* think more of their own interests and pleasures than the happiness of their subjects. If Homer was not to be consigned to deepest Tartarus or the inferno, one possibility remained: allegory. Homer's work, on this account, showed not the forthright speech of the soldier but the allegorical language of mysticism.

THE MIRACLES OF ALLEGORY

Homer does resort to allegory on one occasion. Voltaire rightly admired the scene, which arises out of the narrative with the beauty of a thought taking form in the poet's mind. The elderly Phoenix, one of Agamemnon's ambassadors to Achilles, speaks of Folly or Ruin (*Ate*) and Prayers/Supplications (*Litai*). Prayers, he says, are the daughters of Zeus—limping, wrinkled, and squinting—who avenge themselves on the impious by begging Zeus to send Folly where they have been refused. Folly, by contrast, is "strong and swift" (*Il.* 9.502). Their words are on Phoenix's lips in the scene painted by the young Ingres (cat. no. 24), who had read his Homer closely:

> We do have Prayers, you know, Prayers for
> forgiveness,
> daughters of mighty Zeus . . . and they limp and halt,
>
> trudging after Ruin, . . .
>
> trying to heal the wounds.[59]

Homer's tragic cortege deserved illustration and found it in Flaxman's piteous procession. Ingres's Prix de Rome–winning painting brought to this composition the ambiguous personalities of the ambassadors. In the ninth book of the *Iliad,* the allegory of the seductions of *Ate*, of Folly ruling the world, and of the difficult, vindictive *Litai* provides a counterpoint to the all too human embassy of Agamemnon. It should certainly have discouraged the moralists from attempting allegorical explanations of Homer's shifting and unstable observations. The shifting and unstable, however, offered no reassurance, and so Homer's stories were scrutinized for concealed and intangible moral principles or lies serving an allegorical truth.

Etymology offered a helping hand in this respect. Was Zeus an allegory of the Heavens (the root means "light from the sky") and Hera of the Ether? (The etymology of her name is more obscure.) Even if they were, artists were hard put to make of their embrace on Mount Ida (cat. no. 21) an allegory of the aerial elements.[60] The obscure Heraclitus, presumed author of the *Quaestiones Homericae*, made Homeric allegory his stock-in-trade; for centuries he furnished readings for those who refused to understand Homer. Allegory thus saved the honor of the Homeric gods—indeed of all gods entertained by human misfortune. In the bickering of hate-filled rival gods the allegorists perceived abstract principles. Thus, Ares and Aphrodite are the two principles of Discord and Love that govern this world. "Apollo is opposed to Neptune because heat and wet are eternally at odds; Minerva opposes Mars because wisdom always opposes folly and violence."[61] These abstractions are invariably reducible to allegories of natural forces and primitive struggles. The use of allegorical language, however, does not necessarily weaken artistic interpretation. The world must indeed have begun with elemental hand-to-hand combat, of which the Titans' rebellion is but one reflection and of which sports provide a scarcely more civilized simulacrum in our own day. The physical effort in such struggles fascinated sculptor and draftsman alike, and such scenes were endlessly reproduced in the Academies. Hercules kills the Nemean lion as much for pleasure as for the salvation of humanity. The forces of nature embodied in the gods can be seen in similarly ambiguous terms: as natural forces which mortals can only endure or as oppressors to be resisted in the name of freedom and dignity.

No less allegorical are the combats that unfold in Ulysses' soul.[62] When putting Odysseus on the stage in the early seventeenth century, Pedro Calderón de la Barca and Claudio Monteverdi hesitated between a pagan reading of Homer, spoken by smilingly cynical actors, and Christian allegory voiced by angelic or metaphorical figures. In *Il ritorno d'Ulisse in patria (The Return of Ulysses to His Homeland)* (1640) Monteverdi subordinates his music entirely to the intelligence of the ancient text as evoked and commented upon by his librettist, yet his hero is surrounded by gods and allegories such as Human Fragility, Time, Destiny, and Love. Calderón composed two interpretations of the legend of Circe, one of them profane, the other sacred. In *El mayor encanto amor (The Greatest Enchantment: Love)* he wrote a pagan allegory. In *Los encantos de la culpa (The Enchantments of Sin)* he wrote a Christian allegory. In *El mayor encanto* the charms of female intelligence are celebrated; in *Los encantos* an *auto-sacramental* ("sacred act," a play exalting the presence of God in the Eucharist), the allegorical figures of Sin, Understanding, and Pleasure drive Ulysses into the Vessel of the sovereign Church, accompanied by the music of the Corpus Christi. Like the dramatist and priest Calderón, the allegorized Ulysses wore a monk's habit some days of the week and a hypocrite's smirking countenance on others.

Fortunately poetry and art enriched and diversified the simplistic utterances of allegory and by means of sheer imagination breathed some life into them. In Homer's presentation, Hermes, who escorts the souls of the dead to the underworld, became the bat of Death, weary of his funereal job. In *The Golden Ass* he became the soul's soaring aspiration to purity. Raphael's pupils showed this aspiration to eternal life bursting forth from the frescoed wall of the Villa Farnesina (the Villa Farnesina Mercury, copied by Ingres; fig. 37). Brian's *Seated Mercury* (cat. no. 13) is a paradigm of the most intelligent nineteenth-century Parisian academic work, as intense and vivid as a poem by Alfred de Vigny. Death is tired of killing. He sits down to tie or untie his sandal, gazing at a world full of specters made by his own hand, and he craves the slumber desired by Vigny's

Moses, who wishes "to sleep the sleep of the earth." Hermes did not confine himself to escorting the dead, and the Greeks vaunted the beauty of Argus's executioner, a dangerous young Satan, a liar and thief who delighted in the bloom of blood. They handed this Hermes down to the artists: what could be more fascinating to the painter than an allegory of death renowned for tranquil sadism? The École des beaux-arts possesses many such images.

By contrast, the struggle between the rebirth of spring and the death of nature occupies a wider theater, that of Nature as a whole. Hades, sovereign lord of Death, carries off Persephone (Proserpine), the daughter of the harvest goddess Ceres. The myth created by the *Homeric Hymns* taught painters to combine the charms of a forest clearing with the violence of rape, feminine with masculine elements, and the power of desire with the peaceful life of the seasons (cat. nos. 19, 20). The landscapes painted by the École's nineteenth-century artists seem always aware of the contradictory charms of nature, beneath whose dusky bosks eternal crimes are concealed. The *Quaestiones Homericae* is an attempt to conceal or minimize the multifarious contradictions of the Homeric poems, as if allegory were childish by its very nature and could not "bear very much reality." Myth was wrapped in allegory like a mummy in its bandages. Mythology, however, is too complex to permit such confinement. In the spotlight of visual representation off come the bandages, revealing the body in all its color and sensuality.

MAN MADE THE GODS IN HIS OWN IMAGE

The fact is that the ancient gods did not conceal their desires, however allegorical these may have been. Pseudo-Lucian tells the story of the statue of Aphrodite of Cnidus, so perfect a symbol of sexual desire that devout worshipers often showered it with sperm.[63] The statue has disappeared, but its forms have been imitated ever since. The sculpture that Ingres sent to the École displays these very contours (cat. no. 11). The nineteenth-century students would caress her buttocks on the way to their exams, hoping to be inspired by her exuberant fecundity. We do not know whether, before Homer, the goddesses still clung to a certain modesty. Hera, fable tells us, was never unfaithful to her husband. That seems plausible since even Homer gives her no other lover than Zeus. Jupiter and Juno making love on Mount Ida had, even in antiquity, a certain erotic charge despite the fact that the couple was lawfully wedded (they were, it is true, brother and sister). In the Palazzo Farnese and in the bawdy engravings of their *Loves of the Gods*, Annibale and Agostino Carracci made nothing more of this episode than the *ars amatoria* in action. For all its libertine reputation, the eighteenth century could see nothing in the scene but an active and exhausting night spent—to judge by Jean-Jacques-François Le Barbier's representation (cat. no. 21)—in a very bourgeois and rather sordid alcove.

Homer contrives a number of allusions to the three goddesses who submitted to Paris's judgment. Their appearances in the text are not consistent, and they vacillate between the status, nature, and dignity of women, goddesses, and Graces. In their persons the entire history of art and beauty has departed from the letter and spirit of Homer. Between the *Iliad* and the *Odyssey* Homer transforms his Aphrodite from the gracious spouse of the worthy Hephaestus to the seductive Cypris. In so doing he moves from amiable allegory to cynicism. It is enjoyable to follow in the footsteps of Giordano Bruno and Edgar Wind and compare the three beauteous goddesses to the three Graces, who represent the three forms of pleasure: love divine, intellectual, and human.[64] But one must not forget that these three allegories make strategic use of their charms, which are those of goddesses, women, and lovers. When depicting the Judgment of Paris, not every artist forgot the violent episodes that preceded it: the rape of Thetis and the wedding of Peleus, at which the uninvited Eris (Discord) threw the golden apple inscribed "To the most beautiful" between the three goddesses.[65] Nor are the three candidates' bribes and trickery forgotten. These misogynist fantasies reappear in post-Renaissance figurations.

Was this blasphemy? Although he leaves his tales ambiguous, Homer bestows on the gods a flesh-and-blood existence and a destiny of defeat and death. Aphrodite is a dangerous adviser and an unfaithful wife and lover; Athena's excellent advice is useful but utterly ruthless; and Hera is a fluent and expert liar. If the gods were—as the philosopher would have them—perfect beings, they would lack what artists most require of them, namely, a dense, rich existence, not the hollow and abstract idea far removed from the work of art. Diderot argues the human and artistic inadequacies of Christianity with vertiginous blasphemy:

> If the Virgin Mary had been the mother of pleasure; or if, as the Mother of God, it had been her attractive eyes, her splendid breasts, her beautiful buttocks that had attracted the Holy Spirit onto her . . . ; if the Magdalene had had some kind of affair with Christ; if, at the Wedding at Cana, Christ, somewhat the worse for wear, and just a little nonconformist, had run his fingers over the breasts of one of the bridesmaids and the buttocks of Saint John, wondering whether he should stay faithful to the apostle of the soft chin hair; then you would see what our painters, poets, and sculptors could do . . . and how we should look upon the beauty to which we owe our birth, the incarnation of the Savior and the grace of our redemption.[66]

Audacity, liberty: the blasphemies of Diderot are imbued with the lesson of Homer. It was a further merit of these all-too-human gods that they justified the revolt of reason against belief.

The heavens had struck down earlier blasphemers, such as Don Juan or the lesser Ajax, and Diderot was sometimes afraid that his temerity might earn him a similar fate. Even the most audacious minds preferred to assail the ancient gods, wrapped in their purple cerements, rather than meddle with the current incumbent.

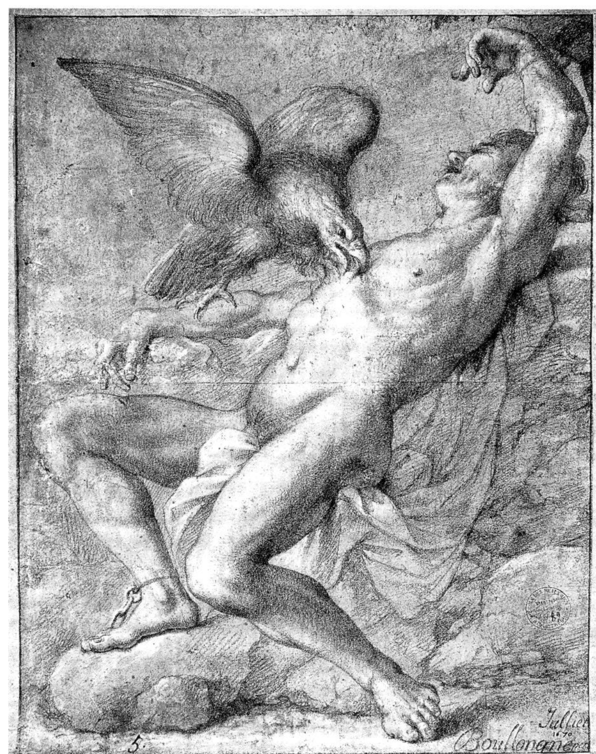

FIGURE 11 | LOUIS DE BOULOGNE THE ELDER (1609–1674), *Prometheus Bound*, 1670. Charcoal with white chalk highlights on paper, 56.2 × 41.8 cm.

The ancient fable was a better match for the aspirations of Enlightenment Europe than Christianity. Those who had come to find gods superfluous wanted myths that implied the death of God, and there was Greek thought, in all its fantasy, to supply them. Prometheus's resounding "No!" to the omnipotent could at last be heard. Like his brother Titans and Goethe's Mephistopheles, Prometheus was seen to escape his chains. Far from seeking Zeus's forgiveness, he sought to bring down the god and all his allies (fig. 11). Niobe, too, denounces the turpitude of those jealous gods who have vented their foul tempers on her innocent children. The injustices suffered by Niobe and Prometheus were also inflicted on Job. No god emerges unscathed from the scrutiny of myth.[67]

In the late eighteenth century, Flaxman and Füssli reverted to the wanton attitude shown to the gods by Primaticcio and the Carracci; indeed, the revolt of mankind against the puerile gods is the principal subject of their drawings. French history painting found this intellectual revolution quite beyond its powers. In France, perhaps under the influence of Caylus, the gods remained gods. They strolled among the clouds or burst forth fully armed from the heavens, bristling with their old-fashioned but indomitable magic. These works, in their way, paid homage to Homer's lucidity. Homer and his more intelligent readers had always known that his tales of their escapades undermined the gods.

"What are the gods of Homer, Aeschylus, Euripides, and Sophocles? The vices and virtues of humanity . . . personified, that is the true theogony; that is how we should view Saturn, Jupiter, Mars, Apollo, Venus, the Parcae, Love, and the Furies."[68] In the second book of the *Iliad* Zeus sends Agamemnon a misleading dream intended to cause the rout of the Greeks: he should attack Troy despite Achilles' absence. If he does, Troy will fall. But this is precisely Agamemnon's "dream" in the metaphorical sense. He would love to bring down Troy unassisted and, with it, Achilles' renown. George Steiner notes: "His dream is so efficacious just because it corresponds so fully to Agamemnon's spoken and unspoken thoughts."[69] Zeus serves to name or sanction Agamemnon's dream because he is that dream. In works of art the gods and monsters of mythology soon show their community with humankind.[70]

The Greeks elaborated a science of mythology, which is set out in Apollodorus's *Bibliotheca,* or *Library.* Apollodorus attempted to establish the common underpinning of Greek myth rather as, two thousand years later, the brothers Grimm did for European beliefs. A man of great imagination and critical acumen, Apollodorus concluded that history is composed of essentially disparate facts to which the historian finds it difficult to ascribe a coherent meaning. Myth, by contrast, is born perfect, spinning itself out as smoothly as the skein from a spindle, with a delicious whirring noise. Into the perfection of naïve belief and primitive myth Homer and the tragic poets inserted beings endowed with conscience and imagination, and these distorted and complicated matters. Herodotus is our witness:

> But it was only—if I may so put it—the day before yesterday that the Greeks came to know the origin and form of the various gods, and whether or not all of them had always existed; for Homer and Hesiod are the poets who composed theogonies and described the powers of the gods for the Greeks, giving them all their appropriate titles, offices and powers, and they [Homer and Hesiod] lived, as I believe, not more than four hundred years ago.[71]

Homer took primitive divinities without substance, desire, or life and made living beings of them; subsequently, his gods, reincarnated in poetic myth, lived with an autonomous life that testifies to the intelligence and critical acumen of the Greeks. There was little or no place for mysticism in these lives. If the gods are the poet's creation, they are also the creatures of the artist, who breathes spirit and life into matter. An artist's vision of a god is what the god was at birth, an agreeable figment of the human imagination. In paintings by academic artists, the sight of Minerva in flight above the head of Achilles is sometimes deemed ridiculous. But it illustrates an important truth: the goddess *was* born directly from the head of the hero. That is why she is in his image, that is, our own.

Homer between Barbarians and Civilization

In France the debate about Homer's morality raged on into the nineteenth century. His French readers were unanimous in condemning his defective sense of propriety. The pedagogues had so often exclaimed on the abundance of divine Homeric tableaux that they felt constrained to read him for themselves. And what did they find? Princes working with their hands, army chiefs serving themselves at dinner, and a queen of the gods (Juno) who washes before receiving Zeus's sexual favors.[72] This was much worse than any divine skullduggery. The rational and *précieux* seventeenth century and the enlightened eighteenth century thought these crude, brawling princes the products of a sordid and barbarous world. Fortunately, this world had since disappeared. Homer's talent had extended only to describing what he had seen; he had not thought to embellish his language and subject matter sufficiently to render it presentable. The defects and contradictions in Homer could now be accounted for by a single explanation.

The result of this ingenuous discovery was the so-called Quarrel of the Ancients and Moderns, which came to a head in the *querelle d'Homère.* On the one side were the Moderns—ranged behind Charles Perrault, their official spokesperson—who were happy to blot Homer out of literary history in floods of purified and civilized ink. The debate rang through the Parisian cafés and is described in Montesquieu's *Persian Letters* (Letter 34). Perrault had an eye for political advantage in accusing Homer of barbarity and praising what Voltaire would later call the "Century of Louis the Great" because, in his own more fortunate times, "the characters that they [the poets] give to their heroes are praiseworthy and heroic. . . . They do not portray them quarreling like market porters. . . ."[73] Why on earth, in so polite a century, should one read these sordid and primitive verses? For the Ancients—led by the good Madame Dacier—Homer's coarseness was excused precisely by the era in which he wrote and did not detract from his nobility. He spoke to us in the words of his barbarian epoch. The *précieuses* and aristocratic women assembled at Versailles or in the Parisian salons, whose purview did not necessarily extend far beyond questions of etiquette and royal love affairs, found it primitive and degrading to hear of princes and princesses undertaking domestic tasks or regaling each other with insults before coming to blows. On this point Voltaire was as satirical as Daumier: "As to what people call coarseness in Homer's heroes, let them laugh their full at the sight of Patroclus, in the ninth book of the *Iliad,* placing three legs of mutton in a pot, lighting the fire and blowing on it, and preparing dinner with Achilles; Achilles and Patroclus are nonetheless splendid."[74] In his very serious *Lettre de M. Eratou à M. Clocpitre* he added that "Princess Nausicaa . . . has nothing in common with the wife or daughter of a church warden."[75] In that case, why did she do the palace washing with her own hands?

FLIRTING WITH HOMER

Since Homer was ignorant of polite taste, he would have to be taught. Around 1700, translations of Homer came thick and fast. Regardless of their attitude toward Homer, they tended to follow the tone set by Paris—a tone that also informed the pictorial conventions. I must therefore single out for praise a Carthusian monk, Bernard Chamony, who reverently preserved the most audacious Homeric epithets in his French translation.[76] Chamony's Zeus was restored to his true Homeric status, namely, that of the "great god who used to herd goats." The godhead a goatherd! All the others, however, softened or purged the images and gestures of the original in accordance with the prescriptions of Antoine Houdar de La Motte, who triumphed as Homeric translator and adapter. A mere day laborer in the vineyard of literature, he set out in verse the guidelines he intended to follow, brazenly placing them in the mouth of Homer himself:

> There were strange gods in my time,
> And heroes swollen with pride.
> Its base kings gloried in crime.
> These things a poet should hide.
> Let decorum rule poet and sage.
> Respect the taste of your age:
> Though it may not to virtue incline
> It knows virtue better than mine.[77]

So no cooking for Achilles in De La Motte's translation. As in the Academy reception pieces, Achilles is dressed to the nines. Madame Dacier was the most illustrious of Homer's defenders, but she was also his most ferocious assassin.[78] Her translation is still more unfaithful to Homer's words than De La Motte's, and she justifies

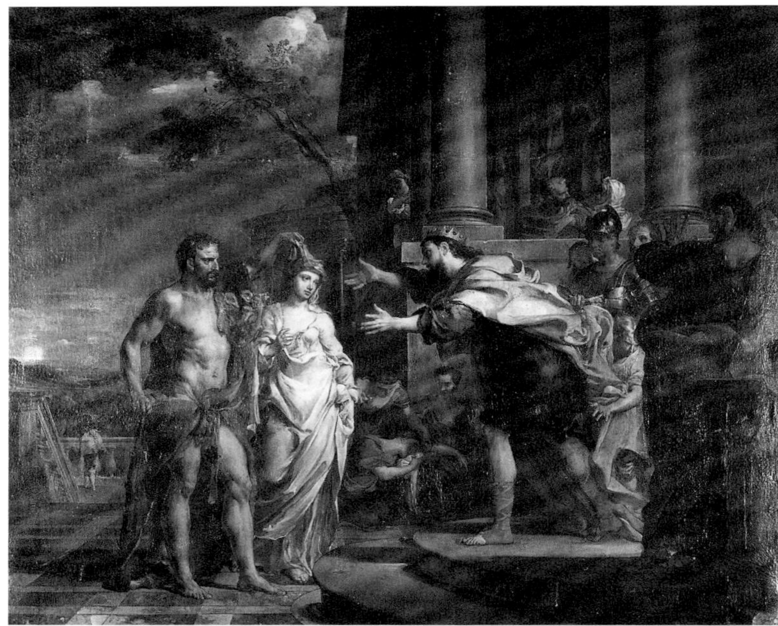

FIGURE 12 | LOUIS GALLOCHE (1670–1761), *Hercules Bringing Alcestis Back from the Underworld to Her Husband Admetus*, 1711. Oil on canvas, 155 × 188 cm. Royal Academy reception piece.

her omissions by commentaries she describes as "historical." In the *querelle d'Homère* the Moderns are the more classical (in today's sense of the word), applying what they thought to be the rules of perfection and beauty. Seeking to defend the authority rather than the liberties of Antiquity, the Ancients were scarcely less rule-bound.

Many painters transposed these principles into their art. One such was Louis Galloche: his Hercules wears a lion skin, it is true, but the *précieuses* whom he visits are arrayed on a country-house terrace that is surely within commuting distance of the Place Royale (fig. 12). In Clément Belle's painting Penelope wears a most fashionable dress (cat. no. 80). Only in Daumier's print is Achilles allowed anywhere near the cooking pots. No one is as badly betrayed, however, as are Ares and Aphrodite—alias Mars and Venus—in the seventeenth and eighteenth centuries. Homer describes them as incautious lovers cuckolding an excessively trusting husband under the eyes of the other gods, who punctuate their guffaws with ribald commentary:

> . . . but Lord Apollo goaded Hermes on:
> "Tell me, Quicksilver, giver of all good things—
> even with those unwieldy shackles wrapped around
> you,
> how would you like to bed the golden Aphrodite?"
>
> "O Apollo, if only!" the giant killer cried.
> "Archer, bind me down with triple those endless
> chains!
> Let all you gods look on, and all you goddesses too—
> how I'd love to bed that golden Aphrodite!"
> —OD. 8.334–42; F 8.377–84

In the time of Louis XIV, whom one could easily identify with Mars, there was no mention of Vulcan and the voyeuristic Rabelaisian gods. Mars then slept with Venus because he was the King of War and had a right to the warrior's furlough.

TROGLODYTE OR NOBLE SAVAGE?

The vanity of the Moderns eventually gave way to its exact contrary—the myth of the noble savage, with its thesis of a primitive temperament unsullied by civilization. The agent of this change, Jean-Jacques Rousseau, formulated a history of the world in which the military virtues were promoted to a starring role. In 1750, the first part of his *Discourse on the Arts and Sciences* celebrated the "heroes who twice vanquished Asia, once before Troy and once defending their homeland."[79] Rousseau deemed these quarrelsome Greeks more virtuous than later generations, who did not sufficiently respect the "defenders of the homeland" and devoted themselves instead to creating "images of every perversion of heart and mind, carefully selected from ancient mythology."[80] He was virulent in his condemnation of fable, which had manifestly been invented by the poets to corrupt precivilized man, of which Ulysses was the last specimen. The mendacious Ithacan passed for a citizen of primitive times, educated by the senses alone, the senses that never lie and equip one to see and act in the darkness of night and illiteracy. He is cited as an example to the young Émile in *Émile, or Education.* Ulysses loves nature and his little house is like the unfenced cottage of the noble savage. Rousseau had Moreau the Younger engrave some Homeric scenes for *Émile.* They include *Thetis Plunging the Infant Achilles in the Waters of the Styx* (bk. 1)—what could be more natural in education than submerging one's child in a river?—and *Ulysses Triumphing over the Spells of Circe* (bk. 5), in which natural man overcomes feminine wiles.

The nineteenth century went even further than Rousseau's contemplation of prehistory, emphasizing the bestiality of gods and kings alike. The perspective of the seventeenth century had been courtly, whereas that of the nineteenth was bourgeois. It had no reason to spare the reputation of Greek princes. It was happy to conclude that Neoptolemus was indeed a brute and deduced that he was therefore an African (see fig. 67 in "Homer's Laughter"). Heroes at this stage had well-developed musculature. The pitying condescension of the bourgeoisie was even more contemptuous than the lofty disdain of the aristocracy; in its view the behavior of the old troopers of antiquity was distinctly working-class. Rousseau, Madame Dacier, and Perrault were all correct in their historical assessment: Homer came after the classical "dark ages."[81] Today's historians have yet to identify the world described by Homer. Was it the much earlier one of the Myceneans, the Late Bronze Age, or simply the Greece of his own time, flavored with the archaic picturesque? No matter. Among the beings created or given life by Homer, not a few would have considered the ages of Louis XIV and Louis XV at least as barbarous as their own.

POLITICAL AND MORAL ANALYSIS

Hepp informs us that the taste for hierarchy in seventeenth-century France explains its difficulties with Homer.[82] Beneath its desire for aesthetic order lurk social prejudice and a craving for authority. The coarseness and viciousness of gods and warriors alike seemed particularly horrid to seventeenth-century readers, given the very courteous and attentive behavior of Homer's servant women and slaves. The upper classes would have had little to reprove if Homer had confined coarseness to the social class in which it was expected. They hoped free-spirited Homer would nevertheless sing the praises of the established order and its authority. Among the translators most respectful of his own social hierarchy was La Valterie. Publishing in 1681, he found it unacceptable that Ulysses' old wet nurse should have recognized Ulysses before his wife.[83] The *Odyssey* (bk. 19) does indeed show Eurycleia in a very good light: she is intelligent, courageous, and great-hearted. Here the painters were less at fault than the translator. Belle's work, for example, contrasts Eurycleia mastering her surprise with the sordid Ulysses, who claps his hand over her mouth (cat. no. 80). La Valterie, meanwhile, has Argos recognized by Odysseus before the dog can reciprocate, and Penelope recognizes her husband before Eurycleia does her former nursling. According to Hepp, "None of the fine contrasts Homer has set up between callousness and subtlety, none of the secret poetry that resides in the relations of men and objects, men and beasts, or masters and servants, is restored, nor is anything lively, vigorous, or unexpected brought in to make up for this loss."[84] Unlike his translators, Homer's illustrators could not afford to attenuate the admirable contrasts that make each character unique. The familiar objects without which no Homeric scene could be understood—Eurycleia's basin, Nausicaa's laundry, the ticks that torment Ulysses' dog, Hector's horsehair crest, Diomedes' statuette, and Philoctetes' bandage—cannot be excluded from painting or sculpture; such attributes inhibit heroes from seeing themselves as heroes. Homer's characters live side by side in their own little world, each no less human than the others.

A MESSAGE FOR THE GREAT

Homer divides humanity into two categories, those who acknowledge their condition and those who believe themselves better than others. Fénelon, in his *Dialogues of the Dead*, allowed Homer to rebuke Achilles' boasting: "Pleasant vanity! for having shed more blood than another, at the siege of a city which was not taken till after thy death!"[85] Voltaire was no less damning in his "Essay on Epic Poetry": "Paris . . . excites our contempt. Agamemnon . . . shocks us with his pride. . . . The fair Helena . . . is insignificant."[86] The dramatic construction of Achilles from legend to the *Iliad*, from war to sulking and grief, leads him from heroism to human awareness. He is born of a goddess and educated for war. One day he discovers humiliation. It teaches him to boycott not only battle but glory and facile happiness. Ulysses is still more wretched a character, a hero-trickster who betrays, connives, avoids combat, and prefers his foe unarmed or unaware.

There came a moment—prefigured in Euripides—in which Homer's readers would no longer lie to protect their gods and princes. It is the weaknesses of these heroes that principally appeal to us since their heroism is peevish at best and their weaknesses are nothing less than heroic. No need to accuse or, for that matter, excuse Homer. It is enough to perceive that he has divided feelings about his characters and is out of sympathy with certain of them. He himself offers an etymology for the name Odysseus that speaks eloquently of his view of the man: *odussamenos*, the man who inspires or feels hatred, hate-filled or odious.[87] He can be perceived as brutal and fragile (Primaticcio) or nervous and clumsy (Baralis, cat. no. 76), but he is always imperfect—and this is his strength. When he becomes the central protagonist and master of the situation, as he does in Boulanger's painting (cat. no. 108), he is ridiculous and invidious.

What is striking about Nausicaa is not her nobility but her laundry work, and Achilles is the more illustrious for his cooking pot. Nausicaa works at the washboard in the historical landscapes of the École des beaux-arts (cat. nos. 72–75), which count among the most agreeable successes of academic painting. The grandeur of these quotidian gestures is magnified by Homer. It, in turn, magnifies an old servant woman who bathes her master's feet and a former king digging the dry earth (cat. no. 83)—in short, the modest harmony of lives devoted to the service of others and to the intelligent use of nature. Such things, engraved by Hephaestus on Achilles' shield, however, meant nothing to the bewigged courtiers portrayed by Saint-Simon or Le Brun. Ulysses is a man proud to have built his own bed and proud to use his own hand to gauge his son's height. As such, he brings to bear on the passing moment the weight of a life's experience, imparting to it the density of a great literary scene.

The message that these heroes must follow is taught by a surprising but eminently Homeric character. He waits until he is beneath the walls of Troy, until Achilles has again taken up arms like the warrior prince he is, but then, as Achilles leaves behind him a trail of blood, a horse speaks up for that very simple value, life: "Yes, we will save your life—this time too— / master, mighty Achilles! But the day of death already hovers near, and we are not to blame." Thus speaks Roan Beauty (Xanthos), the bravest and wisest of Achilles' horses (*Il.* 19.408–9). This honest nag appears in the most conventional or naïve paintings amid the muscle-bound warriors and the trampled, disfigured corpses. It voices Homer's skepticism and compassion as a counterpoint to the action in the foreground. Achilles will, says Xanthos, be overcome by a god "and the strong force of fate." Thus, Lacour and Lebouteux's prize-winning pieces show us Xanthos deploring the folly of Achilles (cat. nos. 32–33). Neither Xanthos nor Homer are great believers in heroism or epic. The eighteenth century could not forgive Homer his Xanthos. It was not the fact that the horse spoke, but that he spoke so much better than his prince and gave him lessons in philosophy. In the midst of the *querelle d'Homère* a man of letters named Gacon—never again to be so inspired— wrote *Homer Avenged* (1715), in which he weighed the glory of the hero against that of his horse and found the former wanting:

> When Homer the wise informs us
> Of horses that speak and reply
> Well, that's not so surprising:
> Frightful asses are writing,
> Why shouldn't a horse learn to talk?[88]

Quite right. Xanthos is a fine horse, and few critics have so clearly illuminated the paintings of Achilles' life.

The Human Condition

What price immortality? Homer's ideal depends on neither eternity nor immortality. His gods dream of living like mortal men. Some even dream of becoming mortal, while others are exiled to the human world; still others perform useful tasks, working metal like Hephaestus or herding sheep like Hermes. Eternity has no attractions for Ulysses, and the solitary Calypso finds it boring. Pseudo-Longinus, the author of *On the Sublime*, is a reverential figure, but he concludes from his reading of Homer that "if men are unhappy, there is always death as a harbor in trouble; what [Homer has] done for his gods is make them immortal indeed, but immortally miserable."[89] Death is spoken of constantly.

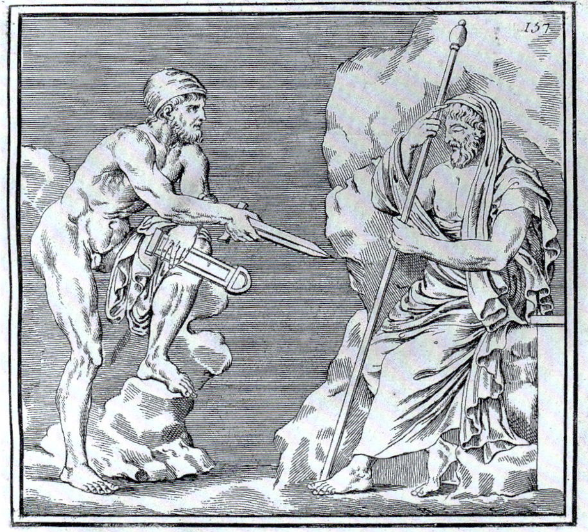

FIGURE 13 | ANONYMOUS, *Ulysses and Tiresias.* Engraving from *Monumenti antichi* (1767–72) by Johann Winckelmann, fig. 157.

Feared and reviled under the terrifying names of Ker, Moira, and Hades, it grimaces hideously at the living. On no other subject was Homer so explicit about his beliefs.[90] He put his words into the mouth not of Death but of the dead. The souls of the dead, as Homer describes them, have put aside their earthly mendacity and speak of the suffering of nonexistence. When Patroclus appears to Achilles or Hector to Aeneas, the dead heroes desire nothing so much as new life. But in Hades, Ulysses encounters two souls quite different from the other shades. The first of these is Tiresias, the seer, a figure who incarnates that combination of ancestor worship and prophecy known as necromancy. Tiresias gorges himself with blood; then, at the prompting of the skeptical Odysseus, he begins a dialogue in which both the living and the dead are haunted by the fear of death. Winckelmann found this so striking a scene that he included it among his *Monumenti antichi* as a subject for artists' meditation (fig. 13).

The second of these two souls, Hercules, raises the most intriguing questions for human beliefs, whether pagan or Christian. Nothing remains of his cremated body but ashes. His wraith remains in Hades (*Od.* 11.601–4) with all his panoply—including the bow he handed on to Philoctetes—but Hercules himself drinks joyfully in Olympus. Plotinus and the Neoplatonics founded a penetrating analysis of human nature on the double soul of the demigod Hercules. The dead Hercules, they thought, survived in two parts: a wraith haunts the dreams of those who knew him, while the purely spiritual part, born of the hero's earthly deeds, has its own abstract life in universal memory. The well-meaning have tended to see in Homer's exploration of the underworld of the human heart a belief in life after death, whereas the reverse is probably true. What remains of a man, Homer informs us, is not his soul but his works.

HOMER'S MATERIALISM

Offered eternal fame in exchange for a short life, the living Achilles accepted. Ulysses in the Underworld praises his choice, but the dead Achilles no longer shares the delusion of the living. His words should finally quash the notion that Homer favored heroism:

> No winning words about death to *me*, shining Odysseus!
> By god, I'd rather slave on earth for another man—
> some dirt-poor tenant farmer who scrapes to keep alive
> than rule down here over all the breathless dead.
> —*OD.* 11.489–91; F 11.555–58

His sentiments were repeated much later by the figure of Hector in Jean Giraudoux's play *The War of Troy Shall Not Take Place* (1935). Hector's pacifism, so memorably voiced by the actor Louis Jouvet, is exemplified in his "Speech to the Dead": "There was one, disemboweled, already turning up the whites of his eyes, and I said to him 'It's not so bad, you know, it's not so bad; you will do all right, old man.' And one with his skull split in two; I said: 'You look pretty comical with that broken nose.' . . . I am happy to give them one final swig of life; it was all they asked for; they died drinking it."[91] Homer's dead Achilles speaks like Giraudoux's life-loving Hector of 1935. Legend mendaciously spotlights the young warrior ready to die for glory and not this entirely Homeric shade, ravenous for the blood of life. Attentive readers, however, also knew that the dying or dead Achilles had gained new insight into the human condition. The mother of Ulysses and all those whom he encounters in Hades give Odysseus another insight, one that concerns not the false eternity of fame but the false eternity of the soul. "Remember all these things / So one day you can tell them to your wife," says Anticlea to her son (*Od.* 11.222). "The breathless dead" is Achilles' description. In his *Dialogues of the Dead* (5.18) Lucian shows himself the heir of Homer's Book of the Dead, but in Lucian's underworld there are no longer even wraiths, merely the rasping of bone on bone:

> MENIPPUS: Tell me Hermes, where are the beauties of both sexes? Show me around, as I'm a newcomer. . . . Show me Helen. I can't pick her out myself.
>
> HERMES: This skull is Helen.[92]

Villon subsequently asked the same question ("Où sont les neiges d'antan?" / "Where are the snows of yester-year?") in his "Ballad of the Beauties of Times Gone By." Ronsard asked the same question after him. There is only one reality for the shades of the departed: the bones of Helen, the skull of Yorick. The remainder of Lucian's dialogue paraphrases the remarks of the old men at the Scaean gates as they gaze on the beauty of Helen. The context has changed, however: "Was it for this, then, that the thousand ships were manned from all Greece, for this that so many Greeks and Barbarians fell and so many cities were devastated?"[93] "Well, Hermes, what does surprise me is this: that the Achaeans didn't know how short-lived a thing they strove for, and how soon it looses its bloom."[94] Not everyone dared to hear this materialism in Homer's lines. It was enough to scare the gods. Translated into painting or sculpture, it has another name—the love of life—and no artist is afraid of that.

"O MY SOUL, DO NOT ASPIRE TO IMMORTAL LIFE" (PINDAR)

Voltaire once poetically remarked that "happiness is like the island of Ithaca, which lay always one step ahead of Ulysses." Ulysses resembles the monsters with which he battles, for like them he dreams of living now and forever. In Greek art the gods come and go above, below, and in the midst of humanity, but Homer is interested only in the condition of the mortal. Internalized in the reader's mind, his subject assumes the endlessly renewed forms of human consciousness, which are not accessible to everyone. The mortal condition is inaccessible to those who are superhuman, that is, much less than human: the gods and demigods. The god overthrowing his predecessor has no further use for him—this is the law of Zeus and the Titans—but it is not the way with humanity. Only humankind is aware, over the intervening centuries, of belonging to one and the same species, for which solidarity is defined by the fact and fear of death. Andromache, heroine of Homer and Jacques-Louis David (cat. no. 42), asks but one word of Hector: the dying man's farewell to the living. There is no answer for Andromache:

> For you never died in bed and stretched your arms
>   to me
> or said some last word from the heart I can remember,
> always, weeping for you through all my nights and
>   days!
> —*IL.* 24.743–45; F 24.875–77

David inscribed part of Andromache's lament in his painting, and her gesture speaks eloquently of this link between the living and the dead.

THE FORMS OF TRAGEDY

Simone Weil provided a Christian commentary to the *Iliad* in her book *The Iliad, or The Poem of Force*. The violence of death was the motif she singled out. "To define force—it is that x that turns anybody who is subjected to it into a thing. Exercised to the limit, it turns man into a thing in the most literal sense: it makes a corpse out of him."[95] The grave digger in *Hamlet*, who had read Homer, agrees, noting that he buries neither man nor woman but a thing. Victims feel themselves reified even before the blow has landed. The paradox is that in visual representations the vanquished weep and by doing so escape reification. Not so the victors. Such is the grandeur of Niobe: surrounded by the corpses of her children and still shadowed by the archer gods, she finds she must eat (*Il.* 24.708–22). Life holds out against tragedy. This resistance, this refusal to give way to the force of things, is characteristic of all Homer's protagonists. It taught tragic grandeur to the emerging Greek civilization. We may be crushed by the universe, it tells us, but the universe is unjust. This refusal to acknowledge the force of events is best reflected in Flaxman and the simplicity of line he learned from Greek vase painting and the Italian Primitives.[96]

Plato perhaps intended a further insult when he called Homer the greatest of the tragic poets.[97] Victor Hugo took up Plato's point almost word for word: "All the ancient tragedians merely divide up Homer. Same fables, same catastrophes, same heroes. All draw from the Homeric river. It is always the *Iliad* and the *Odyssey*. Like Achilles dragging Hector, Greek tragedy revolves around Troy."[98] Like tragedy and opera, epic painting takes a sly pleasure in recounting the injustices of destiny. Andromache and Hecuba both denounce the forces that bear down on them—which is perhaps why the latter was a subject so often set for the École's students during the nineteenth century. The solitude of a woman is quite different from that of a warrior, and this helps us identify with them. They are unbowed by misfortune. The series of handsome oil sketches painted in praise of Trojan women (cat. nos. 56–59) is contemporary with Berlioz's *Trojans*, in which first Cassandra and then Dido proclaim their tragic defiance of death to the doom-laden skies.

BOREDOM AND REVERIE

The human soul is afflicted by yet another form of tragedy: boredom. There is no word in Greek for this, as has often been observed. Yet Homer's characters often stop in the midst of their most epic actions for a moment of inaction or daydreaming. At such times they fear they are wasting their time on earth. They vacillate between stillness and frenzied gesticulation. Rubens, the painter par excellence of movement, brings all his usual vitality to the story of Achilles yet seems to have forgotten that sulking is the essence of his story. Achilles and Ulysses, with their endless hesitations, stand at the origin of the melancholy sentiment dubbed boredom or *spleen* by the modern sensibility. Ulysses is bored because Calypso likes nothing but making love. Anticipating the absence of Ulysses' sweet prattle, Calypso is bored in advance. After how long—and for how long—can a man be bored by a woman? For seven long years Ulysses is bored by the presence of Calypso, while for ten years Menelaus is tormented by the absence of his wife. Do Fénelon and Plato indict the gods for their immorality? Poor gods, they plot and seduce as best they can to avoid an eternity of tedium. The calm of Olympus is boring; they hasten to the banquet or to the vaudeville production staged by Hephaestus and starring Aphrodite and Ares.

What is one to do when things come to a halt and boredom follows? These are times to reflect. The most often read of epic poems is, in this respect, the least epic. Everything that accelerates the action—the rape of Helen, the sacrifice of Iphigenia, the taking of Troy—Homer passes over in silence. The *Iliad* begins with a halt in the action when Achilles refuses to fight. But there is still much interim time to be passed. The warrior Achilles spends his time playing the lyre. The industrious Ulysses similarly spends seven years doing nothing. He at least can dream of his return and invent the term *nostalgia*, which means precisely the tedium of longing for home. The most celebrated scenes in the epic thus concern characters stilled for a decade or a moment during which they can only relive their past and imagine their future. Priam and Achilles seated in the tent around Hector's body fall silent and dream their separate dreams. Odysseus's course is halted by Argos, Eurycleia, and Laertes, and for a moment he meditates upon each of these images from his childhood, like Hamlet before the skull of his childhood friend. Penelope dreams of the past and the future before her loom or at the sight of the beggar whom she perhaps recognizes from the first. Philoctetes is doomed by circumstance to thought and inaction. Orestes at Agamemnon's tomb—driven by his own demons and his sister Electra toward an act of vengeance in which he himself does not believe, and forced to contemplate his own crime in advance—similarly prefigures Hamlet, who knows from the outset that he should refrain. The ever-restless Ulysses is also capable of this distancing perspective, this unexpected inertia. In the moment before battle commences or in the thick of the action, his arm is suddenly suspended. Encountering his mother or the dog Argos, or finding his father at work in the garden, he is plunged into thought, coming to rest in poses admirably suited to the artist's purposes. Hector and Andromache are even more self-aware; before the battle they stand apart, awaiting their stupid and pitiless destiny. They sense that they act in vain, that Hector's commitment to defend his city and his son are futile. Achilles was often represented by Greek artists in attitudes of hesitation. Frozen in thought, Oedipus, Orestes, Achilles, Telemachus, Hector, and Odysseus taught introspection to Montaigne, Hamlet, Don Quixote, and to us.

We have seen that the history painter needs such moments. He finds them in the most original Homeric episodes. Poussin, painter of philosophical or heroic subjects, presents a statuesque *Achilles Among the Daughters of Lycomedes* (fig. 14), with Achilles posing in female costume in an attempt to forestall his fate. His two versions of this para-Homeric episode are paintings of courtly society—anecdotal, static, and antiheroic—yet devoid of either humor or reflection. Poussin modeled his art after antiquity but is blind to Homer's skepticism. These moments of static introspection, however, taught history painters to change the emphasis of their compositions. Women might matter more than warriors, the old be more prominent than the young, and the wounded more vital than the

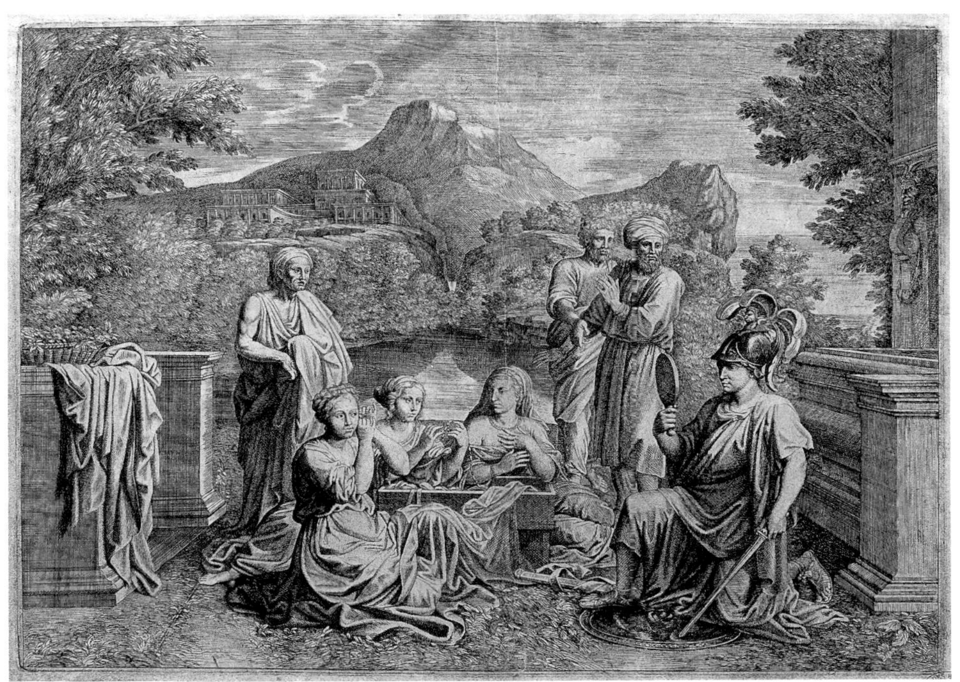

FIGURE 14A | NICOLAS POUSSIN (1594–1665), *Achilles Among the Daughters of Lycomedes*, 1650–51. Engraving by Pietro del Po (1610–1692) after a painting at the Museum of Fine Arts, Boston, 37.5 × 51.3 cm.

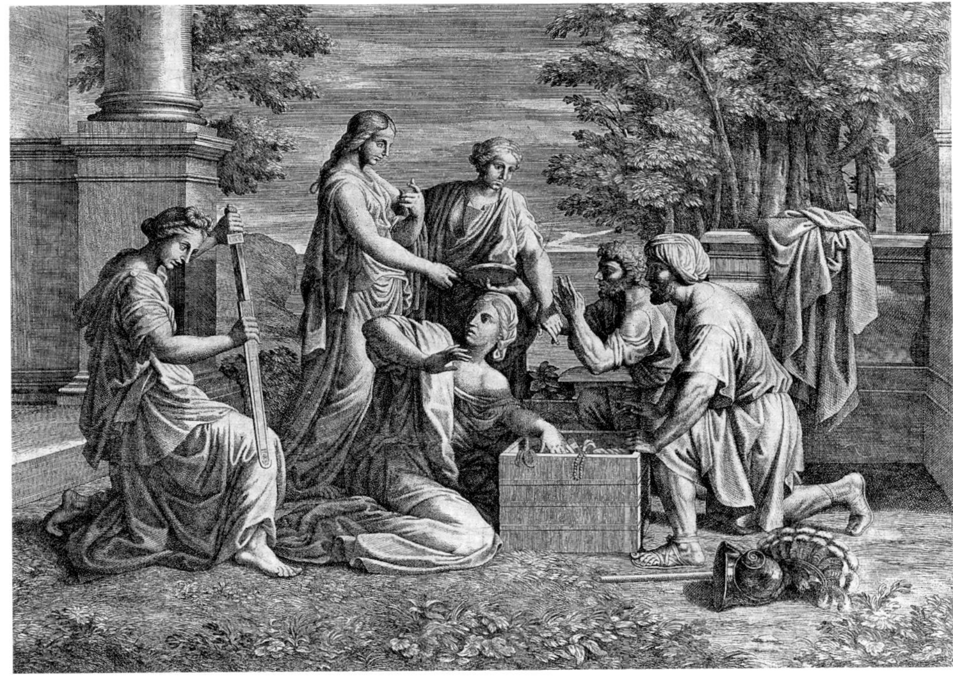

FIGURE 14B | NICOLAS POUSSIN (1594–1665), *Achilles Among the Daughters of Lycomedes*, 1656. Engraving by Pietro del Po (1610–1692) after a painting at the Virginia Museum of Fine Arts, Richmond, 36.5 × 53 cm.

hale. The painters found a particularly successful formula in the early nineteenth century, a form midway between Neoclassicism and Romanticism. At this point the École's sculptors were making figures slightly smaller than life-size, halted in their tracks by some image of past or future, some timeless moment: Hector embracing his son, Ulysses recognizing his dog, or Philoctetes considering his wounded foot.

INDIVIDUAL LIBERTY

The heroic man of action thus chooses inaction. Homer invented the art of surprise, of surprising or contradicting oneself: the art of changing at once one's mind and one's life. The extravagant political or individual eccentricities of certain Greeks demonstrated that a man may sometimes act in defiance of what others expect, against his own interests—indeed, against himself.

Inconsequentiality on this scale is a loophole through which freedom flows. Poor Hercules spent his life obeying orders, and was often mocked for it, but one day he had to choose between virtue and vice. In the history of Western art no scene has been represented more frequently. Needless to say, he chose virtue. Homer's protagonists also make worthy choices but renege on them at the first opportunity. Ulysses promises to help Menelaus whenever the need arises, but when his promise is repeated back to him, he attempts to avoid conscription by feigning madness. This scene was often studied in the École des beaux-arts (cat. no. 69). Achilles, as we have seen, did much the same. Ajax the Great, by contrast, never attains this degree of lucidity. Doggedly clinging to the vanities of war, he condemns himself to suicide. One warrior feigns madness, another actually becomes mad. What kind of saber rattler do you have to be to view the *Iliad* as a heroic poem?

Homer created the first free spirits, the first thinkers, the first of those stubborn and subversive intellectuals who do what no one expects. Ulysses lies when reality disappoints him. Penelope lies to everyone and mistrusts everything. Nausicaa imagines a quite different life for herself. Homer's women play the leading roles in this game of freedom and imagination. It will be objected that women are never free; they are always subject to father, husband, lover, brother, or master. Alcinous's wife is his niece; as heiress and only daughter, she was legally bound to marry her next of kin. True, but servitude has taught her to dominate the stronger sex (cat. no. 76), just as Hera has learned cunning from the might of Zeus. Immortality through heroism is not an option for women, nor would they want it. Yet women are the instigators of both action (Helen) and inaction (Calypso). They alone perceive the forces at work so acutely that they master them (Circe, Penelope, Andromache). Andromache's is perhaps the most interesting case. She knows the value of individuals and actions; she sees her destiny, says so, and then endures and overcomes it. In Wielhorsky's sketch (cat. no. 63) she wears a fashionably long dress as she defies the brutality of Menelaus. The warriors of history painting seem mechanical to the point of absurdity, but none of these women ever looks ridiculous. Their courage is born of their contrariness.

The late eighteenth century made a discovery: human consciousness was embodied in the steady independence of Homer's characters. This—not heroism—is a quality with which readers can identify when confronted with the suffering and grandeur of fictional characters—and Homer knew it. Here we should return to the great dialogue between Homeric and Virgilian heroism. Each states the case for a model life and the principles upon which it is based: happiness or virtue, freedom or order, individual or state.[99] Prince Hector wages war, while Hector the man loves peace. The reader may love either of the two. A painting or sculpture can imply this dichotomy in a meeting of eyes or the tilt of a helmet plume. Hector and Helen exchange just such a glance in the parallel sketches of Auvray and Barye (cat. nos. 39–40). At times characters

OPPOSITE FIGURE 15 | MARIE-GABRIEL-FLORENT-AUGUSTE DE CHOISEUL-GOUFFIER (1752–1817), Map of the Troad, engraved by Barbié du Bocage and Louis-François Cassas, in *Voyage pittoresque en Grèce* (Paris, 1782), vol. 2, pt. 1.

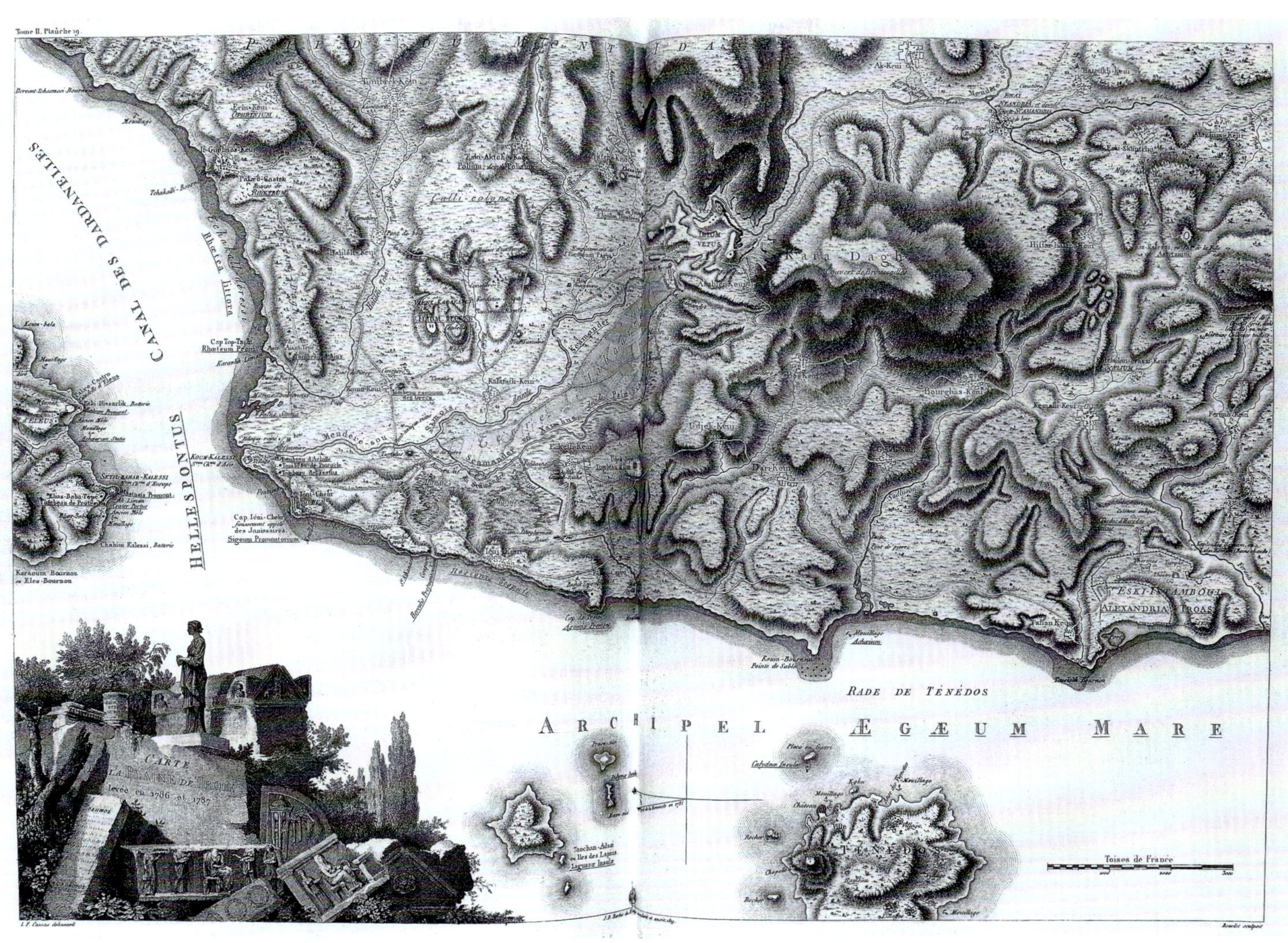
CARTE
DE LA PLAINE DE TROIE
levée en 1786 et 1787
CANAL DES DARDANELLES
HELLESPONTUS
Rhœtea littora
Erin-Keui
OPHRINIUM
Timbrek-Keui
Eski-Aktche-Keui
Calli-colone
Cap Top-Tach
Rhœteum Prom.
Tombeau d'Ajax
Koum-Keui
Tombeau commun des Grecs
Kalafatli-Keui
Simois
Scamander
Mendere-sou
Koum-Kalessi
Tombeau d'Achille
Tombeau de Patrocle
Iéni-Cheir
Cap Iéni-Cheir faussement appelé des Janissaires
Sigeum Promontorium
Seddil-Bahar-Kalessi
Elias-Baba-Tepe
Tombeau de Protesilas
Chahim Kalessi, Batterie
Karaoum Bournou ou Eles-Bournou
Koum-bala
Ida
Eski-Stamboul
Alexandria Troas
Tafian Keui
Mouillage
Achæium
Koum-Bournou
Pointe de Sable
RADE DE TÉNÉDOS
ARCHIPEL ÆGÆUM MARE
Calydnæ Insulæ
Taochan-Adasi ou Iles des Lapins
Lagussæ Insulæ
Château
Mouillage
Rocher
Chapelle
TÉNÉDOS
Toises de France
1000
2000
3000
L. F. Cassas delineavit
Bouclet sculpsit

are reduced to a single thought, act, or speech. This is sufficient if the act is a free and long-meditated one—and no mere convention. It is enough for the character to say "No!" to either universe or self. The absence of gesture (see Hillemacher's Hecuba, cat. no. 56) may be as expressive as a flamboyant gesture (Devambez, cat. no. 59) in communicating an attitude. Audacity of this kind can be the making of a work, conferring a serene grandeur. Works too self-regarding to include this free and futile gesture are engulfed in the vanity of their own insignificance.

"WILD PARADISE"

Homer is neither a moralist nor a historian. He does not reflect the truth of an epoch or a society. Proust and Camus have taught us to seek or perceive in a work the artist's aspiration to construct a world more beautiful than the one by which he is surrounded and disappointed. The world known to Homer—the plain of Troy washed by Mediterranean waters—belonged to a closed domain in which a few people were learning to think and feel. It is this little world, so artificial and yet so intensely alive, that I shall now describe, evoking as I do certain of the most brilliant reconstitutions of that world—those of Primaticcio, Giraudoux, and Joyce. Those in whom a sense of literature—and a sense of grandeur—is innate have always recognized the modest dimensions of the Homeric world in which humans are enlarged to the scale of the universe and the gods perceived through the diminishing lens of skepticism.

Madame Dacier failed to perceive all that the sensibility of Alexander Pope could bring to her own defense of Homer. He summarized his own verdict in a brilliant and very English formula. In the preface to his *Iliad* he describes Homer—his nature, humanity, and art of fable—as a "wild paradise." His image develops Hamlet's perception of the human mind as "an unweeded garden," one "grown to seed" (1.2.135). Pope thus situates all of Shakespeare and Milton in Homer. He places a paradise still in its original state—the forest civilized by the poet's gaze—in a traditional English landscaped garden. "Our Author's work is a wild Paradise. . . . 'Tis like a copious nursery which contains the Seeds and first Productions of every kind."[100] Voltaire summarized Pope's views: "It is a vast but primitive landscape, where there are beauties of every kind, though these do not possess the regularity they would display in a conventional garden; it is a fertile nursery containing the seeds of every fruit, a great tree on which grow superfluous branches, which must be trimmed."[101] One should apply this to the imagination of Homer—in short, to the human soul, for that is the garden from which grow in profusion all the pettiness of grandeur and the grandeur of modesty. Homer, Shakespeare, Pope, Voltaire: wild paradise, unweeded garden, gardens landscaped in the English or French manner—here is a metaphor played out across the centuries through a variety of literary productions; the reader can promenade through its paths as through the circumvolutions of the human brain. After the poet, one should cite the artist, in this case Antoine Coypel, who, in a startling lecture ascribed joint responsibility for the invention of landscape in literature and art to Homer and Plato.[102] This collocation of Homer and Plato is a contradiction only in philosophical terms. Devotees of the "wild paradise" can see that poet and philosopher adopted the same procedure: each is in search of a world harmoniously wild, where the soul seeks its own place amid the gods and other living creatures. Coypel attempted to reconstitute this burgeoning world for a tapestry of the *Iliad*, the designs for which were engraved. Anyone endowed with an unconstrained imagination peoples this "wild paradise" in his or her own fashion. Diderot himself thought of proposing *Tapestry Projects Drawn from Homer.*

Freely re-created, the harmony of the wild paradise lends itself ideally to pictorial representation. This is not true of the historicist or nationalist variety. In his *Dialogues on Eloquence* Fénelon displays unexpected sensitivity and vision when he notes that "in the one as in the other case [the *Iliad* and the *Odyssey*], Homer intended only to paint nature faithfully."[103] He continues: "They are unpretentious things; nature shows herself throughout. [The poet] stakes his reputation upon not appearing at all, . . . as a painter aspires to put before your eyes forests, mountains, rivers, distances and buildings, men, their adventures, their actions, their various passions, without your being able to take notice of the strokes of his brush."[104] Fénelon may indeed have been the first critic to compare the world of Homer with specific painters, discerningly chosen not for their illustrations of Homer but for the way in which they, too, had contrived to make the natural or humanized landscape live and breathe. He evokes Titian for wild landscape and Teniers for festivities and village dances. One of the finest connoisseurs of Homer was Jean Boivin (1663–1726). A contemporary of Fénelon, he was appointed "Professeur royal" of the Greek language in 1705. In his inaugural lecture he showed a similar finesse in explaining the pictorial qualities of Homer:

> The *Iliad* and the *Odyssey* are large pictures of which the *Aeneid* is an epitome, which should be subjected to close examination. Everything in it must be complete. Large pictures must be seen from a distance and not every stroke need be so delicate and even. In a large picture excessive meticulousness is a fault. Adornment and irrelevant ornament are often mistaken for true beauty. Nowhere in even the finest work of the greatest master is there a passage in which nothing could be improved by retouching. Leave it as it is: an excellent original. Alteration may make it more ornate and less beautiful than before.[105]

Rather than draw on Homer for accurate, disciplined history paintings, the painters should have remembered that wild garden from which new flowers bloom. Regularly proposing historical landscape subjects inspired by the *Odyssey*, in which students were free to depict little figures at play beneath large trees, the Academicians showed that they were aware of this. Ulysses covering himself to spare Nausicaa's blushes (cat. nos. 72–74); Hermes discovering the secrets of music or murder (cat. nos. 14–16); Hades carrying off a nymph from a forest clearing (cat. nos. 19–20)—all these show the wild paradise in a new light. In these works the brush delineates, colors, and civilizes primitive nature.

HOMER'S ACADEMY

In Pope's metaphor each of us perceives not just the variety of the human mind but the ambition of artists who, like Homer, set about creating a wild paradise on whatever scale. In the *Iliad* Hephaestus, patron of blacksmiths, creates a harmonious and contradictory world outlined on the shield of Achilles. The sculptor Epeios builds a Trojan horse in which all of Greece's intelligence is concealed. Each creates his own masterful disorder. A dynasty of artists was made to descend from Hephaestus and Homer: Strabo and Alberti decreed Homer the ancestor of all artists, with Phidias, his first and greatest pupil, next in line.[106] This lineage extended down through the centuries to the modern Academies.

Led by Le Brun, the artists who founded the first French Academy of painting and sculpture considered their activity not a trade but a form of intellectual work, with its own doctrine. It was no less noble than the Greek school whose name they adopted; they would treat the same subjects with the same profundity. The innumerable and frankly tedious speeches, treatises, and theories that placed painting and sculpture on a par with poetry—then the benchmark of creativity—dictated the choice of genres, subjects, and styles but left whole areas of ancient sensibility completely out of focus. The collections of paintings and sculptures bestowed on the École by the caprices of history and the generosity of donors illustrate these varying lacunae. Following in the footsteps of the theoreticians, one might have classified the works according to their rhetorical equivalents: expression, passion, convention, erudition, and action. The hierarchy of genres was established by the Academies according to the nobility of the human activity they depicted, with history painting (epic) occupying the loftiest rank and descriptions of everyday life placed very low on the scale. In this it reverses the teachings of Homer, who awards every human his or her own individual and independent universe, along with a license for disorder. In the Homeric poem one never finds two different characters reacting in the same way—nor even the same character reacting twice in the same way. Claiming to reduce this tirelessly inventive creation to formulae and categories, the academic approach betrayed not just Homer but thought, freedom, literature, and art. The translation of the Greek word *mythos* (story) by the Latin term *fabula* (fable) is a perfect illustration of this.

A fable demonstrates a single thesis; a myth demonstrates that the humanity in ourselves cannot be reduced to a single analogy but is as infinite in its variety as human imagination can make it. Was Homer's inheritance fables (*mythoi*) or myths? Whatever it was, he fashioned his poems from it, giving a new sense to the ancient story and a new life to what it contained. Only works that register human variety have any human substance. The gods that exist only in our fears (veiled in mist by Homer) are mere shadows; shadows, too, the dead who have perished from our memories, shadows our prejudices and vanities. What Homer did with the myths he inherited, he did no less with the barbarity of humankind: from its cruelty, suffering, and bloodshed he extracted beauty. Proust once borrowed from Homer a metaphor that summarizes the history of artistic creation: "A hundred characters and a thousand ideas exhort me to give them form like the shades in the *Odyssey* exhorting Ulysses to let them drink a little blood in order to restore them to life, while the hero holds them back with his sword."[107]

Proust's master Anatole France set himself to imagine Homer's career:

> Painted or sculpted figures he had never seen; the altars to the gods of his time were nothing more than crudely sculpted stelae in a sacred grove. . . . Among men who thought only of making war in order to steal women and bronze tripods, he led a life more wretched than that of a minstrel in a village of the Auvergne. Yet within his uncouth and new soul he found tones that will forever resound in generous hearts.[108]

And down through the ages the struggle has continued between those who think only of making war and those who find tones that will forever resound, between those who bring death and those who love new and uncouth beauty. Among the latter, many centuries after the Homeric youth of humanity, we find these young artists of the École des beaux-arts. Sometimes the belligerent ruled the roost and sought to silence the burgeoning artists. Fortunately, the latter like nothing so much as to make themselves heard. The works illustrated here might have been classified according to those two extremes, the blindly heroic and the proudly modest. Instead, the contest rages through each of our subjects, and two camps can again contest the field, much as they did thirty centuries ago beneath the walls of a town that surely never existed. Here again, in the souls of heroes and captives, random events interact with divine barbarity and mortal weakness, love of life encounters the berserk warrior, and humorless ambition menaces freedom of thought.

NOTES

1 Ismail Kadare, *The File on H.*, trans. David Bellos (London, 1997).

2 Quoted in Henri Delaborde, *Ingres: sa vie, ses travaux, sa doctrine, d'après les manuscrits et les lettres du maître* (Paris, 1870), 147.

3 This is an error in the 1544 edition, which confused the initials of Jacques Millet (the most frequent in French onomastics) with those of the author of *Le Roman de la rose.*

4 On Mlle de Scudéry, see Noémi Hepp, *Homère en France au XVIIe siècle* (Paris, 1968), 62. Hepp's book teaches one not only how Homer was read in the seventeenth century in France, but to perceive all the subtleties of a text written for all time.

5 François de Malherbe, *Oeuvres* (Paris, 1862–69), 1:113.

6 See Noémi Hepp, "Homère en France au XVIe siècle," *Atti della Accademia delle Scienze di Torino*, II, Classe di Scienze morali, storiche e filologiche. 96 (1961–62): 445.

7 Ibid., 480.

8 For the lost/destroyed Gallery of Ulysses at Fontainebleau—known through drawings, engravings, and copies—see Sylvie Béguin, Jean Guillaume, and Alain Roy, *La Galerie d'Ulysse à Fontainebleau* (Paris, 1985).

9 Pierre de Ronsard, "ÀMarc Antoine de Muret" (*Isles Fortunées*, 1555), in *Oeuvres complètes* (Paris, 1950), 783–84.

10 Hepp, "Homère en France au XVIe siècle," 482–84.

11 Ibid., 394.

12 Michel de Montaigne, *The Complete Essays*, trans. M. A. Screech (London, 1991), 852.

13 See Jennifer Montagu, "The Painted Enigma and French Seventeenth-Century Art," *Journal of the Warburg and Courtauld Institutes* 31 (1968):328.

14 Ibid., 327.

15 Ibid., 329, n. 103.

16 Both quotations are from Claude-Philipp de Tubière, comte de Caylus, *Tableaux tirés de l'Iliade, de l'Odyssée d'Homère et de l'Énéide de Virgile, avec des observations générales sur le costume* (Paris, 1757), xvi–xviii.

17 The term *picturesque* is derived from *pictura* (painting). On the theory of *ut pictura poesis* (i.e., the parallel between academic painting and narrative poetry), see Rensselaer W. Lee, *Ut pictura poesis: The Humanistic Theory of Painting* (New York, 1967). I shall eschew this analysis of art in terms of rhetoric, which irons out the poetry and humanity of authors and artists alike.

18 Caylus, *Tableaux*, xxx and xxxiv.

19 See, e.g., Articles 5 and 9 of the Regulations for the École des Élèves entretenus par Sa Majesté governing the arts of painting and sculpture, cited in Louis Courajod, *Histoire de l'enseignement des arts du dessin au XVIIIe siècle. L'École royale des élèves protégés, précédée d'une étude sur le caractère de l'enseignement de l'art français aux différentes époques de son histoire, et suivie de documents sur l'École royale gratuite de dessin fondée par Bachelier*, Paris, 1874, 21 and 34.

20 See Étienne-Jean Delécluze, *Louis David: son école & son temps* (1855; rpt. Paris, 1983), 71–73.

21 Ibid., 424.

22 See Norman Schlenoff, *Ingres: ses sources littéraires* (Paris, 1956), 50 and n. 8.

23 See Jean Seznec, *Essais sur Diderot et l'Antiquité* (Oxford, 1957), 61–64.

24 Denis Diderot, "Salon de 1761," no. 17, quoted in Laurent Versini, ed., *Oeuvres*, vol. 4: *Esthétique–Théâtre* (Paris, 1996), 205.

25 Ibid., 224.

26 Diderot, "Salon de 1763," no. 17, in *Ésthétique–Théâtre*, 251.

27 Diderot, "Additions," in *Ésthétique–Théâtre*, 56.

28 Ibid.

29 Denis Diderot, "The Salon of 1765," in *Diderot on Art*, 2 vols., trans. John Goodman (New Haven, Conn., 1995), 1:138–39; my italics.

30 Caylus, *Tableaux*, 26.

31 Diderot, "De la poésie dramatique," 10, in *Ésthétique–Théâtre*, 1305. Diderot's translation is analyzed by Barbara Patzek in "Homère comme idéal de vie en France au XVIIIe siècle," in *Homère en France après la Querelle (1715–1900)*, ed. Françoise Létoublon and Catherine Volphilhac-Auger, Actes du colloque de Grenoble, 1995 (Paris, 1999), 161–77.

32 See Plutarch, *Life of Alexander*, 26, 679d.

33 See Victor Bérard, *Dans le sillage d'Ulysse* (Paris, 1933).

34 See Félix Buffière, *Les Mythes d'Homère et la pensée grecque* (Paris, 1956), 206–12.

35 Quoted by Chantal Grell, "Homère géographe au XVIIIe siècle," in *Homère en France après la Querelle*, ed. Létoublon and Volphilhac-Auger, 262.

36 Lucius Annaeus Seneca, *Epistulae Morales ad Lucilium*, 88.

37 Montaigne, *The Complete Essays*, 662.

38 François Rabelais, *The History of Gargantua and Pantagruel*, trans. J. M. Cohen (Harmondsworth, Eng., 1955), 39.

39 John Milton, *Samson Agonistes*, 80. [Translator's note.]

40 See Denis Diderot and Étienne-Maurice Falconet (January 15, 1766), *Le Pour et le contre: correspondance polémique sur le respect de la postérité, Pline et les anciens auteurs qui ont parlé de peinture et de sculpture*, with an introduction and notes by Yves Benoit (Paris, 1958), 61.

41 C.-H. Watelet and P.-C. Lévesque, *Dictionnaire des arts de peinture, sculpture et gravure*, 5 vols. (1792; rpt. Geneva, 1972), 3:19 (s.v. "Héros").

42 Quoted in Hepp, *Homère en France au XVIIe siècle*, 135.

43 Plato, *Republic*, 2, 378c.

44 See Buffière, *Les Mythes d'Homère*, pt. 1, chap. 1.

45 Plato, *Phaedrus*, 243a–b, 229c–e.

46 See Werner Jaeger, *Paideia: The Ideals of Greek Culture*, 3 vols., trans. G. Highet (Oxford, 1944), 1:213.

47 Theodor Van Thulden, *Les Travavx d'Vlysse, desseignez par le sievr de Sainct Martin, de la façon qv'ils se voyent dans la maison royalle de Fontainebleav* (Paris, 1633).

48 See Hepp, *Homère en France au XVIIe siècle*, 325.

49 Charles de Brosses (1709–1777), known as "le Président des Brosses," wrote in his *Lettres familières écrites de l'Italie en 1739 et 1740* (Paris, 1799) that Bernini had created "a marvelous expression, but frankly much too passionate for a church. If this is divine love, I know it. We see many copies from nature here below." *Lettres d'Italie*, 2 vols., ed. Edmond Pilon (Paris, 1976), 2:68.

50 Simone Weil, "Zeus et Prométhée," *La Source Grecque* (Paris, 1953), 43–46.

51 See Jacques Thuillier, "La Mythologie à l'âge 'baroque,'" in Stella Georgoudi et al., eds., *Mythes grecs au figuré de l'antiquité au baroque* (Paris, 1996), 167–87.

52 The French expression is "saletés des dieux." See Jean de La Bruyère, "De quelques usages," in *Caractères de Théophraste, traduits du Grec, avec les caractères ou les moeurs de ce siècle* (Paris, 1688–89), 17.

53 François de Salignac de la Mothe Fénelon, *Fénelon's Letter to the French Academy*, with an introduction, commentary, and translation by Barbara Warnick (New York, 1984), 105.

54 See Joselita Raspi Serra, "Les Nouveaux Territoires du mythe au XVIIIe siècle," in Georgoudi et al., *Mythes grecs au figuré*, 196.

55 Hepp, *Homère en France au XVIIe siècle*, 600.

56 See Raymond Naves, *Le Goût de Voltaire* (Paris, 1938), 526 n. 410.

57 Quoted in Grell, "Homère géographe," 249.

58 See Robert Rosenblum, "David's *Funeral of Patroclus*," *Burlington Magazine* 115, no. 846 (September 1973), 568; see also Jean Locquin, *La Peinture d'histoire en France de 1747 à 1785: Étude sur l'évolution des idées artistiques dans la seconde moitié du XVIIIe siècle* (1912; rpt, Paris, 1978), 163–64.

59 Homer, *Il.* 9.502ff. Unless otherwise noted, all translations are by Robert Fagles (New York, 1990) and are used by permission. Subsequent references in the text appear as "F," followed by book and line number(s) (e.g., F 9.609–17).

60 See Georgoudi et al., *Mythes grecs au figuré*, 14–16.

61 Hepp, *Homère en France au XVIIe siècle*, 647.

62 See Buffière, *Les Mythes d'Homère*, 374–86, 506.

63 See Kenneth Clark, *The Nude* (London, 1956), 81–83.

64 See Edgar Wind, *Pagan Mysteries in the Renaissance* (1958; rpt. Oxford, 1980), 197.

65 On this subject see Roland Fréart de Chambray, *Idée de la perfection de la peinture démonstrée par les principes de l'art* (LeMans, 1662), 23–40.

66 Diderot, "Essais sur la peinture," in *Esthétique–Théâtre*, 493

67 See Jean Starobinski, "Le Mythe au XVIIIe siècle," *Critique* 366 (1977): 975–97.

68 Diderot, "Entretiens sur le fils naturel," 3, in *Esthétique–Théâtre*, 1180.

69 George Steiner, "The Historicity of Dreams," in *No Passion Spent: Essays, 1978–96* (London, 1996), 219.

70 See Seznec, *Essais sur Diderot*, 61–63.

71 Herodotus, *The Histories*, II, 53, trans. A. de Sélincourt (1954; rev. ed. London, 1996), 106.

72 Hepp, *Homère en France au XVIIe siècle*, 666–67.

73 Charles Perrault, *Parallèle des anciens et modernes en ce qui regarde les arts et les sciences*, cited by Hepp, *Homère en France au XVIIe siècle*, 539.

74 Voltaire, "Essai sur la poésie épique," in *Complete Works of Voltaire* (Oxford, 1996), 3B:414.

75 Voltaire, "Lettre de M. Eratou à M. Clopetre," in *Oeuvres complètes*, 52 vols. (Paris, 1877), 9:498.

76 See Hepp, *Homère en France au XVIIe siècle*, 630.

77 Antoine Houdar de La Motte, *Discours sur Homère avec l'Iliade en vers français* (Paris, 1714), clxxviii.

78 This was the severe verdict of Montesquieu, who compared her to "superstitious priestesses who dishonored the god that they revered and diminished religion by dint of expanding the rites." See *Pensée* 116 in Montesquieu, *Pensées, le Spicilège*, ed. Louis Desgraves (Paris, 1991), 214.

79 Jean-Jacques Rousseau, "A Discourse on the Arts and Sciences," in *The Social Contract* and the *Discourses*, rev. ed., trans. G. D. H. Cole (London, 1973), 8.

80 Ibid., 23.

81 Name given to the period 1200–800 B.C., linking Mycenean civilization to Archaic Greece. Homer's works date from around 800 B.C.

82 Hepp, *Homère en France au XVIIe siècle*, 769.

83 Ibid., 457–58.

84 Ibid., 465.

85 Fénelon, *Dialogues of the Dead; together with some Fables composed for the education of a Prince by the late M. de Féneleon* [*sic*], *newly translated from the French by Mr. Elphingston*; vol. 1: *Dialogues of the Ancients*, "Achilles and Homer" (Glasgow, 1754), 17.

86 Voltaire, "An Essay on Epic Poetry," in *Complete Works of Voltaire*, 3B:318.

87 Homer, *Odyssey* 19.407–9. See W. B. Stanford, "The Homeric Etymology of the Name Odysseus," *Classical Philology* 47, no. 4 (October 1952): 209–13.

88 See Hepp, *Homère en France au XVIIe siècle*, 722.

89 Longinus, *On Sublimity* 9.7, trans. by D. A. Russel, in D. A. Russel and M. Winterbottom, eds., *Ancient Literary Criticism: The Principal Texts in New Translations* (Oxford, 1972), 469.

90 See Buffière, *Les Mythes d'Homère*, 402–9.

91 Jean Giraudoux, *The War of Troy Shall Not Take Place*, trans. Christopher Fry (London, 1983), 47.

92 Lucian, *Dialogues of the Dead*, vol. 7, *Hermes and Menippus*, trans. M. D. Macleod (London., 1961), 21–22.

93 Ibid., 23.

94 Ibid., 25.

95 Simone Weil, *The Iliad, or The Poem of Force*, trans. M. McCarthy (Wallingford, Pa , 1956), 3.

96 On Flaxman see: Robert Rosenblum, *Transformations in Late-Eighteenth-Century Art* (Princeton, N.J., 1967), 185; Dora and Erwin Panofsky, "Romanticism, Classicist and Victorian," in *Pandora's Box* (Princeton, N.J., 1962), 85–113; and Sarah Symmons, "Flaxman and Europe: The Outline Illustrations and Their Influence" [master's thesis, Courtauld Institute of Art] (New York, 1984).

97 Plato, *Republic* 595c and 607a.

98 Victor Hugo, "Preface" to *Cromwell* (1827) (Paris, 1968), 65.

99 This is a paraphrase of the formulations in George Steiner's *Antigones* (Exeter, Eng., 1979).

100 Pope, "Preface" to *The Iliad of Homer, Translated by Alexander Pope*, ed. Steven Shankman (London, 1996), 3. Pope introduces his analogy thusly: "And perhaps the reason why common Criticks are inclin'd to prefer an judicious and methodical genius to a great and fruitful one, is, because they find it easier for themselves to pursue their observations through an uniform and bounded walk of Art, than to comprehend the vast and various Extent of Nature."

101 Voltaire, *Dictionnaire Philosophique*, s.v. "Épique."

102 Antoine Coypel, "Discours prononcés dans les conférences de l'académie royale de peinture et de sculpture" (Paris, 1721), 143 (the manuscript remains in the École's collection); cf. Longinus, *On the Sublime* 13.4; see also Alain Mérot, *Les Conférences de l'Académie royale de peinture* (Paris, 1996), 483.

103 "Dialogue 1," in *Fénelon's Dialogues on Eloquence: A Translation with Introduction and Notes*, trans. W. S. Howell (Princeton, N.J., 1951), 75.

104 "Dialogue 2," 96. See Hepp, *Homère en France au XVIIe siècle*, 599.

105 Hepp, *Homère en France au XVIIe siècle*, 587.

106 See Lee, *Ut Pictura Poesis*, 42, n. 8.

107 Marcel Proust, letter to Antoine Bibesco dated July 1905, in Philip Kolb, ed., *Correspondance*, 21 vols. (Paris, 1970–93), 3:196.

108 Anatole France, *Pierre Nozière* (1899), reprinted in *Oeuvres*, 4 vols., ed. Marie-Claire Bancquart (Paris, 1991), 3:631.

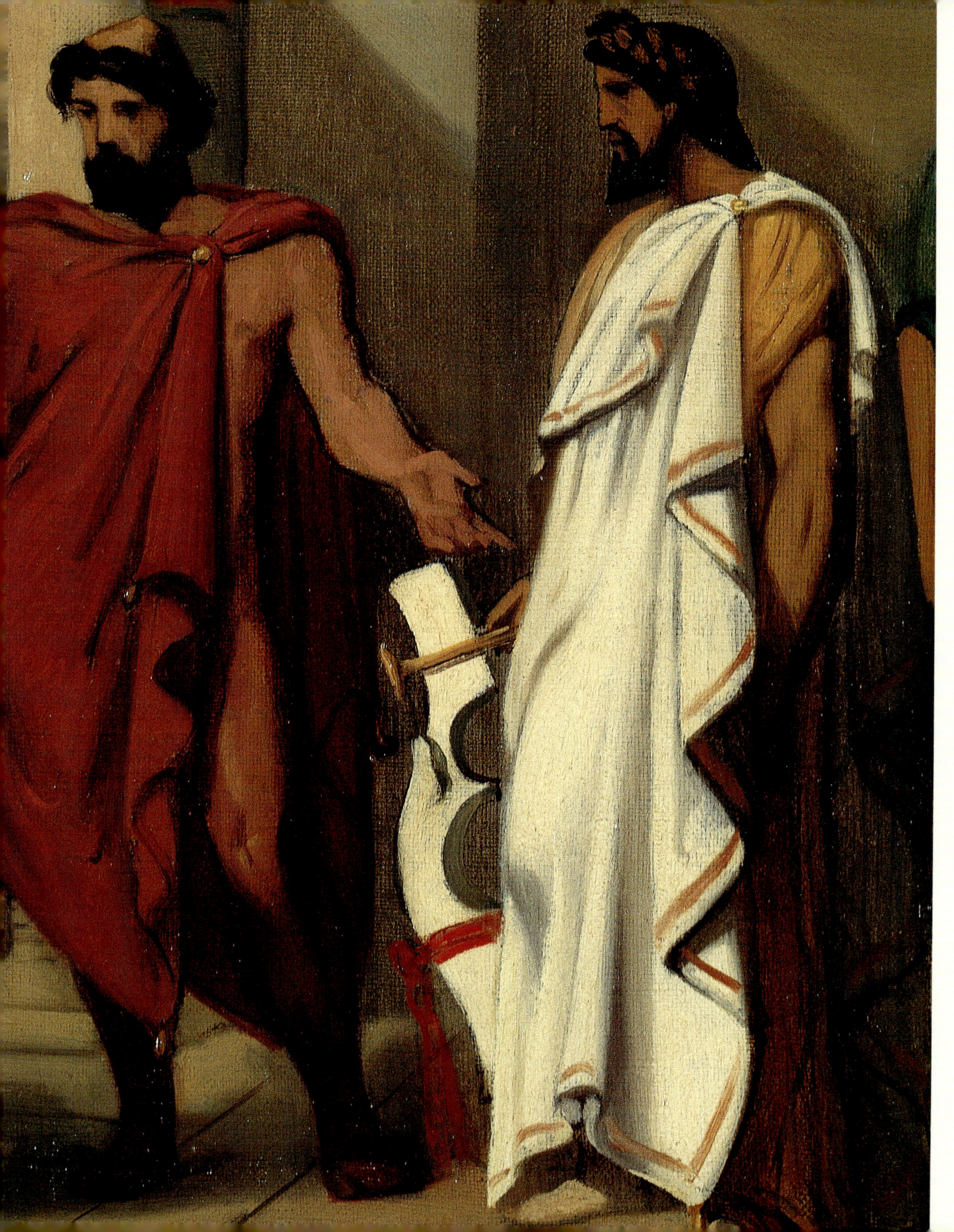

Truth in the Fold | Notes on Drapery in the Ancient Style, 1750–1850

Philippe Sénéchal

"The most beautiful ancient figures are those with the most beautiful drapery."[1] Thus wrote Éméric-David in his *Inquiry into the Statuary Art* (1805). One might have expected him to emphasize the primacy of the nude. Instead, one finds an acknowledgment of the fundamental role played by drapery *à l'antique* in the constitution of a practical and theoretical model for the artists and thinkers of the Neoclassical age.[2] A brief look at the nature of academic teaching on costume seems a useful adjunct to an exhibition on the representation of Homeric legend. Ancient statues were indeed the model for modern sculptors, but what criteria of excellence did they fulfill? Between 1750 and 1850 truth in sculpture was the object of a number of competing notions, and even the most zealous champions of the ancient world could not deny the fact.

Truth in Costume

Until the late nineteenth century, artists training in the academic style usually had to observe the discipline of *costume*, that is, what was known of the customs and habits of the ancient world. This was true of history painters and sculptors alike. The historical detail would permit the spectator instantly to determine the period, place, and circumstances portrayed, along with the rank and sex of the participants. The discipline required artists to know and reproduce religious, military, or quotidian garments and objects—and even the animals associated with particular peoples. Artists and theoreticians of the time tell us that the rule was more or less strictly applied, but it certainly constituted one of the bases of academic teaching and contributed to the production of a large number of treatises intended to help professional artists.[3]

Detail of catalogue no. 70

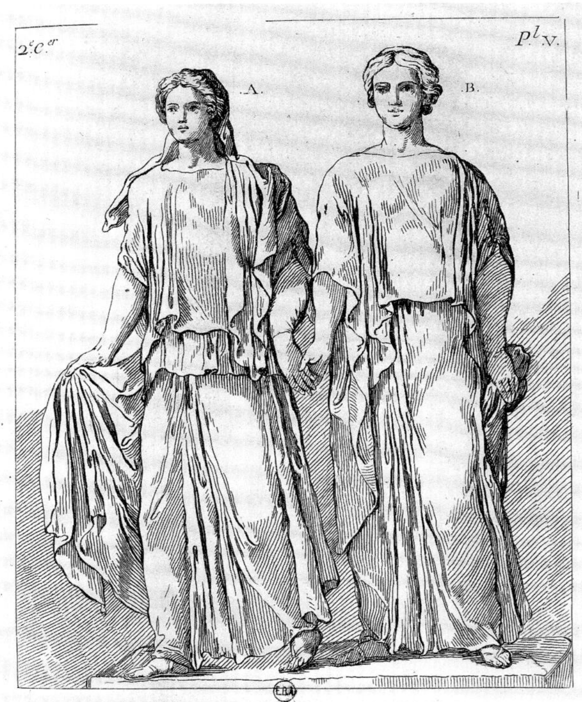

FIGURE 16 | MICHEL-FRANÇOIS DANDRÉ-BARDON (1700–1783), *Two Vestals.* Etching, 22.7 x 17.8 cm., in *Costume des anciens peuples* (Paris, 1772–74), vol. 1, 2nd cah., pl. 5.

There were, however, dissident voices. In a lecture given at the Académie royale de peinture et de sculpture on November 4, 1758, Charles-Nicolas Cochin argued: "Observance of costume is generally necessary but . . . should always be subordinate to the needs of art and the laws of taste; . . . it is not an essential merit, merely a further embellishment, and . . . excessively severe rules in this respect might elicit a pedantry intolerable to the artist and deleterious to the progress of art."[4]

The painter Michel-François Dandré-Bardon was a friend of Cochin's and himself the author of *Costume of the Ancient Peoples* (1772–74). Although an advocate of the *costume* convention, he warned artists against excessive antiquarian scruples, which could inhibit their genius.[5] His treatise—illustrated with vibrant but rather imprecise etchings—relies not only on ancient examples but on models of modern painters like Raphael, Michelangelo, and Le Sueur. Moreover, he sometimes describes ancient clothing in eighteenth-century terms. Thus, his explanation of the costume of two supposed vestals speaks of "two half-tunics of unequal length . . . worn over the rochet, which comes down to their feet" (fig. 16).[6] Eschewing pedantry, he describes the young women's pleated garment in terms of an ecclesiastical ornament of his own time, unabashed by the evident anachronism. Thereafter such lexical approximation was frowned on. Artists were strongly encouraged to know the correct terminology and—more important—the exact form of ancient garments. This more rigorous line prevailed—at least in artistic theory—until the 1830s.

The catalyst for change was the publication of a remarkable treatise by André-Corneille Lens, a painter from Liège, whose *Costume, or Essay on the Clothing and Customs of Several Peoples of Classical Antiquity, as Evidenced by Monuments* (1776)[7] was illustrated with the sober and precise engravings of Pierre-François Martenasie. The fruit of years of research into a very broad spectrum of ancient history and antiquarian scholarship since the Renaissance, it did not merely describe garments but gave their precise form, ending centuries of controversy. Lens correctly described the rectangular shape of the *pallium* and the semicircular form of the *chlamys* (fig. 17) and toga.[8] Several engravings show a draped ancient statue and a diagram of the garment, with letters pinpointing the way in which the cloth was arranged on the figure. For the toga, Lens even provided a step-by-step sketch showing how the garment was worn, enabling the reader to experiment with a piece of cloth cut according to the author's instructions. Previous treatises had confined themselves to reproducing ancient statues without any such diagrams.[9] With Lens the technical know-how extolled by the *Encyclopédie* was extended to the study of costume.[10]

These re-created ancient costumes quickly found their way into theater productions, studios, and society gatherings. In fact, the concern with sartorial authenticity

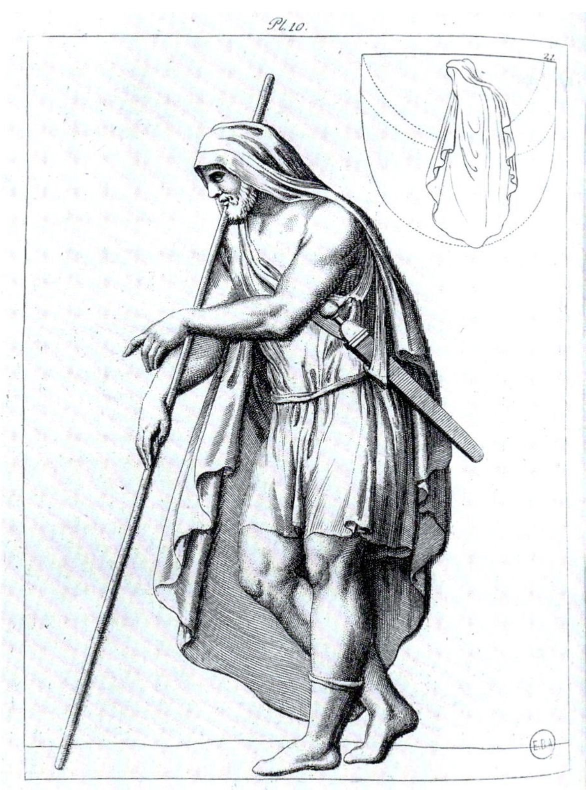

FIGURE 17 | PIERRE-FRANÇOIS MARTENASIE (1729–1789) after André Lens (1739–1822), *Agamemnon Wearing the Short Tunic and Chlamys,* after the Medici Vase in the Uffizi. Etching, 8.3 × 13.5 cm., in André Lens, *Le Costume ou Essai sur les habillements et les usages de plusieurs peuples de l'Antiquité, prouvé par les Monuments* (Liège, 1776), pl. 10, fig. 21.

was strongly associated with two concomitant phenomena. The first was the theater reforms attempted in the last quarter of the eighteenth century[11] by actors and singers such as François-Joseph Talma[12] and Mlle de Saint-Huberti.[13] The second was the fashion for monodramas, attitudes, and *tableaux vivants* that swept through European elite society.[14] Consequently, not only the painter and sculptor but professional and amateur actors were called upon to experiment with drapery in the ancient style. The link between costume history and reflections on the dramatic art is provided by Jean-Charles Levacher de Charnois, who plagiarized Lens in his *Inquiry into the Costume and Theater of Every Nation* (1790). This work features colored engravings by Pierre-Michel Alix after drawings by Philippe Chéry. The treatise reorders the material of Lens's book by imagining the ideal costumes for five tragedies by Racine: *Andromache, Esther, Britannicus, Berenice,* and *Iphigenia.* Levacher de Charnois thus evoked the clothing of the Greeks, Romans, Hebrews, and—rather less accurately—the ancient Persians.[15] He was not simply a plagiarist. His explanations of how to arrange drapery on the figure are, like his illustrations (the diagrams make excellent use of color), even clearer and more detailed than those of Lens, proving that his goal was essentially practical (fig. 18).[16] He consistently linked the world of theater with artistic training, and was indignant that the Royal Academy of Painting showed so little interest in authentic costume, speaking of

> the estimate that it has recently presented to the National Assembly. The low level of interest that it attaches to this study proves that knowledge of this kind is far from being as extensive as it should be. The sum it requests for this purpose would not cover one sixth of the garments of a single people. How does it expect to demonstrate the costumes of the Greeks, Romans, Persians, Egyptians, Assyrians, Medes, Phrygians, and Sarmatians and those of so many other countries (soon to be included in my own work) using one or two cloaks?[17]

The message was reiterated the following year by Antoine-Chrysostome Quatremère de Quincy. In his *Considerations on the Arts of Drawing in France* he argued that the teaching of ancient costume and customs required a course on theory, which should be added to the one on history. "The teacher of this course should create a collection of the garments of every people, based on surviving monuments, and demonstrate them with cloth and on models."[18] In 1849 Prosper Mérimée again argued the case for a course of this kind, to be based on clothes "made up under the

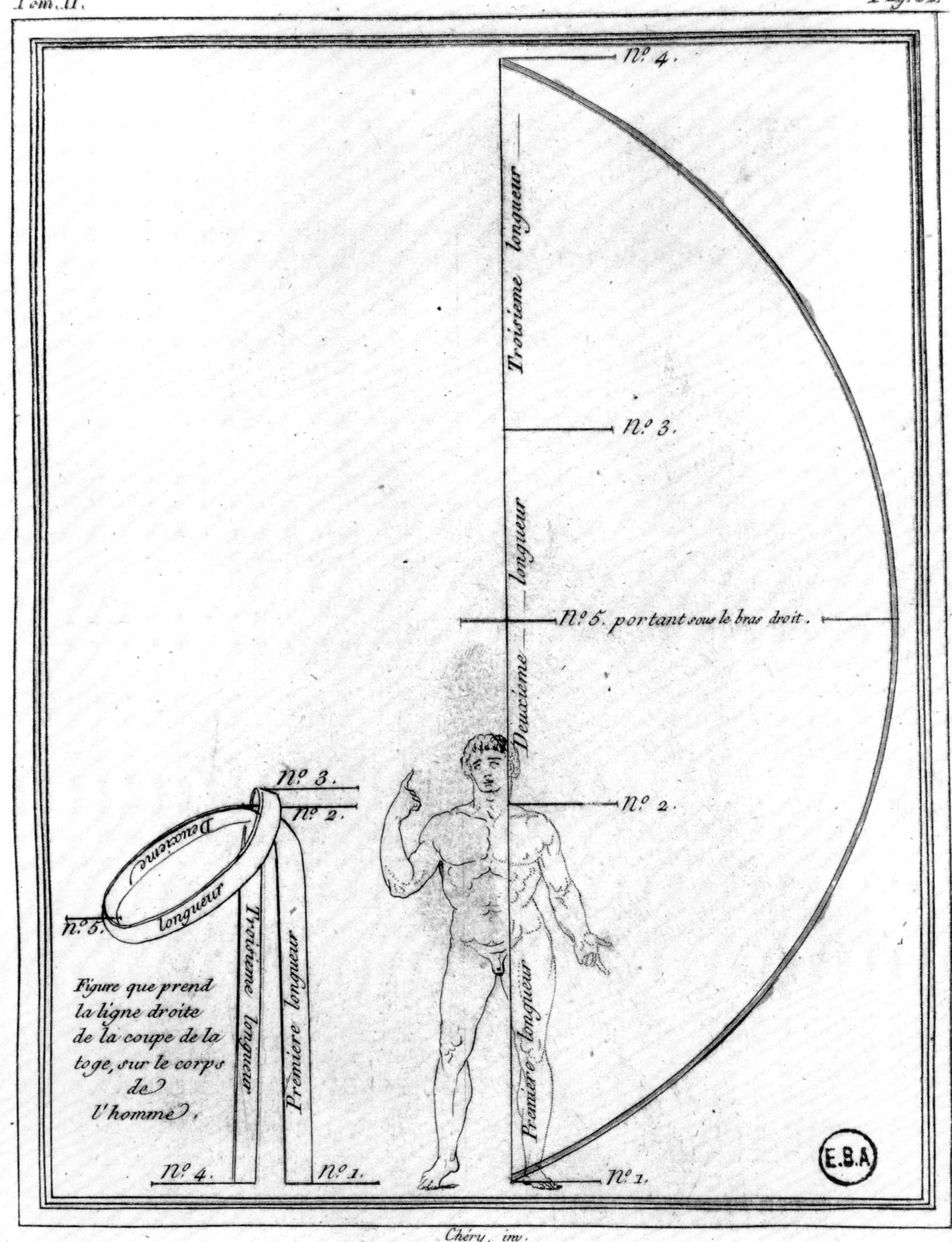

COUPE DE LA TOGE.

guidance of experienced artists and antiquarians."[19] Their endeavors were ultimately rewarded by courses on ancient costume given by the Hellenist Léon Heuzey, who taught at the École des Beaux-Arts from 1863 to 1907.[20] While waiting for the practical demonstrations, however, students continued to study illustrated treatises. These circulated throughout Europe and were particularly prized when not too expensive. One such work was Thomas Hope's *Costume of the Ancients*, first published in London by W. Miller in 1809, followed by a second edition in 1812 containing one hundred new plates. This latter edition included three hundred line engravings and cost only five guineas.[21] Although intended for British artists, Hope's treatise soon found favor on the continent. For example, while staying in Rome between 1824 and 1828 the sculptor Francisque Duret made pen-and-ink copies of several of Hope's Greek and Roman figures.[22]

Timeless Truth?

Artists have never aimed primarily for historical authenticity. They aspire to other kinds of truth. Even ancient monuments do not generally offer an accurate transcription of the fashions of their time. Ennio Quirino Visconti, the greatest antiquarian after Winckelmann, was the first to point out that "garments pertaining to earlier times were used in heroic portraits by Greek sculptors."[23] This, in turn, justified modern poetic license, where the object was to portray esteemed public figures in statuary. Visconti was contributing to a now famous debate about the best way to honor great men in sculpture.[24] Some favored the heroic nude, others argued for ancient costume, while still others insisted on a costume unambiguously evoking the period of the hero's life. Supporters of nudity or ancient costume frequently criticized the use of modern clothing, arguing that fashions soon looked dated and ridiculous, thus undermining the prestige of the model. Besides, modern clothing was constrained and full of petty detail. Visconti declared: "The use of clothing open from top to bottom and attached by buttons—a custom recommended by convenience and indispensable in our climate—nonetheless runs counter to the way in which drapery should be arranged in obedience to the precepts of art. The fact is that our modern garments are too tight and stiff to be compatible with either extensive drapery or, indeed, with variety in pleats and volumes."[25]

Despite ephemeral fashions, the modern garment seemed both limited and monotonous. It was a uniform imprisoning the body. It made provision neither for the infinite variety available in the fall of folds nor for happy accidents or carefully weighed choices in the arrangement of the cloth.[26] By contrast, ancient costume was various and, above all, *natural*. As Quatremère de Quincy put it, "it consisted of a very large piece of cloth" and was "free, inasmuch as the art of the tailor [had] not shaped it."[27] Not having been fashioned by man, it was intrinsically a product of nature. The "art that imitated it thus had nature as its model."[28] This was why drapery in the ancient style could no longer be thought of as specifically Greek or Roman; it was "*ideal by nature* and [could] consequently be the costume of all countries and all times."[29] This "natural" timelessness justified a metaphorical convention: drapery in the ancient style was the only clothing worthy of illustrious men, whose genius transcended their century and made them eternal. "Do not trade in copies of the tailor and bootmaker's craft," Éméric-David exhorted. "Although attentive to the laws of decency, it is rather the man of nature, the man of eternity whom you should present to the centuries to come."[30] This esthetico-philosophical outlook on the representation of great men was upheld at least until David d'Angers and his *Funerary Monument to General Foy* (1831, Père-Lachaise Cemetery).[31]

The natural freedom with which the ancient garment hung was not always considered the key to its beauty. Paradoxically, Quatremère de Quincy found himself speaking for uninhibited naturalism in the rendering of drapery, whereas Éméric-David—rightly

OPPOSITE FIGURE 18 | PIERRE-MICHEL ALIX (1762–1817) after Philippe Chéry (1759–1838), *Cut of the Toga*. Colored etching, 15.8 × 11.7 cm., in Jean-Charles Levacher de Charnois, *Recherches sur les costumes et les théâtres de toutes les nations tant anciennes que modernes* (Paris, 1790), vol. 2, p. 32.

considered a proponent of greater realism in Neoclassical doctrine—emphasized how confused folds might become in nature. He invited the artist to intervene and regulate them, "to produce order without untruth, and so to combine strength and suppleness, method with grace, a broad sweep with a light touch; in short, to create harmony."[32] Éméric-David prized drapery for its capacity to foreground or set off the underlying nude. After analyzing a series of drapes—the cloak on which *Laocoön* is seated, the veil on the vase at the feet of the *Capitoline Venus*, the garment of the *Farnese Flora*, and the *chlamys* of the *Laocoön*—he defines the axes of the compositions, detailing the contrasts of mass and light between flesh and fabric and between the main and secondary folds. He goes on to praise the ancients for their skill in draping or even veiling entire figures without compromising the truth of the nude. The nude remained the supreme principle.[33] Ancient garments could be adjusted so that they were both varied and authentic. Nothing of the kind was true of modern dress, which presented the sculptor with a difficult challenge. He was not obliged to respect the cut of the garment; on the contrary, he should boldly alter folds and outlines in order to reveal the body beneath the suit.[34]

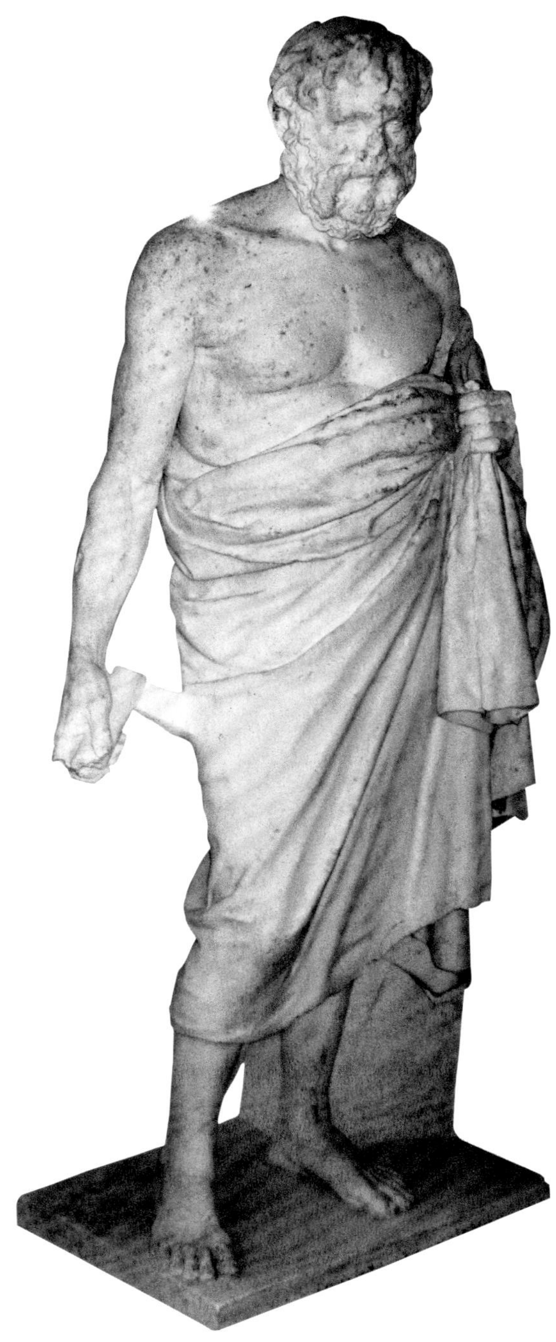

FIGURE 19 | LOUIS-PIERRE DESEINE (1749–1822), *Ancient Philosopher, Known as Zeno*, after an ancient original, 1781. Marble, 183 cm. Musée de la Marine de Loire, Châteauneuf-sur-Loire.

The Relative Merits of Ancient Drapery and Modern Folds

The garments of more recent times were thus rejected. But what of the means by which sculptors had rendered drapery since the Renaissance? There was no general condemnation. There is plenty of evidence to show that late-seventeenth-century sculptors, although passionate in their study of antiquity, also sought to learn from more recent examples. Several theoreticians acknowledged that certain modern sculptors showed a particular talent for large-scale drapery. Bernini's fluttering kirtles were often criticized, but the drapery folds of Algardi, Duquesnoy, Angelo de' Rossi, Le Gros, and Rusconi found favor in the eyes of Falconet and were eulogized by Dandré-Bardon in his *Essay on Sculpture*

(1765).[35] Neither of these authors wished to clip the sculptor's wings, to confine him to *drapé mouillé* and eliminate forms of technical virtuosity that might advance the sculptor's art. Falconet wished to proscribe "only what might be cold, clumsy, extravagant or out of place." True, *drapé mouillé* had a great advantage in that it allowed the movements of the nude to remain visible, and it did so with exquisite naturalness.[36] But "since sculpture's object of imitation is nature as a whole, and nature has more than one kind of beauty, why should a sculptor fetter himself to a particular kind of drapery, whose employment was dependent on time, climate, and circumstance?"[37] Moreover, Dandré-Bardon felt that since Michelangelo, sculptors had made huge progress relative to the ancients in the representation of fabric, in the variety of textures, and consequently in light effects.[38] There would be little point in abandoning these for the sake of antiquarian purism.

In defending the need for large-scale drapery, these two artist-theoreticians also appealed to ancient art, pointing out that Greek and Roman sculptors had not confined themselves to *drapé mouillé* but had left splendid examples of more expansively arranged material.[39] Both refer enthusiastically to the *Capitoline Zeno*.[40] This is now little known, but the renown it enjoyed until 1820 might have earned it a place among the "favorites" listed by Francis Haskell and Nicholas Penny.[41] The statue represents an athlete of the intellect. With his left hand he pulls tight a thick cloak, which falls in broad folds, stretching down over his right leg and leaving his powerful shoulders bare. This work was frequently drawn.[42] A plaster cast was taken for the Académie de France in Rome, and the statue itself was seized by the French and exhibited in the Musée Napoléon before being restored to Rome in 1815.[43] It inspired Giuseppe Angelini's sculpted portrait of *Piranesi* (1780, Rome, Santa Maria del Priorato)[44] and was copied by Louis-Pierre Deseine and Louis-Léopold Chambard, both winners of the Prix de Rome. Deseine's copy, made between 1782 and 1784, has been deposited by the Louvre with the Musée de la Marine de Loire in Châteauneuf-sur-Loire (fig. 19). Chambard made his copy in 1838; it was for a time displayed in the second courtyard of the École des beaux-arts but has since disappeared.[45] Zeno even appeared in biscuitware among the centerpiece figures of the emperor's dinner service, produced by the imperial manufacture at Sèvres.[46] The infatuation with this work had several causes: the prestigious presumed identity of the model; the combination of the nude with a broad, velvety, varied drape; the solid, noble simplicity of the pose; and a certain analogy with plastic solutions practiced by the Baroque masters, who were still discreetly if not openly admired. In fact, when Pajou sculpted his *Buffon* (Paris, Muséum national d'histoire naturelle, 1776; fig. 20), he had in mind not only the *Capitoline Zeno*[47] but the *Saint*

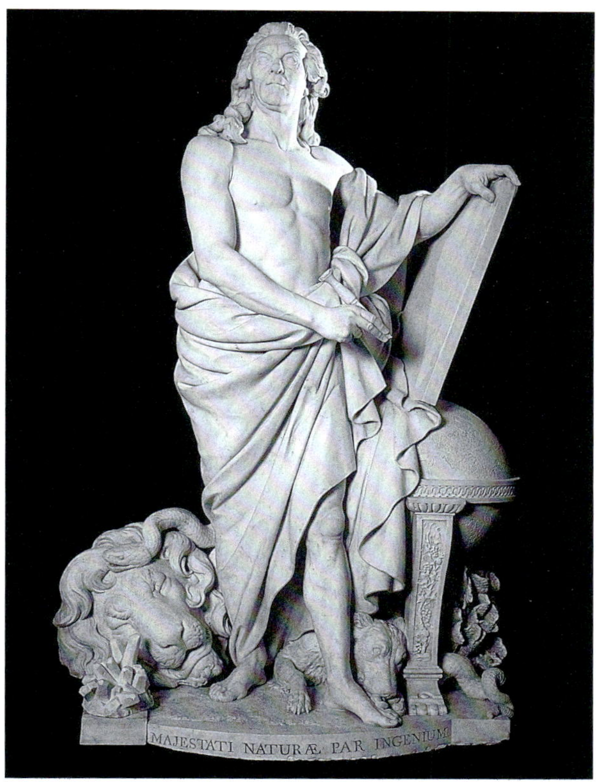

FIGURE 20 | AUGUSTIN PAJOU (1730–1809), *Monument to Buffon*, 1776. Marble, 290 × 135 cm. Muséum national d'histoire naturelle, Paris.

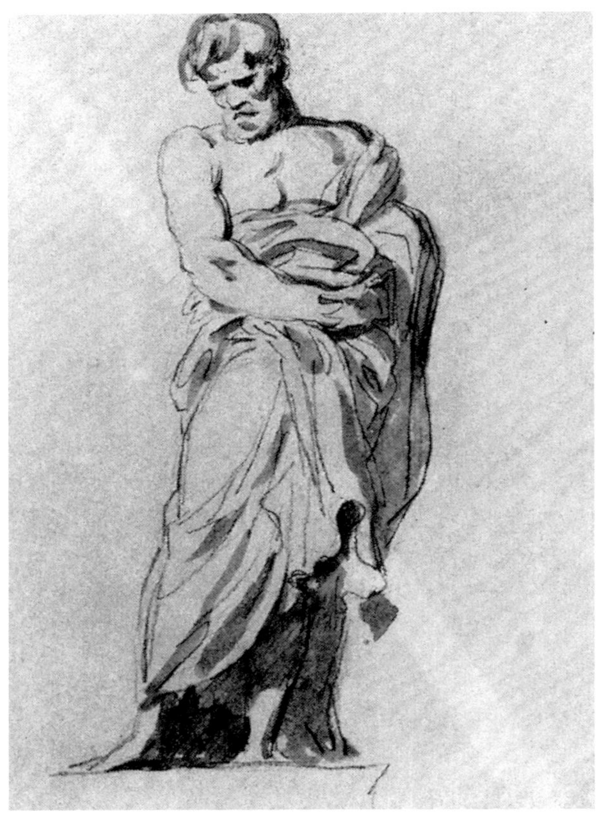

FIGURE 21 | AUGUSTIN PAJOU (1730–1809), *Saint Nilamon*, 1752–56, after Lazzaro Morelli. Graphite and gray wash on paper, 18.1 × 13 cm. Private collection, Paris (photo: Marianne Roland-Michel).

Nilamon carved from travertine in 1667–68 by Lazzaro Morelli (after a drawing by Bernini) for the colonnade of Saint Peter's. Pajou had drawn the sculpture during his stay in Rome in 1752–56 (fig. 21).[48] Simplistic definitions of Neoclassicism are badly exposed by such original syntheses of ancient and modern.

Drapery: Emblem and Language of Emotion in Allegory

In Pajou's *Buffon* one recognizes one of the great pieces of heroic portraiture. This genre plus allegory and heroic portraiture accounted for the majority of draped figures. Allegorical statues were for the most part female and proliferated in public monuments and in funerary sculpture. Whether standing or seated, allegorical figures tended to be draped in the ancient style.[49] This was sufficient to bestow on them an essence and a time scale distinct from the figures around them. Ancient costume was still more essential where two different levels of allegory were present and the artist needed to differentiate, say, an eternal virtue—which would necessarily be clothed *à l'antique*—from a personification belonging to a more recent period, whose costume had to evoke times closer to those of the spectator. Louis-Charles-Henri Dupaty first sketched his *Allegory of the Birth of the duc de Bordeaux* in a neo-Flaxmanian style, with a tearful city of Versailles in Greek costume and the figure of Hope represented as an angel in archaic drapery. The monument was intended for the chapel to the memory of the assassinated duc de Berry in the square Louvois (the chapel was destroyed in 1830) and is now in the crypt of the basilica of Saint-Denis (fig. 22).[50] By the time he made the definitive marble relief (1821–25), Dupaty had changed his mind and accentuated the difference between his two female figures. He bestowed on the weeping duchesse de Berry—who symbolized a bereaved France—a typical Restoration gown with short, bouffant sleeves. Hope, meanwhile, acquired the hairstyle and peplos of one of the *Borghese Dancing Women*. She holds an anchor (the traditional attribute of Hope) like a scepter, and with her left index finger she points to the new shoot—the child of the miracle—growing beside the broken lily of the Bourbon line.[51] The *Borghese Dancing Women*, a relief of the second quarter of the second century B.C. (fig. 23) acquired by Napoleon I in 1807 along with the Borghese collection, had been one of the most celebrated antiquities in Rome since around 1520. It then became one of the most prized possessions of the Musée Napoléon (renamed the Musée Royal in 1814).[52] The quotation is the more explicit because Dupaty also imitated the rhythmic background formed by the partly fluted

OPPOSITE FIGURE 22 | LOUIS-CHARLES-HENRI DUPATY (1771–1825), *The Hopes of the French Realized by the Birth of the duc de Bordeaux*, 1821–25. Marble. Saint-Denis, crypt of the Basilica (photo: Bernard Vitry).

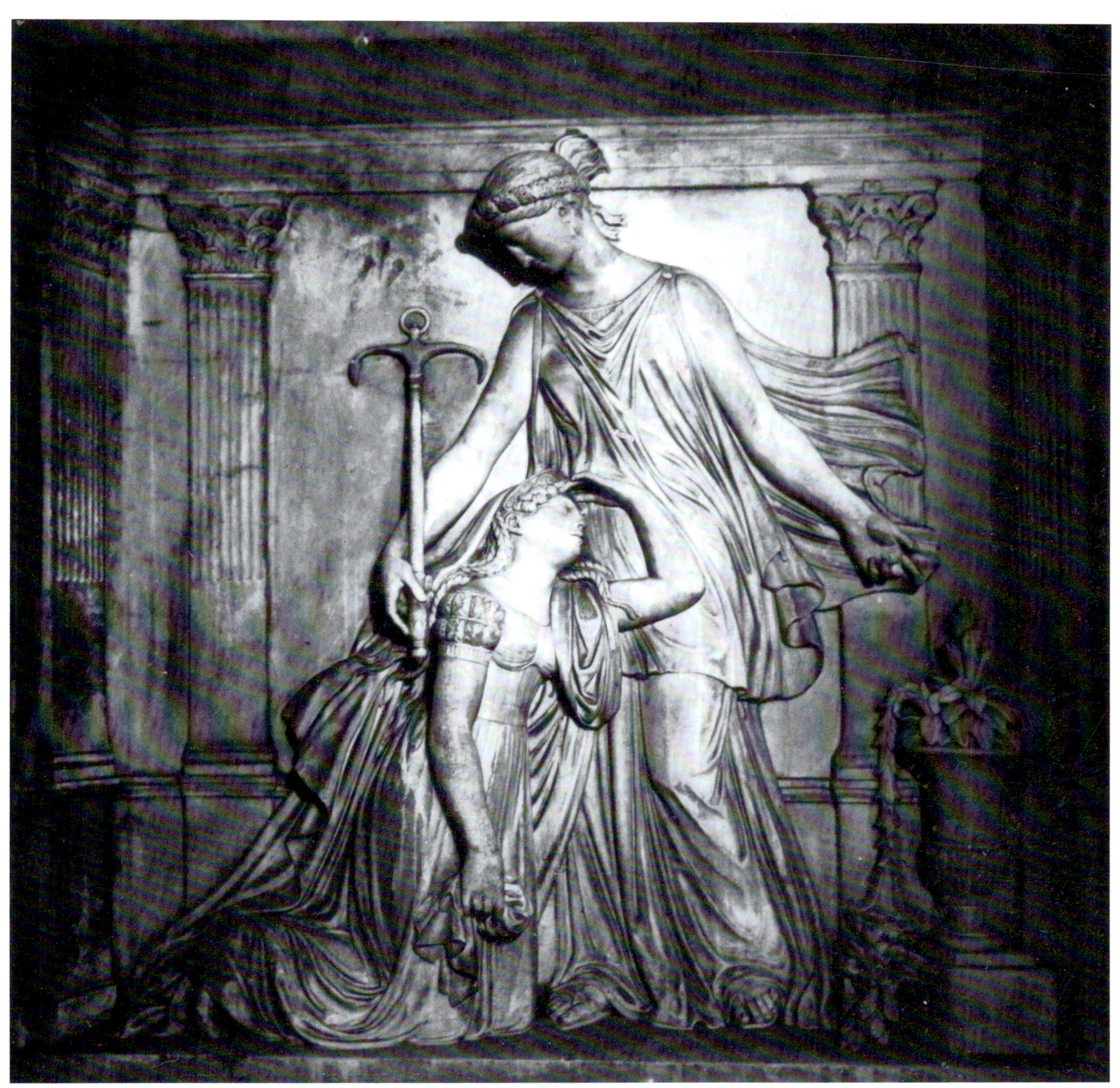

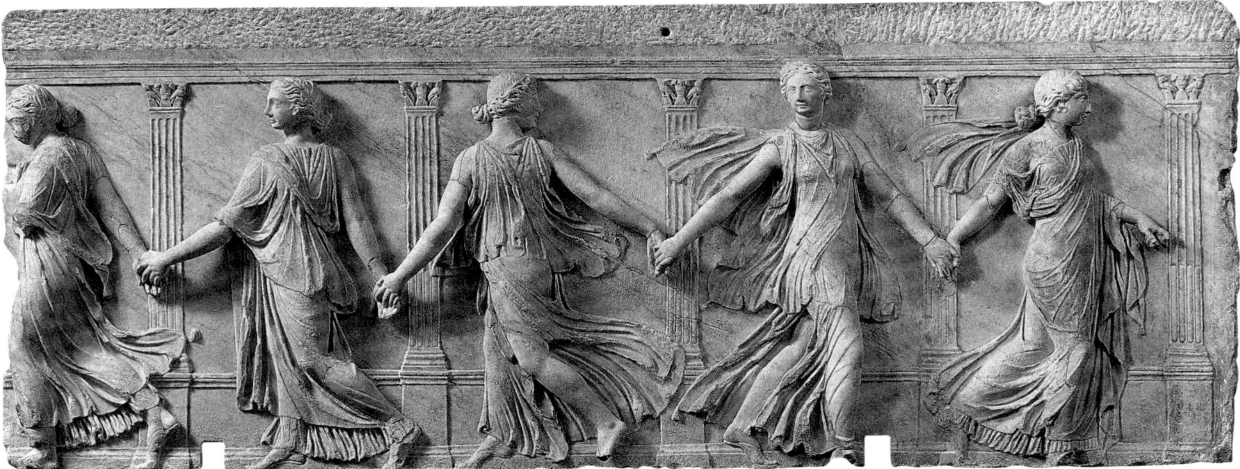

FIGURE 23 | *Borghese Dancing Women*, Roman, second quarter of second century B.C. Marble, 73 × 185 cm. Musée du Louvre, Paris (photo: RMN).

Corinthian pilasters over which the back of the peplos lightly floats.[53] In an effort to convey the joy to be felt by the French nation, a pagan dancing girl thus became a theological virtue. Antiquity, however, could justify anything—in this case an infringement of Quatremère de Quincy's doctrine about the natural quality in ancient drapery. Unless this touching scene took place in a light breeze, there is no obvious reason why Hope's peplos should be thus fluttering behind her when she herself is standing still. One cannot therefore speak of the natural fall of the garment. But there are two reasons why Dupaty needed this incongruity, with its concomitant rejection of realism. On the one hand, he wished to reinforce the allusion to the Roman relief and, on the other, to signify in plastic and poetic manner the resurgence of joy. The latter is expressed in the billowing of the light fabric, which contrasts with the heavy cloak wrapped around the kneeling figure of France. Scholarship, convention, and expression combine. Emotion formulas of pathos—*Pathosformeln*, to use Aby Warburg's term—are often those of costume.

This brief survey confirms that French sculpture of a Neoclassical tendency should not be too rigidly defined. Taught first by illustration and later by example, the requirements of costume were endlessly reaffirmed, yet they were never absolutely inflexible. Historical authenticity in statues was a secondary consideration relative to aesthetic truth and, indeed, to timeless symbolic truth. Moreover, so striking were the technical achievements of the moderns in the rendition of fabric and drapery that artists of the late eighteenth and early nineteenth centuries were unwilling to abandon them. True, artists of the stature of Clodion and Marin gave new life to *drapé mouillé* in their emulation of Roman masterpieces like the *Farnese Flora*. But the ancient sculptors' talent for broad folds received no less emphasis from the theoreticians and was frequently recommended as a model for young artists. Finally, borrowings from famous compositions were not merely scholarly references for the initiate but elements of a coded expressive vocabulary. Drapery *à l'antique* had an inherent authenticity derived from its natural freedom, but this could be sacrificed when it was made to serve poetic purposes entirely at odds with realism.

NOTES

The author would like to thank Catherine Dupraz-Plantiveau, Daniela Gallo, Gérard Hubert, Antoinette Le Normand-Romain, Philippe Malgouyres, and Marianne Roland Michel for their help in the preparation of this essay.

1 Toussaint-Bernard Éméric-David, *Recherches sur l'art statuaire, considéré chez les Anciens et chez les Modernes, ou Mémoire sur cette question proposée par l'Institut national de France: Quelles ont été les causes de la perfection de la Sculpture antique, et quels seroient les moyens d'y atteindre* (Paris, year XIII [1805]), 372. The work was first conceived around 1800.

2 There have been a number of studies focusing on the theories of nature, antiquity, and the rendering of flesh in sculpture that arose in mid-eighteenth-century France. They include: Martial Guédron, *De chair et de marbre: Imiter et exprimer le nu en France, 1745–1815* (Paris, 2003); and Aline Magnien: *La Nature et l'Antique, la chair et le contour: Essai sur la sculpture française du XVIIIe siècle* (Oxford, 2004).

3 For an excellent study of these treatises, see Sylvain Amic and Sylvie Patry, "Les Recueils de costumes à l'usage des peintres (XVIIIe–XIXe siècles): un genre éditorial au service de la peinture d'histoire?" *Histoire de l'art*, no. 46 (June 2000): 39–66.

4 Charles-Nicolas Cochin, "Du costume dans la peinture," in his "Discours sur la connoissance des arts fondés sur le dessin, & particulièrement de la peinture," *Mercure de France* (March 1759): 171–94; reprinted in *Recueil de quelques pièces concernant les arts* (Geneva, 1972), 3–43, esp. 43. See also Christian Michel, *Charles-Nicolas Cochin et l'art des Lumières* (Rome, 1993), 262–65. Diderot was likewise opposed to absolutism in rules of costume. See, e.g., his remarks in *Essais sur la peinture: Salons de 1759, 1761, 1763* (Paris, 1984), 63–64; and in E. M. Bukdhal, A. Laurenceau, and G. May, eds., *Pensées détachées sur la peinture, la sculpture, l'architecture et la poésie, pour servir de suite aux Salons* (*Salons IV: Héros et martyrs. Salons de 1769, 1771, 1775, 1781*) (Paris, 1995), 445. Diderot's views were influenced by Christian Ludwig von Hagedorn's *Betrachtungen über die Malerei*, which was published in Leipzig in 1762 and translated into French in 1775 under the title *Réflexions sur la peinture*.

5 Michel-François Dandré-Bardon, *Costume des anciens peuples*, 2 vols. (Paris, 1772–74), 34; commentary on pl. 1, 5th cahier.

6 Dandré-Bardon, *Costume*, 12, and 2nd cahier, pl. 5. [Rochet: "a white linen vestment resembling a surplice with close-fitting sleeves worn esp. by bishops and privileged prelates" (*Merriam-Webster's Collegiate Dictionary*, 11th ed.). Trans.]

7 On this treatise, in addition to Amic and Patry ("Les Recueils de costumes," 45–46), see the contributions by Alain Jacobs in D. Coekelberghs and P. Loze, eds., *1770–1830: Autour du néo-classicisme en Belgique*, exh. cat., Musée communal des Beaux-Arts, Ixelles (Ixelles, 1985), 69–73; and A. Jacobs, *A. C. Lens, 1739–1822*, exh. cat., Musée Royal des Beaux-Arts, Antwerp (Antwerp, 1989), 69–72. Though criticized on points of scholarship, Lens's treatise was well-received throughout Europe and in particular in Germany. Georges-Henri Martini, Rector of the St. Nicolas College in Leipzig, who translated it into German, revised this translation in 1784, and produced a revised French edition, which appeared in Dresden in 1785. In this 1785 edition, the work was enriched with vignettes and culs-de-lampe taken from the *editio princeps* of Winckelmann's *Geschichte der Kunst des Alterthums* (Dresden, 1764), and three plates taken from the first Italian translation of Winckelmann's *History* (Milan, 1779, 3 vols.). See André Lens, *Le Costume des peuples de l'Antiquité, prouvé par les Monuments. Nouvelle édition, corrigée, rectifiée & considérablement augmentée par G. H. Martini* (Dresden, 1785), p. xxvi. Lens's treatise was thus clothed in the authority of the greatest antiquarian and theoretician of the time.

8 On the *pallium*, see André Lens, *Le Costume ou Essai sur les habillements et les usages de plusieurs peuples de l'Antiquité, prouvé par les Monuments* (Liège, 1776), pl. 4, fig. 11; on the *chlamys*, see pl. 10, fig. 21; on the toga, see pl. 36, fig. 110. The semicircular form of the toga has been confirmed in fairly recent works by historians of antiquity. See Hans Rupprecht Goette, *Studien zu römischen Togadarstellungen* (Mainz, 1990), 3–4 and figs. 1–3. To represent the *chlamys* Lens uses the figure of Agamemnon on the Neo-Attic krater known as the *Medici Vase* in the Uffizi (inv. 307); see Guido A.

Manselli, *Galleria degli Uffizi: Le Sculture* (Rome, 1958), 1:189–92, no. 180, fig. 180b. See also Francis Haskell and Nicholas Penny, *Taste and the Antique: The Lure of Classical Sculpture, 1500–1900* (New Haven, Conn., 1981), 316, no. 82.

9 One should except Ottavio Ferrari's *De re vestiaria*, first published in Padua in 1642 and reprinted several times, though its claims were frequently contradicted by later antiquarians.

10 Nicolas-Xavier Willemin was quick to grasp this point. In his *Choix de costumes civils et militaires* he uses scholarly terms for the components of Greek dress and also provides the reader with diagrams. For example, for the variants of the *peplos*, see Nicolas-Xavier Willemin, *Choix de costumes civils et militaires des peuples de l'Antiquité, leurs Instrumens de Musique, leurs Meubles, et les Décorations intérieures de leurs Maisons, d'après les Monumens antiques, avec un Texte tiré des Anciens Auteurs*, 2 vols. (Paris, year VI [1789]–year X [1802], 1:97 and pls. XLV and XLVI, after the bronze statues found in the Villa dei Papiri (Herculaneum), now in the Museo Archeologico Nazionale of Naples. See also Amic and Patry, "Les Recueils de costumes," 46–47, and fig. 3.

11 See Amic and Patry, "Les Recueils de costumes," 47.

12 See Mario Fazio, *François-Joseph Talma, primo divo: teatro e storia fra Rivoluzione, impero e restaurazione* (Milan, 1999).

13 See Jean-Charles Levacher de Charnois, *Recherches sur les costumes et les théâtres de toutes les nations, tant anciennes que modernes; Ouvrage utile aux Peintres, Statuaires, Architectes, Décorateurs, Comédiens, Costumiers, en un mot aux Artistes de tous les genres; non moins utile pour l'étude de l'Histoire des temps reculés, des Moeurs des peuples antiques, de leurs Usages, de leurs Loix, et nécessaire à l'Éducation des Adolescens*, 2 vols. (Paris, 1790), 1:35–36.

14 See Kirsten G. Holström, *Monodrama. Attitudes. Tableaux vivants: Studies on Some Trends of Theatrical Fashion, 1770–1815* (Stockholm, 1967); see also Bernard Vouilloux, *Le Tableau vivant: Phryné, l'orateur et le peintre* (Paris, 2002).

15 The work of Levacher de Charnois was, in turn, imitated by the engraver and man of letters Sergent-Marceaux, who lived first in Brescia and then in Milan. A passionate supporter of theatrical reform, in 1813 he began publishing an essay on the history of costume in the form of installments of colored prints. The history was based on Alfieri's tragedy *Virginia*, the ballet *Il ritorno d'Ulisse in Itaca*, and *Ginevra di Scozia*, a "serious heroic drama for music in two acts by Signore Giovanni Simone Mayr," which allowed him to include examples of troubadour dress. See Antoine-Louis-François Sergent-Marceau, *Costumi dei popoli antichi e moderni in diverse figure incise e colorite con discorsi analoghi sulla forma degli abiti e la maniera de vestirli arrichiti di osservazioni storiche critici appoggiate all'autorità degli scrittori classici antichi. Opera utile ai Dilettanti di Teatro, ai Commedianti, ai Impresarj, ai Pittori di Scene, agli Statuarj e Pittori di Storia e generalmente a tutti gli amatori delle Belle Arti* (Brescia, 1813; subsequently published in installments in Milan, at the author's address, until 1817).

16 See, in particular, passages on the *pallium* (Levacher de Charnois, *Recherches sur les costumes*, 1:28–31, and plate representing *Orestes*, 28); on the *chlamys* (1:117–18 and plates representing *Asaph, Officer of Ahasuerus* and *2nd Plate of Authorities*, 1:115 and 116); and on the toga (2:28–42, and plates representing *Burrhus, Narcissus*, 28, and the *Cut of the Toga*, 32).

17 Levacher de Charnois, *Recherches sur les costumes*, 2:114.

18 Antoine-Chrysostome Quatremère de Quincy, *Considérations sur les Arts du dessin en France. Suivies d'un plan d'Académie, ou d'École publique, et d'un système d'encouragemens* (Paris, 1791), 132.

19 See his article, "De l'enseignement des beaux-arts," which first appeared in the *Revue des Deux Mondes* in 1849, was republished in *Mélanges historiques et littéraires* (Paris, 1855), and was reprinted in *Les Beaux-Arts, de l'Académie aux Quat'z'arts: Anthologie historique et littéraire*, ed. Annie Jacques (Paris, 2001), 319–34, esp. 323.

20 See Lyne Therrien, *L'Histoire de l'art en France: Génèse d'une discipline universitaire* (Paris, 1998), 117–26; Amic and Patry, "Les Recueils de costumes," 56–59 and figs. 8 and 9; and Jacques, ed., *Les Beaux-Arts*, 131, 142–43, 165–66.

21 See Sandor Baumgarten, *Le Crépuscule néo-classique: Thomas Hope* (Paris, 1958), 135–39, 260.

22 The present whereabouts of these drawings is unknown. They were formerly in the Cot Collection, Paris. See Antoinette Le Normand-Romain, *La Tradition classique et l'esprit romantique: Les Sculpteurs de l'Académie de France à Rome de 1824*

à 1840 (Rome, 1981), 36 n. 106, 56 n. 90, and figs. 22 and 24, which does not give a precise source.

23 Ennio Quirino Visconti, "Lettre au cit. Denon, membre de la Légion d'honneur, de l'Institut national, directeur du Musée Napoléon, de la Monnaye des Médailles, etc. sur le costume des statues antiques, Paris, ce 15 floréal an XII," *La Décade philosophique*, an XIXe, 1804, no. 24, 3e trim., 30 floréal, 338–46, esp. 338.

24 See, among others: Judith Colton, *Monuments to Men of Genius: A Study of Eighteenth-Century English and French Sculptural Works* (Ann Arbor, Mich., 1976); idem, "From Voltaire to Buffon: Further Observations on Nudity, Heroic and Otherwise," in Moshe Barasch and Lucy Freeman Sandler, eds., *Art, the Ape of Nature: Studies in Honor of H. W. Janson* (New York, 1981), 531–48; the entry by Guilhem Scherf on Clodion's *Montesquieu* in Anne L. Poulet and Guilhem Scherf, eds., *Clodion, 1738–1814*, exh. cat., Musée du Louvre (Paris, 1992), 279–86; David Bindman and Malcolm Baker, *Roubiliac and the Eighteenth-Century Monument. Sculpture as Theatre* (New Haven, Conn., 1995); Alison West, *From Pigalle to Préault: Neoclassicism and the Sublime in French Sculpture, 1760–1840* (Cambridge, 1998), 16–42, 91–93, 100, 113–25; and Daniela Gallo, "Pouvoirs de l'antique," in Jean-Claude Bonnet, ed., *L'Empire des Muses: Napoléon et les arts* (Paris, 2004), 317–29, 439–43. A similar controversy, known as the *Kostümstreit*, took place in Germany from 1786 to the mid-nineteenth century concerning the form to be given to the *Monument to Frederick II* in Berlin. This was finally commissioned from Christian Daniel Rauch and inaugurated on May 31, 1851. See Jutta von Simson, *Das Berliner Denkmal für Friedrich den Großen: Die Entwürfe als Spiegelung des preußischen Selbstverständnisses*, with a contribution by Friedrich Mielke (Frankfurt, 1976); idem, "Wie man die Helden anzog: Ein Beitrag zum 'Kostümstreit' im späten 18. und beginnenden 19. Jahrhundert," *Zeitschrift des Deutschen Vereins für Kunstwissenschaft*, 43, no. 2 (1989): 47–63; and *Christian Daniel Rauch. Oeuvre–Katalog* (Berlin, 1996), 286–312, nos. 179–88.

25 Visconti, "Lettre au cit. Denon," 344.

26 "Thus, everything about our clothes is symmetrical, stiff, and uniform. A thousand suits will only ever produce the same suit a thousand times over," one reads in Quatremère de Quincy, *De l'imitation*, with an introduction and notes by Léon Krier and Demetri Porphyrios (1823; reprint, Brussels, 1980), 421. Though they are rarely cited by sculpture specialists, the final pages (400–429) are among the most powerful and rigorous expressions of the Neoclassical ideal, notably in relation to costume and the nude.

27 Quatremère de Quincy, *Considérations sur les arts du Dessin*, 121.

28 Ibid., 422.

29 Ibid., 429 (my italics).

30 Éméric-David, *Recherches sur l'art statuaire*, 526. On Éméric-David see, in particular, Meredith Shedd, "Éméric-David's 'Anatomical Vision': A French Response to the Elgin Marbles," *Gazette des Beaux-Arts*, 6e période, 102 (Nov. 1983): 158–64; idem, "A Neoclassical Connoisseur and His Collection: J. B. Giraud's Museum of Casts at the Place Vendôme," *Gazette des Beaux-Arts*, 6e période, 103 (May-June 1984): 198–206.

31 On this monument, see Antoinette Le Normand-Romain, *Mémoire de marbre: La Sculpture funéraire en France, 1804–1914*, exh. cat., Bibliothèque historique de la Ville de Paris (Paris, 1995), 73–76, 345–47. David d'Angers set forth his aesthetic principles in his notebooks; see *Les Carnets de David d'Angers*, ed. André Bruel, 2 vols. (Paris, 1958), 1:19 (carnet 2, 1828), 171 (carnet 16, 1831–32), 181 (carnet 17, 1831–32); 2:251 (carnet 45, 1846–48), 287 (carnet 47, 1848–49), 445–46 (carnet 55, 1855). Théophile Thoré, who had seen in David d'Angers the future of French sculpture, considered the latter's choice of ancient costume a betrayal and revised his opinion of the artist in light of this. See Théophile Thoré, "Études sur la sculpture française depuis la Renaissance: Musée de sculpture moderne au Louvre. 1er article. XVIe siècle," *Revue de Paris* 25 (January 31, 1836): 330–54, esp. 332.

32 Éméric-David, *Recherches sur l'art statuaire*, 371.

33 Ibid., 373–77.

34 Ibid., 526.

35 See Étienne-Maurice Falconet, *Réflexions sur la sculpture*, in *Oeuvres complètes, . . . troisième édition, revue et corrigée par l'auteur* (1808; rpt. Geneva, 1970), 3:41; see also M.-F. Dandré-Bardon, *Traité de peinture, suivi d'un essai sur la sculpture. Pour servir d'Introduction à une Histoire Universelle, relative à ces Beaux-Arts*, 2 vols. (1765; rpt. Geneva, 1972), 2:24–28.

36 Falconet, *Oeuvres complètes*, 3:40; see also Dandré-Bardon, *Traité de peinture*, 2:15–16.

37 Falconet, *Oeuvres complètes*, 3:40–41.

38 Dandré-Bardon, *Traité de Peinture*, 2:27–28. Falconet acknowledged this technical superiority but wished to step back from the detail of textural rendering and return to the overall conception of drapery. He thought it much more intelligently distributed in ancient statues, for "in the observations one might make about drapery in ancient works, we should not confuse workmanship with the order and choice of folds. The workmanship may at times lack taste, intelligence, and truth, but the order and choice in ancient works are almost always masterful and the most sublime lessons can be learned from them." Falconet, *Oeuvres complètes*, 3:41; see also 44. Thus, for Falconet there was a truth more important than that of visual appearance, namely, the truth of rigorous and grandiose composition.

39 Dandré-Bardon, *Traité de Peinture*, 2:7; Falconet, *Oeuvres complètes*, 3:41; see also his essay "Du Moïse de Michel-Ange et de son Bacchus" (1808), 148. Falconet had never been to Rome and therefore must have based his judgment on Carlo Gregori's print after a drawing by Giovanni Domenico Campiglia in the catalogue of the Museo Capitolino either in its Italian version or in the Latin translation. See Giovanni Gaetano Bottari, *Del Museo Capitolino, tomo primo* (Rome, 1741), vol. 1, pl. 90; and *Musei Capitolini tomus primus, Philosophorum, poetarum, oratorum, virorumque illustrium Hermas continens, cum animadversionibus italice primum nunc latine editis* (Rome, 1750), vol. 1, pl. 90.

40 On this statue, which was found in 1701 in the Villa of Antoninus Pius and bought by Clement XII Corsini from Cardinal Alessandro Albani in 1733–34, see Henry Stuart Jones, ed., *A Catalogue of the ancient sculptures preserved in the municipal collections of Rome: The sculptures of the Museo Capitolino by members of the British School at Rome*, 2 vols. (1912; rpt. Rome, 1969), 347–48, *Stanza del Gladiatore* 8, pl. 86.

41 Haskell and Penny, *Taste and the Antique*.

42 One might cite drawings by Pompeo Batoni (Windsor, Eton College Library). See Hugh Mackandrew, "A Group of Batoni Drawings at Eton College, and some Eighteenth-Century Italian Copyists of Classical Sculpture," *Master Drawings* 16, no. 2 (summer 1978): 131–50 and pls. 1–25; 147, n. 16, and pl. 6. One could also cite drawings by Charles de La Traverse (Musée des Beaux-Arts et d'Archéologie, Besançon, inv. no. D. 4270); see Jean-François Méjanès, "La Traverse et Pajou," in Guilhem Scherf, ed., *Augustin Pajou et ses contemporains,* Actes du colloque, Louvre, Nov. 7–8, 1997 (Paris, 1999), 367 and 388, fig. 30. One could similarly cite drawings by Louis-Pierre Deseine (Musée du Louvre, Département des Arts graphiques, RF 6059, f° 50) and by Francisque Duret—who shows the statue front and profile (Paris, Cot coll., present whereabouts unknown); see LeNormand, *La Tradition classique*, fig. 21. One could cite a drawing from Jacques-Louis David's Album no. 10, whose authenticity is not, however, certain (present whereabouts unknown); see Pierre Rosenberg and Louis-Antoine Prat, *Jacques-Louis David, 1748–1825. Catalogue raisonné des dessins*, 2 vols. (Milan, 2002), 1:685, no. 1046 [leaf 7d], repr., and 2:775, no. 3; for the tracing of this drawing see 2:838, no. C 83).

43 It was exhibited in the Hall of Illustrious Men. See Louis Petit-Radel, *Les Monuments antiques du musée Napoléon, dessinés et gravés par Thomas Piroli*, 4 vols. (Paris, 1804–6), 4:97–98 and pl. 49.

44 See Leopoldo Cicognara, *Storia della scultura, dal suo risorgimento in Italia fino al secolo di Canova . . . per servire di continuazione alle opere di Winckelmann et di D'Agincourt*, vol. 7 (Prato, 1823–24), 76; Carlo Pietrangeli, "Sull'iconografia di G.-B. Piranesi," *Bollettino dei Musei Comunali di Roma*, nos. 3–4 (1954): 40–43; Gérard Hubert, *La Sculpture dans l'Italie napoléonienne* (Paris, 1964), 55–56; and Antonia Nava Cellini, *La Scultura del Settecento* (Turin, 1982), 67, reprod.

45 Measuring 1.83 meters in height, Deseine's statue (MR 1833) was exhibited in the Musée des Antiques at the Louvre, where it was still to be found in 1796. The installation of the copy thus preceded and prepared the way for the confiscated original. Much later, in 1894, it was deposited at the Château de Versailles, receiving the inventory no. MV 6263. In 1939 it was placed in the gardens of Châteauneuf-sur-Loire's town hall. Restored in 2000, it is currently in the Musée de la Marine de Loire, Châteauneuf-sur-Loire. On Deseine's copy, see Georges Le Chatelier, *Louis-Pierre Deseine statuaire* (Paris, 1903), 8–9; and, above all, Anne-Marie de Lapparent, *Pierre-Louis Deseine statuaire (1749–1822)*, Mémoire de l'École du Louvre, 2 vols. (Paris, 1985), 1:4–6 and 2:467–69; on Chambard's copy, see

LeNormand, *La Tradition classique*, 286, no. 140.

46 On the statuette made in 1808 after a plaster model by Pierre Petitot, see the essay by Tamara Préaud in Marie-Anne Dupuy, ed., *Dominique-Vivant Denon: L'Oeil de Napoléon*, exh. cat., Musée du Louvre (Paris, 1999), 304, no. 298.

47 See James David Draper and Guilhem Scherf, eds., *Pajou Sculpteur du Roi, 1730–1809*, exh. cat., Musée du Louvre (1997–98) and New York, The Metropolitan Museum of Art (1998) (Paris, 1997), 397.

48 On the Vatican statue, see the contribution by Laura Falaschi in Valentino Martinelli, ed., *Le Statue berniniane del Colonnato di San Pietro*, Rome, 1987, 86–7, no. 28 and Jennifer Montagu, *Roman Baroque Sculpture: The Industry of Art* (New Haven and London), 1989, 146–47. For Pajou's sanguine drawing, formerly in the Cailleux Collection, currently in a Parisian private collection, see Marianne Roland Michel, "Dessiner à Rome au temps de Pajou," in Scherf, ed., *Augustin Pajou*, 285–308, 292 and 299, fig. 2. For the other drawings of his stay in Italy, which also mix copies from ancient and baroque statues, see J. D. Draper and G. Scherf, "Augustin Pajou dessinateur en Italie 1752–1756," *Archives de l'art français*, nouvelle période, 33, Nogent-le-Roi, 1997, and Roland-Michel, "Dessiner à Rome," above.

49 The rule applied equally to male allegorical figures; *Crime* in Louis-Pierre Deseine's *Monument du duc d'Enghien* (1816–24, Vincennes, castle chapel). The figure is half-covered with a broad and vaguely Roman cloak that partly veils his knife. See Le Normand-Romain, *Mémoire de marbre*, 85–86 and fig. 66. On standing and seated female statues, see Karina Türr, *Zur Antikenrezeption in der französischen Skulptur des 19. und frühen 20. Jahrhunderts* (Berlin, 1979), 43–53, 64–73; on allegory in nineteenth-century funerary statues, see LeNormand-Romain, *Mémoire de marbre*, 268–96.

50 The subject of the marble relief became *The Hopes of the French Realized by the Birth of the duc de Bordeaux* or *The duchesse de Berry Born Again to Hope*. For the history of the monument, see François Macé de Lépinay, "Un monument parisien éphémère: la chapelle expiatoire du duc de Berry," *Bulletin de la Société de l'Histoire de l'Art français* (1973–74): 283–98; see also Le Normand-Romain, *Mémoire de marbre*, 86–92 and fig. 74. The pen-and-ink drawing, made around 1821 and now in a Parisian private collection, represents *The Town of Versailles Lamenting the Death of the duc de Berry. Hope Comes to Console Her and Shows Her a Bud on the Branch of the Lily that She Covers with Her Wing*. See Le Normand-Romain, *Mémoire de marbre*, 91, fig. 73.

51 The shoot represents the duc de Chambord, the grandson of the deposed Charles X of France. The *légitimiste* pretender to the French throne, Chambord was "miraculous" in being born after his father's death. In 1832, his mother instigated a brief insurrection against Louis-Philippe in an attempt to put Chambord on the throne and thus restore the Bourbon line. [Trans.]

52 See D. Gallo's contribution in Dupuy, *Dominique-Vivant Denon*, 203–4, no. 208, repr.

53 However, he differs from the ancient format and Canova's notion of relief in placing the pilasters at right angles to the background in order to suggest depth. On this point, see Macé de Lépinay, "Un monument parisien éphémère," 293. This insistence on the imitation of the ancient architectural format in the background of high-relief allegory continued up to the mid-nineteenth-century. Evidence for this is found in the six allegorical figures draped *à l'antique* (1859–65) carved in stone by Augustin Dumont (*Prudence* and *Truth*), Francis Jouffroy (*Punishment* and *Protection*), and Jean-Louis Saley (*Equity* and *Strength*) between the semi-columns of the west portal of the Palais de Justice in Paris, designed by Duc. As Türr has observed, these reliefs, though on a much larger scale, are clearly inspired by the *Provinces* of the temple of the Divine Hadrian in Rome, founded in A.D. 145, and by their framing in that temple. Of the thirty-eight figures originally in the *cella*, only sixteen survive, now dispersed throughout many different collections (Naples: Museo Archeologico Nazionale; Rome: Palazzo dei Conservatori on the Capitol, the Farnese and Odescalchi Palazzi, the Villa Doria-Pamphili, the Temple of Hadrian in the piazza di Pietra, and the Musei Vaticani). See Jocelyn M.C. Toynbee, *The Hadrianic School: A Chapter in the History of Greek Art* (1934, rpt. Rome, 1967), 152–59 and pls. xxxiv–xxxvi; see also Türr, *Zur Antikenrezeption*, 168–69, fig. 151–52.

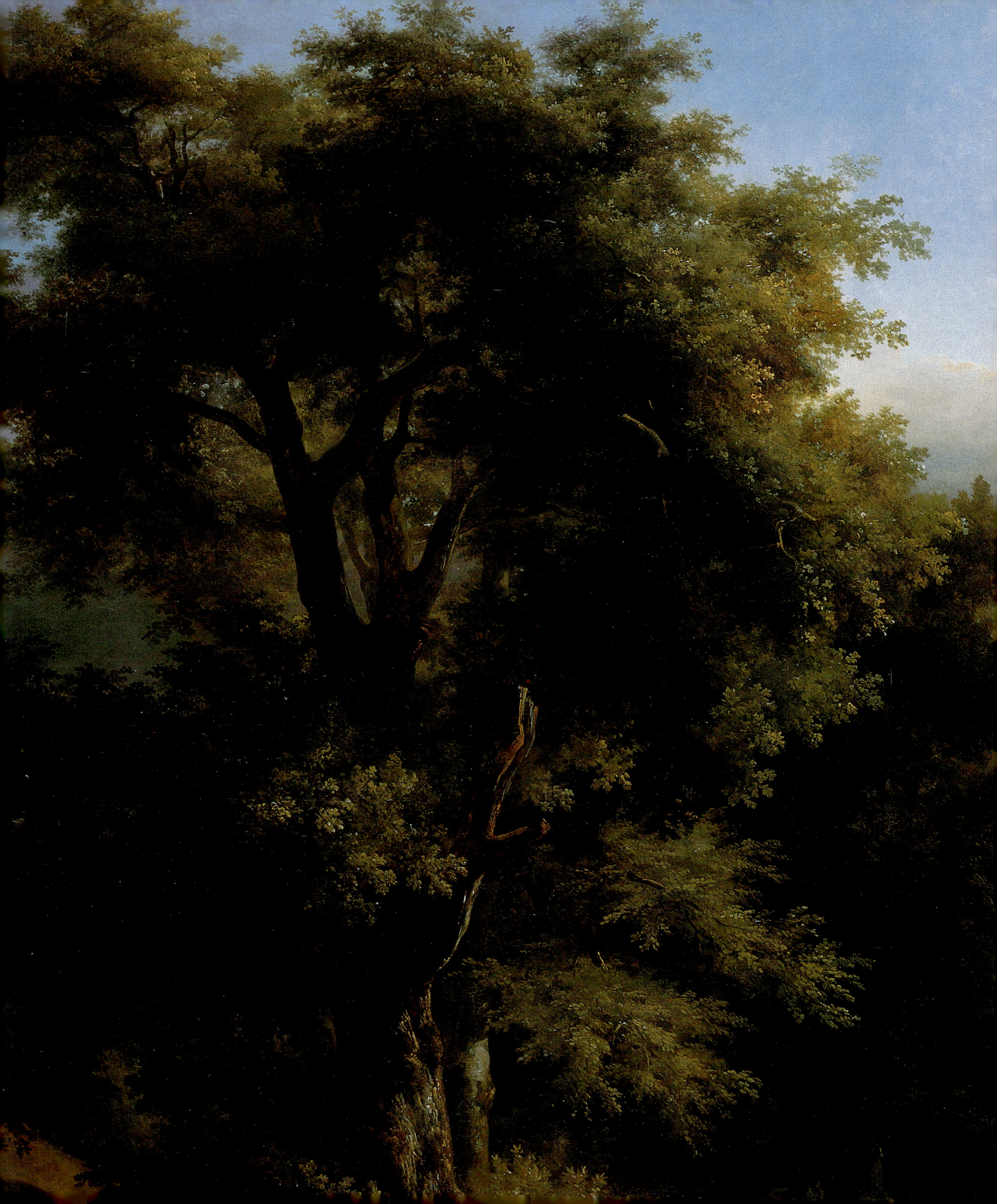

A Brief Administrative and Artistic History | Teaching Art in Paris

Emmanuel Schwartz

THIS PUBLICATION CELEBRATES AN ARTISTIC ENTERPRISE BEGUN IN 1648 WITH THE founding of the Académie royale de peinture et de sculpture and continued in the École des beaux-arts. It was undertaken by young artists at the outset of their careers and by others already recognized by their peers. It comprised a quest for humanism and truth in art and was performed under the tutelage of one of the subtlest and most celebrated poets of all time—Homer. Though there were many hesitations and doubts, the works that it produced demonstrate a continuity of themes, modes, and ideals over many generations. A nineteenth- and even an early-twentieth-century student of the École des beaux-arts might justifiably claim that, when it came to reading Homer, he or she was a direct descendant of Charles Le Brun (fig. 24). Despite revolutions and coups d'état, the acquisition of a new name, new premises, and being placed under the auspices of different ministries, until 1968 the École kept faith with the way art was practiced in the seventeenth century. For most of its history the administrative, pedagogical, and artistic practices of the École were little affected by politics and acknowledged no aesthetic evolution.

Administrative History

The seventeenth century inherited the principles of the medieval *maîtrise*, or craft guild. The status accorded to painters and sculptors was that of practitioners of a mechanical or base art, assimilating them to manual workers or traders. Some artists considered the conditions for entering the maîtrise—and therefore for practicing their art—humiliating. They thought of themselves as servants of noble arts and had long ago requested and obtained from the king individual dispensations that placed them outside the guild structure. In 1647 the Fronde set the corporations and the nobility against monarchical power. Taking advantage of this, the artistic guild

DETAIL OF CATALOGUE NO. 20

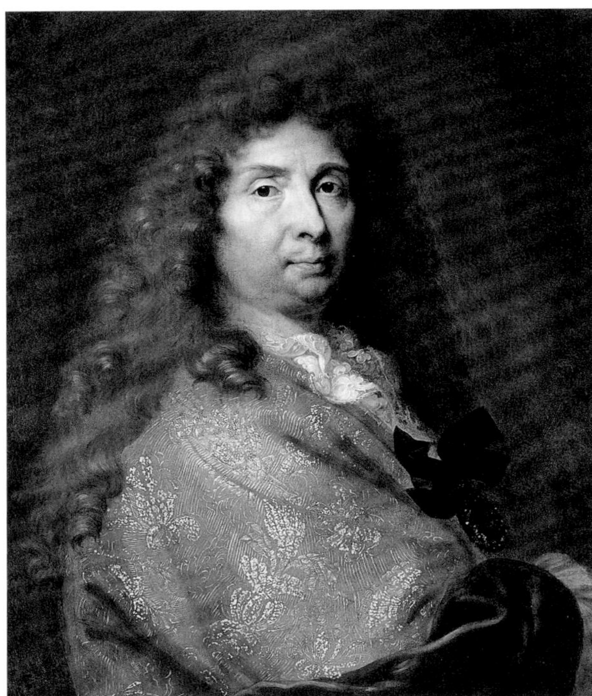

FIGURE 24 | NICOLAS DE LARGILLIÈRE (1656–1746), *Portrait of Charles Le Brun*, ca. 1683. Oil on canvas, 75 × 59 cm.

obtained from the Parliament of Paris a decree prohibiting the painters and sculptors of the king and queen from working for private clients.

THE SCHOOL OF THE ROYAL ACADEMY OF PAINTING AND SCULPTURE

In 1648, early in the reign of Louis XVI, a group of artists centered around Charles Le Brun, the Testelin brothers, and Justus van Egmont obtained a royal privilege to leave the trade guild and form an association under the auspices of the king. In conformity with the Italian model, which referred to the philosophical school of Plato, this was to be called an Academy. The academicians declared themselves practitioners of a liberal and intellectual art distinct from the commercial vocation of the guild's apprentices, journeymen, and masters. The twelve founders were dubbed *Anciens* (Elders).

From the date of its founding on February 1, 1648, the Academy provided drawing classes for all who could afford them. Each Elder taught the class for one month a year, and a nude male model was provided. An attempt was made to provide free classes, but the king declined to subsidize them. The teaching dispensed by the Royal Academy was soon competing with that of the guild, which had founded its own academy (the Academy of Saint Luke). For a time, during the Fronde (1651–55) the two schools were combined. The atmosphere that resulted is unlikely to have favored cooperation since the members of the two rival institutions hated and despised each other.

In 1655 the academicians introduced new statutes and the Academy was granted by letters patent the right to style itself *Académie royale*. Moreover, it was decreed that only Royal Academicians could become painter or sculptor to the king or queen. The prime minister, Cardinal Mazarin, became the first patron of the Academy. It was awarded an annual income of one thousand livres, which the finance minister, Jean-Baptiste Colbert, raised to four thousand in 1668. In 1671 a Royal Academy of Architecture was created. It offered classes and awarded prizes but remained independent of the Academy of Painting and Sculpture until the French Revolution.

The Academy's statutes provided for a *concours* (competition) in *dessein* (literally "drawing," but in this sense referring to an oil sketch).[1] The *dessein* was intended to celebrate "the heroic actions of the king." Since this decision was essential both to the teaching of art in France and to the collections of the École des beaux-arts, it is quoted here in full. On January 27, 1661, it was decreed:

> Prizes will be offered to the students of the Academy who have been chosen in the examination conducted every Saturday on the basis of the drawings they have done from the model. To this end, every year on the last Saturday of March, the Academy will give all the students a subject bearing on the heroic actions of the

> king, so that each will do a *dessein* to be submitted three months later, at which time a prize will be awarded; then it will be ordered that this subject be executed in painting, the picture to be submitted six months later, at which time the *grand prix Royal* will be awarded to the best picture; the said painting, of course, will remain at the Academy. For the judgment of such prizes, each will be required to submit his reasons on paper as briefly as possible, these to be examined and resolved by four Rectors. The winner should receive a reward, along with the authorization to choose his own place in the life class.[2]

In 1663 the minister decided that the *grand prix* (first in painting, then in sculpture, and finally in architecture) should comprise a salaried stay in Rome. (The École still possesses the oldest prizewinning piece extant, Pierre Monier's *Conquest of the Golden Fleece*, an homage to one of Louis XIV's victorious campaigns [cat. no. 100], which won in 1663.) In the early days of the Academy, this *concours* was open to teachers as well as students, but later the teachers took care to avoid competition with those inspired and ambitious young artists, their students.

In 1663 the Royal Academy obtained a monopoly in teaching art; it alone had the right of providing models for students (this was withdrawn in 1705). A hierarchical structure of twelve teachers (one per month) and four rectors took charge of teaching. Certain of these teachers were designated Officers, the highest-ranking of whom was the Protector, a position occupied throughout the eighteenth century by the Director General of the King's Buildings. Below him was a Director. Assistants replaced the teachers when needed and eventually succeeded them. The painter Le Brun, a protégé of Colbert, was appointed the first director. Colbert had succeeded Mazarin and Chancellor Séguier as the official Protector of the Académie.

Each academician was permitted to give private teaching lessons and employ models—male or female—to pose in his studio. Art lovers possessing no technical artistic attainments were also admitted to the Academy. At least one of these, the comte de Caylus, exercised considerable influence over the École's teaching methods (a point to which I shall return). The Academy occupied various premises. From 1656 to 1661 it was located in the Louvre, first in the rooms of the sculptor Jacques Sarrazin and then in those of the tapestry weaver Pierre Dubourg. From 1661 to 1692 it was housed in the Palais-Royal (Palais Brion). Then it returned to the Louvre, initially in the first-floor rooms. In 1702 it moved to the Salon Carré, and in 1711 to the ground floor. It returned to the first floor in 1721 and expanded over the course of the century until, in 1763, it had absorbed the Galerie d'Apollon, where its reception pieces were hung.

The Academy also held *Salons* (exhibitions) in the Louvre to display the latest works of the academicians. Most Academy reception pieces and certain prizewinning works, however, were featured in these exhibitions. In 1667 Colbert decided that they should be held during Holy Week every other year. The critics were invited, and from 1673 on, the occasion was marked by the publication of brochures. Interrupted for long periods, under Louis XV they took on a form of ritual. Beginning in 1751 the exhibition was held in the Louvre's Salon Carré, from which such exhibitions derived the name *Salon*. By opening on August 25, the feast day of Saint Louis, the exhibition paid homage to Louis XI and, perhaps more significantly, to all the other kings who, over the course of the Academy's existence, bore this name.

During the eighteenth century the Academy of Saint Luke continued to offer free classes. The Royal School merely enjoyed a monopoly in the award of the Grand Prix (which was not yet called the Prix de Rome). To qualify for the Grand Prix an artist had to attend the École. The latter was divided into the Lower École (École d'en bas), where the teacher's drawings were copied, and the Upper École (École d'en haut), a life class where students drew from a nude model. Admission to the Lower École required the recommendation

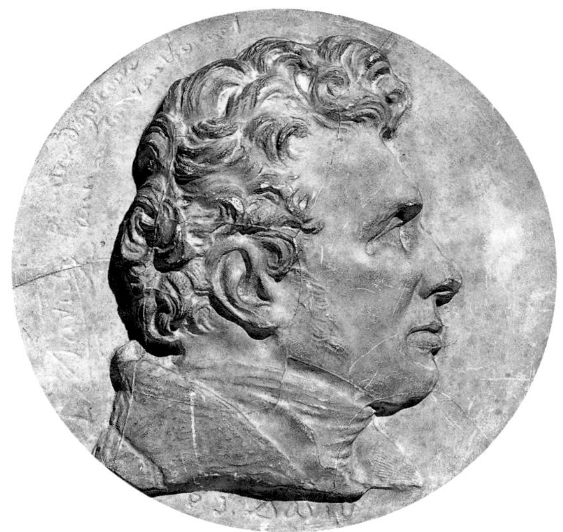

FIGURE 25 | PIERRE-JEAN DAVID D'ANGERS (1788–1856), *Portrait of Jacques-Louis David*, 1828. Plaster medallion, 13 cm. diam.

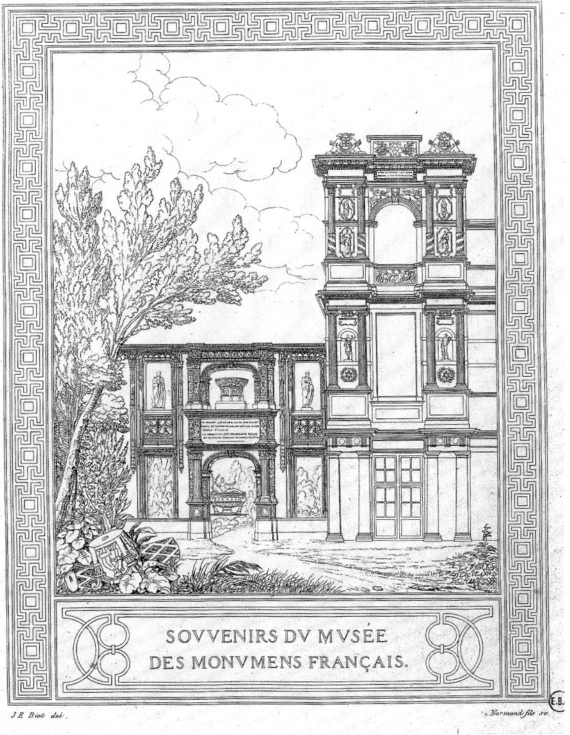

FIGURE 26 | J.-E. BIET, *Musée des monuments français* (1821), in J.-P. Brès, *Souvenirs of the Musée des monuments français*, engraved by Normand the Younger.

of an academician; no other form of selection was practiced. Thereafter *concours de place* governed the order in which students entered the life class; quarterly *concours* (known as the *petits prix*, or little prizes) in life drawing or low-relief sculpture established a hierarchy among the students. Courses in perspective, anatomy, and history were given, although they seem to have been organized and attended in rather haphazard fashion. In 1749 Superintendent of Buildings Lenormant de Tournehem, Protector of the Academy, noted that the education of the students—specifically their knowledge of Latin and Greek literature—left much to be desired. He decided that before leaving for Rome, the Grand Prix winners should complete their literary and historical studies at the Royal School of Protected Pupils.

THE REVOLUTION AND THE EMPIRE

In 1789 privileges and guilds were abolished and, with them, the Academies. The painter Antoine Renou (1731–1806) now defended the hierarchical organization of the Academy against the demands of egalitarianism. The archaeologist Antoine Quatremère de Quincy (1755–1849), although not himself an academician, suggested uniting all the schools that taught drawing: the Academic School of Painting and Sculpture; the Free Royal School of Drawing (for apprentices); the School of Architecture; and School of Bridges and Highways (civil engineering). This attempted centralization was prevented by Renou. In these times of political turmoil, the history of the École came to be linked with Jacques-Louis David, a man as anxious to abolish the old administrative framework as he was to found a new artistic vision (fig. 25).

Initially a Jacobite and regicide and then a Bonapartiste, David was to die in 1825 in exile after the Restoration. In 1793 an artist applying for membership in the Academy committed suicide following his rejection and David seized on the occasion to have all the academies closed. (His hatred of the system may have been personal, for he had long been refused a Grand Prix.) Only a few months later, however, the

Convention reversed its decision. The fall of Robespierre put an end to David's tyranny over the arts. In 1794 the École's drawing *concours* were reinstated under the direction of Renou. In 1795 the National Institute of Science, Literature, and Arts (Institut de France) was founded, and in 1797 the Grand Prix was reestablished. But under whose authority should the École now be placed? The influence of the artist-members of the Institut (David not least among them) soon outweighed that of Renou since the Grand Prix was theirs to award. The choice often fell on David's pupils, although he himself was not a teacher at the École. Between 1801 and 1807 the Institut and École were moved to the quai de Conti, specifically to the Collège des Quatre-Nations building that now houses the Institut de France. Renou died in 1806 and was succeeded as permanent secretary to the École by the painter Léonor Mérimée, father of the more famous Prosper, the novelist and short-story writer. The Institut was now divided into three and, later, four classes. In 1803 responsibility for the award of prizes in painting, sculpture, architecture, and—unexpected innovation—engraving and musical composition was transferred from the members of the Institut as a whole to the new Fine Arts Class (Classe des beaux-arts). The teachers, however, hoped to restore their status as Officers of the Royal Academy. In 1819 the Royal Special School of Fine Arts (École royale et spéciale des beaux-arts) was founded. Although its major decisions—notably appointments—were subject to the approval of the minister, responsibility for teaching now reverted de facto to the Fine Arts Academy, the "classe" of the Institut that had taken the old name of Academy in 1816.

THE NINETEENTH CENTURY

Events of a very different kind now influenced the history and development of the École. It acquired new premises formerly occupied by the Museum of French Monuments, which earlier had displaced the suppressed convent of the Petits-Augustins (fig. 26). Alexandre Lenoir, the curator of the museum, had saved many sculptures from revolutionary vandalism, and the exhibitions that he organized have been a constant source of inspiration to the new institution. The architects and curators of the École were never to forget that on this site had stood a Romantic museum that evoked—through tombs artfully fabricated from medieval remains—the long history of France.

Before 1863 there were no painting studios in the École des beaux-arts. The buildings were occupied by an immense collection of plaster casts and paintings (originals or copies), most of which have long since been allocated to museums or consigned to the basement. As in the eighteenth century, the students learned to paint, sculpt, and build in the private studios of their masters. It was advisable to choose an influential master irrespective of whether he taught at the École. The master then wrote a letter of recommendation permitting the aspiring student access to the École to draw there and prepare for the competitive entrance exam (*concours d'entrée*).

Until 1863 the methods of the twelve teachers of painting and sculpture remained those of the eighteenth century. They corrected the students' drawings of ancient artefacts—plaster casts and sculptures—and of the life model. Passing the biannual drawing *concours* gave the student access to the École for the next six months. These *concours* also established the order of precedence in the life class. *Concours d'émulation* in painting and sculpture brought financial rewards and advantages in the other competitions. Courses included anatomy, perspective, history, and antiquity. There were different courses for the students of architecture, who far outnumbered the other students, until their departure from the École after 1968.

AFTER 1863

The architect Viollet-le-Duc, the writer Prosper Mérimée, and others attempted a radical reform. They wanted to curb the influence of the Académie des beaux-arts, strip it of its authority to award the Prix de Rome, and shorten the period of study (one could study until age thirty in Paris and thirty-five in Rome). Until then pedagogical matters had come under the

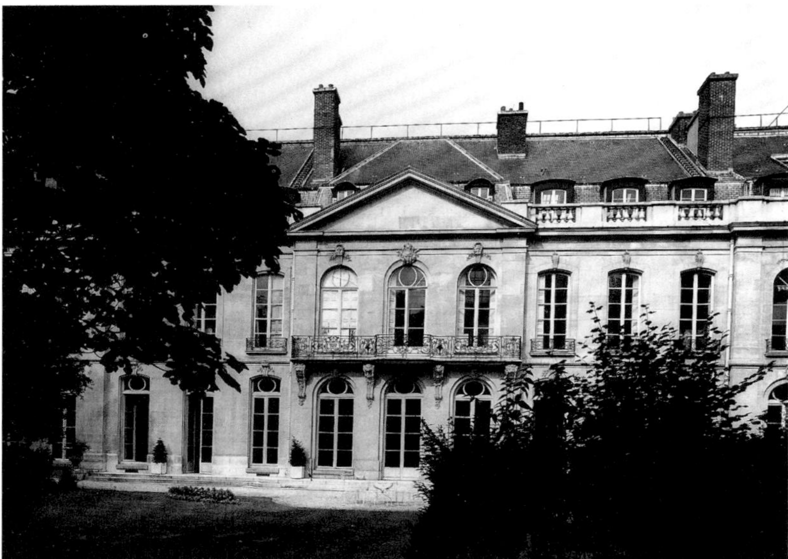

FIGURE 27 | DEBIAS-AUBRY (François Aubry, d. 1755), Hôtel de Chimay (formerly Hôtel de Bouillon), garden facade, 1744–47.

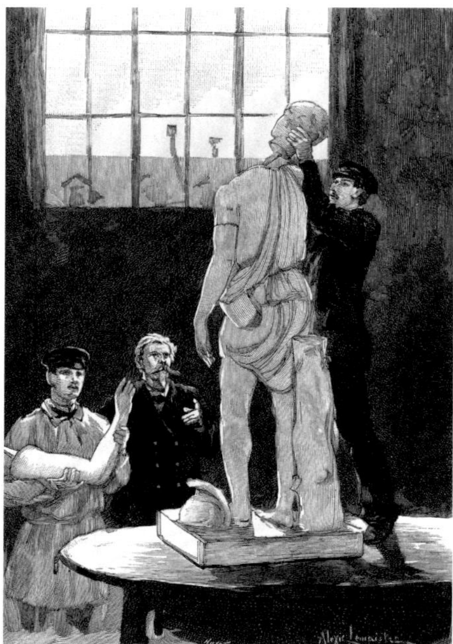

FIGURE 28 | ALEXIS LEMAISTRE (1873–1889), "Posing in the Ancient Style" (1889), in *L'École des beaux-arts dessinée et racontée par un élève.*

authority of the president, who had been elected by the assembled teachers. Now the president was to be appointed. Many of the proposed reforms, however, were overturned by the combined opposition of teachers and the student body. In 1871 the Académie des beaux-arts regained control of the panel that awarded the Prix de Rome. The Higher Council responsible for organizing the Prix de Rome did little to change either the subjects or the criteria for the prize. The only real innovation was the installation of studios within the precincts of the École. Directed by studio heads, they attracted ever larger numbers of students. As a result, the École's collections of sculptures, maquettes, and paintings had to be moved, lent out, or disposed of. New buildings were acquired or constructed, among them the Hôtel de Chimay, formerly the Hôtel de Bouillon, on the quai de Malaquais (fig. 27). Designed in the seventeenth century by François Mansart and decorated by Charles Le Brun, it originally had a garden laid out by Le Nôtre. Although the studio heads were, almost without exception, academicians, many students continued to attend outside studios, especially when preparing for entrance exams (fig. 28). In 1883 a new reform created the Teaching of the Three Arts, which forced students to take simultaneous courses in painting, sculpture, and architecture and transformed the entrance exam into a long succession of tests.

History of the École's Collections: The Works

The provenances of the works in the École's collections are inseparably linked to the history of the École itself and its predecessor, the Royal Academy, and thus with the entire history of art instruction in France. The provenances of the objects are, for the most part, highly institutional: the criteria of format, subject, and composition that the competition pieces were required to meet has imparted a recognizable tone or style. Precise regulation of the way a subject was illustrated led artists to assume a particular view of *history* and *fable*, and their perspective does much to explain the successive forms of academic art in France. (See the short, individual analyses later in this essay.) Since the organizing principle behind this catalogue is mythological rather than chronological, the works exhibited are not grouped according to stylistic affinity. What follows is a simplified account of the ways the different categories of works exhibited entered the collections of the École. The mode of acquisition is specified in the entry for each individual work.

PROVENANCES: FORMER COLLECTION OF THE ROYAL ACADEMY OF PAINTING AND SCULPTURE

Royal Academy Reception Pieces

Before its abolition in 1793, the Royal Academy had its premises in the Louvre and possessed various collections linked to the selection process for new academicians. The first step in acceptance was to present samples of one's work to the Academy. Upon acceptance, the artist was granted the right to exhibit in the Salon du Louvre and was required to produce a reception piece within a certain time frame—normally one year, although this was often extended. It had to be based on a subject agreed upon in advance. In the case of the minor genres of portrait and still life, two pieces were required. The reception piece could be rejected, but once accepted it remained the property of the Academy and was exhibited within its premises. In 1793 the reception pieces were either handed back to the living academicians or deposited with the new Museum (the Musée du Louvre). A few sculpture reception pieces went first to the Musée des Monuments français (see later discussion) and then to the École. In 1872 the Musée du Louvre deposited a certain number of paintings with the École, and they were incorporated by the architect Jacques-Félix Duban into his design for the library. For the most part these were history paintings drawn from fable. (The present exhibition draws heavily on this category.) David withdrew his own reception piece, *Andromache Mourning Hector* (cat. no. 42), when he turned against the Academy, but it was donated to the École by his descendants. It was deposited with the Louvre in 1971, but it has been included in this overview of the École's collections and Homeric inspiration.

The Royal Academy Grand Prix in Painting

Before the Revolution, little care was taken to keep together the paintings that had won the Grand Prix of the Royal Academy. Those currently in the École's collection were either repossessed by their authors at the time of the Revolution and subsequently returned or assigned to the École by the ministry on which it depended. The works exhibited were painted under conditions much like those of nineteenth-century Prix de Rome entries (see later discussion). These conditions had evolved gradually. According to one eyewitness account:

> The Grand Prix *concours* opens some days before the first Saturday in April. Students who think themselves good enough to compete assemble on a given day in one of the halls of the Académie. The teacher for that month is locked in with them. He sets them a subject, often chosen from the Bible. They compose [an oil sketch] on this subject without leaving the room. Their sketches are presented at the next assembly [of the teachers]. The Academy then keeps the best of them, up to a maximum of eight. Next the sketches are executed full-size in the *loges*[3] that have been built in the Academy to exclude external help. They are judged on the last Saturday of August by the vote of the assembled Academicians.[4]

In 1768, a figure painting was also required between the initial sketch and the sketch of the definitive composition. Provisions for impartiality soon entered the regulations: subjects were kept secret until the day of the exam; competitors were required to paint in the *loges*; and entries were anonymous. The dimensions of the entries were fixed by the Royal Academy session of March 5, 1768: "Painters may use canvases up to the size of twenty-five sols."[5] The regulations anticipated attempts at cheating, and students and teachers duly

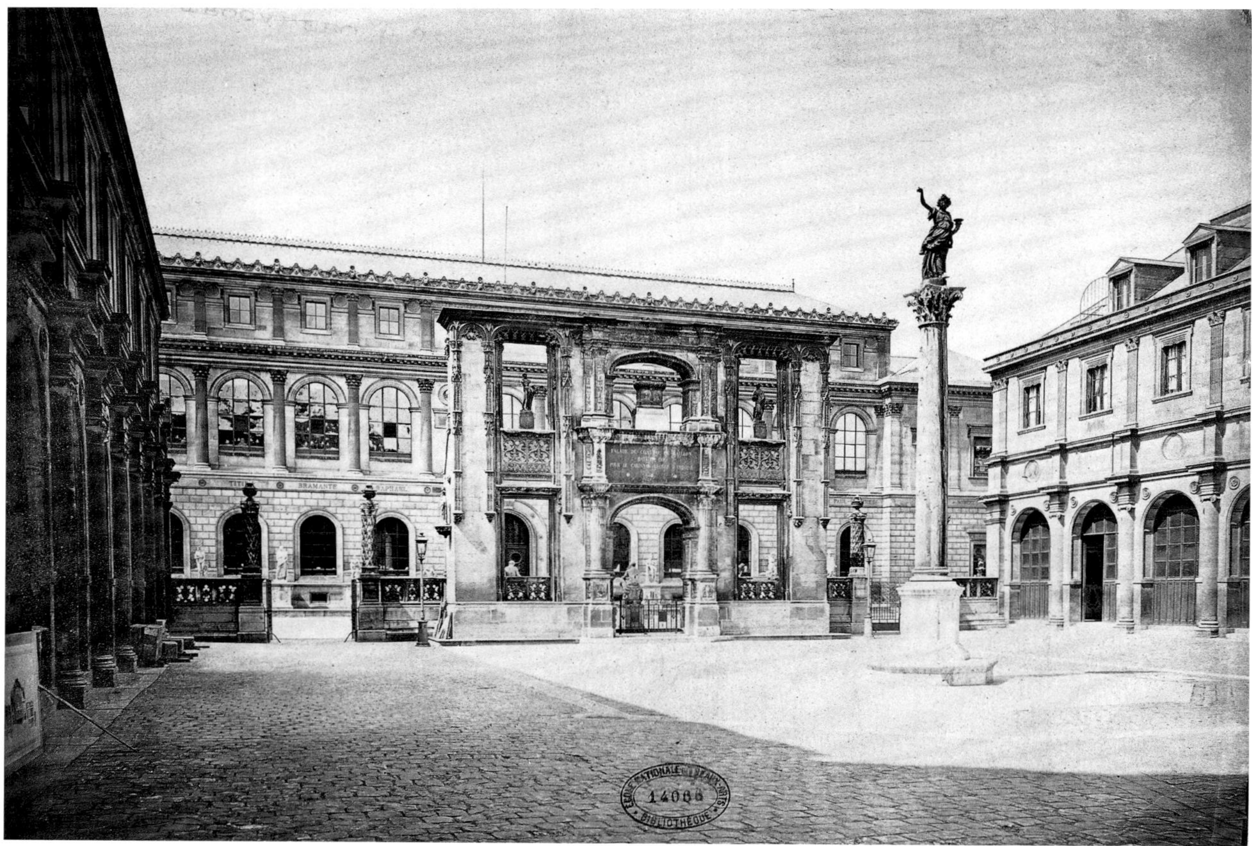

FIGURE 29 | ANONYMOUS, *Courtyard of the École des beaux-arts*, photograph, ca. 1880.

obliged. Irregularities were occasionally reported by the students and sometimes even sanctioned, but in general the École was as indulgent of the students' abuses as of its own failings.

THE MUSÉE DES MONUMENTS FRANÇAIS

During the Revolution, the Musée des Monuments français occupied the former convent of the Petits-Augustins. There Alexandre Lenoir collected sculptures from many sources, the majority French. After the closure of the museum in 1817, the most important works were returned to the buildings from which they had been taken or transferred to the Louvre. Nevertheless the École des beaux-arts still possesses hundreds of relics of the Musée des Monuments français. They include sculptures that were Academy reception pieces and Pierre II Legros's *Combat of Athletes* (cat. no. 44), a work which reproduces the kind of poses favored by the Academy's models.

REGULATION DEPOSITS WITH THE ÉCOLE DES BEAUX-ARTS (AFTER 1797)

Winning a grand prix or medal or being highly placed in a *concours* brought with it financial reward. In exchange, the student was invited to cede the prize work to the École, where it was exhibited. This tradition goes back to the school of the Royal Academy. Between the seventeenth and twentieth centuries, *concours* were increasingly funded by private foundations. The competitions were abolished in the educational reforms of 1968, but the income from the funds donated to the École made it possible to continue the policy of financial prizes (under new names) and thus to keep the prize works. The following section presents a simplified description of the different *concours* cited in this catalogue.

SKETCHES

Oil Sketches on a Historical Subject

Founded in 1816, this *concours* was held every six months until 1843, when it became quarterly. In some cases the exam required the completion of the sketches within twelve hours. In others there was a second stage, in which the sketch had to be realized on a larger scale within a month.

Oil Sketches of a Historical Landscape

Founded in 1822 as an annual *concours*, it became quarterly in 1843.

Sculpture Sketches

Compositions were based on the same subject as the oil sketch *concours* until 1828, except for 1821. From 1816 to 1831 the *concours* was held every six months, after which it was held on a quarterly basis. Beginning in 1832 it alternated between low relief and sculpture in the round. After 1863 it took place six times a year, with different formats.

Architectural Sketches

This *concours* was for advanced students (*première classe*). There were six *concours* per year. The exam was taken in the *loges* and lasted twelve hours.

ACADEMIC *CONCOURS*

Expressive Head

The *concours de la tête d'expression* was created by the comte de Caylus in 1760. Candidates had to depict an expression enacted by a model over several sittings. At first, entries could be submitted in any medium, but in the nineteenth century the *concours* was divided into sculpture and painting competitions on the same subject. The expression was sometimes combined with a classical reference: *Philoctetes, or Anger mingled with contempt.*

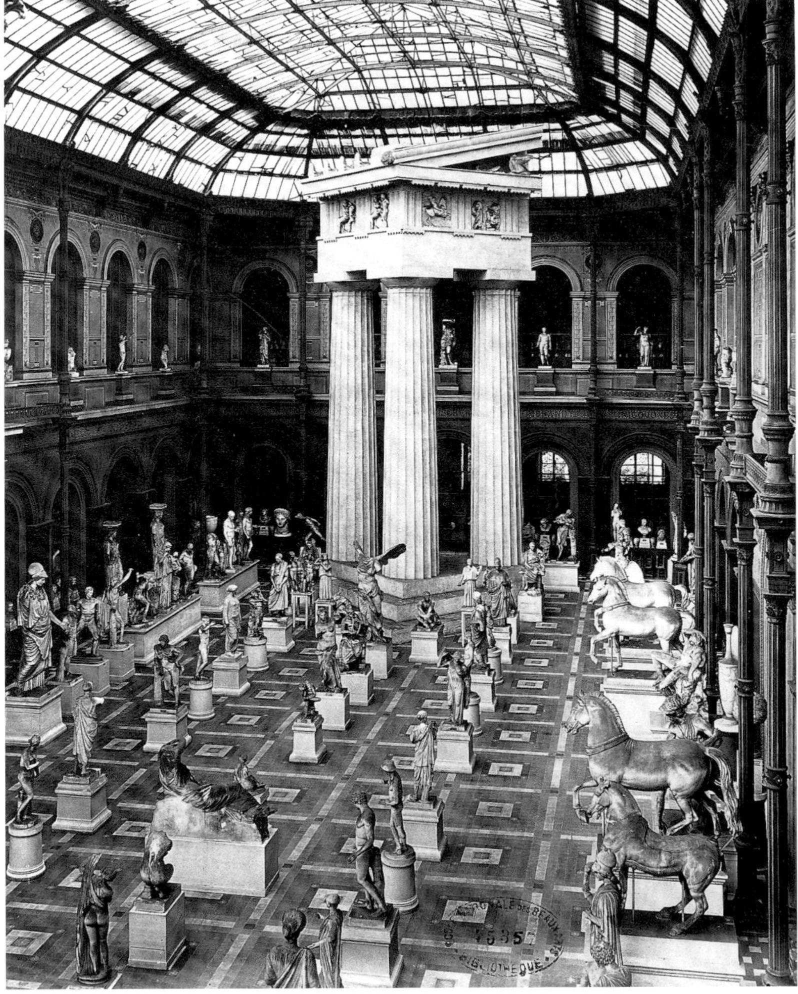

FIGURE 30 | ANONYMOUS, *The Glazed Courtyard of the École des beaux-arts*, photograph, ca. 1920.

Grand Prix de Rome in History Painting

This was also an annual *concours*. The following conditions applied to all disciplines: the artist had to be under thirty, single, and (beginning in 1810) of French

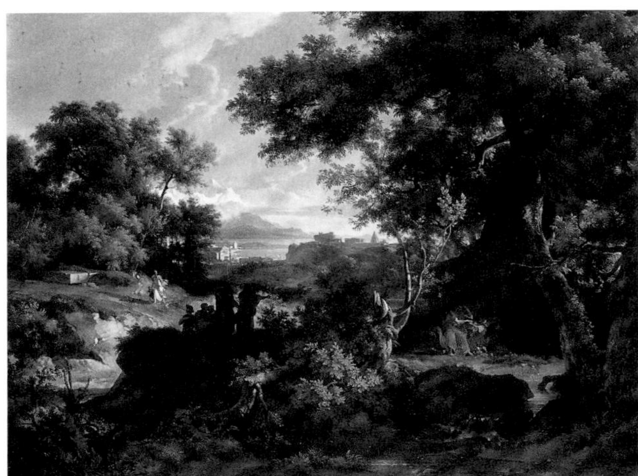

FIGURE 31 | ACHILLE-ETNA MICHALLON (1796–1822), *Democritus and the Abderites*, 1817. Oil on canvas, 115 x 145 cm. Prix de Rome in Historical Landscape.

nationality. The Rome scholarship only came into being after the Revolution, so Grands Prix awarded before the dissolution of the Royal Academy are not Grands Prix de Rome. Moreover, the consolation Grands Prix (second Premier Grand Prix, and even first and second Deuxième Grand Prix [!]), which did not confer the Rome scholarship, should not be described as Prix de Rome. A series of qualifying rounds led to the definitive *concours*, which was undertaken in separate *loges* (hence the term *logiste* for finalist). Former finalists and students who had already won important *concours* were spared the initial qualifying round. All others were required on one day in spring to sketch a history composition in oils on a canvas measuring 32.5 by 40.5 centimeters. Twenty candidates at most were selected for the second eliminating round, the life study, which was painted in four sittings, for a total of seven hours. Ten candidates at most were then invited to paint a subject in the space of a single day. The surviving candidates then had seventy-one days to paint a picture of specified size—normally 113.5 by 146.5 centimeters—based on the sketch composition, of which a tracing had been made for the purpose of comparison. In addition to the Premier Grand Prix, second prizes and distinctions could be awarded for outstanding entries. If the annual crop was particularly weak, the Premier Grand Prix could be held over until the following year. Although the procedures remained unaltered in the twentieth century, the size of the final work was no longer specified.

Grand Prix de Rome in Historical Landscape Painting

This competition took place every three years between 1817 and 1863. The procedure was analogous to that of the history painting *concours*. It was invented for the purpose of awarding a Roman scholarship to Achille-Etna Michallon (fig. 31), the great hope for the revival of French landscape painting of his time and master to a pupil older than himself—Camille Corot. The historical landscape required the *logiste* to imagine a landscape in which figures from fable appeared, although these were strictly limited in their dimensions. The qualifying rounds included the drawing of a tree since the painting in the final *concours* was often organized around a handsome tree in the manner of the Dutch landscape painters. In accord with the subjects, however, the students naturally tended to evoke the light, the seas, and mountains of the Mediterranean landscapes. The meeting of Ulysses and Nausicaa was frequently set, combining as it did all the required components.

Grand Prix de Rome in Sculpture

This resembled the painting *concours*. The first qualifying round (twelve hours) took place on the second Thursday in May and involved a sketch of a historical or mythological theme. Of the sixteen candidates selected, an additional eight were eliminated in the next round, a sketch of a figure from life. These two rounds determined whether the candidates' abilities in composition and anatomy qualified them for the final round, in which the *logistes* received a classical, biblical, or mythological subject. Beginning in 1806, low relief alternated with sculpture annually. Candidates had twelve hours to create a clay sketch, then seventy-one days to make a relief measuring 1.14 by 1.46 centimeters, or a sculpture standing a meter high. Works that diverged from the initial sketch were eliminated. Late-nineteenth-century sculptures tended to be life-size. Starting in 1816, the École paid for plaster casts of the winning work to be made. In 1902 plaster casts were made for several earlier works whose original casts had been lost. For example, a *surmoulage* (a cast of a cast) was made from the cast of James Pradier's relief, which was preserved in Geneva (the town of his birth), since the École's cast had been partly destroyed by a fire in the storeroom where it was kept (cat. no. 49). These works have not been much studied and their very fragile material (plaster) has exposed them to damage. The analysis of the sketches presented in this catalogue provides a fresh perspective on these interesting works.

Grand Prix de Rome in Engraved Medallions or Semiprecious Stones

Founded in 1805, this *concours* took place every three years. After the qualifying rounds (*concours d'essai*), candidates were required to make a low-relief sketch on a subject drawn from the Bible or ancient history. They then had ninety-seven days in which to make a steel medal or a low relief on semiprecious stone. The École kept dies, plaster proofs, pewter casts, or wax impressions either identical in size to the prizewinning medal or in a larger format. Every other year a copperplate engraving *concours* was also held.

PRIX JAUVIN D'ATTAINVILLE

Founded in 1877, this annual prize was awarded for history and landscape painting. After eliminating rounds, a maximum of ten students worked in their *loges* throughout September on a subject sometimes inspired by classical antiquity.

DISPATCHES FROM ROME (ENVOIS DE ROME)

Holders of the Prix de Rome generally spent five years at the French Academy in Rome. Every year they were required to send to the Institute a consignment of work based on the exercises set in Rome, one example of which entered the École's collection. For a long time the convention prevailed that it had to be a copy of an Italian painting or a classical sculpture. The most impressive is Ingres's copy of the Farnesina *Mercury* by Raphael or his studio (1809 Dispatch; fig. 37). The winners of the Prix de Rome in architecture sent studies they had drawn of an ancient building: surveys, plans, elevations, and, above all, reconstructions showing the putative or imaginary original state of the edifice. These spectacular hypotheses influenced the École's vision of the ancient world. Thus, Charles Garnier's *Reconstruction of the Temple of Aegina* (1852; cat. no. 8) forms part of the École's collection.

DONATIONS AND LEGACIES

The donors of some of the works are listed below:

> In 1876, Madame Duchenne de Boulogne donated studies (photos and casts) used by her husband, Dr. Guillaume-Benjamin Duchenne, who was known as Duchenne de Boulogne (1806–1875).
>
> In 1879, the great republican Victor Schoelcher (1804–1893), deeming the École, with its democratic principles, worthy of his sympathy, donated a fine collection of prints.
>
> Jacques-Édouard Gatteaux (1788–1881), a sculptor and engraver of medals, left various paintings and drawings to the École, among them Poussin's *Mercury, Herse, and Aglauros* (cat. no. 17).
>
> In 1885, the architect Joseph-Frédéric Debacq (1800–1892) gave the École a collection of antiquities acquired during his archaeological expeditions in southern Italy with the duc de Luynes.

ADMINISTRATIVE ALLOCATIONS

For a long time, the government allocated works to the École on the basis of their artistic and pedagogical value. In 1841, Ingres, then director of the French Academy in Rome, sent three ancient statues to the École. Two remained there (*Torso of Venus, Torso of Mars*; cat. nos. 11, 12), while the third (the *Medici Minerva*) was allocated to the Louvre in 1913. In 1864 the French

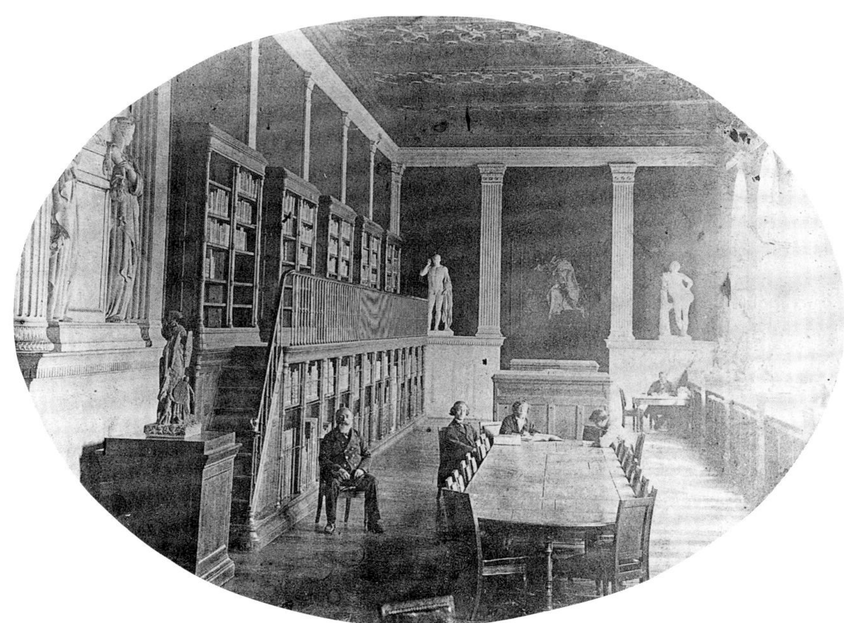

FIGURE 32 | ANONYMOUS, *The Library of the École des beaux-arts*, photograph, ca. 1880.

state commissioned a bronze cast of Brian's *Mercury* (cat. no. 13) and allocated it to the École des beaux-arts. These works remain the property of the state, which may at any time deem their presence in the École superfluous and allocate them to another institution. This occurred with the plaster casts of ancient works, most of which returned to the École from the Louvre in the nineteenth century but were removed in 1970 from the Palais des Études to the Petites Écuries at Versailles. In 2002 they came under the auspices of the Department of Greek, Etruscan, and Roman Antiquities of the Musée du Louvre, as they are now considered relevant to the history of taste.

ACQUISITIONS

In 1978 the École bought Georges Rochegrosse's painting *Le Bal des Quat'z'arts* (cat. no. 128) at auction. It occasionally buys works linked to the history of teaching or to the academic tradition, such as the set of engravings comprising Daumier's *Histoire Ancienne* (cat. nos. 109–27), which was purchased in 2001.

The Future of the Collections

This book is illustrated almost exclusively with works belonging to the École des beaux-arts. This gives the reader a notion of the artistic and intellectual coherence of the collection and makes it clear why the École was long considered a museum of art history and of the teaching of art.

For a long time, the majority of these works were on view: display cases, revolving bookcases, and entire rooms were devoted to the prizewinning works. Books, engravings, and photos that had been bought or given by donation or bequest were arranged in series and were frequently consulted by the students.

The large room for the library, now named after Stratis Andreadis (fig. 32), perpetuates this tradition to the present day. This gallery crowns the facade of the Palais des Études and dominates the central courtyard, aligned in perspective with numerous works from the French Renaissance. It forms part of the sacred itinerary, the *Gradus ad Parnassum*, leading from the monumental porch to the amphitheater in which the

Grands Prix were awarded. Designed with the proportions of the Royal Academy reception pieces in mind, this gallery, a classified historical monument, offers erudition in its books and an artistic model in its paintings, while its statues and busts prompt one to reflect on history. Here architecture defines and illustrates pedagogy. The increasing numbers of on-site studios, requirements of security and conservation, and evolution of taste have gradually made it difficult to see the greater part of the École's collections. This book pays homage to this intelligent, discreet, and all but forgotten museum. It may perhaps not have transmitted to successive generations an understanding of all the riches it contains, but its collections are still inhabited by the students' passionate loyalty to their school.

RECEPTION PIECES IN HISTORY PAINTING

Painters were accepted by the Academy for a specific genre. Relying on artistic ideals, ossified but little contested, the Academy accorded first place to history painting, that is, paintings representing scenes borrowed either from ancient history or from ancient literature (the latter was divided into Fable and Bible). The priority of history painting remained unassailable even to so free a spirit as Diderot. This was a humanist tradition in which the representation of the human figure was considered the supreme goal of artistic creation. Le Brun was the dominant figure in the Academy at the outset, but the king subsequently placed it under the authority of the General Director of the King's Buildings. In 1727, Louis-Antoine d'Antin, son of Louis XIV's mistress, Mme. de Montespan, organized a History Painting Competition in which twelve academicians participated. Under the directorship of Philibert Orry (1737–1745), this lofty genre fell out of favor. Beginning in 1745, however, the personalities and commitments of the successive directors were determining factors in the development of an academic art founded on history painting. The general directors were Lenormant de Tournehem (1745–51), uncle of the marquise de Pompadour (the mistress of Louis XV); the marquis de Marigny (1751–74), brother of Mme de Pompadour; and the comte d'Angiviller under Louis XVI. Each promoted history painting systematically in accordance with his own aesthetic notions.

GRAND MANNER AND *PETITE MANIÈRE*

The history painting reception pieces studied here represent a little over a century (1663–1787) of official royal depictions of the classical world. The changing tastes of that century are evident in the subjects chosen. At first the gods of Ovid reign supreme (they are also those of the *Homeric Hymns*). Their only rival is Hercules, the great hero of the Homeric warriors who came after him. Le Brun's disciples, such as René-Antoine Houasse and Jean-Baptiste Corneille, depicted Hercules in simplistic political allegories relating to the king's recent activities, showing little sensitivity to the narratives upon which they drew. Hercules' strength is merely physical, and even when he crushes chthonic powers (such as Antaeus in a painting by Verdot), or the Titans (Leblond, cat. no. 18), there is little to distinguish the hero from his victims. By contrast, Louis Galloche's 1711 painting (fig. 12) illustrates Euripides' *Alcestis* in an unexpectedly fresh manner, at once detached and worldly-wise in its bright-toned elegance.

Charles de la Fosse, François de Troy, and François Lemoyne—along with members of the next generation, such as Louis-Michel Van Loo and Carle Vanloo—emphasized the harmony of landscape and gods with a sensuality and understanding of myth worthy of the *Homeric Hymns* interpreted by Ovid. The nature they depict is alive with gods, and one might say the same of their painting. In the reception piece of Charles de la Fosse (1673) the influence of the Italians is clearer than that of his master Le Brun. Several years later La Fosse played a leading role in introducing the art of Rubens (*colorisme*) into France. Rubens's taste for color ran counter to the most sacred principles of the Academy of Le Brun's day, in which line reigned supreme. *Colorisme* illuminated and enlivened history painting for a number of years thereafter.

The *Apollo and Daphne* by Louis-Michel Van Loo (1733) and the *Apollo and Marsyas* (1735) by his nephew Carle Vanloo both feature swirling figure compositions. Although the figures are inspired by the very classical *Apollo Belvedere*, they are unleashed into violent movement by the pleasures of cruelty and the chase; intelligent use is made of the heritage of the late Baroque. Toward the middle of the century the tone changes. In 1744, Jean-Charles Frontier made use of the academy (male model drawn from the life) in his depiction of Prometheus (cat. no. 106), whom Hesiod and Aeschylus had established as humanity's spokesman against the all-powerful gods. The gods of fable now lost their allure, replaced by precise references to Homer and other great writers of antiquity, the interpretation of whose thought and inspiration offered new and enriching perspectives.

The evolution of the academic style is a much-studied topic, and Jean Locquin's overview of history painting has established itself as a classic.[6] While Boucher's rococo *petite manière* was at the height of its influence, in the years 1730 to 1750 the Grand Manner, or *grand goût*, often turned for inspiration to Poussin, the seventeenth-century Bolognese painters, and also, more simply, toward the last surviving participants in the foundation of the École—Louis Galloche, for example. The influence of Poussin deserves a book-length study in itself. The École possesses two early copies of Poussin: *The Triumph of Pan*, copied by Poussin's friend Jacques Stella (1596–1657), and *The Death of Germanicus*, copied in Rome in 1765 by Jean-François Sané (1732?–1779). They offer examples of Poussin's interpretations of fable and history, which successive generations variously interpreted as poetic and political. The first lecturers of the Academy devoted much of their time to commenting on the work of Poussin, as the École's many surviving manuscripts testify.

Carle Vanloo was then at the height of his very considerable fame. He and other Lemoyne pupils learned much from their master's decorative mastery, though they sometimes also succumbed to Boucher's superficiality. It has already been stated that in his *Apollo and Marsyas* Carle Vanloo referred to a number of classical statues. The ambition of such painters was fueled by a marvelous wealth of sources. The Enlightenment now brought to the reading of classical texts the scrupulous attention of the historian, judging gods and heroes with the instruments of critical philosophy. At the heart of the Academy, the comte de Caylus played the role of a French Winckelmann.

DIDEROT AND CAYLUS

Two art lovers—two irreconcilable enemies—have left a lasting mark on our vision of history painting in their time. The comte de Caylus was a scholarly antiquarian and archaeologist, a highly influential member of the Royal Academy of Painting and Sculpture, and a member of the French Academy of inscriptions and belles-lettres. Denis Diderot was a writer, art critic, and de facto editor of the *Encyclopédie*. The judgment of both was constrained by their time, and their taste was shaped by the same points of reference: ancient statuary and Homer. But Diderot, in his *Salons*, was infinitely more successful than Caylus in suggesting the form that might be assumed by a Greek sensibility revised for modern times. In a series of delightful critical judgments, he reviewed and then reinvented the academicians' attempts to illustrate the poems of Homer and other classical subjects. Those whom Diderot loved to revile, the practitioners of Boucher's rococo manner, are not represented in the collection of the École precisely because in Diderot's eyes and in those of the École's teachers and curators only the most ambitious and serious pieces were worthy of study. (Seriousness and ambition did not, of course, mean they were the best.) Such were the pieces chosen to decorate the École's austere library in 1873. Caylus has often been cited in this catalogue, and he did indeed inspire many of the subjects set in the *concours* of the École. Diderot's influence on his own time was less decisive, but today art lover and critic alike rejoice in his unbridled fantasy, rakish intelligence, and visual imagination. In 1759 Caylus founded a *concours* that long underpinned the École's teaching: the Expressive Head (cat. nos. 43, 48, 55). This emphasized the representation of simplified emotions, never really transcending the lifeless schemata drawn up by Le Brun in his *Method for Learning to Draw the Passions* (1698). The Academy and École were the principal destinations of Caylus's *Pictures Drawn from the Iliad and Odyssey of Homer and the Aeneid of Virgil* (1757), in which he described theatrical compositions of a kind that the *concours* adjudicators prized above all others for the next century and a half.

VIEN AND DAVID

The death of Louis XV ushered in a new epoch of taste whose official personification was Charles-Claude de Flahaut d'Angiviller, the new Director General of the Royal Buildings. The libertine mythologies of Boucher were now forbidden. One recognizes in the reception piece of a protégé of Caylus, Joseph-Marie Vien's *Daedalus and Icarus* (1754), and especially in David's *Andromache Mourning Hector* (1783; cat. no. 42) two important staging points in the gradual discovery of a severe and philosophical image of classical antiquity. Subjects involving heroism in action now gave way to scenes of more universal import. For Vien and his student David, Daedalus (inventor of flight and encaustic painting) and the tragic Andromache symbolized this new reading of antiquity. While the Rome-based Scottish painter Gavin Hamilton was creating large, well-populated scenes, the French preferred to limit their compositions to a small number of figures. They interact intensely with one another. Although freighted with meaning, like allegories, in their suffering or joy they remain creatures of flesh and blood, as the classical imagination had created or intended. Interpreters of antiquity in the manner of Fénelon were rarely considered worthy subjects for reception pieces, although Nicolas-Guy Brenet's *Theseus* (1769; cat. no. 103) is a submissive son and lacking in political fire.

If the Royal Academy played a paternal role in David's career, it found in him a parricidal son. He has been accused of petty malice, of cloaking personal vengeance in political principles. What does it matter, when his paintings (for example, *Andromache Mourning Hector*; cat. no. 42) have the stylistic and political density of Montesquieu and depict human tragedy with the violence and nobility of Homer and Poussin, Corneille and Racine? Compared with the work of David, the antiquarianism of his master Vien soon seemed cold, finicky, and affected. Vien was not alone in being unable to sustain the comparison with David. Other artists, including Jean-Jacques-François Le Barbier (*Jupiter in the Toils of Sleep* [1785]; cat. no. 21) celebrated the ancient gods in tones of libertine disabuse, their mockery sapping religious authority at a time when David was overthrowing monarchical interpretations of ancient myth with increasingly seditious works.

Painting Prizes in the Eighteenth Century: Iconographic and Stylistic Tendencies

For the students of the École royale there was both a doctrine and a teaching method: history painting (or sculpture) naturally constituted the ultimate goal of their training, even though painting was taught only in the studios of the masters, not at the École itself. Prizeworthy entries were judged in terms of the requisites of history painting: references to the ancient world; mastery of perspective, expression, and composition; and quotations from Poussin and Raphael. It is important to note that whereas the academicians' reception pieces were exhibited and probably served as models, over the years the successive Grand Prix–winning works tended to be forgotten. It seems that students did not generally attempt to imitate the methods that had succeeded the previous year. The prizewinning entries often exhibit the freshness and sincerity of artists in search of a style. Efforts were occasionally made to favor the study of color. In 1749 the Royal School for Protected Pupils was founded in order to foster the literary inspiration of the best students. Winners of the Grand Prix needing to improve their historical and literary culture before their stay in Rome received room and board in this institution.

The subjects set in the seventeenth century were political in nature, as were certain reception pieces. Pierre Monier's Jason (cat. no. 100) holds the Golden Fleece aloft as Louis XIV would display his emblem, the sun. From 1674 to 1761, subjects were systematically drawn from the Bible. Then fashions literary, sartorial, and artistic changed. In 1762 the academicians set the first subject taken from the classical world: the death of Socrates (for sculptors it was the death of Germanicus). Thereafter the subjects alternated between *exempla virtutis* (examples of political virtue) and sanguinary or worldly scenes derived from antiquity. On occasion the insolent inquiries of the *Encylopédie* can be seen to have left their mark. Here again Caylus's suggestions and the edicts of D'Angiviller were decisive. The general director of Louis XVI closed the School for Protected Pupils and reestablished the authority of the French Academy in Rome, notably by appointing Vien to direct it. It was there that Vien received his pupil David. In Rome, David discovered the principles of a new form of painting, in which his examples of political or spiritual heroism drew their conviction from the sense of human weakness overcome or sublimated. When he returned to Paris, he painted *Andromache Mourning Hector* (cat. no. 42).

Prizewinners such as David brought back from Rome a passionate admiration, both heroic and philosophical, for classical antiquity, occasionally expressed in the somber perspective of the Italian painters of the seventeenth century (essentially the Bolognese school). They imparted this admiration to their successors. Today the works of winners of the Grand Prix in the second third of the eighteenth century often seem more innovative than the reception pieces of their maturity. The heroes and great men of antiquity increasingly tended to adopt solid Neoclassical poses, their heroic nudity and republican virtues disposed amid an austere architectural framework. This continued until 1793, when David contrived the abolition of the Academy. In 1795 the National Institute of Sciences, Belles-Lettres, and Arts was founded, and when the *concours* resumed in 1797, the students of David and Jean-Baptiste Regnault dominated the roll call of winners. Both were past winners of the prize. David had obtained the prize in 1774 with his *Antiochus and Stratonice.* Regnault had triumphed two years later with a bold and intelligent interpretation of *The Meeting of Alexander and Diogenes,* in which the encounter of monarch and free man is made to symbolize the rise of bourgeois individualism and the death throes of monarchic absolutism.

The Oil Sketch at the École

Adjudicators examining oil sketches for a *concours* used very specific criteria, awarding marks or places for literal conformity with the set text, on the one hand, and with prescriptions as to the number and dimensions of the figures, on the other. Today we tend to look for something quite different: effects of light, color, impasto, and movement. The best historian of nineteenth-century French academicism perceives in the sketch the source of the modern schools that triumphed everywhere but in the École itself.[7] Certainly the exponents of Romanticism and Impressionism were often, however fleetingly, students of the École. Although soon repelled by the prevailing academicism, Delacroix spent a year at the École and his history paintings show him adapting the rapid strokes of the oil sketch to his own Romantic lyricism. Within the École these rapid strokes imparted to many epic scenes a violence, vitality, and dreamlike poetry that were steadily eliminated as the full-sized work progressed. One objection to this argument can be summarized in the terms of another *concours*, namely, the historical landscape oil sketch. Specifying small figures, a large tree, an ancient city, a detailed foreground, and a distant landscape, it therefore limited the artist to a heavily constrained vision of nature. Themes drawn from Fénelon were particularly favored in this *concours* and leached all vitality from the entries. By contrast, the most successful historical landscapes made use of the surrounding landscape to imbue the scene with its poetic atmosphere.

In the late nineteenth century—when originality was in short supply among winners of the Prix de Rome—many sketches exhibited a humorous tendency and considerable sensitivity. The sculpture sketches often registered ironic situations in a highly intelligent fashion. This was partly due to the sculpture teachers, who were wise enough to set subjects as fertile as the cunning of Odysseus, the coquetry of Helen, or the petty cowardice of Paris. Outstanding examples include the delicate *relievo stiacciato* sculpted by Barye in 1820 (cat. no. 40) and the cumulative picturesque effects carved ten years later by Théophile Caudron (cat. no. 69).

NOTES

1 The spelling *dessin* gradually gained its specifically artistic sense ("drawing") over the course of the eighteenth century, thus differentiating itself from the homophone *dessein*, or "intention."

2 Louis Vitet, *L'Académie royale de peinture et de sculpture* (Paris, 1861), 269.

3 This term refers to the small enclosed studios within the École to which the candidates were confined while painting their entries for *concours*. [Trans.]

4 Jacques-François Blondel, *Architecture française* (1756), quoted by Pierre Rosenberg, "La Peinture," in *Louis XV: un moment de perfection de l'art français*, exh. cat. (Paris, Hôtel de la Monnaie, 1974), 101.

5 Anatole de Montaiglon, *Procès-verbaux de l'Académie royale de Peinture et de Sculpture, 1648–1793*, 10 vols. (Paris, 1875–92), 7:384. [Price was used to specify size. Trans.]

6 Jean Locquin, *La Peinture d'histoire en France de 1747 à 1785: Étude sur l'évolution des idées artistiques dans la seconde moitié du XVIIIe siècle* (1912; rpt. Paris, 1978).

7 See Albert Boime, *The Academy and French Painting in the Nineteenth Century* (London, 1971). For a detailed history of the École and its teaching, see Annie Jacques, *Les Beaux-Arts, de l'Académie aux Quat'z'arts: anthologie historique et littéraire* (Paris, 2001).

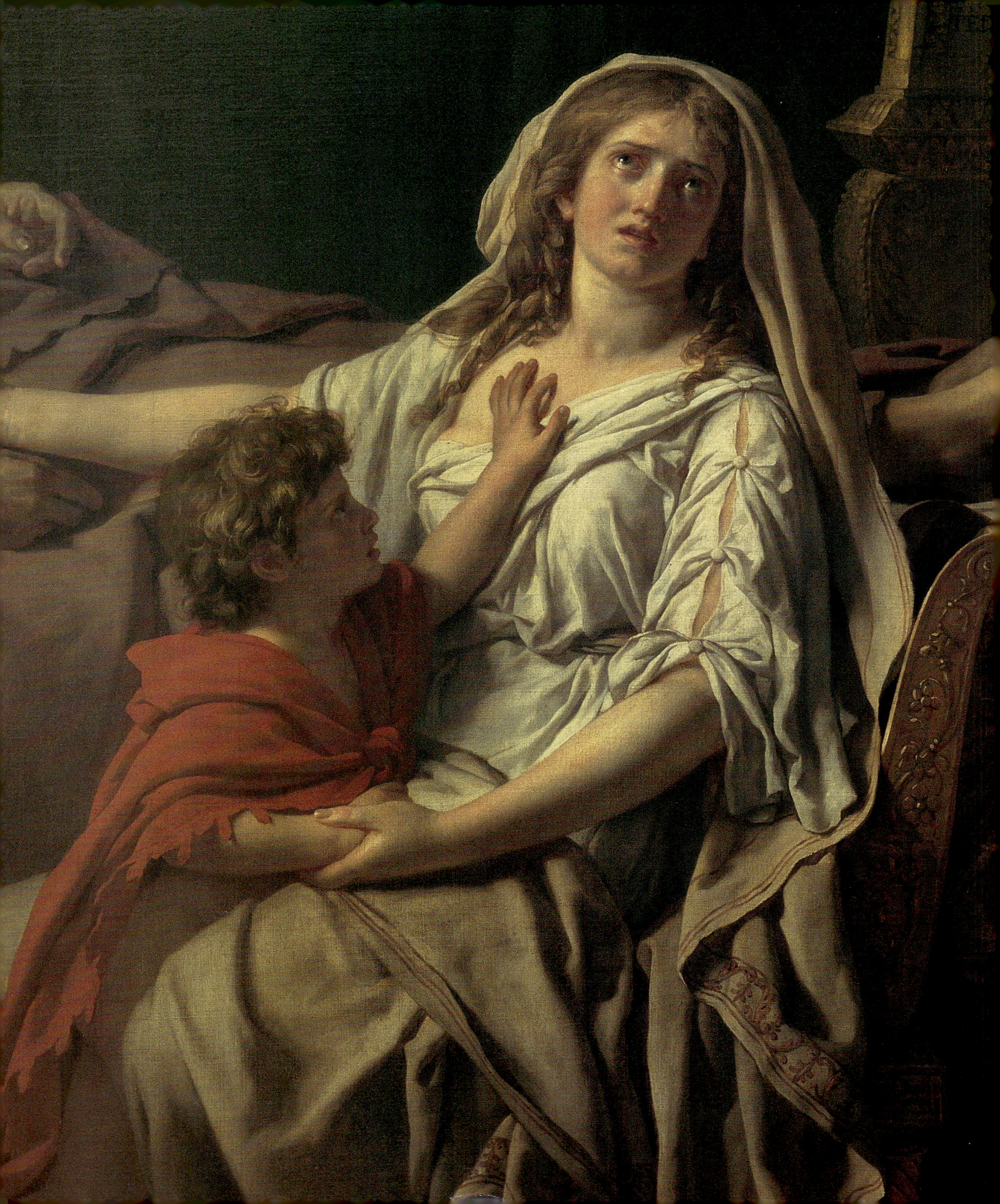

Catalogue

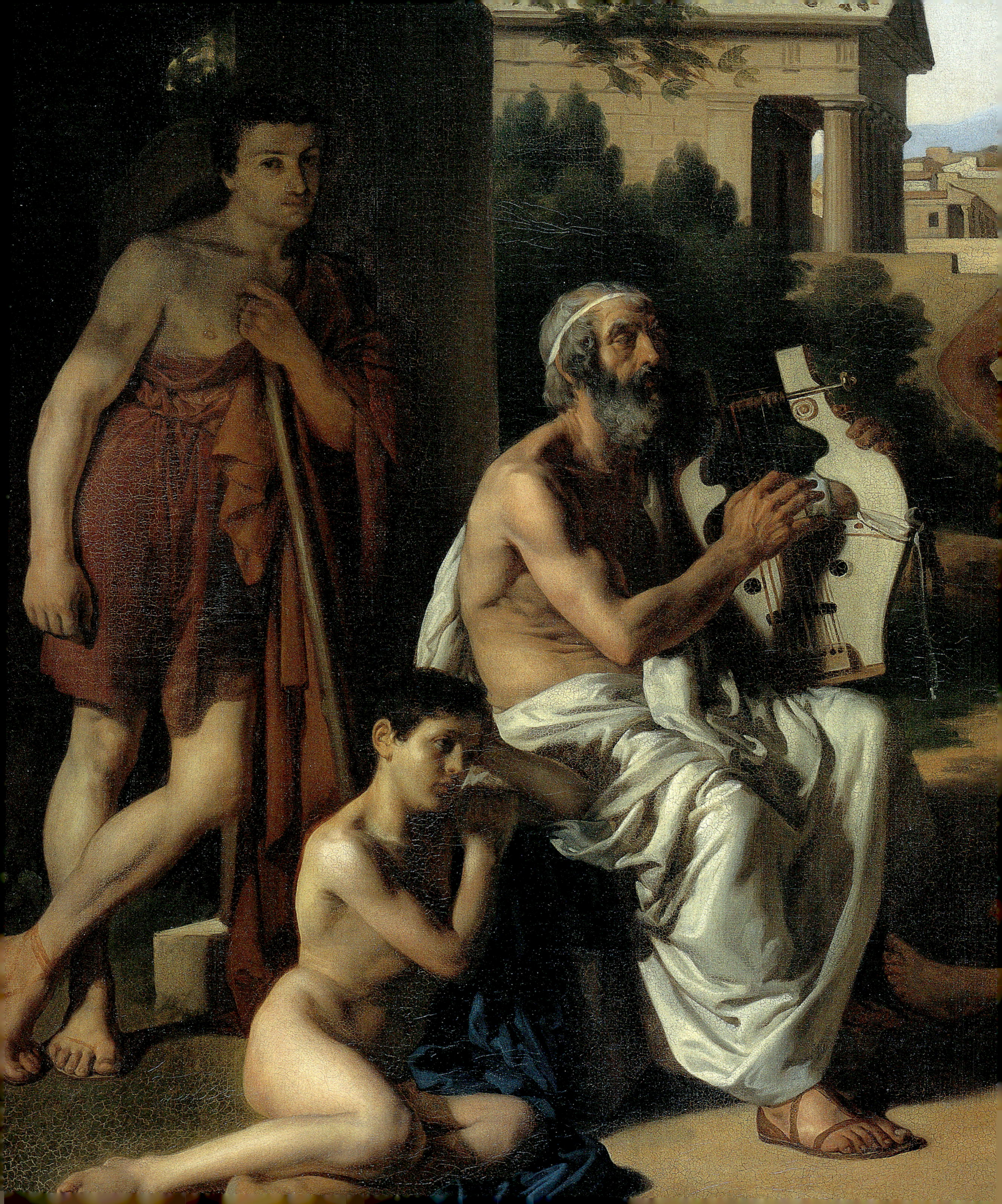

THE HISTORICAL BACKGROUND AND THE HOMERIC WORLD

It might now seem the height of absurdity to endow Homer with a biography and place of birth, attributing the two most famous poems in history to a man of flesh and blood. The man is the work, and Homer is therefore the Trojan War. "We have lost the Trojan War," exclaimed Moses Finley, one of the best and wittiest specialists of the Mycenaean world.[1] Yet archaeologists long pored over the remains of Troy and Mycenae, finding in the latter the golden funerary mask they dubbed the "mask of Agamemnon." Thucydides (1.10) strongly suspected Homer of having embellished the Trojan War. Subsequent travelers, more naïve than Thucydides, set out in search of the Trojan War. They ranged from Alexander the Great in ancient times to Choiseul-Gouffier (fig. 15) and Heinrich Schliemann, who excavated Troy from its successive layers of tombs while consulting his own "map" of the epic city. All these men sought to raise Ilion (Lat. Ilium) from its bed of earth. A few photos of Mycenaean and Cyclopean ramparts give us some idea of what was—and still is for the historian—the architecture of the times described by Homer (fig. 33). Artists were more circumspect than scholars, however, and for long periods were more interested in Homer than in the war he narrated. They read the poems and ignored the archaeology.

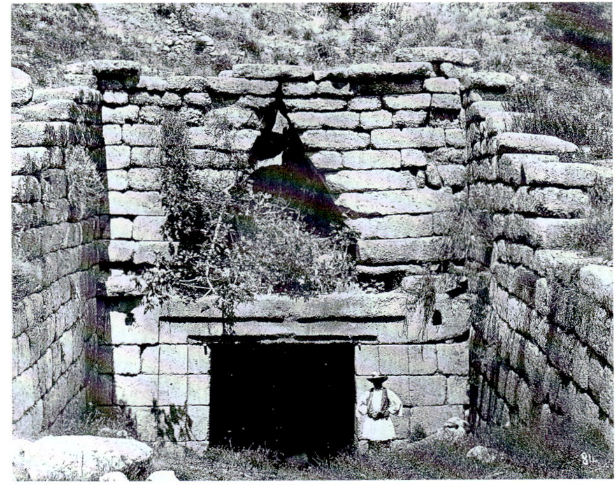

FIGURE 33 | ANONYMOUS, *Mycenae: The Tomb of Agamemnon*, photograph, 19th century.

The Ancient Historians

The question was first raised in antiquity. Herodotus and Thucydides, the founders of Western history, saw themselves as continuing Homer's work to slightly higher standards. They therefore read him as one might read an earlier historian. His creative powers bestowed historical conviction on the product of his poetic imagination. All the ancient representations of Homer himself, both written and visual, merely extrapolate from the Homeric text. It was soon concluded that if the Bard described a bard, it must be a self-portrait. The *Odyssey* features two bards, the first of them described in considerable detail:

> In came the herald now,
> leading along the faithful bard the Muse adored

above all others, true, but her gifts were mixed
with good and evil both: she stripped him of sight
but gave the man the power of stirring, rapturous
song.
Pontonous brought the bard a silver-studded chair,
right amid the feasters, leaning it up against
a central column—hung his high clear lyre
on a peg above his head and showed him how
to reach up with his hands and lift it down.
And the herald placed a table by his side
with a basket full of bread and a cup of wine
for him to sip when his spirit craved refreshment.
All reached out for the good things that lay at hand
and when they'd put aside desire for food and drink,
the Muse inspired the bard
to sing the famous deeds of fighting heroes—
the song whose fame had reached the skies those days:
The Strife Between Odysseus and Achilles, Peleus'
Son . . .
how once at the gods' lavish feast the captains
clashed
in a savage war of words, while Agamemnon, lord of
armies,
rejoiced at heart that Achaea's bravest men were
battling so.

The herald returned and placed the ringing lyre now
in Demodocus' hands, and the bard moved toward
the center,
flanked by boys in the flush of youth . . .

—OD. 8. 62–78, 261–64; F 8.71–92, 295–97

Blindness gave Demodocos a physical identity, while his success with the young conferred on him a lasting social function; he created *Paideia*, Greek education, announcing himself publicly as the teacher of the young (among whom one should include the young artists of the future academies). The irony and political skepticism with which Homer's entire corpus is imbued are present in his description of Demodocos. Here is the insolent poet who tells of princes who insult and exploit one another. Since classical antiquity, the lineaments of Homer have been traced in his description of Demodocos. André Chénier's poem "The Blind Bard" is a classic example. This hypothetical figure of the artist stoically enduring his infirmity has been promoted at the cost of Homer's humor and intelligence.

Various "lives" of Homer emerged in antiquity. They were fathered on two outstanding authors: Herodotus, the father of history, and Plutarch, the father of biography. From the two given elements—sightlessness and immediate, immense success—they composed a figure easily grasped by the public, the penurious poet delivered up to a merciless world. In these ancient biographies infirmity was combined with the status of the beggar to construct puerile anecdotes useful to moralizing pedagogues. According to Pseudo-Herodotus, the blind Homer composed the *Iliad* and received a triumphant reception in Cyme, in Ionic Asia. Cyme is also the setting for the story of the cobbler Tychios, before whom the poet is said to have improvised magnificent verses. Homer is said to have written the *Homeric Hymns* while living in Tychios's house. Next the poet leaves for Chios (Khios) to denounce an impostor claiming authorship of the Homeric corpus. Upon arrival, he is attacked by the dogs of a shepherd named Glaucos, who rescues the bard and makes him tutor to his children. In other versions Homer is abandoned by the sailors who brought him ashore and is lost or asleep when young shepherds find him. In repetitive episodes he hops from island to island, visiting Samos, Smyrna, Skyros, and Syros. The impostor eventually flees. Homer opens a school, prospers, marries. One day he embarks for Athens, only to die en route on the little island of Ios. Madame Dacier adapted these stories in an appendix to her translation of the *Iliad* (1699); although unhistorical, they continued to inspire artists until the end of the eighteenth century. While his genius was admired, both his partisans (Ancients) and detractors (Moderns) criticized the bard for his misfortune or carelessness in having been born into a barbaric age. There was little point in dwelling on the man and his life, work, and times. Better to modernize his poems and forget a poet who had proved unable to civilize his contemporaries.

The Wandering Poet

The apocryphal commentators having fabricated their Homer on the basis of his own creations, it should come as no surprise that his adventures simply follow the plot of the *Odyssey.* Sharing the naïveté of modern biographers, the pseudohistorians deemed their author incapable of imagining any story other than his own. From the eighteenth century onward, modern artists and poets took their turn at reconstructing Homer's character and life story. Flaxman, for example, juxtaposed three poets inspired by the same lyre. Homer humbly hears out the Muse, who dictates those familiar lines "Rage—Goddess, sing the rage of Peleus' son Achilles" or "Sing to me of the man, Muse, the man of twists and turns." A coincidence, no doubt, that Ulysses is moved at hearing his inspired biographer Demodocos sing his praises to the Phaeacians (*Od.* 8.499). In Ithaca, however, the suitors listen to Phemios, the other bard of the *Odyssey,* who sings the lay of Achilles and that of Odysseus himself (*Od.* 1.337) while the latter lies in wait in the shadows, intent on massacre. There can be no denying that the historical bard liked to represent himself, but in fantastical form: blind among the Phaeacians but clearsighted enough in Ithaca, where he mixes with the servant women guilty of collaborating with the suitors.

History painting covets mythological or literary subjects as much as it does authentic reference. In the "historical" Homer invented by the pedants of antiquity, Neoclassicism discovered a very handsome and virtuous subject. Jacques-Louis David, imprisoned in Brumaire of Year III (1794), drew on the pseudo-Homeric lives in a composition that combines the myths of the mendicant Homer and those of Tasso the poet and prisoner.[2] Homer's discovery by the shepherds or his performance in roadside towns—those adventures in which episodes of the *Odyssey* fuse with the apocryphal lives of Homer—established themselves as commonplaces of poetry and painting. This was the period of Chénier's "Blind Bard," although Chénier borrowed from a source purer than the apocryphal lives—the "Homeric Hymn to Apollo," which states: "A blind man is he, and dwells / On rugged Khios; all of his songs are hereafter supreme."[3] The hymns display the uneven talents of their authors, who wrote, if not in the spirit of Homer, at least in his rhythm (the dactylic hexameter). Their vision, unlike their master's, was more descriptive than ironic. Chénier drew on them for his "Subjects for Paintings and Poems": "Homer singing in a village; men, women, and children bring him fruit, while other men and women hasten to hear him."[4] The subject of the 1864 Prix de Rome (cat. no. 2) was inspired by Chénier's verses on the subject: the shepherd children mistake the blind man for a God, while he, in turn, fears their mockery.

> The penniless stranger's suspicions are not relieved;
> He thinks they have come to make fun of his infirmity,
> To abuse him. "Why compare me to the immortal gods?
> Grey and wrinkled as I am, enveloped in eternal night,
> Look, are these the features of one who dwells above?"

For the 1864 *concours* the teachers copied out the opening lines of Chénier's poem:

> God of the silver bow, god of Claros, hear me,
> Apollo-Smintheus, for I shall surely die
> Unless you guide this blind vagabond.
> So the blind man said his prayer and sighed,
> Walked faltering steps by the forest's edge,
> Then sat on a rock to rest. Three young shepherds
> followed him, locals summoned by the wild
> Barking of their dogs, who guard the bleating flock.
> They held back the furious dogs to protect
> The anxious and defenseless old man. Then,
> Hearing his words from a distance, asked:
> Who is this blind old man with no one to help him?
> Is he not some inhabitant of the celestial realm?
> There is greatness and pride in his looks, and from
> His rustic belt there hangs a battered lyre, while at his voice
> The very air and waters, sky and woods are moved.[5]

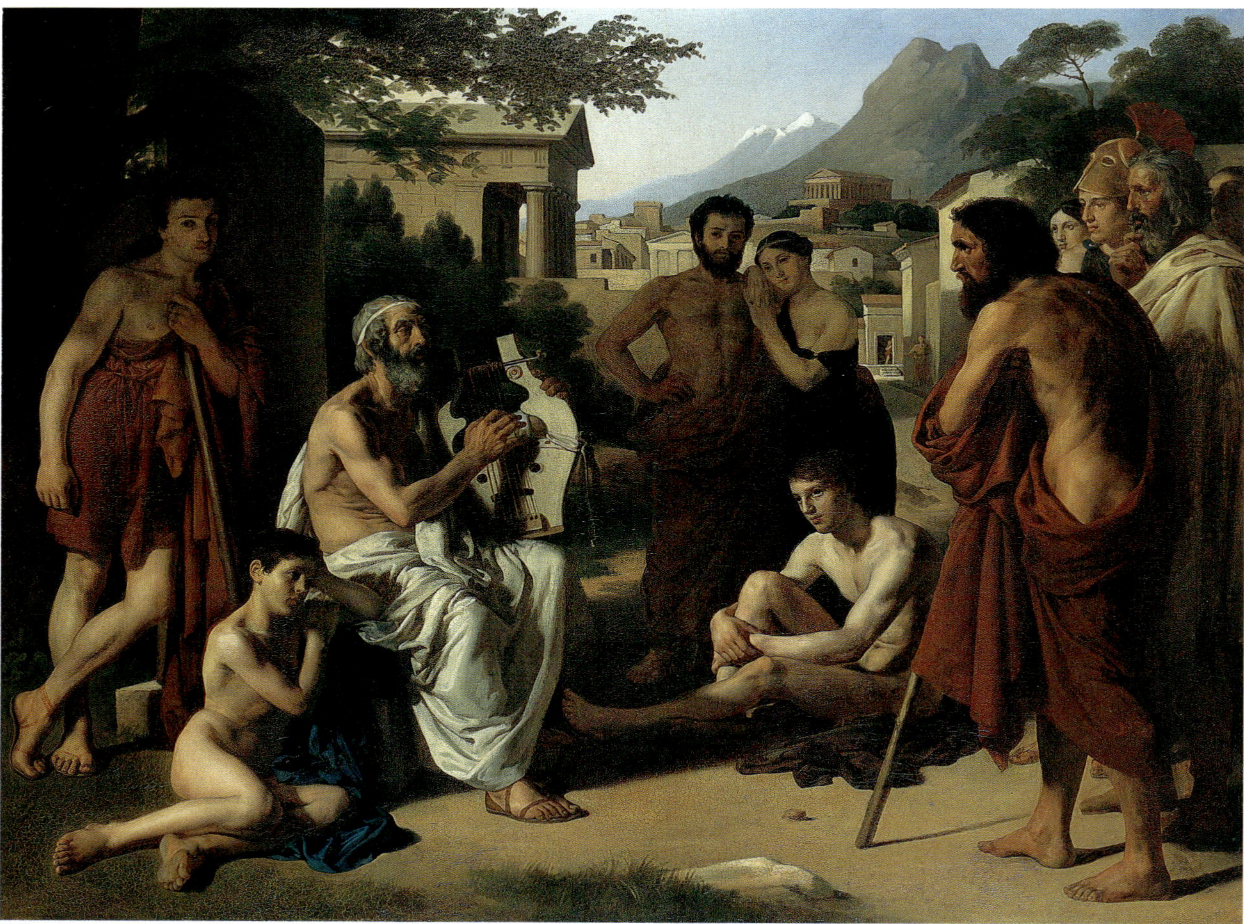

CATALOGUE NO. 1 | PAUL JOURDY (1805–1856), *Homer Travels through the Cities of Greece, Singing His Poems*, 1834. Oil on canvas, 114.1 × 116.5 cm.

The figure of the persecuted poet came triumphantly to the fore in Romanticism. The poet is persecuted by the greed of mediocrities, powerful or envious, but the people always adore him. In this role Homer increasingly eclipsed Torquato Tasso, the old favorite, while the careers of Thomas Chatterton and the unfortunate Chénier himself, guillotined in 1794, offered a similar pathos. In 1834, the subject for the Grand Prix was *Homer Travels through the Cities of Greece, Singing His Poems* (cat. no. 1); most of the competitors depicted him as an invalid and beggar, at once penniless and revered. The episode of Glaucos, the naïve shepherd with a taste for poetry, thus paved the way for two visions of Homer that were especially prevalent in the École des beaux-arts. In the first of these, the poet appeared to advantage in Historical Landscape (the "Bucolic," to use Chénier's term). In an urban landscape Homer stood center stage in a moralizing composition of a historical, dramatic, and romantic nature: the citizens honor Homer's blindness before discovering his wisdom. These scenes were again echoes of the *Odyssey*, that is, of Odysseus's story: he, too, is woken by young women after a shipwreck (bk. 6) or by Athena disguised as a shepherd after he has been abandoned on the shore (bk. 13), and he likewise is attacked by dogs (bk. 14).

The Poet-Pedagogue

A further thread in the "Homer story" was his literary vocation as the teacher of Greece. This is exemplified in the child who accompanies the bard and receives alms in his name. The subject set for the 1834 Prix de Rome *concours* did not explicitly require the competitors to depict Homer as the master philosopher of his time, but Paul Jourdy set about the task anyway (cat. no. 1). All ages are represented in the audience that surrounds his Homer; they belong to the period of Greece's greatest glory and stand at the foot of an ideal city. One of the spectators wears the helmet of Pericles, and their sculptural attitudes bear the stamp of attention and meditation, offering a very Greek perspective on what was most respectable in humanity. The subject illustrated by Louis-Hector Leroux and Clément-Amédée Bidot (cat. nos. 3–4) is, in principle, *Homer Requesting Hospitality*, but the only vestige of this title is the evening twilight. The rest of the picture—the attention of his hosts (especially the women), the lyre, the attitude of the beggar and his guide—simply describes the function of the poet: he who interprets nature through the miracle of words and song. His auditors, men and women alike, display elegant, pensive silhouettes.

In 1864, the Prix de Rome judges gave first place to a Homer too weary to play his lyre, while around him shepherds posed like Parisian models (cat. no. 2). The center of attention is no longer the heroic, inspired poet of Neoclassicism but the Greek shepherds so often evoked by Chénier, popularized by Delacroix, and now visualized with naïve realism. These sympathetic street urchins wear the most charming hats. Alert of face and gaze, they love to hear tales of far-off places told by a stranger. The dogs—one spaniel in particular—have that moist and profoundly human gaze canines affect when seeking to convince us that they follow human speech. The landscape is entirely subordinated to human genius; more and more spectators come running from its depths. Although the parents of Diogène-Ulysse-Napoléon Maillard must have been lovers of antiquity to have named their son so resoundingly, the painter himself seems to have forgotten that the weary old man he has painted owes less to Homer than to Chénier:

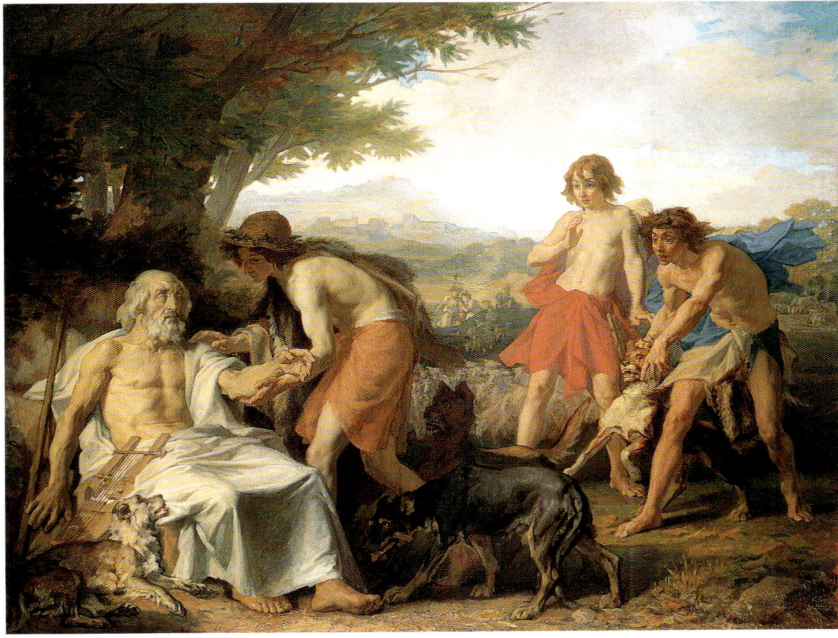

CATALOGUE NO. 2 | DIOGÈNE-ULYSSE-NAPOLÉON MAILLARD (1840–1926), *Homer on the Island of Scyros*, 1864. Oil on canvas, 113 × 145 cm.

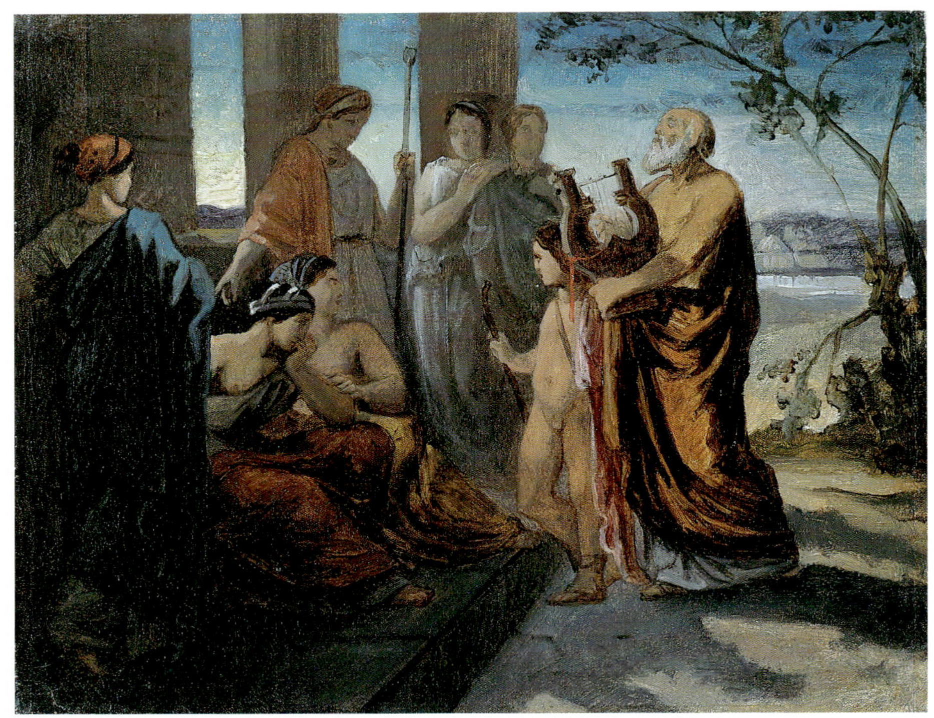

CATALOGUE NO. 3 | LOUIS-HECTOR LEROUX (1829–1900), *Homer Requesting Hospitality*, 1855. Oil on canvas, 32.5 × 40.5 cm.

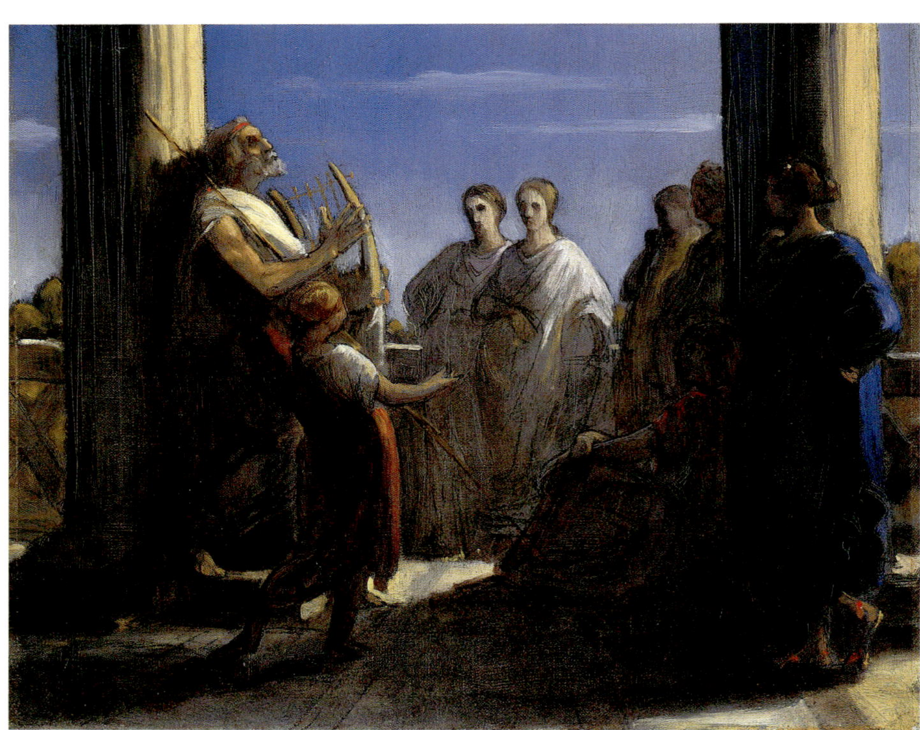

CATALOGUE NO. 4 | CLÉMENT-AMÉDÉE BIDOT (1833–?), *Homer Requesting Hospitality*, 1855. Oil on canvas, 32.5 × 40.5 cm.

> There is greatness and pride in his looks, and from
> His rustic belt there hangs a battered lyre, while at his voice
> The very air and waters, sky and woods are moved.

In 1875, the subject was again set for the Prix de Rome, this time for sculpture (fig. 34). Dominique-Jean-Baptiste Hugues carved a Homer who inspires as much enthusiasm in his audience as the rhapsodes of whom Plato speaks in the *Ion* (535e). As if he, too, were joining the ranks of Chénier's commentators, in 1895 Anatole France published a short story entitled "The Singer of Cyme," where one reads: "When he woke, he saw, drawn up in respectful ranks before him, the children of Cyme, to whom he taught poetry and music as his father had done. Several of them were blind." The École des beaux-arts students doubtless aspired to be the distant descendants of this lineage of masters and disciples.

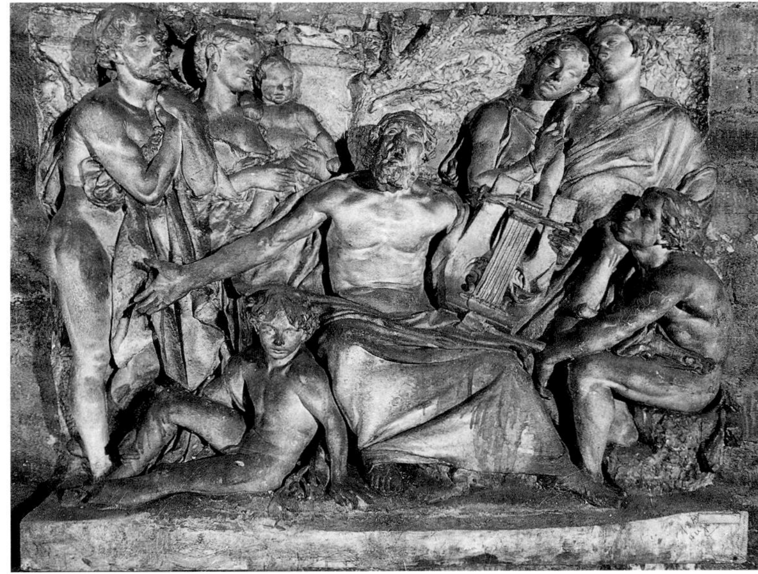

FIGURE 34 | DOMINIQUE-JEAN-BAPTISTE HUGUES (1849–1930), *Homer Sings in a Greek Town*, 1875. Plaster, 127 × 154 cm. Prix de Rome in Sculpture.

Homeric Architecture, Homeric Landscape

Of all the École's students, those who thought most sensitively about the nature of classical antiquity were the Prix de Rome–winning architects. They took their example from the architect Joseph-Frédéric Debacq (1800–1892), who assisted the duc de Luynes in his excavations in Magna Graecia. The magnificent terracotta lion's head that he brought back from Italy is still in the collection of the École; it is a part of the *acroterion* of the sanctuary of Apollo Lycaeus—then known as the "chiesa di Sansone"—at ancient Metapontum (cat. no. 10). Sculpted around 530 B.C., it has a twin in the collections of the Bibliothèque nationale de France. This is a common decorative component in both Greek architecture and Homer's poetry. Since in Greek art the most fearsome animal seems always to smile with fully human intelligence, let me compare Debacq's lion—its wide eyes, hungry mouth full of sarcastic eloquence, flamboyant mane, and bright colors—with a marvelous Homeric simile. Here is Odysseus, naked following his shipwreck, encountering a gathering of young Phaeacian women:

> And out he stalked
> as a mountain lion exultant in his power
> strides through wind and rain and his eyes blaze
> and he charges sheep or oxen or chases wild deer
> but his hunger drives him on to go for flocks,
> even to raid the best-defended homestead.
> So Odysseus moved out . . .
> about to mingle with all those lovely girls,
> naked now as he was, for the need drove him on.
> —*OD*. 6.130–36; F 6.142–50

Greek humor is at work in this comparison: the exultant lion is no more intimidating than Ulysses' nudity, and when he bares his teeth in a ferocious snarl, there is always a young Nausicaa to consider the spectacle with detached amusement.

Two of the École's greatest teachers summarized in paint their thoughts about the place of Greece and Homer in human art. In his *Apotheosis of Homer* (Louvre, 1827; fig. 4) Ingres presents the Homeric period as

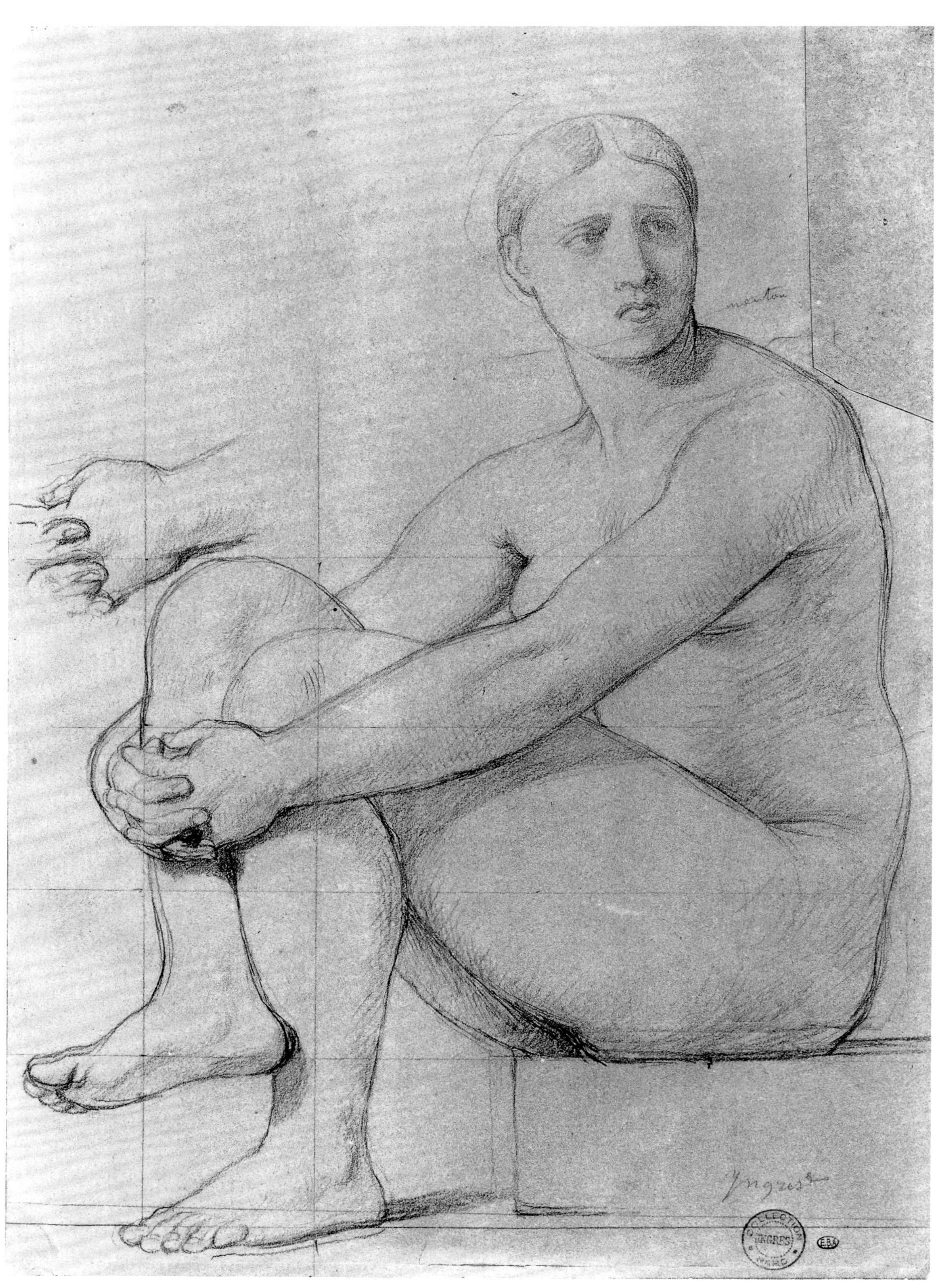

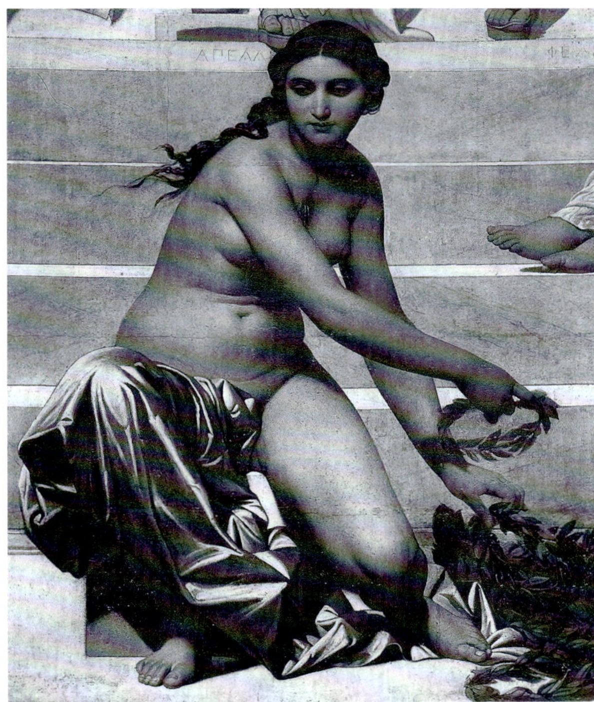

FIGURE 36 | PAUL DELAROCHE (1797–1856), *The Genius of the Arts Distributing Crowns*, central detail of *The Hemicycle*, 1837–41. Oil on canvas.

preeminent in the history of art. The pioneer is Homer, and Raphael and Michelangelo follow in the footsteps of Apelles and Phidias as they lead the arts down the path he has traced. The École possesses a preparatory drawing for the allegorical figure of the *Iliad*, which sits in the foreground of the *Apotheosis* (fig. 35). Ingres wrote: "At Homer's feet [sits] the *Iliad*, her air proud and martial, her arms wrapped around her knees. Her clothing and slightly disheveled hair suggest both Achilles disguised in the garb of Lycomedes' daughters and the angry Achilles withdrawn into his tent."[6] Following Ingres's normal practice, the model is drawn nude. The second of these prestigious teachers is Paul Delaroche, who decorated the École's amphitheater with an homage to Greek, Roman, Renaissance, and Gothic artists. No poets are admitted to this celebration of the fine arts, but the figure of Renown sits in front of the greatest geniuses of Greek art—Phidias, Ictinus, and Apelles—assuming both the pose of Ingres's *Iliad* and her allegorical significance (fig. 36). In the background of these two great paintings, classical architecture forms a temple to Homer and Greek art.

Further tributes to Homer came from the pen of two young architects, one of whom, Félix Thomas, subsequently won a Grand Prix. They are entries for a sketch *concours* of 1844, and both are indebted to Ingres and Delaroche. Alexandre-Adolphe-Gustave Levasseur honors Homer with a temple (cat. no. 5) representative of the genius of Greece. It is as if nature—the mountains and ocean of Greece—were carried on columns of thought. The thoughts are those of Homer, seated in the shadow of the sanctuary. The spectator's gaze rises toward this statue, ascends the mountain, and finally comes to rest on the sea, "that tranquil roofline where the doves promenade." (Paul Valéry's famous line from "The Cemetery by the Sea" shows him wonderfully imbued with the spirit and landscape of Greece.) Levasseur's colleague Thomas has Homer's statue enthroned before a *bouleuterion*, a council chamber or courthouse (cat. no. 6). A frieze of human figures runs around the chamber, while above it opens a natural amphitheater. Here is architecture designed for debate, in which democracy, justice, and theater—the Greek taste for argument and contradiction—are seen to derive from the vivid, multifarious intelligence of Ulysses and Homer. For centuries the ideal of the intellectuals who read Homer remained Greek politics set in the cities and landscape of Greece.

Such were the architects who left for Rome and, in particular, Greece. They did not confine themselves to drawing tediously abstract colonnades; rather, they brought back *reconstructions*, visions of the past recreated in the imagination, flavored with the eternal smile of the Aegean and the anfractuous coastline of Greece. One of the "Neo-Greek" styles that frequently came into being during the nineteenth century owed its birth to this seductive vision of cities arising directly from the landscape, and it left its traces in various École

OPPOSITE FIGURE 35 | JEAN-AUGUSTE-DOMINIQUE INGRES (1780–1867), *The Iliad*, preparatory drawing for *The Apotheosis of Homer*, ca. 1827. Graphite on paper, 31.2 × 21.4 cm.

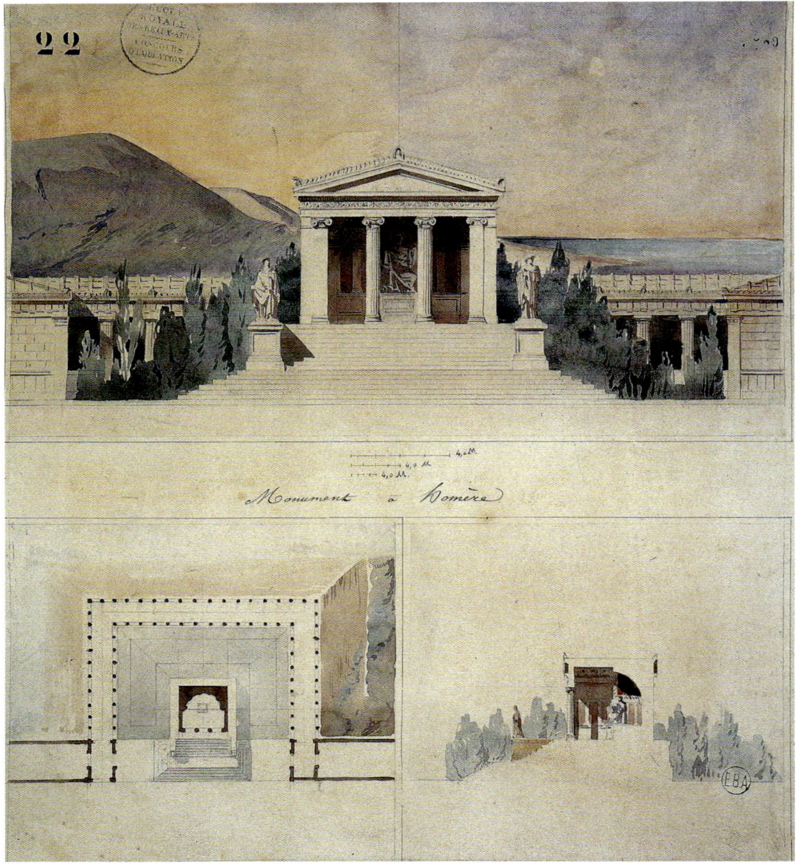

CATALOGUE NO. 5 | ALEXANDRE-ADOLPHE-GUSTAVE LEVASSEUR (1808–?), *Monument to Homer.* Elevation, plan, and section, 1844. Watercolor, 32.5 × 26.3 cm.

paintings, notably Jourdy's work of 1834 (cat. no. 1). In 1851, the young writer Edmond About—fresh from the École normale supérieure—the architect Charles Garnier, and the painter Alfred de Curzon discovered and reinvented a Greece mingling the modern and the classical,[7] enlivening the mountain landscape with their school learning and their school learning with mountain landscapes. With what joyful enthusiasm Garnier reconstituted in 1852–53 one of the pediments of the temple of Aphaia in Aegina (cat. no. 8), which had long been repatriated to Munich's Glyptothek! I believe he mixed the elements of two different pediments in his restoration, creating a palimpsest of the two Trojan Wars. A generation before the conflict narrated in Homer, Hercules the Archer waged the first Trojan War. His ally was Telamon, the father of the great Ajax, who, having entered the city before his commander, escaped with his life only by placing the first stone of an altar to the Victorious Hercules before retribution could follow. In the fifth book of the *Iliad* Hercules' son Tlepolemus delivers an encomium on his father's prowess and the lineage of Zeus.

These were times of legend, the period of ancient Europe's attempted conquest of Asia. After wars, invasions, and Crusades, the situation was reversed by the fifteenth century, when the Ottoman Turks captured Greece. In the newly liberated Greece of the nineteenth century, the young Charles Garnier bestowed on the ancient heroes a new enthusiasm marked by vibrant colors. A frieze of warriors occupies the triangular heaven of the pediment, while the sky above is devoid of Olympians. Those who know the site of the temple of Aphaia in Aegina know that there, as in the theater of Segesta in Sicily or in the whole site of Delphi, Greek architecture seized upon an edenic landscape and sowed stones of beauty.

Homer and Apollo

The ancient world was also in awe of Homer. Honoring poetry as something divine, it acknowledged in Homer the qualities that he often refused the gods: beauty and truth. Hymns dedicated to the gods and written in the same rhythms as the *Iliad* and the *Odyssey* were therefore deemed Homeric. Moreover, the ancients preferred the gods who most resembled Homer. Hermes and Apollo both claimed credit for having invented the lyre—the soul and emblem of poetry—just as many Greek towns contested the title of Homer's birthplace.

In the "Homeric Hymn to Apollo" the god claims to have invented his instrument: "May the lyre and curving bow be possessions to call my own, / And for humans let me proclaim the unerring counsel of Zeus."[8] In 1837, setting a subject for the Historical Landscape prize, the Academicians took Apollo's part against Hermes: "Apollo, Shepherding the Flocks of Admetus, King of Thessaly, Invents the Lyre." The figure painted by Eugène-Ferdinand Buttura (cat. no. 7) is thus the god of the sun, temporarily exiled to the shadowy earth for slaying the Cyclops—and Hermes' claims are forgotten.

The first "Homeric Hymn to Hermes" tells a very different story:

> He found a tortoise there, and vast good fortune gained:
> Hermes it was who made the tortoise a singer first.
> At the courtyard gates she met him, grazing in front of the house
> On the thickly flourishing grass, and moving with waddling steps.
> The speedy son of Zeus with a laugh at the sight at once said:
> "But where
> Did you get this beautiful toy, a glimmering shell to put on,
> You tortoise who live in the mountain?"[9]

Thus presented as a figure surrounded by the natural world upon which his presence alone confers a meaning, Hermes invents not merely the lyre (music) but something more modest: the Historical Landscape as conceived by the Parisian academicians of the nineteenth century.

> In this way he spoke, and raising her up with both of his hands
> He returned back into the house, the lovely toy in his grasp.
> There tossing her up, with a knife of iron grey he scooped out the flesh
> Of the tortoise that dwelt in the mountains, and like the quick passing of
> thought
> Through the mind of a care-haunted man, or the whirling of gleams from
> eyes,
> No sooner said than done was what glorious Hermes devised.
> Cutting reed shafts to measure, he fitted them, piercing the back

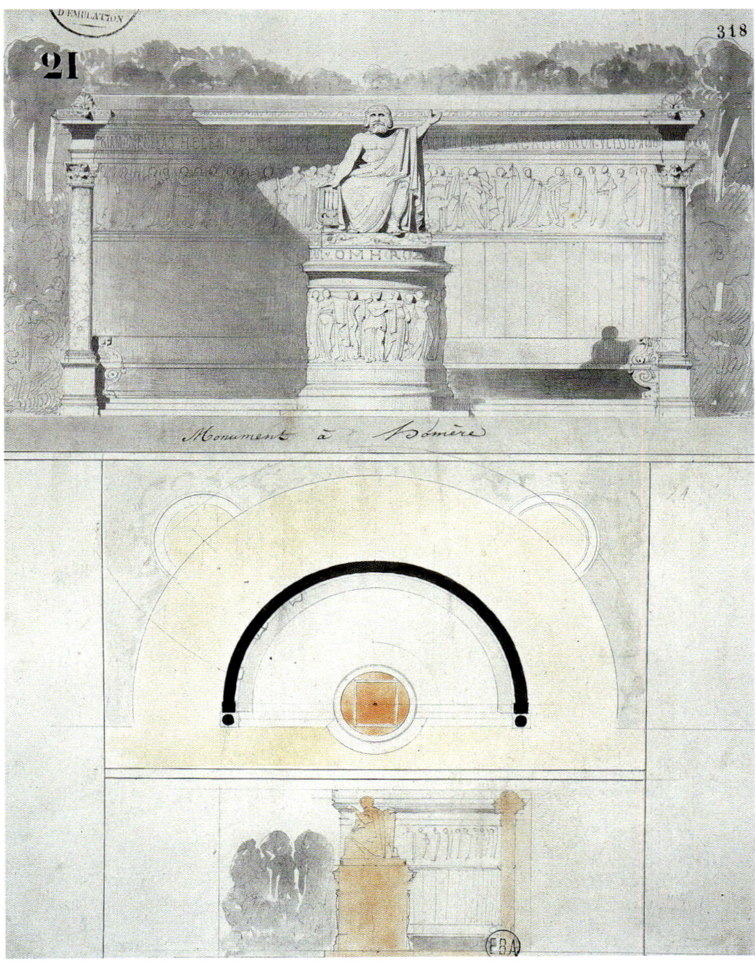

CATALOGUE NO. 6 | FÉLIX THOMAS (1815–1875), *Monument to Homer*. Elevation, plan, and section, 1844. Watercolor, 34.5 × 29.7 cm.

> Through the shell of the tortoise; about it he stretched with his cunning the hide
> Of a cow, affixed the arms and fastened the yoke to them both,
> Then stretched seven cords of sheep's gut to serve as harmonious strings.
> But when he had finished, he tried with the plectrum string by string
> The lovely toy that he bore, and beneath his hand it made
> An astonishing sound.[10]

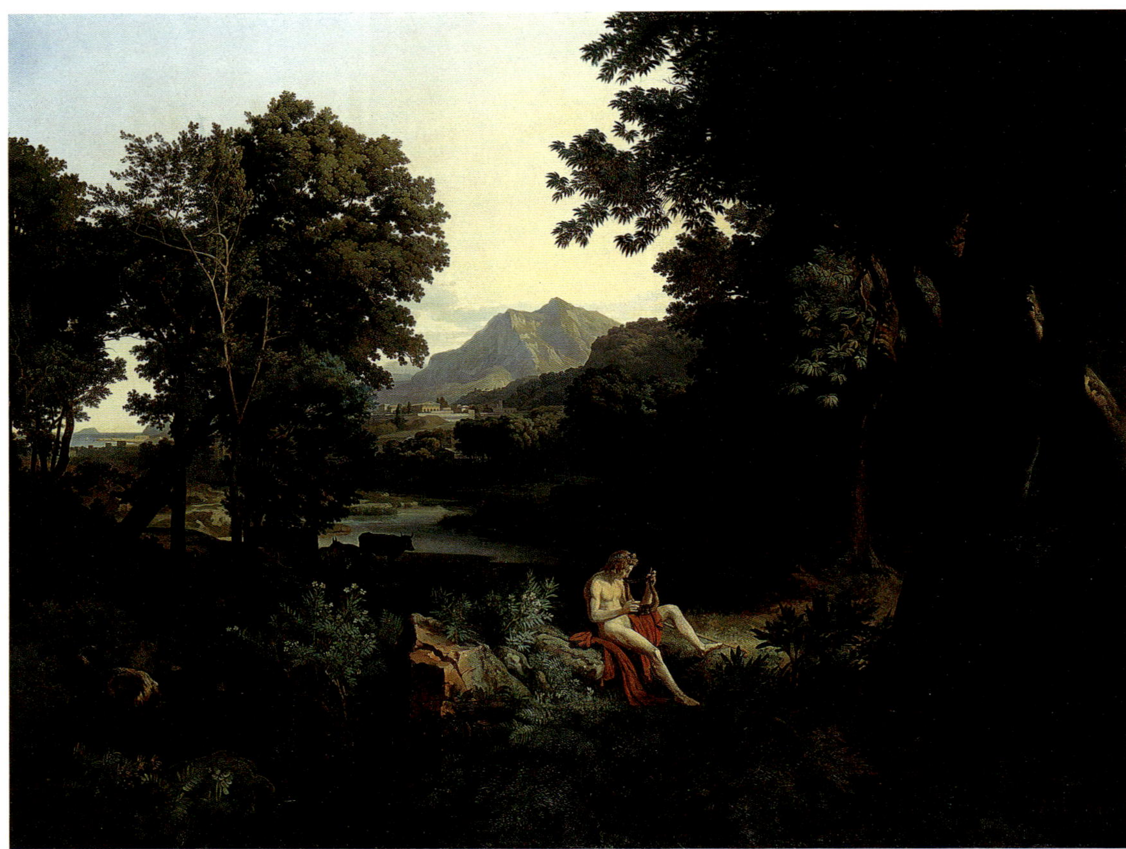

CATALOGUE NO. 7 | EUGÈNE-FERDINAND BUTTURA (1812–1852), *Apollo, Shepherding the Flocks of Admetus, Invents the Lyre*, 1837. Oil on canvas, 115 × 146 cm.

Satisfied with his invention, Hermes sets off at once to rustle the cattle of Apollo. The Archer comes after him seeking revenge but is appeased by the sight and sound of the new instrument. Hermes exchanges the tortoise for Apollo's flocks and friendship. Apollo turns out to be something of a prodigy on the instrument: "Beneath his hand it made / An astonishing sound, and the god sang a beautiful song to the tune" (ll. 499–500). The "Homeric Hymn to Hermes" does not tell us whether some passerby, hearing the Apollonian plectrum, mistakenly ascribed the art of melody to the divine Archer. In any event, the Robber-God was bilked of his own invention, not least by the subject set in 1837. Buttura was reluctant to lavish his talents on a tortoise and reestablished the truth. In his painting, Apollo does not invent the lyre but rather discovers his own creative powers, plying the strings with his delicate fingers. Hermes was the first lute maker, but Apollo was the first virtuoso.

The light is Italian and the trees are Dutch, so there is nothing very Greek about the landscape, but all too often the principal objection to the École's Historical Landscapes is the presence in the foreground of entirely conventional figures. In Buttura's painting the banality of the god distracts the gaze toward the lyre, expertly drawn in the arc of Apollo's arms so that its sides are parallel to the tree trunks. In the distance, an ox—Apollo is neglecting his duties as a cowherd—turns its head toward the pastoral musician, raising an ear to the first chords ever sounded on a musical instrument. To the left, a goat, less sensitive, turns its back on the god. Apollo and Buttura have long since forgotten Hermes' tortoise. All that remains is the lyre, the god, and the musical ox. This unexpected trio fills

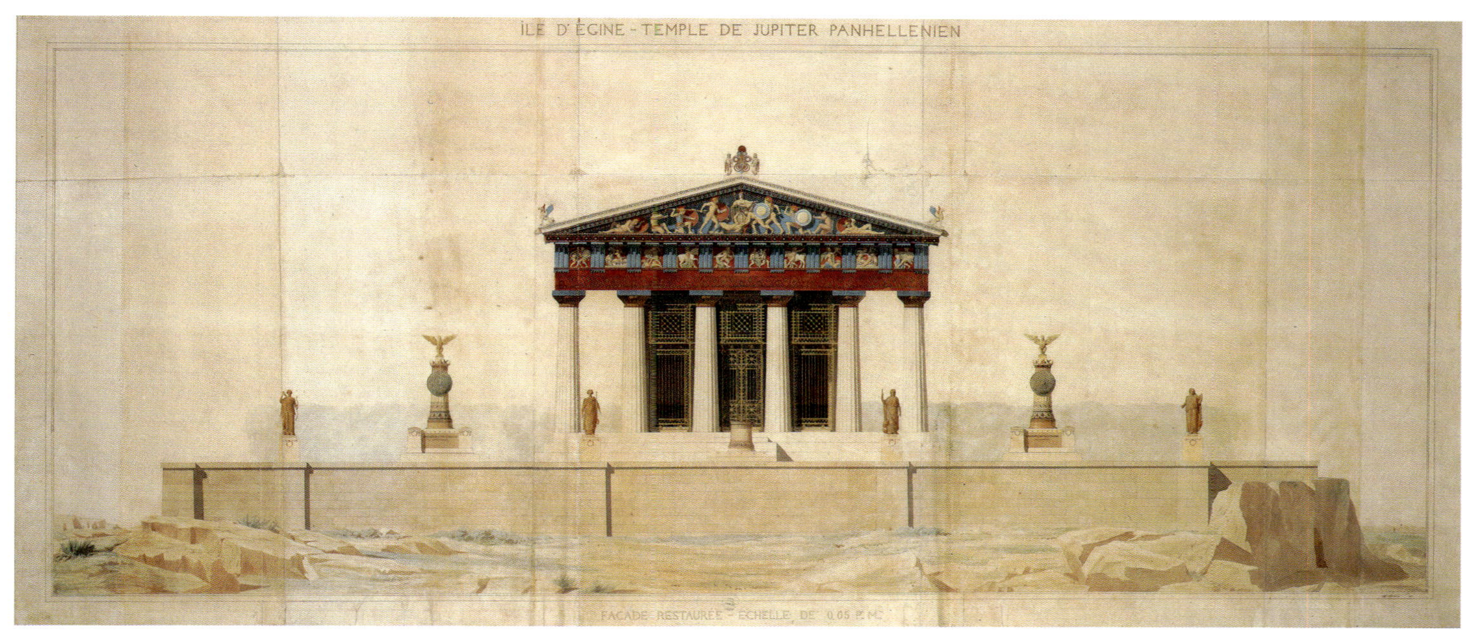

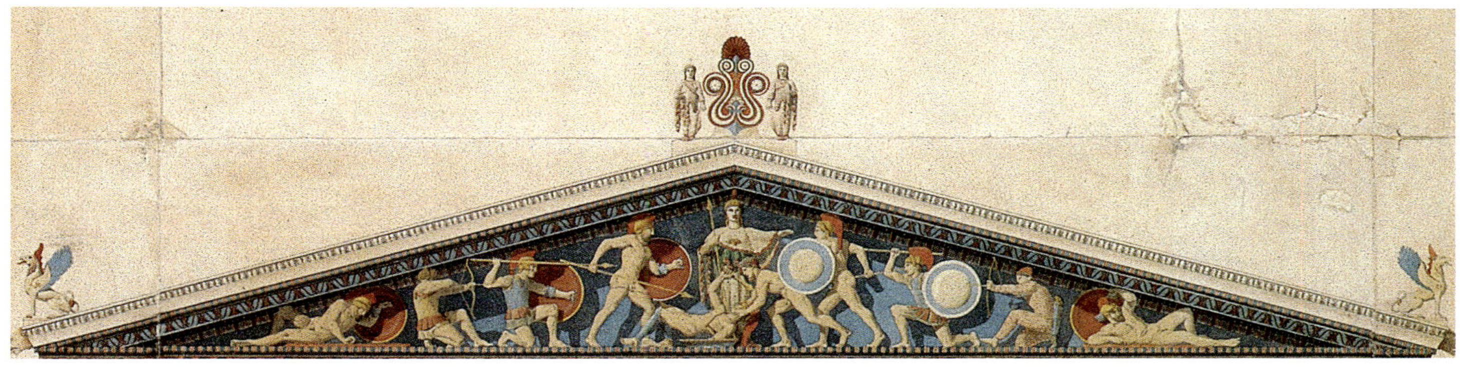

CATALOGUE NO. 8 | CHARLES GARNIER (1825–1898), *Temple of Panhellenic Jupiter or Athena, Aegina.* Facade, reconstruction, 1852. Watercolor over India ink, 136 × 281.5 cm.

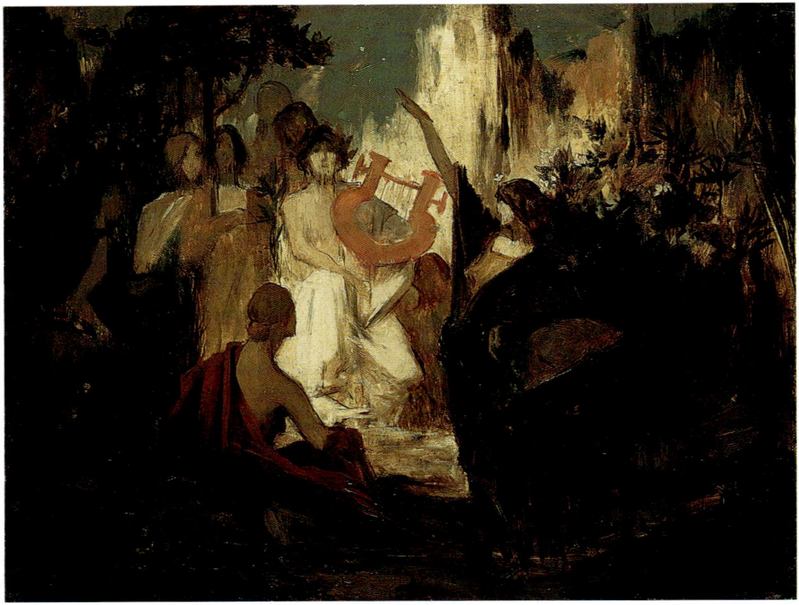

CATALOGUE NO. 9 | PIERRE-AMÉDÉE-MARCEL BÉRONNEAU (1869–1937), *The Scene Takes Place on Parnassus*, 1894. Oil on canvas, 32 × 41 cm.

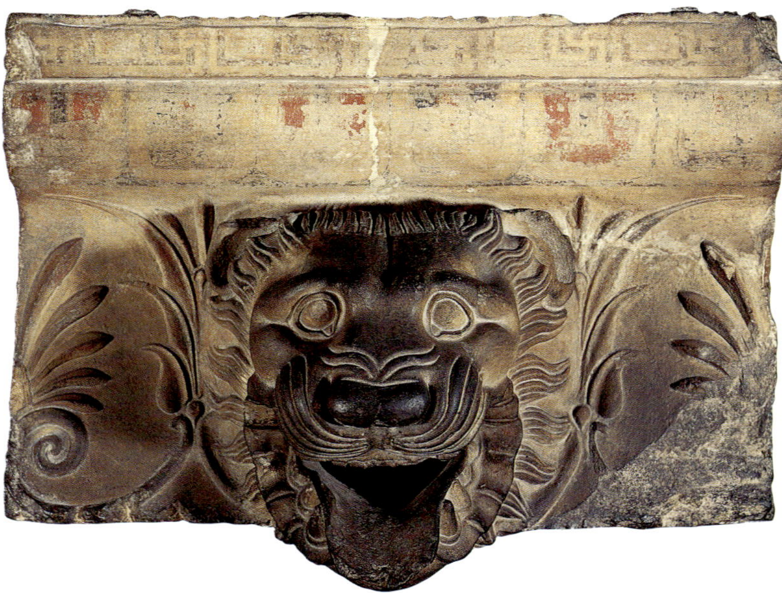

CATALOGUE NO. 10 | Element from an *acroterion* with lion's head, ca. 530 B.C. Terracotta, 40 × 56 × 36 cm.

the Greek landscape with an ironic melody that echoes the false naïveté of these legends.

As poet and servant of the lyre, Homer often sings Apollo's praises. In these descriptions Apollo resembles Homer's alter ego Demodocos:

> That hour then
> and all day long till the sun went down they feasted
> and no god's hunger lacked a share of the handsome banquet
> or the gorgeous lyre Apollo struck or the Muses singing
> voice to voice in choirs, their vibrant music rising.
> —*IL.* 1.601–5; F 1.723–27

Joy, laughter, and the poetic art that embellishes human life and abolishes misfortune through the ages: these summarize Homer's teaching. In the vaguely Symbolist oil sketch *Parnassus* (1894) by Marcel Béronneau, a pupil of Gustave Moreau, gods at the feast are no longer the same: they are all muses or goddesses (cat. no. 9). But the lyre still resounds. Center stage, Apollo has the posture and blind gaze of Homer, while men sit before him listening like the children of Chios to the aged poet. Urania, the Muse of Astronomy, gazes on Apollo but points upward to the sky; like the astronomer, the poet interprets the movements of the stars. The ancient world attributed universal knowledge to Homer, granting him mastery of natural laws, history, and human crafts. Since the Renaissance, the leader of the muses and god of light has taught that harmony and truth govern the sciences no less than arts and letters. Artists tended to forget the cruel Apollo who took part in the battle for Troy and massacred the children of Niobe, while the poet deplored the futility of the bloodshed by man and god alike. Sometimes, however, the god and the poet were one and the same.

Hermes invented the lyre, Apollo created music, and Homer spread the musicality of words and lyricism of song throughout the human world. The path we follow through the works of the artists and their students runs from Olympus down to the mortals. Let us first hear from the gods.

NOTES

1 This is the title of a French volume, wittily translating the title of Finley's essay "Lost: The Trojan War," in *Aspects of Antiquity: Discoveries and Controversies* (London, 1968), 24–38.

2 See Jon Whiteley, "The Artist and the Writer in France," in F. Haskell, A. Levi, and R. Shackleton, eds., *Essays in Honour of Jean Seznec* (Oxford, 1974), 40–51.

3 "Homeric Hymn to Apollo," ll. 172–73, in *The Homeric Hymns,* trans. M. Crudden (Oxford, 2001), 29.

4 André Chénier, "Sujets de tableaux et de poèmes," in *Oeuvres complètes* (Paris, 1958), 603.

5 André Chénier, "L'Aveugle," in *Oeuvres complètes*, 43. See Édouard Guitton, "André Chénier et Homère," in *Homère en France après la Querelle (1715–1900)*, Actes du colloque de Grenoble (October 23–25, 1995), Université Stendhal-Grenoble 3 (Paris, 1999), 333–45.

6 Henri Delaborde, *Ingres: sa vie, ses travaux, sa doctrine, d'après les manuscrits et les lettres du maître*, Paris, 1870, 202.

7 See Bruno Foucart, "La Modernité des néo-grecs," in *Paris-Rome Athènes*, exh. cat. (Paris, 1982), 49–60.

8 "Homeric Hymn to Apollo," in *The Homeric Hymns*, l. 131, p. 27.

9 "Homeric Hymn to Hermes," in *The Homeric Hymns*, ll. 24–29 and 33, p. 44.

10 Ibid., ll. 39–54, pp. 44–45.

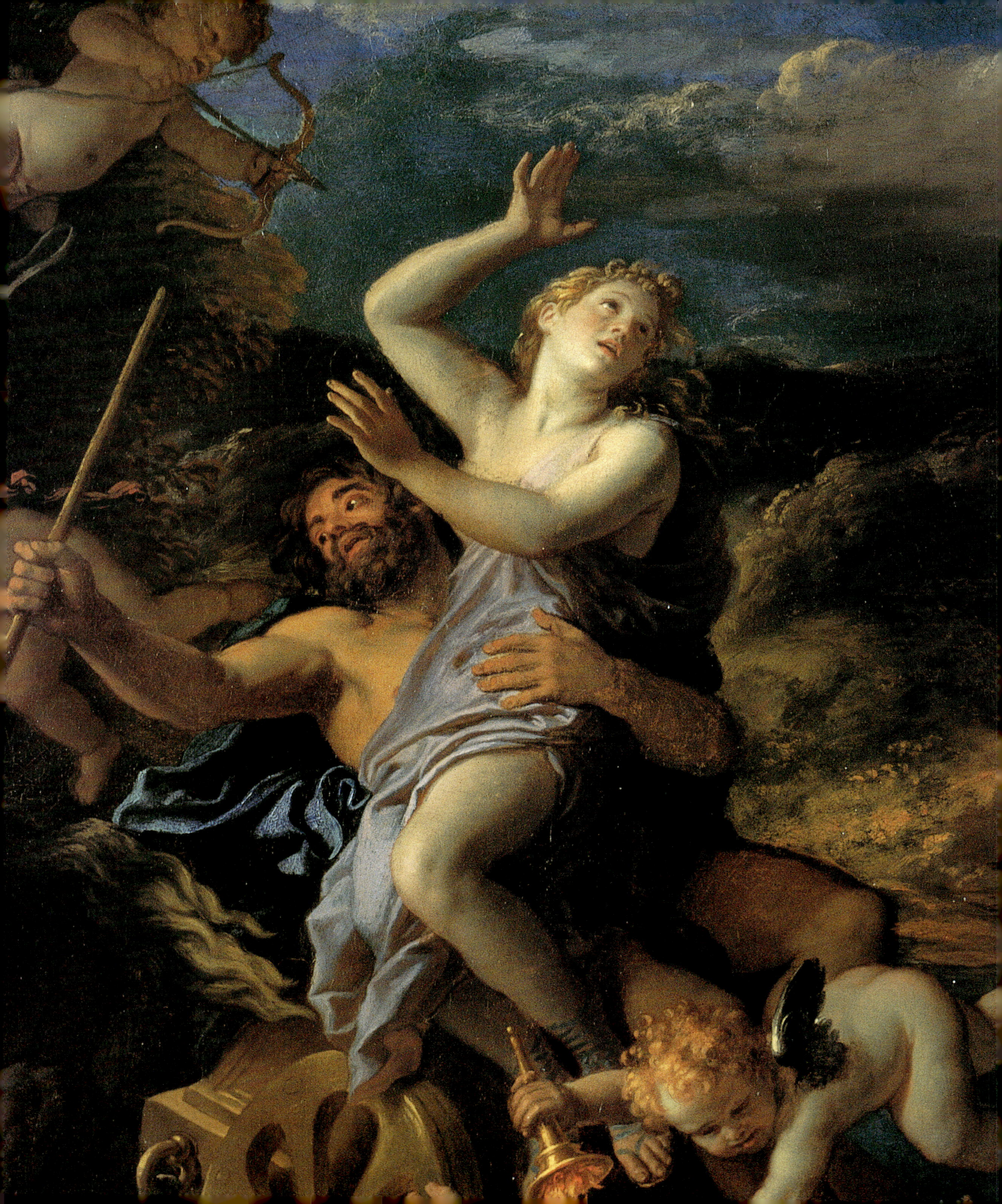

THE GODS

In Homer's world the gods exhibit personalities no less various and mutable than those of mortals. So close is the resemblance that one cannot help but perceive the Olympians as an image—at times even a caricature—of humanity. No god or immortal attains perfection except perhaps in pettiness. But there are distinctions. Circe and Calypso are second-rank divinities who must comply with the behest of the Olympians. Intelligent mortals exploit this gap in status, insinuating themselves into a deity's favor by intriguing, flattering, and seducing. They exploit gods and goddesses while seeming to serve them. Poets and artists, as one might expect, also make use of the immortals: they make stories about them.

Ares and Aphrodite

Two ancient statues impress upon École students the primary lesson all the gods (Hephaestus excepted) can claim to teach: that of physical beauty. One of them, a male torso, is probably a first century B.C. Roman copy of a Greek bronze original probably dating from the second quarter of the fourth century B.C. This mutilated torso (cat. no. 12) is now thought to be that of an athlete placing the victor's crown on his head. A brother to the athletes sculpted by Polyclitus, it displays a strikingly powerful muscularity, emphasized by the accidental coloration of the marble, rendered polychrome by its long burial in Italian soil. Ingres sent it to Paris in 1841, when he was director of the French Academy in Rome. He identified it as Mars (Greek: Ares, god of war). Students were still copying works of classical antiquity from casts, and the torso was accepted as an authentic Greek original.

Ingres very likely assumed that study of this marmoreal work would clarify the representation of volume in the drawings he demanded of his disciples. In fact, a plaster cast of the torso was finally installed in the glazed courtyard where draftsmanship was practiced, at the entrance to the Palais des Études (the Cast Gallery) beside the torso of Aphrodite (cat. no. 11), to which Ingres had married it as if in illustration of the legend of divine adultery. The *Medici Minerva* formed part of the same consignment, but early in the twentieth century it crossed the Seine to join the collections of the Louvre. In exchange, a plaster cast was made and long presided over the École's central courtyard and the passage leading to the main amphitheater.

Since it was flanked by Aphrodite, with Minerva above, the male torso could hardly be other than Ares—at least in the view of the École—for the god of war was both the lover of Aphrodite and Athena's failed adversary. The female torso represented one of the innumerable variations on the form of the *Cnidian Venus* (fourth century B.C.). In his book *The Nude*[1] art historian Kenneth Clark brilliantly evokes the melancholy mystery of the *Aphrodite of Cnidus*, a creation of Praxiteles subsequently betrayed by so many Venuses

DETAIL OF CATALOGUE NO. 19

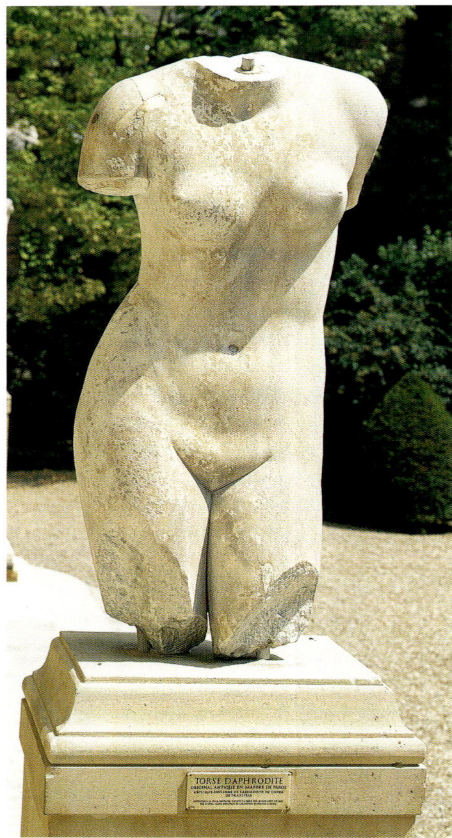

CATALOGUE NO. 11 | Feminine Torso, Roman copy after the *Aphrodite of Cnidus* by Praxiteles (340 B.C.). Marble, stone base, 103 × 46 × 32 cm.

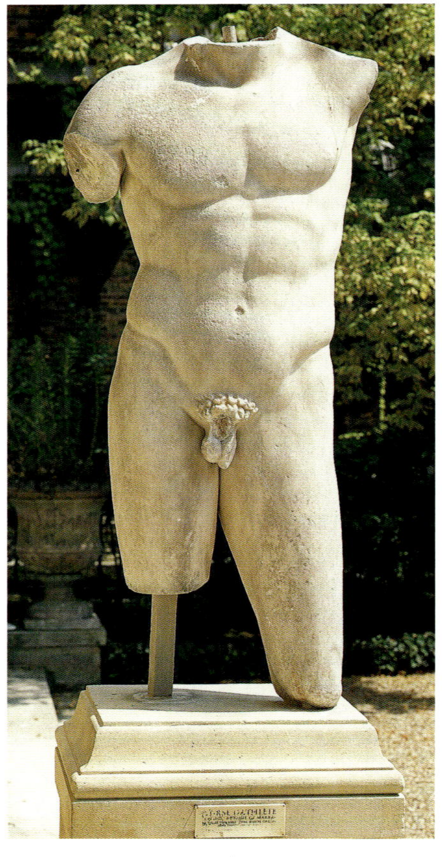

CATALOGUE NO. 12 | Masculine Torso, or Torso of an Athlete (or of Mars). First century B.C., after a Greek original of the fourth century B.C.? Marble, stone base, 133 × 60 × 37 cm.

derived from but utterly unworthy of her, notably the *Medici Venus* and *Capitoline Venus.* He notes that in Praxiteles' pose the "disposition of balance has automatically created a contrast between the arc of one hip, sweeping up till it approaches the sphere of the breast, and the long, gentle undulation of the side that is relaxed. . . . It is almost a geometric curve; and yet . . . it is a vivid symbol of desire." We know from Pseudo-Lucian that it filled male visitors to Cnidus with desire. At all events, the buttocks of this variant became a mixture of idol and good-luck charm for those in the École's *concours.* Students caressed it before going to meet their fate, and visitors can see on the callipygous goddess the traces of their sweaty fingers.

Homer sometimes makes Aphrodite's name a synonym for desire, and she certainly bears most of the responsibility for the outbreak of the Trojan War. Ares is merely her instrument, and though he *is* war and therefore kills as war kills, Apollo and Poseidon are more active on the front line. Let us, then, follow the nineteenth-century École and admit that this hypothetical Ares, who for two centuries has stood by his woman, must have applauded her victory in the Judgment of Paris. Even if one puts aside their adultery and capture by Hephaestus, narrated with such relish in the *Odyssey,* Ares and Aphrodite play unflattering roles in the war. Aphrodite is manipulated by Hera, while Ares, docile as a soldier, is a pawn in Apollo's hands. Moreover, these divine adulterers protect the least courageous warriors. Aphrodite carries Paris to safety when he is defeated by Menelaus in single combat, although it was agreed that the prize of the duel was Helen.

Despite their godhead, both Ares and Aphrodite are wounded by Diomedes, the fiercest Achaean warrior. In Homer's view, love and war have little enough personality. In the history of humanity, other motives—the ambition and intelligence of Athena among them—exert a greater sway. But Homer bestowed on Aphrodite a piece of luck she made the most of: a son named Aeneas, whom Virgil would make a hero (see "The *Aeneid*").

Mercury / Hermes

Homer calls Hermes "messenger" and "killer of Argus" (*argeiphontes*). These are the two functions of Hermes upon which the artists concentrate. Hermes as messenger accompanies the shades to the Underworld; in this function he is *psychopompe*, "leader of souls" (*Od.* 11.626 and 24.1–14). Following classical tradition, Caylus proposed this subject to the Royal Academy in his *Pictures Drawn from . . . the Odyssey*: "Mercury with his golden rod, at the head of the [dead] suitors like a shepherd leading his flock." Homeric epithets are rich in philosophical implications and visual detail: Hermes is generally shown with his staff, the caduceus, winged feet, and a cortege of dead souls on a frieze around his helmet.

Chance acquisitions have made Hermes one of the more privileged guests of the École des beaux-arts. The spirit and history of both place and institution speak out eloquently in the many famous sculptures and paintings in which he features. The most prestigious student and most influential teacher of the École, Ingres enjoyed the salaried stay in Rome conferred by the eponymous prize and sent back a copy of the Farnesina *Mercury* by Raphael (and studio) (fig. 37). This is a vivid illustration of the strange narrative of Psyche in Apuleius's Latin "novel" *The Golden Ass.* The heroine's name means "soul," and Psyche's poetic and erotic adventures are a transposition of the soul's errant quest for Truth, which Apuleius identifies with divine love (Eros). In this quest, it is the "leader of souls," the *psychopompe* Hermes, who naturally leads Psyche to Eros, her divine lover.

Although Apuleius's symbolic narrative has its roots in Platonic or Neoplatonic philosophy, comparison with the Homeric image remains startling. For Homer, the *pyschopompe* governs the transition between life and death. Moreover, this death is very different from the Platonic ascent:

> Now Cyllenian Hermes called away the suitors' ghosts,
> holding firm in his hand the wand of fine pure gold
> that enchants the eyes of men whenever Hermes wants
> or wakes us from sleep.
> With a wave of this he stirred and led them on
> and the ghosts trailed after with high thin cries
> as bats cry in the depths of a dark haunted cavern,
> shrilling, flittering, wild when one drops from the chain—
> slipped from the rock face, while the rest cling tight . . .
> So with their high thin cries the ghosts flocked now
> and Hermes the Healer led them on, and down the dank
> moldering paths and past the Ocean's streams they went
> and past the White Rock and the Sun's Western Gates and past
> the Land of Dreams, and they soon reached the fields of asphodel
> where the dead, the burnt-out wraiths of mortals, make their home.
>
> —OD. 24.1–14; F 24.1–15

Homer's imagination speaks to our own—indeed, perhaps he created it. We can easily imagine that the threshold of the Underworld is a bat-haunted cave. The bat-in-chief, the winged Hermes, wakes his fellow beings from their black slumber, but he also wakes the souls of the suitors whose bodies are piled high in the palace, along with those of the servants hanged by Odysseus's order. The souls fly here and there like birds flung about by a high wind. Homer's Hermes is a mere god, and the Homeric gods did not concern themselves overmuch with metaphysical questions. His gestures are mechanical:

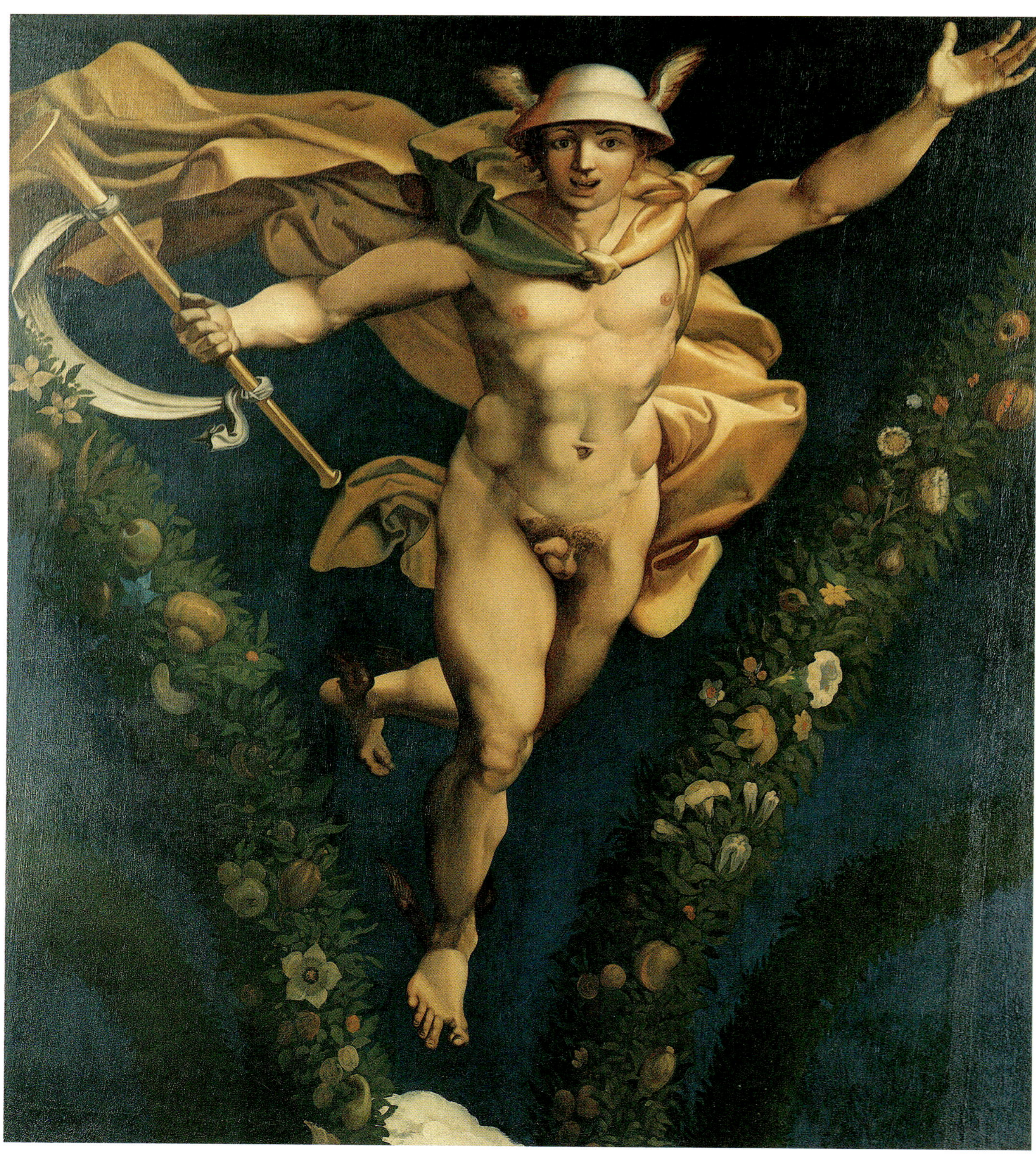

FIGURE 37 | JEAN-AUGUSTE-DOMINIQUE INGRES (1780–1867), *Mercury*, after the fresco by Raphael in the Loggia of the Farnesina, 1809. Oil on canvas, 245 × 212.5 cm. Rome Dispatch in Painting.

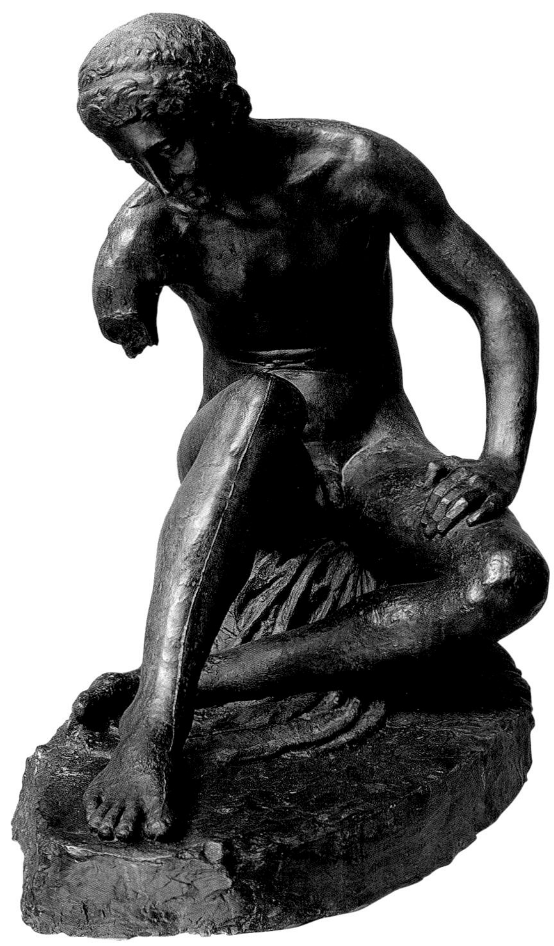

CATALOGUE NO. 13 | JEAN-LOUIS BRIAN (1805–1864), *Seated Mercury* (unfinished). Bronze, 93 × 100 cm. Cast from a plaster model (exhibited at the 1864 Salon) by the metal-founder Henri-Léon Thiébault (or Thiébaut).

> Quickly under his feet he fastened the supple sandals,
> ever-glowing gold, that wing him over the waves
> and boundless earth with the rush of gusting winds.
> He seized the wand that enchants the eyes of men
> whenever Hermes wants, or wakes us up from sleep.
> That wand in his grip, the powerful giant-killer,
> swooping down from Pieria, down the high clear air
> plunged to the sea and skimmed the waves like a tern.
> —OD. 5.43–51; F 5.48–55)

Seen full face amid festoons of flowers, Ingres's and Raphael's Hermes bursts forward in foreshortened form, eyes wide, toes spread, his torso and winged *petasus* (broad-brimmed hat) angled forward. He crashes through the picture plane, smashing the architectural triangle of the Farnesina pendentive. No fanfares to immortality from the trumpet he holds (replacing the staff Homer describes). On the contrary, he flees the light of life like some nocturnal predator. The bizarre function of the *psychopompe* forces the hand of Ingres and Raphael as it had that of Homer, resulting in an uncanny image of striking precision.

The *Seated Mercury* by Jean-Louis Brian (cat. no. 13), tightening his missing sandals absent-mindedly with his right hand (also absent), has entered the (self-flattering) legends of the École as the unfinished and posthumously cast work of a sculptor exhausted by his own labors and dying for his art. His last breath served to animate this figure. Brian died before finishing Mercury's arms, and the feet too are only sketchily modeled. The tradition of Mercury tying his sandals is an ancient one, illustrated by Lysippus in antiquity and by Jean-Baptiste Pigalle in modern times. Rather than paraphrase, let me quote the "Homeric Hymn to Hermes":

> But once at the sands of the sea
> With withies he plaited sandals beyond the description of speech,
> Beyond the grasp of mind, miraculous works that he made
> By mixing tamarisk stalks together with myrtle-like shoots.[2]

Brian's work revises with weary elegance the models of Pigalle, which were themselves inspired by the images in the Loggia di Psyche at the Farnesina. It also carries echoes of the *Hermes in Repose*, whose pose is preserved by the copy in the Naples Archaeological Museum. A cast of this was long copied by students; the École possesses a fine marble copy made by the

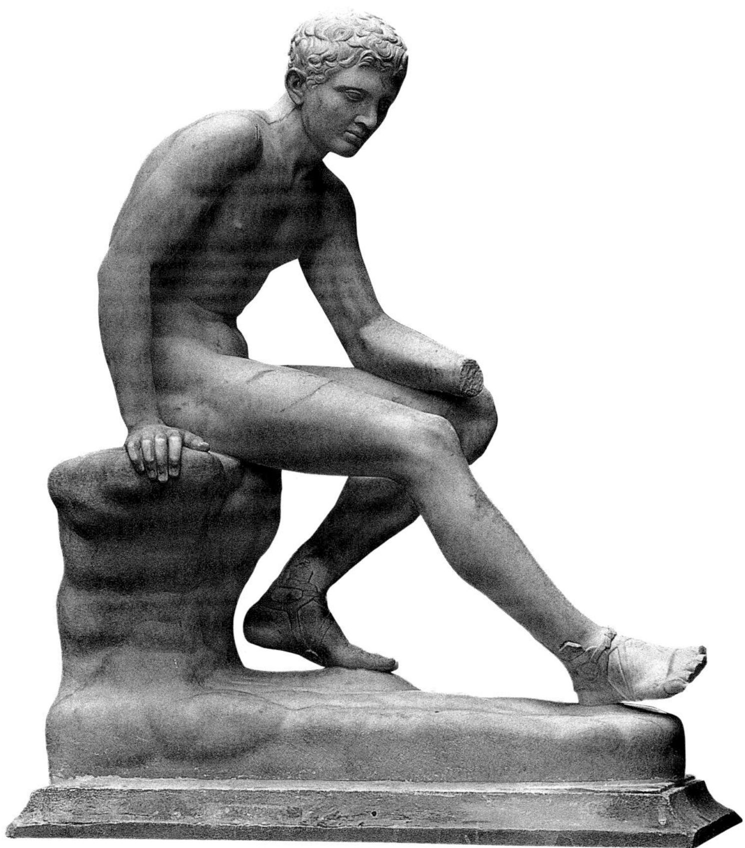

FIGURE 38 | PIERRE-ANTOINE-HIPPOLYTE BONNARDEL (1824–1856), *Seated Mercury;* copy of an ancient statue in the Naples Museum, 1854. Marble, 121.5 × 47 × 84 cm. Rome Dispatch in Sculpture.

unfortunate Pierre-Antoine-Hippolyte Bonnardel, who won the Prix de Rome for sculpture but died during his residence there (fig. 38). Clearly Hermes was a mortal omen for winners of the Prix de Rome, accompanying too many of them to their last resting place. Bonnardel's divinity is caught in a moment of repose, stretching out one leg and bending his back, which no longer bears the fearful burden of the *psychopompe.* This Hermes would be hard put to convince the dead that happiness and truth await them in the Underworld.

The Hermes of Raphael/Ingres and Brian illustrate verses from Homer. They are supplemented with *Mercury Overcomes the Vigilance of Argus* (1674; cat. no. 14), the reception piece painted by François de Troy upon his acceptance into the Royal Academy of Painting and Sculpture, and a treatment of the same subject by Eugène Lepoitevin (1828; cat no. 15) in a historical landscape sketch. Both works recall the second formulaic epithet bestowed on Hermes, *argeiphontes*, which the ancients understood to mean "killer of Argus." Before introducing the unfortunate Argus, I should point out that some modern translators take a different view of the etymology of the word, preferring to interpret it as "he who shows by making radiant" (*argos* means "shining"), thus distancing us considerably from the messenger of death and Raphael's batlike *Mercury.* In this view, the febrile imagination of amateur etymologists incorrectly reinterpreted the root, thus conceiving a monster named *Argos* whom Hermes the killer (*phoneus*) had to dispatch.

Artists and poets make what use they like of legend. In their view, and following the dubious etymology of *argeiphontes*, Hermes was ordered by Zeus to kill the abominable Argus because Argus, in his turn, had been ordered by Hera to use his one hundred eyes to keep watch over Zeus's lover Io. Zeus had taken the precaution of turning the pregnant Io into a heifer to protect her from Hera's jealousy. Hera was therefore ensuring that Io remained in this form, which held little appeal even for the insatiable Zeus. De Troy makes a classical shepherd of Argus, whom Hermes prepares to run through with a sword. Dutch artists, by contrast, sometimes presented him as old and fat, perhaps seeking to render his murder more acceptable. Zeus's beloved heifer sees her chance and makes off. Three Naiads avert their gaze; according to Ovid, who propagated the legend in his *Metamorphoses*, they are Io's sisters.[3] Under the influence of Flemish painting, De Troy treats the subject as a peasant scene, presided over by the majestically voluptuous rump of the cow. The freshness of the scene, imparted by De Troy's sensitive imagination and colors, is at one with the Greek spirit, although only the masculine figures conform to academic criteria. The elegance of the human presence in the picture, the animal solidity, and pleasing vegetation all combine to create a tranquil effect. Hermes' next act

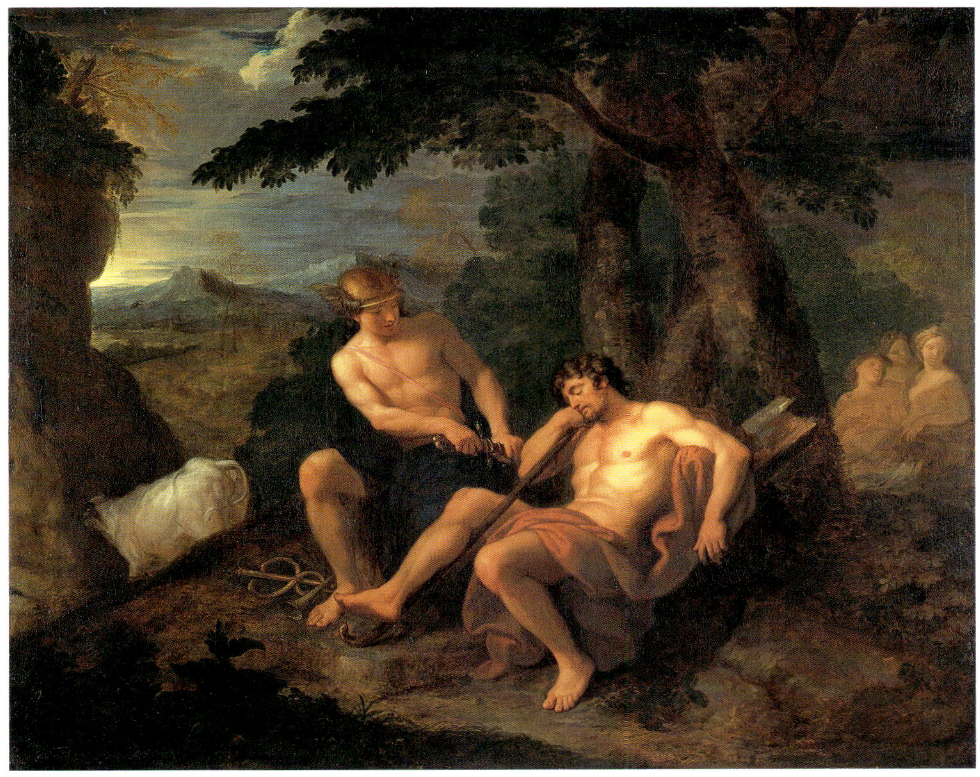

CATALOGUE NO. 14 | FRANÇOIS DE TROY (1645–1730), *Mercury Overcomes the Vigilance of Argus*, 1674. Oil on canvas, 148 × 177 cm.

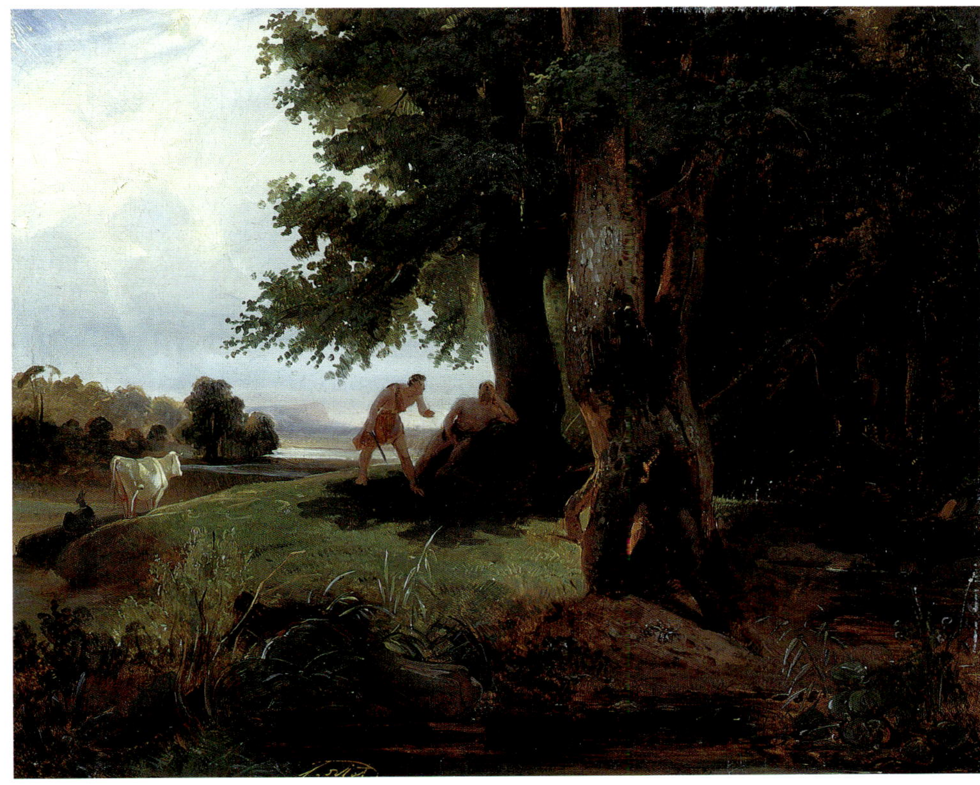

CATALOGUE NO. 15 | EUGÈNE-MODESTE-EDMOND LEPOITEVIN, 1806–1870, *Mercury Lulls Argus to Sleep and Kills Him*, 1828. Oil on canvas, 37.5 × 46 cm.

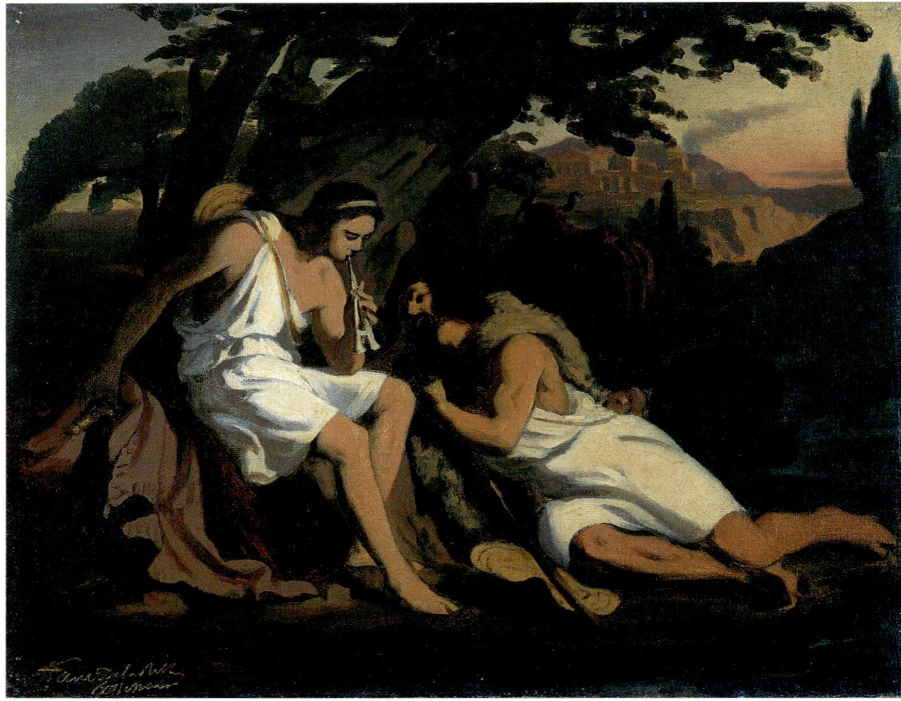

CATALOGUE NO. 16 | VICTOR-FRANÇOIS-ÉLIE BIENNOURY (1823–1893), *Mercury Lulls Argus to Sleep and Kills Him*, 1842. Oil on canvas, 32.4 × 40.5 cm.

will be to tear out Argus's eyes and present them to Hera. She consoles herself by scattering them on the plumage of that redoubtable "hundred-eyed" guard bird, the peacock.

In 1828 the student Eugène Lepoitevin showed scrupulous respect for the subject and constraints of the historical landscape sketch *concours* (a large tree and small figures were required), although he evidently had trouble placing his figures in the landscape. The ironic emphasis on the spreading white rump of Io must surely be involuntary. This cow is not—as in François de Troy's painting—making off while she can. She is ruminating, a patch of white amid the rich Norman grassland. She turns her head to observe the antics of the humans, while the subtle Hermes of fable sports a clumsy silhouette unworthy of his reputation (cat. no. 15). The beauteous heifer has grown considerably more discreet by 1842, when the same subject was set for the *concours* in history painting proper. Victor-François-Élie Biennoury (cat. no. 16) conceals the cow's ample rear in the shadow of a tree. Argus, too, is transformed, having become something of a caveman, while the eye rests on Hermes, the elegant flute player. Nevertheless, his right hand is on his sword. An impassive killer with a taste for music, Hermes here embodies the cold malice of the divinity rather than the humane executioner weary of escorting the souls of the dead.

Hermes the bat and the assassin of peacocks: these are not the only Homeric epithets for the god represented in the École's collections. There was a further aspect to Hermes, less frequently cited in Homer but one in which Ovid revels, namely, Hermes the concupiscent. Poussin, too, was attracted to it. *Mercury, Herse, and Aglauros*—the only painting in the École's collection attributed to Poussin (cat. no. 17)—records an episode also painted by Veronese. Ovid's story suits the flying, thieving, cruelty of Mercury. In Poussin's picture he enters the room of his lover, Herse, naked as a Greek god. Athena—the sexless goddess, jealous of her brother Hermes—has infected Herse's sister

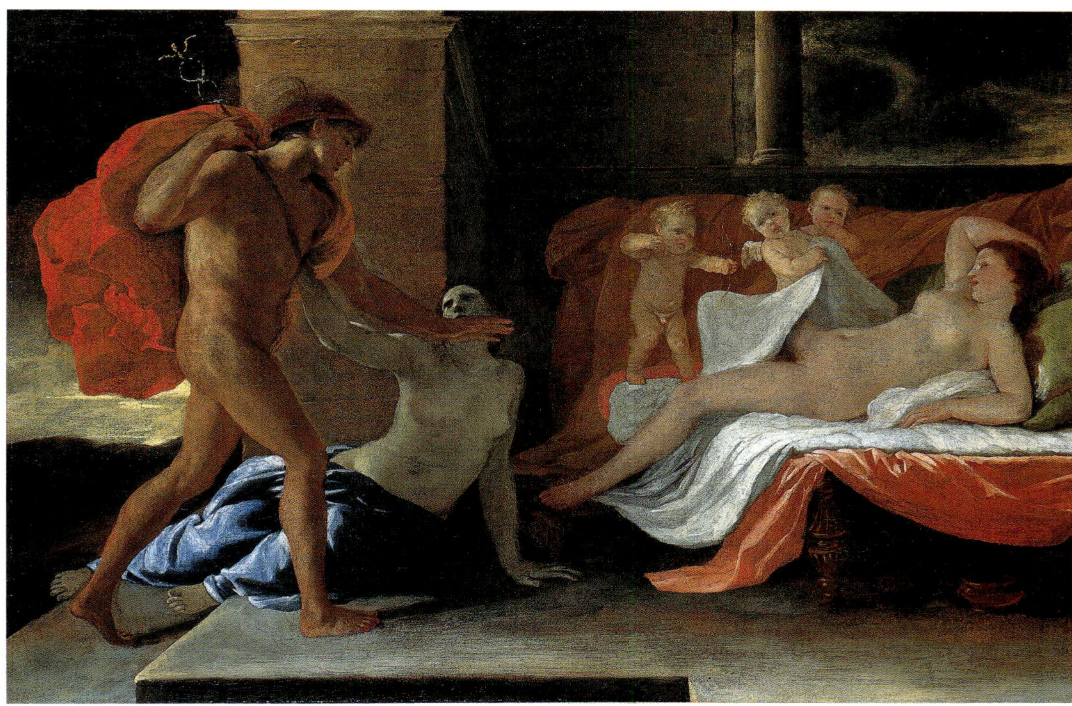

CATALOGUE NO. 17 | NICOLAS POUSSIN (1594–1665), *Mercury, Herse, and Aglauros*, ca. 1625. Oil on canvas, 53.5 × 77.5 cm.

Aglauros with her own jealousy. When Aglauros attempts to prevent his sport, the furious Mercury transforms her into a stone statue.[4] This youthful piece is often said to show the influence of Venetian sensuality transformed by cold Northern Mannerism, but the glacial cruelty of these naked bodies—their provocative poses and controlled gestures—are all drawn from Ovid's description. Such lethal premeditated eroticism is remote from the Homeric world. Everyone in Homer is weak, and his indulgent and skeptical smile embraces gods and mortals alike. The Mercury painted by Poussin is quite unacquainted with doubt, and doubt is the source from whence Homer's humanity flows.

The Wrath of Zeus

When Homer speaks of divine vengeance or retribution, every word is imbued with sympathy for mortals and distrust of the pseudojustice inflicted from above:

That very instant storming Zeus dispatched Apollo:

"Go, my friend, to the side of Hector armed in
bronze.
The god of the quakes who grips and pounds the
earth
has just this moment plunged in his own bright sea,
diving away from all my mounting anger. Just think
what the gods would have heard if we had come to
blows,
even those beneath the ground who circle Cronus."

—*IL.* 15.223–26; F 15.262–68

"My mounting anger," says Zeus, who invariably speaks of might rather than right. The battle between the Titans and the Olympians (Homer's gods) inspired not merely the brief allusion in the *Iliad* but the weighty, noble verses of Hesiod's *Theogony* (seventh century B.C.). The Titans were the sons of the primitive Earth and their leader was Zeus's own father, Cronus.

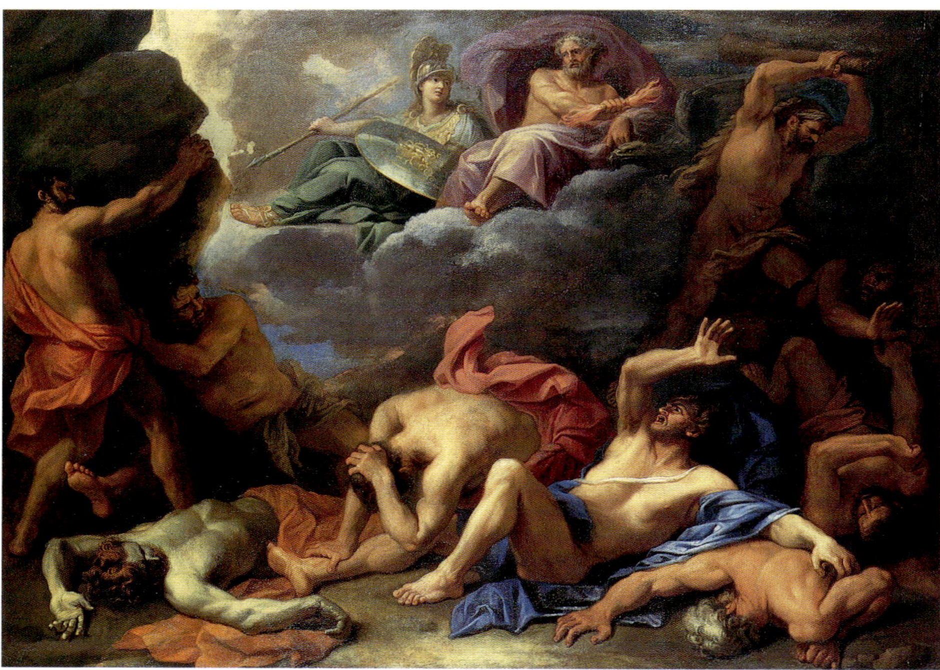

CATALOGUE NO. 18 | JEAN LEBLOND (1645–1709), *The Titans Crushed by Jupiter's Thunderbolts*, 1681. Oil on canvas, 146 × 199 cm.

By reputation they were gods of an inhuman religion still in thrall to the brute forces of nature, who were overthrown by the "civilized" gods of Olympus. The fall of the Titans is depicted by the obscure painter Jean Leblond in his 1681 reception piece (cat. no. 18); its agents are Zeus and Athena rather awkwardly seated in their cloud fortress, guarded by Heracles. Homer shows no great confidence in the Olympians' ability to assume the values of civilization. No triumphant victor is ever free of arrogance, and Homer loves only the vanquished. This is the lesson taught us, however unwittingly, by the men who give battle in the plain of Troy and the all-powerful gods above them, who have the prickly vanity of generals remote from the fighting.

Homer—especially the Homer of the tragic poets and Aristotle—has imparted to the West a new perspective on the defeated: the vanquished are never entirely in the wrong and victors—especially immortal victors—are never entirely in the right. Moralists cannot accept that power has driven the gods of Homer mad. Homer never believed in absolute good and bad and thinks no less of the vanquished Titans than of their ferocious conquerors. Plato condemns him for this in the second and third books of the *Republic*, saying nothing should be so strictly forbidden to children as the *Gigantomachia* (the war between the Giants and the Olympians).[5] The Giants shared the fate of their brothers the Titans and their fall was often illustrated by artists avid for spectacle (for example, Giulio Romano in Mantua's Palazzo del Te and Perino del Vaga in Genoa's Palazzo Doria Pamphili). Ancient sculptors often carved gigantomachies in temple pediments with upright combatants at the center and Titans falling into the acute angles of the corners. Modern depictions of the event, like the Homeric poems, invariably respect the victims of Olympus, for a being in free fall combines movement and suffering and therefore attracts both our gaze and our sympathy. The egotistical satisfaction of the supine victors can hardly do other than repel. The most modestly talented artist has only to follow Homer to make of the formless Titans—the "wretched of the earth"—figures who live, suffer, and die, and in the process move the spectator much more than the invincible gods.

Persephone Raped by Hades

More sensual even than mortals, Homer's gods love wine, women, and food. They lacked for none of these at their banquets, which were termed *Homeric*. The contemporaries of Rabelais and Ronsard read Homer avidly for this rambunctious joy, whose secret was subsequently forgotten. Here I will confine myself to a few examples of divine debauchery. Two École paintings (cat. nos. 19–20) describe the abduction, ravishing, or rape of Persephone (Proserpine) by Hades (Pluto). The formidable Persephone, goddess of death and the dead, appears in the eleventh book of the *Odyssey*, the Book of the Dead, which describes Ulysses' descent to the Underworld. Her legend was propagated in one of the Homeric hymns written during the centuries that followed in rhythms borrowed from Homer. Their inspiration is Homeric, but they bestow on the gods' persons and functions a cult significance, whereas in the Homeric poems the immortals take few or no pains to unite the city of men around them. These divine adventures subsequently spread to modern iconography through works of other authors entirely devoid of the naïve religiosity of the hymns, in particular the Roman poet Ovid. The connections between the irreverent Homer and the pictorial interpretation he was given by the students of the École des beaux-arts are therefore somewhat indirect, and the Greek hexameter is less their source than a poetic commentary. Here are some verses from the "Homeric Hymn to Demeter":

> With fair-tressed Demeter, the sacred goddess, my song begins,
> With herself and her slim-ankled daughter, whom Aïdoneus once
> Abducted . . .
> She was joining with Ocean's full-bosomed daughters in play,
> And amidst a soft meadow-field was plucking flowers . . .
>
> . . . But broad-pathed Earth gaped wide
> On the Nysion plain, where the lord, the Receiver of Many, rushed forth
> With his deathless horses, Kronos' son who has many a name.
> He seized her against her will, and aboard his golden car
> Carried her off, lamenting; she uttered a piercing scream.
>
> While the goddess viewed earth and starry sky, and the strong-flowing sea
> Teeming with fish, and the rays of the Sun, she still hoped to behold
> Her dear mother again . . .
>
> The mountains' peaks and the depths of the sea rang out at the sound
> Of her deathless voice.[6]

Thus, the daughter of Demeter (goddess of Earth, fertility, and harvests) is carried off by the god of the Underworld. Hades/Pluto compromises, ceding his wife to her mother and the world of the living for six months of every year. This symbolism—the opposition of the seasons, the struggle between the principles of life and death—was projected back onto the *Iliad* and *Odyssey* by the ancient critics. But in the combats beneath the walls of Troy, the gods are no more able to oppose Ker or Moira—Thanatos, as she is known in contemporary times—than are the mortals. Both are creatures of life and pleasure. This endless struggle, which pervades every belief system and all religious fears, was illustrated by the vision of humanist artists.

The power of myth and bounty of nature have vanished from the reception piece by Charles de La Fosse (cat. no. 19), replaced by the Ovidian picturesque. He borrows Ovid's sleeping waters of Lake Pergus, on

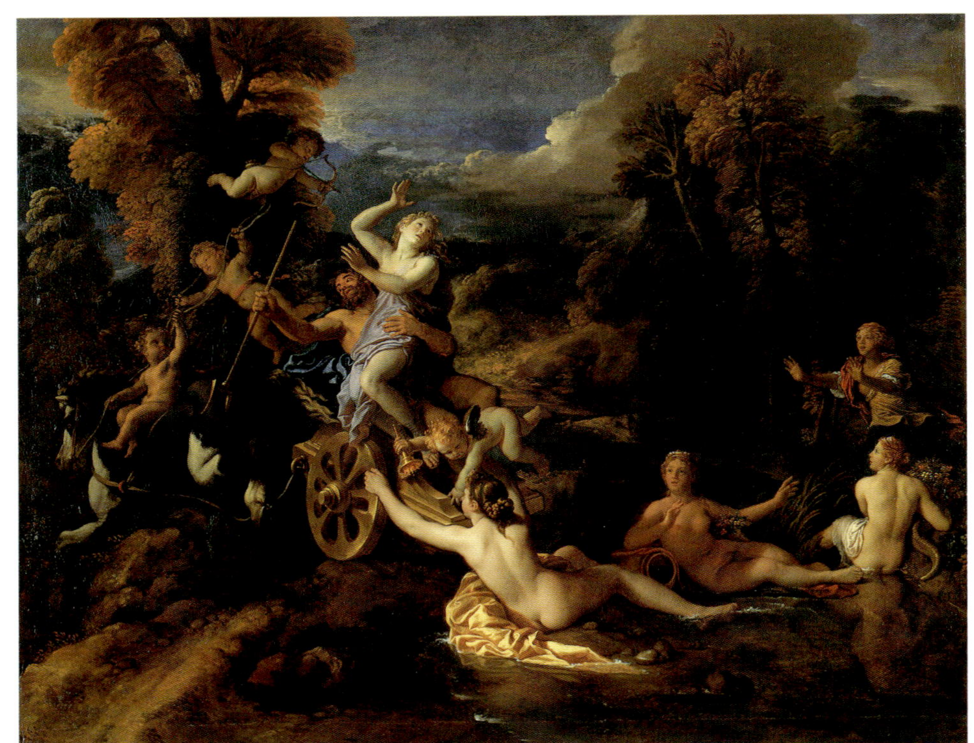

CATALOGUE NO. 19 | CHARLES DE LA FOSSE (1636–1716), *The Rape of Persephone*, 1673. Oil on canvas, 145 × 181 cm.

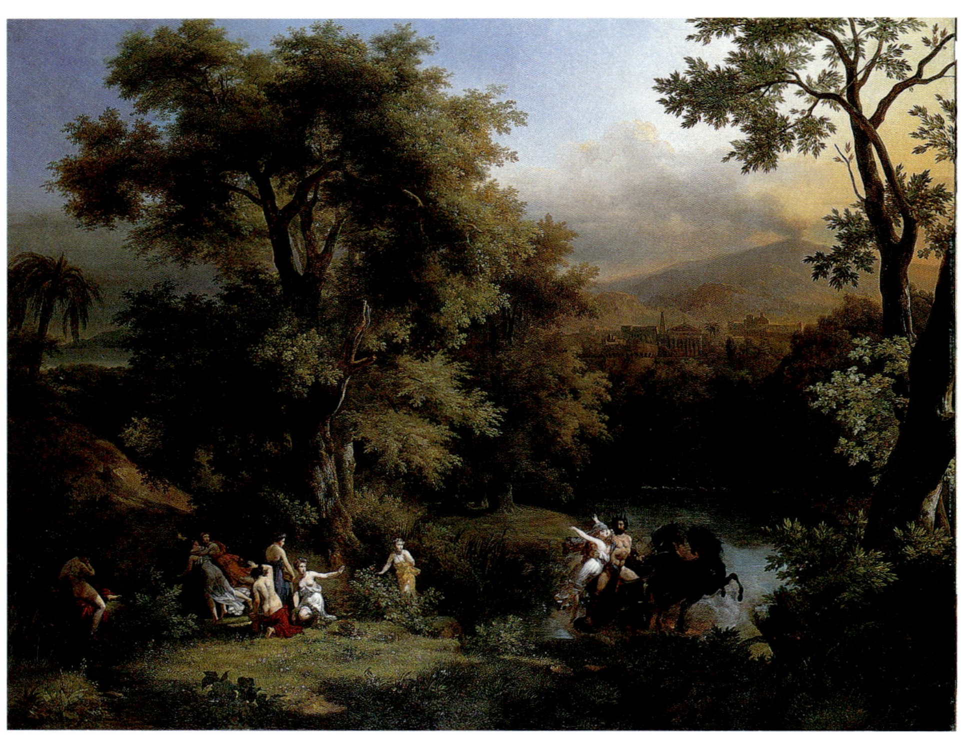

CATALOGUE NO. 20 | JEAN-CHARLES-JOSEPH RÉMOND (1795–1875), *The Rape of Persephone*, 1821. Oil on canvas, 114 × 146 cm.

whose banks the rape takes place. Before our eyes Hades opens a chasm in the earth with his scepter and into it carries his new wife. The painter has added the naked nymphs in the foreground, one of whom vainly tries to hold back the infernal chariot. The winged Cupids, fluttering in very dubious taste above Persephone's head, are likewise his own invention, as is the weeping mother in an elegiac and artificial landscape. The poses come from Gianlorenzo Bernini's sculpture and Italian painting, benefiting little or not at all from the presumably fresh spring water and cool shade of the trees. Too many outstretched arms, too many expressions full of pious conviction learned from Poussin and Le Brun run counter to the supposed violence of the rape. The young Jean-Charles-Joseph Rémond won the historical landscape prize in 1821 (cat. no. 20) with a more adroit mixture of Italian landscapes, dominated by a smoking volcano and the discreet silhouette of the god of the Underworld, all seen in the complex light of an eruption: Hades will no doubt return to the Underworld through the molten crater. Rémond's trees have a coolness, his leaves a naïve accuracy unknown to De La Fosse. In the historical landscape, the small scale of his protagonists was obligatory. The gods are reduced to what Homer saw in them: mere supernumeraries compared to the mortals who traverse these landscapes in their exploration of the face of the earth. Far from paralyzing the young artists, the requirement that one paint a tree helped to suggest—without pedantry—the simple and universal landscape of this hymn to Earth and Life. It also revived the cool mythological descriptions of Ovid.

Zeus Raped By Hera

The rape of Persephone as presented in the Homeric hymn undoubtedly belongs to the universal symbolism of natural forces. By contrast, when Homer creates a dramatic scene to suit the purposes of his narrative, nothing remains of the allegorical origins of the gods but what his skepticism chooses to conserve. It was not Homer who sought to marry Zeus and Hera by means of allegory. The others who did so had recourse to etymology, playing with the names *Zeus*, whose root meaning is "light of the sky," and *Hera*, a word of uncertain origin. Since classical antiquity, the fourteenth book of the *Iliad*, with its long description of the coupling of the Olympian principals, has given rise to conflicting interpretations.[7] That the book displayed an irreverently humorous attitude toward matters religious was completely unthinkable. Among the moralists, some, like Plato, were both fascinated and scandalized.[8] Others, led by one Heraclitus—who probably wrote his *Quaestiones Homericae* during the century of the Roman emperor Augustus—explained Homer's story in terms of a very moral allegory, screening the divine couple from sight in a cloud of natural metaphors. The site of this coupling was the heights of Gargaron, one of the summits of Mount Ida, which looks down on Troy. Now, Heraclitus perceives nothing less on Gargaron than the fusion and uniting of the masculine and feminine principles of the world: air-Hera with her brother ether-Zeus. But when it comes to painting, one must of necessity descend from the heavens to more earthly beds and acknowledge the spectacle of Zeus and Hera, as Heraclitus puts it, "lying down on the mountainside, like beasts."[9] Let us, then, descend to our animal origins.

Homer dealt with these immense if rather vacant questions in a scene worthy of the variety theater, were it not so deliberately pornographic. The fourteenth book of the *Iliad* is not written to honor any being, human or immortal. Zeus, at the request of Achilles' mother, Thetis, has ordered the gods not to intervene in Trojan affairs; but Achilles steadfastly refuses to fight, and the Greeks are routed by Hector's attack. So Poseidon disobeys his brother's order. Zeus's wife—sister, sister-in-law, and ally of Poseidon—conceals the latter's rebellion by means of a stratagem suspect from both moral and marital points of view:

> What could she do?—
> Queen Hera wondered, her eyes glowing wide . . .
> how could she outmaneuver Zeus the mastermind,
> this Zeus with his battle-shield of storm and
> thunder?

At last one strategy struck her mind as best:
she would dress in all her glory and go to Ida—
perhaps the old desire would overwhelm the king
to lie by her naked body and make immortal love
and she might drift an oblivious, soft warm sleep
across his eyes and numb that seething brain.
So off she went to her room,
the chamber her loving son Hephaestus built her,
hanging the doors from doorposts snug and tight,
locked with a secret bolt no other god could draw.
She slipped in, closing the polished doors behind her.
The ambrosia first. Hera cleansed her enticing body
of any blemish, then she applied a deep olive rub,
the breath-taking, redolent oil she kept beside her . . .
one stir of the scent in the bronze-floored halls of
   Zeus
and a perfumed cloud would drift from heaven down
   to earth.
Kneading her skin with this to a soft glow and comb-
   ing her hair,
she twisted her braids with expert hands, and sleek,
   luxurious,
shining down from her deathless head they fell,
   cascading.
Then round her shoulders she swirled the wondrous
   robes
that Athena wove her, brushed out to a high gloss
and worked into the weft an elegant rose brocade.
She pinned them across her breasts with a golden
   brooch
then sashed her waist with a waistband
floating a hundred tassels, and into her earlobes,
neatly pierced, she quickly looped her earrings,
ripe mulberry-clusters dangling in triple drops
and the silver glints they cast could catch the heart.
Then back over her brow she draped her headdress,
fine fresh veils for Hera the queen of gods,
their pale glimmering sheen like a rising sun,
and under her smooth feet she fastened supple sandals.
Now, dazzling in all her rich regalia, head to foot,
out of her rooms she strode and beckoned Aphrodite
away from the other gods and whispered, "Dear child,
would you do me a favor . . . whatever I might ask?"

—*IL.* 14.159–90; F 14.194–233

Hera asks the goddess of desire for one of her aphrodisiac charms, serving up a transparent lie as pretext. Why should Aphrodite believe that Hera wants to reconcile Thetis and Oceanus, a couple who have, as Hera herself declares (206–7), long since given up marital intercourse? Aphrodite is quick enough to suspect Hera of plotting against the Greeks under other circumstances, and the reconciliation of Oceanus and wife can hardly have motivated Hera to dress and make up like a courtesan. In any event, Hera obtains from the Trojan's staunchest ally

the breastband,
pierced and alluring, with every kind of enchantment
woven through it. . . . There is the heat of Love,
the pulsing rush of Longing, the lover's whisper,
irresistible—magic to make the sanest man go mad.

—*IL.* 14.214–17; F 14.257–61

Hera then purchases the assistance of Sleep—Hypnos or Morpheus. She promises him a fine solid-gold seat, but, thanks to his bargaining powers, he raises the ante to a young Grace. Now Hera can set off for the residence of Oceanus. But—quite by chance—she comes across Zeus, a god famously willing to raise any passing skirt—even his wife's.

Modestly Hera insists that they go to her bedchamber, constructed by Hephaestus in a golden cloud, protecting them from indiscreet eyes and, incidentally, preventing Zeus from seeing the plain:

With that the son of Cronus caught his wife in his
   arms
and under them now the holy earth burst with fresh
   green grass,
crocus and hyacinth, clover soaked with dew, so thick
   and soft
it lifted their bodies off the hard, packed ground. . . .

Folded deep in that bed they lay and round them wrapped
a marvelous cloud of gold, and glistening showers of dew
rained down around them both.
And so, deep in peace,
the Father slept on Gargaron peak, conquered by Sleep
and strong assaults of Love, his wife locked in his arms.
—*IL.* 14.347–53; F 14.413–21

Thus the gullible husband blindfolds himself. Like Romeo, he wakes rather too late in the action—one book later—when the golden, dewy mist has finally dissipated. He is greeted by the spectacle of the routed Trojans, Poseidon triumphant, and Hector wounded by the greater Ajax. He threatens to hang his wife from the heights of Olympus, but the wrath of the lascivious husband comes too late.

A woman who seduces her husband; a husband who performs his matrimonial duty: this is by no means an allegory of air and ether, but is it immoral? The Carracci brothers paid homage to the athleticism of the royal couple, who are permitted one of the more recondite positions illustrated in *The Loves of the Gods.* Zeus is ridiculous not because his performance is less than masterful but because he is overmastered by his wife. His weakness for women is a confirmed trait and not simply a recompense for sexual favors. Ingres illustrated the (nude) supplication of Thetis, who has come to request exactly what Hera wishes to avert, namely, the defeat of the Greeks, who have insulted Thetis's son Achilles. Granting the request, Zeus anticipates and dreads Hera's angry reaction, but he does not foresee her stratagem. How ridiculous can a husband be? He surreptitiously acts contrary to his wife's interests (secretly sending a dream to Agamemnon), and so his wife, predictably, takes the next available opportunity to deceive him. Never has a god had his chin so absurdly stroked as Zeus in Ingres's *Jupiter Petitioned by Thetis* (1811; Musee Granet, Aix-en-Provence). But this absurdity was inherent in Homer's account and the relations of the omnipotent Zeus with his divine spouse.

How does Zeus court his wife, thinking he fills her with desire, when it is he who has been caught? Like some comedic Don Juan, he combines boorishness with stupidity, comparing her to a catalogue of his former mistresses, giving them marks for beauty and recording the progeny he sired with them (314–28). The list is excessively long and Zeus's memory nevertheless defective. The catalogue, however, supplied the engravers of lubricious stories with abundant matter. True, Hera's correspondent in this affair was her own husband, but if Zeus was really in the habit of rehearsing all his love affairs to his wife, any reciprocal action undertaken by Hera can only be applauded. In 1699 Antoine Coypel painted a Zeus still energetically lascivious,[10] and over the course of the following century the subject was frequently revived. As might be expected, it elicited some of Diderot's most pointed remarks. Thus, reviewing a work by Lagrenée in the 1767 Salon (no. 20 in the Salon catalogue), he states: "A good lesson for you, husbands of Paris, everywhere in the world. Beware of your wives when they go out of their way to make themselves attractive to you. Look out for the request that's coming." Diderot, of course, indulges in his customary revisions, this time undressing the goddess: "But tell me if it makes any sense to clothe her, and modestly at that. Don't you know what she's up to here? She should be nude, completely nude, I tell you. . . . And you call that the pleasure of the master of the gods, and of the first among the goddesses!"[11]

The reception piece of Jean-Jacques-François Le Barbier (cat. no. 21) allows Zeus still less nudity, virility, and dignity. He is clearly worn out after the embrace. His right arm gestures wearily toward Hera's accomplice, the winged god of Sleep, who holds a candle to the scene; seeming to garland Zeus's amorous triumph, he in fact ensures his continued torpor. Nor is Zeus's eagle immune to the soporific influence, drowsing at his master's feet like a lapdog. Hera smiles, no doubt satisfied (with the trick she has played on him). She

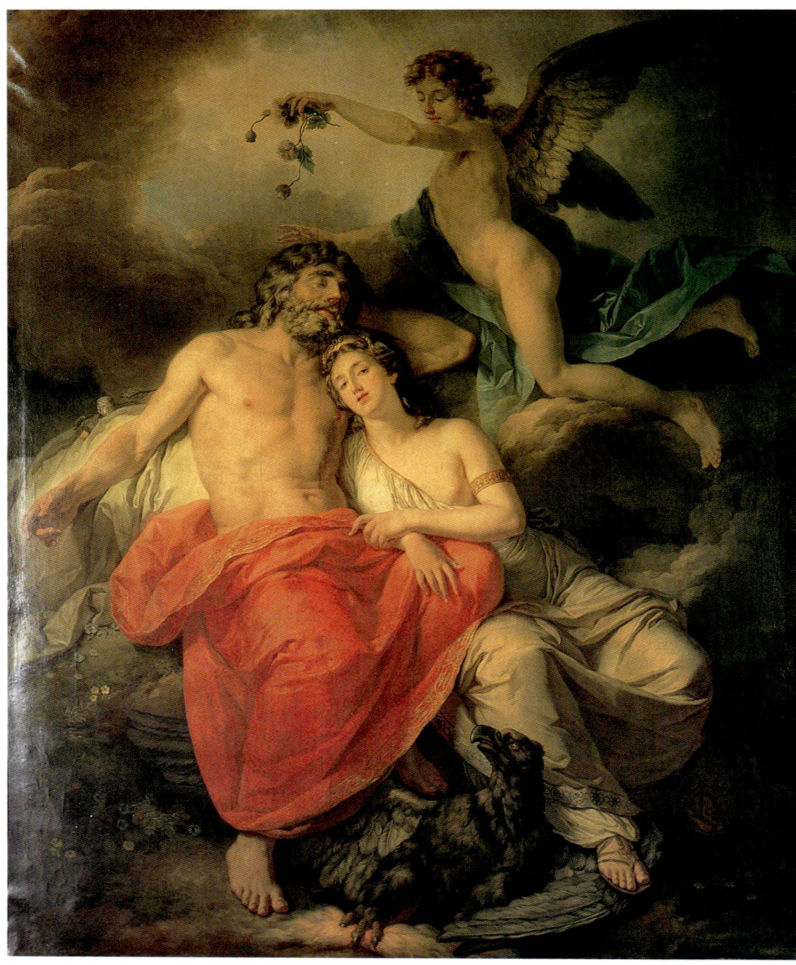

CATALOGUE NO. 21 | JEAN-JACQUES-FRANÇOIS LE BARBIER (1738–1826), *Jupiter in the Toils of Sleep*, 1785. Oil on canvas, 260 × 194 cm.

looks not at her royal lover but downward, an indication she is thinking not of the matrimonial embrace but of the Greeks she favors. The painting was exhibited at the 1785 Salon and gave rise to very bawdy criticism, which, ignoring the legend, subtly analyzed Homer's presentation of the Olympian royal couple: "Well, when first I saw the picture, I took Juno for one of the nymphs of the Palais Royal [notorious for its prostitutes], who, generously remunerated by a foreigner, dares not leave his side while he sleeps; but who consoles herself for this constraint by daydreaming of some handsome hairdresser or a dashing lackey on whom she has set her heart." And again: "This painting presents an ingenious satire of Marriage: the heedless husband sleeps, while his old, malignant yet seductive wife gracefully pinions one wing of the eagle with her foot as if to tell you that, in this marriage, pleasure is somewhat drooping and earthbound."[12]

I shall, in due course, speak of *Les Aventures de Télémaque*, in which Fénelon christianizes gods and goddesses and systematically confronts Telemachus with carnal temptations, so that Ulysses' son becomes a young prig full of Christian sentiments. A grim and very moral destiny awaits every religion, from Homer to the god of modern times: that of becoming thoroughly tedious. It is therefore easy to see why the painters of the Royal Academy frequently appealed to Homer to waken their art from its slumber. They were lucky enough to perceive in him what the excessively serious Heraclitus of the *Quaestiones* could not, namely, "one huge joke."[13] Plato, Homer's censor, and Heraclitus, his exegete, were unanimous on one point: when they discussed Homer's morality, they ascribed to him not a single religious sentiment. For Plato, Homer places his irreverence at the service of an entirely amoral invention and rejoicingly scabrous verse. For Heraclitus, Homer's narratives are extended metaphors of the physical universe. Plato is undoubtedly closer to the truth, and I am happy to concur with him that the more libertine and immoral poetry becomes, the more attractive it is. Jean-Jacques Rousseau believed that Homer—born to a world as yet unacquainted with writing or civilization but peopled with gods—displayed in his poems the religious virtues of the earliest representatives of humankind.[14] But any Parisian painter of the eighteenth century could read his Homer better than the naïve Rousseau: the great weakness of the male Olympians is women. They are not, then, very different from men.

NOTES

1 Kenneth Clark, *The Nude* (London, 1956), 71–93.
2 "Homeric Hymn to Hermes" (ll. 79–81) in *The Homeric Hymns*, trans. M. Crudden (Oxford, 2001), 45–46.
3 Ovid, *Metamorphoses* 1.583–748.
4 Ibid., 2.708–832.
5 Plato, *Republic* 2.378c.
6 "Homeric Hymn to Demeter" (ll.1–6, 17–21, 33–34, 38–39), in *The Homeric Hymns*, trans. Crudden, 4–5.
7 See Félix Buffière, *Les Mythes d'Homère et la pensée grecque* (Paris, 1956; rpt. 1973), 106–15.
8 Plato, *Republic* 3.390c.
9 Heraclitus, *Quaestiones Homericae* 39.1.
10 See Helge Siefert, *Themen aus Homers Ilias in der französischen Kunst, 1750–1831* (Munich, 1988), 333.
11 Denis Diderot, *Salons,* vol. 2, *The Salon of 1767* (no. 20), trans. J. Goodman (New Haven, Conn., 1995), 54.
12 Quoted in Siefert, *Themen aus Homers Ilias*, 337–38.
13 *Quaestiones Homericae* 39.1.
14 See Jean-François Perrin, "Comment Rousseau écrivait-il avec Homère," and Barbara Patzek, "Homère comme idéal de vie en France au XVIIIe siècle," in F. Létoublon and C. Volpilhac-Auger, eds., *Homère en France après la querelle*, Actes du colloque de Grenoble, 1995 (Paris, 1999), 161–77 and 289–303, resp.

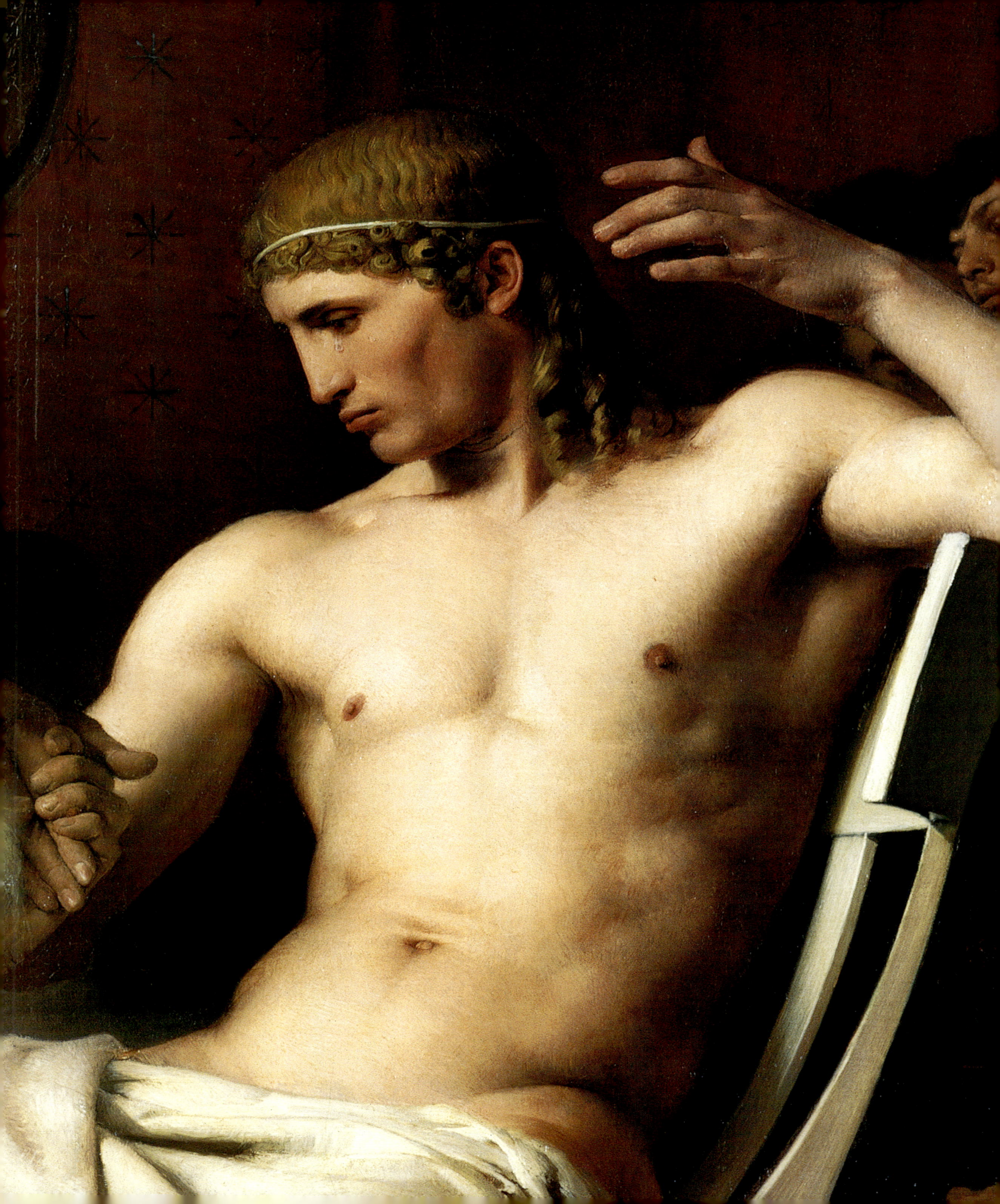

Achilles

The career of Achilles begins well before the Trojan War, and he has a very limited influence over its course; battles are lost and the war is won without him. Between his fabled origins and almost incidental death—an arrow strike to his heel—Homer singles out and spotlights (invents?) a famous moment of bad humor, "The Wrath of Achilles." This is the *Iliad*'s principal subject, but it is irrelevant to the outcome of the war.

Adventures in Youth and Childhood

Achilles is the son of the goddess Thetis. Zeus longed to bed her, but having learned (from Prometheus, says Aeschylus) Thetis's son would be more powerful than his father, he had her raped by the mortal Peleus. In the interests of his present and future power, the king of the gods could not permit her to be impregnated by a god. Thetis, however, rendered her son quasi-immortal by immersing him in the waters of the Styx, the river of the dead. Only the heel by which she held him remained vulnerable. It became the target of Paris's fatal poisoned arrow (cat. no. 51).

The goddess attempted to avert her son's tragic destiny, explaining that he must choose between a long and obscure existence and a brief life followed by eternal renown. It is easy to imagine what any mother would prefer, and even godlike Achilles may have hesitated. His prewar apprenticeship is evoked here for the skeptical light it casts on his subsequent exploits at Troy.

Achilles' education was confided first to the centaur Chiron, redoubtable sportsman and virtuoso of the lyre, and then, on the island of Scyros, to the daughters of Lycomedes, those virtuosos of sensual refinement. Achilles was not exclusively devoted to male friendship, and his son Neoptolemos was born of Deidamia, one of Lycomedes' daughters. Thereafter he divided his time between ancillary love affairs and virile friendships. Let us not forget that the motive presiding over his introduction into the *gynaeceum* of Lycomedes' house was by no means heroic. The warrior-hero Achilles lived in women's attire among King Lycomedes' daughters to escape recruitment into the Greek army. Achilles among Lycomedes' daughters was a gift to ancient artists, in particular Polygnotus,[1] who liked to depict the warrior in female garments. Homer spares Achilles that disguise, confining himself to the image of a warrior playing the cithara while his companions die in combat. Ulysses, who had attempted to avoid recruitment by feigning madness, was dispatched to Scyros to bring back the young hero. Presenting himself at the court of Scyros as a vendor of embroideries, he mixed arms with his merchandise, and when one of the young "ladies" seized upon the weapons, Ulysses left with the invincible warrior. Although these

DETAIL OF CATALOGUE NO. 36

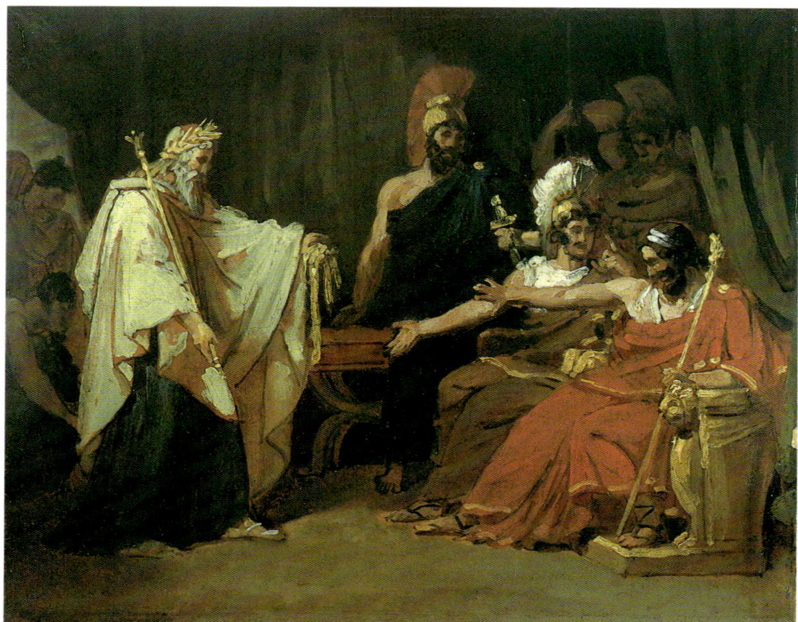

CATALOGUE NO. 22 | ÉLOI-FIRMIN FÉRON (1802–1876), *Chryses Asks Agamemnon to Return His Daughter*, 1822. Oil on tracing paper mounted on canvas, 33 × 40.5 cm.

inglorious episodes inspired numerous drawings, paintings, and engravings, it was not morally desirable that the students of the École take too close an interest in the ambiguities of heroism; for them the epic of Achilles began and ended on the dusty plain of Troy.

Achilles and Women

Achilles' career as leader of the Myrmidons of Thessaly began in female guise, and it remained under the control of three young women, mortals all: the charms of Helen, Chryseis, and Briseis led the young man to his fate. In this dance the most powerful was Agamemnon, in Homer's ironic presentation the least intelligent of men and the first to fall victim to womanly wiles. Helen was the most beautiful of mortals, and her Greek suitors had all sworn to come to the aid of the chosen prince should he suffer the misfortune liable to befall husbands whose wives are too pretty. When Menelaus lost his newly wedded Helen to Paris, it fell to his brother, Agamemnon, to organize the expeditionary force. Meanwhile Agamemnon's wife, Clytemnestra, remained in Greece, opening the marital bed to Aegistheus, a most ambitious lover, as we shall see. In Troy, Agamemnon declared himself master and owner of the insignificant Chryseis, daughter of a priest of Apollo named Chryses, who was part of the plunder from a brief campaign against Troy's allies:

> Yes, Chryses approached the Achaeans' fast ships
> to win his daughter back, bringing a priceless ransom
> and bearing high in hand, wound on a golden staff,
> the wreaths of the god, the distant deadly Archer.
> He begged the whole Achaean army but most of all
> the two supreme commanders, Atreus' two sons,
> "Agamemnon, Menelaus—all Argives geared for war!
> May the gods who hold the halls of Olympus give you
> Priam's city to plunder, then safe passage home.
> Just set my daughter free, my dear one . . . here,
> accept these gifts, this ransom. Honor the god
> who strikes from worlds away—the son of Zeus,
> Apollo!"
>
> And all ranks of Achaeans cried out their assent:
> "Respect the priest, accept the shining ransom!"
> But it brought no joy to the heart of Agamemnon.
> The king dismissed the priest with a brutal order
> ringing in his ears: "Never again, old man,
> let me catch sight of you by the hollow ships!
> Not loitering now, not slinking back tomorrow.
> The staff and the wreaths of god will never save you
> then.
> The girl—I won't give up the girl. Long before that,
> old age will overtake her in *my* house, in Argos,
> far from her fatherland, slaving back and forth
> at the loom, forced to share my bed!
> Now go,
> don't tempt my wrath—and you may depart alive."
>
> —*IL.* 1.12–32; F 1.13–37

Arrogant Agamemnon: Apollo and Chryses had their revenge. The École teachers liked this story, the only case in all of Homer in which a captive woman escapes the sexual slavery to which her new master has condemned her. Clearly Homer singled out the glorious Agamemnon, "leader of men," highest-ranking Greek prince, for humiliation. Agamemnon's discomfiture was the subject set for the Painting and Sculpture prizes in 1812 (François Rude took part, but his maquette, alas, has been lost) and again in the Oil Sketch *concours* of 1822. The little sketch on tracing paper by Éloi-Firmin Féron (cat. no. 22) offers a subtle vision of the world of Agamemnon and Chryses. The young woman is not even present at the discussion of her fate. Aggrieved father and offended king, arms raised in gestures they suppose imperious, succeed only in bringing disaster on all who witness their bickering—and ridicule on the head of Agamemnon. Two Greek warriors, anonymous representatives of the Achaean army, look on in mortified astonishment: it is foolhardy to threaten a representative of Apollo. The god promptly unleashes an epidemic that can only be halted by Chryseis's return, as the soothsayer Calchas declares. This transaction is undertaken by Ulysses, who is seen restoring Chryseis to the priest and bringing gifts to the god in Justin-Chrysostome Sanson's relief (Grand Prix in Sculpture, 1861; fig. 39).

Chryseis, under the name Cressida in modern times, continued to expose princes to derision in the many works she inspired, from the medieval continuations of the *Iliad* to Shakespeare's *Troilus and Cressida.* A king of kings cannot be the only one to give up his "share of honor," as the French expression has it. The remainder of the first book of the *Iliad* deals with Agamemnon's anger. Out of disappointment in love or piqued vanity, he demands another warrior's captive. He doesn't care who makes the sacrifice—Achilles, Ulysses, Ajax, or Idomeneus. He has learned from Chryseis that any slave woman is preferable to the redoubtable Clytemnestra, who stayed behind in Greece, steeped in fury after Agamemnon sacrificed their eldest daughter, Iphigenia, in the supposed interest of the army. Since only Achilles is foolish enough to reproach Agamemnon for his selfishness, and since Achilles spontaneously threatens to leave the plain of Ilion, the order comes for the maladroit hero to renounce Briseis, one of his captive women. Achilles' response is his wrath, perhaps an invention of Homer. In any case, it gave to the legendary traditions of the Trojan War a new and inexhaustible meaning. "The Wrath of Achilles" *is* the *Iliad.* Nor does its significance end there, for it is all those sulking heroes of European literature, those warriors who dream or sleep through battles instead of marching out against the enemy, from Voltaire's Candide to Stendhal's Fabrice del Dongo:[2]

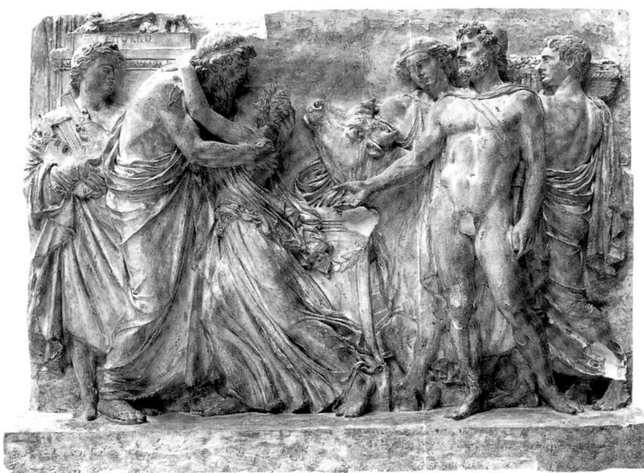

FIGURE 39 | JUSTIN-CHRYSOSTOME SANSON (1833–1910), *Chryseis Restored to Her Father by Ulysses*, 1861. Plaster, 125 × 160 cm. Prix de Rome in Sculpture.

> He broke off and anguish gripped Achilles.
> The heart in his rugged chest was pounding, torn . . .
> Should he draw the long sharp sword slung at his hip,
> thrust through the ranks and kill Agamemnon now?—
> or check his rage and beat his fury down?
> As his racing spirit veered back and forth,
> just as he drew his huge blade from its sheath,
> down from the vaulting heavens swept Athena,
> the white-armed goddess Hera sped her down:
> Hera loved both men and cared for both alike.
> Rearing behind him Pallas seized his fiery hair—
> only Achilles saw her, none of the other fighters—
> struck with wonder he spun around, he knew her at
> once,
> Pallas Athena! the terrible blazing of those eyes,
> and his winged words went flying . . .
>
> —*IL.* 1. 188–201; F 1.222–36

The impulsive intervention of Achilles—the molten anger falling into impotence—offered a perfect exercise for artists of every temperament, from the Baroque of Rubens and Antoine Coypel to the cold theoreticians, extending to David and his school. Anger, then dejection; fury followed by hesitation: in the Achilles of the visual arts, close on the heels of heroism comes despair. As ever, the gods—especially the goddesses—greatly contribute to the confusion. Here, though, it is most apparent in the minds of the young artists required to illustrate the scene. For an École student, an invisible protagonist could hardly be depicted as a simple mortal. Ronsard's *Odes* hit just the right tone for this marriage of man and immortal, of Achilles and Athena. It is anything but serious, especially where "The Wrath of Achilles" is concerned:

> Have you not seen, reading Homer
> How when Achilles with burning choler
> Raged furious against his king,
> Pallas Athena, goddess and warrior
> Grasping his locks from behind,
> Left him foolishly mumbling
> His anger lost in the air?
> Already his dagger was drawn,
> So goaded he was by his ire
> To make an end of Atreus's son;
> Without her, it would have been done.
> She sent him back to his ship
> There to calm his anger's fire.
> How often Achilles refused
> Agamemnon's offers of peace,
> His presents and his pleas
> That Achilles' anger cease.[3]

Athena is the doctor who attends to his ire, who makes him swallow it. His character tends not to impassioned anger but to pique.

One cliché predominates in the representation of this scene: Athena bursting forth from a cloud. Martin Drölling, who won the Prix de Rome in 1810 (cat. no. 23) makes play with Athena's cloak, sending it billowing over the anachronistic sails, while Achilles and Athena make excessively dramatic gestures. All of Drölling's Greeks evoke pictorial or sculptural models; his master was David, and in his Achilles we recognize the gesture of David's Leonidas from *Leonidas at Thermopylae*, while his Agamemnon reproduces the pose of Marius in *Marius at Minturnae* by Jean-Germain Drouais, another David pupil (both paintings are in the Louvre). Athena, holding back the sheathed sword Achilles has already raised in defense of Briseis, promises him a terrible revenge if he will only be patient. The soothsayer Calchas, who first revealed the epidemic to be due to Apollo's anger, holds forth vainly in the background. The tedious old Nestor, in turn, is about to preach to these two monsters of pride. No matter. No one is listening to the old scolds anyway.

On ten different occasions in the *Iliad* a god or goddess intervenes to impede or provoke the gesture of a mortal. These are not interventions of immanent justice. They occur with the speed of desire and the discretion of thought. Aphrodite, whose very name means sexual desires, arises in the minds of Paris and Helen. Athena, who has never been young (she sprang from Zeus's head fully formed), arrives with excellent advice when it is time to pass beyond doubt and hesitation to decision. So many other gods, known for their violence or stupidity, accompany the poor humans who wait only for arousal by forces that master or transcend them before unleashing their instincts, the only gods they venerate. In the nineteenth century, Achilles' repertory of gesture is gradually reduced to that of a marionette. His strings are held by the gods, who are themselves confined to the frozen movements of those bland statues and casts that were, in 1810, first suffering comparison with the living figures of Phidias. Heroic playthings in the hands of the gods: such is the grim vision of man in certain of the École's prize paintings.

The entry by Louis-Édouard-Paul Fournier for the 1881 prize provides a logical conclusion to this tendency (fig. 66). Against a background of totem poles, Greek urns (absurd in every particular), and flags abandoned on the ground, black heroes are found wearing white sandals and geometrically patterned loincloths; the

OPPOSITE CATALOGUE NO. 23 | MICHEL-MARTIN DRÖLLING (1786–1851), *The Wrath of Achilles*, 1810. Oil on canvas, 113 × 146 cm.

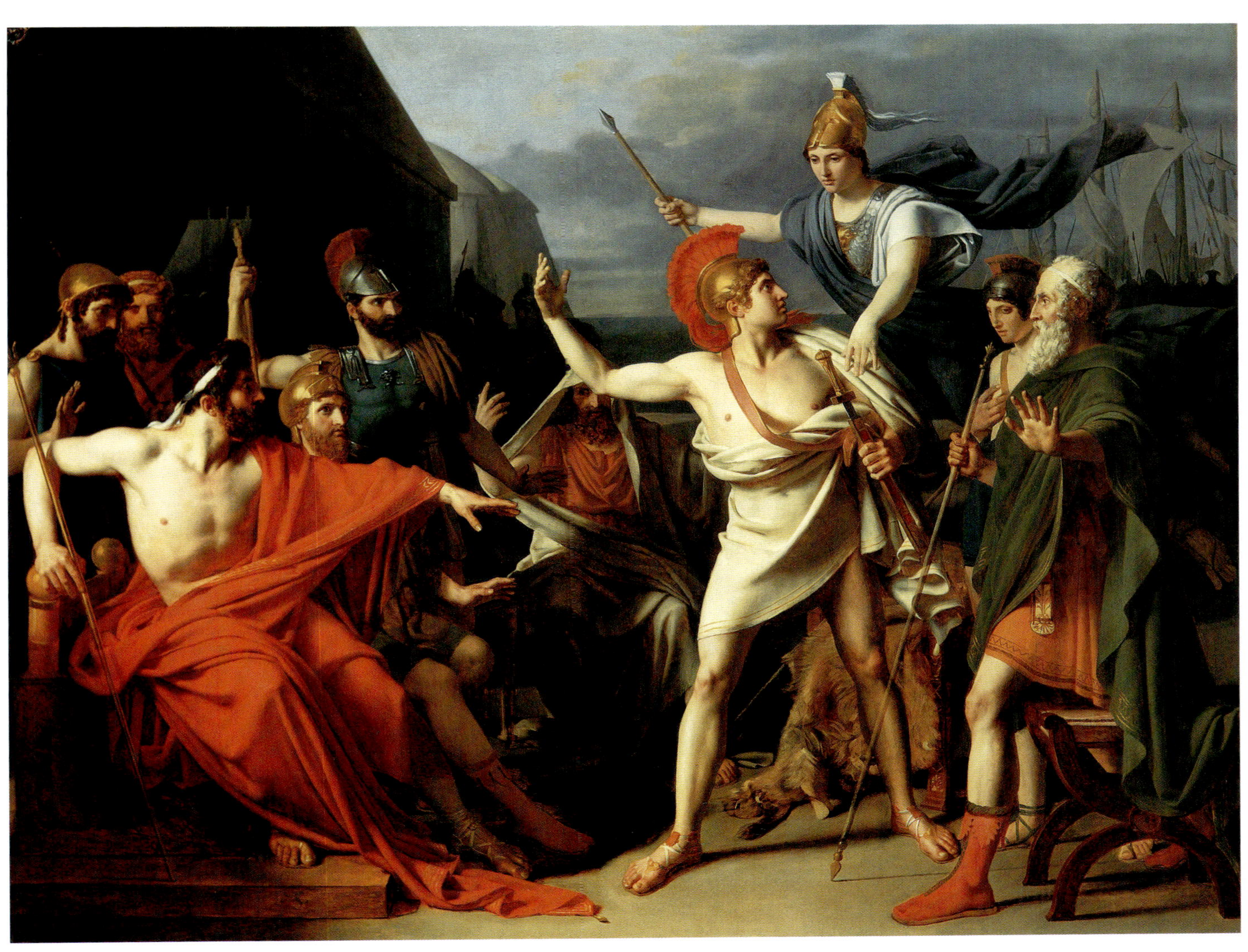

goddess herself is blue. Mortals and goddess alike seem figures from a cartoon strip, moved by supposedly invisible forces and wholly lacking in human depth. It might be said that as early as 1793 Flaxman had presented a view of the Homeric world equally primitive and lacking in depth. In fact, however, his evocation of Greek vase painting imparts to this world an abstract dignity clearly absent in Fournier, who simplifies until his scenes are reduced to the confrontation of two indistinguishable groups. As such, they are a betrayal of Homer, who always tends to see the individual as a free spirit while identifying each group as the sum of very different individuals. Flaxman's austere line may lack warmth, but it animates phantoms like those Ulysses meets in the Underworld, not so much minds as tragic destinies and inconsolable witnesses of inevitable catastrophe. Homer's Achilles fails to act because he thinks too much. The Achilles of the nineteenth-century academic student fails to act because he does not think for himself; professors and students alike believed that gods were the true agents of the war. They were not: they are the conscience and unconscious of mankind. The teachers did not sufficiently attend to the most famous of their number, he who, at twenty, at the dawn of the nineteenth century, won the Grand Prix by placing before the judges a group of men who repudiated any divine order and trusted only to their own intelligence.

Ingres: *The Ambassadors*

After a few inconsequential successes, the Greeks suffer their first defeat since the loss of their most redoubtable warrior (bk. 8). A few days have passed since the quarrel, which is not yet perceived as irreconcilable. Agamemnon now perceives that he needs Achilles' strength in battle, and that without him the war (and his own position at the head of the Greek army) is at stake. He therefore sends envoys to Achilles, hoping to convince him to rejoin the Greek ranks. But it is precisely Achilles' constant taste for inaction that Ingres spotlights in his prize-winning painting of 1801 (cat. no. 24), the most famous work ever composed by a student while still at the École des beaux-arts. It is the picture that best explains and denounces the scholastic aspects of French academicism because as the century wore on French, academicism increasingly took Ingresque form. By 1801 Ingres had already adapted to his own vision the lessons his master David had learned from antiquity. As has often been pointed out, *The Ambassadors* combines a number of much-quoted ancient statues with a relief composition derived from Flaxman (*Iliad*, bk. 9, engraving 14). What we are looking for in Ingres's piece is an homage to Achilles the sybaritic warrior and harpist.

At the most unexpected moments Homer's words evoke not action but the mind's ability to dwell on the pleasures and spectacles of the moment. Dispatched by Nestor and preceded by the elderly Phoenix, Ajax and Ulysses bring Achilles the news of Agamemnon's capitulation or repentance; he is ready to give up Briseis as he has already been forced to give up Chryseis:

> So Ajax and Odysseus made their way at once
> where the battle lines of breakers crash and drag,
> praying hard to the god who moves and shakes the
>   earth
> that they might bring the proud heart of Achilles
> round with speed and ease.
> Reaching the Myrmidon shelters and their ships,
> they found him there, delighting his heart now,
> plucking strong and clear on the fine lyre—
> beautifully carved, its silver bridge set firm—
> he won from the spoils when he razed Eetion's city.
> Achilles was lifting his spirits with it now,
> singing the famous deeds of fighting heroes. . . .
> Across from him Patroclus sat alone, in silence,
> waiting for Aeacus' son to finish with his song.
> And on they came, with good Odysseus in the lead,
> and the envoys stood before him. Achilles, startled,
> sprang to his feet, the lyre still in his hands,
> leaving the seat where he had sat in peace.
> And seeing the men, Patroclus rose up too
> as the famous runner called and waved them on:

OPPOSITE CATALOGUE NO. 24 | JEAN-AUGUSTE-DOMINIQUE INGRES (1780–1867), *Achilles Receives the Ambassadors of Agamemnon*, 1801. Oil on canvas, 113 × 46 cm.

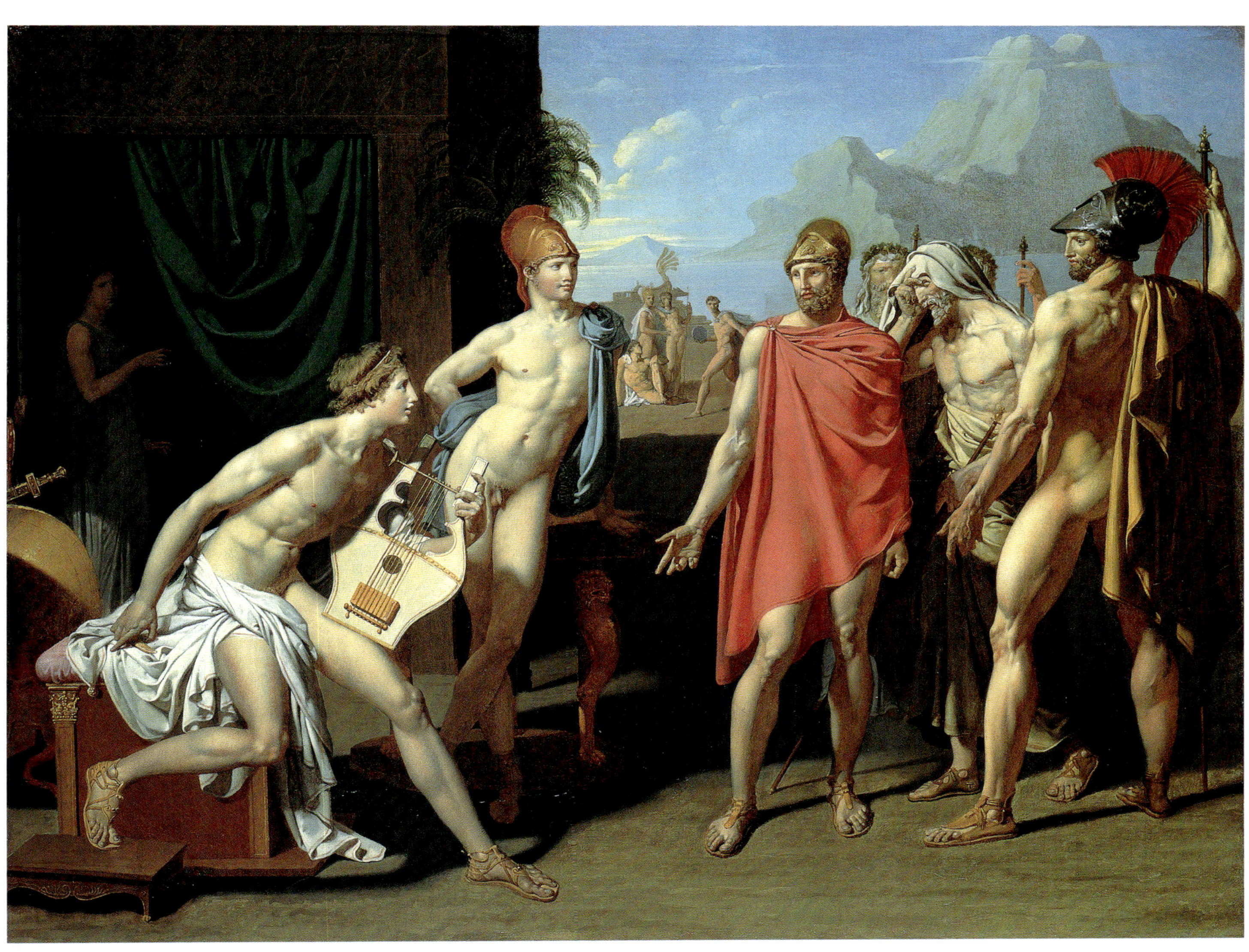

"Welcome! Look, dear friends have come our way—
I must be sorely needed now—my dearest friends
in all the Achaean armies, even in my anger."

So Prince Achilles hailed and led them in,
sat them down on settles with purple carpets
and quickly told Patroclus standing by, "Come,
a bigger winebowl, son of Menoetius, set it here.
Mix stronger wine. A cup for the hands of each
guest—
here beneath my roof are the men I love the most."
—*IL.* 9.182–98; F 9.217–45

The time was soon to come when, in the École's *concours*, word-for-word translation would set in stone the poses of Homer's protagonists. In 1801 Ingres's models step briskly enough along the seashore. Ingres knew Flaxman's composition, in which the five ambassadors (three princes and two heralds) and two hosts face each other in profile. The embassy comes to an abrupt halt, those at the back all but colliding with their leaders. Ingres's ambassadors are subtler than Flaxman's. Attempting to avoid the frozen gestures of statues, they do not paraphrase Homer but offer a commentary on his text. The two musical warriors rise from their singing as Ulysses arrives, partly obscuring the discus throwers he has passed in his walk along the shore. Their effeminate or peaceable gestures are lit by the light reflected from Mount Ida, from the sea—and from the captive women within the dark tent, whose role it is to remind them that the truth of life is not to be found in fighting beneath city walls. Homer tells us the melodious names of these two women:

. . . Achilles slept with
the woman he brought from Lesbos, Phorbas' daughter,
Diomede in all her beauty sleeping by his side.
And over across from him Patroclus slept
with the sashed and lovely Iphis by his side . . .
—*IL.* 9.664–67; F 9.811–14

If we take the Homeric narrative literally, the two ambassadors fail because Achilles will not pardon Agamemnon, because what Ulysses promises is insufficient, and because the tedious Phoenix, who raised Achilles, wastes time invoking the calamitous example of Meleager, who, for good reasons, likewise took umbrage and long refused to come to the aid of his fellow citizens. Since Achilles is unwilling to fight, Phoenix asks, why does he remain? But Achilles is no more able to make the decision to leave than he is to return to the ranks of the army. Ingres does not make Achilles into a Hamlet absorbed in existential considerations, as certain wonderful ancient vase paintings do. The Achilles of 1801 likes nothing so much as idleness. He plays music with Patroclus, he likes to share the sports of the Myrmidons on the beach behind the tents, and, within the tents, the joys of sex with his two pretty captive women and his handsome and inseparable friend. Achilles all languid indolence among the busy ambassadors, Achilles unwilling to hear political sermons: this is the figure who lives again in Ingres's painting.

Homer certainly believes in the need for a political system or order. In both epics it is Ulysses who sets out the case for authority (and thus for the states that came into being some centuries after his demise). He argues it to Achilles and the calamitous Agamemnon and in justification of his conduct toward the suitors. In Sophocles he argues it to Philoctetes and Neoptolemus. Homer—or, rather Hephaestus, in the shield he makes for Achilles—seems almost to claim democratic credentials. But Homer is also aware that in the burgeoning cities everyone feels an individual aspiration to live, as Achilles does, outside the city, or at least, like the captive women, to think and suffer alone. Take a look at Ingres's Achilles, how he lets the ambassadors speak, polite but distracted because in his ear and nimble fingers he retains the lasts notes of a tune. This Achilles wishes to live happily and obscure in a Greece already civilized, governed, and orderly. He has no desire to bring down the established order. Looking forward some twenty or thirty years after the competition of 1801, we find that the heroes of the nineteenth-century novel are close kin to Ingres's Achilles, attempting without conviction to confront civil society before removing themselves from its ambit.

For Drölling and Fournier the sea is a plain covered with ships. For Homer and Ingres the susurration of its myriad smiling waves covers the sound of human agitation and cradles dreamlike vessels in its mists. The blue depths of ocean, sky, and mountain distract our attention from the ambassadors, from Ulysses posed like the ancient statue of the Athenian general Phocion, Ajax all muscle, and Phoenix a pitiful old man. The two Thessalians, meanwhile, inhabit the languid poses of Alexandrian statuary. Only later would their enervated attitudes be transformed into unhealthy gesticulations and soulless muscularity. In Homer's ironic poem, the wrath of Achilles causes many catastrophes, but wrath has never since been so voluptuously described. Ingres was barely twenty years old when he contrived at a stroke to capture the indolence of youth, the ambiguity of decadent statues, and the indulgent smile with which Homer considers his two favorite characters, Achilles and Ulysses.

Achilles enjoyed dressing as a young girl in the *gyneceum* of Lycomedes of Scyros and moving among the king's sensuous daughters; he fathered Neoptolemus with Deidamia, one of Lycomedes' daughters, and wept at the loss of Briseis. Shakespeare's Achilles may also love women, but it is by no means an exclusive love.[4] The ambassadors depicted by Ingres are given life in *Troilus and Cressida*: Achilles has given up battle, says Ulysses, because he prefers to spend time in bed with Patroclus.[5] No such hypothesis for Plato, who believed that the gods would grant Achilles eternal bliss for avenging his friend.[6] The embassy scene as treated by Shakespeare and later by Ingres also serves to explicate Ulysses' secret thoughts and methods. In *Troilus and Cressida* he wants to tempt Achilles back into battle by playing on his vanity, eulogizing Ajax, whose increasing renown now threatens to eclipse that of Achilles. His failure is easily explained by Achilles' character: calming the choleric is child's play for a diplomat, but how was the sybaritic musician portrayed by Ingres to be cajoled out of his apathy? The cithara is a distant ancestor of the violin that Ingres proverbially loved, and one can understand Ingres loving Achilles the indolent musician. The ambassadors return empty-handed.

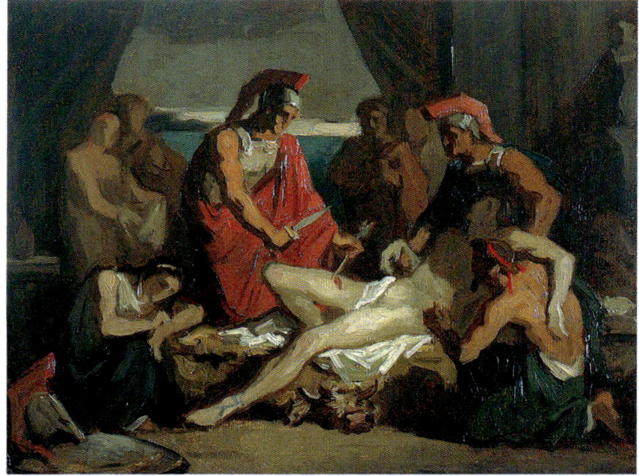

CATALOGUE NO. 25 | JACQUES-FERDINAND HUMBERT (1842–1934), *Eurypylus Wounded*, 1863. Oil on canvas, 32.5 × 41 cm.

Obscure Exploits

In the absence of Achilles, the fate of the Greeks is sealed by the humane and valiant Hector, the bulwark of Troy. The gods permit the Greeks a few illusory successes; then the rout begins, marked by a new series of combats and deaths, which inspired few artists and interests few modern readers. True, during this episode the important events take place elsewhere, among the gods who intervene discreetly between the heroes and their friends. In these rightly celebrated scenes Homer is the true founder of humanist individualism in literature. (I have devoted a separate section to them, thus freeing them of the piles of cadavers that accumulate on the plain of Troy.) The teachers of the École des beaux-arts in the nineteenth century wisely avoided subjects involving random combat (with one exception for the year 1831; see the painting by Henri-Frédéric Schopin, cat. no. 34). The École's collection seems to include only a single work (Jacques-Ferdinand Humbert's oil sketch of 1863; cat. no. 25) paying homage to these almost anonymous combatants, in this case Eurypylus, the "illustrious" son of Euaemon. "Illustrious" is a nice example of Homer's humor; the *Iliad* abounds with Eurypyli, each more obscure than the next. Paris shoots an arrow into the thigh of this particular Eurypylus (*Il.* 11.582). Our "unknown soldier" cries out in piercing tones. His courage tells him to remain at the side of the greater Ajax. Instead, he limps to the rear. There, a better doctor than warrior, he explains to Patroclus how he should operate, hoping all the while that Patroclus has learned from his beloved Achilles the rudiments of surgery imparted to the latter by the centaur Chiron.

Statius wrote in his *Achilleid*: "His, quaerenda salus, / Quinetiam succos, atque auxiliantia morbis/ gramina . . . / edocuit" (5.159–60). Achilles the man slayer learns the simplest remedies of nature, "those by which health must be sought. [Chiron] taught him the juices and the herbs effective against maladies." Now Patroclus takes on the mantle of the healer:

> And bracing the captain, arm around his waist,
> he helped him toward his shelter. An aide saw them
> and put some oxhides down. Patroclus stretched him
> out,
> knelt with a knife and cut the sharp, stabbing arrow
> out of Eurypylus' thigh and washed the wound clean
> of the dark running blood with clear warm water.
> Pounding it in his palms, he crushed a bitter root
> and covered over the gash to kill his comrade's pain,
> a cure that fought off every kind of pain . . .
> and the wound dried and the flowing blood stopped.
> —*IL.* 11.842–48; F 11.1006–15

The statues of decadent Greece so frequently copied by the academic painters often fix suffering with marmoreal complacency. The furious brush strokes of Humbert, on the contrary, evoke the gestures of a nervous and incompetent first-aid team stifling a wounded man with their excessive attention. Patroclus holds the arrow and the scalpel, two assistants hold Eurypylus still, and a woman brings linen to dry the wound.

Among the many corpses of the *Iliad* brought back from the battlefield, two have gained a permanent place in the affections and sensitivity of all Europe. The first of these is Patroclus, Achilles' much-loved friend, and the second is Hector, Andromache's attentive husband. They are killed in succession, one for killing the other. The "bulwark of the Trojans," Hector is for a time also their vanguard. Patroclus knows that many Achaeans have died at Hector's hands, and he can see the fury of the combats approach the tents and ships as the would-be besiegers are themselves beleaguered. Since the reasons that make a spectator of his companion and lord do not apply to Patroclus, he asks Achilles' permission to fight. Unwilling to refuse his dear friend, Achilles lends him his own armor. The man slayer does not come to the aid of those who have humiliated him, but his *kagemusha* does. Suddenly the tables are turned. The Trojans see the armor of Achilles and imagine that the greatest of the Greeks has returned to combat. Patroclus dreams of being a shadow Achilles. The gods and Hector quickly and literally bring him back to earth; he is not a man but a faceless warrior, a suit of armor uninhabited by a soul. Hector swiftly kills him. So it is almost invariably the dead Patroclus who is seen in art, his disarmed body again a thing of flesh and suffering. By contrast, Hector, who kills him, and Achilles, who avenges him, exist in their own right even when they are far from the field of battle.

The Tears of Achilles

The body of Patroclus (the subject of reliefs sculpted by the two Grand Prix winners of 1851, Gustave-Adolphe-Désiré Crauk [fig. 40A] and Pierre-Antoine-Hippolyte Bonnardel [fig. 40B]) becomes the background for a series of scenes in which mourning is transfigured by Homer into an analysis of human weakness. In the eighteenth century, the revenge of Achilles was frequently taken up throughout Europe; one could find one's way through the narrative of that revenge with no other guide than the École's prize-winning paintings, from the low-key *petite manière* of the eighteenth century to the bourgeois Academic style of the Third Republic.

Although Hector and the Trojans strip Patroclus of his arms, the Greeks recover the body and bring it back to the camp. Achilles mourns his friend and lover in

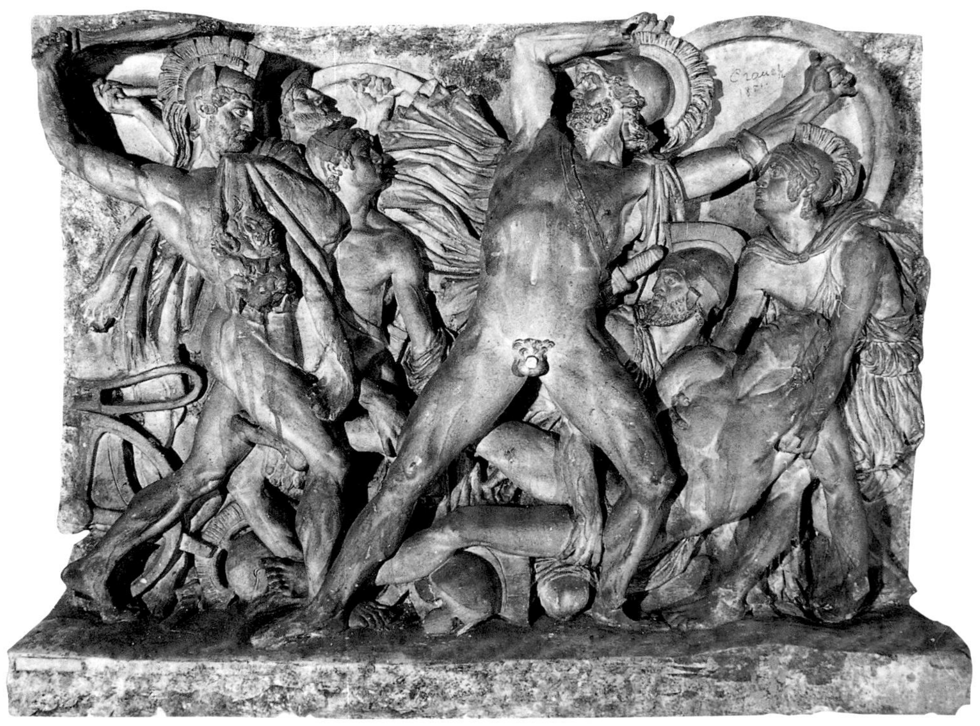

FIGURE 40A | GUSTAVE-ADOLPHE-DÉSIRÉ CRAUK (1827–1905), *The Greeks and Trojans Fight Over the Body of Patroclus,* 1851. Plaster, 120 × 150 cm. Prix de Rome in Sculpture.

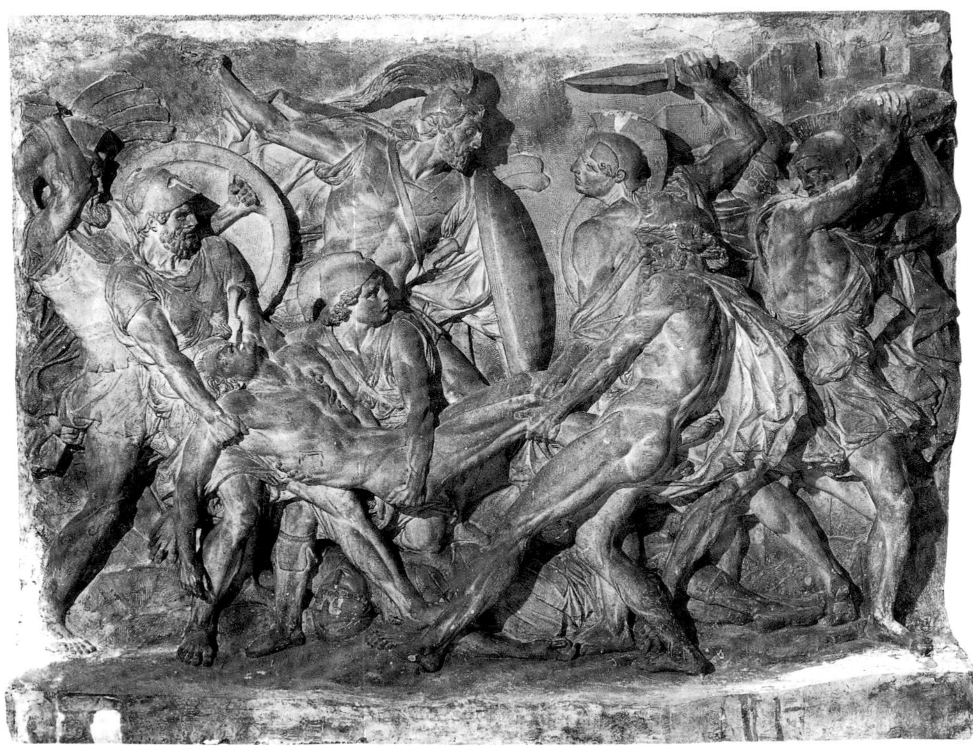

FIGURE 40B | PIERRE-ANTOINE-HIPPOLYTE BONNARDEL (1824–1856), *The Greeks and Trojans Fight Over the Body of Patroclus,* 1851. Plaster, 119 × 156 cm. Prix de Rome in Sculpture.

several famous scenes, his cries waking the captive women and his distant mother:

> Achilles suddenly loosed a terrible, wrenching cry
> and his noble mother heard him, seated near her
> father,
> the Old Man of the Sea in the salt green depths,
> and she cried out in turn.
>
> So Thetis cried
> as she left the cave and her sisters swam up with her,
> all in a tide of tears, and billowing round them now
> the ground swell heaved open. And once they reached
> the fertile land of Troy they all streamed ashore,
> row on row in a long cortege, the sea-nymphs
> filing up where the Myrmidon ships lay hauled,
> clustered closely round the great runner Achilles . . .
> As he groaned from the depths his mother rose before
> him
> and sobbing a sharp cry, cradled her son's head in her
> hands
> and her words were all compassion, winging pity:
> "My child—
> why in tears? What sorrow has touched your heart?
> Tell me, please. Don't harbor it deep inside you.
> Zeus has accomplished everything you wanted,
> just as you raised your hands and prayed that day.
> All the sons of Achaea are pinned against the ships
> and all for want of you—they suffer shattering losses."
>
> And groaning deeply the matchless runner answered,
> "O dear mother, true! All those burning desires
> Olympian Zeus has brought to pass for me—
> but what joy to me now? My dear comrade's dead—
> Patroclus—the man I loved beyond all other
> comrades,
> loved as my own life—I've lost him—Hector's killed
> him,
> stripped the gigantic armor off his back, a marvel to
> behold—
> my burnished gear! Radiant gifts the gods presented
> Peleus
> that day they drove you into a mortal's marriage bed
> . . .
> I wish you'd lingered deep with the deathless sea-
> nymphs,
> lived at ease, and Peleus carried home a mortal bride.
> But now, as it is, sorrows, unending sorrows must
> surge
> within your heart as well—for your own son's death.
> Never again will you embrace him striding home.
> My spirit rebels—I've lost the will to live,
> to take my stand in the world of men—unless,
> before all else, Hector's battered down by my spear
> and gasps away his life, the blood-price for Patroclus,
> Menoetius' gallant son he's killed and stripped!"
>
> But Thetis answered, warning through her tears,
> "You're doomed to a short life, my son, from all
> you say!
> For hard on the heels of Hector's death your death
> must come at once—"
> "Then let me die at once"—
> Achilles burst out, despairing—"since it was not my
> fate
> to save my dearest comrade from his death! Look,
> a world away from his fatherland he's perished,
> lacking me, my fighting strength, to defend him.
> But now, since I shall not return to my fatherland . . .
> nor did I bring one ray of hope to my Patroclus,
> nor to the rest of all my steadfast comrades,
> countless ranks struck down by mighty Hector—
> No, no, here I sit by the ships . . .
> a useless, dead weight on the good green earth—
> I, no man my equal among the bronze-armed
> Achaeans,
> not in battle, only in wars of words that others win."
>
> "But now I'll go and meet that murderer head-on,
> that Hector who destroyed the dearest life I know.
> For my own death, I'll meet it freely—whenever Zeus
> and the other deathless gods would like to bring it on!
> Not even Heracles fled his death, for all his power,

favorite son as he was to Father Zeus the King.
Fate crushed him, and Hera's savage anger.
And I too, if the same fate waits for me . . .
I'll lie in peace, once I've gone down to death.
But now, for the moment, let me seize great glory!—
and drive some woman of Troy or deep-breasted Dardan
to claw with both hands at her tender cheeks and wipe away
her burning tears as the sobs come choking from her throat—
they'll learn that I refrained from war a good long time!
Don't try to hold me back from the fighting, mother,
love me as you do. You can't persuade me now."

The goddess of the glistening feet replied,
"Yes, my son, you're right. No coward's work,
to save your exhausted friends from headlong death.
But your own handsome war-gear lies in Trojan hands,
bronze and burnished—and Hector in that flashing helmet,
Hector glories in your armor, strapped across his back.
Not that he will glory in it long, I tell you:
his own destruction hovers near him now. Wait—
don't fling yourself in the grind of battle yet,
not till you see me coming back with your own eyes.
Tomorrow I will return to you with the rising sun,
bearing splendid arms from Hephaestus, god of fire!"
—*IL*. 18.35–37, 65–106, 112–13; F 18.39–42, 74–125, 134–62

This is not the first time that Achilles has called upon his mother for help. In the first book of the *Iliad*, deprived of Briseis and raging against Agamemnon, he had already summoned her to ask her for the Greeks to be defeated while he laid down his arms.

During the second visit Thetis promises her son a new panoply, to be ready the following day. The grief of Achilles is not merely for his friend but for the arms stripped from his fallen friend's body by his nemesis, Hector. Homer places these two losses on the same footing:

Hector's killed him,
stripped the gigantic armor off his back, a marvel to behold—
my burnished gear! Radiant gifts the gods presented Peleus
that day they drove you into a mortal's marriage bed . . .

The attentive mother is at her son's side when arms are required. She obtains a new panoply from Hephaestus:

And once the god had made that great and massive shield
he made Achilles a breastplate brighter than gleaming fire,
he made him a sturdy helmet to fit the fighter's temples
beautiful, burnished work, and raised its golden crest
and made him greaves of flexing, pliant tin.
—*IL*. 18.609–13; F 18.96–99, 710–14

These arms are delivered early in the nineteenth book of the *Iliad*, on Thetis's third visit to her son:

As Dawn rose up in her golden robe from Ocean's tides,
bringing light to immortal gods and mortal men,
Thetis sped Hephaestus' gifts to the ships.
She found her beloved son lying facedown,
embracing Patroclus' body, sobbing, wailing,
and round him crowded troops of mourning comrades.
And the glistening goddess moved among them now,
seized Achilles' hand and urged him, spoke his name:
"My child, leave your friend to lie there dead—
we must, though it breaks our hearts . . .
The will of the gods has crushed him once for all.
But here, Achilles, accept this glorious armor, look,

a gift from the god of fire—burnished bright, finer
than any mortal has ever borne across his back!"
Urging,
the goddess laid the armor down at Achilles' feet
and the gear clashed out in all its blazoned glory.
A tremor ran through all the Myrmidon ranks—none dared
to look straight at the glare, each fighter shrank away.
Not Achilles. The more he gazed, the deeper his anger went,
his eyes flashing under his eyelids, fierce as fire—
exulting, holding the god's shining gifts in his hands.
And once he'd thrilled his heart with looking hard
at the armor's well-wrought beauty,
he turned to his mother, winged words flying:
"Mother—armor sent by the god—you're right,
only immortal gods could forge such work,
no man on earth could ever bring it off!
Now, by heaven, I'll arm and go to war.
But all the while my blood runs cold with fear—
Menoetius' fighting son . . . the carrion blowflies
will settle into his wounds, gouged deep by the bronze,
worms will breed and seethe, defile the man's corpse—
his life's ripped out—his flesh may rot to nothing."

But glistening-footed Thetis reassured him:
"O my child, wipe these worries from your mind.
I'll find a way to protect him from those swarms,
the vicious flies that devour men who fall in battle.
He could lie there dead till a year has run its course
and his flesh still stand firm, even fresher than now . . .
So go and call the Argive warriors to the muster:
renounce your rage at the proud commander Agamemnon,
then arm for battle quickly, don your fighting power!"

With that she breathed in her son tremendous courage
then instilled in Patroclus' nostrils fresh ambrosia,
blood-red nectar too, to make his flesh stand firm.
—*IL.* 19.1–39; F 19.1–45

Achilles is blinkered by his intended revenge just as he was by the wrath that preceded it. He dwells as much on the arms as on his friend's body: he loves the arms not for what they are but for the blood they will shed. In this he differs from his mother, Thetis, his captive concubines, and even the whinnying horses, all of whom lament the loss of the dead rather than celebrate their sacrifice. Homer's characters are clearly divided into two categories: those who love death and those who hate it. Among the latter, there are some courageous if despairing warriors, notably Hector. Achilles is of quite another kind.

The oil sketch by Jules-Joseph Lefebvre (1858; cat. no. 26) avoids or overlooks the question of arms. He painted Thetis's second visit, and although the presence of a helmet at Achilles' foot is anomalous, at least the gestures of Thetis and Achilles are profoundly coherent, the man's powerful arms giving even greater weight to the efforts and support of the goddess. The hero holds his head in his hand, seized not with regret but with remorse: How could he have let Patroclus enter the battle alone? There is nothing of the divine in this intelligent sketch. Thetis and her naiads have arrived on their shells, which Lefebvre makes poetic shadows and melancholy gondolas. Joseph Brian's plaster sketch of 1829 clearly shows Thetis bearing her son's helmet, but the famous shield, whose very decoration is a plea for peace, is nowhere to be seen (cat. no. 27). The sketch is full of mourning gestures and weeping. The moment chosen by Brian precedes the delivery of the new arms, allowing him to borrow from Jean Alaux's painting of 1815, which depicts a slightly later moment (cat. no. 28). This is the point at which we are given some of the noblest verses in all of Homer (*Il.* 19.287–302). They are spoken by Briseis the captive—at last restored to Achilles—and by her companions in misfortune. To their calm and lucid eloquence I devote the following digression.

The Tears of Briseis

Briseis mourns Patroclus with greater sincerity than either Achilles or Thetis. Her tears are at the heart of Jean Alaux's prize-winning work:

And so Briseis returned, like golden Aphrodite,
but when she saw Patroclus lying torn by the bronze
she flung herself on his body, gave a piercing cry

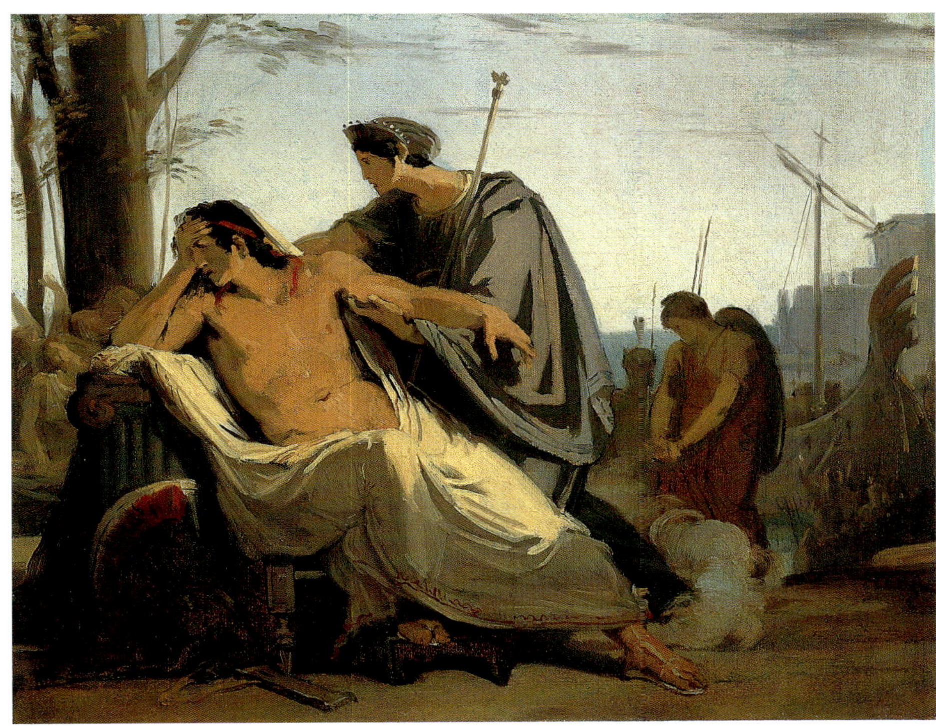

CATALOGUE NO. 26 | JULES-JOSEPH LEFEBVRE (1834– 1912), *Thetis Consoling Achilles*, 1858. Oil on canvas, 32.5 × 40.5 cm.

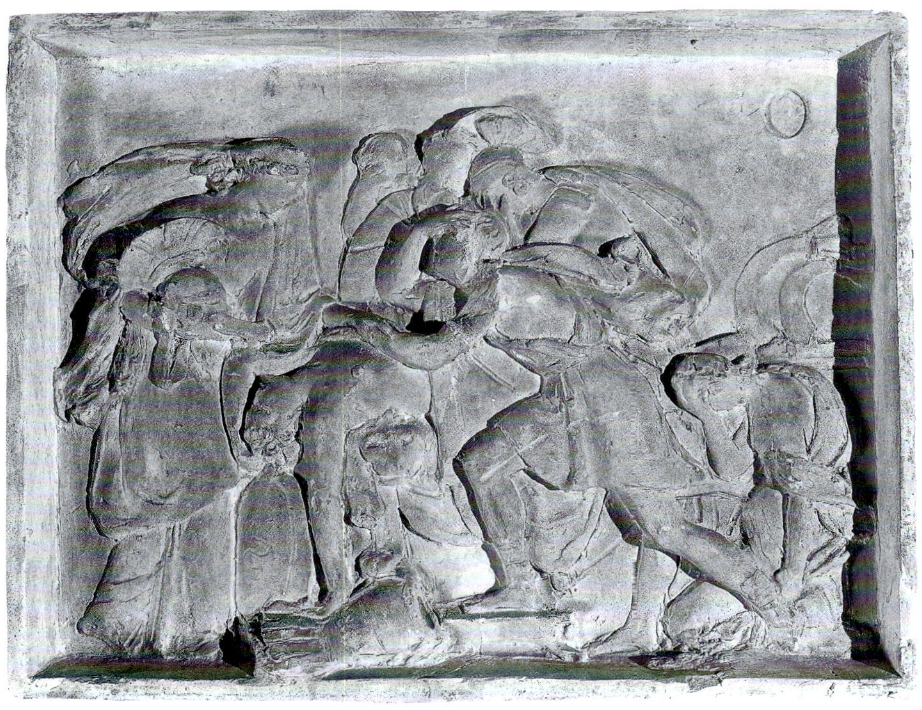

CATALOGUE NO. 27 | JOSEPH BRIAN (1801–1861), *Thetis Brings Achilles the Arms Forged by Vulcan*, 1829. Plaster, 40 × 47 cm.

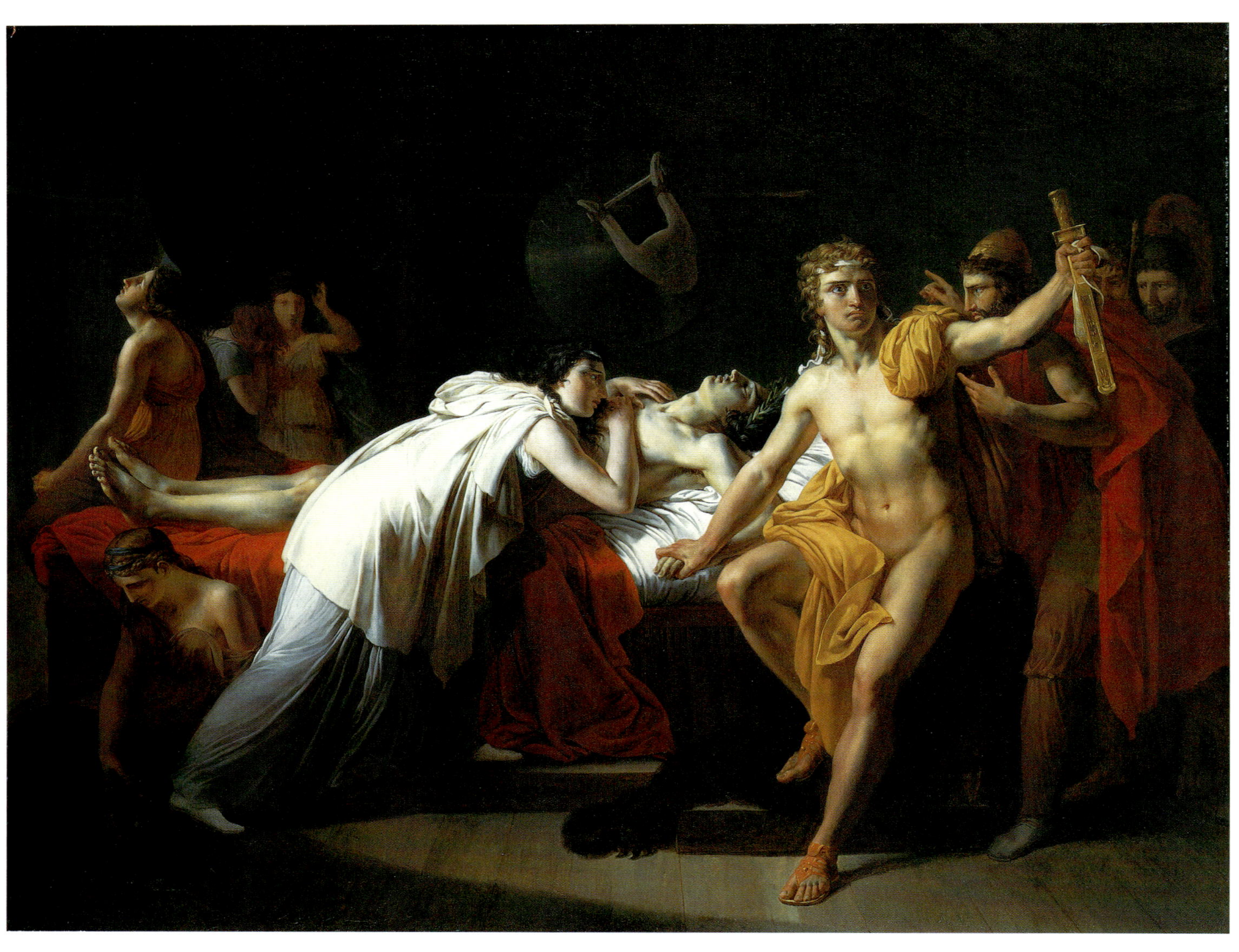

and with both hands clawing deep at her breasts,
her soft throat and lovely face, she sobbed,
a woman like a goddess in her grief, "Patroclus—
dearest joy of my heart, my harrowed, broken heart!
I left you alive that day I left these shelters,
now I come back to find you fallen, captain of armies!
So grief gives way to grief, my life one endless sorrow!
The husband to whom my father and noble mother
  gave me,
I saw him torn by the sharp bronze before our city,
and my three brothers—a single mother bore us:
my brothers, how I loved you!—
you all went down to death on the same day . . .
But you, Patroclus, you would not let me weep,
not when the swift Achilles cut my husband down,
not when he plundered the lordly Mynes' city—
not even weep! No, again and again you vowed
you'd make me godlike Achilles' lawful, wedded wife,
you would sail me west in your warships, home to
  Phthia
and there with the Myrmidons hold my marriage
  feast.
So now I mourn your death—I will never stop—
you were always kind."
                    Her voice rang out in tears
and the women wailed in answer, grief for Patroclus
calling forth each woman's private sorrows.
But Achaea's warlords clustered round Achilles,
begging him to eat. He only spurned them, groaning,
"I beg *you*—if any comrade will hear me out in this—
stop pressing me now to glut myself with food and
  drink,
now such painful grief has come and struck my heart!
I'll hold out till the sun goes down—enduring—
fasting—despite your appeals."
  —*IL.* 19.282–308; F 19.333–65

This is the true quality of Homer's genius, "grief for Patroclus / calling forth each woman's private sorrows." The captive Briseis—pathetic object of an absurd quarrel, sad hostage of a sordid negotiation—counts for nothing in the history of the world and for everything in the poet's regard. No need to cite the rest of the Homeric text, in which Achilles, in his turn, laments, then takes up the arms brought by Thetis. Homer does not vouchsafe whether he again embraces the body of Patroclus. His fury is now expressed by his grinding teeth, and neither painter nor sculptor can do much with this information. Alaux sought to combine two scenes—the modest grandeur of the captive and the self-advertising wrath of Achilles—depicting them both beneath a shield decorated with a stylized lyre: to the left the captive women; to the right Achilles and some Greek princes. The sincerity of the Homeric text transpires more clearly in Brian's modest sketch, organized as it is around elbows, knees, and plaster right angles. Alaux's rhetoric of pathos places the male characters in the foreground, sadly obscuring the subject, which is here the misery of the captive women. The lyre that glimmers in the chiaroscuro contributes its own clear and intelligent note; these two friends sang together to its accompaniment a mere day or two earlier. Now the song has died, and the silence of the dead singer alternates with the cries of the mourning women. A sketch by Léon Cogniet (cat. no. 29) for the same *concours* spotlights Briseis's gesture, reiterates it

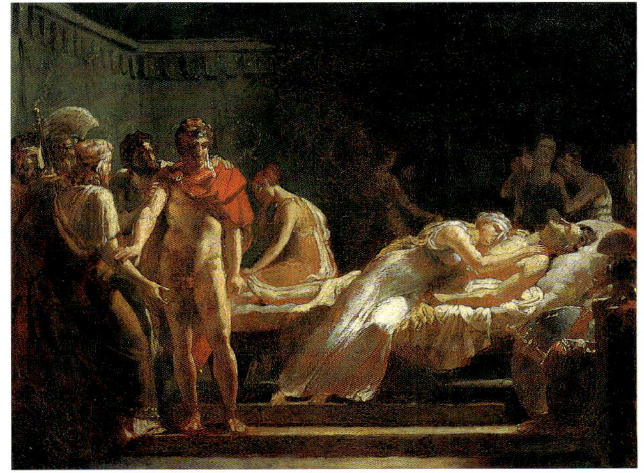

CATALOGUE NO. 29 | LÉON COGNIET (1794–1880), *Briseis Mourning Patroclus*, 1815. Oil on tracing paper mounted to canvas, 29.5 × 37.5 cm.

OPPOSITE CATALOGUE NO. 28 | JEAN ALAUX ("THE ROMAN") (1786–1864), *Briseis Mourning Patroclus*, 1815. Oil on canvas, 113.1 × 146 cm.

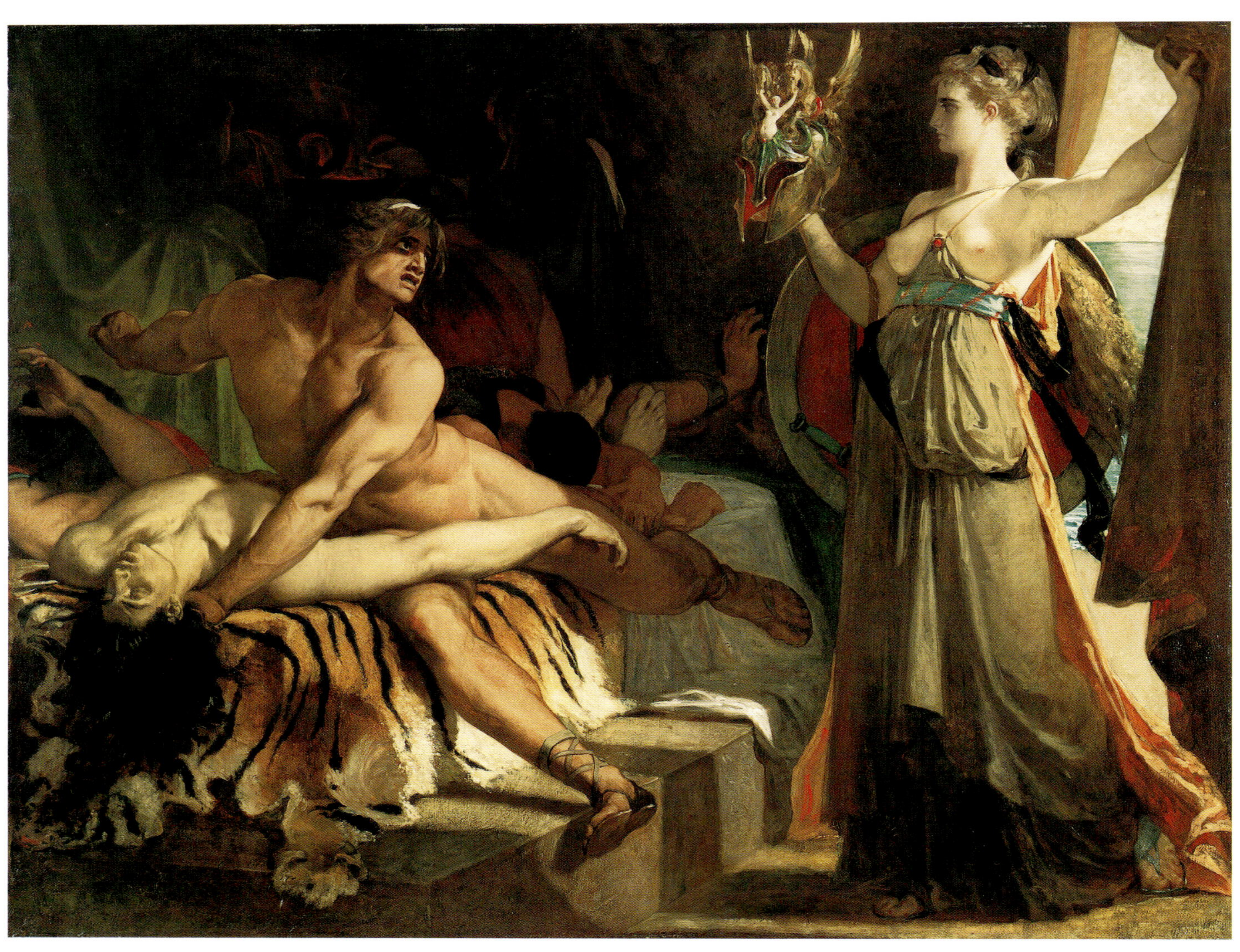

in the careworn back of one of her companions in misfortune, while Achilles stands obscured amid a group of Myrmidons. A composition in which the hero is eclipsed by his concubine and slave! No Prix de Rome rewarded Cogniet's audacity in 1815.

In 1866 Henri Regnault (cat. no. 30) carried off the prize. Claiming fidelity to a text that he misunderstood, he replaced Achilles center stage. Killed in the Franco-Prussian War of 1870, Regnault attained eternal renown (the Prix de Rome) before dying an Achilles-like death, cut down by Prussian machine-gun fire. Thetis is more goddess than mother; indeed, she is a Second Empire goddess straight out of Offenbach (Regnault's model and mistress was a celebrated singer). She presents Achilles with a helmet fresh from the goldsmith's window, while the breasts that nourished our hero conceal the shield that cannot defend him. Achilles is bursting with a rage not childish nor even adult but simply animal. The captive women have been swallowed up in the shadows—although from behind the funeral bed we see a hand contorted with grief. Humans have given way to brutes, and melancholy, relief-like compositions are replaced by indications of foreshortened muscle. Presumably in quest of historical realism, the École's teachers have fallen afoul of literary truth. Some things were, at the time, axiomatic: a Homeric warrior was a mountain of muscle whose only thought was war, and an epic poem could mention nothing but battle. This was a danger to which sculpture—particularly sculpture in the round—was less susceptible. The lack of a pretentiously historical background and the impossibility of combining the picturesque with the academic nude tended to reduce the sculptors to a single pose or finite number of gestures. In the early nineteenth century these gestures were compact and thoughtful; during the second half of the century their balance was disturbed by anger and "Neo-Baroque" virtuosity. Constant-Ambroise Roux, who won the Prix de Rome in 1894 for his *Enflamed with Anger Following the Death of Patroclus, Achilles Dons the Armor Brought by His Mother Thetis* (cat. no. 31), was clearly inspired by the *Discobolus.* Achilles is strapping on his handsome greaves and imagining his revenge:

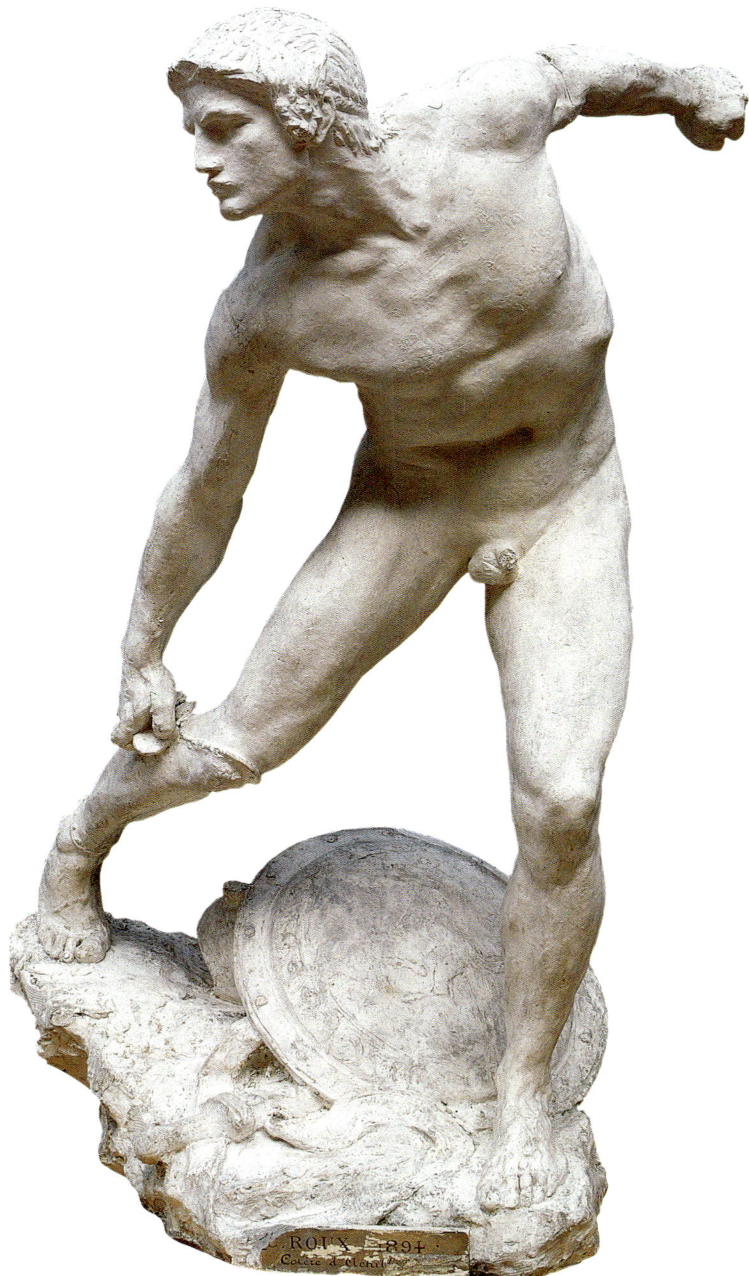

CATALOGUE NO. 31 | CONSTANT-AMBROISE ROUX (1865–1929), *Enflamed with Anger Following the Death of Patroclus, Achilles Dons the Armor Brought by His Mother Thetis*, 1894. Plaster, 142 × 89 × 89 cm.

OPPOSITE CATALOGUE NO. 30 | HENRI REGNAULT (1843–1871), *Thetis Brings Achilles the Arms Forged by Vulcan*, 1866. Oil on canvas, 113 × 146 cm.

And in their midst
the brilliant Achilles began to arm for battle . . .
A sound of grinding came from the fighter's teeth,
his eyes blazed forth in searing points of fire,
unbearable grief came surging through his heart,
and now, bursting with rage against the men of Troy,
he donned Hephaestus' gifts—magnificent armor
the god of fire forged with all his labor.
First he wrapped his legs with well-made greaves,
fastened behind his heels with silver ankle-clasps,
next he strapped the breastplate round his chest
then over his shoulder Achilles slung his sword,
the fine bronze blade with its silver-studded hilt,
then hoisted the massive shield flashing far and wide
like a full round moon—

—*IL.* 19.364–74; F 19.429–43

Homer's description continues with a profusion of detail, which Roux leaves to one side. But the forged arms—the enormous shield, the greaves, and the sword—are all there on the ground (the plinth). Roux's Achilles is at once a young hero and an athlete, entirely caught up in his vision of revenge. Unlike Regnault's Achilles, he aspires to life and action before consenting to suffer and die.

The Horses of Achilles

Nonsense is less offensive than bad taste. Homer never considered his heroes demigods or aristocratic fops. These are merely the very different faces bestowed on them by interpretations of successive epochs. Achilles and Patroclus think and act like impulsive adolescents, selfish and inconstant. The demigods and fops by whom they are represented in pre-Revolutionary painting are similarly immature. The winners of the 1769 Prix de l'Académie royale show them as vain courtiers. Although they lack grandeur, they have not succumbed to mere bestiality.

The scene depicted by Joseph-Barthélemy Lebouteux (cat. no. 32) and Pierre Lacour (cat. no. 33) allowed them to combine several interpretations of Homer then current:

. . . but Achilles still would not dismiss his Myrmidons,
he gave his battle-loving comrades strict commands:
"Charioteers in fast formation—friends to the death!
We must not loose our teams from the war-cars yet.
All in battle-order drive them past Patroclus—
a cortege will mourn the man with teams and chariots.
These are the solemn honors owed the dead. And then,
after we've eased our hearts with tears and dirge,
we free the teams and all take supper here."
All as one
the armies cried out in sorrow, and Achilles led the chant.
Three times they drove their full-maned stallions round the body . . .

Achilles led them now in a throbbing chant of sorrow,
laying his man-killing hands on his great friend's chest:
"Farewell, Patroclus, even there in the House of Death!
Look—all that I promised you once I am performing now:
I've dragged Hector here for the dogs to rip him raw—
and here in front of your flaming pyre I'll cut the throats
of a dozen sons of Troy in all their shining glory,
venting my rage on them for your destruction!"
So he triumphed
and again he was bent on outrage, on shaming noble Hector—
he flung him facedown in the dust beside Patroclus' bier.

—*IL.* 23.4–15, 17–26; F 23.4–14, 20–29

The Academicians perhaps chose this subject—the first taken from Homer in the history of the Grand

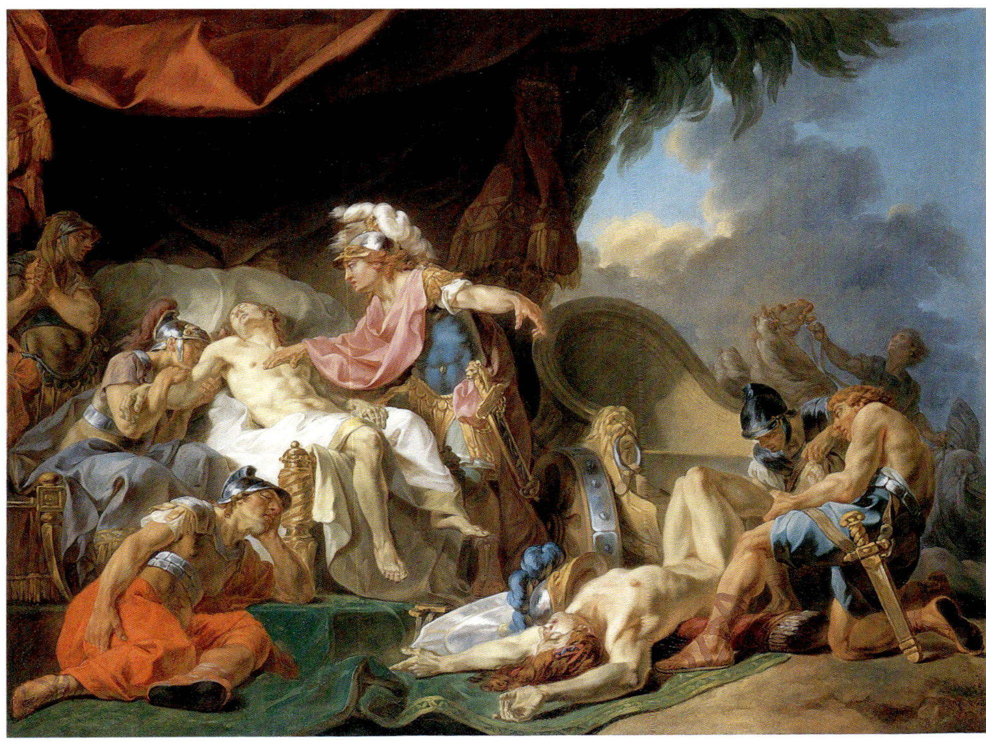

CATALOGUE NO. 32 | JOSEPH-BARTHÉLEMY LEBOUTEUX (1742–?), *Achilles Places the Body of Hector at the Feet of the Dead Patroclus*, 1769. Oil on canvas, 111 × 147 cm.

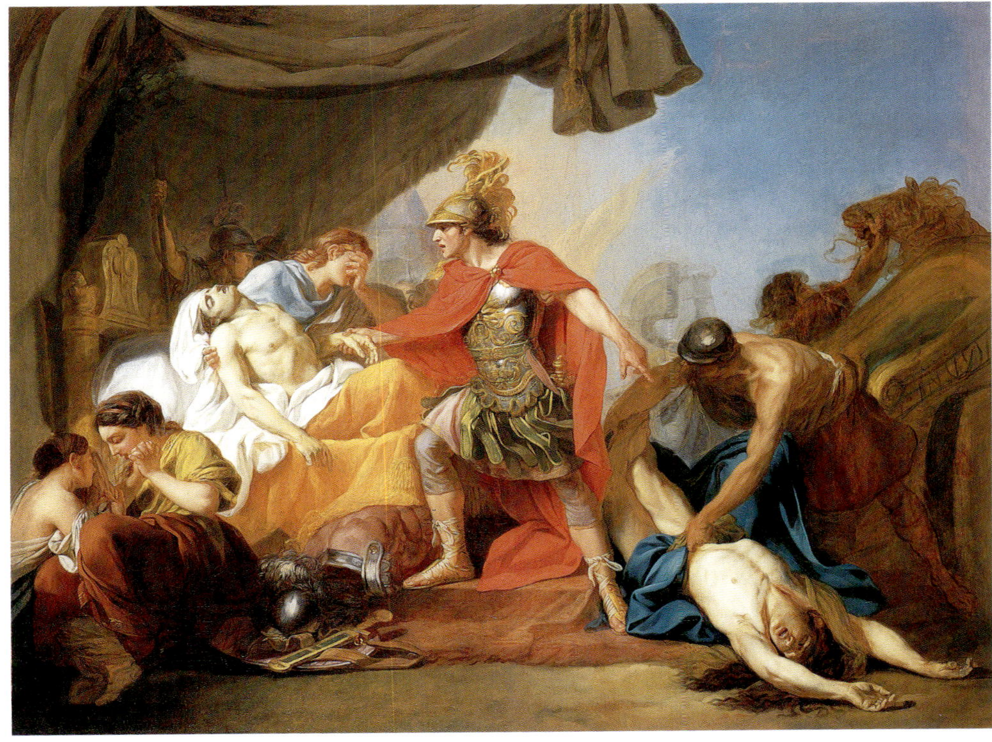

CATALOGUE NO. 33 | PIERRE LACOUR (1745–1814), *Achilles Places the Body of Hector at the Feet of the Dead Patroclus*, 1769. Oil on canvas, 111 × 147 cm.

Prix—because it resembled that of Poussin's *Death of Germanicus* of 1626–28. (There was also a closer precedent in Gavin Hamilton's version of the Homeric scene, ca. 1765.) They hoped to judge the candidates on their knowledge not of Homer but of Poussin, and on the sense of nobility and historical reconstruction that students would necessarily learn from Poussin's oeuvre. In fact, the decor of the two paintings, with their strangely collapsed canopies, shows little concern for archaeological accuracy. The sense that Lacour and Lebouteux are painting by the schoolbook, however, is clear in their studies of the nude and their references to Poussin. Lacour uses the curtain from *The Death of Germanicus* as an elegant screen; in his treatment, the tapestry covers with tasseled fringes are not so much shroud as ornament, echoing the rich garments worn by the courtly Achilles. Nothing in Lacour's painting gives any sense of the nobility of Achilles: not the sand in the foreground; nor the luminous bed on which Patroclus lies; nor the insulted and maltreated body of Hector; nor the arms of Achilles, which passed from Patroclus to his killer, Hector, and which have here returned to pay a final homage to the faithful friend, the incompetent warrior. The "frieze" in Poussin's *Germanicus* rigorously aligned the standing warriors with their spears, raised to the indifferent vaults. Heedless of his example, the prizewinners of 1769 multiplied poses and points of view. In spite of Homer's description, they contrast the musculature of the Myrmidon in the foreground and the corpse of Hector, elongated from having been dragged around the walls of Troy, with the still supple body of Patroclus and shimmering colors of the armor of Achilles.

Better, then, to look into the background, where the heads of Achilles' horses rear up against the sky, clearly exasperated to have been forced to do what a horse never does, namely, trample a corpse. When the furious Achilles was still donning his armor, these same animals had sought to restore him to reason. Whinnying and rearing is a constant in the representations of these equine philosophers. The students of 1769 depicted Achilles as vain and childish. Achilles' horses share their view.

Achilles and the River Flowing with Blood

We have met Achilles the musician, the fop, sulking, capricious, and vain. We have even encountered Achilles in love. It is time we confronted a more warlike version of the son of Peleus. The subject for 1831 was *Achilles Pursued by the River God Xanthos*. The subject is neither exclusively heroic nor altogether sanguinary. Achilles, attacking the Trojans, finds he cannot kill his adversary, the River Scamander or, rather, its long-bearded river god Xanthos, an ancestor of Priam, the king of Troy, and therefore no friend to Achilles:

> The more he vaunted the more the river's anger rose,
> churning at heart for a way to stop his rampage,
> godlike Achilles, and stop the Trojan's rout.
>
> . . . still more Paeonian men the runner would have killed
> if the swirling river had not risen, crying out in fury,
> taking a man's shape, its voice breaking out of a whirlpool:
>
> "All my lovely rapids are crammed with corpses now,
> no channel in sight to sweep my currents out to sacred sea—
> I'm choked with corpses and still you slaughter more,
> you blot out more! Leave me alone, have done—
> captain of armies, I am filled with horror!"
>
> —*IL.* 21.136–68, 211–13, 218–21; F 21.156–58, 237–39, 246–50

But Xanthos is wasting his time. It takes more than a god in human guise to halt a beast in the guise of man:

> When he heard *that*
> Achilles the famous spearman, leaping down from the bluff,
> plunged in the river's heart and the river charged against him,
> churning, surging, all his rapids rising in white fury

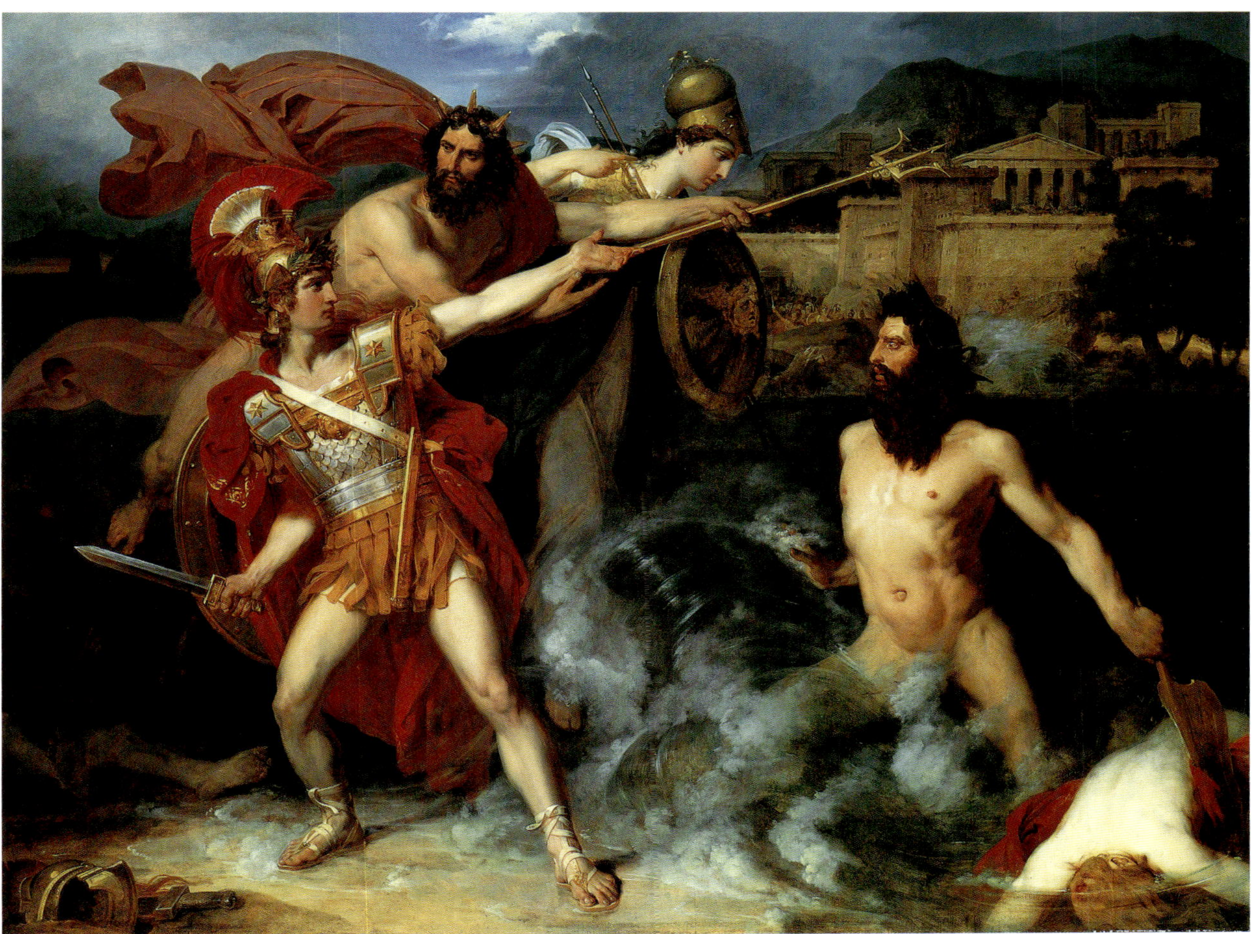

CATALOGUE NO. 34 | HENRI-FRÉDÉRIC SCHOPIN (or Chopin) (1804–1890), *Achilles Pursued by the River God Xanthos*, 1831. Oil on canvas, 113 × 146 cm.

and drove the mass of corpses choking tight his
 channel,
the ruck Achilles killed—Scamander heaved them up
and bellowing like a bull the river flung them out
on the dry land but saved the living, hiding them
 down
the fresh clear pools of his thundering whirling
 current . . .
 —*IL.* 21.233–39; F 21.263–71

A deus ex machina must inevitably seem ridiculous on canvas: this thought was clearly on the mind of Henri-Frédéric Schopin, winner of the 1831 Grand Prix (cat. no. 34). A few decades later, the fear itself would seem ridiculous. Homer clearly says that the gods Achilles summons for assistance—Athena and Poseidon— take human form. Schopin prefers to give them their usual godly appearance, but they are not excessively sublime. Achilles, meanwhile, has the

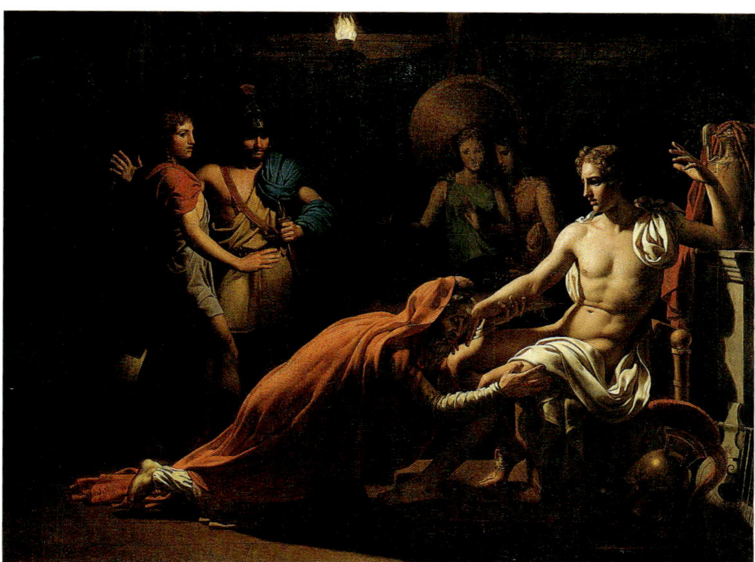

CATALOGUE NO. 35 | JÉRÔME-MARTIN LANGLOIS (1779–1836), *Priam at the Feet of Achilles*, 1809. Oil on canvas, 113 × 146 cm.

physiognomy of a little boy, and his inexperience elicits some sympathy. Things conspire to restrain him: the beautifully ornamented trident of Poseidon; the shield of Athena; and the civilization that covers the hill of Troy. In this bizarre battle between gods and waves, Homer's sympathies clearly lie with the dead and wounded. For all the energy exhibited by the river god, he is doomed to occupy the slightly absurd pose—often ridiculed by Diderot—of a half-submerged bather with water running down his chest.

Priam and Achilles

Encouraged by the gods, Priam enters the Greek camp to offer Achilles a ransom in exchange for the body of his son, which Achilles has daily been dragging behind his chariot around the walls of Troy. This act of cruelty, this insult to the dead and to the human condition in general, long disqualified Achilles from the ranks of those models of virtue the artists were required to depict. But then they discovered the wrath of Achilles entered a new phase following revenge, namely, that of compassion and weariness. Around 1750 it was finally admitted that history and war are not always consistent with order and courtesy. The subject of Priam and Achilles was much favored by Scandinavian artists and was often set in the nineteenth-century *concours*.

In 1809, the Academy of Fine Arts specified the subject precisely: "The body of Hector must be represented on the ground outside the tent of Achilles. The chariot that bore Priam and his presents, driven by Ideus, may also be represented. With the exception of Alcimes and Automedon, the other friends of Achilles may be omitted. Priam's costume should be Phrygian; the tent was made of wood and covered in reeds."[7] The artists had to make a choice: on the one hand, rhetorical expressions, costumes, chariots, and historical bric-à-brac; on the other, everything else—everything that constitutes an analysis of human conflict and inner conflict. The winner was Jérôme-Martin Langlois (cat. no. 35).

What Hector means to Andromache, Patroclus and Briseis to Achilles, and in this scene Achilles to Priam is something more than merely a reason to live and love. Homer's humanity quite transcends the attachment of one human being to another. The process of mourning takes Homer's characters through hatred of those they perceive as their enemies to sympathy with those they perceive as their fellow men. The scene that shows Priam begging for the body of his son from Achilles serves no purpose in the unfolding military situation. It is the crowning moment of the *Iliad*, which finishes not with the end of the war but with this meeting of the two principal adversaries and the two greatest victims of the war, the two literary figures of king and hero, both doomed and impotent in the face of events. They discover that each is to the other an image of what he most loves or has loved: a father and a son. How can so simple a lesson be conveyed in so complex a drama? Homer proceeds slowly, his successive explorations of the mind of each interrupting his descriptions of their words and gestures:

OPPOSITE CATALOGUE NO. 36 | JOSEPH WENCKER (1848–1919), *Priam at the Feet of Achilles*, 1876. Oil on canvas, 145 × 113 cm.

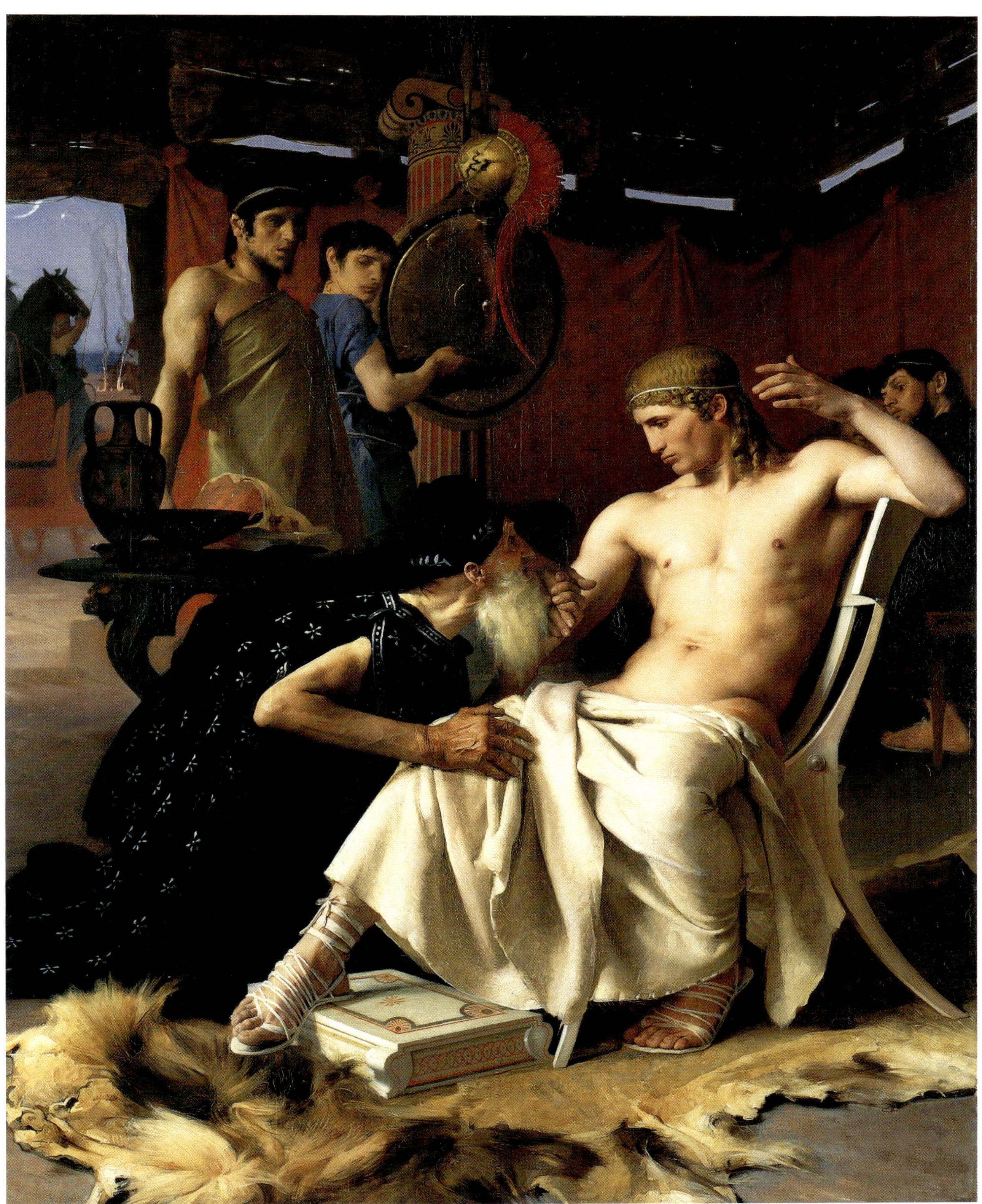

The majestic king of Troy slipped past the rest
and kneeling down beside Achilles, clasped his knees
and kissed his hands, those terrible, man-killing
hands
that had slaughtered Priam's many sons in battle.
Awesome—as when the grip of madness seizes one
who murders a man in his own fatherland and flees
abroad to foreign shores, to a wealthy, noble host,
and a sense of marvel runs through all who see
him—
so Achilles marveled, beholding majestic Priam.
His men marveled too, trading startled glances.
But Priam prayed his heart out to Achilles:
"Remember your own father, great godlike Achilles—
as old as *I* am, past the threshold of deadly old age!
No doubt the countrymen round about him plague
him now,
with no one there to defend him, beat away disaster.
No one—but at least he hears you're still alive
and his old heart rejoices, hopes rising, day by day,
to see his beloved son come sailing home from Troy.
But I—dear god, my life so cursed by fate . . .
I fathered hero sons in the wide realm of Troy
and now not a single one is left, I tell you.
Fifty sons I had when the sons of Achaea came,
nineteen born to me from a single mother's womb
and the rest by other women in the palace. Many,
most of them violent Ares cut the knees from under.
But one, one was left me, to guard my walls, my
people—
the one you killed the other day, defending his
fatherland,
my Hector! It's all for him I've come to the ships now,
to win him back from you—I bring a priceless
ransom.
Revere the gods, Achilles! Pity me in my own right,
remember your own father! I deserve more pity . . .
I have endured what no one on earth has ever done
before—
I put to my lips the hands of the man who killed
my son."

Those words stirred within Achilles a deep desire
to grieve for his own father. Taking the old man's
hand
he gently moved him back. And overpowered by
memory
both men gave way to grief. Priam wept freely
for man-killing Hector, throbbing, crouching
before Achilles' feet as Achilles wept himself,
now for his father, now for Patroclus once again,
and their sobbing rose and fell throughout the house.
—*IL.* 24.477–512; F 24.559–99

The subject was treated by François Doyen in a painting shown in the 1787 Salon, by Jérôme Langlois in the 1809 *concours* (cat. no. 35), and by Joseph Wencker in 1876 (cat. no. 36). Each was faced with the complex, symmetrically opposed thoughts of the two men. Achilles and Priam hold each other responsible for their respective bereavements and see in each other the image of what they mourn: Achilles hates in Priam the father of Patroclus's killer; Priam fears in Achilles the killer of his son. But Achilles remembers his father, Peleus, and Priam appeals to Achilles' filial love. After their initial explanations, their dialogue is conducted in the form of thoughts that remain unspoken, and resembles Rembrandt's biblical scenes in its greatness; although the subdued light and deep shadows depicted by the two students owe much to Homer's description, there are undeniable overtones of the Dutch seventeenth-century master. The artists dared not depart from Homer's words, and so two Myrmidons witness the scene, which centers on Priam's suppliant gesture. Langlois remembers that Priam came wreathed in darkness, while Wencker's attempts at historical reconstruction pile up around the figures. In 1809 and 1876, Achilles' pose is that of a statue of Sulla, as popularized in the theater by the actor François-Joseph Talma. In Langlois's painting there is something memorable about the luminous torso of Achilles and the expressiveness of his face and right hand—anger mingled with compassion, as the *concours* subjects tended to put it. At this point Achilles does not see himself as either master or judge of Priam; he dreams and he understands. But the more powerful character, Priam, accepts the conventional pose, kneeling with hand outstretched in supplication.

In Wencker's work, the mass of historical detail seems predominant. The eyes of the two men reveal little of their memories or of the way in which each comes to contemplate in the other an aspect of his own situation. If we now look back over the Homeric scenes by which artists have been inspired, we realize that none are based on a particular historical or moral fact. Faced with his fellow man, each Homeric character is entirely himself, individual in purpose and sensibility. Homer's protagonists are never the plaything of conventions or custom. In the Homeric text the meeting of Achilles and Priam is no exception to this rule: the thoughts and words of the two men occupy dozens of lines, while their pose is described in a single line that immediately precedes their parallel, silent monologues. Like the captive women in Achilles' tent, the two men see in the other's sadness only the image of their own. They are both desperately alone. Langlois and Wencker lacked the imaginative power to give expression to the hidden thoughts of the heroes. A more vigorous artist was needed to express the "tragic sense of life." One such was Rembrandt, as we have seen. Another was David, Langlois's master, who presides over the next section.

NOTES

1 Pausanias, "Attica," in *Description of Greece* 1.22.6–7.

2 Candide is the eponymous hero of Voltaire's *Candide* (1759); Fabrice del Dongo is the hero of Stendhal's *Charterhouse of Parma* (1839). [Trans.]

3 Pierre de Ronsard, *Oeuvres*, 2 vols. (Paris, 1950), 1:563–64.

4 See *Troilus and Cressida*, esp. 2.2.116 and 3.3.215–20, 237–40.

5 Ibid., 1.3.147.

6 Plato, *Symposium* 179–80.

7 See Marcel Bonnaire, *Procès-verbaux de l'Académie des beaux-arts*, 3 vols. [published for the Société de l'histoire de l'art français] (Paris, 1937–43), 3:230, 256.

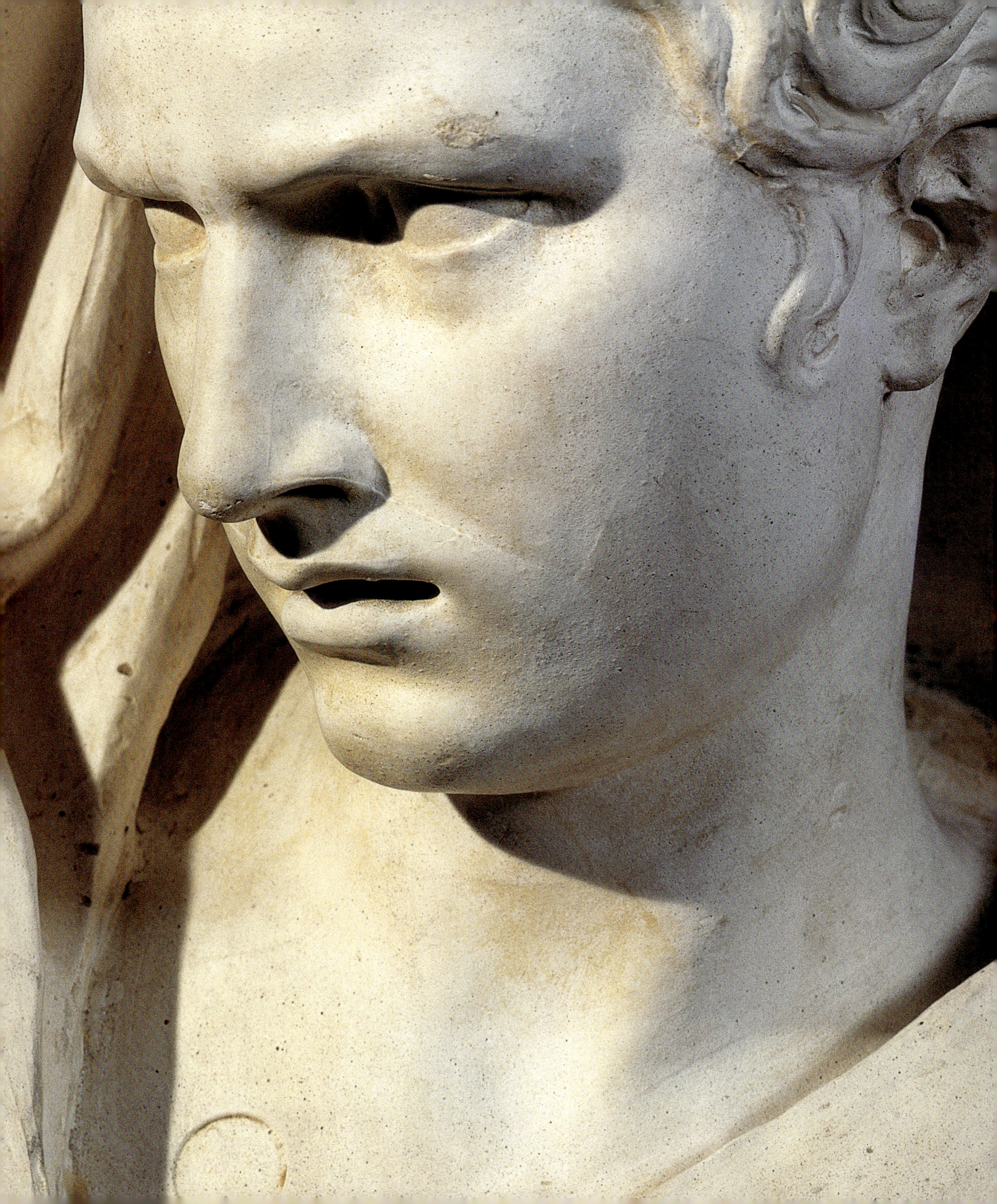

Far from Combat | The Great Scenes

Two cocks lived together like peas in a pod.
Now see a hen alight.
War breaks out in a trice.
Love, you were the ruin of Troy. Yours the vice
Whence this bitter fight,
Whence Xanthos stained with the bright
Blood even of the gods.

—LAFONTAINE, "THE TWO COCKS," VII, 12

Helen: To Die For?

If La Fontaine's lines do not summarize the entire course of the Trojan War, they at least circumscribe its primary cause: women. Let me begin with Helen and Clytemnestra, the two daughters of Zeus and Leda. Helen seemed so beautiful to the Greeks that all their princes sued for her hand, promising if she were later carried off by some seducer, her husband would have the support of her former suitors. Helen's choice fell on the blond Menelaus, king of Sparta. Among the rejected was his brother, Agamemnon, king of Argos, who promptly sought consolation by marrying Helen's sister, Clytemnestra. Alas, on the other shore of the Aegean, the Trojan prince Paris (also called Alexander) was to women what Helen was to men: beauty to a catastrophic degree. One of Priam's fifty sons, Paris had been exposed at birth on Mount Ida in deference to an oracle declaring he would be the ruin of his native land. He was saved by well-meaning shepherds, however, and grew up the most handsome among them, thus qualifying for a task too heavy for him. The goddess Discord (Eris), furious that she had not been invited to the wedding of Peleus and Thetis, rolled a golden apple marked "To the Most Beautiful" between Hera, Athena, and Aphrodite. Zeus nominated the blond Paris to judge the contest, and Hermes was sent to fetch him. It was a good-humored affair and was often drawn as such, almost invariably on the model of a well-known Marcantonio Raimondi print after Raphael. Ronsard sets the scene:

Then Paris, seated on a tree hard by,
Strumming, saw descending from the sky
Three goddesses, all naked to the eye.[1]

This unusual shepherd, judge by chance, chose Aphrodite. The judgment was rigged, for each goddess offered a magnificent bribe. Paris scorned Hera's offer to rule all Asia; Athena's offer of wisdom and military success meant nothing to him. But Aphrodite's proposal—possession of the world's most beautiful woman—suited him perfectly.

Destiny and character did the rest—and perhaps might have done so whether or not the goddesses had been involved. Paris carried off Helen—or, rather, Helen allowed herself to be carried off. Later she persuaded her husband and one or two artists—those whose taste in art ran to violence rather than seduction—that she had been abducted. Many artists,

DETAIL OF CATALOGUE NO. 43

however, among them Guido Reni (Musée du Louvre) and Daumier (cat. no. 113), take it for granted that Helen carried off Paris. Menelaus therefore summoned his allies. Achilles and Ulysses were reluctant. (Their stories are related in separate sections.) Appointed to head the expedition, Agamemnon gathered his forces and flotilla at Aulis, in Boeotia, across the Aegean Sea from Troy. To obtain favorable winds, he was obliged to sacrifice his eldest daughter, Iphigenia. He made his departure in this way, and for ten years forgot everything, wife and daughter included. Clytemnestra forgot nothing and for ten years awaited the return of Agamemnon, a sword in her hand, in the company of her lover. Meanwhile, the goddesses rejected by Paris swore to bring down Paris, Troy, and the Trojans. Aphrodite naturally sided with Paris.

These episodes were known to one and all long before Homer ever sang and are evoked only in passing in the *Iliad* and *Odyssey*. But in the imagination and literary culture of Europe—in its iconology—they have infinite resonance. Analogies were interwoven between the goddesses and the Three Graces (*Charites*), the chaste daughters of Zeus: Euphrosyne, Thalia, and Aglaia, each of whom embodied one of the forms of philosophical love, namely, *Castitas, Pulchritudo*, and *Voluptas* (Chastity, Beauty, and Pleasure). For the Neoplatonic Humanists the beauty of Aphrodite would be imperfect without the wisdom of Athena and the majesty of Hera. But it required considerable ingenuity on the part of the poets to transform Hephaestus's adulterous spouse—a goddess happy to prostitute Helen for the prize in a village beauty contest—into an image of moral perfection. Homer himself balked at this, changing the name of the spouse of Hephaestus to Charis (Grace) in the *Iliad* but remarrying him to the faithless Aphrodite in the *Odyssey*.

The *Iliad* celebrates scenes of war but hymns moments of peace. The traditional legend abounded in scenes of combat and massacre. Homer inserts long conversations between these outbreaks of mayhem, conversations for which there is no narrative requirement but which remove his characters from fable into the more complex life of literature. The wellspring of the *Iliad*, if not its subject, is Helen and her lovers rather than battlefield duels. How many warriors were quick to sense that they would die not for their own renown but for that of Helen? Ulysses long refused to fight for so futile a cause, preferring to stay on his little island-kingdom with his wife and son. The poem's supposed heroes are less than heroic when we see them away from the battlefield with their wives, mistresses, and children.

By contrast, those who most hate war suddenly find within them "an irresistible need to kill," as Hector puts it in Giraudoux's play *The War of Troy Shall Not Take Place*.[2] Paris presents the most complex case. In the third book of the *Iliad*, proud as a peacock in the handsome armor he has meticulously ornamented, he meets the gaze of the flouted husband Menelaus on the plain of Troy. The handsome lover takes discretion to be the better part of valor. A few deeply felt insults from Hector are, however, sufficient to rouse his shrunken vanity: "Paris, appalling Paris! Our prince of beauty— / mad for women, you lure them all to ruin! / Would to god you'd never been born, died unwed. // . . . you have no pith, no fighting strength inside you" (*Il.* 3.9, 44–45). Then the raging armies are suddenly stilled and a duel is arranged between Menelaus and Paris. As Homer and the gods know only too well, however, it takes more than the blood of two men to restore peace between warring peoples: the duel comes to nothing. Athena and Aphrodite intervene. Divine purposes overwhelm human foresight.

Helen at the Scaean Gates

Homer, meanwhile, shows the quarrels of men and gods in an ever more ironic light. He first describes the scene through the eyes and voice of Helen. She approaches the spectacle high on the walls of Troy, near the Scaean gates. Before coming, she has suffered a moment of nostalgia for her old husband and home, the "live tears welling" (3.142), as Homer puts it with a hint of misogyny. All the same, she takes pleasure in her entourage of beautiful women, less beautiful than herself, and in the appreciative audience comprised of the old men of Troy, who rehearse the judgment of Paris in ironic or pitiful counterpoint of old age to youth. The eighteenth century argued strenuously over how this scene should be portrayed, bearing in mind that the ancient painter Zeuxis had inscribed lines from the third book of the *Iliad* at the bottom of one of his paintings. In the second of his *Pictures Drawn from the "Iliad," the "Odyssey," and the "Aeneid,"* Caylus describes the scene thus:

> Helen, wearing a white veil, appears amid a number of old men, among whom is Priam, distinguished by the marks of Royalty. The Artist must endeavor to make clear the triumph of beauty by the avidity of the glances and by all the signs of admiration inscribed on the faces of these men, whose ardor time has cooled. The scene takes place above one of the gates of the city. I believe that the background of the sky would be better than the buildings of the city; it will at least be more audacious, although either would be suitable.[3]

Lessing rejected this proposal, preferring to fill the eye with Helen's beauty rather than the lubricious faces of the senile. "Let us imagine this picture executed by the greatest master of our own day, and then let us place it beside that of Zeuxis. Which one will show the true victory of beauty? The first, where I feel it for myself, or the second, in which I must deduce it from the grimacing admiration of bearded old men?"[4] Like Lessing and Paris (and the Trojan elders), most artists concentrated on Helen rather than her tired old admirers. Lessing acutely identifies the prudishness of Caylus's tableau: he reminds us of the wisdom of Homer's old men, who, having once sated their eyes, would like Helen returned to Menelaus.

Better, therefore, to represent them as Homer did, watching Helen parade along the walls, and hear them as they happily contradict themselves:

> And with those words
> the goddess filled her heart with yearning warm and deep
> for her husband long ago, her city and her parents.
> Quickly cloaking herself in shimmering linen,
> out of her rooms she rushed, live tears welling,
> and not alone—two of her women followed close behind,
> Aethra, Pittheus' daughter, and Clymene, eyes wide,
> and they soon reached the looming Scaean Gates.
>
> And there they were, gathered around Priam,
> Panthous and Thymoetes, Lampus and Clytius,
> Hicetaon the gray aide of Ares, then those two
> with unfailing good sense, Ucalegon and Antenor.
> The old men of the realm held seats above the gates.
> Long years had brought their fighting days to a halt
> but they were eloquent speakers still, clear as cicadas
> settled on treetops, lifting their voices through the forest,
> rising softly, falling, dying away . . . So they waited,
> the old chiefs of Troy, as they sat aloft the tower.
> And catching sight of Helen moving along the ramparts,
> they murmured one to another, gentle, winged words:
> "Who on earth could blame them? Ah, no wonder
> the men of Troy and Argives under arms have suffered
> years of agony all for her, for such a woman.
> Beauty, terrible beauty!
> A deathless goddess—so she strikes our eyes!
> But still,
> ravishing as she is, let her go home in the long ships
> and not be left behind . . . for us and our children
> down the years an irresistible sorrow."
>
> —IL. 3.139–60; F 3.167–94

They nevertheless find an excellent pretext to bring her beauty close to their decrepitude; since Helen knows both Greeks and Trojans, she can supplement their weary eyes by commenting on the duel. To appreciate at its full the windings of Homeric irony, of that ineffable smile that illuminated all Greek culture, one has only to think of scenes drawn from other ancient authors. Compared to Homer's heart-warming cicadas, the old men who spy on Susannah are voyeurs.

Giraudoux does not betray the spirit of Homer in his use of natural metaphor:

> Beautiful Helen, Helen of Sparta,
> With a beautiful breast, with a noble head,
> May the gods keep us from your parting
> Toward your Menelaus anew.

In his play the old men run beneath a raised passageway on which Helen complacently exposes her legs and "two charming buttocks." They applaud with the passion of old age: "One, two, three! Long live Helen!"[5] Equally inspired by the spirit of Homer, in 1880 two students of the École, Louis-Édouard-Paul Fournier and Jean-Baptiste Marty (cat. nos. 37–38), sketched a sort of dance in which the old men seek a clear view over the battle raging below the city walls, while hoping that Helen's elegant outline will come between them and the spectacle (cat. no. 38). Drawing their eyes to her, the sunshade protects Helen from the sun only to expose her to their desire. On one point at least, Caylus was right: the silhouette of Helen does indeed stand out admirably against the sunlit sky. The rays of the Mediterranean sun pour through the diaphanous fabric of Helen's robe, caressing her skin and, in the process, dissolving the Caylus-Lessing debate. In Helen's promenade at the Scaean gates—as in the rakish grace of the lace-clad warriors of the eighteenth century and the grandeur of twentieth-century peace conferences—we recognize the "privileges of the great," who, Giraudoux reminds us, prefer "to watch catastrophes from a terrace."[6] Homer and these brilliant sketches tell us better than Caylus and Lessing of the pleasures afforded the great by a distant prospect of war, especially when a beautiful woman displays her charms on a terrace high above the tumult. The parapet, chairs, and sunlit walls of the walkway sketched by Fournier and Marty are most agreeable foils for Helen of the white arms and the transparent veils.

Two Brothers: Paris and Hector

Exchanging the red mist of battle for quiet conversation with friends, warriors have profound things to say about the most subtle contradictions of human life. In the private scenes of the *Iliad* men and women loose their constraints and deliver uninhibited verdicts on the justice of this world. Warriors reassume their civilian status and express doubt about the need for war; women denounce the world of men; and mortals invite the gods to meditate on their responsibilities. All speak the language of Homer. Brilliantly simple, these scenes are the work of a humanist genius. If we except those artists who sought no more in epic than lessons in military heroics—*exempla virtutis*—these were the scenes most frequently imitated, discussed, and illustrated by the artists who read Homer. Thanks to their profoundly original structuring and placement, they have the power to impress the Homeric vision of this world even on younger artists, from whom it is normally concealed beneath descriptions of battle.

Homer has set every imaginable obstacle to fraternal affection between those unlikely brothers Paris and Hector. A contented husband and attentive father, Hector has nothing in common with his sibling, exposed at birth in anticipation of his future misdeeds. When the Trojans suffer serious reverses, the two men react in very different ways. Paris mopes at Helen's side, while Hector rallies the Trojan troops, only to perceive his brother's absence:

> Hector approached the halls of Paris, sumptuous halls
> he built himself with the finest masons of the day,
> master builders famed in the fertile land of Troy.
> They'd raised his sleeping chamber, house and court
> adjoining Priam's and Hector's aloft the city heights.
> Now Hector, dear to Zeus, strode through the gates,
> clutching a thrusting-lance eleven forearms long;
> the bronze tip of the weapon shone before him,
> ringed with a golden hoop to grip the shaft.
> And there in the bedroom Hector came on Paris
> polishing, fondling his splendid battle-gear,

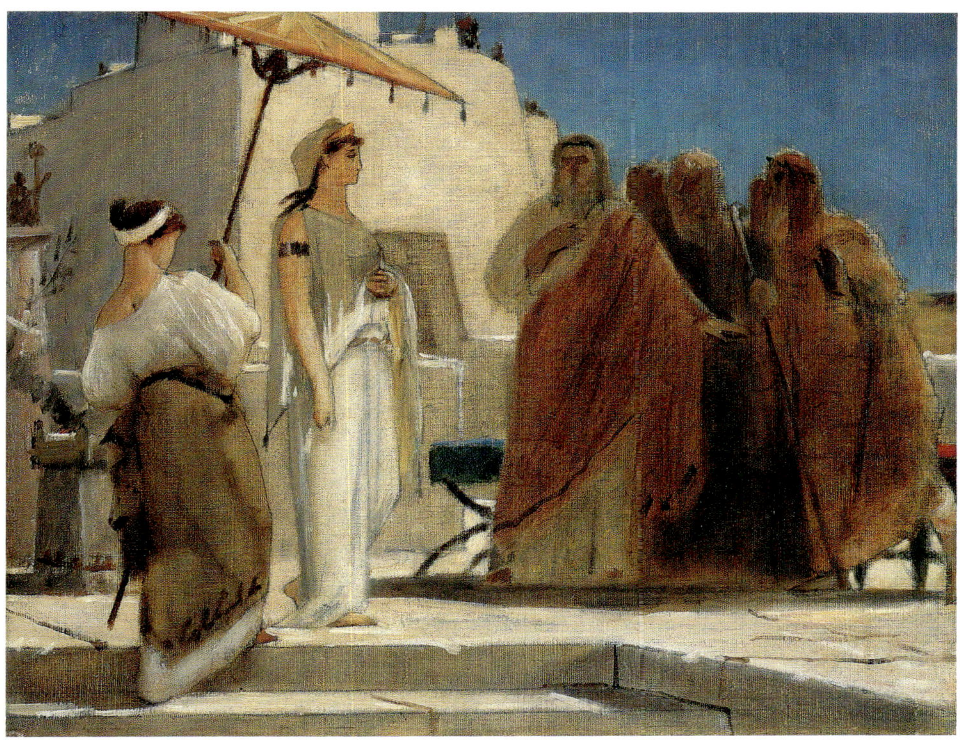

CATALOGUE NO. 37 | LOUIS-ÉDOUARD-PAUL FOURNIER (1857–1913), *Helen and the Elders (The Triumph of Helen)*, 1880. Oil on canvas, 32.5 × 40.5 cm.

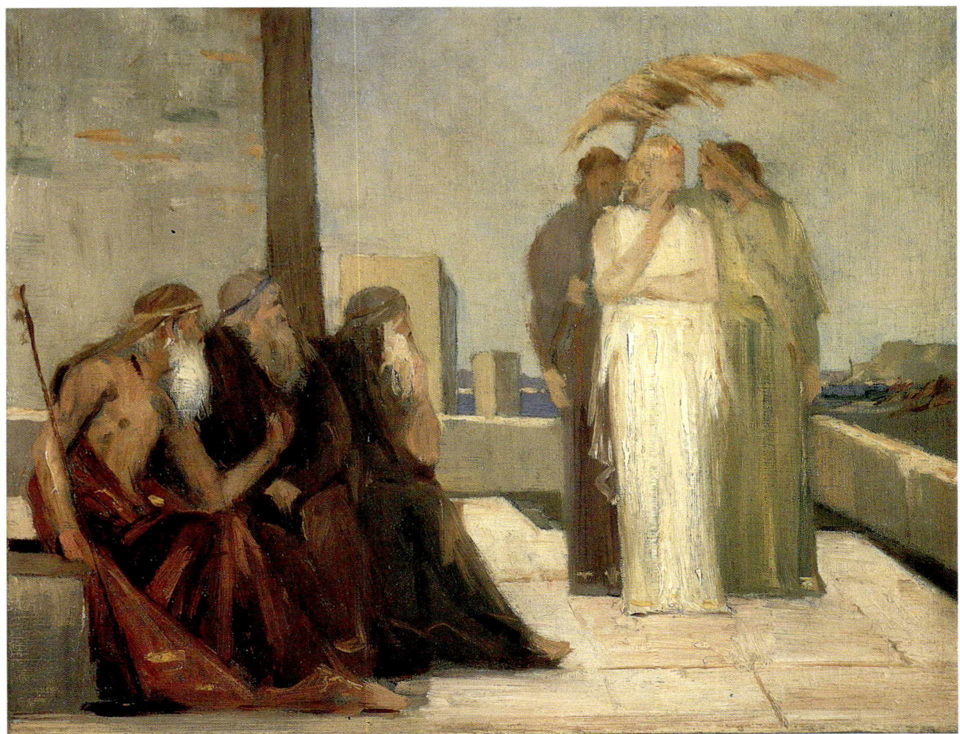

CATALOGUE NO. 38 | JEAN-BAPTISTE MARTY (1857–?), *Helen and the Elders*, 1880. Oil on canvas, 32.5 × 40.5 cm.

his shield and breastplate, turning over and over
his long curved bow. And there was Helen of Argos,
sitting with all the women of the house, directing
the rich embroidered work they had in hand.
Seeing Paris,
Hector raked his brother with insults, stinging taunts:
"What on earth are you doing? Oh how wrong it is,
this anger you keep smoldering in your heart! Look,
your people dying around the city, the steep walls,
dying in arms—and all for you, the battle cries
and the fighting flaring up around the citadel.
You'd be the first to lash out at another—anywhere—
you saw hanging back from this, this hateful war.
Up with you,
before all Troy is torched to a cinder here and now!"
—IL. 6.313–31; F 6.368–91

Homer's treatment of Paris—and of Helen, the other witness to this tense exchange—shows greater sensitivity than modern readers have acknowledged. The sensual Helen encourages Paris to go and fight, while the virtuous Andromache attempts to keep Hector back, but it is Helen who is accused of sapping her man's courage. Paris is willing to accept the challenge of a duel, but the goddesses remove him from danger at once and Aphrodite quickly restores him to Helen's arms. It has been said that in Homer the gods are personifications of mortal desires, and that the less virile desires take the shape of goddesses.

What did the Greeks think of these two lovers, who brought down the world upon their heads? For many Helen's beauty was sufficient excuse. Only the blind were immune to seduction. The ancient poet Stesichorus was struck blind when he spoke ill of Helen; his sight was restored when he revised his verdict in a palinode. Artists, priests, and other lovers of beauty naturally made a goddess of her. The most celebrated of all ancient paintings was Zeuxis's portrait of Helen, called *Helen Hetaira* or *Helen the Courtesan*, which showed her preparing to receive Paris after he had been whisked to safety by Aphrodite; it was the first nude in the history of Western painting. No other ancient work inspired so many *ekphraseis* nor so many attempts at reconstruction. (The well-known anecdote of how Zeuxis selected the best features of five beauties can be consulted in Livy.) This lascivious subject was commissioned by the temple of Hera Lakinia at Crotona.[7] An erotic painting for a temple! Not just any temple, moreover, but that of Hera, who never commits adultery, and detests in equal measure Aphrodite and Helen, the goddess of desire and her mortal embodiment. One might well ask whether Greek thought in its maturity acknowledged nothing beyond the religion of beauty and pleasure. Homer's vision is subtler, if less adult. Might makes right, as Paris understood when facing Menelaus in the battle La Fontaine saw as little more than a village cockfight (see the epigraph to the present section).

It was easier for the moralists to deem Paris a rake and praise Hector as the heroic defender of his country, if not a saber-rattler. The scene between Paris and Helen in the third book of the *Iliad* was unknown as a subject until Gavin Hamilton devoted a cycle of paintings on the ceilings of the Villa Borghese in Rome to the story of Paris (1780–85); David then painted the lovers (Salon of 1789, Musée du Louvre). The scene is a riot of sensuality and pleasure liable to enflame the imagination of the students; it was thought better to bring on the virile Hector and have Paris shamed by him. The École students thus gave evidence of their various temperaments as they succumbed to either virtue or eroticism. The sketch by Félix-Henry Auvray (1823; cat. no. 39) imitates David's work in showing an idle and effeminate Paris—whereas Homer describes him polishing his arms—while Helen's transparent robe is distinctly First Empire in style. Like the École's ever more languid models, Paris is led on by a Helen increasingly conscious of the powers of her femininity in transparent veils. Perhaps the scene is set after Aphrodite has passed by? We know that in Homeric Greek the goddess's name was a synonym for the sexual act.

Antoine-Louis Barye's plaster sketch in low relief (cat. no. 40) won a prize in the same year as Auvray's painting. It has no moral lesson to teach; the influence of Flaxman (who treated this subject in the *Iliad*, bk. 6, engraving 10) was important in this respect, for his style

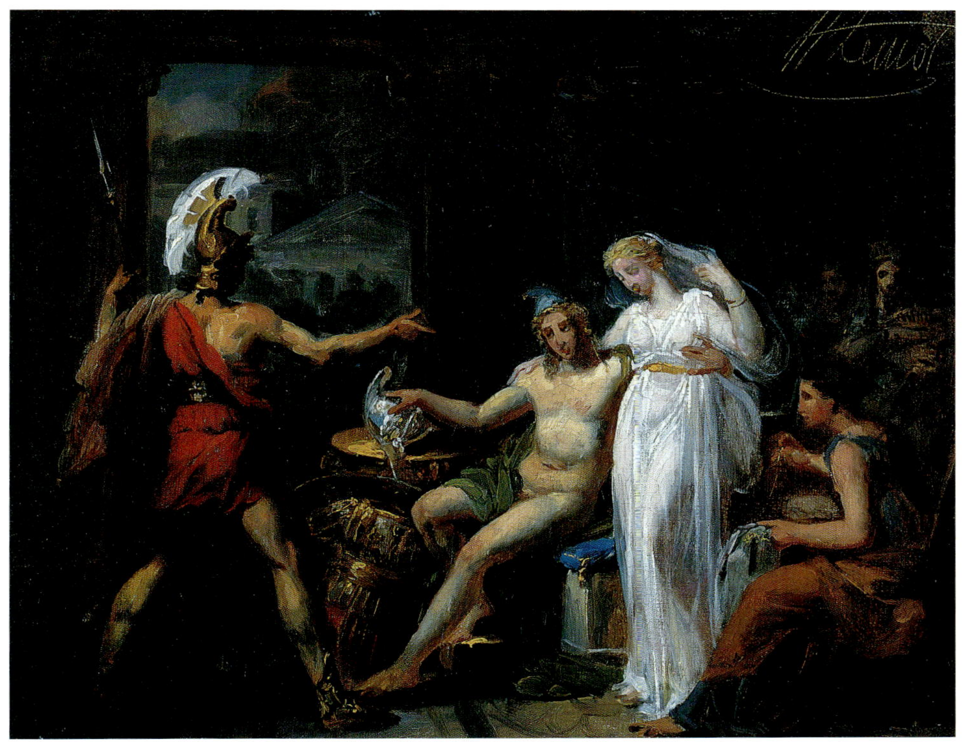

CATALOGUE NO. 39 | FÉLIX-HENRY AUVRAY (1800–1833), *Hector Reproaches Paris*, 1823. Oil on tracing paper mounted on canvas, 32.5 × 40.5 cm.

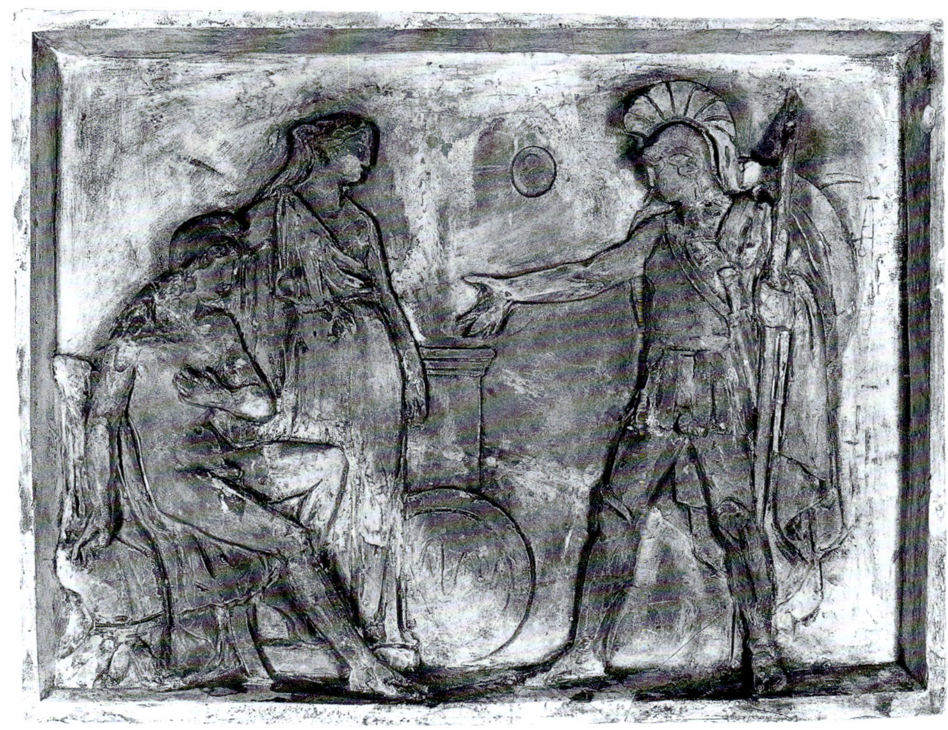

CATALOGUE NO. 40 | ANTOINE-LOUIS BARYE (1796–1875), *Hector Reproaches Paris*, 1823. Plaster, 33.5 × 45 cm.

remains reserved even at its most moving and shielded the sculptors from too sentimental or moralizing an approach. The three protagonists are rather lifeless; it is hard to imagine this is a conversation about war. Helen listens, Paris is defiant, and Hector assumes as much weight and conviction as his two interlocutors combined. The expression of sensuality—Ovid's reading of Homer—was the province of painting. Sculpture—in this case a very lightly incised relief—inherited for two long centuries the rhetoric Virgil imposed on Homer. The confrontation between Hector and Paris is thus governed by the duel between the two principal descendants of Homer, Ovid and Virgil. When the two winning sketches were exhibited side by side, the École teachers could congratulate themselves. The combination of these two perfectly contradictory visions constituted an equivalent of Homer's verses. For in Homer, too, the lovers' words indicate their acquiescence in Hector's recrimination, while their bodies and poses tell quite another story, as do the gods who animate them.

Hector and Andromache

Before returning to the fray, Hector wishes to see his wife and son. Let us follow him as he twice crosses the city, first to his palace, which he finds empty, then to the Scaean gates, where his anxious wife is hoping to see the battle. In the very place where Helen had shown herself to the crowds a few days earlier, Hector briefly stands apart from the fracas of war and remote from the time of men and gods:

> She joined him now, and following in her steps
> a servant holding the boy against her breast,
> in the first flush of life, only a baby,
> Hector's son, the darling of his eyes
> and radiant as a star . . .
> Hector would always call the boy Scamandrius,
> townsmen called him Astyanax, Lord of the City,
> since Hector was the lone defense of Troy.
> The great man of war breaking into a broad smile,
> his gaze fixed on his son, in silence. Andromache,
> pressing close beside him and weeping freely now,
> clung to his hand, urged him, called him . . .
> —*IL.* 6.339–406; F 6.471–82

Husband, wife, and child: as if demarcating scenes for future artists, Homer has each, in turn, take the stage. Andromache begs her husband to stay out of harm's way. Hector knows he cannot comply, that his duty condemns her to widowhood and slavery. Servitude and solitude are his terrifying predictions. In Homer premonitions of disaster are invariably realized, whereas expectations of happiness come to nothing. Hector's pessimism is expressed in a gesture: he holds out his arms for his son. Gazing at his child, is he thinking of the future to which he has just condemned him or does he seek solace from those thoughts in the embrace of a child to whom the cruelty of the world is still unknown? A few steps below them Europe and Asia angrily collide; here two sensitive adults—in the time it takes to speak a few words—create their own little world of reason and peace. The reaction of a babe at the breast, his parents' laughter, the plume on a shiny helmet—in these things the human condition is forever summed up:

> In the same breath, shining Hector reached down
> for his son—but the boy recoiled,
> cringing against his nurse's full breast,
> screaming out at the sight of his own father,
> terrified by the flashing bronze, the horsehair crest,
> the great ridge of the helmet nodding, bristling terror—
> so it struck his eyes. And his loving father laughed,
> his mother laughed as well, and glorious Hector,
> quickly lifting the helmet from his head,
> set it down on the ground, fiery in the sunlight,
> and raising his son he kissed him, tossed him in his arms,
> lifting a prayer to Zeus and the other deathless gods:
> "Zeus, all you immortals! Grant this boy, my son,
> may be like me, first in glory among the Trojans,
> strong and brave like me, and rule all Troy in power
> and one day let them say, 'He is a better man than his father!'—

when he comes home from battle bearing the bloody
gear
of the mortal enemy he has killed in war—
a joy to his mother's heart."
—*IL.* 6.466–81; F 6.556–74

The spite shown by the Greek gods to mortals is notorious. None of Hector's wishes for Astyanax will be realized, and nothing could be less predictable than Andromache's destiny: a long life combining the worst misfortunes with eventual domestic contentment. The gods, however, will soon relish the sight of the son of Achilles hurling the son of Hector from the ramparts of Troy. No man can trust the future, which belongs to the immortals alone and can only be wrested from their hands by cunning. Their petty jealousy is triggered by so little: a man who holds his son in his arms and wishes he will grow to be a brave man. Hector's words echo vainly in the void of his future, but his gestures speak forever to the artist's heart.

The scene has often been illustrated in French art from the seventeenth century onward.[8] No painter dared be less than serious,[9] particularly since the scene follows Hector's reproaches to Paris. Caylus subtly analyzed the difference in subjects for painters and sculptors. He divided the scene into two tableaux: "The picture of Hector, Andromache, and the nurse who carries Astyanax is simple and full of interest; the location of the scene at the foot of the wall of a battlefield makes it still more touching." He continues: "The farewell of Hector; the intimate pain of a husband and wife, varied as they are by sex and character; the fear of the child at the sight of the plume—all these things produce a composition that has been seen more than once but which will always merit the attention of painters. . . . [I]t cannot be too often undertaken."

Sculptors surely found it easier than painters to show how the child assures the equilibrium of gestures, glances, and feelings of this tripartite meeting. The young Jean-Baptiste Carpeaux, winner of the Prix de Rome for Sculpture in 1854 (cat. no. 41), perfectly grasped the sculptural nature of Caylus's second

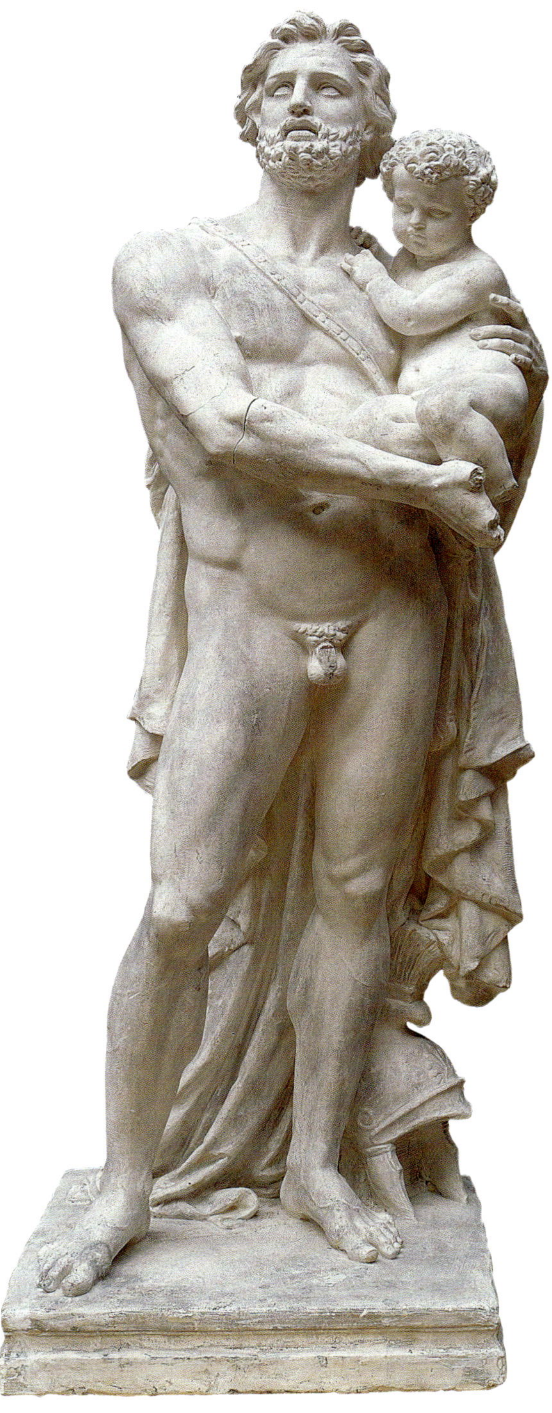

CATALOGUE NO. 41 | JEAN-BAPTISTE CARPEAUX (1827–1875), *Hector Holding His Son Astyanax in His Arms*, 1854. Plaster, 131 × 51 × 48 cm.

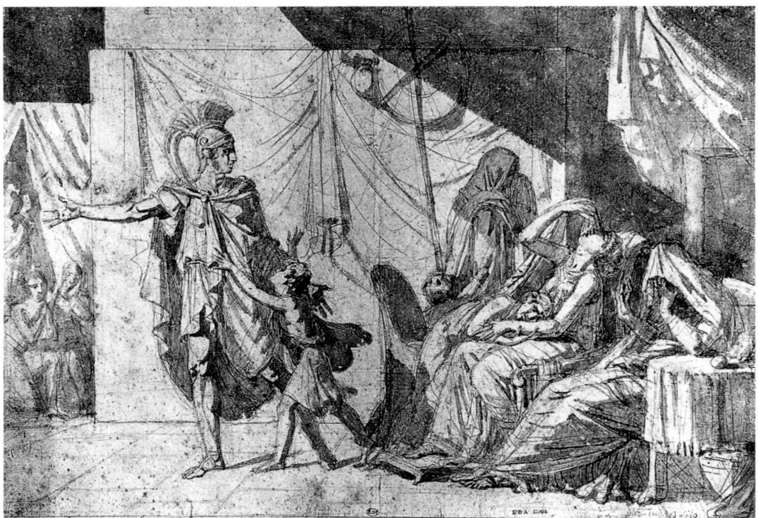

FIGURE 41 | JEAN-AUGUSTE-DOMINIQUE INGRES (1780–1867), *Hector and Andromache*, 1801. Graphite and ink on paper, 35.3 × 51 cm.

picture. The fluttering of the helmet plume frightens not just the child but the sculptor; a poet of immobility, he cannot accommodate its movement. But a moment later, motion has ceased, the warrior's helmet is put aside, and the son is hugged to a warrior's body, now crowned by the familiar features of the father. Although the menacing sounds of battle still float over the city walls, catastrophe is momentarily held at bay. For comparison, a clumsy drawing by Ingres shows how far one can go in attenuating Homer's thought (fig. 41). Linked to Ingres's first attempt at the Prix de Rome (1801), it shows little Astyanax holding back his helmeted father (not, as Homer says, flinching away from him), while Andromache and the nurse weep where they sit. Everything is lacking: laughter, intelligence, and sensitivity. Ingres is not even faithful to the text, which continues:

> So Hector prayed
> and placed his son in the arms of his loving wife . . .
> Hector aflash in arms
> took up his horsehair-crested helmet once again.
> And his loving wife went home, turning, glancing
> back again and again and weeping live warm tears.
> —*IL.* 6.482–83, 494–95; F 6.575–77, 589–92

There is realism enough in Ingres's drawing of a child clutching at his father's clothes and a wife sitting disconsolate at home, but they have nothing to do with Homer, whose outdoor tête-à-tête with babe in arms offers a telling denunciation of both war and the weapons by which a father accidentally terrifies his son. Leaving his mother's lap, Ingres's Astyanax is unabashed by his father's helmet, while his mother imitates the mourning gestures of a greater Andromache, the one painted by Ingres's master, David. Poor Hector, meanwhile, gesticulates like a general in an operetta. Carpeaux's success is first and foremost that of Homer, to whom he has carefully attended. He paid scant attention to the judges' instructions, which insisted on Hector's heroic address to the gods. In this scene Homer transforms the ingredients of epic, turning them into emotion and beauty. Our fate may be in the hands of the gods, but in Homer's vision an object like the helmet, a speech like Hector's prayer, and a stance like that of a laughing father picking up his child are sufficient to show the gods that the present moment is all our own.

Andromache and the Body of Hector

With Hector's departure to fight and kill Patroclus, Achilles resumes the starring role. He kills Hector. Dragged in the dust by Achilles' chariot, cast to the dogs, protected by the immortals, lamented by the women, Hector's body becomes the center of the poem, the very image of human tragedy. Priam brings the body back to Troy. The funeral car is met by Hector's mother Hecuba, his sister Cassandra, and his wife Andromache in a public and official display of grief that long predominated in the artists' visions. Then Hector's body is laid out in his palace, where Homer gives the mourning scenes a private and poetic tone echoing the warrior's farewell to his family in the sixth book.

In that scene Hector and Andromache foresaw that death would soon sever their destinies. Now the grim prediction has been fulfilled. To the immortal scene of the waving plume succeed the lamentations of women mourning the dead. The mother and child who testified to the dignity of life can now, in David's painting, do no more than bewail the tragic fate of all mortals (cat. no. 42). This is one of the most supremely tragic paintings in the history of art. Although the first artist to restore this subject to life was probably the Scottish painter Gavin Hamilton in his *Iliad* cycle on the ceiling of the Villa Borghese, in 1783 David gave it a denser and more Homeric form.

> Once they had borne him
> into the famous halls, they laid his body down
> on his large carved bed and set beside him singers
> to lead off the laments, and their voices rose in grief—
> they lifted the dirge high as the women wailed in
> answer.
> And white-armed Andromache led their songs of
> sorrow,
> cradling the head of Hector, man-killing Hector
> gently in her arms: "O my husband . . .
> cut off from life so young! You leave me a widow,
> lost in the royal halls—and the boy only a baby,
> the son we bore together, you and I so doomed.
> I cannot think he will ever come to manhood.
> Long before *that* the city will be sacked,
> plundered top to bottom! Because you are dead,
> her great guardian, you who always defended Troy,
> who kept her loyal wives and helpless children safe,
> all who will soon be carried off in the hollow ships
> and I with them—
> And you, my child, will follow me
> to labor, somewhere, at harsh, degrading work,
> slaving under some heartless master's eye—that,
> or some Achaean marauder will seize you by the arm
> and hurl you headlong down from the ramparts—
> horrible death—
> enraged at *you* because Hector once cut down his
> brother,
> his father or his son, yes, hundreds of armed
> Achaeans
> gnawed the dust of the world, crushed by Hector's
> hands!
> Your father, remember, was no man of mercy . . .
> not in the horror of battle, and that is why
> the whole city of Troy mourns you now, my Hector—
> you've brought your parents accursed tears and grief
> but to me most of all you've left the horror, the
> heartbreak!"
> —*IL.* 24.719–45; F 24.845–74

The poet then describes the tears of Hector's mother, his slaves, and even those of Helen. As in every scene of lamentation, these mourners grieve as much for themselves as for their hero, as much for their future as for their present loss. Death itself has lost much of its horror; the gods have protected the body from either disintegrating as it was towed around Troy by Achilles or decomposing thereafter. The body tortured by the chariot of Achilles but cleansed by the gods has stiffened and no more aspires to immortal life than do his widow and son. All strain toward life, Hector in his last convulsion, his wife and son in their mutual love. To the warrior is left nothing but an ironic laurel crown honoring the vanquished, while his widow calls on the onlooker to bear witness to the injustice of the gods. Echoing the millenarian funeral traditions of the Mediterranean, Homer's mourning scenes are more hectic than the moments of happiness over which calm presides. At moments when everything seems to celebrate life, Homer senses the presence of death. But in the presence of death David follows in Homer's footsteps and recalls the beauty of life. In the scene of lament Homer effectively evokes the entire history of his characters. By presenting Andromache's memories within the composition, David does the same.

His work refers to Raphael, Poussin, Greuze, and an ancient sarcophagus relief of *The Death of Meleager*. This display of erudition, however, does not diminish the tragic eloquence of the reliefs painted on the deathbed. They depict Hector and Andromache's

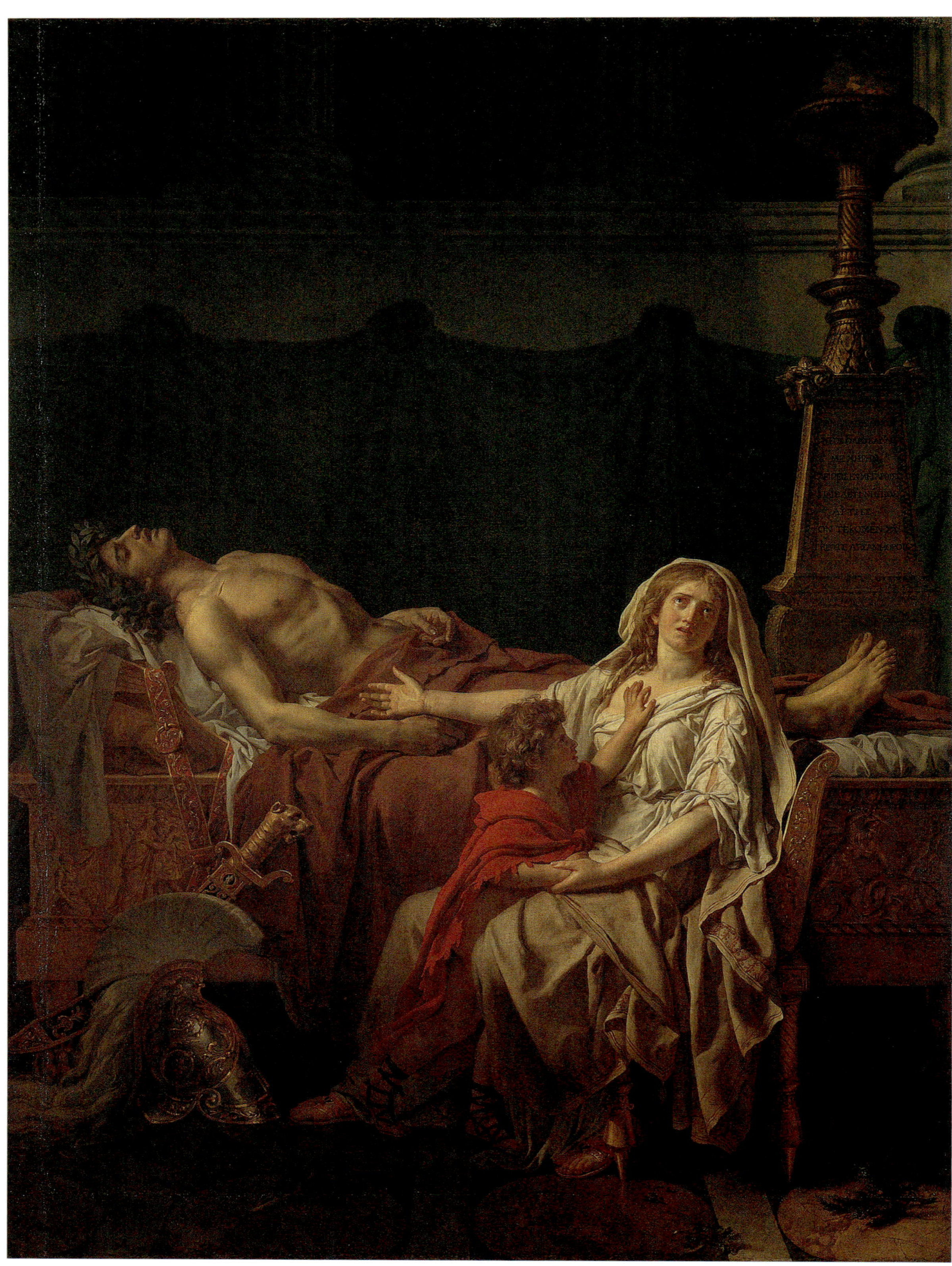

farewell and the death of Hector; thus, along with the subject of the painting, they present the three scenes that Homer devoted to the most humane couple of the *Iliad*. The inscriptions scattered in the painting discreetly proclaim the grandeur of the tragedy. The ever more sober and concentrated techniques of expression employed in the age of David contrast with the bitterly precious eloquence of Racine. The three protagonists are imprisoned in the grid of tiles, curtains, and columns. Everything external weighs down on and crushes the deformed torso of the corpse. Conversely, everything private—the plumed helmet, the bed, and the gestures of mother and child—recalls family scenes, above all the one described earlier. This is the meaning of tragedy: the confrontation between the world of others and individual happiness threatened or (as here) destroyed. David the reader of Homer brings his own commentary to David the painter, inscribing on the candleholder verses 725–27 of the twenty-fourth book of the *Iliad*:

ΑΝΕΡ ΑΠΑΙΩΝΟΣ
ΝΕΟΣ ΩΛΕΟ ΚΑΔΔΕ
ΜΕ ΧΗΡΗΝ
ΛΕΙΠΕΙΣ ΕΝ ΜΕΓΑΡΟΙΣΙ
ΠΑΙΣ ΔΕΤΙ ΝΗΠΙΟΣ
ΑΥΤΩΣ
ΟΝ ΤΕΚΟΜΕΝ ΣΥ
ΤΕΓΩ ΤΕ ΔΥΣΑΜΜΟΡΟΙ

[O my husband . . .
cut off from life so young!
You leave me a widow,
lost in the royal halls—
and the boy only a baby,
the son we bore together,
you and I so doomed. (F 24.852–55)]

Present, past, father, mother, child, and destiny: David here attempts in painting what Aeschylus, Sophocles, and Euripides had accomplished in drama. He extracts from the words of Homer the very essence of tragedy.

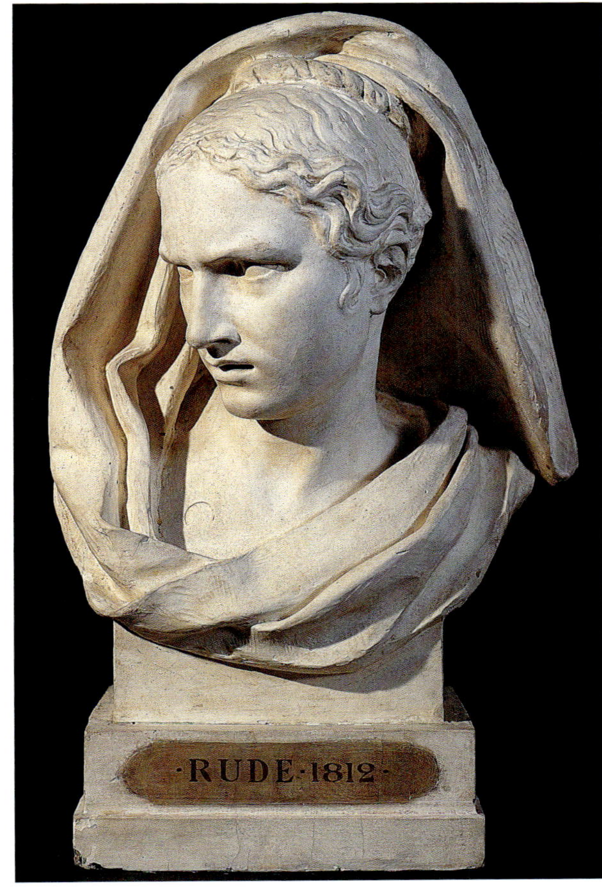

CATALOGUE NO. 43 | FRANÇOIS RUDE (1784–1855), *Attention Mingled with Fear (Andromache)*, 1812. Plaster, 66.5 × 39.5 × 31 cm.

A few years later, François Rude took part in the Expressive Head *concours* of 1812. The subject of his plaster bust (cat. no. 43) was *Attention Mingled with Fear*. The live model who posed for this test no doubt deliberately assumed the role of Andromache meditating on the fate of her son. Or perhaps Rude himself imagined the destiny of Andromache, the better to animate his study of apprehension. Comparison with a bust of Andromache by François Milhomme (now in the Louvre, RF 3521) suggests that in the minds of cultivated artists, tragedy as a whole now assumed the features of Andromache, just as Achilles embodied heroism. Taking his cue from Homer, Euripides

OPPOSITE CATALOGUE NO. 42 | JACQUES-LOUIS DAVID (1748–1825), *Andromache Mourning Hector*, 1783. Oil on canvas, 275 × 203 cm.

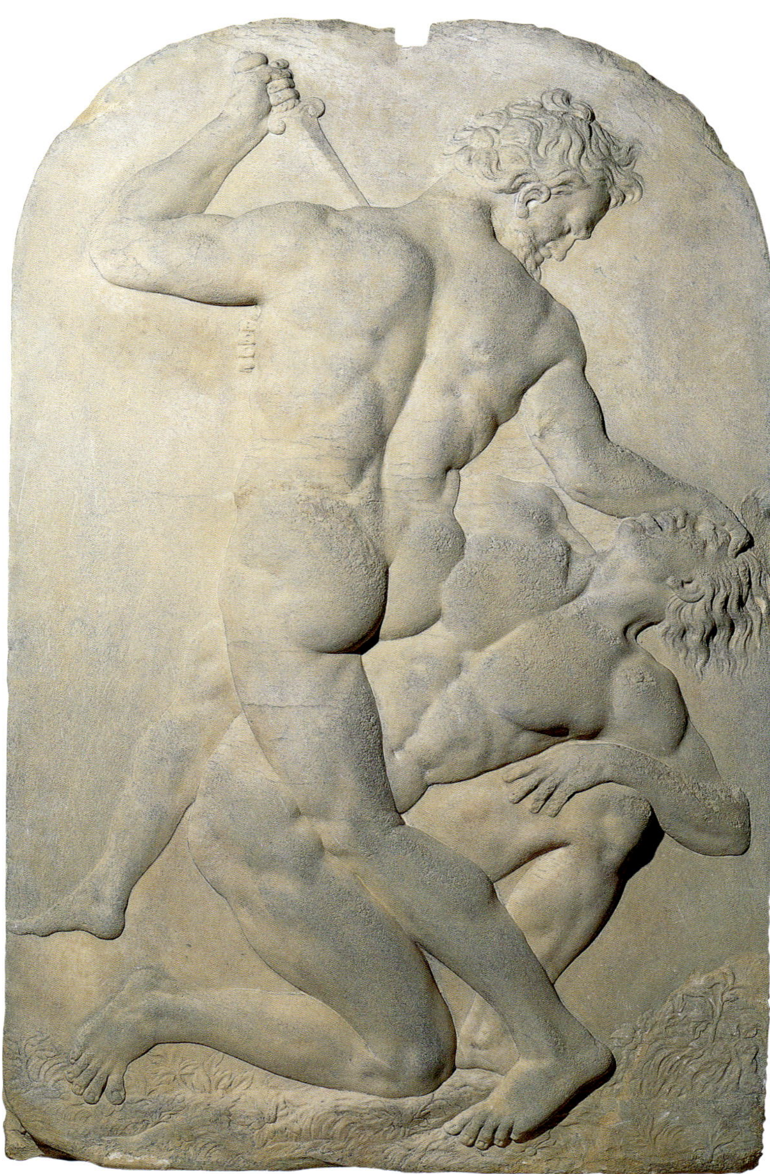

CATALOGUE NO. 44 | PIERRE II LEGROS (1666–1719), *Combat of Athletes or Gladiators* (or *Combat of Hercules and Antaeus*). Marble, 80 × 50 cm.

brought to life on the stage the lucid grief of the captive Trojan women. The actress who interpreted *Attention Mingled with Fear* for Rude—or Rude himself—now read the subject of the *concours* as Euripides read Homer. The lineaments of his Andromache articulate an impulse of revolt; suffering and intelligence have lent a far-seeing quality to her eyes, which fearfully contemplate the suffering to come. In art and poetry alike, warriors' widows know all there is to know of human tragedy.

Sports and Contenders

Ajax, son of Telamon, plays a grotesquely heroic role in the *Iliad*—that of a warrior unable to make the most of his physical advantages. His successive disappointments are tabulated in legend and Homer repeats them. On several occasions the great Ajax—he who wounded Hector during the wrath of Achilles, when everything seemingly favored the Trojan; he who recovered Patroclus's body from the enemy—had to face an enemy more redoubtable even than Hector: the jealousy of his friends.

Ajax takes part in all the games organized beneath the walls of Troy. Although he never wins, his defeats are always the product of his opponents' cunning rather than their valor. The first such combat takes place at the games for Patroclus's funeral. In the wrestling match

> . . . Odysseus never missed a trick—
> he kicked him behind the knee, clipping the hollow,
> cut his legs from under him, knocked him
> backward—
> —*IL.* 23.726–27; F 23.806–8

Whether or not Odysseus is the better wrestler, Achilles, judge and referee of the contest, deems it prudent not to name a winner. The next contest is with the pike, and Ajax is pitted against Diomedes. Stop the contest! Ajax is nearly disemboweled. The obscure Polypoetes defeats Ajax at the discus. The worst humiliation, however, still awaits him. After the fall of Troy, Achilles' mother, Thetis, offers his arms to the Greek who inspired the greatest fear in the Trojans. Ajax, who had come so close to killing Hector, was the obvious candidate; but he was foolish enough to allow the verdict to be entrusted to the Trojans, who took revenge on their worst surviving enemy by nominating someone else. Thus, the cunning Odysseus came by Achilles' arms. Literally maddened by this judgment, Ajax massacred the cattle of the Greeks under the delusion that they were his Trojan enemies and fell on his sword when he awoke from his illusion the following day. When he met the tragic Ajax in the Underworld, Odysseus attempted in vain to explain his absurd death to him:

> Now the rest of the ghosts, the dead and gone
> Came swarming up around me—deep in sorrow there,
> each asking about the grief that touched him most.
> Only the ghost of Great Ajax, son of Telamon,
> kept his distance, blazing with anger at me still
> for the victory I had won by the ships that time
> I pressed my claim for the arms of Prince Achilles.
> —*OD.* 11.541–46; F 11.617–23

I like to read the representations of this infantile squabble, this contest of human simulacra, as continuous with one trend in Greek poetry—that which, from Homer to Euripides, sees half the poets denouncing the stupidity of sporting competitions while the other half follows Pindar's lead in celebrating the victors.

Ajax was better served in subsequent art and literature than in Homer. Sophocles ennobled his madness, and in the sixteenth century his glory rivaled that of Achilles to the point where, in Shakespeare's *Troilus and Cressida*, it even serves to belittle Achilles. His madness came to have greater resonance than even that of Orestes since it taught him to perceive the world through the eyes of solitude, unconstrained by vengeance or remorse. Engravings often illustrated the Shakespearean sentiments spoken by Sophocles' mad warrior:

> Strangely the long and countless drift of time
> Brings all things forth from darkness into light,
> Then covers them once more. Nothing so marvelous
> That man can say it surely will not be.[10]

Madness teaches Ajax what neither fury nor bereavement can instill in Achilles: the sense that his existence is linked to that of others. He looks into his own heart, and what he sees there drives him—like Hamlet, Macbeth, or Richard II—to seek his own destruction. In comparison with Odysseus, the man of action, and Achilles, the master of indecision, Ajax, the least intelligent of the three, asks the most vertiginous questions.

Ah, happy times, when sport gave rise to such profound contemplation! The athletic, literary, and even poetic posterity of these first sporting contests is all too evident—from the ancient games to the poetry of Pindar, the *Medici Wrestlers* (Galleria degli Uffizi, Florence), and innumerable academic studies of wrestling models. An example of the latter is a marble relief probably sculpted by Pierre II Legros (cat. no. 44). Academies loved the gratuitous drama of wrestlers, the pitiless tension of the muscles barely veiling the handsome futility of their efforts. We do not know the provenance of the École's splendid wrestlers, but we can be sure that their origins lie in the *Iliad*'s sporting contests, and that behind them a raucous crowd of spectators both mortal and immortal is cheering them on. Legros's wrestlers take up poses worthy of Homer; their daggers might belong to royal musketeers, and their nudity is clearly that of Academy models. The tragic power of these straining muscles is no doubt bestowed by mythology, by the combat of man and earth, figured, for example, in the hand-to-hand combat of Hercules and Antaeus. The standing wrestler crushes his victim beneath a series of sinuous curves, while his victim molds his body to the rock, the better to draw from it the strength to rise again.

When by chance Ulysses stumbles into the village discus-throwing competition of the Phaeacians, he enjoys a powerful advantage: the assistance of the

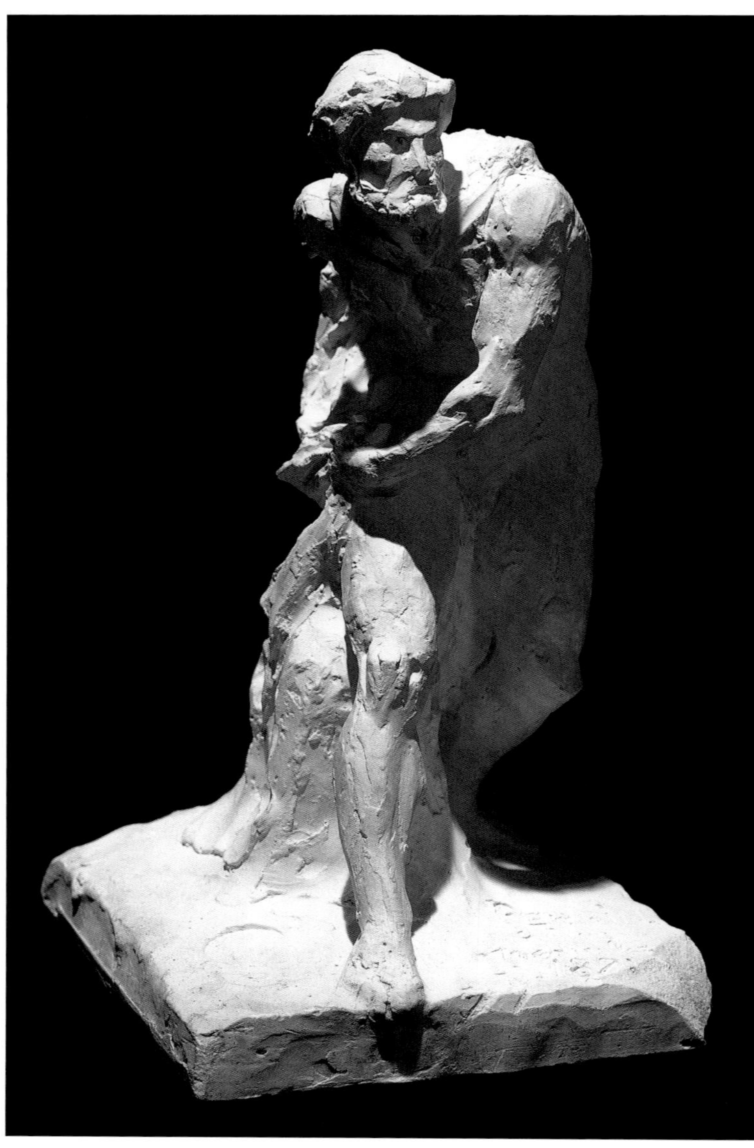

CATALOGUE NO. 45 | JACQUES PERRIN (1847–1915), *Ulysses Throwing the Discus*, 1871. Plaster, 36 × 20.5 × 21 cm.

goddess Athena. He cannot resist the chance to shine among these poor provincial athletes:

> "I'm no stranger to sports—for all your taunts—
>
> But now I'm wrestled down by pain and hardship, look,
> I've borne my share of struggles, cleaving my way
> through wars of men and pounding waves at sea.
> Nevertheless, despite so many blows,
> I'll compete in your games, just watch. Your insults
> Cut to the quick—you rouse my fighting blood!"
>
> Up he sprang, cloak and all, and seized a discus,
> huge and heavy, more weighty by far than those
> the Phaeacians used to hurl and test each other.
> Wheeling round, he let loose with his great hand
> and the stone whirred on—and down to ground they went
> those lords of the long oars and master mariners cringing
> under the rock's onrush, soaring lightly out of his grip,
> flying away past all the other marks . . .
> —*OD.* 8.179, 182–93; F 8.207–23

Homer, however, records the significant detail that Athena was measuring the throws. No wonder he wins with such ease! In Jacques Perrin's *Ulysses Throwing the Discus* of 1871 (cat. no. 45) there is inadvertent humor in the damage done to Odysseus's boasts by the shrinking of the plaster. The muscles have been tightened, but the face of the improvised discus thrower has wrinkled. With the aid of his suborned referee, the great talker Odysseus has for two millennia convinced us he was a true athlete. A little later he turned from the discus to archery, but that takes us back to the sanguinary concerns of epic.

NOTES

1 Pierre de Ronsard, "Gayetez" (Gayeté III), in *Oeuvres complètes*, rev. ed., 2 vols., ed. Jean Céard (Paris, 1994), 1:329.

2 Jean Giraudoux, *The War of Troy Shall Not Take Place*, trans. Christopher Fry (London, 1983), 71.

3 Comte A.-C.-P. de Caylus, *Tableaux tirés de l'Iliade, de l'Odyssée d'Homère et de l'Énéide de Virgile, avec des observations générales sur le costume* (Paris, 1757), 26.

4 Gotthold Ephraim Lessing, *Laocoön: An Essay on the Limits of Painting and Poetry*, rev. ed., trans. E. A. McCormick (Baltimore, Md., 1984), 115 (chap. 22).

5 Giraudoux, *The War of Troy Shall Not Take Place*, 25, 14, 15. [The verses cited are eccentric, as Hector himself observes in the play, and Christopher Fry's translation reflects this. Trans.]

6 Ibid., 67.

7 Cicero, *De Inventione* 2, 1, 1.

8 See Dora Wiebenson, "Subjects from Homer's 'Iliad' in Neoclassical Art," *Art Bulletin* 46, no. 1 (March 1964): 27.

9 See Helge Siefert, *Themen aus Homers Ilias in der französischen Kunst (1750–1831)* (Munich, 1988), 113–20.

10 Sophocles, *Ajax*, trans. D. Grene, 646–48, in *The Complete Greek Tragedies*, vol. 3, *Sophocles: Ajax, The Women of Trachis, Electra, and Philoctetes* (1957; paperback rpt. Chicago, 1969), 31–32.

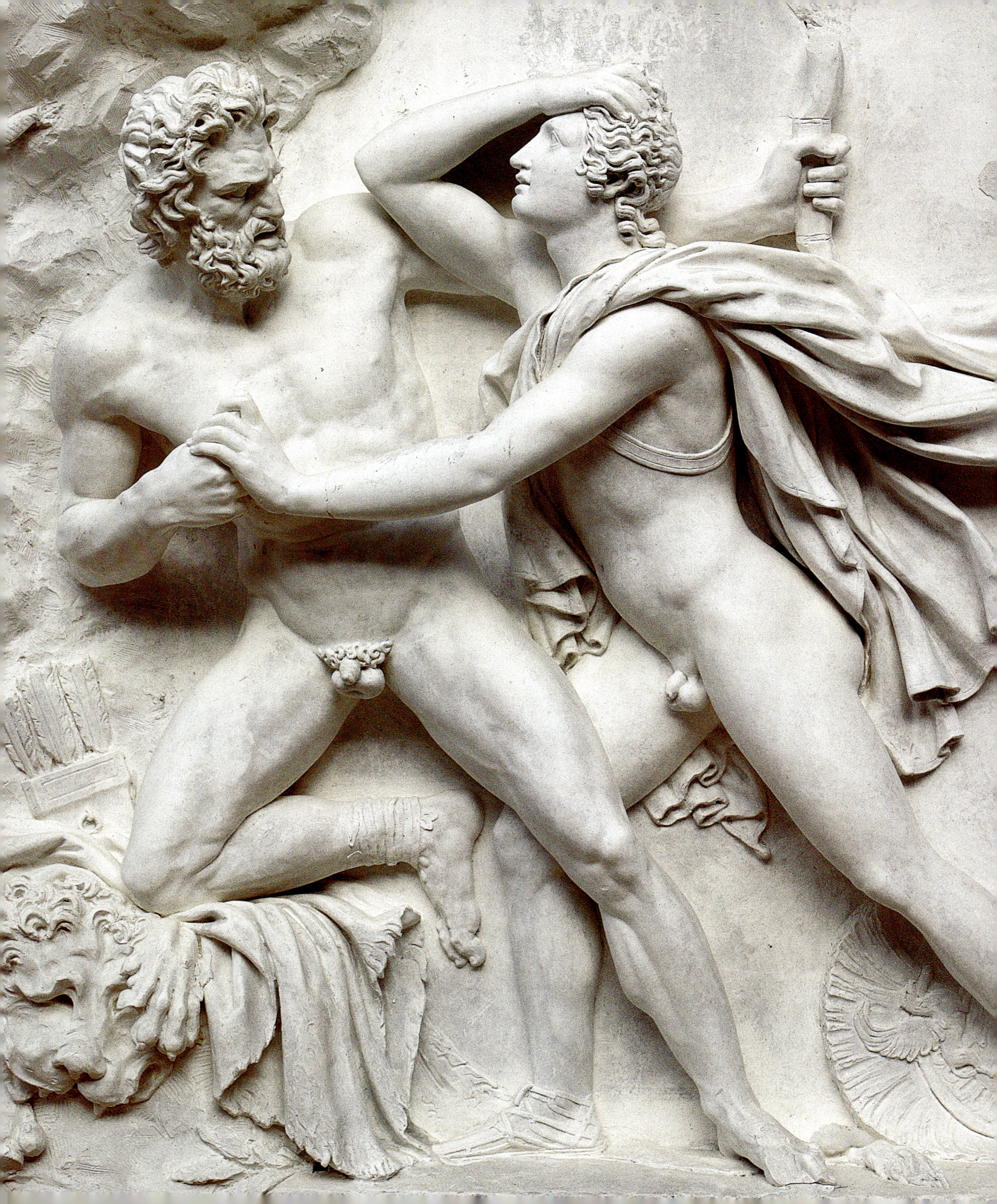

Philoctetes

Not all Greece decamped to the plain of Troy. In the Greek palaces remained the parents, wives, and children of the princes. Ten years passed, during which some of them died, while others grew bored or consoled themselves for the absence of the head of the family.

Among the great absentees of the *Iliad*, Homer dramatically isolated that jinxed and maladroit warrior, the archer Philoctetes. In the second book of the *Iliad* Homer sets out his fate with characteristic irony and verve:

> Then men who lived in Methone and Thaumacia,
> men who held Meliboea and rugged ridged Olizon:
> Philoctetes the master archer had led them on
> in seven ships with fifty oarsmen aboard each,
> superbly skilled with the bow in lethal combat.
> But their captain lay on an island, racked with pain,
> on Lemnos' holy shores where the armies had marooned him,
> agonized by his wound, the bite of a deadly water-viper.
> There he writhed in pain but soon, encamped by the ships,
> the Argives would recall Philoctetes, their great king.
>
> —IL. 716–25; F 2.817–26

Homer's allusive lines suggest that the legend of Philoctetes was already well established. Philoctetes had inherited his bow from Hercules as a reward for having kindled the pyre on which Hercules, suffering horribly from the tunic soaked in Nessus's blood, had ended his own life. The bow was Philoctetes' reward and made him the best Achaean archer, for in this specialization he exceeded Odysseus himself (*Od.* 8.219). Hercules' last request was that the place of his death should never be known. Philoctetes broke his promise and spent ten years expiating his sin. Having sued for Helen's hand, he, too, set sail to restore her to Menelaus but was wounded en route either by a hydra, a serpent, or one of his own poisoned arrows (on this point the traditions vary). Because his wound stank, or because his cries offended the sensitive ears of Odysseus and the Achaeans, he was marooned on the desert island of Lemnos. Odysseus doubtless instigated this dereliction. Priam's son Helenus—a prophet like his twin sister Cassandra—was another of Helen's suitors. Disappointed in love, he betrayed his city ten years later (the duration of the siege) by revealing to the Greeks that they could take Troy only with the aid of Hercules' bow. The noblest literary portrayal of Philoctetes is provided by Sophocles' tragedy of that name and recounts the attempts of Odysseus, ever the Hellenic ambassador, to recover Hercules' invincible weapon. Odysseus's companion was Achilles' son, Neoptolemus. They were carefully chosen envoys. The expeditionary force that marooned Philoctetes had set sail before Neoptolemus was of military age; his presence would

DETAIL OF CATALOGUE NO. 49

counterbalance that of the totally cynical Ulysses, who had first suggested abandoning the archer and could hardly expect a favorable reception. It was agreed from the start that if Philoctetes refused to hand the bow over, some fraud would be contrived.

Sophocles bestowed on Philoctetes a grandeur like that of the Athenian democracy, at a time when it was establishing the historical paradigm of the free city-state. According to the playwright, the archer was wounded by one of his own arrows, which Hercules had dipped in the blood of the Lernean Hydra. But his spirit, too, is wounded. For ten years he nurses his resentment of the comrades-at-arms who have deserted him, and when they reappear he has not the slightest desire to oblige them, instead rejoicing at their defeat. Odysseus recognizes the archer's rancor and withdraws in favor of Neoptolemus. The younger man does indeed win the archer's trust. Having promised to return Philoctetes to his native country, he receives the bow. He even prepares to take him onto the ship, which will take him not to Greece but to Troy. Philoctetes has a sudden intuition of his own naïveté. Discovering that the ship is that of his archenemy, he refuses to set sail. Neoptolemus is struck with remorse and returns the bow and arrows, whereupon Odysseus steps forward to meet the hatred of Philoctetes. The bow is aimed at the man who has duped him twice, but Hercules, purged of mortality on the pyre, looks down from Olympus and persuades his friend to rejoin the Greek army. Philoctetes therefore sets sail. In Troy his wound is treated by Machaon (see the relief by Jean-Antoine Idrac, Grand Prix winner in 1873; fig. 42) and his bow proves instrumental in the eventual victory of the Greeks. His arrow kills Paris and, according to the *Odyssey*, Philoctetes joyfully returns to his native city.

No one attaches any importance to the *Hercules ex machina* of Sophocles' *Philoctetes*, and, with the exception of that episode, the course of Philoctetes' life owes nothing at all to the gods; it is comprised entirely of his own deeds and those of others. No other Homeric figure combines heroism with physical weakness. None is so profoundly alone. Only Philoctetes is consumed with pain and rancor.

In the eighteenth century, when sensitive souls delighted as much in their own tears as in those of others, Philoctetes seemed the most touching of classical warriors. But the archer bellowing and writhing with pain was soon eclipsed in artistic contemplation by the silent suffering of Laocoön. Lessing nevertheless devoted the first and fourth chapters of his legendary study not to Laocoön, a character largely without literary resonance, but to the imprecations Philoctetes hurls at his fellow men: "High as Homer raises his heroes above human nature in other respects, they still remain faithful to it in their sensitivity to pain and injury and in the expression of this feeling by cries, tears or invectives."[1] It is not clear whether Lessing thought that Homer's characters were elevated "above human nature" only in combat, when it would be more appropriate to describe them as debased below common humanity. Certainly Philoctetes' cries drive his companions to flight more quickly than his arrows could, and they impart to him two forms of Promethean grandeur entirely lacking in Laocoön, namely, solitude and revolt.

Painters found in this solitary figure, silhouetted against his island seascape, a most satisfactory subject. Philoctetes on Lemnos and his archenemy Odysseus on the island of Calypso are the two products of Greek genius who suffer most from that melancholic self-loathing later known in French as *le spleen*. Philoctetes discovered this sentiment, little known to the Greeks, by focusing on the suffering of his own wounded body. In contrast to Odysseus, however, his solitude is defined not by boredom but by tragic obsession. The verses from the *Iliad* cited earlier must have read like a challenge to the Greek tragic poets. They perceived the nobility of our castaway and overheard in Homer's compassionate account the birth of "the individual" torn between the reassuring world of the city and the

FIGURE 42 | JEAN-ANTOINE IDRAC (1849–1884), *Philoctetes, Brought to the Camp of the Greeks by Ulysses and Neoptolemus, Is Attended by Machaon*, 1873. Plaster, 125 × 158 cm. Prix de Rome in Sculpture.

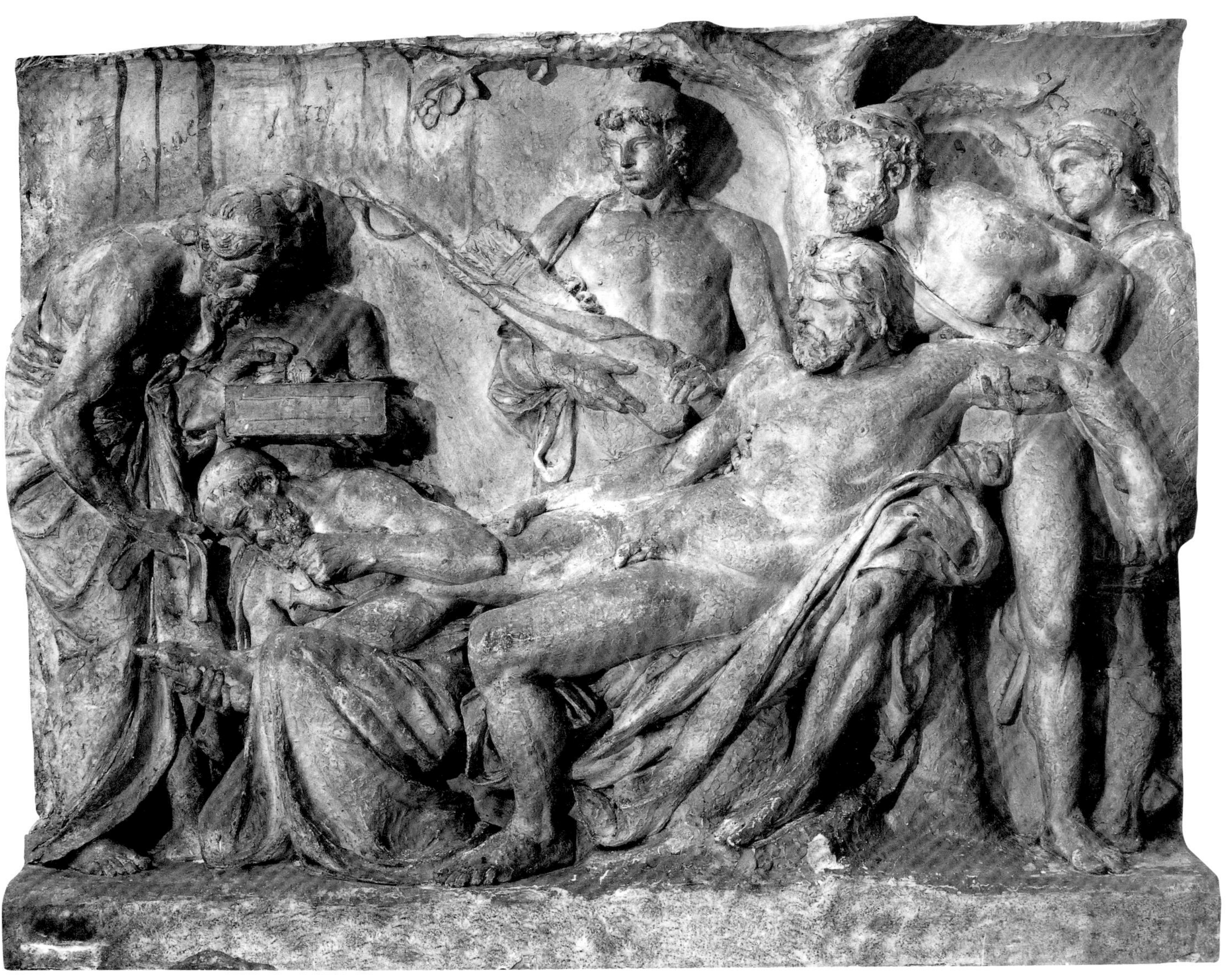

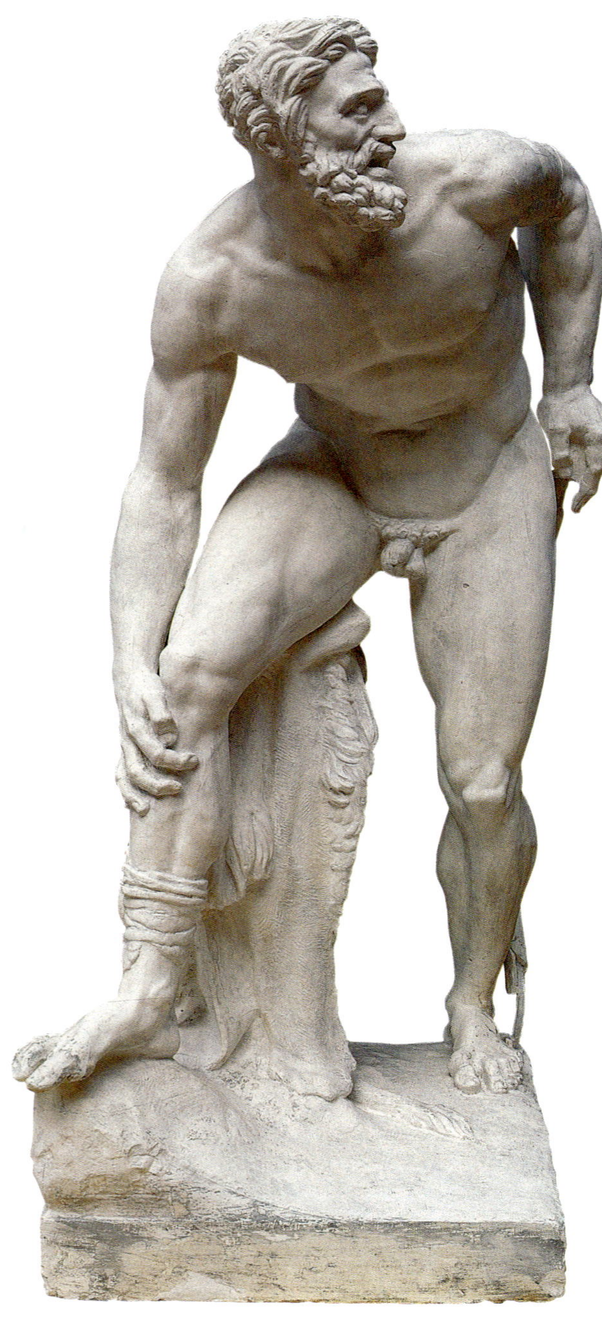

CATALOGUE NO. 46 | PIERRE-FRANÇOIS-GRÉGOIRE GIRAUD (1783–1836), *The Wounded Philoctetes on the Island of Lemnos*, 1806. Plaster, 96 × 37 × 43 cm.

vacant pride of solitude. Philoctetes stood at the heart of classical teaching in the Paris School; he was the subject of several *concours*, a strange figure in the pose of a wounded warrior, a silhouette romanticized by endlessly reawakened resentment. Having won the Grand Prix de l'Académie in 1784, Jean-Germain Drouais painted a monstrous and grotesque *Philoctetes* (1788; now in the Musée de Chartres) while still on scholarship in Rome. His archer is a veritable assemblage of disabilities, apparently combining the lameness of Philoctetes with the blindness of Homer and the suffering of Laocoön.

The evolution of sculpture at the École des beaux-arts during the first half of the nineteenth century is suggested by a succession of five images of Philoctetes. The hesitant young artists, influenced by changing fashions, contrived for Philoctetes an attractive but mutable appearance. Grégoire Giraud (1806, cat. no. 46) shows a man wounded but full of energy, whose rage is rooted not only in misanthropy but in physical pain. We see these pangs pass from the injured muscle to the clenched right hand, spreading through the powerful thigh until they find expression in the violent movements of the torso. The intelligence of the three Hellenistic sculptors of the *Laocoön* is conjoined with a reminiscence of Pierre Puget's *Milo*. The fate of the archer resembles that of the famous athlete, who similarly fell victim to the weaknesses of a body he had thought invulnerable. In the suffering of Milo of Crotona—his hand imprisoned by a tree he had rent apart in an act of sheer bravado—we see only the hubris of a fatuous sporting challenge. In Philoctetes, the poet and the young artist alike perceived suffering transmuted into energy, hatred, and inner freedom.

In the 1813 *concours* the young Genevan artist Jean-Jacques (James) Pradier was required to treat the last scene of Sophocles' tragedy, in which Philoctetes, perceiving Odysseus's wiles, brandishes his bow. He produced a harmonious sequence of refined figures in low relief (cat. no. 49). Neoptolemus is almost feminine; his legs intersect with those of Philoctetes, whose weight rests gingerly on his injured knee, while their arms push in opposite directions. Although bow and arrows are neatly disconnected from these interlocking limbs, the two nude figures embody a debate between youth and maturity, realpolitik and honor: two urban moralities. The cynical Ulysses, his intelligence ageless, stands to one side, his strength frozen, immobile, withdrawn from the passage of time. This sculptural staging places the solitude of each protagonist in harmonious opposition, creating through the medium of plaster the tension produced in the theater by means of language. At the bottom left, the head on the Nemean lion's skin—also bestowed on Philoctetes by the dying Hercules—affords an ironic counterpoint, a still life that is almost a *vanitas*.

The intelligence of his three classical protagonists inspired in Pradier a reconstituted and reinterpreted dramatic scene, denser even than the successive debates that punctuate Sophocles' drama. The scene would lack coherence if the opposing gazes of Odysseus and Philoctetes, both weighing on the young Neoptolemus, were not reflected in the latter's pose. At this point in his career Pradier makes the most of the rigor imparted by his study of classical statuary: the protagonists are all on one level, their heads forming a line in which they confront one another dramatically and psychologically.[2] Neoptolemus comes between the two enemies: one informs him of his duty as a Greek, while the other appeals to his conscience. His left hand detains Philoctetes and his right hand is raised to his own brow. The characterization of the three heads and the tension between the firmness of Odysseus and the anger of Philoctetes create a visual and psychological equilibrium that go beyond mere theatrical anecdote. In fact, they illustrate Lessing's penetrating remark: "Philoctetes . . . brings Neoptolemus back to his natural self by his own complete naturalness."[3] Lessing's moral lesson derives from his aesthetic teaching. He argued that only action reduced to a single moment could be imitated in painting, and that pure beauty was therefore the preserve of sculpture. Here the very sculptural Philoctetes, himself

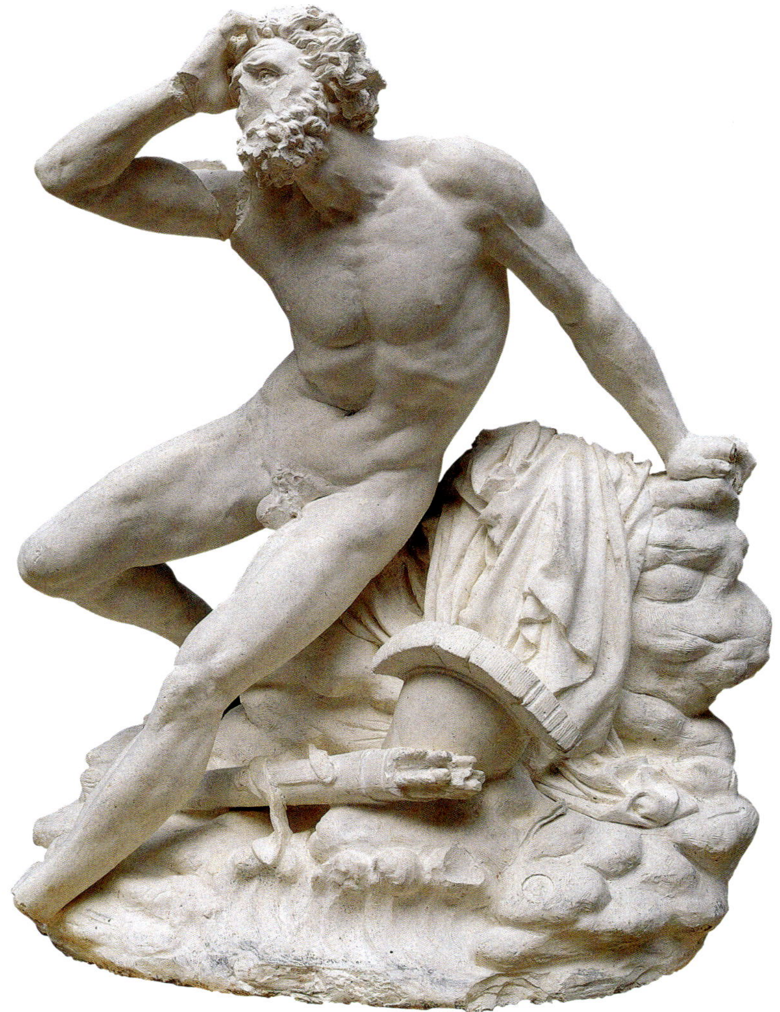

CATALOGUE NO. 47 | ALFRED-ÉDOUARD LEPÈRE (1827–1904), *The Wounded Philoctetes on the Island of Lemnos Surrenders to His Sorrows*, 1852. Plaster, 103 × 85 × 53 cm.

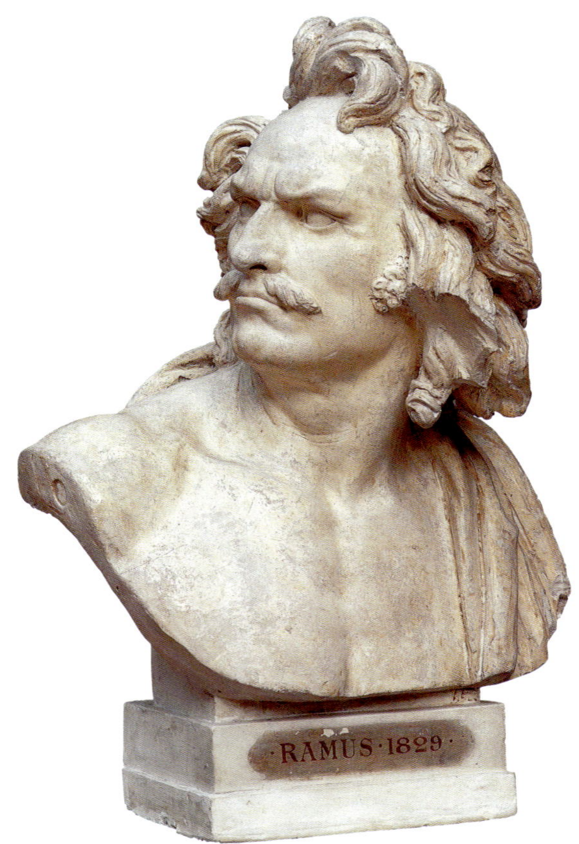

CATALOGUE NO. 48 | JOSEPH-MARIUS RAMUS (1805–1886), *Anger Mingled with Contempt (Philoctetes Faces Ulysses)*, 1829. Plaster, 77.5 × 51 × 34 cm.

not unlike Laocoön, is coupled with a more pictorial Neoptolemus. Pradier thus illustrates Lessing's aesthetic theory: sculpture (Philoctetes) teaches painting (Neoptolemus) how calm and noble beauty should be. The parallel between morality and aesthetics, between political vision and Neoclassical style, can be extended further: realpolitik first alienates and then reunites the sovereign and the citizen, the politician and the man of action. For all their contradictions, the passionate gestures of the figures ultimately achieve an equilibrium.

Later in the same century André Gide brought this trio to the stage in a spirit close to that of Pradier. In his *Philoctetes* (1899), Ulysses embodies *raison d'état* and is faced with a Philoctetes almost entirely detached from life. Throughout the nineteenth century, however, the intellectual and political debate constructed by Sophocles was less important than the central figure of the raging archer. In 1829 the pitiful Philoctetes reappeared in the *concours* for a sculpted Expressive Head. Founded by Caylus, this competition involved a title and a subject: the title customarily resembled a hollow allegory—in this case *Anger Mingled with Contempt*—and was supplemented by the subject—here "Philoctetes Faces Ulysses." The teachers thus presented an unexpectedly simple interpretation of our hero. The winner, Joseph-Marius Ramus, transposed these qualities onto his model, who sported the long whiskers then fashionable (1829; cat. no. 48). Since the purulent wound stood well outside the compass of this *concours*, Ramus carried the day by exploiting every expressive technique to excess: hair on end; face creased with fury; grimace of hatred; and eyes wide and vacantly staring. This is not a man of sorrows; his violence is not that of the wounded but rather of a Hernani, a Porthos, or a Vercingetorix. The Romantic ideal of the time was action, and a resentful or sulking Philoctetes was inconceivable. Instead, one perceives the sturdy warrior long fettered by his wound, who is soon to arise and put the Trojans to flight.

The invincible archer competed for the Prix de Rome in Sculpture in 1848 and again in 1852. In 1848 he is willing to depart for Troy and gazes calmly and heroically into the future. The statue by Gabriel-Jules Thomas (cat. no. 50) intelligently reinterprets the classical contrapposto to accommodate Philoctetes' handicap; the bent leg is, of course, the wounded one and is balanced by the bow on which he leans as if on a staff. In a phrase of magnificent ambiguity from *Laocoön*, Lessing suggested that Philoctetes' bow was his staff: "This is the kind of pity that we feel for Philoctetes, and we feel it most strongly when he is deprived of his bow, the only thing that could [support] his wretched life."[4]

OPPOSITE CATALOGUE NO. 49 | JEAN-JACQUES (JAMES) PRADIER (1790–1852), *Neoptolemus Prevents Philoctetes from Loosing His Arrows Against Ulysses*, 1813. Plaster (cast, 1901), 128 × 154 cm.

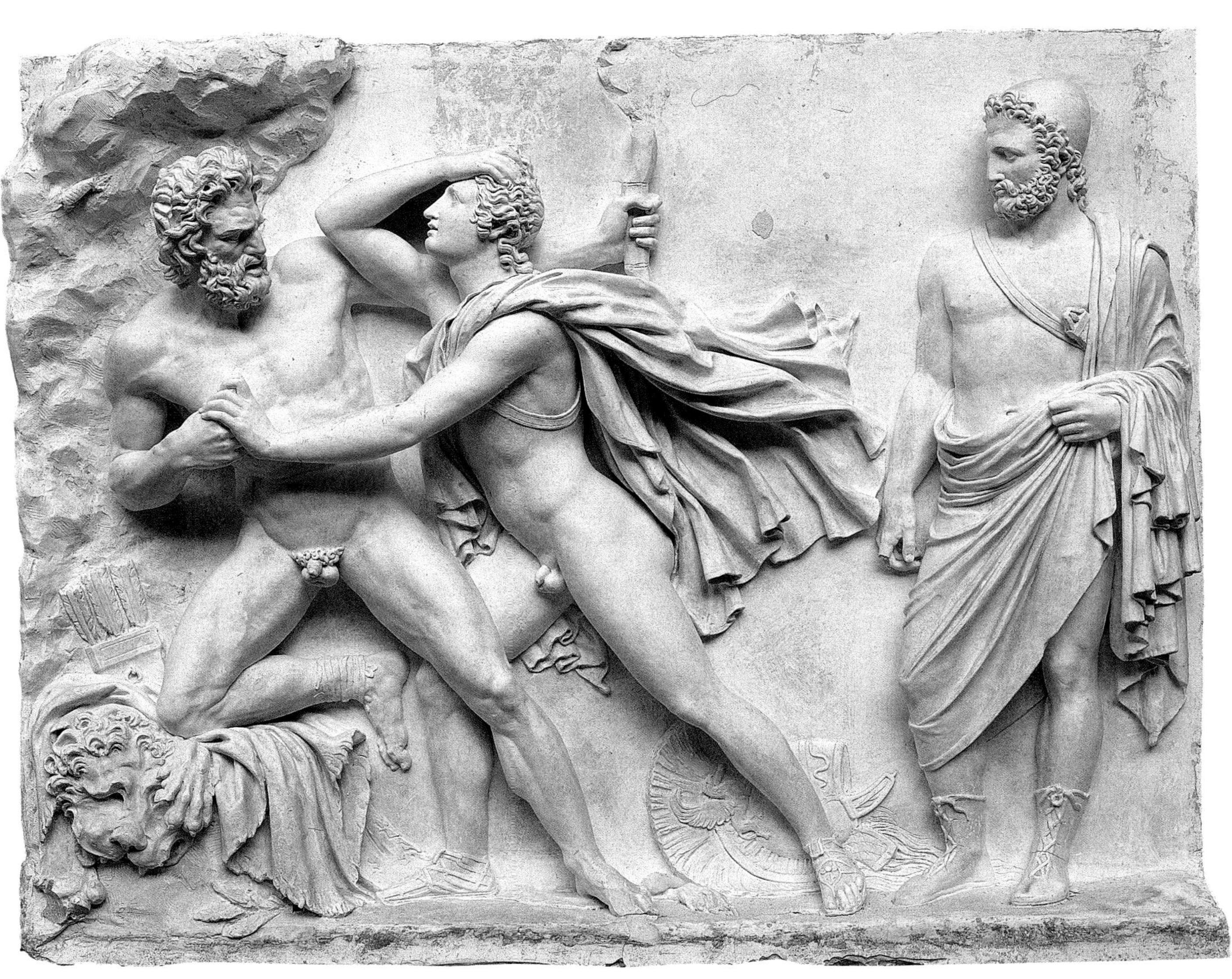

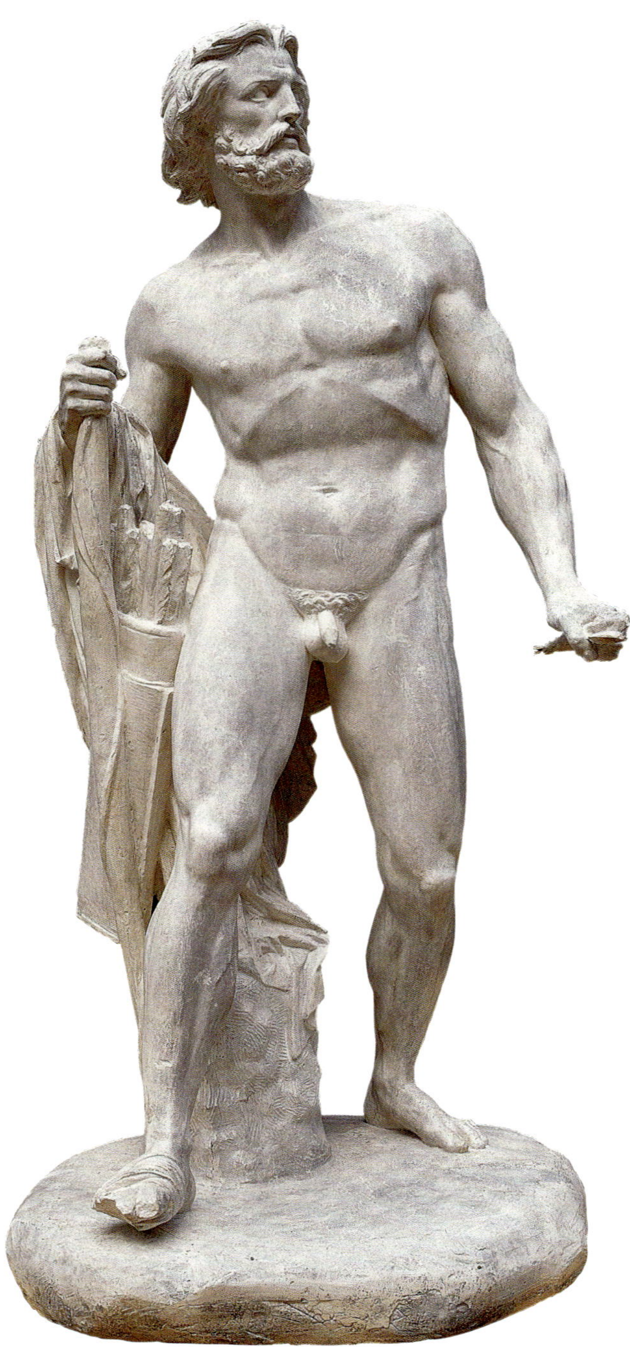

CATALOGUE NO. 50 | GABRIEL-JULES THOMAS (1824–1905), *Philoctetes Leaves for the Siege of Troy*, 1848. Plaster, 127 × 57 × 62 cm.

But when Philoctetes recovers both his bow and the desire to ply it in anger, his supporting leg projects backward like the left arm, while the arrow seeks its Trojan target. The hero's gaze, head, and torso become as firm as those of Pradier's Odysseus. The art historian Philippe Durey summarized his view of Parisian sculpture around 1850 with the words "the severe style."[5] At a time when painting at the École illustrated the ancient world, sculptors such as Thomas and Brian (cat. no. 13) were bringing their intelligence to bear on the Greek texts that inspired them.

This acute interpretation of myth, in which thought and action are fused, was rejected by some in favor of pure, undiluted passion. Four years after Gabriel-Jules Thomas's *Philoctetes* won the Prix de Rome competition, the subject set by the examiners was *Philoctetes on Lemnos*, an episode that took place ten years earlier in Greek history, before the siege of Troy: "Philoctetes, wounded in the foot, is abandoned on the island of Lemnos by the Greek army. Indignant at this desertion, in agony from his wound, the hero gives himself up to his grief." The winner was Alfred-Édouard Lepère (cat. no. 47). Never have the movements of a Philoctetes been so contradictory. Which is the injured leg? Why is his pain thus redirected as though to the head? The lines inscribed on this torso seem to run amok. The conditions under which it has been preserved in the basements of the École have compounded the ancient wound with many new infirmities, fracturing the face and amputating the wounded leg, leaving the last of the *Philocteteis* with a horrifying gaze. The violence of his contortions resembles that of Barye's wild animals; the combined effects of pain (by which even the most handsome face is distorted) and of random vandalism have wrested Sophocles' hero back into the world of Laocoön. For Philoctetes is, according to Lessing, a soulmate to Laocoön, but one whose wounds are self-inflicted, whose serpents are self-created, and whose suffering is not merely physical pain but furious resentment against others, against himself, and against his own blundering errors.

NOTES

1 Gotthold Ephraim Lessing, *Laocoön: An Essay on the Limits of Painting and Poetry*, rev. ed., trans. E. A. McCormick (Baltimore, Md., 1984), 9. Lessing here uses Homer's lines to comment on Winckelmann's formulation ("Laocoön suffers like the Philoctetes of Sophocles") from the first chapter of his *Reflections on the Painting and Sculpture of the Greeks*.

2 See Guilhem Scherf, "'De la malignité d'un microbe': l'antique et le bas-relief moderne, de Falconet à David d'Angers," *Revue de l'Art*, no. 105 (3rd trim. 1994): 19–32; see esp. p. 25.

3 Lessing, *Laocoön*, 31.

4 Ibid., 27. [The translation cited runs "save his wretched life": "support" has been substituted to restore the ambiguity present in the French *soutenir*, metaphorically "sustain" or physically "support." Trans.]

5 Philippe Durey, "Le Néo-classicisme," in *La Sculpture française au XIXe siècle*, exh. cat. (Paris, 1986), 300–302.

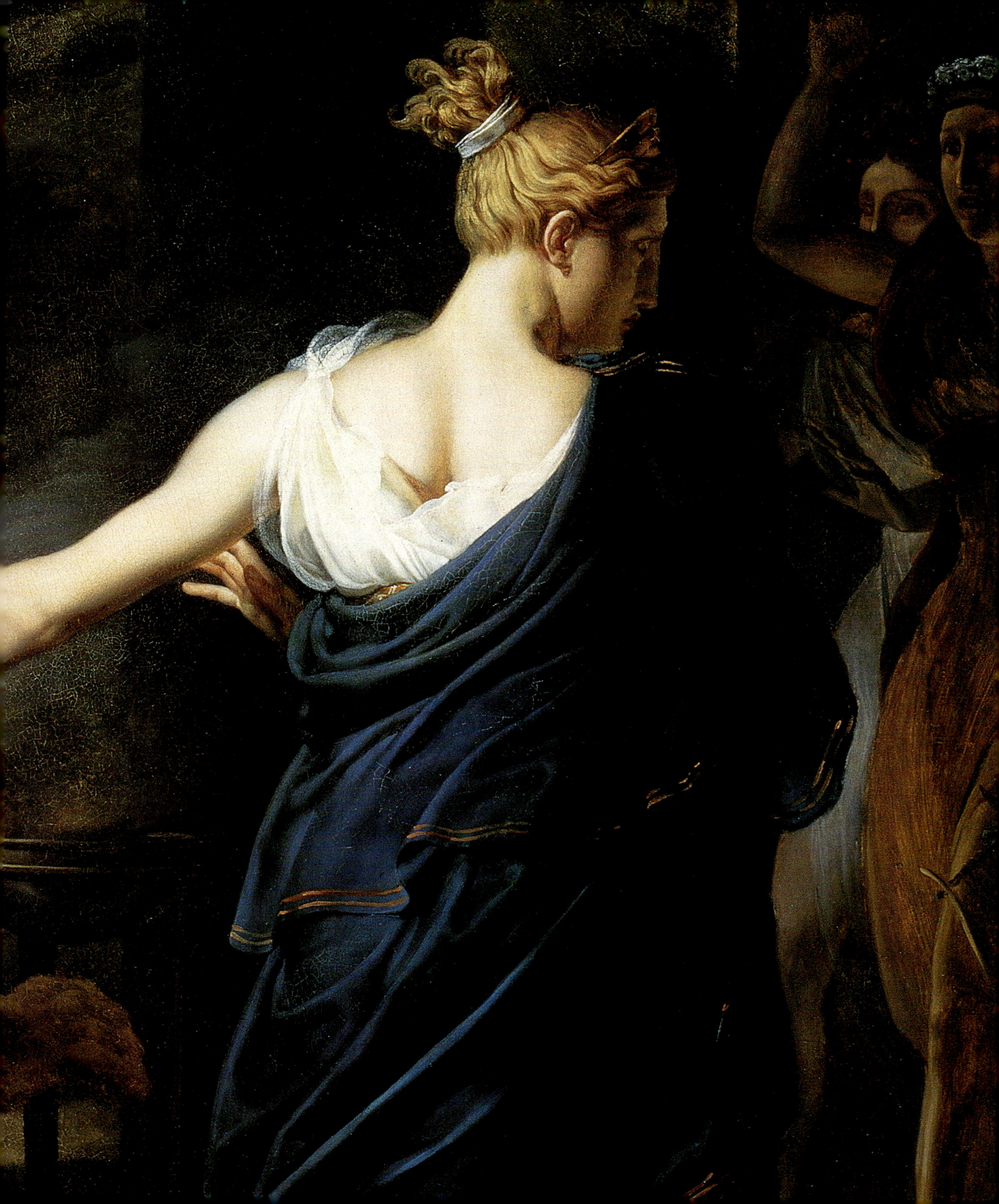

THE FALL OF TROY

The most striking image in a narrative is often the last: the hero's triumph or death; the final catastrophe or redemption. Homer no doubt felt the tradition of the Trojan War as he received it from anonymous storytellers was too well known to bear retelling. For fear of boring his audience or out of a very Greek sense of paradox, he omitted the familiar events from his poem. He alludes to the fall of Troy only in the words of some survivors or victims in the Underworld, who recall their terrestrial lives, and in the songs of the bard Demodocos (*Od.* bk. 8), which reduce Odysseus to tears. Reported stories, digressions, flashbacks, painful memories: through these complex means Homer created literature and broke the thread of his narrative. He focused on those who were reliving (or reinventing) their exploits and ordeals, preferring to hymn their memories, regrets, hopes, and dreams rather than rehearse adventures endlessly repeated by legend. He invited his audience, brought up since childhood on narratives of suffering and dying heroes, to give in to their emotions only at moments chosen for their dramatic or poetic qualities.

Between the end of the *Iliad* and beginning of the *Odyssey* many years pass that are rich in events. Achilles dies. The Greeks understand Troy will fall to them only with the aid of Philoctetes and the arrows of Hercules, and by the cunning of Odysseus and his wooden horse. They take Troy and raze it to the ground, then set out again across the seas to return to their wives and children. They live or die. Almost all of this—the essential, in a word—the two Homeric poems exclude. Instead, they focus on prolonged (relative) inaction: Achilles' sulking beneath the walls of Troy; Odysseus's boredom on Calypso's island. In the background of these private scenes the epic continues: massacres proliferate; in Argos, Crete, and Epirus terrible events occur. Homer's audience hears only some fading echoes of these tragedies.

The Death of Achilles

The most decisive deaths, the catastrophies, occupy a few paltry lines. How does Achilles die? His mother had failed to make him wholly invulnerable; she dipped him in the Styx head first, and the heel by which she held him was never submerged. Two verses from the *Iliad* warn him, for, predestined by the gods and his own choice to live a short but glorious life, he hears his dying victim, Hector, prophesy the hour of his death:

> But now beware, or my curse will draw god's wrath
> upon your head, that day when Paris and lord
> Apollo—
> for all your fighting heart—destroy you at the Scaean
> Gates!
> —*IL.* 22.359–60; F 22.422–24

Driven mad by his successes, one day Achilles, hot on the heels of the fleeing Trojans, profanes the temple of Apollo; the archer god takes his revenge through the arm and bow of Paris. The arrow penetrates the soft

DETAIL OF CATALOGUE NO. 53

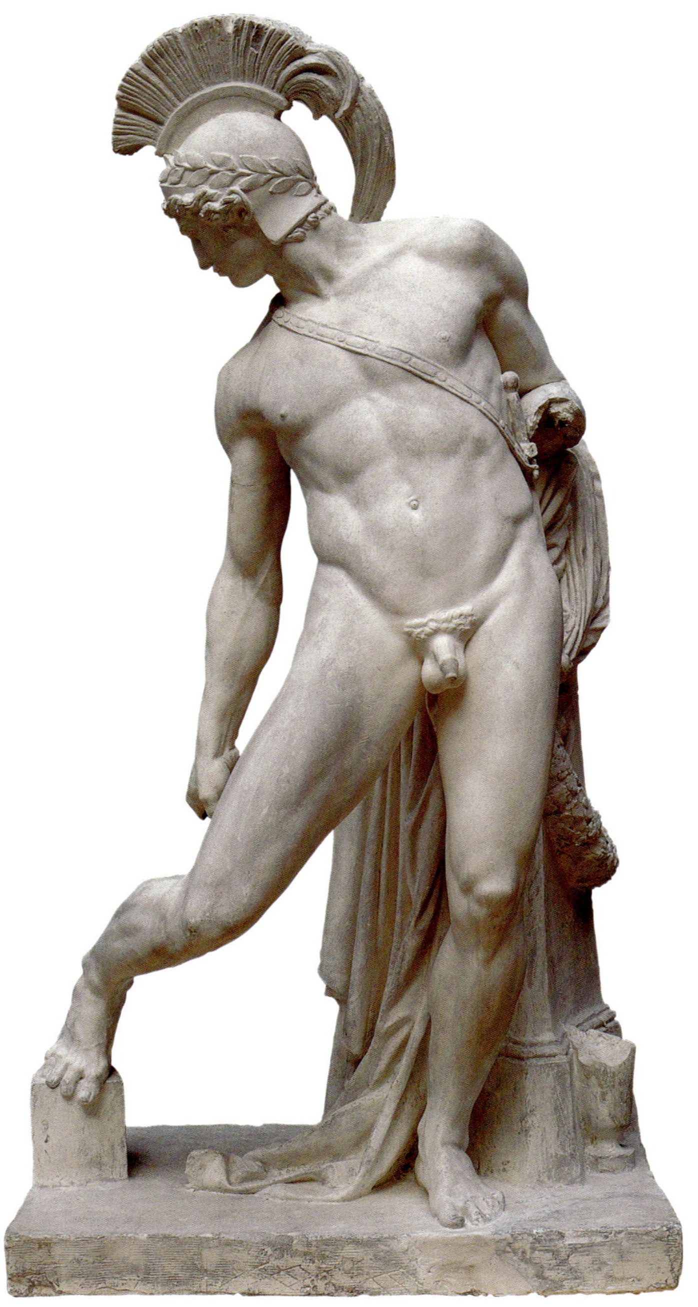

CATALOGUE NO. 51 | CHARLES-ALPHONSE-ACHILLE GUMERY (1827–1871), *Achilles Wounded in the Heel by Paris*, 1850. Plaster, 128 × 65 × 60 cm.

heel, there to deliver its poison. The statue by Charles-Alphonse-Achille Gumery entitled *Achilles Wounded in the Heel by Paris* (cat. no. 51) was made for the 1850 Grand Prix. Such a wound, normally painful rather than life-threatening, is here reduced to an elegant gesture. Achilles is portrayed as a very young adolescent, wearing a crest several sizes too large for him, who casually stoops to pluck the arrow from the wound. He is forced to stop and lean on his spear, looking behind him at the earth that will soon cover him. He thus stoops to contemplate his past, his fatal wound, and its predestined site—his heel. The glorious Achilles already contemplates nothingness, although it is not yet that of death. He is merely dreaming. Achilles likes to dream. He has not yet made the connection between Hector's prediction, the wound caused by this arrow sped from he knows not what bow, and the distant memory of his mother bathing him all but completely in the Styx.

He has chosen to die young, in the flower of his renown, rather than live a long, obscure life. Now that he faces the reality of his death, however, like anyone else he would change his mind if he could. Glory and vainglory are nothing to him now; the young think they are immortal, but the blood on his heel tells a different story and robs him of this illusion. Homer's poems offer little encouragement to believe in either an afterlife, that unreal world populated by mindless beings, or immortal glory. As he considers the wound that will wrest his life away, Achilles has already ceased to be the braggart who chose glory, becoming a mere mortal who cannot face the fact of his death.

The Death of Paris

Paris does not survive long after his victory over Achilles. Greek irony clearly required that the two most dissimilar protagonists of the Homeric narrative be struck down by the same weapon. When still a mountain shepherd, Paris had loved the nymph Oenone.

She sought to prevent Paris's courtship of Helen by revealing his destiny: he would one day receive an arrow wound only she could cure. When Paris was indeed struck by one of Heracles' poisoned arrows, shot by Philoctetes, Oenone refused to tend the wound. Then, struck with remorse, she returned to find Paris dead and killed herself on his body, like a Juliet immolating herself upon an unworthy Romeo. Unlike Gumery, the painter Antoine-Jean-Baptiste Thomas (Prix de Rome, 1816, cat. no. 53) turns a deaf ear to Homer's indulgent and rational skepticism, depicting a ridiculous Paris in the throes of his well-deserved death. Effeminate, proud of his gleaming sandals, he is seen just as the more superficial readers of Homer imagine him, imploring the forgiveness of the woman he has betrayed. There is nothing about this figure to remind us of Alexander (his warrior name in the *Iliad*), a man forever aware that the gods have doomed him to a role beyond his strength. On the other hand, the young women painted by Thomas show a real sensitivity to Raphael's vision of the ancient world: powerful forms, elegant gestures, and dreamlike draperies. In the background, behind the columns of Troy, rises the mountain where Paris first seduced Oenone, offering the dying youth and his former paramour a final view of a place of pleasant memories.

The Palladium

After the deaths of Hector and Achilles beneath the walls of Troy, the leading role falls to Odysseus. Two narrators confer this honor: the bard Demodocos, in the eighth book of the *Odyssey*, and later—as expected—Odysseus himself, who narrates the following three books in the first person. Perhaps he promotes himself over more courageous combatants with inferior gifts for making their valor known; we have already seen how Ajax allowed the arms of Achilles to escape him. Now Diomedes, who raids Troy to steal the Palladium—a divine statue of Pallas bestowing protection on the city where it resides—nearly loses it, and with it the prestige of his feat, to the cunning Odysseus. This episode undoubtedly predates Homer, and it prefigures the stratagem of the wooden horse. The Greeks knew it through the *Little Iliad*, a compilation from the seventh century B.C. that summarizes the episodes passed over by Homer in the *Iliad*. The Palladium affair is certainly worth telling: it is highly amusing, and Homer can only have neglected it for the very dishonorable light in which it shows Odysseus. Always happy to highlight the dishonesty of Ulysses, Virgil gives the best-known version of the affair (*Aen.* 2.162–75). The Trojan soothsayer Helenus, having been captured by Odysseus and turned traitor, had revealed that Troy could not be taken while it held the Palladium. Odysseus and Diomedes therefore set out together, under the cloak of night, steering by the stars as they attempt to wrest the statue from its sanctuary. They succeed, and Odysseus encourages Diomedes to carry the statue while plotting to stab him in the back and carry off the trophy as his own. Diomedes, however, glimpses on the ground the bright reflection of a sword, turns, puts down the statue, and urges Odysseus to fight honorably. Odysseus declines. The arch-deceiver was surely put out to find his treachery exposed, but he knew if once a piece of trickery had failed, there was no point in wading ever deeper in lies. No, confess and change the subject. This is the moment shown in the statue by Pierre-Jules Cavelier (Prix de Rome, 1842, cat. no. 52). Diomedes' right eye is directed behind him, and the statue is concealed in his arms, but his powerful legs are frozen in mid-pace; arm, glance, and leg pull in three different directions, stilling his gesture in its carapace of plaster. Thereafter, Diomedes had Odysseus walk ahead of him, driving him on with the flat of his sword. We must therefore imagine that behind Diomedes stalks the treacherous Odysseus; his foresight precedes him, and above him looms Odysseus's sword arm. The whole scene has a pervasive flavor of Greek irony and cynicism, symbolized here in the little statue of Athena. One suspects that it wears the ghost of a smile, which Diomedes cannot see but which Odysseus is well qualified to appreciate.

Laocoön

Odysseus is a fine publicist for his own merits and never misses an opportunity to recount and (as Athena points out) embroider upon his own exploits. So what part did he play in the famous Trojan horse episode, which has entered the language as a paradigm of Greek cunning? The Greeks sailed out of the bay, leaving on the sands a vast, hollow wooden horse in which were concealed the most valiant of their warriors. The Trojans breached the fortifications of the citadel to bring this poison gift within its walls. In the fourth book of the *Odyssey*, Menelaus and Helen inform Telemachus of the foresight and exploits of Odysseus, who claimed credit for devising the horse and was taken within its belly. When Helen, comprehending, knocked on the walls of the horse, those who wished to respond were forbidden by Odysseus: Helen might be accompanied by a Trojan spy or might be playing a duplicitous role. The merit of devising and executing the stratagem—and thus the fall of Troy—was, he says, all his own. "Again, when our champions climbed inside the horse / that Epeus built with labor . . . I held full command" (*Od.* 11.523–24) he reminds Achilles in the Underworld, while the hero's shade questions him on the conduct shown by his own son, Neoptolemus, who was also enclosed within the wooden beast. By the time Odysseus is received at the Phaeacian court, this version has become official. He can ask the bard Demodocos to eulogize his unrecognized self:

> Sing of the wooden horse
> Epeus built with Athena's help, the cunning trap that
> good Odysseus brought one day to the heights of
> Troy . . .
> —OD. 8.492–95; F 8.552–54

Like Menelaus, Demodocos describes this masterpiece of cunning as the work of all the Greek warriors.

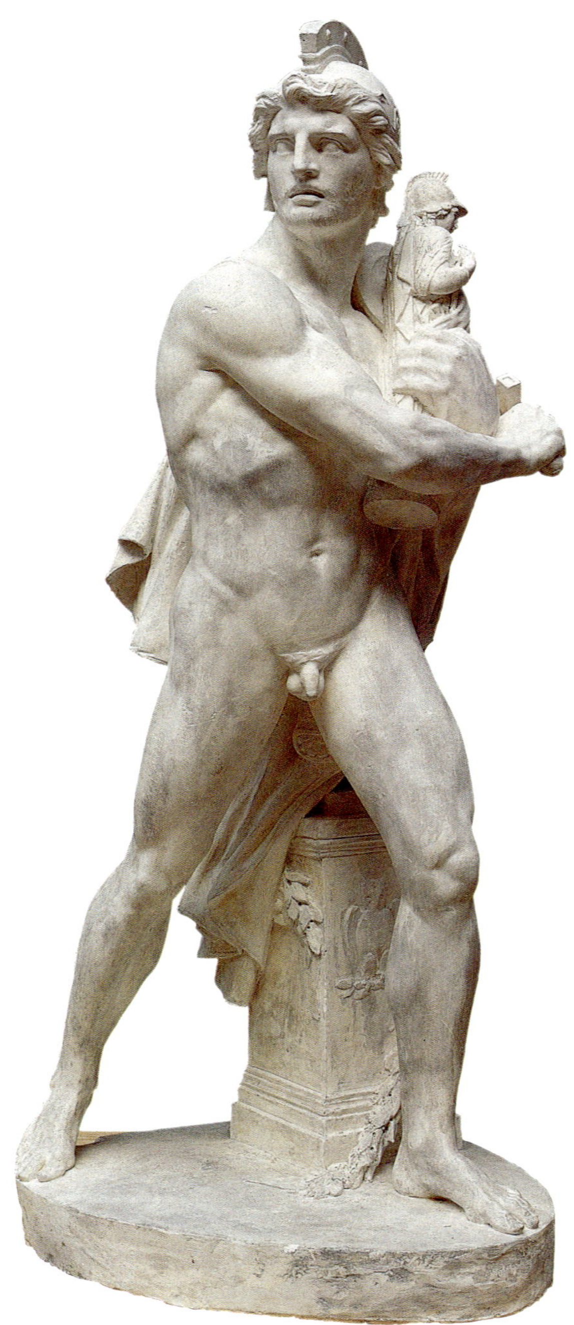

CATALOGUE NO. 52 | PIERRE-JULES CAVELIER (1814–1894), *Diomedes Carrying Off the Palladium*, 1842. Plaster, 119 × 40 × 54 cm.

OPPOSITE CATALOGUE NO. 53 | ANTOINE-JEAN-BAPTISTE THOMAS (1791–1834), *Oenone Refuses to Aid the Wounded Paris*, 1816. Oil on canvas, 114 × 146 cm.

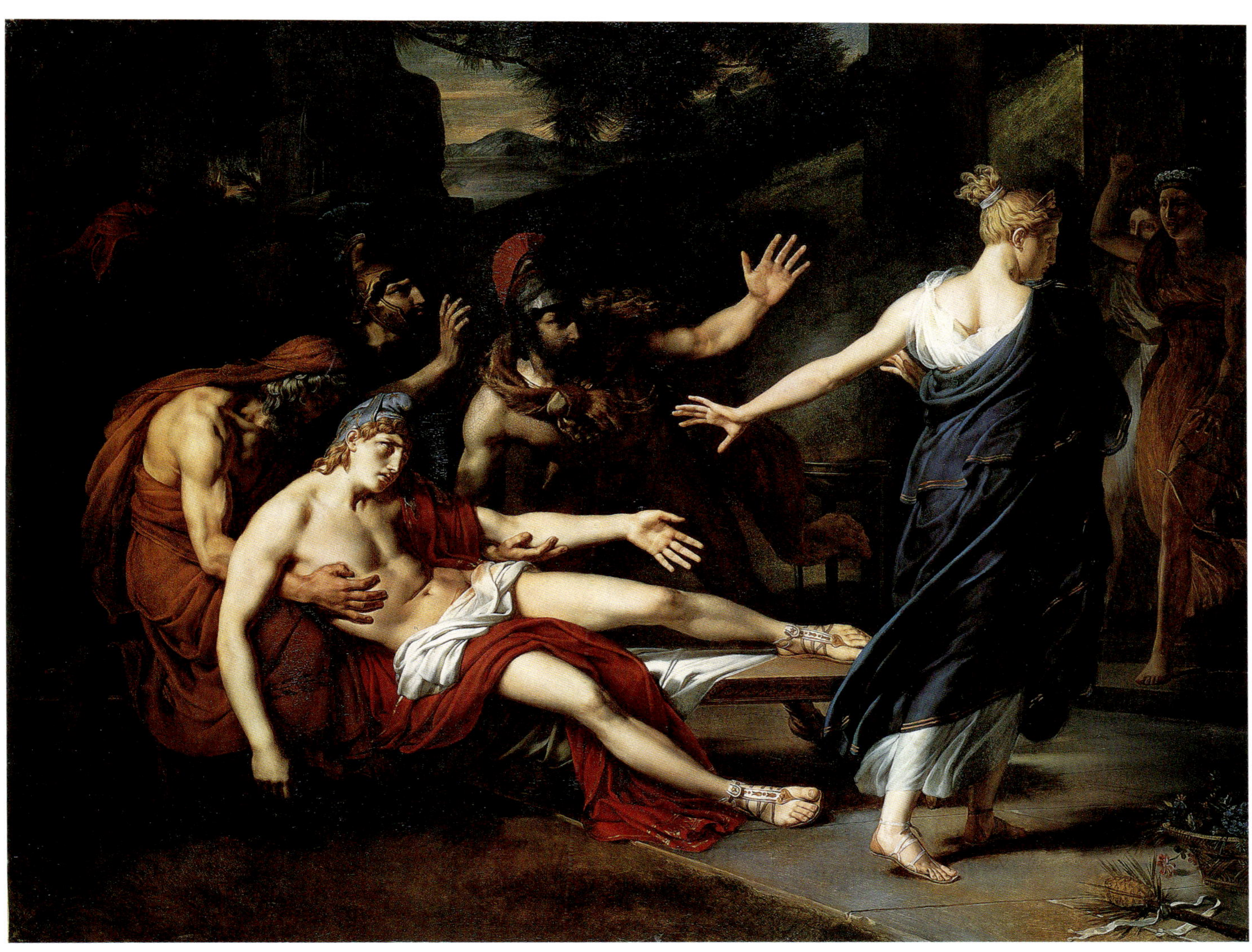

He does not explain the ruse in detail, nor does he attribute it exclusively to Odysseus:

> Stirred now by the Muse, the bard launched out
> in a fine blaze of song, starting at just the point
> where the main Achaean force, setting their camps
> afire,
> had boarded the oarswept ships and sailed for home
> but famed Odysseus' men already crouched in
> hiding—
> in the heart of Troy's assembly—dark in that horse
> the Trojans dragged themselves to the city heights.
> Now it stood there, looming . . .
> and round its bulk the Trojans sat debating,
> clashing, days on end. Three plans split their ranks:
> either to hack open the hollow vault with ruthless
> bronze
> or haul it up to the highest ridge and pitch it down the
> cliffs
> or let it stand—a glorious offering made to pacify the
> gods—
> and that, that final plan, was bound to win the day.
> —OD. 8.500–510; F 8.559–72

Other storytellers, notably Virgil (*Aeneid,* bk. 2) further diminish the role of Odysseus in favor of a Greek double agent, the perfidious Sinon, who feeds the Trojans an absurd fantasy they swallow whole. The naïve Phrygians are led to believe that in the wooden horse they have a substitute for the stolen Palladium; that Pallas was much exercised by the theft of her statuette; and that the statue of the horse will take over her role in protecting their citadel. That is why the Greeks have made it too big to enter the city walls. The Trojan priest Laocoön "fears the Danaeans and still more their poison gifts" [Timeo Danaos et dona ferentes] (*Aen.* 2.49). Bellowing his distrust of the horse, he hurls his javelin at its side, whereupon two monstrous serpents arise from the deep and swallow up the priest and his sons, as if to persuade the Trojans that Athena was punishing the blasphemous gesture. The serpents were, in fact, punishing Laocoön for a quite different transgression (he had failed to observe the requirement of chastity imposed by his function), but the gods undoubtedly wanted the Trojans to misunderstand the serpents' mission. Odysseus passes lightly over these episodes, for not only does he play no active role in them but he is surpassed in the matter of duplicity and perfidy by some obscure extra (Sinon). The visual arts have nevertheless taken up precisely these scenes for their symbolic, tragic, and blasphemous power, qualities remote from the character of the king of Ithaca.

As for Laocoön, the marble group with him at its center had already attained mythical status in antiquity and was rediscovered in Rome in the sixteenth century. Thereafter it served as evidence for all kinds of artistic theories, notably in the debate concerning the kinship or disparity of the poetic and visual arts. In arguably the most decisive study of all Western aesthetics, Lessing cited the *Laocoön* group as proof that the verbal and visual arts follow different paths. Three millennia earlier Homer's trust in the fable and character of Laocoön was not unbounded; he who so often painted the sufferings of the humblest slaves, the victims of princes and their henchmen, has almost nothing to say about the high priest of Troy. Yet Homer is never reluctant to show the vanity of prediction and ineffectuality of soothsayers. No doubt physical suffering made no impression on his spiritual grandeur; he describes death and moral suffering, but not simple pain. If one excepts a being like Elpenor—a member of Odysseus's crew who dies of drunkenness in the tenth book of the Odyssey—when men or women die in Homer's works, they think not of their own bodies but of those they will never see again. A French academic tradition, deriving from Charles Le Brun, argued the contrary, namely, that the soul's suffering dictated the expressions of physical pain, which were mere reflections thereof. Hence the excessive gestures and grimaces found in the compositions of the École's teachers and students alike. We have already seen Philoctetes assuming the mask of Laocoön.

The expressiveness of Laocoön's features left their mark on the *concours* founded by the comte de Caylus in 1759, which required the student to draw, paint, or

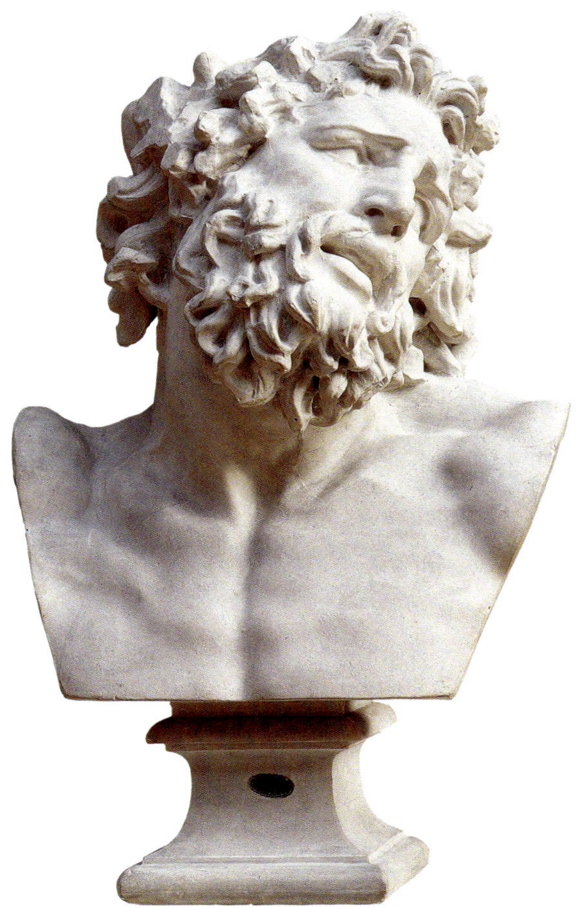

CATALOGUE NO. 54 | GUILLAUME DUCHENNE DE BOULOGNE (1806–1875), *Laocoön, Contraction of the Superciliary*, 1856–57. Corrected plaster cast, 65.5 × 39.5 × 32.5 cm.

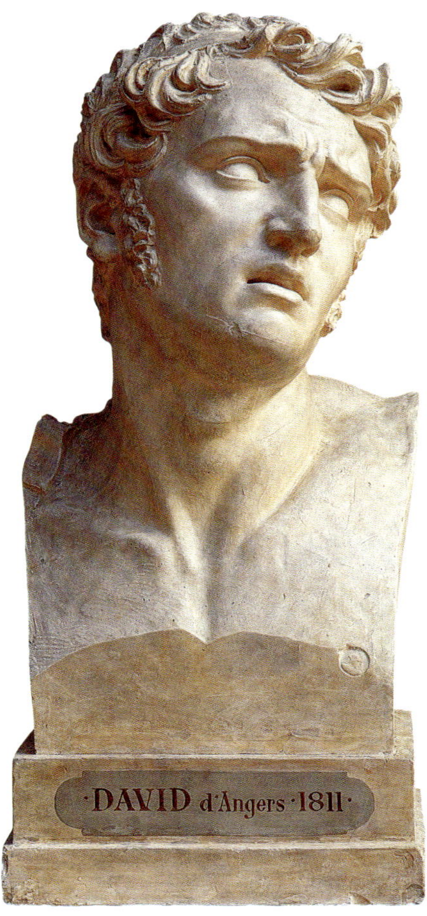

CATALOGUE NO. 55 | PIERRE-JEAN DAVID, KNOWN AS DAVID D'ANGERS (1788–1856), *Pain (Variation on the "Laocoön")*, 1811. Plaster, 67.7 × 30.5 × 26 cm.

sculpt an *expression*. David d'Angers studied *Laocoön* long and hard and often wrote about it. When tackling the subject of the 1811 *concours*, an expressive head depicting *Pain* (cat. no. 55), he gave his work not only the pitiful and schematic traits of Laocoön but the facial traces of a long life of moral ordeals. In this bust the image of Laocoön is not simply overlaid with David d'Angers's customary anatomical precision. The sculptor clearly hesitated between the timelessness of his subject and the reference to contemporary fashion implicit in the form of the sidewhiskers; he attempted to connect the pained gaze and the source of pain; he also followed Lessing's recommendation in seeking the "pregnant moment" in a display of passion, when suffering has not yet reached its paroxysm; and in the wrinkles he evoked a conscience that bears the scars of past tribulations. David d'Angers subsequently devoted his life to teaching this complex understanding of antiquity. Others, meanwhile, discovered in the example of antiquity solutions that were merely simplistic.

In 1856–57 Guillaume Duchenne de Boulogne, a doctor of medicine fascinated by the physical expression of the emotions, also made use of the face of the *Laocoön*. He made a fresh cast of it and then corrected the anatomical errors—for example, in the "contraction of the superciliary" (cat. no. 54). His goal was to teach young artists the true face of suffering by means of the *Mechanism of human physiognomy or electro-physiological analysis of the expression of the emotions.* This was the title of one of his publications, and his collection of casts and photographs—partially donated to the École des beaux-arts—offered a lesson in science to the students of the arts. One of his rectified casts can be compared to David d'Anger's *Pain;* it served as an end point in the teaching of expression. In the pedagogy of the École, scientific methodology now replaced literary inspiration.

The Crimes of Pyrrhus

Homer scrupulously distinguished the most pitiful of the victims of the destruction of Troy from those who had enjoyed their share of power and happiness and therefore could not expect unlimited compassion. He does not so much as allude to the death of King Priam, whose horrifying fate it was left to Virgil to describe. In the massacre that follows the fall of the city, Priam, his wife Hecuba, his daughters, and his son Polites—one of the few sons whose death he has not already witnessed—take refuge by an altar. Pyrrhus (or Neoptolemus in Greek), son of Achilles, bursts in and kills Polites. Priam upbraids him:

> "If there is any goodness in the heavens
> to oversee such acts, for this offense
> and outrage may you find your fitting thanks
> and proper payment from the gods, for you
> have made me see the murder of my son,
> defiled a father's face with death. Achilles—
> you lie to call him father—never dealt
> with Priam so—and I, his enemy;
> for he had shame before the claims and trust
> that are a suppliant's. He handed back
> for burial the bloodless corpse of Hector
> and sent me off in safety to my kingdom."
> The old man spoke; his feeble spear flew off—
> harmless; the hoarse bronze beat it back at once;
> it dangled, useless now, from the shield's boss.
> And Pyrrhus: "Carry off these tidings; go
> and bring this message to my father, son
> of Peleus; and remember, let him know
> my sorry doings, how degenerate
> is Neoptolemus. Now die." This said,
> he dragged him to the very altar stone,
> with Priam shuddering and slipping in
> the blood that streamed from his own son. And Pyrrhus
> with his left hand clutched tight the hair of Priam;
> his right hand drew his glistening blade, and then
> he buried it hilt-high in the king's side.[1]

In Homer it is Odysseus who carries to Achilles' shade the message confided to Priam by the bloodthirsty Pyrrhus. In the Underworld he recounts the exploits of Achilles' son, passing over that particular episode as unworthy of the civilized words exchanged (over the body of Hector) by Priam and Achilles. The École teachers, however, delighted in such horrors.

The horror of the sack of Troy was illustrated with little or no imagination by Jean-Georges Vibert (cat. no. 60), in his oil sketch of 1861, and by Jules-Joseph Lefebvre (cat. no. 61), who won the Grand Prix that same year. We see blood, writhing bodies, and violence; the suffering of the father who witnesses the slaughter of his last remaining son (in both paintings Priam bears traces of Laocoön's features); we see a wife watching her husband murdered. Here are dark deeds accomplished under the veil of night and a ruinous blaze fit to mark the end of the world. Everywhere among the coursing bodies is expressionism of face and gesture. One can contrast this Virgilian arsenal with scenes of genuinely Homeric construction. Homer leaves war to one side; it is seen only through the eyes of women or warriors weary of the slaughter. This is how Eugène-Louis Lequesne understood the question in his relief (Grand Prix de Rome of 1844; fig. 43). Three women despairingly witness the murder of Priam, while the three divine spectators display that criminal indifference of which Homer so often accused the gods.

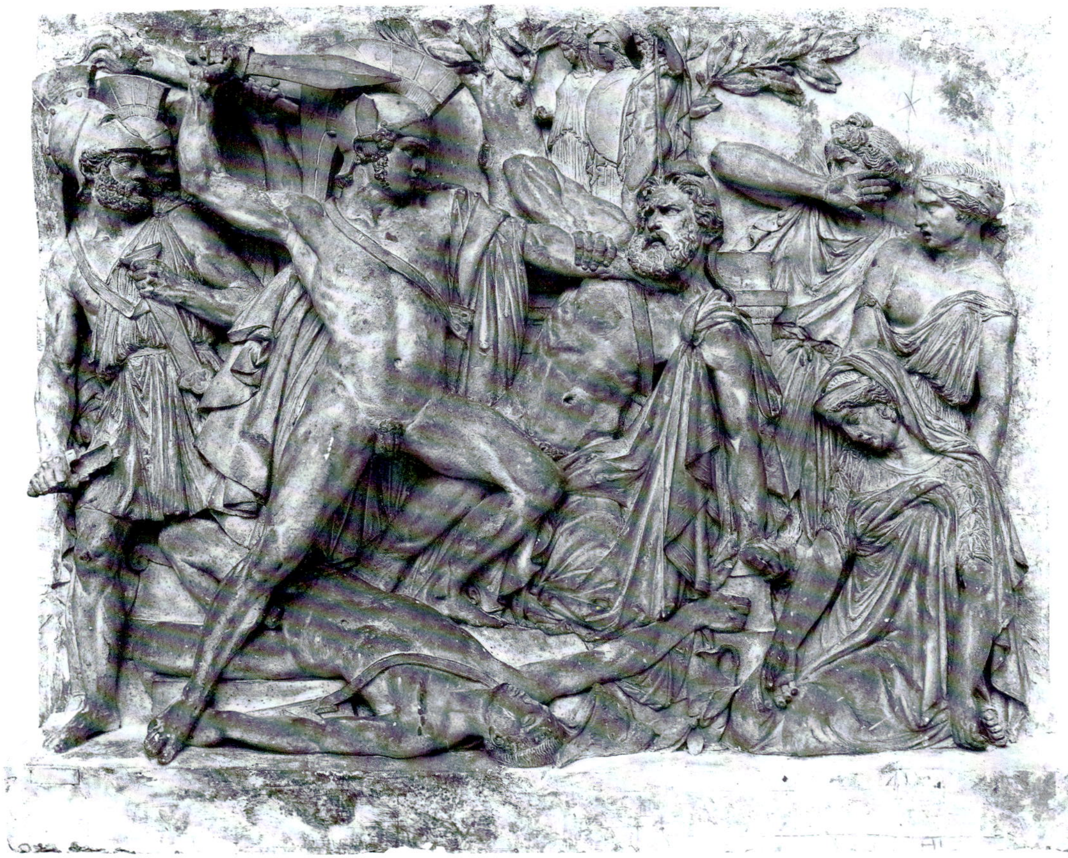

FIGURE 43 | EUGÈNE-LOUIS LEQUESNE (1815–1887), *Pyrrhus Killing Priam*, 1844. Plaster, 120 × 150 cm. Prix de Rome in Sculpture.

The fate of the child Astyanax was constantly foreseen by his mother. Andromache practiced *apotropaism*, a form of Greek cunning difficult to explain, in which those who fear a catastrophe seek to *avert* it by declaring it inevitable. Vexed at this second-guessing, the immortals then attenuate the "inevitable" woe.

> Think, even if he escapes
> the wrenching horrors of war against the Argives,
> pain and labor will plague him all his days to come.
> —*IL.* 22.487; F 22.572–74

Thus cries Andromache, her gaze on a child young enough to be frightened by his father's helmet crest. Homer's audience knew the boy's fate; the purpose of this device is to sound character rather than to wring hearts. The tragedians, however, stepped in to show what Homer had merely foreshadowed. Aristotle and his commentators have taught us that we take an ambiguous pleasure in horror; human solidarity has a part in this, as does the cowardly relief of those who see others suffer while they themselves remain unharmed, and the unhealthy fascination excited by the sight of flowing blood. There is none of this in Homer, although all of Greek tragedy is drawn from his work. In the wake of the Homeric account comes Euripides' *Trojan Women*, in which Odysseus unearths Astyanax from his hiding place and

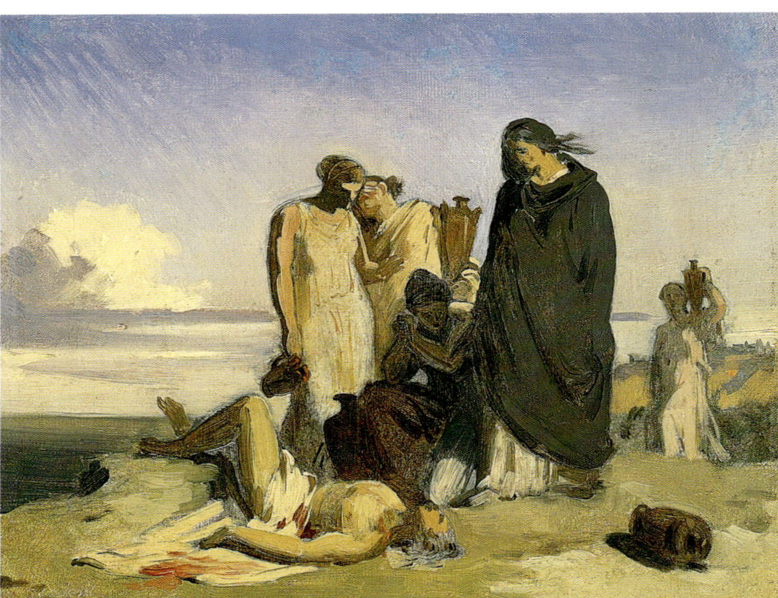

CATALOGUE NO. 56 | EUGÈNE-ERNEST HILLEMACHER (1818–1887), *Hecuba Discovering the Corpse of Her Son Polydorus*, 1840. Oil on canvas, 32.5 × 40.5 cm.

condemns him to be hurled from the ramparts. Pyrrhus executes the sentence. Indeed, Euripides' tragedy is one long hymn to Homer's humanism, for the horrors that it presents—illustrated in this section—all have the same effect: they condemn the victor and ennoble the vanquished, the captive Trojan women. The painters of the École des beaux-arts did not always grasp this principle. What remains of Homer's and Euripides' protests in the strange painting that won the 1868 Prix de Rome for Édouard Blanchard? (see "Homer's Laughter"; fig. 67). In the background the solid fortress is silhouetted against menacing glimpses of sea and sky. But the contortions of the adolescent, the predictable maternal supplications, and the African executioner clad in animal hides make of the ancient tragedy a Romantic melodrama. A series of modest sketches put this Grand Prix in its place; they pay homage to the victims of history, the heroines of this human tragedy.

The murder of one of Priam's and Hecuba's daughters, Polyxena, is another incident that Homer omits. In subsequent legends (taken up by Euripides in *The Trojan Women*) it was ascribed to Greek barbarity, Polyxena being sacrificed on the tomb of Achilles. In 1846 Victor-Alfred Latapie showed Polyxena resigned to her fate and Neoptolemus carrying the body of his victim toward the altar (cat. no. 62). In the shadows the captive women appeal for mercy. In another Euripidean tragedy, *Hecuba*, it is Odysseus who demands this sacrifice of the Greeks. Polyxena refuses to plead for mercy, offering up her breast to the sword of the executioner (again Neoptolemus).

In Euripides' *Hecuba* the heroine loses yet another of her sons: Polydorus. Before the culmination of the Trojan War, Priam had entrusted his son and his son's wealth to Polymestor, the king of the Chersonesus. Polydorus was forthwith dispatched by Polymestor and consigned to the sea, which washed him up on the shore of Troy at Hecuba's feet after the fall of Troy. These terrible subjects were several times set in the École's oil sketch *concours*, presumably to test the candidate's expressive techniques. They often imparted considerable verve to their sketchy silhouettes and lowering skies. In 1840 Eugène-Ernest Hillemacher (cat. no. 56) soberly depicted the corpse of Polydorus: a blood-stained veil partly covers the body, whose knees stand out against the flat maritime horizon. It is a moving image of the mortal condition. The captive women have come to the shore to fetch water for their masters, bearing on their shoulders the amphorae that contain every earthly woe. Arrayed on the shore, they are frozen and ghostly in their horror. Hecuba's amphora alone has fallen to the sand, and its shadow and hers cast a pall across the violet sea. Their faces are not sketched in, but the power of their poses is eloquent.

No such restraint was shown some fifty years later in the *concours* of 1885. The affliction of the weeping women, however, as depicted by Cresswell, Croizé, and Devambez (cat. nos. 57–59), is clear enough beneath their cold skies swirling with thunderclouds. The revolt of Euripides against the injustice of men and gods survives in these figures. In *Hecuba* he crowns Hecuba's despair with vengeance: the betrayed mother puts out the murderer's eyes and exterminates his children. These three sketches from the same year

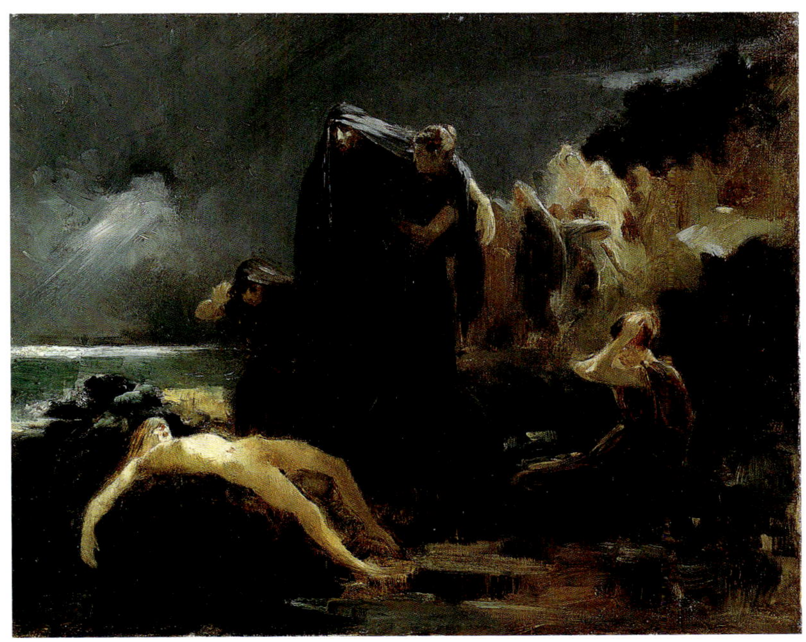

CATALOGUE NO. 57 | JEAN-ALBERT CRESSWELL (1864–1936), *Hecuba Despairs at the Sight of Her Murdered Son*, 1885. Oil on canvas, 38.5 × 46 cm.

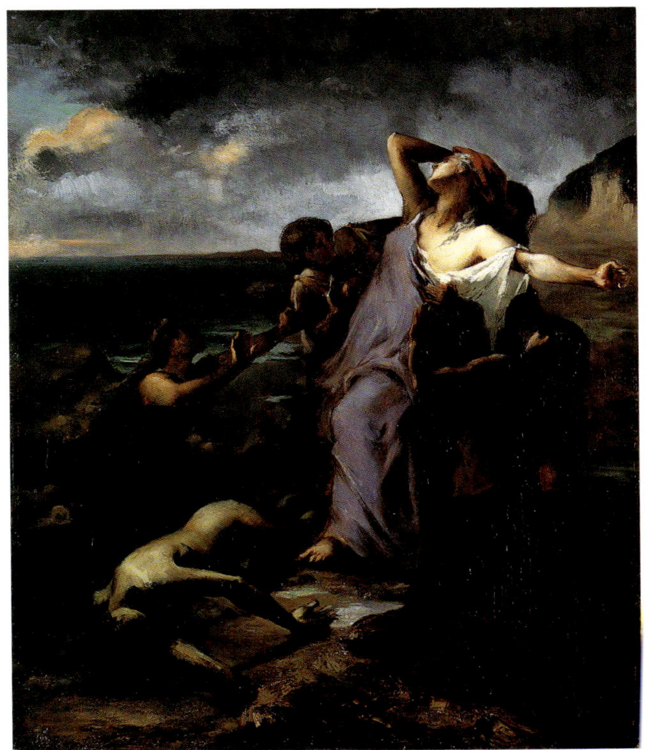

CATALOGUE NO. 58 | EMMANUEL-PIERRE-LOUIS CROIZÉ (1859–?), *Hecuba Despairs at the Sight of Her Murdered Son*, 1885. Oil on canvas, 46 × 38.5 cm.

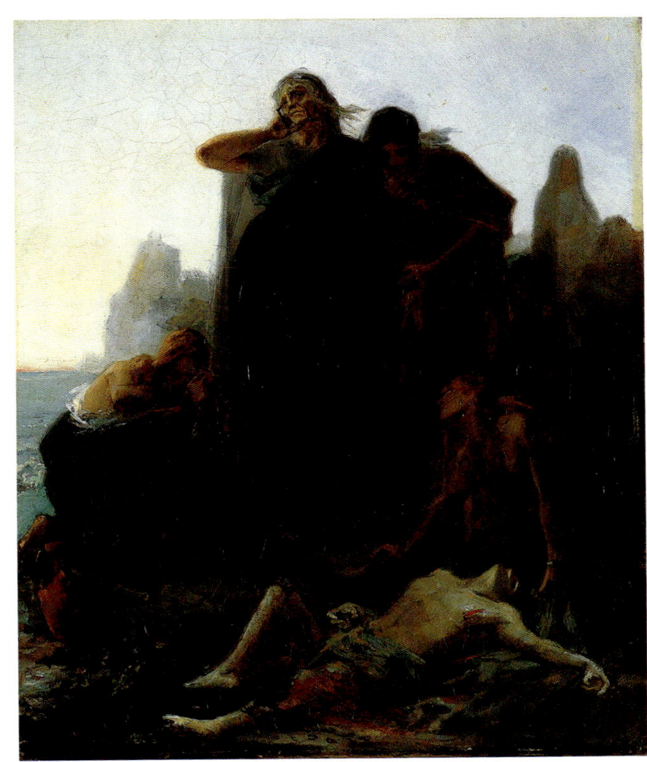

CATALOGUE NO. 59 | ANDRÉ-VICTOR-EDOUARD DÉVAMBEZ (1867–1943), *Hecuba Despairs at the Sight of Her Murdered Son*, 1885. Oil on canvas, 46 × 38.5 cm.

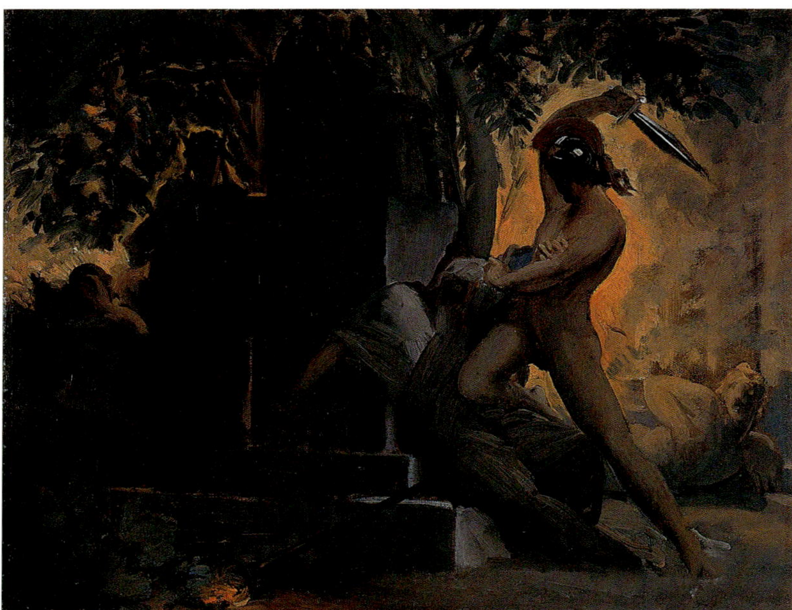

CATALOGUE NO. 60 | JEAN-GEORGES VIBERT (1840–1902), *The Death of Priam*, 1861. Oil on canvas, 32.5 × 40.5 cm.

articulate three protests raised by women against the world they live in. In Cresswell's sketch rays of light seem to rise from the cortege of newly enslaved women, from the arm of the woman on the ground, and even from the sea and the sky: brilliant rays of light express the rage and revolt of the defeated women. Croizé makes play with cadaverous colors, the green of the drowned body combining with strident, glacial blues and violets. The opposite strategy is seen in Devambez's sketch, where the dark mass of the women seems to emanate directly from the corpse and impose its grief on sea and sky alike.

Andromache

Euripides' *Andromache* burdens the widow of Hector with new misfortunes. She is the slave and concubine of Neoptolemus (Pyrrhus), who has finally acquired a measure of humanity in her shadow. But when he leaves his kingdom, his wife Hermione and her father Menelaus attempt to kill his mistress. They are prevented from doing so when she seeks refuge in a temple, but Menelaus stumbles on the hiding place of Molossus (Andromache's son by Pyrrhus) and threatens to kill him unless Andromache quits the inviolable sanctuary of the temple. (He knows the gods are very touchy about murders committed against those they protect.) Achilles' father, Peleus, great-grandfather to Molossus, at last saves mother and child. The pessimism of Euripides creates ever more entangled destinies for the Homeric heroes; abandoned by the gods in whom they no longer believe, they alone are now responsible for their crimes. The oil sketch by Jules-Casimir Wielhorsky entitled *Menelaus Forces Andromache to Quit the Sanctuary* (cat. no. 63) was painted for the 1896 *concours*. It does not attain the rational pessimism of the tragedian. The arguments with which the last great tragedian's heroines defy their executioners are more substantial than a grandiloquent gesture and an evening dress. Presided over by none other than Adolphe-William Bouguereau, the Academicians met on November 5, 1896. They understood that their subject was little known and might disconcert their candidates, so they offered their own translation of Euripides:

> ANDROMACHE: Beset with fear, I have come to seek sanctuary in the temple of Thetis, hoping that she will save me from death. I embrace the statue of the goddess as a supplicant, and my tears fall like water from the rock, drop by drop.
>
> MENELAUS *(ARRIVING WITH ANDROMACHE'S YOUNG SON)*: Woman, if you do not of your own accord leave this temple, your child will die in your stead. Up then! Leave the temple of the goddess!

The contrast between the décolletage of the supplicant and the metal-girded torso of this very Roman-looking Greek is delectable. But the blasphemies of the text of Euripides, the description of the crime in a temple that lies at its very core, have vanished. The heart of 1900 is summarized in a gown and a helmet, a society hostess and a fireman.[2]

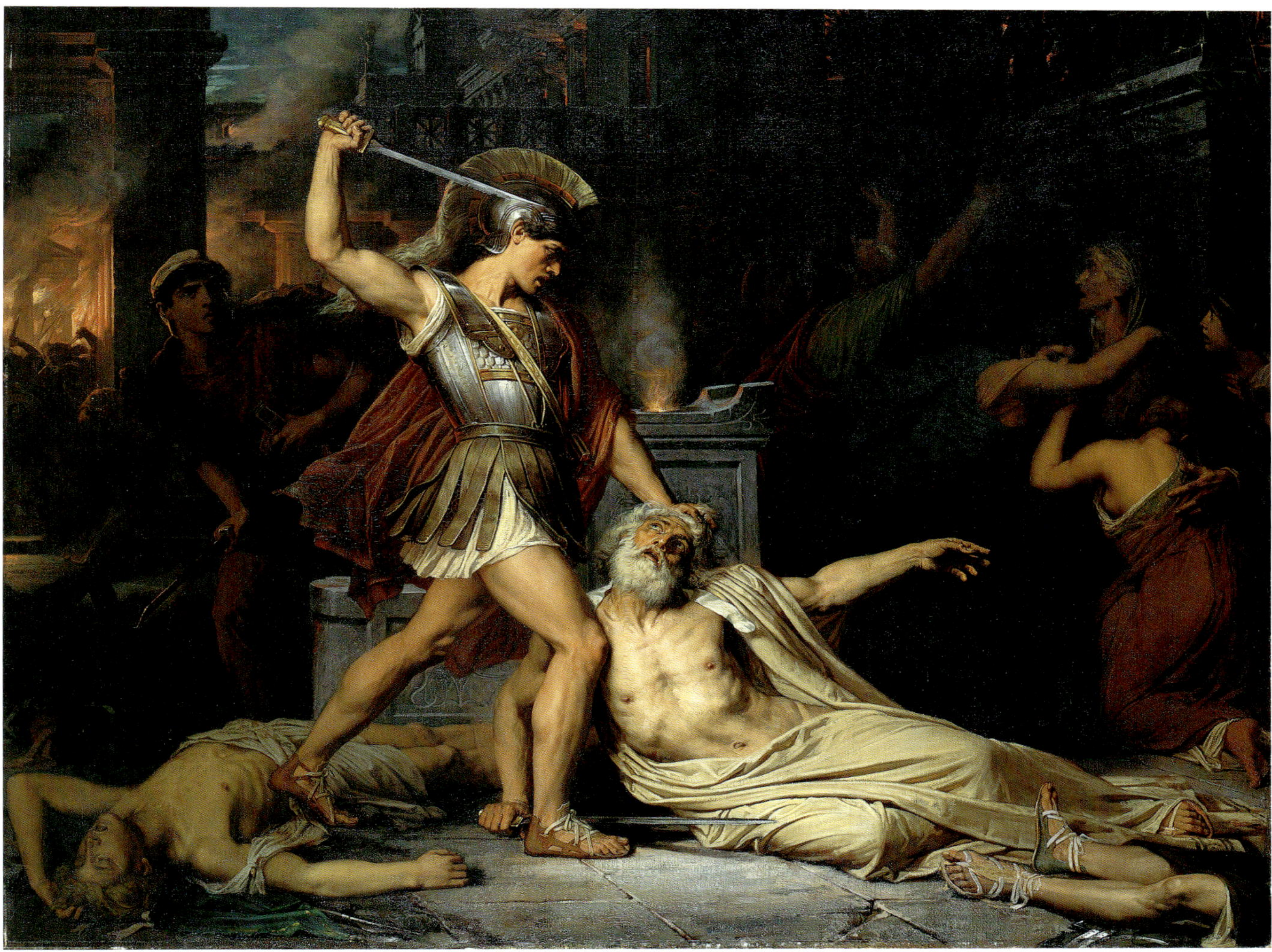

CATALOGUE NO. 61 | JULES-JOSEPH LEFEBVRE (1834–1912), *The Death of Priam*, 1861. Oil on canvas, 114 × 146 cm.

The Death of the Lesser Ajax

In 1872 the Prix de Rome jury set a rarely illustrated subject: "Ajax defying the gods is struck down by a thunderbolt. Minerva having sunk Ajax's fleet near the rocks of Caphareus, a promontory of the island of Euboea, the intrepid warrior gained the safety of a rock and arrogantly declared: 'I shall escape despite the gods.' He was struck down on the instant by a thunderbolt."

The son of Oileus was no weakling, although Homer humorously refers to him as "the lesser Ajax" to distinguish him from the son of Telamon. Indeed, his violence forced both gods and poet to meditate on questions affecting the divinities' immortal status. Wishing to secure Cassandra for himself at the sack of Troy, Ajax tore her from the statue of Athena she embraced at the temple altar, thus compounding his rape with violation of the divine image. Outraged by

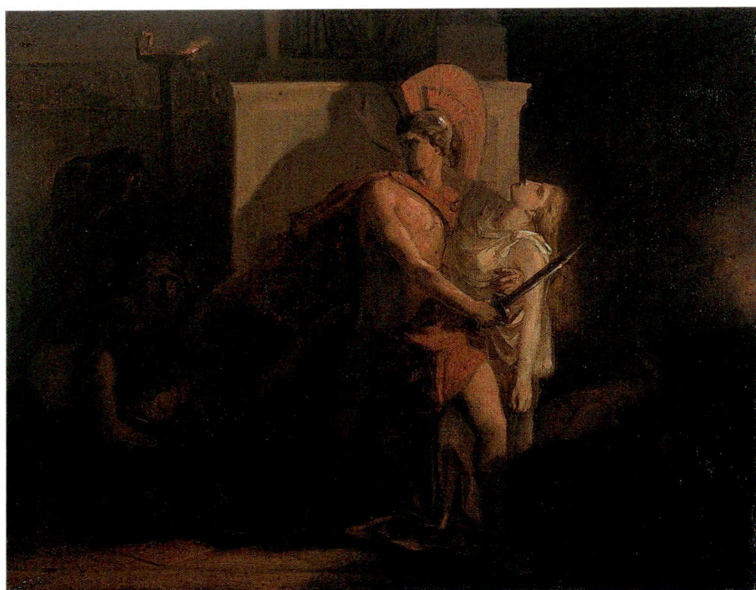

CATALOGUE NO. 62 | VICTOR-ALFRED LATAPIE (1823–?), *The Abduction of Polxyena*, 1846. Oil on canvas, 33 × 41 cm.

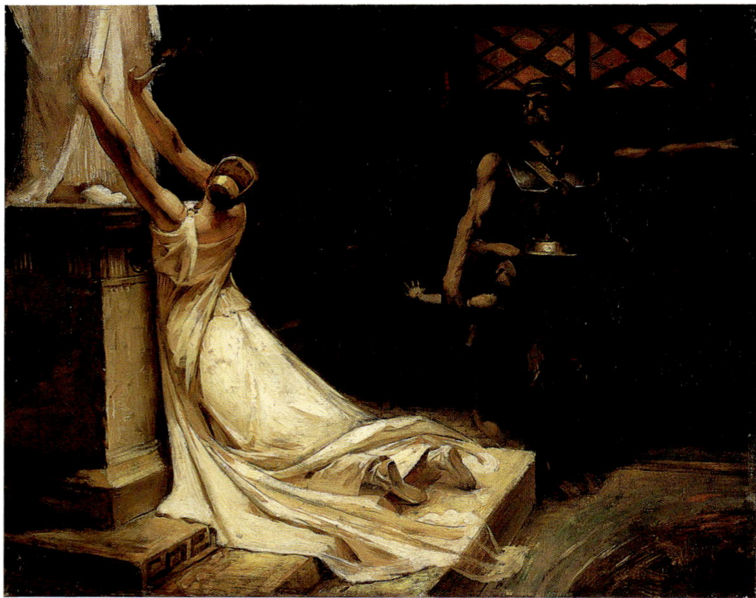

CATALOGUE NO. 63 | JULES-CASIMIR WIELHORSKY (1875–?), *Menelaus Forces Andromache to Quit the Sanctuary*, 1896. Oil on canvas, 38 × 46.5 cm.

his blasphemy, the Greeks would have stoned him to death had he, in turn, not sought the protection of Athena's altar. One recognizes in this an ingenious development of the scene, described earlier, in which Menelaus forced Andromache to abandon the sanctuary of a temple. Mindful of Ajax's pollution of her temple and cynical invocation of her sanctuary, Athena caused the wreck of his ship as he returned to his kingdom of Locris. Homer does not mention Ajax's crime but recounts his terrible punishment:

> Ajax, now, went down with his long-oared fleet.
> First Poseidon drove him onto the cliffs of Gyrae,
> looming cliffs, then saved him from the breakers—
> he'd have escaped his doom, too, despite Athena's hate,
> if he hadn't flung that brazen boast, the mad blind fool.
> "In the teeth of the gods," he bragged, "I have escaped
> the ocean's sheer abyss!" Poseidon heard that frantic vaunt
> and the god grasped his trident in both his massive hands
> and struck the Gyrean headland, hacked the rock in two,
> and the giant stump stood fast but the jagged spur
> where Ajax perched at first, the raving madman—
> toppling into the sea, it plunged him down, down
> in the vast, seething depths.
> —*OD.* 4.499–510; F 4.560–72

In the second century A.D., Philostratus noted that the painter of this scene would finish up with more spume than shipwreck on his canvas.[3]

Jules-Félix Coutan, winner of the 1872 Prix de Rome in sculpture, provided an ingenious commentary on the Homeric text (cat. no. 64). The exacerbated violence of his work should not be confused with the madness of Ajax the Great, nor the solitary revolt of Prometheus. Coutan combined the contradictory movements of defiance (the right arm) and collapse (the body pivots; the legs give way; the face is contorted with pain). The

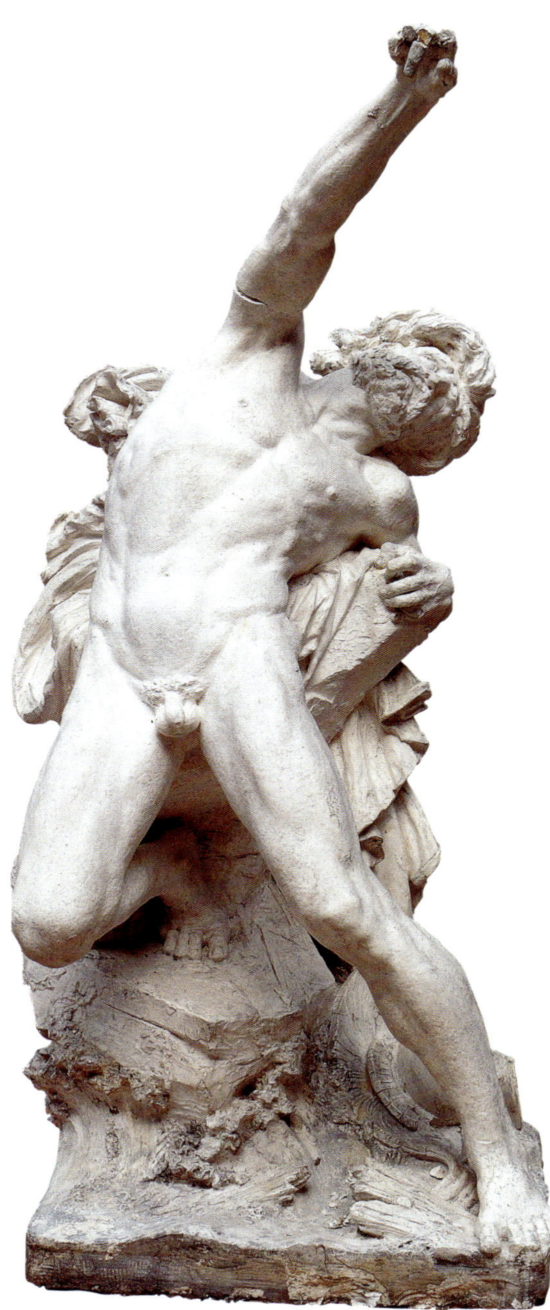

CATALOGUE NO. 64 | JULES-FÉLIX COUTAN (1848–1939), *Ajax, Defying the Gods, Is Struck by Lightning*, 1872. Plaster, 128 × 67 × 67 cm.

Greeks had little enough respect for the gods and invented many mythical instances of blasphemy. In Ajax's struggle with the gods, there is no heroic grandeur, and no reader takes his part even though he is one of the vanquished. Nor do the gods seem any the greater or more amiable in victory. Ajax is a brute. He is punished not for the rape of Cassandra but rather because he involved the gods in his act without their consent and thus offended the masters of the world. The power bearded by the shipwrecked Ajax is neither better nor worse than he is. It fell to Niobe and Prometheus to show how far inferior to the martyred human this power was, just as the Trojan women in their misery seem superior to the Greeks, their new masters.

Homer recounts the fall of individuals rather than of a city or civilization. This is a grim victory from which none of the victors emerge unscathed. The *Iliad*, or the birth of tragedy: Hugo put the matter in a nutshell when he remarked: "Like Achilles dragging Hector, Greek tragedy revolves around Troy."[4]

NOTES

1 Virgil, *Aen.* 2.535–53. Unless otherwise noted, all translations of the *Aeneid* are by Allen Mandelbaum, *The "Aeneid" of Virigil*, 2nd ed. (Berkeley, Calif., 1981), and are used by permission. Subsequent references appear in the text as "M," followed by book and line number(s) (e.g., M 2.718–43).

2 [The Academic painters were known as *peintres pompiers*. This was associated in the public mind with their use of burly models wearing helmets—like firemen—although the adjective is thought to derive from the French for "pomp." Trans.]

3 Philostratus, *Imagines* 2.13.

4 Victor Hugo, "Preface" to *Cromwell* (1827) (Paris, 1968), 65.

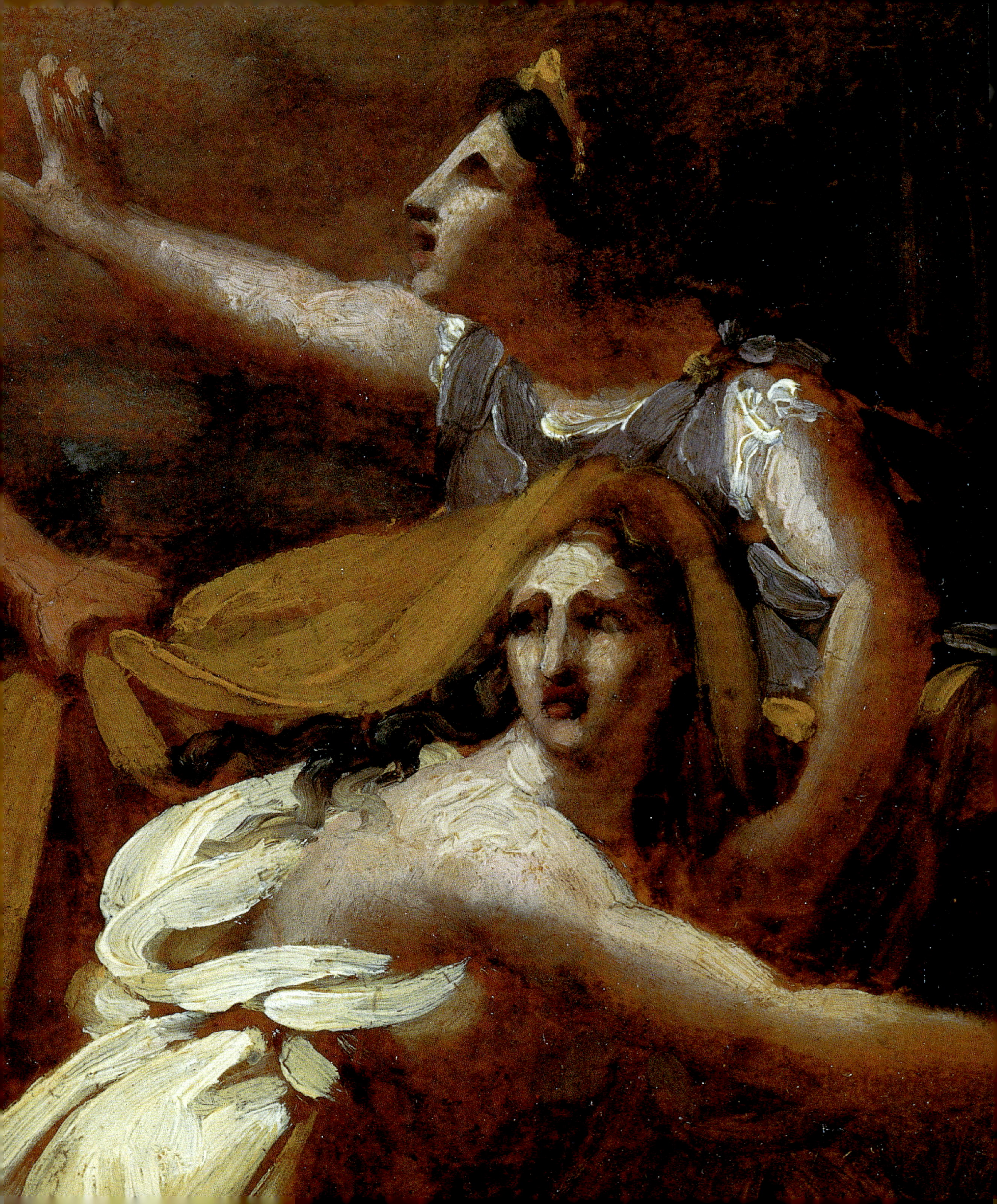

THE *ORESTEIA*

The *Iliad* tells the story of two peoples, the *Odyssey* one man's adventures. Both poems create a vivid relationship between individuals and the world that surrounds them, and therein lies a part of their literary merit. A few centuries later, Greek drama made this relationship its staple. No two tragic characters, however close, react in identical fashion to the forces—city, gods, war, and social divisions—by which they are oppressed. Family supplied the most striking instance of this law. Homer and the tragedians inherited from tradition a number of family cycles—notably those of the Atreidae and Pelopidae—which were necessarily diluted in epic but were reborn within the structuring principles of Athenian tragedy: city, democracy, and citizen.

During the Trojan War, family revenge and marital discord receded into the background. The Greeks had left their wives far behind and could give themselves up to infidelity without fear of a conjugal scene when they returned home in the evening. When the time came for explanations, family affairs were variously settled, some in comic and some in tragic form. Vaudeville, variety theater, and the crude farce of cuckolded husband and adulterous wife had a common backdrop in the world of the gods, where their wives made laughingstocks of Zeus and Hephaestus. The time is ripe for tragedy when the man of the house returns and the characters of the drama "declare themselves," as Giraudoux puts it in his *Electra*. Nostalgia—the desire for *nostos*, or homecoming—is a constant among Homer's characters. The lost cycle of *Nostoi* poems recounted the return of the Greek princes to their hometowns. Nothing, however, is more painful than the moment of reunion in the arena of the hate-filled family, the mirrored hall of dynastic revenge. Each family bears the name of an ancestor who, long ago, triggered the vendetta that repeats itself generation after generation, no longer honor-driven but a congenital defect to be concealed beneath the mounting pile of corpses. The most hideous of these founding fathers is Atreus, whose children are the Atreidae, born to slaughter, cannibalism, infanticide, and parricide. On this dunghill of violence and stupidity flowered two of the greatest achievements of Greek genius, those sibling consciences Orestes and Electra. A parallel, symmetrical or complementary, to the long voyage of Ulysses, the sanguinary return of Agamemnon to Argos is the true sequel to the events narrated in the *Iliad*. It founded Greek and European theater, defining the sense of tragedy in art as the cunning of Ulysses defined artistic intelligence.

These events, to which Homer alludes several times, are only loosely connected to the adventures of Ulysses and are therefore reported to him (and Telemachus) when occasion provides, as negative examples carrying their own counsel. Left behind in Argos, Agamemnon's wife Clytemnestra has forgiven

DETAIL OF CATALOGUE NO. 65

and forgotten nothing. She still rages at the fate of her daughter Iphigenia, sacrificed at Aulis when the Greek allies offered her to the gods in exchange for a favorable wind. She knows that the campaigning Agamemnon found comfort with Chryseis and Briseis before consoling himself with Cassandra, and that among the returning king's plunder is this sexual slave. Cassandra the soothsayer drags her heels, knowing only too well the fate that awaits her and her master, but he doesn't listen. (Her fate is to speak the truth unheeded.) The slighted wife and mother Clytemnestra has chosen a most bourgeois revenge, taking as her lover a cousin of the king, Aegisthus, born of a branch of the family alienated by the ancient blood feud that divides the family of the Atreidae. It is Agamemnon's shade that tells Ulysses of the reception that awaits him in his palace in Argos: Aegisthus slaughtered Agamemnon and his companions at arms while Clytemnestra put an end to Cassandra's prophesying.

The vendetta therefore passes into the hands of the children of this doomed marriage, Electra and her young brother Orestes, the latter placed out of harm's way by his sister and his tutor till the hour of justice is nigh:

> Seven years he [Aegisthus] lorded over Mycenae rich in gold,
> once he'd killed Agamemnon—he ground the people down.
> But the eighth year ushered in his ruin, Prince Orestes
> home from Athens, yes, he cut him down, that cunning,
> murderous Aegisthus, who'd killed his famous father.
> Vengeance done, he held a feast for the Argives,
> to bury his hated mother, craven Aegisthus too,
> the very day Menelaus arrived, lord of the warcry,
> freighted with all the wealth his ships could carry.
> —*OD.* 3.304–12; F 3.344–52

The Homeric text, much disputed on textual grounds, dictated to both tragedians and artists the logic of the drama, with its three unities of time, place, and action. In one family and one palace between dawn and dusk of a single day, the murder of the murderous mother and lover is committed by her children, capped by the arrival of the brother and sister of the doomed parents: Menelaus, brother of Agamemnon, and Helen, sister of Clytemnestra. Close family; distant relatives; those who remain; those who return; those who are passing through—everything is now prepared for the *Oresteia*, for the vengeance of Electra and the brutal revelation of two characters bred by the distant past for a pitiless future. The heroes of the tragic generation find themselves alone against the rest and forever deprived of the peace they have so long awaited.

Barely limned in those few lines from the *Odyssey*, the *Oresteia*—strictly speaking, the tragedy of Orestes—is known to us principally from the plays of Aeschylus, Sophocles, and Euripides, which bestow on Orestes (and his overweening sister Electra) a vertiginous profundity born of his abysmal hesitations. Here is an irrationality quite unknown to Homer, one that leads on to Shakespeare and the modern soul.

The Return of Menelaus, Helen, and Orestes

The most famous return from Troy must be postponed while we shift our attention to Ithaca, where everything is turning out for the best. Ulysses massacres half his people, is reunited with his son and wife, and rules happily until his son by Calypso arrives to kill him. On the whole, Menelaus made a less laborious crossing. True, the conviction that Helen had never really been unfaithful required the production of numerous miracles, of a kind easily credited by cuckolded husbands anxious to keep or retrieve errant wives. Since they ultimately led this ill-assorted couple to Orestes' Argos (a subject in the 1820 oil sketch *concours*), and the poets have so often composed apologetic paeans of praise to the beauteous Helen, let us find out what these miracles were. Ronsard was not the last to dwell on this theme:

> See Helen after the Greeks set Troy alight;
> See how she flatters her sweet-natured man,
> And he pardons her sin for the sake of her bright
> Eyes still aglow with Paris's amorous might.[1]

Only the most attractive excuses would do for Helen. Homer is the first to let us hear why she could hardly help but follow the handsome Paris onto his ship. By the third book of the *Iliad* she is already regretting her "sweet-natured man" when she spies him from the Scaean gates, but Aphrodite has no difficulty returning Helen to her lover. In the twenty-fourth book, Helen pays sincere tribute to the dead Hector, who should have been her worst enemy but to whom Homer (and, later, Giraudoux) bind her in subtle complicity; both are remote from hatred and ugliness alike, he out of nobility and she because she cannot abide a fool. An entire post-Homeric literature debated the extent of Helen's sins, but it required a great deal of imagination on the part of Euripides (and others) to clear her of all imputations and make a goddess of her. The *Helen* of Euripides is a sort of Stesichorean palinode: Helen was abducted not by Paris but by the gods, who immured her in an Egyptian palace for the duration of the war, while a simulacrum of her elegant body took her place in Paris's arms and served as a target for men's hatred. Menelaus, clearly "the ideal husband" in every respect, happily swallows this fable and good-naturedly carries his wife back to Argos. There he arrives at the worst possible moment, that is, at the height of a magnificent tragedy.

The Beauty of Madness

Having dwelt on cycles of epic, I turn to cycles of tragedy. In the Athenian theater a character's destiny was confided not to one play but to three, to which was added a satirical work, the satire play—although these have mostly been lost. The multiplicity of modern versions of the myth is partly explained by the survival of the plays devoted to Orestes and Electra by Aeschylus, Sophocles, and Euripides. Throughout her youth Electra nurses the idea of avenging her father and killing her mother. Orestes, removed from Argos after the murder of his father, returns as an adult to the city to place an offering at the tomb of Agamemnon. Electra recognizes her brother by this gesture, meets him, and persuades him to kill her mother and Aegisthus. The goddesses of vengeance and remorse, serpent-haired Eumenides, bellowing their hatred in Orestes' ears, drive him from remorse into madness. He seeks refuge and counsel in Delphi, where Apollo refers him to the Athenian court, the Areopagus. The decision is inconclusive. A casting vote is needed, and Athena, presiding over the court, absolves the matricide; some trials will redeem the criminals. In the nineteenth century a number of *concours* required the still innocent students of the École to study this painful initiation of the young into the meaning of responsibility for their acts.

All the works discussed were created for the Prix de Rome. They treat different moments in the story of Orestes—his meditation on vengeance; the trap closing around him; his appeal to Apollo; the intervention of Athena—thus summarizing the destiny of their protagonist. On three occasions artists of modest abilities attempted to wrest from plaster the gaze of a mind apprised of its own aberration. The Orestes of Louis-Joseph Convers (1888), sword in hand for the futile murder, grieves at the tomb of Agamemnon—a conventional monument, as required by the subject (fig. 44). The jury had not asked for a hero on the brink of madness. Their subject was as follows: "Back in Argos after the murder of his father, Orestes at the tomb of Agamemnon gives himself up to his grief." Convers goes beyond the expression of grief, however, to show Orestes grasping the weapon of his revenge. His arms and legs are petrified by the vision of the act for which he yearns. He barely sees the grave. His gaze is turned

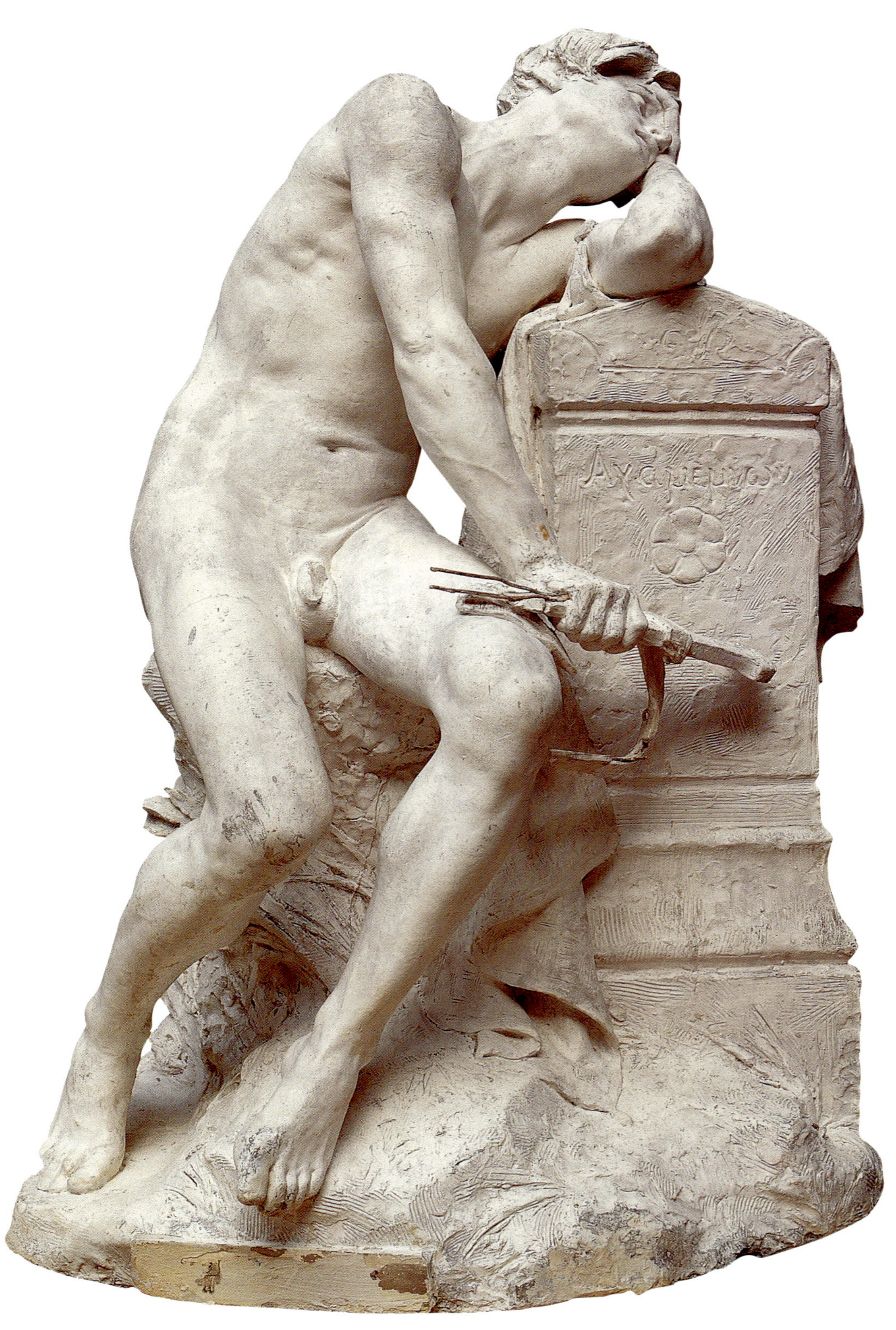

FIGURE 44 | LOUIS-JOSEPH CONVERS (1860–1915 [1919?]), *Orestes at the Tomb of Agamemnon*, 1888. Plaster, 126 × 83 × 65 cm. Prix de Rome in Sculpture.

inward, dwelling on the curse of the Atreidae, which compels him to kill his mother. The three Athenian tragic poets also have Orestes grieving at his father's tomb, in the process leaving there a lock of his own hair, which becomes a linchpin of the drama. The simplicity and grandeur of this motif were such that only Aeschylus dared take it up directly, which he did in the *Choephori*, the second play of his *Oresteia* trilogy. There Electra deduces Orestes' presence from his offerings: a lock of hair stained with the blood of the Atreidae; a piece of cloth that she herself once wove; his footprints. The different degree of realism learned by Sophocles and Euripides has affected their dramatic methodologies, and they prefer to have two witnesses report to Electra the visit of the anonymous bearer of offerings. Twenty-five centuries later, the picturesque humanity of these details is of no interest to the young Convers, for whom there is only the madness of Orestes preparing to kill the woman who brought him into the world. Agamemnon's son bewails his own, not his father's, fate. Even before the act, the matricide is filled with remorse.

In the Homeric poems there is no individual responsibility below princely rank. The lower classes are playthings in the hands of royalty or divinity, but kings and queens live and act—kill and are killed—as they decide or merit, always fully responsible for their acts. Madness and remorse are therefore no mitigation when catastrophe strikes. The *Odyssey* does not record Orestes' delirium or Electra's paeans of hatred, simply informing us that the mother died at her son's hand. In contrast, Aeschylus, Euripides, and Sophocles show that crime of crimes, matricide, with all its train of the madness and remorse of the murderer.

In Euripides' version of *Orestes*, the miasma of distrust and hatred dividing man, woman, and divinity is enough to make one despair of humanity. Euripides seizes upon Homer's idea of a single day on which everything coincides and all the old scores are settled. Helen arrives in Argos immediately after Orestes and Electra, having murdered Clytemnestra, are condemned by the people to be stoned to death. To

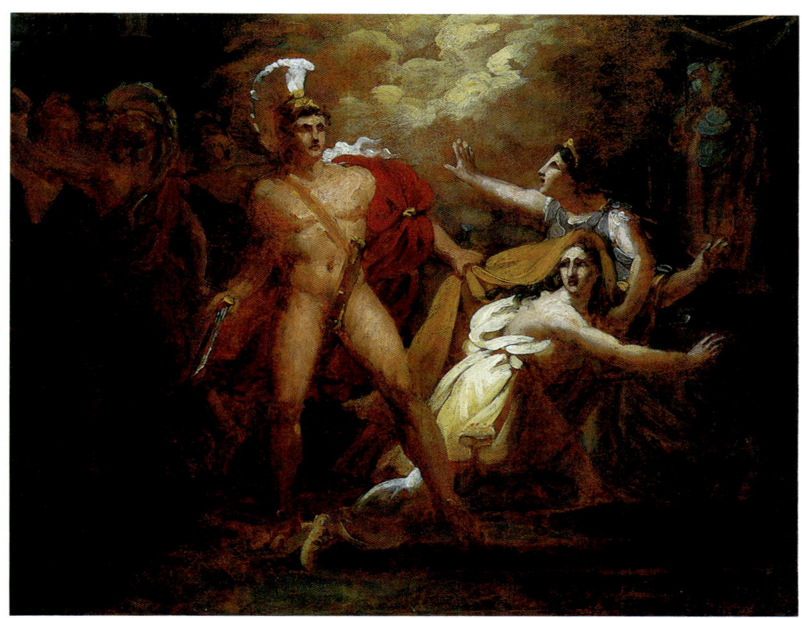

CATALOGUE NO. 65 | HENRY-AUGUSTE-CALIXTE-CÉSAR SERRUR (1794–1865), *Orestes and Pylades Desire Helen's Destruction*, 1820. Oil on tracing paper mounted on canvas, 32.5 × 40.5 cm.

escape their fate, Electra, Orestes, and his inseparable friend Pylades decide to kill Helen, who can easily be blamed for the murder of Clytemnestra and made the scapegoat of all the catastrophes that have afflicted Argos. They also plan to abduct Hermione, daughter of Helen and Menelaus. Apollo, however, saves Helen by concealing her in a cloud, ordering the matricide Orestes, mad with remorse, to seek a verdict from the Areopagus, then return and marry Hermione.

How can an academic sketch convey the pessimistic imagination of Euripides? In the oil sketch painted in 1820 by Henry-Auguste-Calixte-César Serrur, Orestes is alone in his heroic, luminous nudity (cat no. 65). Incapable of focusing on his victims Helen and Hermione, he drowns in the dark fumes of his nascent madness, while Pylades holds back the people who crowd forward like waves of remorse. The two women cling convulsively to each other, their arms, glances, and profiles interwoven. Surely Electra can be heard offstage, hurling her fulminations from some vantage point to the right. Serrur's contemporary, Delacroix,

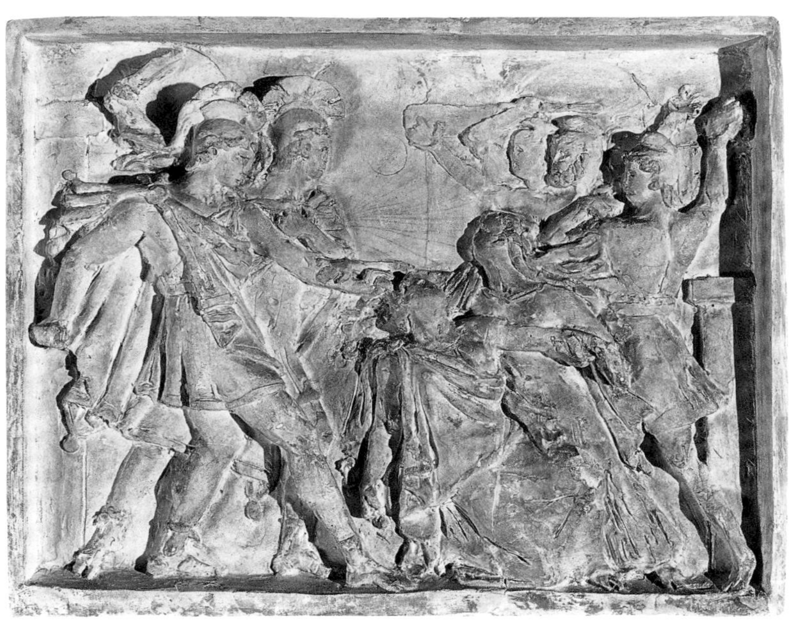

FIGURE 45 | CHARLES-MARIE-ÉMILE SEURRE (1798–1858), *Orestes and Pylades Wish to Immolate Helen*, 1820. Plaster, 36 × 44 cm. Sculpture Sketch *concours*.

The questions asked of the gods by Aeschylus, the first of the three great tragedians, still haunt humanity. The subject set for the medal-engraving *concours* of 1884 was inspired by Aeschylus: "Orestes pursued by the Eumenides [Furies] after the murder of his mother Clytemnestra seeks refuge at the foot of a statue of Apollo." The *Eumenides* is the end point of Aeschylus's trilogy and its quest for divine justice. Apollo had first ordered him to kill his mother, so Orestes flees to the Delphic sanctuary of Apollo and there requests the god and his favored intermediary, the Pythian Sybil, to protect him from the goddesses of Vengeance, the Erinyes, those bestial incarnations of remorse whose claws lacerate his face. Too terrible to name, they are known to humankind as the "Eumenides" or "Gracious ones." In the mind of the Greeks the internal hierarchy of the gods was several times overthrown. The Eumenides are allegorical divinities, born before either civilization or the Homeric world, and they are ignorant of Justice's hesitant and scrupulous proceedings. By Homer's time, if the gods intervene in human affairs, they must bear

read and reread the great myths; like him, Serrur interprets the Greek imagination in the light of Shakespeare and the Romantics. In his relief sketch of the same year Charles-Marie-Émile Seurre sculpts a knowing assassin, armed from head to foot and seconded by his accomplice; they are repelled by a largely female crowd, which stones Orestes from the right of the composition (fig. 45). In Serrur's oil sketch, Apollo may yet burst onto the scene. There is no indication of a deus ex machina in the plaster sketch. A comparison of these very different compositions revives the debates instigated by the Greek theater and distinguishes the different media: painting shows us the nightmare of madness and the hoary old pretext "compelled by the gods," while in three dimensions we see no more than the brutal reality of a crime dividing two clans of a doomed family. Greek tragedy thus plays with motivations psychological, political, and religious.

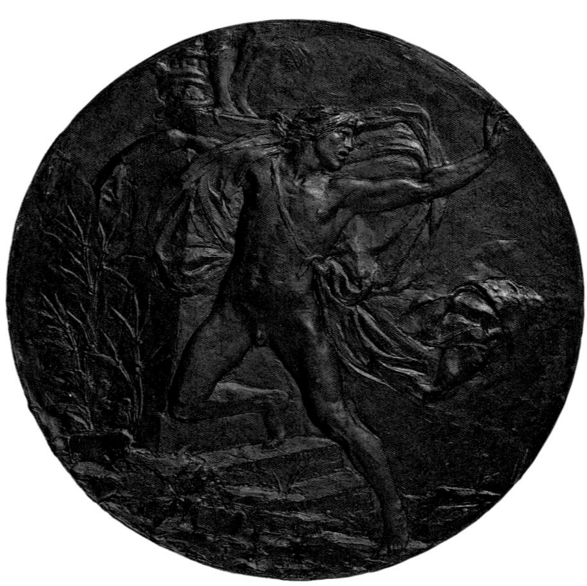

CATALOGUE NO. 66 | HENRI NAUDÉ (1859–?), *Orestes Seeks Refuge at the Statue of Apollo*, 1885. Wax, diam. 50 cm.

responsibility for their acts. With Orestes and the tragic poets everything changes yet again. The Prix de Rome winner, Henri Naudé (1885; cat. no. 66), and Raymond Barthélemy (1860; cat. no. 67) show Orestes as a suppliant to Athena, the goddess of the city, civilization, and Aeschylus. The Athena who protected Ulysses and founded Athens now presides over a jury. Thus, Aeschylus's Orestes makes justice an integral part of both the divine order and civic governance.

In their modest way, both Naudé and Barthélemy have enriched the subject set by the jury. For Barthélemy the subject was: "After the murder of his mother, Orestes, pursued by the Eumenides, takes refuge in the temple of Minerva, clasps his arms around the altar and begs the goddess to protect him (The *Orestes* of Aeschylus's *Eumenides*)." In both 1860 and 1885 the candidates were required only to portray Orestes, but in the range of his expression, his wild gaze, and frenzied gestures, they contrived to suggest the terrors by which he is haunted. In two illustrations of the works of Aeschylus (engravings 21 and 23), John Flaxman shows, behind the hero, the image of his nightmares. In the two prize-winning works, we see their reflection in his rolling eyes.

The Eumenides at Orestes' heels demand revenge. The gods ahead of him, Apollo and Athena, are founding civic justice. Neither Homer nor Athena can conceive of a world in which reason and *polis* weigh light in the scales compared to madness. Twenty-five centuries of progress have taught us the fragility of reason. Orestes and Oedipus are neither unjust nor irrational, but they are haunted by murder and incest, just as one day the soul of Hamlet will be. Orestes and his melancholy soulmate Hamlet—each doomed to avenge his father on his mother—have, with the passage of centuries, come to symbolize the absurdity of action in a world in which reason and justice cannot prevail. The young, naïve Orestes, as portrayed by Barthélemy and Naudé, first longs to act and then longs to undo what he has done. The starting eyes and haggard gestures no longer implore the help of the gods but rather denounce them for abandoning their victim to the toils of a madness they have inflicted but cannot cure. The heroes of epic, Achilles or Odysseus, often seem to be tempted by inertia and inaction, and when they finally decide to act, they are psychologically unaffected by the catastrophes that follow. Orestes is the first to anticipate the consciousness of modern man, as embodied in Hamlet, Faust, and Lorenzaccio. He discovers and confronts two contradictory truths: action enhances the world by the meaning it bestows but destroys those bold enough to act.

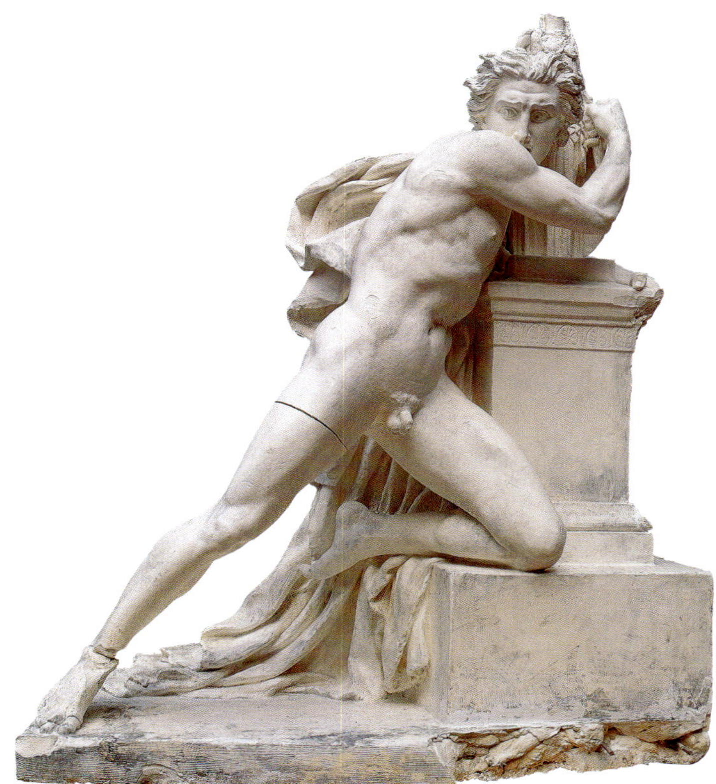

CATALOGUE NO. 67 | RAYMOND BARTHÉLEMY (1833–1902), *Orestes Seeks Refuge at the Altar of Minerva*, 1860. Plaster, 132 × 107 × 52 cm.

NOTES

1 Pierre de Ronsard, "Amours de Marie," in *Oeuvres complètes*, 2 vols. (Paris, 1994), 1:113–14.

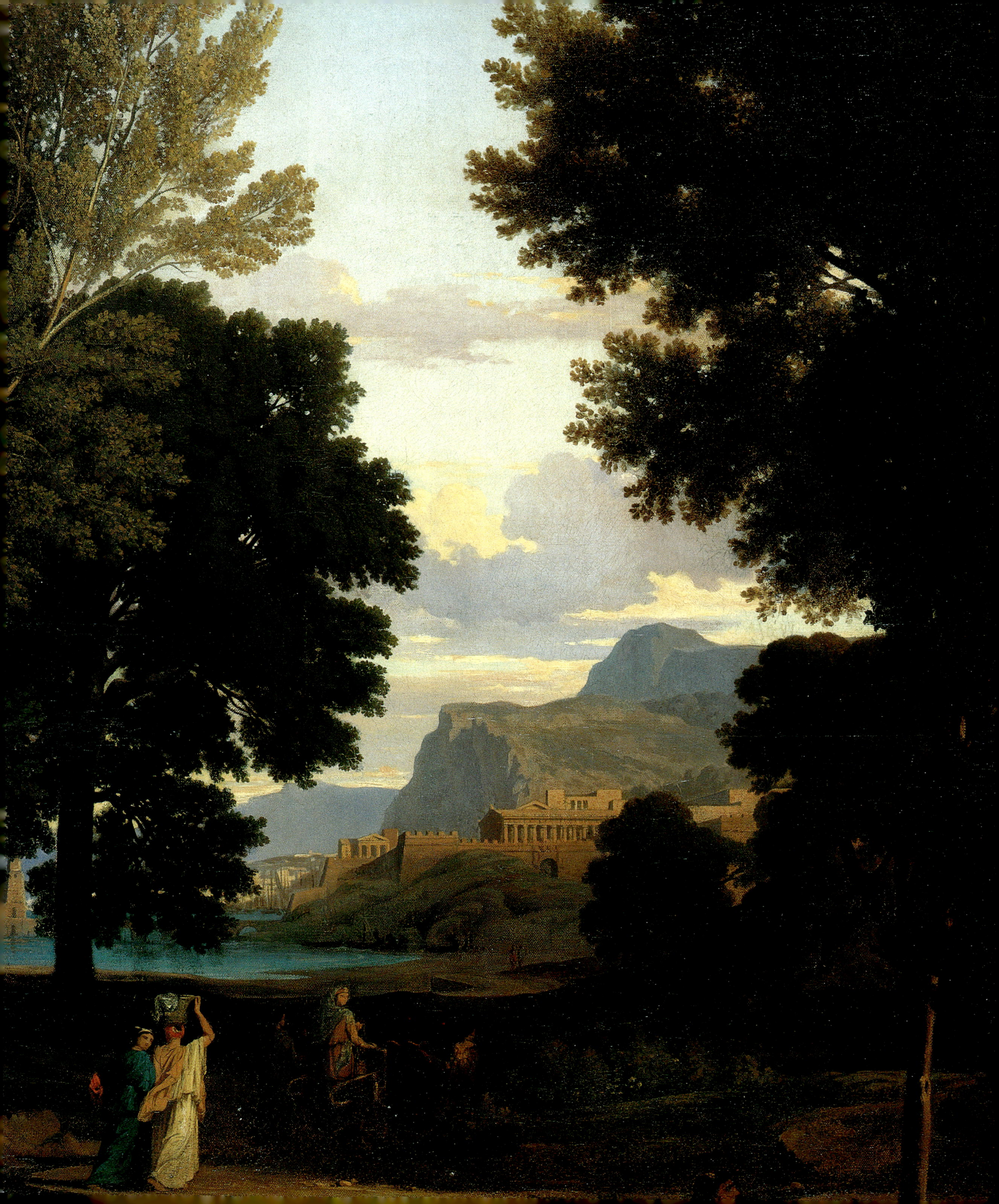

THE VOYAGES OF ULYSSES

Introduction: From the *Iliad* to the *Odyssey*

A much-cited poem from the *Palatine Anthology* anticipates the myriad faces assumed by Ulysses in the history of art and literature: "The sea will always be cruel to the Laertiad. The waves have flowed over his portrait and effaced his features from the tablets. What then? In the pages of Homer his portrait is indelibly incised."[1] The eloquent Odysseus, brined in every billow of the Mediterranean, did not always emerge from history in the most favorable light. Posterity gave him so many different faces that one should evoke some of the earlier ones before turning to those bestowed on him by the students and teachers of the École des beaux-arts.

From the *Iliad* to the *Odyssey*—from Agamemnon to Ulysses—Homer changes, and with him so do the world and the gods themselves. From the *Odyssey* to James Joyce and ourselves, Ulysses has embodied these changes. Homer did not conceive his second epic as an austere and respectful chronicle of the world as he found it. In Odysseus's own account and that of the bard Demodocos, the immortals are portrayed much as the *Iliad* depicted them. Crime paves their way to pleasure. Most of them are hostile toward Odysseus. His only loyal ally is Athena. The gods he encounters are forced to accede to his caprices, which are even more numerous, contradictory, and frivolous than those of Achilles. Odysseus attracts only goddesses. Male gods are of little interest to him, and he therefore spends his time exasperating them. He sometimes regrets his casual treatment of Poseidon, god of the sea, or Eolus, god of the winds, not because he respects them but because, faced with the wind and the sea, he must depend on his own physique, which is no match for these elements. This is galling to a man who relies entirely on his mental resourcefulness. In moments of extremity, when he fears the violence of the natural world, he entreats the relevant divinities and thanks them if his prayers are answered, making the occasional modest offering. (This is the subject for the Rome Prize for sculpture in 1902; see fig. 49.) More often he admires the beauty of the natural world, of land and seascapes: the wine-dark sea; the marvelous choir of the Sirens; and the attractive greenery of a creek. A new form of history painting and sculpture was required to accommodate Odysseus's personality, one in which beings, landscapes, and things weighed heavier in the scale than mere gods.

Odysseus's Adventures and Avatars

In a sonnet famous throughout the world, Joachim du Bellay records the hopes and regrets of a Renaissance Ulysses. The first stanza is, in the image of the cunning warrior, insolent and mendacious:

> Happy the man like Ulysses
> Or he who sought the Golden Fleece,

DETAIL OF CATALOGUE NO. 75

Who's traveled far and wide:
His voyage made, he now retires
To friends and kin, learned and wise
To wear the years out at their side.[2]

A *beau voyage*, that endless shipwreck in which all but the captain perished? Little enough happiness was restored in the wake of Odysseus or Jason, each of whom returned to preside over or suffer further massacres. Why these seductive lies? Other, less familiar sonnets, no less true to the spirit of Homer, answer this question. Du Bellay is not as hostile to distant adventures as he claims. Sorceresses and libertine goddesses are more attractive than a calamitous return to the native land:

I had escaped, I thought, from vice,
from Circe and the Sirens' voice.
But after those long years of pain,
No rest now I'm at home again:
A myriad cares my heart repeats,
I have no hope of their surcease.[3]

Du Bellay experienced humanism—the rediscovery of ancient thought—as Homer experienced the discovery of poetry and humanity. Ulysses and Telemachus tour the emergent Mediterranean world with curiosity, skepticism, boredom, and irony. In their hopes and disillusions they invent the critical eye, at once creative and destructive, which endlessly embellishes reality with lies, sensitivity, and imagination. Return to the native land marks a return to the banality of everyday life. By contrast, distant perils have a certain poetry about them. What, after all, do the Sirens sing in order to inveigle the seaman onto the rocks? Nothing less than the *Iliad* (*Od.* 12.184–91).

Ulysses is the opposite of Aeneas; he acknowledges no master, morality, or god. Racine was for a time smitten with his subtlety (see *Remarks on Homer's Odyssey* [1662]), but *Iphigenia* (1674) made him a villain darkly plotting against the noble Achilles, the innocent Iphigenia, and the legitimate king Agamemnon. In 1699 Fénelon rehabilitated Ulysses, eliciting from his most pitiful victim, Philoctetes, the recognition that Ulysses invariably acted for the good of the state (*Les Aventures de Télémaque*, chap. 25). Fénelon thought this was for the best, but it proved catastrophic for Ulysses, art, and literature. Many artists believed that Ulysses was a good, honest soldier who knew only discipline and *raison d'état*, and it is this version of the wily Odysseus that appears in certain Prix de Rome paintings of the nineteenth century.

The Form of the Human Condition

In his successive ordeals Odysseus travels in quest of wisdom with precisely the humanist intelligence one finds in the sonnets of Du Bellay. Ulysses's tricks had long been recognized as the ruses employed by humanity against gods, destiny, and the human condition[4] in general. Ulysses the trickster is no hero, athlete, or force of nature but rather a spokesman for intelligence in all its forms. Plato, in the conclusion of the *Republic*, authorizes Homer's characters to choose the form in which they will be reincarnated. Their order having been decided by lot, each chooses his own avatar. Ajax wishes to sport a lion's mane, Agamemnon the talons of an eagle, while Thersites, Ulysses' enemy and a model of physical and moral ugliness, chooses the body of an ape. "And it so happened that it fell to the soul of Odysseus to choose last of all. The memory of his former sufferings had cured him of all ambition and he looked around for a long time to find the uneventful life of an ordinary man; at last he found it lying neglected by the others, and when he saw it he chose it with joy."[5] In Plato's view, Ulysses asked to become one with the man in the street, and in the finest artistic incarnations of Odysseus dating from the Middle Ages and the Renaissance, his sociable and practical intelligence peeps out from under the carapace of insolence.

The very structure of the *Odyssey* implies that Ulysses is a fidgety character, never happy in one place. His is not simply a distaste for the static condition: he is in search of something. Peace in the home? Why, then, would he put his questions to the shade of Tiresias, who knows the secrets of death? Circe counsels him to choose between two courses, that of Scylla or Charybdis. Of course, he tries both, twice over. He returns to the sorceress, who has so much to teach him. Why does he risk listening to the Sirens? That is perhaps the Ulysses revealed by Dante: in the *Divine Comedy* (*Inferno*, canto 26), the inventor of the wooden horse is condemned to the circle of fraudsters and the thief of the Palladium to that of the blasphemers. It is, moreover, the puritanical Virgil who pronounces these verdicts. Then Dante lets Ulysses speak for himself. He describes his earthly self, speaking of

> the ardor which within me glowed
> to gain experience of all lands that be
> and man's nature whether good or bad,

exhorting his comrades to

> Think of your breed: nature did not intend
> mankind to live as brutes, but to pursue
> virtue and knowledge to the very end.

He recounts how a whirlwind struck his ship, spinning it round four times: "at the fourth—for thus / another willed— . . . the sea closed over us."[6] That "other" is the god of the Christians. Dante's Ulysses affirms the freedom of a Greek hero against the Virgilian and, later, Christian ideal of subordination to authority.

Let us move on to modern times, to June 16, 1904: Bloomsday. The rambling, labyrinthine itinerary James Joyce traced for his *Ulysses* (1922) led him through Catholic Dublin rather than the pagan Mediterranean. Leopold Bloom is still Ulysses as he becomes the Wandering Jew. His Telemachus is Stephen Daedalus, and together they reconstitute the Odyssean duality of curiosity and intelligence, confronting all the questions asked of humanity since Homeric times.

The grand compositions of Dante and Joyce stand well outside my present purpose. Let me turn for guidance to the modest Clément Marot, for whom the greatest deed of Ulysses was to reject the immortality offered by Calypso:

> Odysseus was reported wise,
> He did well to turn aside
> The chance to be immortal.
> Death had no sting at all
> He said, if once he might
> Taste his country's air again
> And be granted sight
> Of cottage and the village lane,
> Smoke rising in the light.[7]

Immortality is nothing compared to a well-filled human life: this is surely what Ulysses discovers. Did he choose the mortal condition, like Molière's Don Juan, "for love of humanity"[8] or for the love of Penelope alone? Faced with this alternative, painters and sculptors have mostly settled on the latter option.

In-Laws of Odysseus

Who knows of Odysseus's earlier journey, a much shorter round-trip to Sparta to carry Penelope off from her tearful parents? She was the daughter of Icarius, who is several times cited in the *Odyssey*, being the brother of Tyndareus and therefore Helen's uncle. When the time came for Tyndareus to give away his much-coveted daughter to a Greek prince, Ulysses of course offered his hand, probably without much hope. According to certain legends, however, it was he who suggested to Tyndareus that all suitors for Helen's hand must promise not only to accept her choice but to come to the assistance of the chosen man if his wife should be taken from him. This notion allowed Tyndareus to avoid any dispute, and he thanked Ulysses by arranging his marriage to Penelope. It is easy to believe that Ulysses, an unlikely suitor to Helen in any case, had always had this in mind. Her cousin's taste, wit, and foresight made Penelope a much more suitable match. The episode is little known. In 1892 the subject set for the oil sketch *concours* was "Ulysses and

Penelope Depart for Ithaca," with the following commentary: "Ulysses marries Penelope, daughter of Icarius, whose brother is king of Sparta. He must now return to Ithaca. At the moment of departure, seeing the grief of his father-in-law, he allows his young bride to choose whether to remain in her family or go with him. Penelope's only response is to lower her veil and move toward Odysseus. *Odyssey*, Book 16." The reference to book sixteen is incorrect. Homer constantly makes use of Penelope's patronymic but gives no information at all about the life of Icarius. Pausanias tells the story but is sparing with the details.[9] He does not tell us whether Odysseus had always sought to return to Ithaca with the sage Penelope rather than her dangerous cousin Helen. Ulysses at least knew it was no easy thing for a man of his character to live with the parents of his wife, especially when they were richer and more powerful than he. He therefore refused Icarius's self-seeking offer to let him stay in Sparta, suspecting that his father-in-law saw in his sagacious son-in-law the guarantee of a prosperous and comfortable old age. Icarius and his wife, Periboeia, were insistent and even tearful. Ulysses and Penelope nevertheless continued to hold the view that a life shared with his in-laws in their own palace and city would be intolerable.

This very bourgeois—or very antibourgeois—subject has inspired few paintings. The prizewinner Jean-François Auburtin successfully captured the banal modernity of the anecdote in a few sketchy outlines (cat. no. 68). Faceless and silent as these figures are, they are rich in personality and presence. The two parents hide their pain or fury—feigned or real—in their hands. As the legend requires, Penelope veils her blushes and says nothing. Ulysses is no more forthcoming. The parents' answer comes in the couple's first eloquent steps toward a quite different future, suggested in the attenuated colors of the horizon on the right of the little painting, as the newlyweds turn their backs on the imposing statue looming over the great city and set out for their little village. It is said that here, on the road leading to Ithaca, Icarius raised an altar to Modesty. This is perhaps what Auburtin depicts behind the pitifully grieving parents. As to the young couple, they show themselves more adult than the previous generation, putting behind them the statue of Modesty for which they currently have not the slightest use.

Ulysses' Plough

As we have seen, at Ulysses' suggestion the Greek kings swore that they would all come to the aid of the man who won Helen's hand. When Menelaus lost his wife, enthusiasm for honoring this oath was not boundless. The triumph of the blond prince of Sparta had won him few friends. Odysseus's response is discreetly evoked by Homer in the *Odyssey*. Agamemnon in the Underworld remembers the visit he made to Ithaca to

> . . . urge Odysseus to sail with us in the ships
> on our campaign to Troy?
>
> That's how hard it was to bring him round,
> Odysseus, raider of cities.
>
> —OD. 24.116–17, 119; F 24.126, 128–29

By an irony of fate, Ulysses' oath came back to haunt him. Attempting to shirk a duty that was to cost him twenty years of peaceful family life, he feigned madness, appearing before the Greek ambassadors in a ridiculous hat consisting of half an eggshell and sowing salt behind a plough drawn by a donkey and an ox. Palamedes, one of the ambassadors, placed the young Telemachus under the plowshare. Ulysses at once gave up his agricultural playacting. This picture of peasant cunning shipwrecked on parental love cannot help but appeal to the modern reader, summarizing as it does the tradition of Ulysses' character as known from Homer to Du Bellay. The subject was twice set for the sculpture sketch *concours* and once much later in the century for the oil sketch, inspiring in the three prizewinners some subtle variations on this anything but heroic hero.

The sculpture sketch by Théophile Caudron (1830, cat. no. 69) shows an animated and picturesque scene verging on pathos. A dog licks the child beneath the plowshare, while accusations and windswept drapery

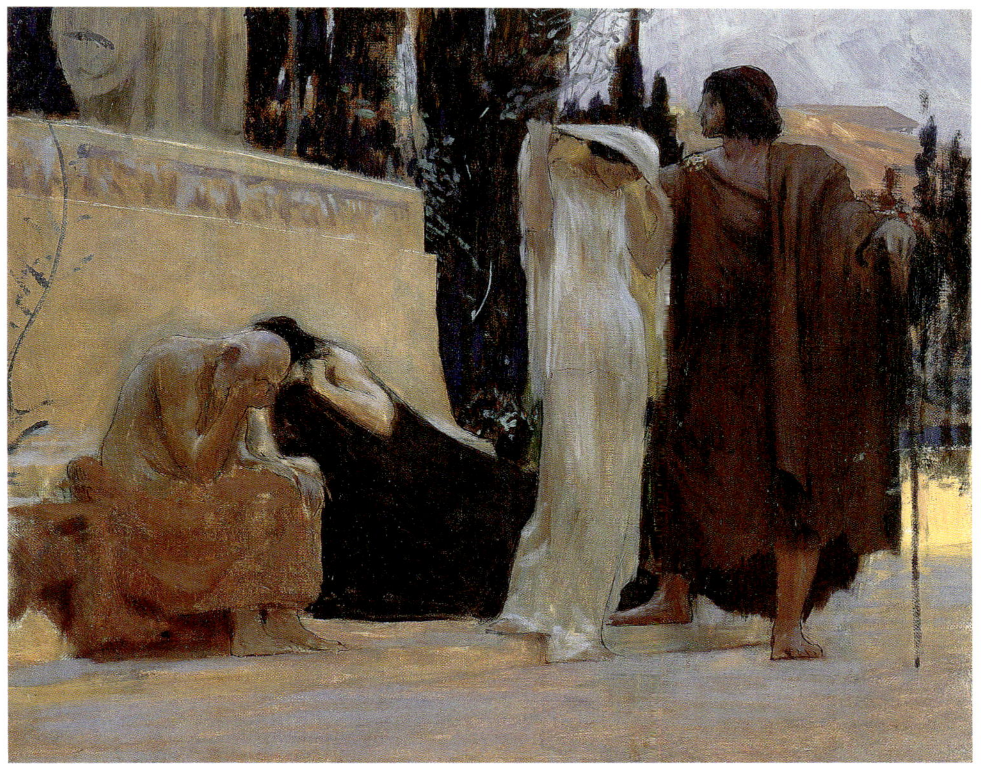

CATALOGUE NO. 68 | JEAN-FRANÇOIS AUBURTIN (1866–1930), *The Departure of Ulysses and Penelope for Ithaca*, 1892. Oil on canvas, 36.5 × 43 cm.

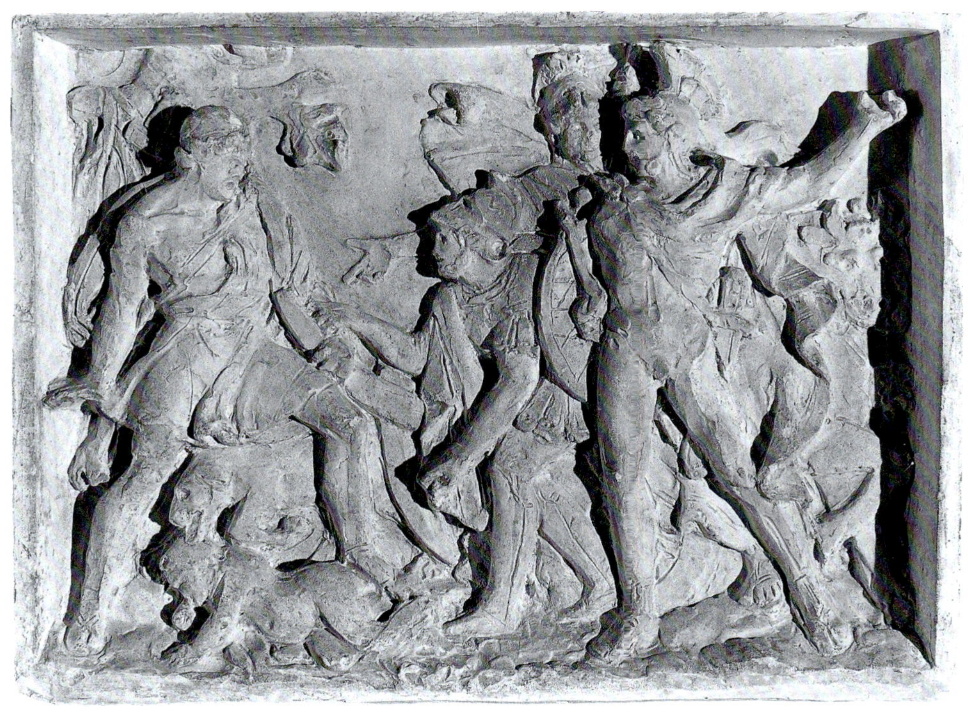

CATALOGUE NO. 69 | THÉOPHILE CAUDRON (1805–1848), *Ulysses Feigns Madness*, 1830. Plaster, 35 × 47 cm.

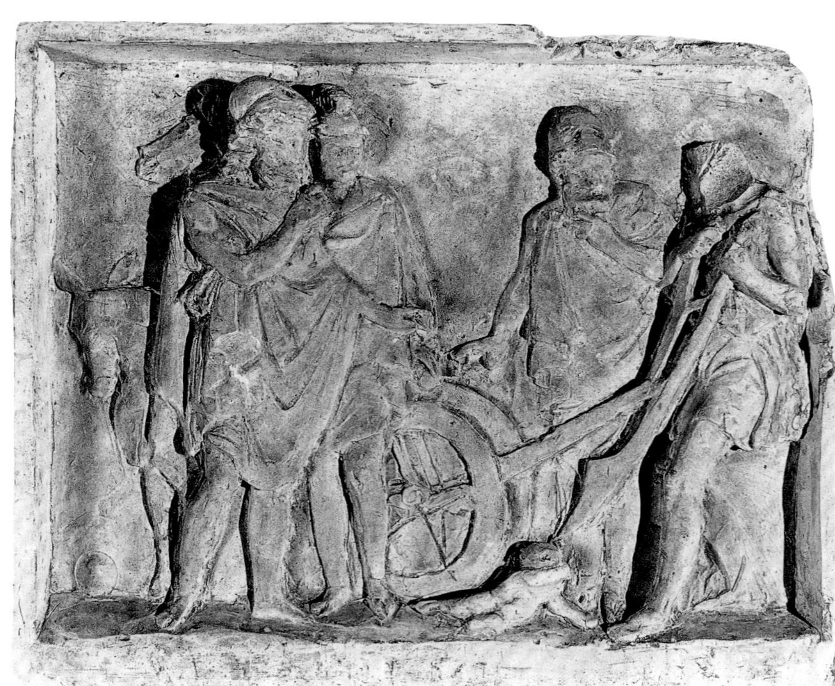

FIGURE 46 | JACQUES-EUGÈNE CAUDRON (1818–1865), *Ulysses Feigns Madness*, 1842. Plaster, 36.4 × 43.2 cm. Sculpture Sketch *concours*.

fly. The beasts in this hybrid team wonder—with good reason—why Odysseus has yoked them together. Jacques-Eugène Caudron's relief of twelve years later schematizes the poses and freezes the protagonists (fig. 46). Even before Odysseus betrays himself, the drama has declined into ceremony, and the genre scene takes on the kind of rustic nobility that occasionally illuminates the *Odyssey*. Late in the same century, the young painter Eugène Cadel gave the scene a humorous treatment in the oil sketch *concours* (1889; fig. 47). Ulysses is clearly overdoing his role as madman to the point where no one takes him seriously—not the child swinging on the yoke, not even the two draft animals who pull in opposite directions, exhibiting their lumpen cruppers. Palamedes placidly attends the dénouement. The ambassadors are like a pantomime audience, warning of infanticide but doing nothing to prevent it. Here are three versions of Ulysses' mendacity: our hero is not inhibited by scruple, vanity, or peer judgment.

Ulysses thus has no choice but to join the army, and in the oil sketch by Jean-Nicolas-Alphonse Isambert (1846; cat. no. 70) he resolves to do so. Palamedes is reduced to a background silhouette, a presumably ironic observer under whose gaze Ulysses entrusts the education of his son to Penelope and Mentor (who holds the lyre). This scene is not unlike the encounter of Hector, Andromache, and Astyanax at the Scaean gates. Human society is defined by the education adults give their children, and legend bestowed on Homer himself the status of teacher: he is always shown surrounded by young disciples. The noble immobility of the four protagonists is threatened by the presence of the old trooper bulking large against the gates. Everyone would like to remain within the safe urban colonnades and attend to the lessons of Mentor and the songs of Homer, but Palamedes' weapons bristle against the sky. The outwitted Odysseus had his revenge when the Greeks, relying on evidence fabricated by our hero, stoned Palamedes to death as a traitor.

Ulysses' Mother

Hard as it was to persuade Odysseus to leave for Troy, it proved harder still for him to return, and the

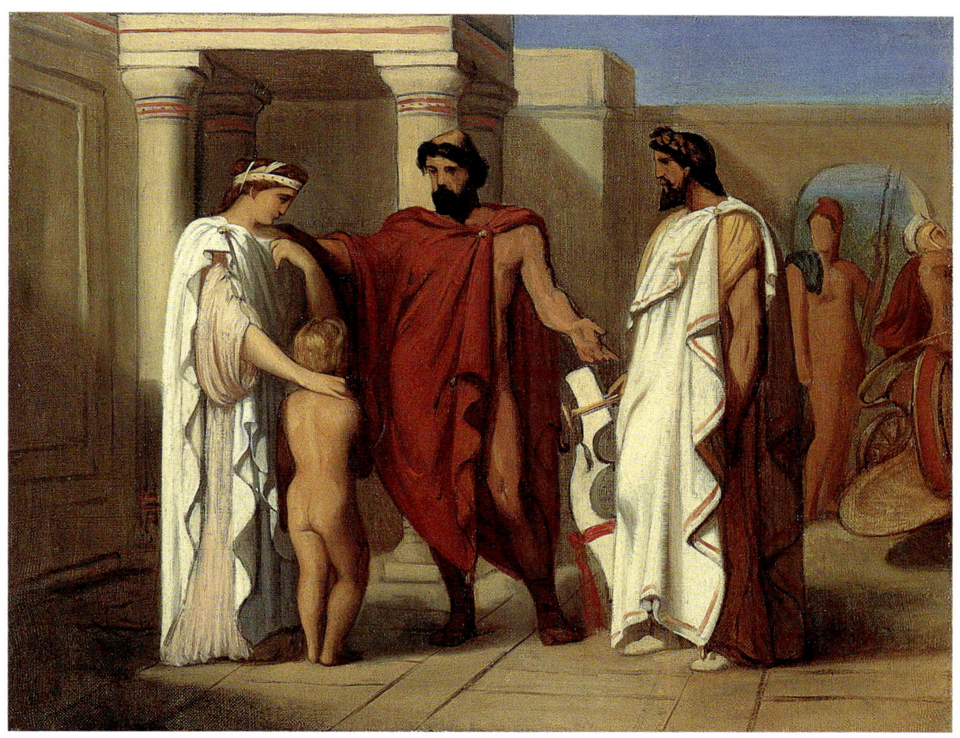

CATALOGUE NO. 70 | JEAN-NICOLAS-ALPHONSE ISAMBERT (1818–?), *The Departure of Ulysses*, 1846. Oil on canvas, 32 × 40.5 cm.

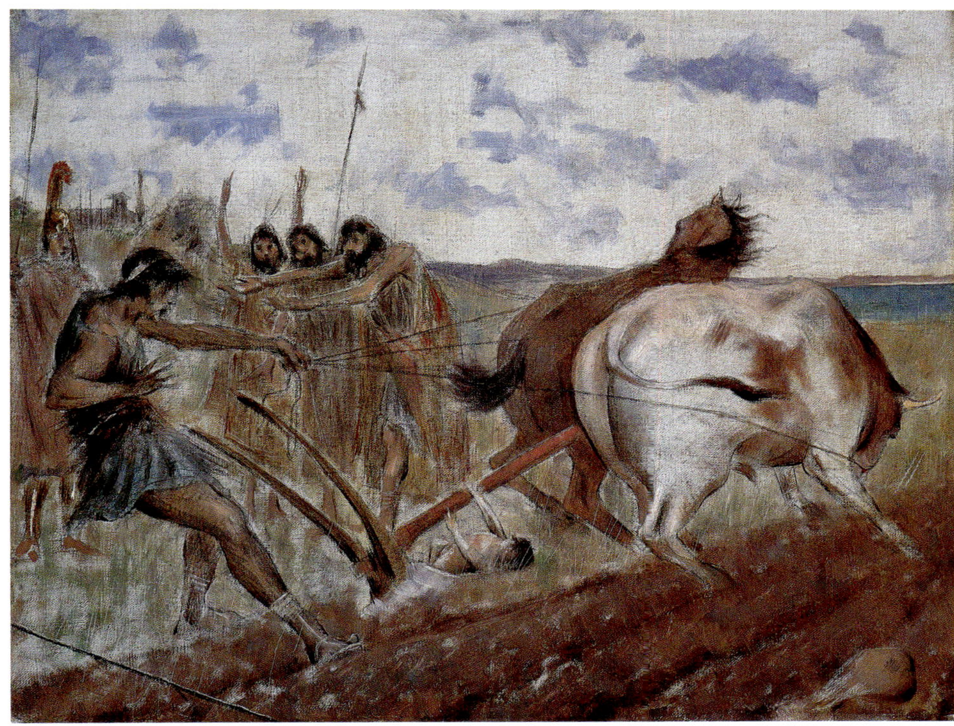

FIGURE 47 | EUGÈNE-CASIMIR CADEL (1862–1940), *Ulysses Feigns Madness*, 1889. Oil on canvas, 32 × 40.5 cm. Painted Sketch *concours*.

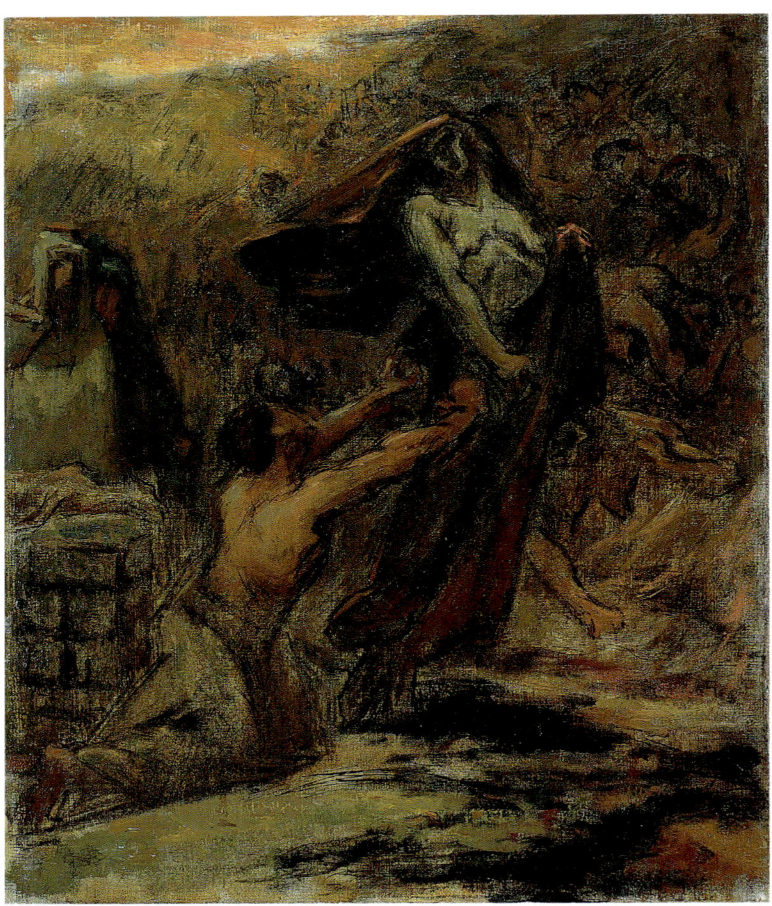

CATALOGUE NO. 71 | GUSTAVE-AUGUSTE CORLIN (1875–1924), *Ulysses and the Shade of His Mother*, 1901. Oil on canvas, 46 × 38.5 cm.

difficulties inspired Homer's second poem. The *Odyssey* offers a complex mixture of ancient stories and more strictly Homeric scenes, placing the heroes in situations as completely alien to epic and legend as any we have seen in the *Iliad*. The poet is the narrator of the first books, in which Ulysses ingloriously leaves the tedious Calypso. Our hero himself then takes up the story during the feast at the court of Alcinous, king of the Phaeacians. Thus, in the more unlikely sequences, Homer allows Odysseus to speak in the first person, occasionally remarking on his tendency to embroider upon his exploits. Modesty is not Ulysses' forte. He ranges over three years of adventures full of fantastical events and divine intervention, ending with his stay on the island of the unfortunate Calypso, whom he had abandoned only three weeks earlier after a stay of seven years. Everything changes with his return from the island of the Phaeacians to his native land. There follows a series of hostile or distrustful meetings between the hero and his son, swineherd, dog, wife, rivals, and father. The poet returns to the rostrum. Faced with these modest interlocutors, Odysseus the third person cuts a much less dashing figure than in his own narration.

For some two hundred years the members of the Royal Academy (and then the post-Revolutionary Institute) tended—consciously or not—to put aside Ulysses' heroic adventures in favor of less flattering scenes. The fabulous or monstrous—Cyclops and Sirens—were studiously ignored. In 1901, however, the examiners set their students to meditate on the meeting of "Ulysses and the Shade of His Mother," one of the episodes Odysseus himself recounts. Gustave-Auguste Corlin won the prize (cat. no. 71) with a very noble depiction of Ulysses' mother, Anticleia; she becomes an all but invisible incarnation of death and destiny, swirling in the wind of time and forbidden to gaze on her son. To the left we see the once blind soothsayer Tiresias, who has recovered his sight in the Underworld. He alone could tell Ulysses how to return to Ithaca; he alone among the dead has the right to gaze upon the living. As Circe puts it: "Even in death—Persephone has given him wisdom, / everlasting vision to him and him alone . . . the rest of the dead are empty, flitting shades" (*Od.* 10.494–95), avid to drink the blood of life that Ulysses parsimoniously offers them. When Tiresias finally leaves mother and son together, their dialogue is more complex than any rhetorical disquisition on mortality.

Did Corlin know that his sketch sounded a distant echo of the most famous painting in ancient Delphi, Polygnotus's *Nekuia* ("Descent to the Realm of the

Dead")? In 1761 a strange debate took place between Diderot, the sculptor Falconet, and the comte de Caylus, the latter having commissioned an engraving from Louis-Joseph Le Lorrain (fig. 48).[10] The engraving follows fairly accurately the long and precise description of Polygnotus's work by Pausanias (*Description of Greece* 10.28–31). Caylus adapted this description for one of his *Tableaux Taken . . . from the Odyssey*: "The victims, that is, the black sheep, their throats cut in the square ditch at the base of a rock, on the edge of one of the rivers of the underworld. We see the palace of Pluto in the distance. . . . The souls come thronging around."[11] Polygnotus clearly attempted to include the whole *nekuia* of the *Odyssey* in his painting and not simply the moment of Odysseus's conversation with Tiresias, which most directly raises the question of the eternal soul. This ancient *Divine Comedy* or Last Judgment presented the dead as filled with memories of their past lives. The modern engraving, by contrast, is a didactic procession of all the inhabitants of the Underworld. There is a certain innocence about the *Odyssey* so literally interpreted, as if it were a sacred text. Homer no doubt added this descent to Hades to Ulysses' story in order for our hero to encounter his memories and remorse there—just as, on his return to Ithaca, he meets with the memories of his now ancient youth.

The merest evocation of Anticleia's brief, melancholy replies to Ulysses is more eloquent than the longest visual paraphrase by Le Lorrain. The words and gestures of mother and son as Homer imagined them have to encompass not death, of which only Tiresias knows the secrets, but our hatred of death. Ulysses needs the advice of Tiresias, and at first keeps back the shade of his mother, who anxiously awaits her draught of blood:

> But look, the ghost
> of my mother came! My mother, dead and gone
> now . . .

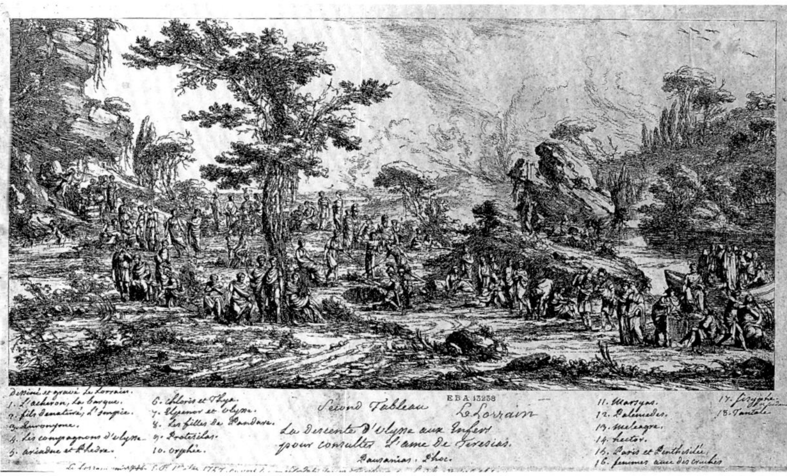

FIGURE 48 | LOUIS-JOSEPH LE LORRAIN (1715–1759), *Ulysses Descends to the Underworld to Consult the Shade of Tiresias*, 1757. Etching, 22.8 × 38.7 cm.

> Anticleia—daughter of that great heart Autolycus—
> whom I had left alive when I sailed for sacred Troy.
> I broke into tears to see her here, but filled with pity,
> even throbbing with grief, I would not let her ghost
> approach the blood till I had questioned Tiresias
> myself.
> —OD. 11.84–89; F 11.93–99

Odysseus is alive, and his primary responsibility is to his own and his mariners' fates. He thinks first of life, then laments the dead, and finally confesses to the guilt of the survivor. Anticleia's words, after the long conversation between Ulysses and Tiresias, are made up of a mother's reproaches and a son's remorse. It was not "some hateful illness" that struck her:

> No, it was my longing for *you*, my shining Odysseus—
> you and your quickness, you and your gentle ways—
> that tore away my life that had been sweet.
> —OD. 11.200–203; F 11.230–32

For the survivor, death takes the form of memories of his nearest and dearest, "sifting away, / like a shadow, dissolving like a dream" (*Od.* 11.206–7) or like the image of his mother that Odysseus three times vainly tries to embrace. Two years before Corlin won his prize, Anatole France had translated and commented upon this very scene in the *Odyssey*. His surprise at finding in a narrative full of superstition and primitive barbarity the voice of reason and sentiment was no doubt also experienced by Corlin. Here is France's translation:

> She had spoken. Her son wished to take her in his arms. Three times he sprang forward, his heart burning to grasp her; three times, she vanished from his arms, like a shadow, like a dream.

Then, his heart transfixed with pain, he said: "Mother, why do you not wait for me when I wish to embrace you, so that here, in the Underworld, we may sate ourselves with tears in each other's arms?"

And his venerable mother replied:
"Alas, my child! Such is the state of humankind when dead: the sinews are bare of flesh and bone, the fierce fire consumes them as soon as the spirit leaves the white bones, and the soul, like a dream, floats, fluttered away."[12]

Ulysses and Homer together assert the intensity of our desire for life and the immense vacuity of death. Ulysses perceives that this void of death into which Circe has briefly sent him after he succumbed to the charms of the sorceress indeed inspires tears but not a shred of hope (*Od.* 10.501–2). The dead exist only in the spirit of those who remember them before dissolving into the shadowy, monochrome oblivion that the young Corlin depicted. Like Ulysses, Corlin attempts to fix the elusive shade in paint, as the subject of the *concours* required. Like his mother, Ulysses sees the bodies writhe around him, sees them mingle with the earth as memory of them is dissolved. It is no easy thing to paint the craving of the dead and their nostalgia for life, but the magic of the sketch conveys above all the materialism of Homer's vision. The rest of the poem expresses the desire to make the most of life, to bathe in its warmth, to travel and to escape for as long as possible the immobility of death. To Achilles an eternity of glory if he wants it, but everyone else prefers free use of this world. The dead possess nothing but a specter devoid of strength and energy, unconnected to life and the living.

This pitiless lesson is taught by a mother—by the shade, the memory of that mother. Her son knows that nothing is left of her, but her words are still everything to him. It is sometimes said that civilization was born when humankind first buried its dead in order to remember them the better. Every reader of the eleventh book of the *Odyssey*—from Diderot and the obscure Corlin to the refined Anatole France—has learned how wrong we are to think of ourselves as more civilized than Bronze Age man. Homer's poetry is "more enduring than bronze," and no one knew better how to contemplate and record the long conversation that has, throughout the history of the human race, conjoined the living with the unforgotten dead who were buried in the earth or consumed on the pyre.

Ulysses' Mistress

The immortals cannot, by definition, experience the feelings of life and death. The goddess Calypso admits the shipwrecked mortal to her island and her bed. She loves to abandon herself in the arms of her lover, while he, after seven years, longs for just one thing: to return to Penelope. The goddess believes she can retain him with the offer of immortality—an eternity of boredom. She cannot understand Ulysses' desire to live the life of a mortal man.

Let us remind ourselves of the situation. Like all the other gods, the sea god Proteus is a voyeur who likes to watch the love affairs of one or another of his fellow gods, and he has been to Ogygia, as he tells Menelaus: "I saw him once on an island, weeping live warm tears / in the nymph Calypso's house—she holds him there by force" (*Od.* 4.555–57). Homer later affords us a glimpse of the evening's entertainment on Ogygia:

Off he sat on a headland, weeping there as always,
wrenching his heart with sobs and groans and
anguish,
gazing out over the barren sea through blinding tears.
—*OD.* 5.82–84; F 5.93–95

The intervention of the gods, who decide to split up the lovers, provokes a grand separation scene. Hermes arrives with orders for Calypso to free her captive forthwith. The immortal repines:

Hard-hearted
you are, you gods! You unrivaled lords of jealousy—
scandalized when goddesses sleep with mortals,
openly, even when one has made the man her
husband.
—*OD.* 5.118–20; F 5.130–33

She seeks out Odysseus for one last desparate effort to avoid separation:

The queenly nymph sought out the great Odysseus—

and found him there on the headland, sitting, still,
weeping, his eyes never dry, his sweet life flowing away
with the tears he wept for his foiled journey home,
since the nymph no longer pleased. In the nights,
true,
he'd sleep with her in the arching cave—he had no
choice—unwilling lover alongside lover all too
willing . . .
[The Greek phrase is οὐκ ἐθέλων ἐθελούσῃ.]
—*OD.* 5.151–58; F 5.165–72

Here, then, is the model for all European love literature: the boredom of one lover; the rage of the other; the scene of separation despite the wishes of one or the other. Suetonius rehearses Homer's ironic rhythms in recounting the amours of Titus and Berenice but gives them a tragic reciprocity—*dimisit invitus invitam*—a divorce sought by neither but inflicted on both.[13] Racine followed in Suetonius's footsteps, constructing his *Bérénice* around the same paradox.

Calypso at last lets her Prince Charming prepare for his departure. The construction of a raft restores him to himself: Ulysses the engineer, the artisan, the indefatigable mariner lulled to sleep during the last seven years. Calypso's regrets receive special attention in Daumier's *Calypso's Despair* (cat. no. 124).

Nausicaa

No sooner has Ulysses risen from his seven-year Ogygian slumber, no sooner has he put to sea in his self-constructed raft, than his adventures (as if they, too, had been drowsing) resume with a vengeance. His old enemy, the sea-god, targets his raft, and Ulysses' return to Greece takes place over two acts and two Adriatic islands. The sea first throws Ulysses up on the island of the Phaeacians (today's Corfu). This short stop provides an agreeable backdrop for subtle and amusing scenes. Poor Odysseus thinks he has escaped the domination of women. Calypso let him depart with a few gifts, no doubt intended to instill guilt rather than assist him in his journey, which, in any case, are swallowed up by the sea soon afterward. Poseidon's long-awaited vengeance for his son Polyphemus can now be effected: in a few trident blows, the ocean tears the raft apart and Ulysses is forced to swim for land. The coast is unknown to him. His sole remaining possession, a scarf, was bestowed on him by another goddess, the Nereid Ino, a bit of fabric that serves as a loincloth. The current of a river thrusts our swimmer back toward the sea, but a prayer becalms the current, and the shipwrecked sailor finally gains the shore, there to sink into exhausted slumber. How can he thank the marine deities for sparing his life? He returns Ino's scarf:

. . . he regained his breath and rallied back to life,
at last he loosed the goddess' scarf from his body,
dropped it into the river flowing out to sea
and a swift current bore it far downstream
and suddenly Ino caught it in her hands.
—*OD.* 5.458–62; F 5.507–11

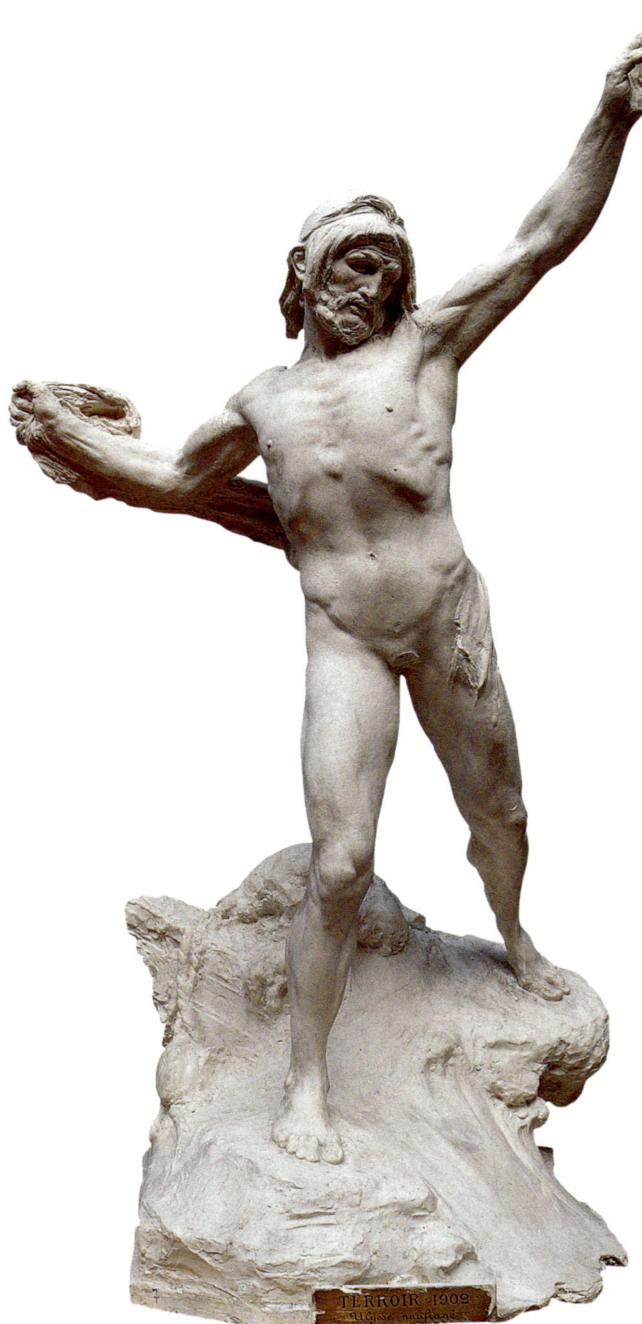

FIGURE 49 | ALPHONSE-CAMILLE TERROIR (1875–1955), *The Shipwrecked Ulysses Throwing the Scarf of the Goddess into the Sea*, 1902. Plaster, 178 × 100 × 86 cm. Prix de Rome in Sculpture.

Now Ulysses' limbs are at last free of the ties woven by the goddesses; he need no longer fear humiliating imprisonment by woman. He is, however, naked as the day he was born, as he is shown by Alphonse-Camille Terroir (1902 Prix de Rome in Sculpture; fig. 49). Sporting nothing but a little cap, he removes the scarf, throwing it into the wine-dark sea. This grand gesture is supposed to recall Raphael's immortal image of Galatea; only goddesses and the forces of nature should see his noble deed. But Homer is fertile in irony: a few hours later Ulysses awakens to regret the useful loincloth he has so improvidently abandoned when a new Circe, a new Calypso, appears in the company of her pretty handmaidens. This is the young Nausicaa, daughter of Alcinous. (He himself describes his position as follows: "There are twelve peers of the realm who rule our land, / thirteen counting myself" [F 8.435–36].) Briefly crossing Ulysses' path as he arrives and departs, Nausicaa is one of Homer's subtlest inventions. Her personality and intelligence singled her out in classical times either as the future wife of Telemachus or as the real author of the *Odyssey*, a tradition to which Goethe also pays homage. Ulysses stumbles from Calypso to Nausicaa, from a woman he quits with relief to one he must decline with regret.

The young laundry girls play ball while their washing dries, and the game wakes the castaway. Odysseus knows women well and shows himself equal to this delicate situation. We hear his thoughts:

> "Listen: shouting, echoing round me—women, girls—
> or the nymphs who haunt the rugged mountaintops
> and the river springs and meadows lush with grass!
> Or am I really close to people who speak my language?
> Up with you, see how the land lies, see for yourself now . . ."
>
> Muttering so, great Odysseus crept out of the bushes,
> stripping off with his massive hand a leafy branch
> from the tangled olive growth to shield his body,
> hide his private parts. And out he stalked

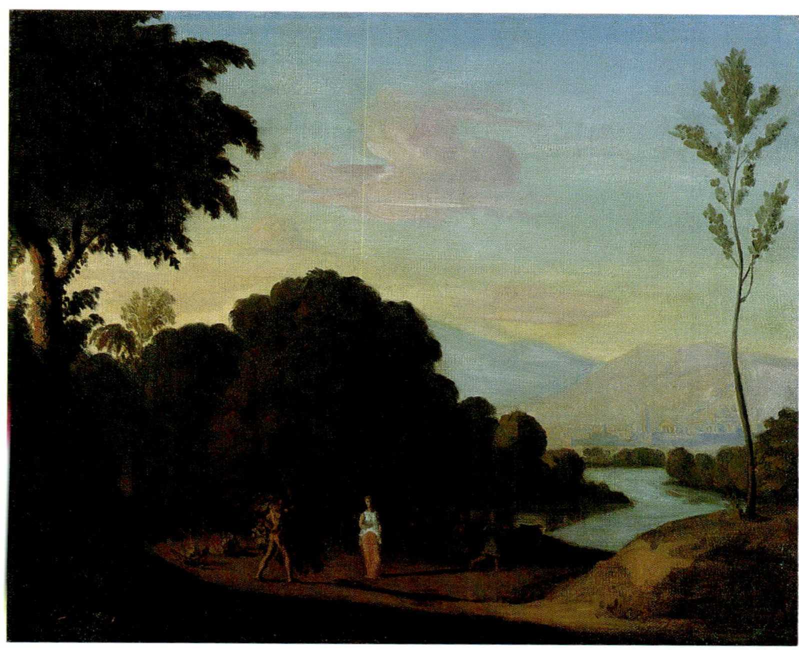

CATALOGUE NO. 72 | PAUL FLANDRIN (1811–1902), *Ulysses and Nausicaa*, 1832. Oil on canvas, 38.5 × 46 cm.

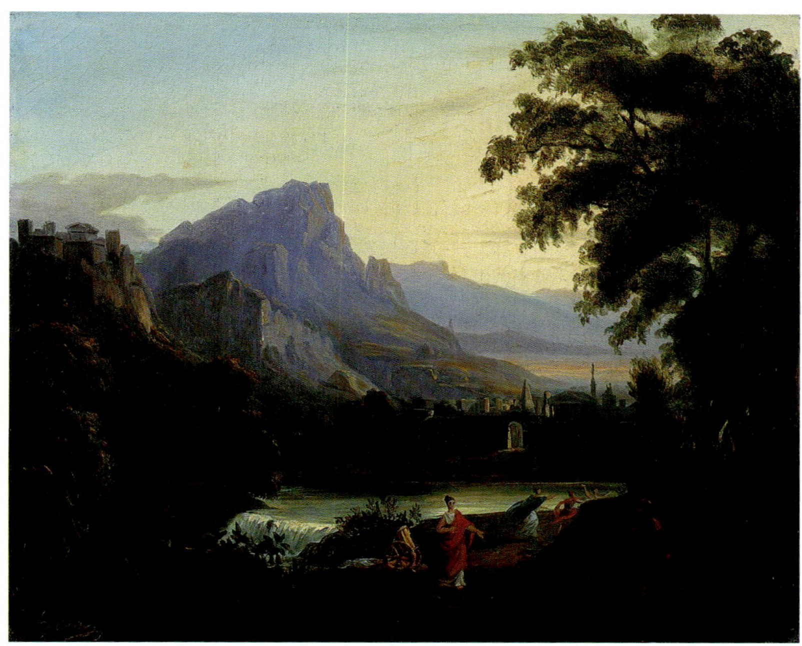

CATALOGUE NO. 73 | THÉODORE-FRANÇOIS-ALEXIS LEDIEU (1806–?), *Ulysses and Nausicaa*, 1832. Oil on canvas, 37.5 × 45.5 cm.

as a mountain lion exultant in his power
strides through wind and rain and his eyes blaze
and he charges sheep or oxen or chases wild deer
but his hunger drives him on to go for flocks,
even to raid the best-defended homestead.
So Odysseus moved out . . .
about to mingle with all those lovely girls,
naked now as he was, for the need drove him on,
a terrible sight, all crusted, caked with brine—
they scattered in panic down the jutting beaches.
—*OD.* 6.122–40; F 6.134–52

Perspicacious Ulysses: he guessed that in the group of young Phaeacian girls at least one would have some curiosity. He was right to cast Ino's veil to the waves, and he strides out handsome as the lion of Metapontum (cat. no. 10). His humor is intelligent and displays exactly the false humility that women most love. He fashions an elegant compliment to the pretty princess: she is more beautiful than any other woman, than any of the goddesses. His cajoling charm detains her long enough for him to improve his appearance and even be admired:

At first he seemed appalling, I must say—
now he seems like a god who rules the skies up there!
Ah, if only a man like *that* were called my husband . . .
—*OD.* 6.242–44; F 6.268–70

This is a very varied scene, lasting from dawn to dusk, and the École has many representations of it. They tend to concentrate on the flight of the serving women and the meeting of the two main protagonists. In the 1832 oil sketch *concours* and the 1833 Grand Prix the subject was handled this way by every one of the competitors. Paul Flandrin's sketch (cat. no. 72) makes best use of the dawning day: the misty light is reflected on the water and the long shadows it casts bring together protagonists who seem determined to maintain their distance. The young women flee into the shade. For Alexis Ledieu (cat. no. 73), the scene occurs somewhat later and the shadows have already thinned. This is a bright, cool place where it is a pleasure to meet

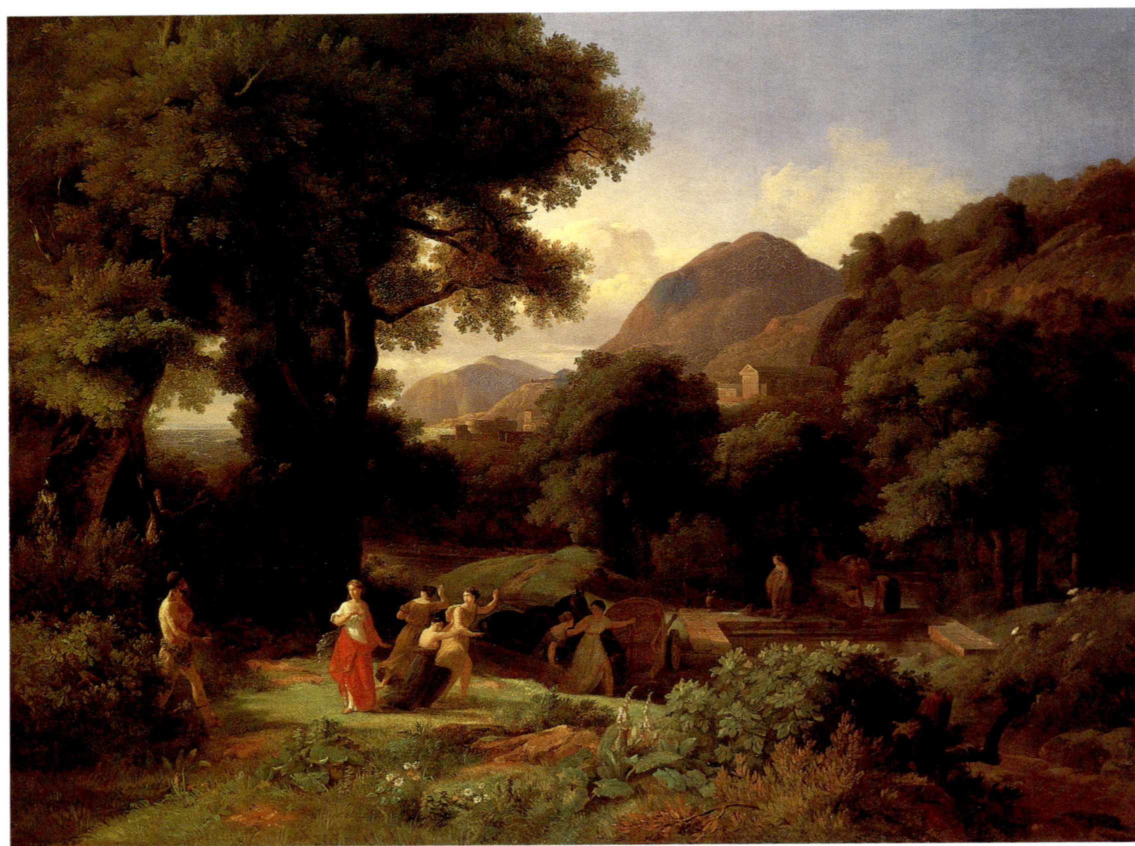

CATALOGUE NO. 74 | ROMAIN-ÉTIENNE-GABRIEL PRIEUR (1806–1879), *Ulysses and Nausicaa*, 1833. Oil on canvas, 114 × 146 cm.

and talk. Ledieu is more ironic than Flandrin: the princess's friends, caught in flight, are lit to great advantage. For Flandrin, by contrast, the massy dark shadows in which Ulysses lurks like a satyr become a foil for the frail tree and the no less frail Nausicaa. The winning entry in the 1833 Landscape Prize, that of Gabriel Prieur (cat. no. 74), exhibits quite excessive historical precision, as the rules required. We can see the town better than the water and the servant girls better than Nausicaa. Odysseus, however, might indeed attract the eyes of a young lady by this triumphal entrance into the dappled light of a clearing.

In accordance with the subject set in 1845, Achille Benouville (cat. no. 75) describes a later stage of the action and the day. The serving girls have returned, and Nausicaa has dressed the shipwrecked hero in clean clothes—the wash having already dried. The heat of the day has come and gone, and the morning's excitements are already just a memory. The task was to paint the aspiration of Nausicaa to seem decisive and reasonable in the eyes of a man clearly weary of sentimental mistresses. He and she are to make their separate ways to the town, she on the cart, he some distance behind, for they must avoid any gossip, as she rightly points out—just the kind of wisdom that would attract and reassure this mature man. A few hours later, in the presence of Nausicaa's father, Alcinous, Ulysses claims credit for this initiative, which might have appeared too knowing

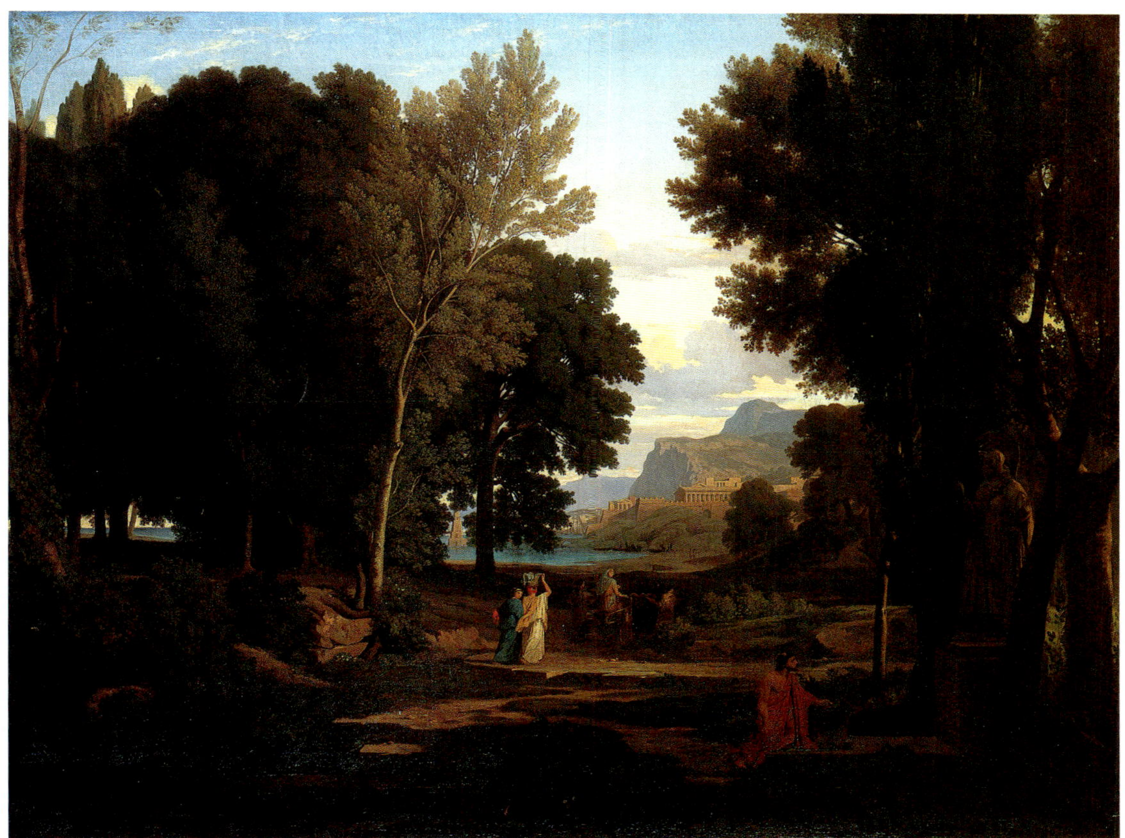

CATALOGUE NO. 75 | ACHILLE BENOUVILLE (1815–1891), *Ulysses and Nausicaa*, 1845. Oil on canvas, 114 × 146 cm.

on the part of a young girl. We hardly thought him so tactful. She, moreover, has had time to direct a few deeply felt compliments to the visitor concerning his handsome looks. The psychological finesse that requires Ulysses to distance himself from Nausicaa just so much and no more is beyond Benouville's reach. He was asked to paraphrase these isolated verses:

> At that she touched the mules with her shining whip
> and they quickly left the running stream behind.
> The team trotted on, their hoofs wove in and out.
> She drove them back with care so all the rest,
> maids and Odysseus, could keep the pace on foot . . .
> —OD. 6.316–20; F 6.346–50

In this crepuscular scene, with its columns of light falling on sea, temples, and mountains, how can we make out the deft, nervous movements of the young Nausicaa?

With her nimble intelligence and measured audacity, Nausicaa makes a mockery of philosophical and mythological interpretations.[14] In her case, ancient critics were forced to abandon the symbols with which they had weighed down Ulysses' three other encounters with women, namely, Circe, Calypso, and Penelope. Goethe set down in a few splendid verses his project for a tragedy, in which Ulysses seduces Nausicaa during his stay with the Phaeacians, promising her Telemachus's hand in marriage by way of compensation, and then

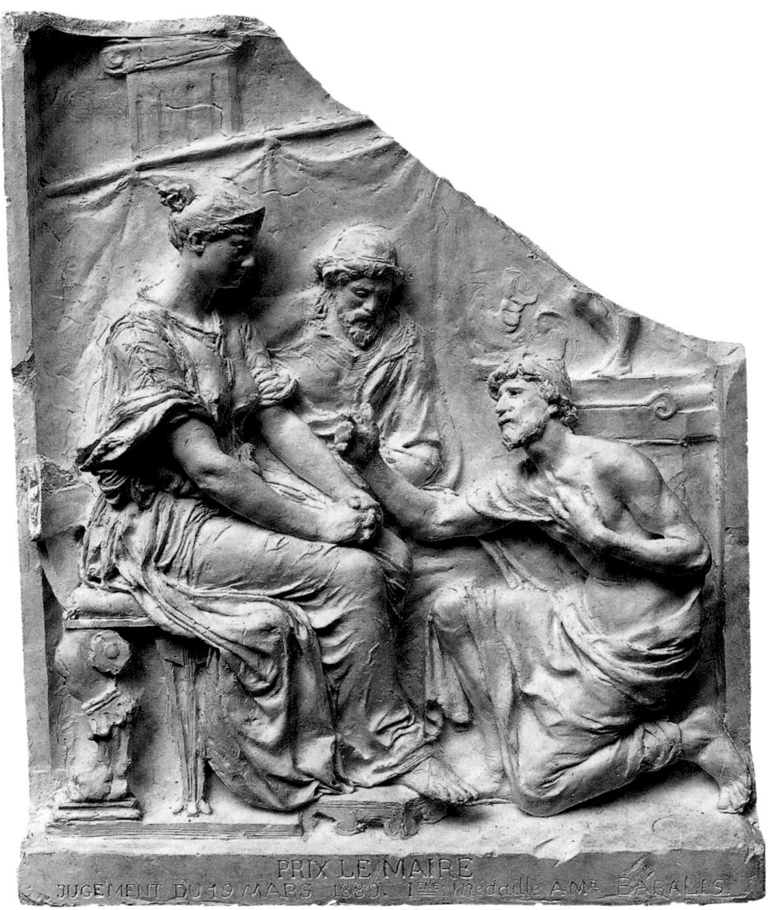

CATALOGUE NO. 76 | LOUIS-AUGUSTIN BARALIS (1862–?), *Ulysses in the Palace of Alcinous*, 1888. Plaster, 79 × 61 cm.

departs, leaving her no choice but suicide—the pattern, in short, of Aeneas's relationship with Dido in the *Aeneid*. Homer's story also left its mark on Alfred de Musset's play *Young Girls Dreaming*. There is no better subject for a classical landscape than this fragile young woman who refuses to let her destiny be dictated, and with miraculous grace chooses forever to remain an immobile silhouette on a background of wooded landscape and bracing sea air.

I shall speak elsewhere of Daumier's *Nausicaa*, which so perfectly conforms to the Homeric model. The subject for the 1888 Prix de Rome was again Nausicaa. Jean Veber covered her in a sort of transparent vapor of clearly Symbolist provenance. Her red lips and matching red ball contrast with Odysseus's large, hairy paw, emphasizing the vacuity of bourgeois taste. Daumier's *Nausicaa* came much closer to Homer's essential humanity. Even the Academy examiners acknowledged this, refusing to award a Grand Prix. Perhaps an echo of Homer's laughter reached Veber as he contemplated his entry, for shortly afterward he turned to caricature.

The sculptor Louis-Augustin Baralis is less well known than Daumier, but his entry for the Prix Lemaire of 1888 (cat. no. 76) ingeniously interleaves the unspoken thoughts of three characters who enhance one's idea of humanity: Ulysses and the royal couple Arete ("Virtue") and Alcinous, parents of the absent Nausicaa. Alcinous is both Arete's uncle and husband, having married her, as custom required, following the death of her father; Greek society sought to protect the orphaned daughter (and her inheritance) by giving her another father as close as possible to the one she had lost. The third protagonist is the unknown foreigner Ulysses. We find him in the unexpected pose of a suppliant, humble and embarrassed. The subject of the *concours* was simple: "Ulysses in the Palace of Alcinous." Nausicaa's absence is essential to Homer's complex account of their relations. The hosts turn away from their ritual sacrifice to Hermes to examine the shipwrecked mariner wearing his borrowed clothes, a most moving and discreet recommendation. He is no mere vagabond; he knows all about them, addressing the wife, imploring the husband:

> And then,
> . . . he flung his arms around Arete's knees . . .
>
> ". . . Arete, daughter of godlike King Rhexenor!
> Here after many trials I come to beg for mercy,
> your husband's, yours, and all these feasters' here."
> —*OD.* 7.142, 146–67; F 7.167–68, 173–75

And each responds with the intelligence upon which Odysseus was counting. Alcinous considers the proud humility of this prudent orator, this imposing beggar, and suspects that a god kneels before him. Already he bows modestly and avoids Odysseus's gaze. Barely allowed adult status in the world of men, the wife-and-niece Arete is more perspicacious, not for a moment mistaking Odysseus for a god. Her eyes are on his clothes:

> The white-armed Queen Arete took the lead;
> she'd spotted the cape and shirt Odysseus wore,
> fine clothes she'd made herself with all her women . . .
> —OD. 7.233–35; F 7.269–71

Lacking the king's prejudices, Arete is willing to admit that a beggar may be intelligent without being a god but also knows only her daughter could have clothed the suppliant thus.

The thoughts of husband and wife turn to their absent daughter, so present in their hearts that a scenario is taking shape there: their daughter will love and marry this man about whom they know nothing except that Nausicaa has deemed him worthy to be her husband. That is enough for them. It is a pleasure to see how closely the obscure Baralis has observed Homer's stage directions and his focus on attentive sympathy. As is so often the case, Homer's sensitivity is best reflected in the expression of the woman: her honest, perceptive gaze and her clasped hands, which alternately fold and unfold as her reflections and mother's love alternate in her heart. From her alert foot to her Roman chignon, she seems all intelligence. Ulysses, by comparison, is a lightweight. Clearly unaccustomed to kneeling, he looks awkward and unstable. The athlete soon to crush his provincial adversaries lacks muscle; his gaze shows more hesitation than cunning; and his cap—seen in profile—attracts the eye less than the headgear of Alcinous and Arete. His feigned humility seems all too real.

NOTES

1 *Palatine Anthology*, 13.2.

2 Joachim du Bellay, "Heureux qui, comme Ulysse, a fait un beau voyage," *Les Regrets*, in *Oeuvres Poétiques*, vol. 2, ed. Henri Chomard (Paris, 1910), 76.

3 "Et je pensois aussi ce que pensois Ulysse," ibid., 130.

4 The title of this section refers to a quotation from Montaigne that is often cited in the definition of humanism: "Every man bears the whole Form of the human condition" (3.2); see Michel de Montaigne, *The Complete Essays*, trans. M. A. Screech (London, 1991), 908. [Trans.]

5 Plato, *Republic* X 620c, trans. D. Lee (Harmondsworth, Eng., 1987), 454.

6 Dante, *L'Inferno, La Divina Commedia*, canto 26, ll. 97–99, 118–20, 141–42.

7 Clément Marot, "A la Royne de Navarre," from *Les Épistres*, in *Oeuvres poétiques complètes*, ed. Gérard Defaux (Paris, 1993), 122.

8 Molière, *Dom Juan*, 3.3. [Don Juan will reward a hermit if he blasphemes. When he refuses, Don Juan tips him anyway "for love of humanity." Trans.]

9 Pausanias, "Laconia," *Description of Greece* 20.10–11.

10 See Jean Seznec, "L'Ombre de Tirésias," in his *Essais sur Diderot* (Oxford, 1957), 43–57.

11 Claude-Philipp de Tubière, comte de Caylus, *Tableaux tirés de l'Iliade, de l'Odyssée d'Homère et de l'Énéide de Virgile, avec des observations générales sur le costume* (Paris, 1757), 205.

12 Anatole France, chap. 5 of *Pierre Nozière* (1899); reprinted in vol. 3 of *Oeuvres complètes*, 4 vols. (Paris, 1991), 631.

13 Suetonius, "Titus," in *De vita Caesarum* 7. [lit. "he (unwilling) sent her (unwilling) away." Trans.]

14 See Félix Buffière, *Les Mythes d'Homère et la pensée grecque* (1956; rept. Paris, 1973), 388.

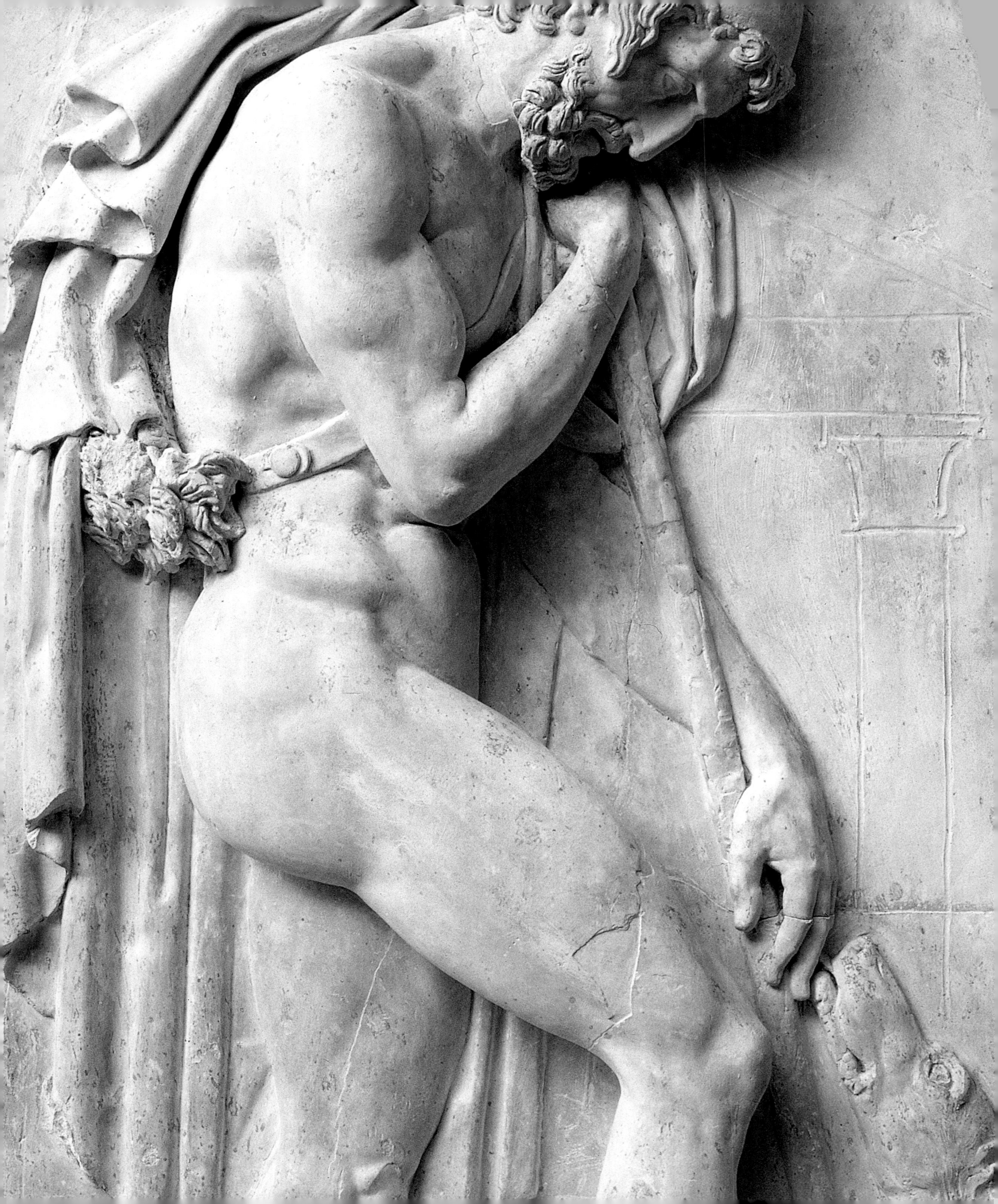

Ulysses in Ithaca

The spacious halls of the Phaeacian palace are the setting for several ensemble scenes bringing together Ulysses, Nausicaa, Alcinous, and Arete: the mature man thrown up by the sea; the sensitive and intelligent young girl; and those fine judges of human nature, her parents. The appearance of a bard hymning the exploits of the Achaeans at Troy adds to the literary density of their relations. Homer leaves the stage to the bard Demodocos. Is Demodocos the reflection of his creator and the first self-portrait of a poet? Ulysses hears his own tale told by a blind singer whom posterity was quick to identify with Homer himself. André Chénier used Demodocos to create the first image of the poet as doomed outcast. Our hero weeps, reveals his name, and launches into a less than modest account of his finest adventures—which I have necessarily evoked in chronological order in defiance of the *Odyssey's* complex construction.

It is not for us to denounce the braggart in Odysseus. In the *Odyssey* Athena makes this reproach when, in the thirteenth book, the Phaeacian mariners have dumped the sleeping Odysseus onto the Ithacan shore. Glorious homecoming! They want to be rid of the passenger their king has imposed on them and cannot wait for him to wake.

From now on Odysseus attempts—for the most part unsuccessfully—to hide his identity from everyone he meets, beginning with Athena. Nausicaa did not know him, yet intuited his nature. Odysseus now faces a series of recognition scenes with the most modest of Ithaca's inhabitants—serving women; domestic animals; old and outcast men; defenseless women and children—all of whom have led their obscure lives in the shadow of the king, whether present or far away, and know him better than he knows either them or himself. The scale of these scenes is derisory. The town in which they take place is barely larger than a village on the little island kingdom of Ithaca. Yet a whole society is present, with a people that joins its voice to that of the bard, and a village aristocracy weary of the power of its absentee monarch. Let us leave the study of this Homeric and pre-Homeric world to the historians. Within the circle of his family Odysseus requires no historical context.

When Odysseus arrives in Ithaca, he takes it into his head to go about incognito. Needless to say, the first person he meets believes not a word of his absurd tale. Unlucky in his choice of dupe, Ulysses was talking to Athena.

Let us again acknowledge that this Athena is an allegory of Ulysses' cunning:

> Approaching, closer, now she appeared a woman,
> beautiful, tall and skilled at weaving lovely things.
>
> . . . the gods don't show themselves to every man alive.
> Odysseus saw her, so did the dogs; no barking now,
> they whimpered, cringing away in terror through the yard.
>
> —OD. 16.157–58, 161–63; F 16.178–79, 182–84

DETAIL OF CATALOGUE NO. 79A

Homer multiplies contradictory and arbitrary notations, metamorphosing the divinity into a creature of dream. For as long as they were instructed and raised on Homer's imagination, European artists of modern times showed little concern for realism. The gods were, in theory, only half visible but became fully visible to those who needed them, mingling quite naturally with the beings of flesh and blood from whose imaginations they had sprung. In the passage cited, the divinity means less than nothing to the dogs, but it is they who cower and whimper while the hero maintains his silence. Nothing could be more natural than the encounter of Athena, Ulysses, and Telemachus as described by Homer. The son wants only to see the father he has awaited for twenty years. Ulysses, as one might expect, sees Athena, who points out that if he wishes to pass incognito, he shouldn't turn up clean and proud. She outfits him as a beggar, allowing him to tell Eumaeus an incomprehensible story that the swineherd neither believes nor resents. If Athena is an allegory of intelligence, she is also an allegory of futile precautions since Ulysses continues to disguise himself and his acquaintances continue to unmask him at first sight. The only exception is his son Telemachus.

Ulysess and His Son

In his prize-winning painting *The Recognition of Ulysses and Telemachus* (1880; cat. no. 77), the painter Henri-Lucien Doucet reconstructs the scene by inverting the parable of the prodigal son: here it is a prodigal father who returns, but Doucet keeps the son in the position of humility. Around them a goddess, very much in the Third Republic mode and dressed in a muslin gown, protects an embrace (which the Homeric text compares to the cries of birds) between the muscular father and son. Here is what Homer says:

> At that
> Odysseus sat down again, and Telemachus threw his arms
> around his great father, sobbing uncontrollably
> as the deep desire for tears welled up in both.
> They cried out, shrilling cries, pulsing sharper
> than birds of prey—eagles, vultures with hooked claws—
> when farmers plunder their nest of young too young to fly.
> —*OD.* 16.213–18; F 16.243–48

I have often characterized the greatness of Homer: it is expressed in his indifference to power or wealth and his interest in those capable of understanding the suffering of others. In the lines cited, the unexpected comparison of two warriors with chirping birds is the poetic expression of this attentiveness, comprised of tenderness and humor. It should destroy any effect of mawkishness. Painters more than sculptors, however, give in to the temptation of sentimentalism in scenes of recognition. All of the episodes from the sixteenth book onward are variations on the same theme. They are evidence of grafts that have been made by a storyteller onto a reduced narrative plotline. Ulysses returns to his country to reclaim his wife and massacre his enemies. The bard thought it better to substitute for this brutal homecoming, this confrontation of two clans with no justification except their respective force, the revelation of the complex and subtle human relationships between the master and his subjects, through their accidental or deliberate encounters.

Ulysses and His Dog

First a son and a swineherd, next a dog and an old wet nurse, and finally a distrustful wife: in these protagonists, the reader discovers both the nobility of the poor and the pictorial wealth of Homer's scenes. Ulysses always proceeds in the same way, telling rambling stories to those he encounters while scrutinizing their reaction. Few hear him out. Antinous, the leader of the suitors, replies by throwing a stool at his head. One being on whom Ulysses does not inflict one of his childish tales is the dog Argos, who nonetheless recognizes him:

OPPOSITE CATALOGUE NO. 77 | HENRI-LUCIEN DOUCET (1856–1895), *The Recognition of Ulysses and Telemachus*, 1880. Oil on canvas, 145 × 113 cm.

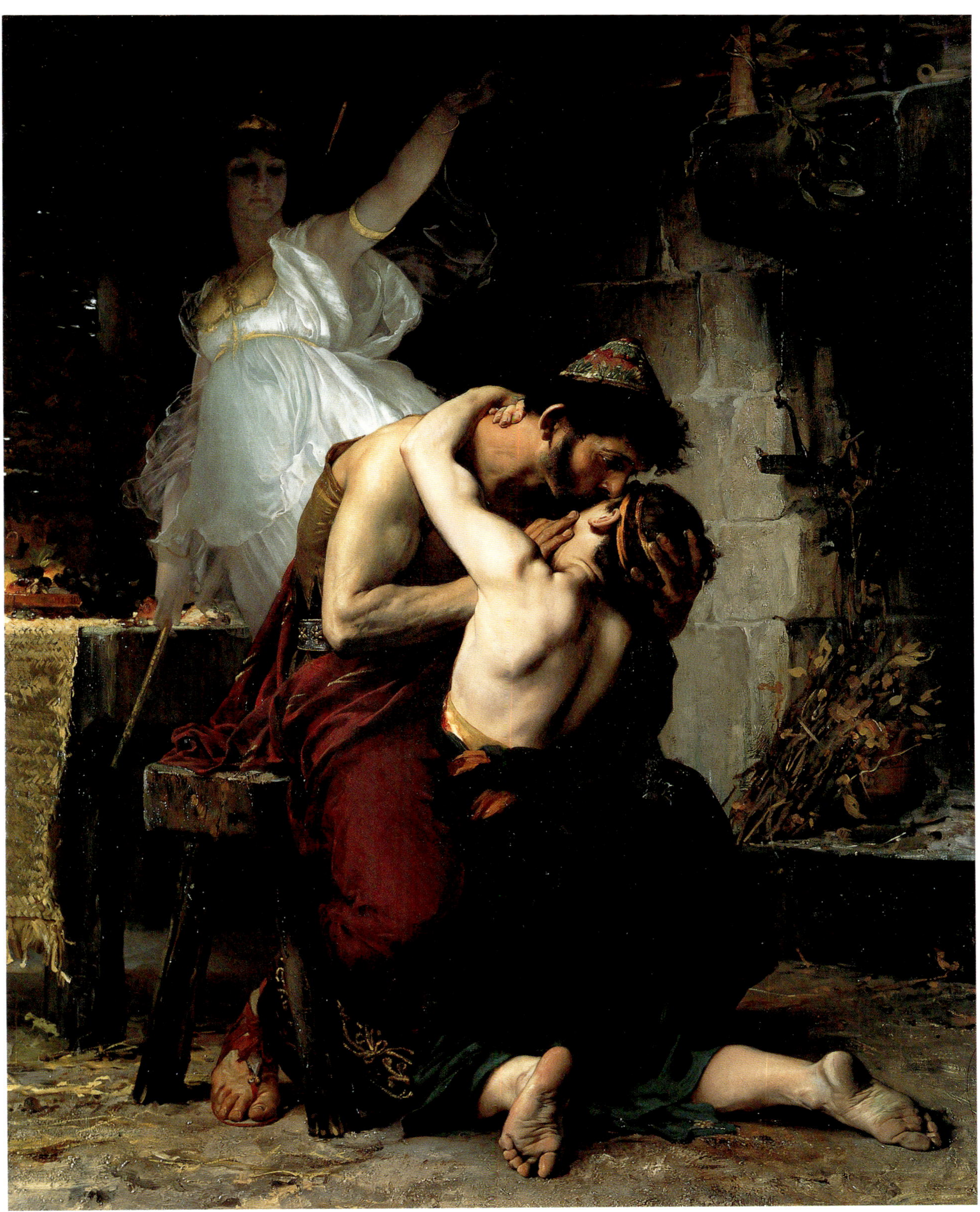

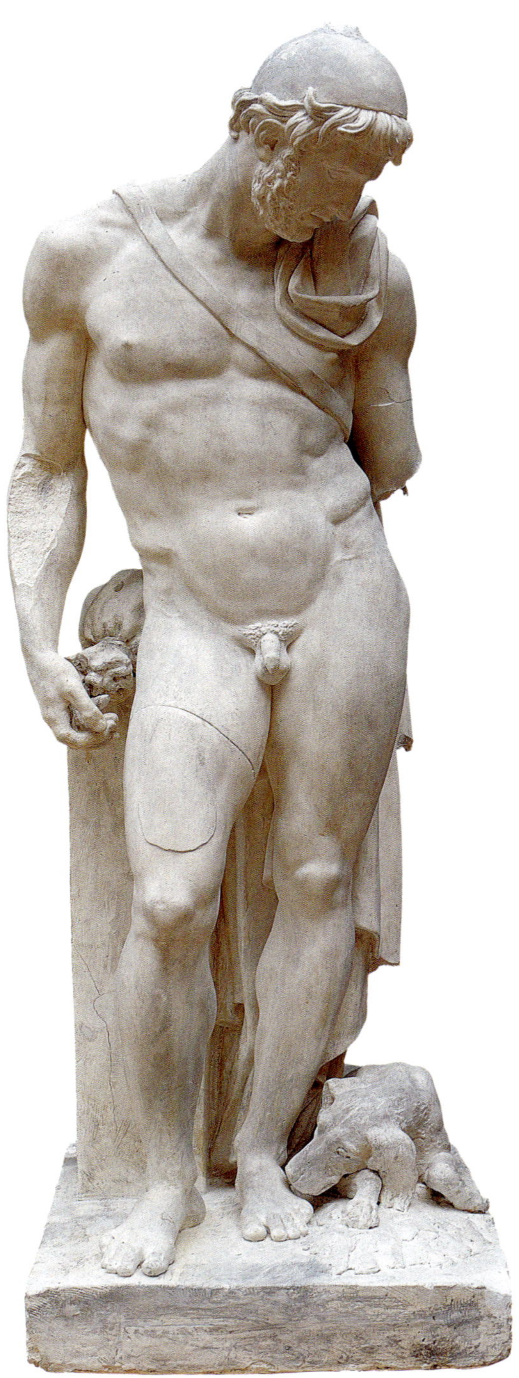

CATALOGUE NO. 78 | ÉTIENNE-JULES RAMEY (1796–1852), *Ulysses Recognized by His Dog*, 1815. Plaster, 109 × 44 × 39 cm.

Now, as they talked on, a dog that lay there
lifted up his muzzle, pricked his ears . . .
It was Argos, long-enduring Odysseus' dog
he trained as a puppy once, but little joy he got
since all too soon he shipped to sacred Troy.
In the old days young hunters loved to set him
coursing after the wild goats and deer and hares.
But now with his master gone he lay there, castaway,
on piles of dung from mules and cattle, heaps
collecting
out before the gates till Odysseus' serving-men
could cart it off to manure the king's estates.
Infested with ticks, half-dead from neglect,
here lay the hound, old Argos.
But the moment he sensed Odysseus standing by
he thumped his tail, nuzzling low, and his ears
dropped,
though he had no strength to drag himself an inch
toward his master. Odysseus glanced to the side
and flicked away a tear, hiding it from Eumaeus,
diverting his friend in a hasty, offhand way:
"Strange, Eumaeus, look, a dog like this,
lying here on a dung-hill . . .
what handsome lines! But I can't say for sure
if he had the running speed to match his looks
or if he was only the sort that gentry spoil at table,
show-dogs masters pamper for their points."

You told the stranger, Eumaeus, loyal swineherd,
"Here—it's all too true—here's the dog of a man
who died in foreign parts. But if he had now
the form and flair he had in his glory days—
as Odysseus left him, sailing off to Troy—
you'd be amazed to see such speed, such strength.
No quarry he chased in the deepest, darkest woods
could ever slip this hound. A champion tracker too!
Ah, but he's run out of luck now, poor fellow . . .
his master's dead and gone, so far from home,
and the heartless women tend him not at all. Slaves,
with their lords no longer there to crack the whip,
lose all zest to perform their duties well. Zeus,

the Old Thunderer, robs a man of half his virtue
the day the yoke clamps down around his neck."

With that he entered the well-constructed palace,
strode through the halls and joined the proud suitors.
But the dark shadow of death closed down on Argos'
eyes
the instant he saw Odysseus, twenty years away.
—*OD.* 17.290–327; F 17.317–60

Here is a scene combining daily life and fantasy, a recognition scene that moves everyone and reduces animal lovers to tears. Odysseus and Eumaeus ironize upon the puerile egotism of humankind. Perhaps Argos does the same. Ulysses deplores the breeding of toothless, discontented indoor dogs. His swineherd explicitly accuses him of casting aside an animal in which he once took pleasure.

Faithful to an undeserving master, Argos found an unexpected ally in the sculptor Étienne-Jules Ramey, whose very likable sketch won the Prix de Rome in Sculpture in 1815 (cat. no. 78). Ramey combined Homeric poetry with the spirit of Alexandrian statuary. Noble nudity and sculptural *déhanchement* are transformed by these two influences into a pose and dimension that are minutely human. As Homer tells us, the dog is no longer the brilliant hunter of his youth. Reduced to a lapdog, an ankle-high basset, he can only just reach the feet of his master, who does not reject this homage of licks and ticks. In Homer, Ulysses is briefly moved as he goes about his business. In 1815, Ulysses gazes at the wretched beast and sees his childhood. The medal with which Pierre-Amédée Durand won his Grand Prix in 1810 (cat. no. 79B) transcribes the same ironic emotion in its touching small-scale precision. But the dog in the medal still has the strength to raise its head and neck elegantly, perhaps dreaming of returning to the hunt. In 2003 I stumbled upon the plaster sketch for this medal (cat. no. 79A). The larger scale does not alter Durand's intelligent and mocking reading of Homer: Ulysses suddenly discovers the Age of Sentiment. Memory is born of this filthy, sickly animal that communicates its melancholy like the chance discovery of some forgotten toy. Homer's Ulysses says nothing of this, but his eye wells up with a tear, which he hides. In the early nineteenth century the École's sculptors were fashioning animal lovers rather than adamantine warriors.

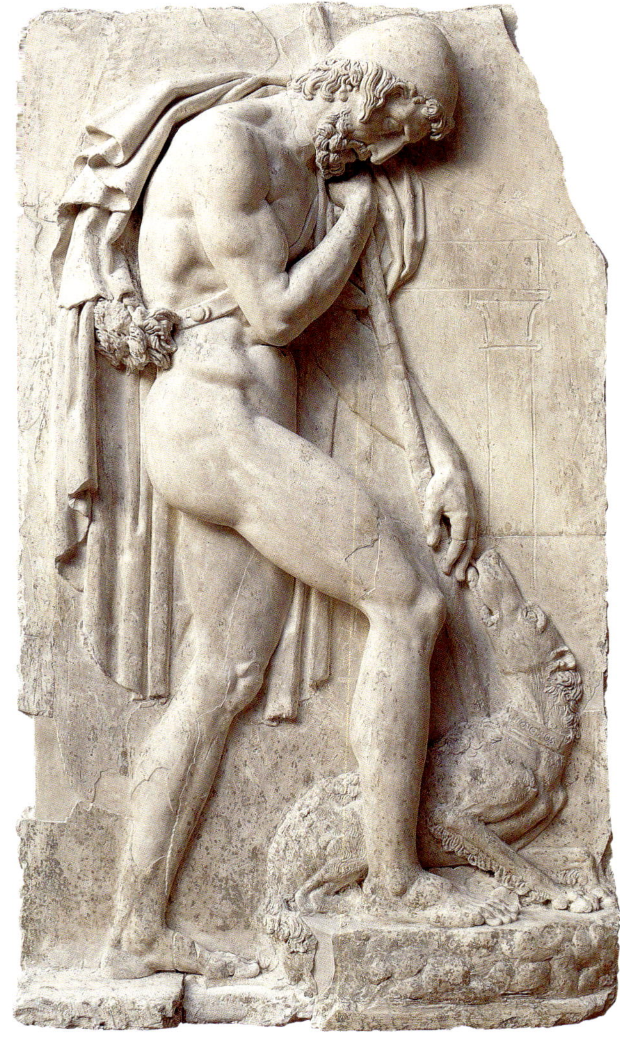

CATALOGUE NO. 79A | PIERRE-AMÉDÉE DURAND (1789–1873), *Ulysses Recognized by His Dog*, 1810. Plaster, 113 × 69 cm.

Ulysses and His Wet Nurse

What Argos the dog expresses in the minor key—the infinite weakness of the great Ulysses—an old woman states without fear or hesitation. The nineteenth book of the *Odyssey* places the characters in situations where lies are close kin to the truth. Ulysses enters his palace still unrecognizable in his beggar's costume. There he finds disorder, debauchery, and treachery—and, at the center of it all, his wife. Distrustful, he does not reveal himself to her. He plays the role of Tempter:

> I'll stay here behind
> to test the women, test your mother too.
> She in her grief will ask me everything I know.
> —OD. 19.45–46; F 19.47–49

he tells Telemachus. Penelope mistrusts the stranger. Surrounded by enemies and spies, she has been forced to avow her deceit: she had promised to marry a suitor when she finished the tapestry she worked on all day. She had long undone by night what she wove by day. The function of this tapestry is often forgotten: it was to be the shroud of Laertes, her husband's aged father. The suitors uncovered her stratagem and forced her to finish the shroud. Now she is obliged to choose a husband, that is, to betray both Ulysses and herself.

The stranger at her side makes her weep by claiming to know her husband, to have shared his misfortunes, and to be ruined, as is Odysseus. She questions him carefully, intuiting his lies, and he replies with disturbing—almost excessive—accuracy. He intensifies her doubts by refusing a bath, afraid as he is to wash off his disguise and stand revealed. Speaking of the invented Ulysses he claims to have met in foreign climes, Homer (or Ulysses himself) portrays a liar entangled in his own inventions. But now the smooth-tongued man who claims to have been Ulysses' friend and equal begins to betray himself. He will accept only a footbath, and he can accept only the attentions of an old woman. Humility suits his station, he says. The excuse is not convincing, but the minor concession to hygiene should stave off exposure. A man cannot be recognized simply on the basis of his feet, even if they are clean—or so he believes. But the woman who bathes his feet, the Magdalene of Ulysses, was once his wet nurse.

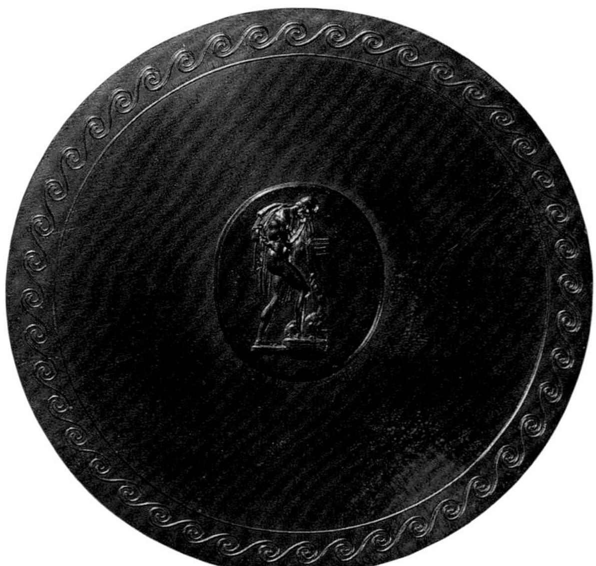

CATALOGUE NO. 79B | AFTER PIERRE-AMÉDÉE DURAND (1789–1873), *Ulysses Recognized by His Dog*. Modern steel casting, diam. 8 cm.

Penelope gives the order:

> Up with you now, my good old Eurycleia,
> come and wash your master's . . . equal in years.
> Odysseus must have feet and hands like his by now—
> hardship can age a person overnight.
> —OD. 19.357–60; F 19.406–9

Even before she touches his heroic feet, Eurycleia makes things worse:

> . . . never, I swear, has one so struck my eyes—
> your build, your voice, your feet—you're like
> Odysseus . . .
> to the life!
> —OD. 19.379–80; F 19.431–33

The liar's invention is failing him:

> "Old woman," wily Odysseus countered,
> "that's what they all say who've seen us both.
> We bear a striking resemblance to each other,
> as you have had the wit to say yourself."
> —*OD.* 19.382–85; F 19.434–36

He has already invented one coincidence—that of the beggar who has met Ulysses. Now comes another, still less likely, compounding the first. Thus, the poet gradually transfers the cunning, intelligence, and stage management of the scene to Penelope and then to the serving woman, whom Ulysses takes care to flatter. Bad luck indeed to have come across one of these old folks whose sight is as clear as ever! The arrogant hero and dynastic king has forgotten that in Homer's world everyone, irrespective of birth, shares the full range of human faculties. Homer reminds him. It is the old woman who unmasks him before he has recognized her, although he is heavily disguised and famously cunning, and she never lies and has nothing to hide.

It is an astonishing scene—all lies—and every lie transparent. In terms of psychology, expression, and dramatic tension, it is one of those pregnant moments so beloved of eighteenth-century theoreticians of painting. Homer adds his own humorous lesson—one that has passed over the heads of scholars and artists alike—about greatness, here inverted like the situation of Odysseus as he is caught out in his stratagem by an aged slave. The paintings and sculptures of the scene are so many tributes to the ingenuity of Homer's construction. The painter Gustave Boulanger (cat. no. 108), the sole artist in this series to have completely destroyed Homer's composition, now provides a perfect—nay, brilliant—example of the artistic aporia reached by academic teaching in the nineteenth century.

Let us, then, bring on the instruments: the cauldron, the mixture of hot and cold water. Odysseus suddenly remembers a detail that his lie cannot account for:

> Odysseus, sitting full in the firelight, suddenly
> swerved round to the dark, gripped by a quick
> misgiving—
> soon as she touched him she might spot the scar!
> The truth would all come out.
> Bending closer
> she started to bathe her master . . . then,
> in a flash, she knew the scar—
> that old wound
> made years ago by a boar's white tusk . . .
> —*OD.* 19.388–93; F 19.440–48

The poet then takes a malign pleasure in increasing the suspense, recounting over the course of seventy lines the circumstances (wholly without interest) in which Ulysses acquired this scar. Curiously enough, this is not a childhood injury—sparing us sentimentality and psychoanalysis—but a hunting accident, acquired far from Ithaca on Parnassus. (It sometimes featured as a Grand Prix subject—for example, in Joseph Tournois's *Ulysses Wounded by a Boar* of 1857; fig. 50.) Eurycleia did not tend the wound but merely heard Odysseus tell of the accident, proudly displaying the scar on his return to the palace. Homer continues:

> That scar—
> as the old nurse cradled his leg and her hands passed
> down
> she felt it, knew it, suddenly let his foot fall—
> down it dropped into the basin—the bronze clanged,
> tipping over, spilling water across the floor.
> Joy and torment gripped her heart at once,
> tears rushed to her eyes—voice choked in her throat
> she reached for Odysseus' chin and whispered
> quickly,
> "Yes, yes! you are *Odysseus*—oh dear boy—
> I couldn't know you before . . .
> not till I touched the body of my king!"
>
> She glanced at Penelope, keen to signal her
> that here was her own dear husband, here and now,
> but she could not catch the glance, she took no heed,
> Athena turned her attention elsewhere. But
> Odysseus—
> his right hand shot out, clutching the nurse's throat,
> with his left he hugged her to himself and muttered,
> "Nurse, you want to kill me? You suckled me yourself

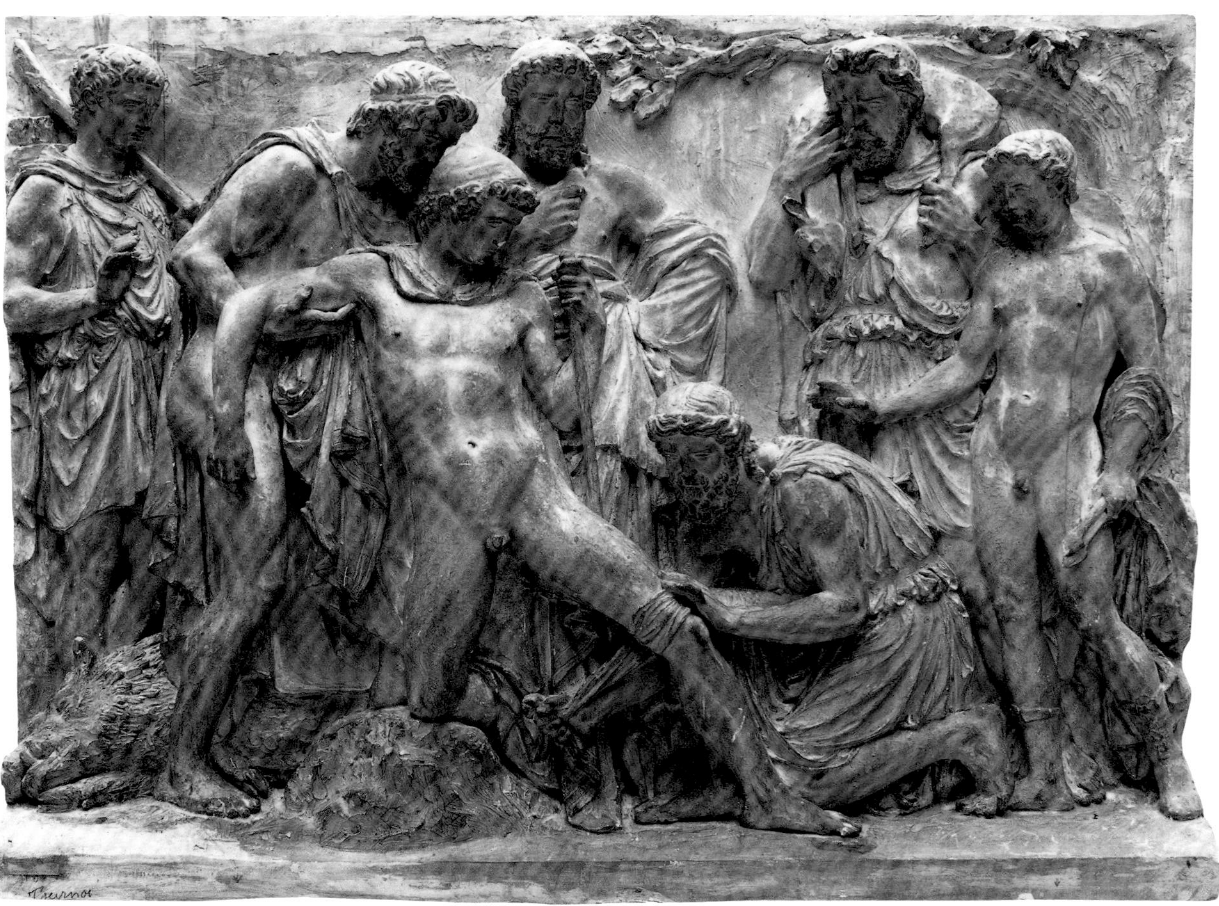

FIGURE 50 | JOSEPH TOURNOIS (1830–1891), *Ulysses Wounded by a Boar*, 1857. Plaster, 120 × 150 cm. Prix de Rome in Sculpture.

at your own breast—and now I'm home, at last,
after bearing twenty years of brutal hardship,
home, on native ground. But now you know,
now that a god has flashed it in your mind,
quiet! not a word to anyone in the house.
Or else, I warn you—and I mean business too—
if a god beats down these brazen suitors at my hands,
I will not spare you—my old nurse that you are—
when I kill the other women in my house."

"Child," shrewd old Eurycleia protested,
"what nonsense you let slip through your teeth!
You know *me*—I'm stubborn, never give an inch—
I'll keep still as solid rock or iron."

—*OD.* 19.467–94; F 19. 528–58

In Homer the crushing superiority of the servant over the warrior—who can speak only with brutal authority and is less humane with his old wet nurse than with his dog—is underscored by the third person in this scene, distracted though she is. Penelope has seen nothing, not because Athena intervened but because she is lost in thought; she is rehearsing a dream, the dream of Ulysses returning to the house. And she is meditating a way out of the dilemma in which her own stratagem has placed her, an elimination test

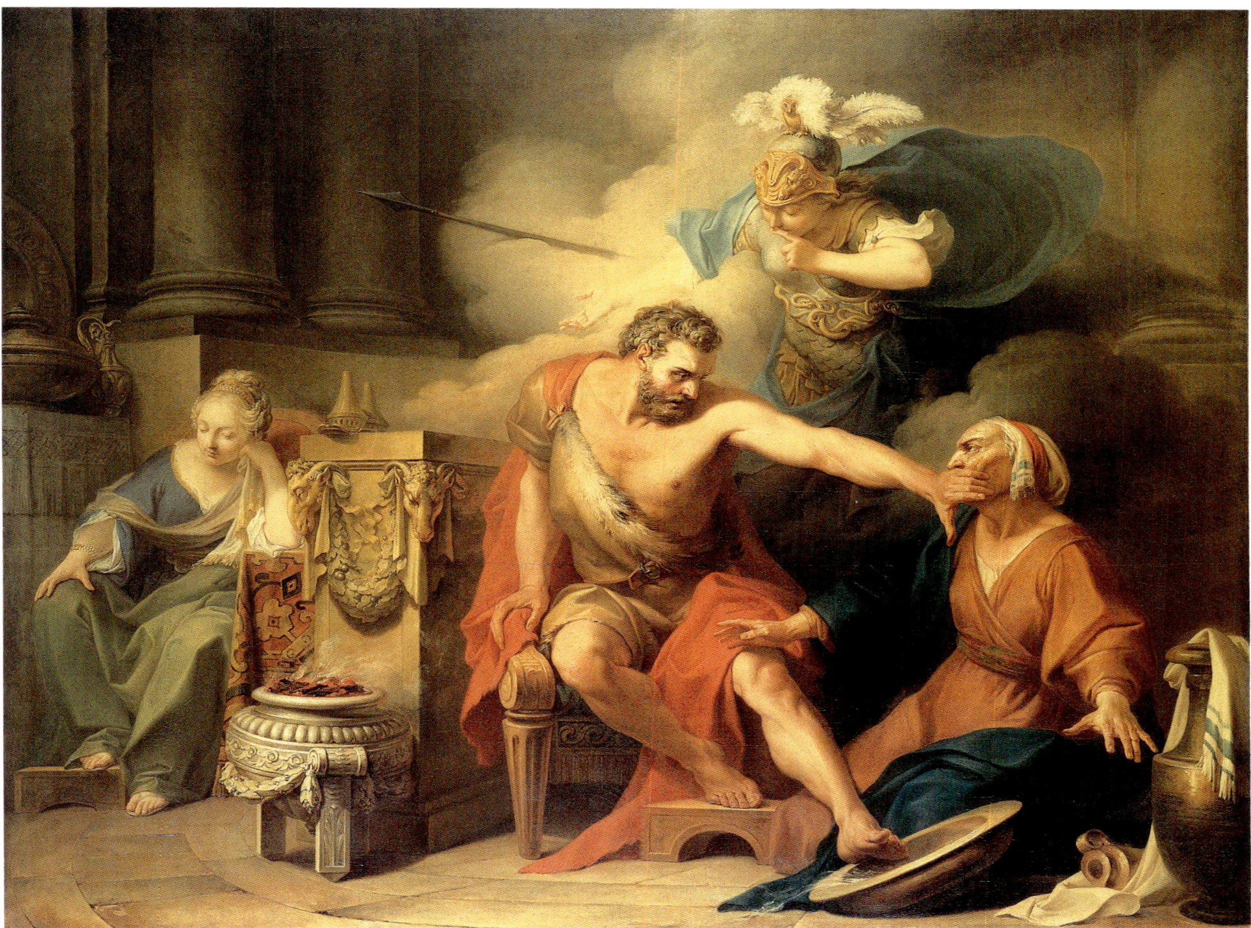

CATALOGUE NO. 80 | CLÉMENT BELLE (1722–1806), *Ulysses Recognized by His Wet Nurse Eurycleia*, 1761. Oil on canvas, 195 × 256 cm.

for the suitors. Will any of them be able to string Ulysses' bow, which no one else in Ithaca has ever been able to bend? Does she guess Ulysses will arrive before those drunkards, seducers of serving women, can master the bow? Probably she counts on all of them being eliminated. At all events, in a painting her meditation serves another purpose. Penelope on the one side and the percipient servant on the other present two faces of lucid and amiable intelligence, while between them the cunning warrior knows nothing but threats and brute force.

The scene has been set at some length. Here are people sunk in thought and suspicion, each of them plotting and planning, every new suspicion prompting further thought. The psychological density of the situation is freighted with a multitude of human relationships, all internalized and therefore independent of historical time. In 1761 the Academician Clément Belle (cat. no. 80) contrived a broad stage and an ingeniously reconstituted time sequence in which to set out the parallel history of these three lives. In the foreground Ulysses has been foolish enough to place himself and his incognito center stage. Neither woman must see Athena, who springs forth, helmet plumes jouncing, from the mind of Ulysses (who does not look at her). She gestures to silence not Eurycleia but the hero himself. In the space of a second, the aged Eurycleia, fifty years of servitude behind her, scrutinizes Ulysses' foot and face, sees them as they once were, touches the scar, hides it, understands, and is silent.

Penelope has no reason to attend to this incident. She is mulling over what she knows and must do. Seneca, whose tragedies include just such complications, suspected Penelope of recognizing her husband in this excessively eloquent beggar who talks so much about Ulysses. In his view, Ulysses nevertheless maintains his role, unmasking only at the massacre of the suitors. Homer, however, generally spells out the thoughts of his characters, and if Seneca is right, the attitude of Penelope must have seemed to Homer sufficiently evident to require no explanation. Penelope's extreme prudence is clear even after the massacre of the suitors; she requires ever more proofs and risks her trump card only when the bet itself serves a purpose. Such, at least, is Belle's commentary in his reception piece: draped in the ancient manner and without artifice, her hair meticulously arranged, Penelope looks, without seeing it, at her right hand, stretched out in her anxiety to act. She combines the subtlety of a sibyl with the easy confidence of a habitué of eighteenth-century literary salons. For the pleasure of a word, one of the most beautiful in the Greek language, let me pay homage to etymology: in Greek *unpicking* is *analusis* (ἀνάλυσις)—analysis. And so Penelope has come to represent philosophy, which picks and unpicks, refines and defines, splitting semantic hairs in defiance of reality. The two women in Belle's painting, captured in poses and reflections of unparalleled originality, entirely eclipse our hero, who can do no better than imitate the *Belvedere Torso.* In his encounter with Nausicaa, Ulysses confessed himself outdone by her finesse, but she did not dominate the scene and surroundings. Faced with these two feudal underlings, wife and wet nurse, Ulysses is no more master in his own palace than a nursling or husband without authority.

In 1826 the subject returned in the oil and sculpture sketch *concours.* The time limit forced the candidates to simplify the reactions of the three characters. Athena falls by the wayside. The Eurycleia painted by Émile Signol (cat. no. 81) has risen and turned away before Ulysses' hand can find her mouth. He imposes silence like a child, finger on lips, while his legs and left arm are tense with anxiety. Penelope is lost in the shadows, as if absorbed by her own sad thoughts. The brush strokes and features ingeniously and distinctly set out the reciprocal relations of each: the faces and glances of the nurse and master are a full ninety degrees apart, while the figure of Penelope closes off the depths of the painting; she neither sees nor hears the exchanges in the foreground. The sculptor Jean-Louis-Nicolas Jaley adapted the confined spaces of his relief to the density of Homer's scene (fig. 51). False beggar and kneeling servant confront each other, the one violent and barely controlled, the other humble yet dignified. This is a combat that only the sensitivity of spectator and reader can decide. Our sympathy must light on either the action of the sturdy seated man or the entire past of this old woman. Is there any choice? The warrior throws the old woman to the floor and prevents her from rising and crying out. To the left, Penelope is all sinuous movement, like an amorous Indian temple goddess. Oblivious of potential spectators, she discovers all the sensuality that languid melancholy can infuse into a body and soul.

In 1849 Gustave Boulanger won the Prix de Rome for a new version of *Ulysses Recognized by Eurycleia* (cat. no. 108). By that date the École's architects—who considered Greece one immense archaeological site—had convinced everyone else of Homer's historical accuracy. Ulysses could be given life only amid archaic columns painted in the Cretan style. Athena is no longer the anxious impulse of a human mind but Truth, a platonic form haloed with azure. Eurycleia is no longer a servant from whom her liegelord has much to learn but rather an allegory of Terror or Old Age. Penelope remains in the shadows, absorbed not in womanly stratagems but in her weaving—which, Homer tells us, the suitors had long since forced her to complete. The rich ambiguities of Homer have given way to certainties—probably because young Boulanger had not read

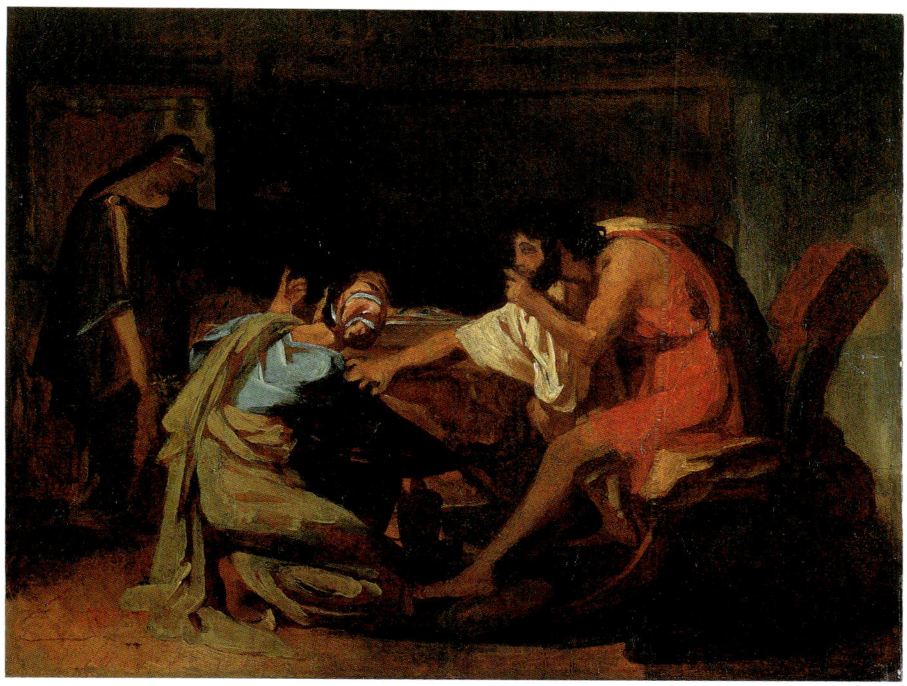

CATALOGUE NO. 81 | ÉMILE SIGNOL (1804–1892), *Ulysses Recognized by Eurycleia*, 1826. Oil on tracing paper mounted on canvas, 32 × 41 cm.

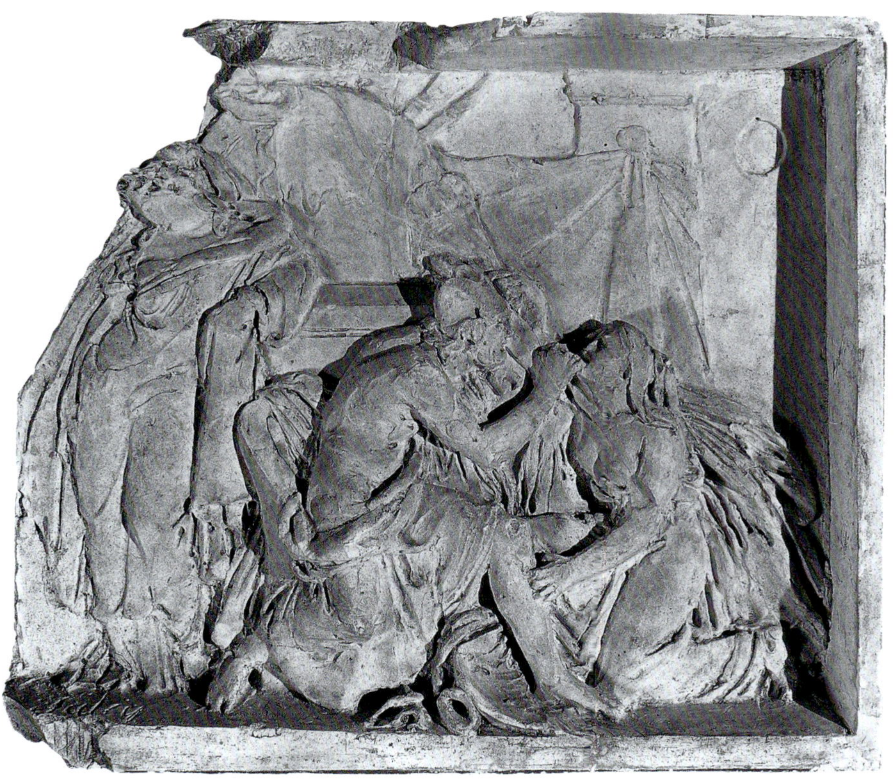

FIGURE 51 | JEAN-LOUIS-NICOLAS JALEY (1802–1866), *Ulysses Recognized by His Nurse Eurycleia*, 1826. Plaster, 35.7 × 40 cm. Sculpture Sketch *concours*.

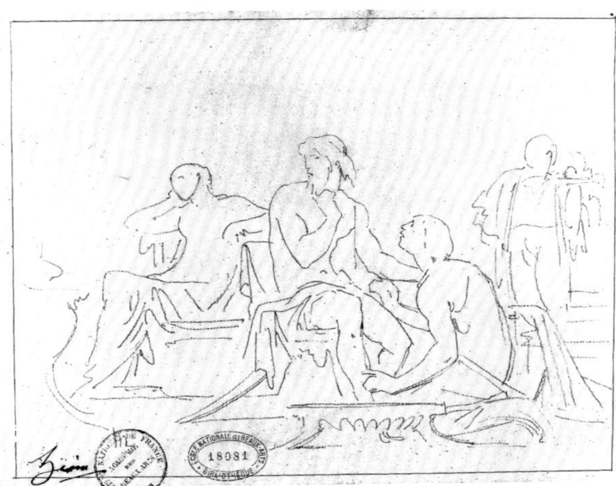

FIGURE 52 | GUSTAVE MOREAU (1826–1898), *Ulysses Recognized by Eurycleia*, 1849. Tracing on paper for the Prix de Rome *concours* in Painting.

his Homer. This painting came to symbolize the triumph of the Academy in the nineteenth century because it is a definition of the academic. When artists think that poetry contains nothing but simple and serious Truth, academicism rules. In the same *concours* Gustave Moreau studied the three characters overwhelmed by their doubts and hesitations (fig. 52). Eurycleia starts in surprise, while the thin, anxious Ulysses glances over his shoulder to see if Penelope has spotted her servant's reaction. Penelope is plunged in shadow and deep in meditation. Moreau's finished picture is lost—stolen long ago from the walls of the École—and only a tracing of it remains as witness to Moreau's sure hand. He was a close observer of human relations and a rigorous and attentive reader of ancient texts. There was no prize for Moreau.

Ulysses' Bow

In the panoply of the Homeric warrior, the defensive arms (shield, cuirass, and greaves) receive the most detailed descriptions. The shield of Achilles is a pacifist proclamation in itself. Among the offensive weapons, only the bow plays a decisive role. Ulysses has received from one of his Spartan hosts a bow that he left behind in Ithaca when he went to war. Penelope announces that the archer who can use this bow to shoot an arrow through the eyes of twelve axe heads in a line shall have Ithaca for his kingdom and herself for his wife.

Telemachus tries to cut the contest short by going first; he wishes to prove that he is the sole heir of his father and has inherited his strength, cunning, and power—and Penelope. He and the weakest of the suitors fail. Antinous, the strongest and most alert among them, suggests they wait until the next day. Then comes the beggar in his rags, Ulysses, whom the suitors reject from the competition. Penelope, however, does not consider him unworthy to be her husband. She is expressing her contempt for the suitors, or perhaps she prefers this mature man, however dirty, to the seducers of Ithaca. Telemachus now assumes the authority denied by the bow, sending her back to the women's quarters—it is not for her to decide her destiny. The suitors have no time to dwell on this transfer of authority from a mother to a son who has already recognized his father. They are alarmed to see the beggar manipulate the bow deftly and authoritatively. Beneath the suitor's eyes, three actions follow in quick succession: the bow is handled, strung, then, quick as a flash, the arrow is put to the bowstring and flighted through the axe heads. At each gesture Ulysses is alone with the bow. The others vanish from his field of vision. Here only a statue of Ulysses is justified, catching that instant of perfect equilibrium between resistance and muscle as the bow is stretched.

The competitors for the 1864 Prix de Rome had to rival the serenity of the ancient sculptors. The prize-winning pieces have been mutilated over the years. Thus, the plaster sketch by Jean-Baptiste Deschamps (fig. 53) has lost its bow and right arm. But Ulysses' gaze is still fixed on the target, and the tension soon to be applied to the bow is present in the face, the slightly thrown-back torso, and the arm that seizes the bow:

> So they mocked, but Odysseus, mastermind in action,
> once he'd handled the great bow and scanned every
> inch,

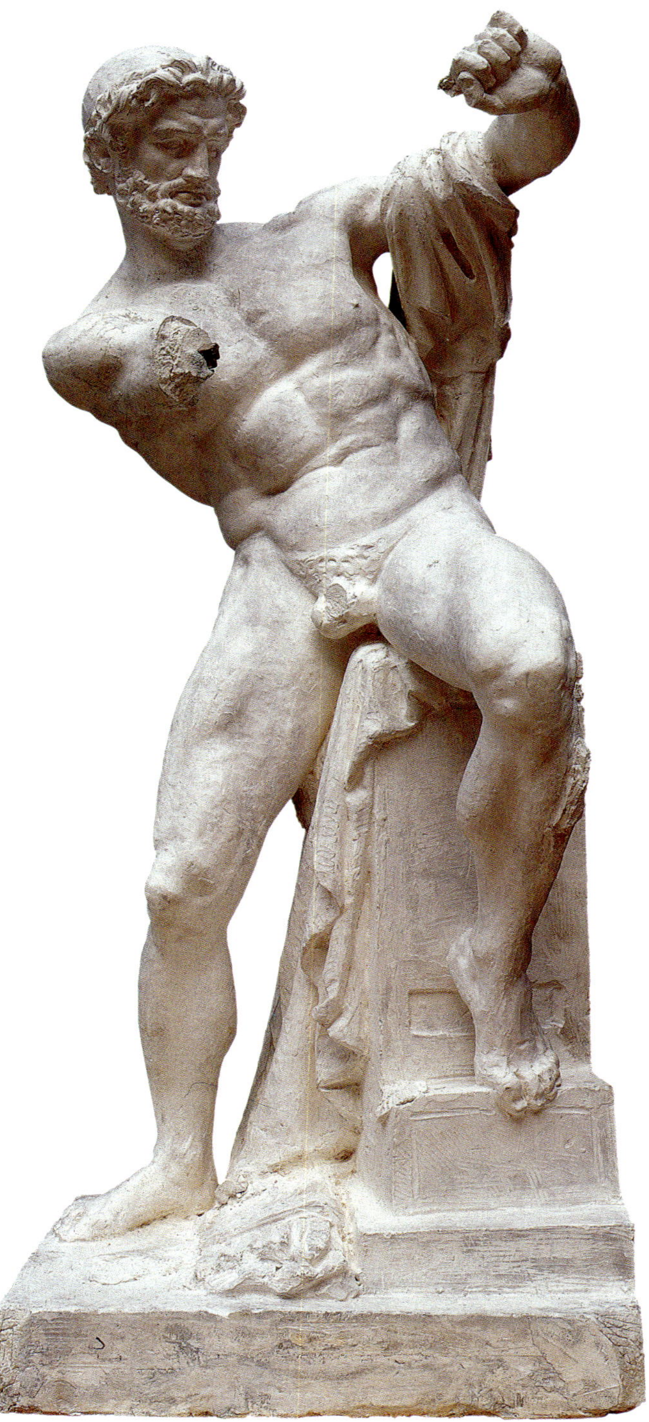

FIGURE 53 | JEAN-BAPTISTE DESCHAMPS (1841–1867), *Ulysses Stringing the Bow*, 1864. Plaster, 118 × 58 × 56 cm. Sculpture Sketch *concours*.

> then, like an expert singer skilled at lyre and song—
> who strains a string to a new peg with ease,
> making the pliant sheep-gut fast at either end—
> so with his virtuoso ease Odysseus strung his mighty bow.
> Quickly his right hand plucked the string to test its pitch
> and under his touch it sang out clear and sharp as a swallow's cry.
> Horror swept through the suitors, faces blanching white . . .
>
> Setting shaft on the handgrip, drawing the notch
> and bowstring back, back . . . right from his stool,
> just as he sat but aiming straight and true, he let fly—
> and never missing an ax from the first ax-handle
> clean on through to the last and out
> the shaft with its weighted brazen head shot free!
>
> —*OD*. 21.404–12, 419–22; F 21.451–59, 466–71

Homer also fixes Ulysses' gaze on the winged arrow that passes through the first ax head. The sound enchants, but the arrow kills: the string's vibration still echoes in everyone's ears as the first suitor falls in his own blood. In Deschamps's sketch, time has stopped and the vibration of the arrow reverberates endlessly through the space scanned by Ulysses' gaze. Painting now takes up the story, with its characters, actions, and objects systematically arranged.

The paintings I will now describe are strictly for moralists, who love to see the hand of justice fall on the malefactor. Ulysses the mariner very seldom kills. An eye put out in the Cyclops's cave; a few poor women strangled—these are minor casualties, and it is his sailors who, through clumsiness or stupidity, slaughter some herbivore beloved of a god. Between combat and shipwreck, Ulysses causes the death of every one of his crewmates, but he kills almost none of his enemies. The man chosen at Troy (with the help of a little trickery) as the greatest Achaean warrior celebrates his election by conducting a sustained and inglorious flight through the Mediterranean. When he reaches home, however, there are victims aplenty for the sacrifice.

Readers of the medieval and classical periods found the massacre of the servant-girl mistresses of the suitors unpardonable. Understandably, this noble deed was rarely depicted.

The blood of the suitors stains all of the twenty-second book. Ulysses' first arrow zooms through the axes; he then casts the others on the floor, where we see them in Louis-Vincent-Léon Pallière's winning entry for the 1812 Prix de Rome (cat. no. 82). Antinous, the leading suitor, has been killed without warning and is already covered by the body of another victim. The combat has several phases. Pallière depicts the first of these, when Ulysses still has arrows to shoot and the suitors are ill-equipped to defend themselves. Rather improbable interruptions punctuate the next stage, in which the two sides form up, arm themselves, and attack. Ulysses is aided by Telemachus (and several servants whom Pallière deems unworthy of inclusion). Homer describes events in detail, but Pallière has not restricted himself to a word-by-word depiction. In Homer's account, Eurymachus alone has time to draw his sword before he is killed by Odysseus. Pallière has him dispatched by Telemachus, who should be spearing Amphinomus in the back. Ignoring individual victims, the artist has shown a crowd routed by an ambush. The effect is not unworthy of Homer's later simile:

> . . . down the hall they panicked—
> wild, like herds stampeding, driven mad as the darting gadfly
> strikes in the late spring when the long days come round.
> The attackers struck like eagles, crook-clawed, hook-beaked,
> swooping down from a mountain-ridge to harry smaller birds
> that skim across the flatland, cringing under the clouds
> but the eagles plunge in fury, rip their lives out—hopeless,
> never a chance of flight or rescue—and people love the sport—
> so the attackers routed suitors headlong down the hall,
> wheeling into the slaughter, slashing left and right
> and grisly screams broke from skulls cracked open—
> the whole floor awash with blood.
>
> —*OD.* 22.302–9; F 22.313–24

The delight of the killers who take pride in their precision; the animal madness of the victims fleeing through the dark palace: in this abominable scene Homer tells us something of his own life. He saw the cruelty of men and the insensibility of beasts, and understood how these apparently distinct worlds come together in the most intense moments of life and the moment of death. In 1812, the École student could do no more than supply his figures with classical gestures. Yet some residue of Homer's inspiration pervades Pallière's picture. The poet's inspiration disperses and animates the fixed poses just as the gadfly or vulture disperses and revives the all too beautiful order of the peaceful flocks.

It now remains for Ulysses to summon Penelope to his bed. She puts the beggar to the test by suggesting that Eurycleia move the marital bed out of its chamber, knowing full well that Ulysses carved their bed from a living olive tree. Husband and wife are reunited by his answer.

Ulysses' Father

Homer has a variety of ways of describing how the world looks in the aftermath of war—that unleashing of brutality and madness when humans set about massacring humans. The suitors descend to the Underworld to explain their slaughter to Agamemnon. They have clearly understood nothing about the political conflict they stirred up. In the world of the living, their fathers vainly attempt to reestablish the power of the aristocracy against the three generations of monarchs: the former king Laertes, the returning king Odysseus, and the incompetent regent Telemachus.

Laertes appears in the twenty-fourth book of the *Odyssey*. Ulysses' father is still sturdy enough to

OPPOSITE CATALOGUE NO. 82 | LOUIS-VINCENT-LÉON PALLIÈRE (1787–1820), *Ulysses and Telemachus Massacre Penelope's Suitors*, 1812. Oil on canvas, 110 × 140 cm.

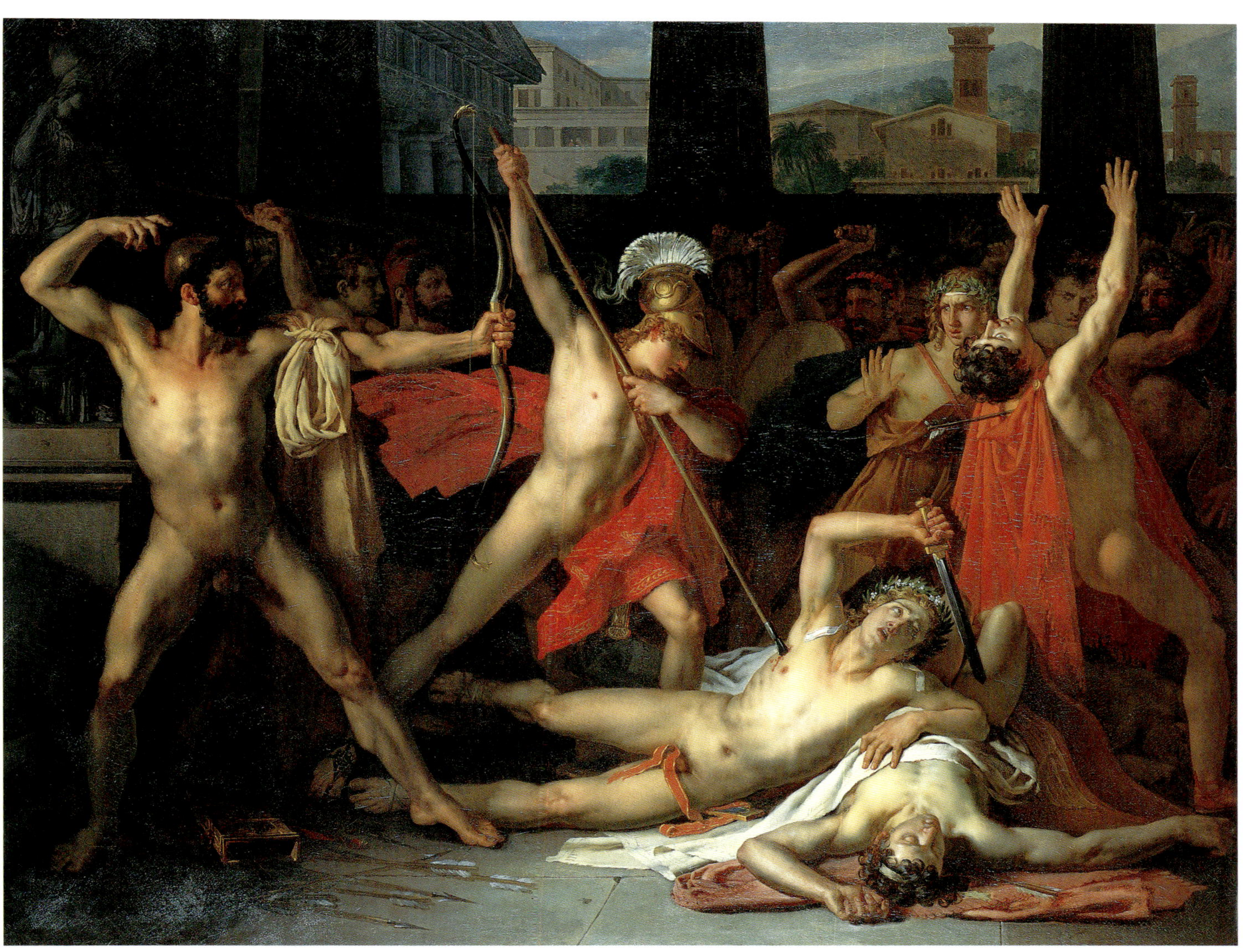

undertake manual work in his garden, but he is living on memories. He raises curious questions. One cannot say why Shakespeare gave his name to Ophelia's brother. In the eleventh book, Anticleia has implied that her husband Laertes is living like a hermit by choice, out of regret for his lost son. It is possible that an interpolator merely developed these remarks in the twenty-fourth book, but it is consistent that Ulysses should approach his father as he did his son, servants, and wife, testing the mettle of each in turn:

> . . . he did find
> his father, alone, on that well-worked plot,
> spading round a sapling—clad in filthy rags,
> in a patched, unseemly shirt, and round his shins
> he had some oxhide leggings strapped, patched too,
> to keep from getting scraped, and gloves on his hands
> to fight against the thorns, and on his head
> he wore a goatskin skullcap
> to cultivate his misery that much more . . .
> Long-enduring Odysseus, catching sight of him now—
> a man worn down with years, his heart racked with sorrow—
> halted under a branching pear-tree, paused and wept.
> Debating, head and heart, what should he do now?
> Kiss and embrace his father, pour out the long tale—
> how he had made the journey home to native land—
> or probe him first and test him every way?
> —OD. 24.226–38; F 24.248–63

Then come verses of vertiginous psychological and dramatic ambiguity:

> But I must say—and don't be offended now—
> Your plants are doing better than yourself.
> Enough to be stooped with age
> but look how squalid you are, those shabby rags.
> —OD. 24.248–50; F 24.274–77

Not content with these insulting remarks, and without even explaining what he is doing in the garden, the unrecognized visitor claims that he has met Ulysses and thus forces Laertes to speak his name and describe the torment of having lost all contact with his son.

Homer's work often testifies to the dignity of slave and serving woman, as well as to the childish pettiness of princes. He also has a predilection for men apparently young, active, and heroic who spend their lives doing nothing and postponing the moment of decision. Achilles, Ulysses himself, Hector, Paris, and Philoctetes all wait for events to force their indolent hands. But in this scene, enriched as it is by the age of father and son, the adult prince is forced to wonder from whence comes so much will power and detachment in this solitary old man? Faced with this rare subject in the 1896 oil sketch *concours* (cat. no. 83), Henri-Achille Zo has taken his stand on the questions Ulysses asks. The old man bends forward as he digs, as though bowing to the trees standing asymmetrically around him. Many aging workers dream of sowing a garden with flowers and welcoming grandchildren into a private Eden. Zo's Laertes, however, cultivates an arid plot, steep and wild. Astonished, Ulysses takes up a pose that echoes that of his humble father. Trees, men, pickax, sloping ground, and fence together trace the acute angle of a triangle that plunges into the sea on the right.

Painted with an austere, peasant naturalism, Zo's pitiless sketch exudes an acute sense of the land. The laborer lives by struggling against the land, and that struggle is his living. This old man was once powerful and now prefers to live in discomfort. But why should he lavish on the soil the care he denies to himself? This is an eccentricity of age, Ulysses concludes. An eccentricity, too, that a man who is still, twenty years after retirement, strong enough to dig his garden should have renounced the throne as did those who came after him, perhaps following his example: Sulla, Cincinnatus, and Coriolanus. Did some weariness overtake him? Homer, so prompt to fathom the soul, says nothing about it. The son has just killed dozens of men and

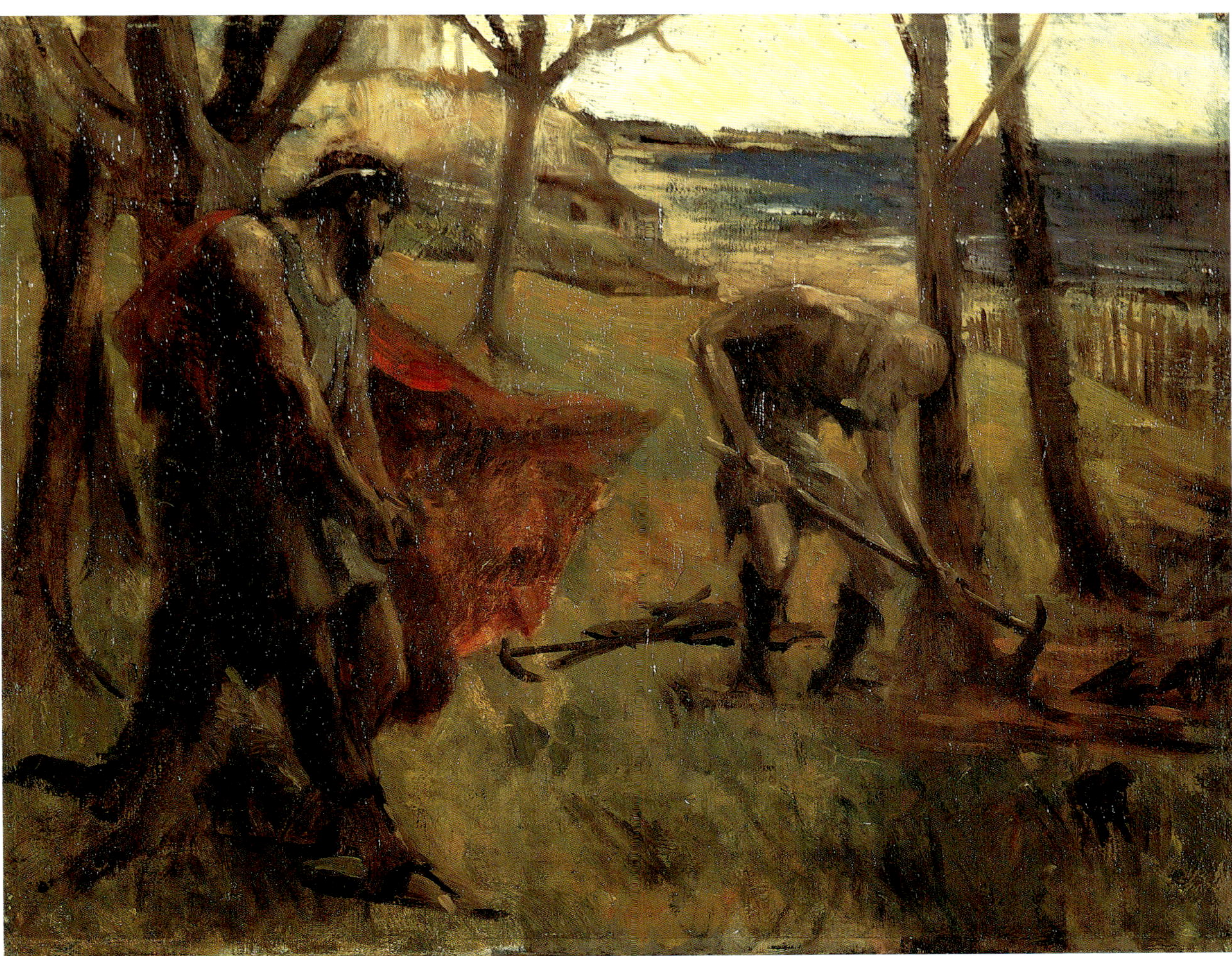

CATALOGUE NO. 83 | HENRI-ACHILLE ZO (1873–1933), *Ulysses and Laertes*, 1896. Oil on canvas, 32.5 × 40.5 cm.

women for the pleasure of reigning. The father has renounced the throne in order to cultivate his garden. While insolent suitors were squandering his wealth, courting his daughter-in-law, and dishonoring his son, he made no attempt to return to power. Ulysses is struck with this sudden insight into human ambition and renunciation as he stands behind a tree in the corner of the garden. Seeing his modest father—who proved able to walk away from power before he had become enslaved by it—the glorious, vainglorious, and catastrophic Ulysses perhaps imbibes a lesson of skepticism or political wisdom. Ulysses, the Greek Macchiavelli, seeing his father the former king of Ithaca, does not know what to say and says nothing. Homer, concluding his work at this point, does the same.

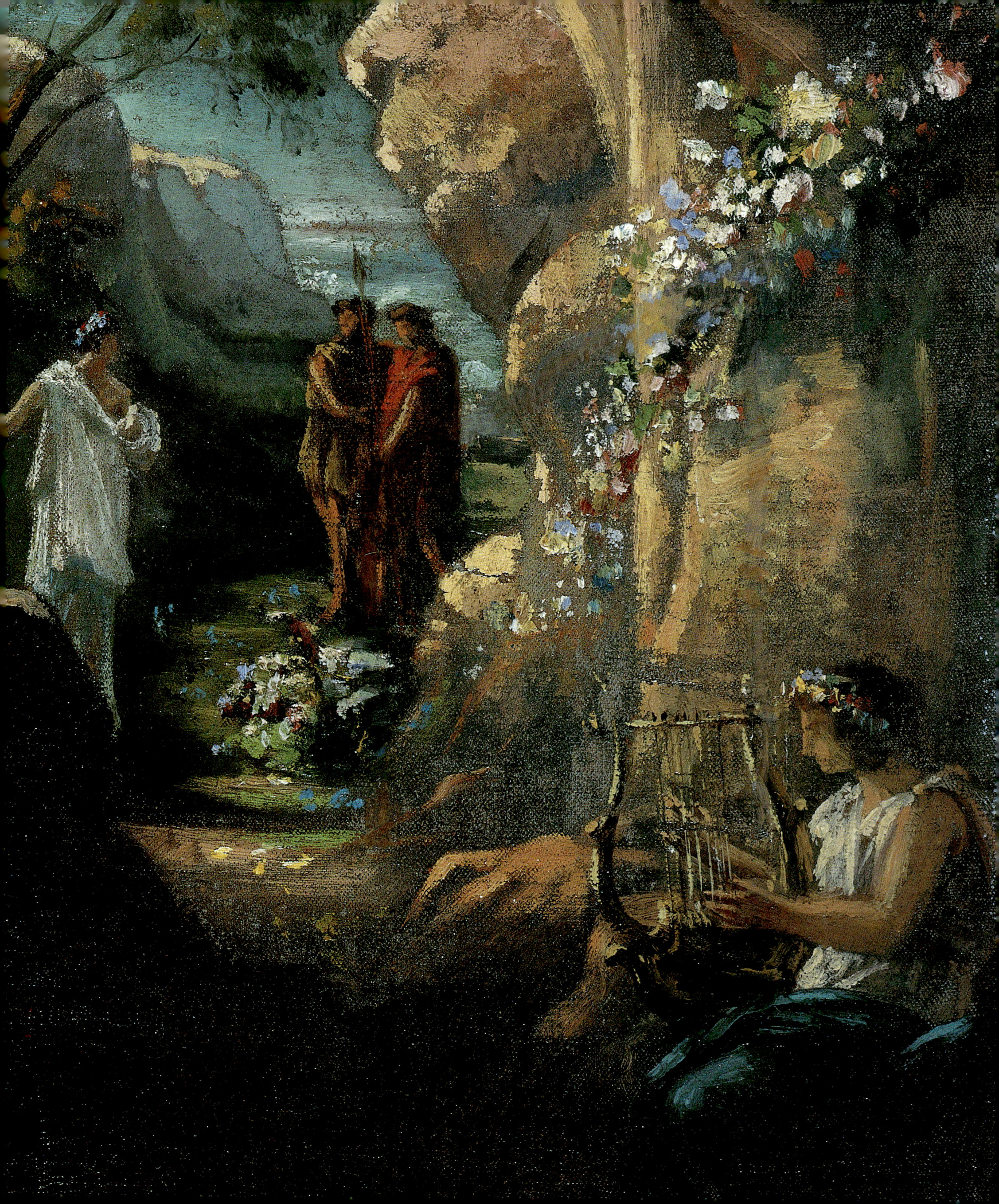

THE ADVENTURES OF TELEMACHUS

François Fénelon's *Adventures of Telemachus* was published in 1699. He wrote it as a manual of education for the duc de Bourgogne, grandson to Louis XIV and future heir to the French throne. At the time, the adaptation of Greek texts had a clear function, enabling readers—especially women—to avoid the rigors and insolence of Homer himself. During the Quarrel of the Ancients and Moderns, Homer was widely viewed as a relic of barbarian times, a dark age in which not merely beggars—who should never have been mentioned in the first place—but even princes and gods killed, blasphemed, lied, and raped. Since Homer had failed to impart any polish to the rough grain of his times, translators rewrote and bowdlerized his work. Instead of a new translation, the archbishop of Cambrai and tutor of the king's grandson wrote a whole new *Odyssey*, creating an epic centered on Ulysses' son. In the *Odyssey* Telemachus lacks authority except in his relations with his mother. Para-Homeric legend granted him an amiable character and married him off to Nausicaa. In Fénelon's work, Athena, bearing the features of Mentor, maintains the tutelary role she occupies in the Homeric original. The following is intended to indicate, through five sketches by École students, the new tone imparted to Homer's narrative by Fénelon.

Calypso Invites Telemachus and Mentor to Rest in a Cave

In Fénelon the colors and flavor of the Homeric landscape are transformed. Divine but wild in Homer, Calypso's island learns order, harmony, and civilization.

The first book of *The Adventures of Telemachus* must have enchanted the entire eighteenth century. Nature as described by Homer in the *Odyssey* overflows with Mediterranean plants, sounds, and scents:

> Thick, luxuriant woods grew round the cave,
> alders and black poplars, pungent cypress too,
> and there birds roosted, folding their long wings,
> owls and hawks and the spread-beaked ravens of
> the sea,
> black skimmers who make their living off the waves.
> And round the mouth of the cavern trailed a vine
> laden with clusters, bursting with ripe grapes.
> Four springs in a row, bubbling clear and cold,
> running side-by-side, took channels left and right.
> Soft meadows spreading round were starred with violets,
> lush with beds of parsley. Why, even a deathless god
> who came upon that place would gaze in wonder,
> heart entranced with pleasure. Hermes the guide,
> the mighty giant-killer, stood there, spellbound . . .
> —OD. 5.63–74; F 5.71–84

DETAIL OF CATALOGUE NO. 84

Even a god, says Homer, appreciates the beauty of nature. The gods, perhaps, but not Ulysses. No dreams of a troglodytic existence haunt *him*, especially if his cave must be shared with Calypso. The Homeric description above is considerably expanded by Fénelon in the first book of *Telemachus*. He adds new sounds and removes everything man-made:

> They came to the entrance of Calypso's grotto, where Telemachus was surprised to see, with an appearance of rural simplicity, all that can charm the eye. There was seen indeed neither gold, nor silver, nor marble, nor columns, nor pictures, nor statues: the grotto was hewn out of the rock, in arches lined with shells and pebbles; its tapestry was a young vine, which extended its pliant branches equally on all sides. Gentle Zephyrs here maintained, in spite of the beams of the sun, a delightful coolness. Fountains, sweetly purling through meadows sown with amaranths and violets, formed, in various places, baths as pure and clear as crystal. A thousand springing flowers enameled the verdant carpets which surrounded the grotto. There was found a whole wood of those tufted trees which bear apples of gold, and whose blossoms, which are renewed in all seasons, shed the sweetest of all perfumes. This wood seemed to crown those beautiful meads, and formed a shade which the rays of the sun could not penetrate. Here nothing was ever heard but the warbling of birds, or the murmurs of a brook, which, rushing from the top of a rock, fell in large and frothy streams, and fled across the meadow.[1]

Fénelon then describes the maritime view paradoxically available to Calypso; perhaps a goddess's vision can penetrate where the rays of the sun cannot. Gods and goddesses take pleasure in Homer's nature, where the birds labor like humans. Moving from the Homeric landscape to Fénelon's nature, we move from Pope's "wild paradise" to the divine order: "The instinct for happiness takes the shape of a dream of harmony."[2] In this case, Charles Baudelaire's "There all is order and beauty, / luxury, calm, and voluptuousness"[3] is shorn of its last element. In the eighteenth century Jean-Jacques Rousseau discovered new pleasure in this perfect if perfectly unimaginative nature, but in 1699 Telelemachus could find in it only a moral satisfaction far removed from the Homeric description.

The inside of the cave is surprising, for although the objects it contains are far removed from luxury, the nymphs within proffer velvety garments and serve exquisite delicacies (simple ones, of course), while spellbinding perfumes waft through the air. Is this Hell or Paradise? Has Telemachus entered a brothel or a prelapsarian world? Daumier showed another episode—Telemachus tempted by women-flowers (*Telemachus a Prey to Love*, cat. no. 121). As the caption of the print puts it:

> When the sun rose in the west
> He plundered for his mistress
> the brightest and the best;
> with his blooms the sorceress
> adorned her satin breast.

Félix-Auguste Clément showed the scene from a vantage point within the grotto for the Historical Landscape oil sketch *concours* (cat. no. 84). He emphasizes Mentor's vain admonitory gesture while his brush caresses the nymphs who await the visitors in the accommodating shadows of the cave. They are preparing garments for the two men, but their own seem less than wholly opaque. Even a reader deeply imbued with the *Odyssey* cannot expect to restitute any flavor of the original by scraping away at the moralizing sediment of Fénelon. The flowers spread in garlands, as if around seventeenth-century Flemish Virgins, and the hesitation of the two men, stationed remote from Calypso and her sophistries, are incorrigibly saccharine. Calypso gestures disconsolately with her right hand as if to acknowledge the impossibility of ever substituting the son for the father, Telemachus for Ulysses. The "swan of Cambrai" has written a new, purified *Odyssey*. In *Ulysses*, on the contrary, James Joyce later composed a *Telemachy* as dark and mysterious as Calypso's grotto.

OPPOSITE CATALOGUE NO. 84 | FÉLIX-AUGUSTE CLÉMENT (1826–1888), *Calypso Invites Telemachus and Mentor to Rest in a Cave*, 1851. Oil on canvas, 46 × 38 cm.

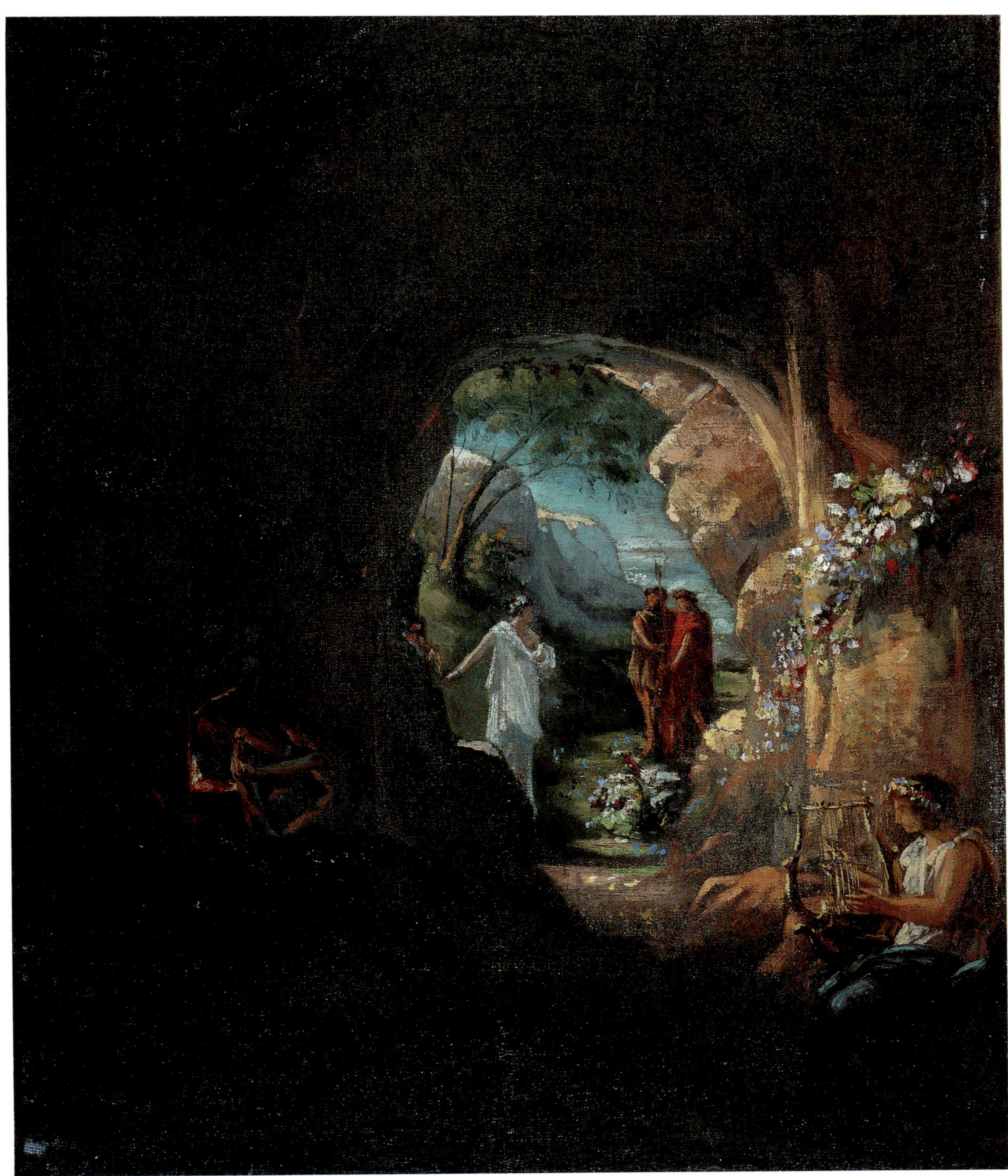

Telemachus Teaching Music to the Shepherds

In the second book of *The Adventures of Telemachus* the hero is enslaved in Egypt. No doubt we should see in this Fénelon's intention to combine in the story of Telemachus the adventures of Ulysses and the misfortunes of Joseph and Apollo (Joseph sold into Egyptian slavery; Apollo condemned to tend the flocks of Admetus). There is further evidence of Fénelon's syncretic ambitions in his invention of a priest of Apollo bearing the fantastic Greco-Egyptian name Termosiris, who tells Telemachus the story of Apollo inventing—with a little help from Hermes—the art of the flute. But he and Fénelon simplify the story, paying little heed to the ancient narratives (see Eugène-Ferdinand Buttura's painting, cat. no. 7) in which those two accomplices in thievery, Hermes and Apollo, alternately steal each other's cattle and musical inventions. Instead, Fénelon's Apollo charms his fellow shepherds by teaching them "the uncorrupted joys that flee the gilded palace."[4] Apollo, Termosiris, and Telemachus all make this seraphic form of music. Here is Termosiris:

> When he was clad in his long robe of shining white, and took his ivory lyre in hand, the tigers, the lions, the bears came to fawn upon him and to lick his feet. The Satyrs came out of the woods to dance around him, the trees themselves seemed to be moved, and one would have thought the affected rocks were going to descend from the tops of the mountains at the charms of his melodious accents. He sang but the majesty of gods, the virtue of heroes, and the wisdom of men who prefer glory to pleasure.[5]

Music has changed its tune. Homer sang of the pettiness of the gods, the sensuality of heroes, and the errors of mankind. Those who hear the harmonies of the Sirens are doomed not to a life of virtue, but to certain death. Here is Telemachus himself:

> Termosiris gave me so sweet a flute, that the echoes of the mountains, which could be heard on every side, soon drew all the neighboring shepherds around. My voice had a divine harmony; I was moved and rapt as it were out of myself. . . . All the shepherds, forgetting their huts and their flocks, stood motionless around me, while I gave them their lessons. These deserts appeared no longer savage; all was pleasant and smiling; the courteous manners of the inhabitants seemed to meliorate the soil.[6]

Were these manners genuinely edifying or merely soporific? It is interesting to compare the 1857 sketch by Clément-Amédée Bidot (fig. 54)—evanescent as the morals and prose of Fénelon—with the 1855 sketches, which are also of indirectly Homeric inspiration (see the commentary for Louis-Hector Leroux and Clément-Amédée Bidot, cat. nos. 3 and 4, resp.). In the eighth book of the *Odyssey* the bard Demodocos sings of Ulysses' deeds at Troy and of the outrage inflicted on Hephaestus. In Bidot's sketch the attention of Termosiris's audience is expressed in the quality of light, but this is shared with the sketches more directly inspired by Homer. In both cases, minds and figures are dissolved in the vagueness of the oil sketch. Only the singer's gaze somewhat disturbs this magical repose. According to legend, the blind Homer was unable to stare down his audience in this way, and his cruel, ironic songs were destined as much for himself as for the listeners who surrounded him. Aware that Fénelon's moralizing was intended less for the shepherds than for Telemachus and ourselves, Bidot directed Termosiris's excessively clairvoyant gaze out of the canvas toward the spectator.

Telemachus Crushes the Lion to Death

Fénelon wanted his Telemachus to imitate the skills of the singer and warrior Achilles, to make him a musician on the level of Orpheus, and an athlete the equal of Hercules. He therefore awarded him a prodigious victory over a lion, inspired by the Herculean labors involving the Nemean lion and the crushing of Antaeus. The episode immediately follows the edifying flute lessons:

OPPOSITE FIGURE 54 | CLÉMENT-AMÉDÉE BIDOT (1833–?), *Telemachus Teaching Music to the Shepherds*, 1857. Oil on canvas, 32 × 40.5 cm. Painted Sketch *concours*.

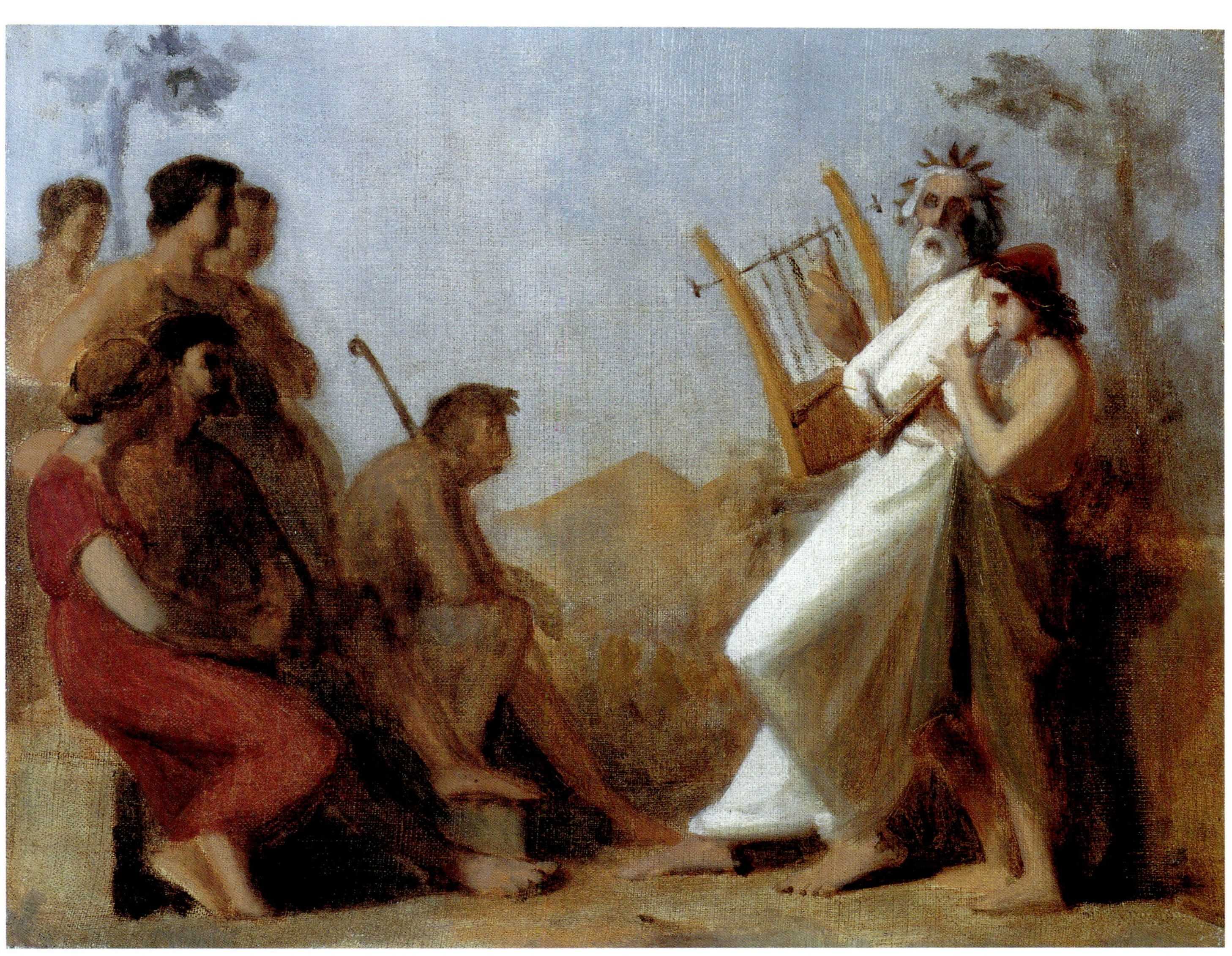

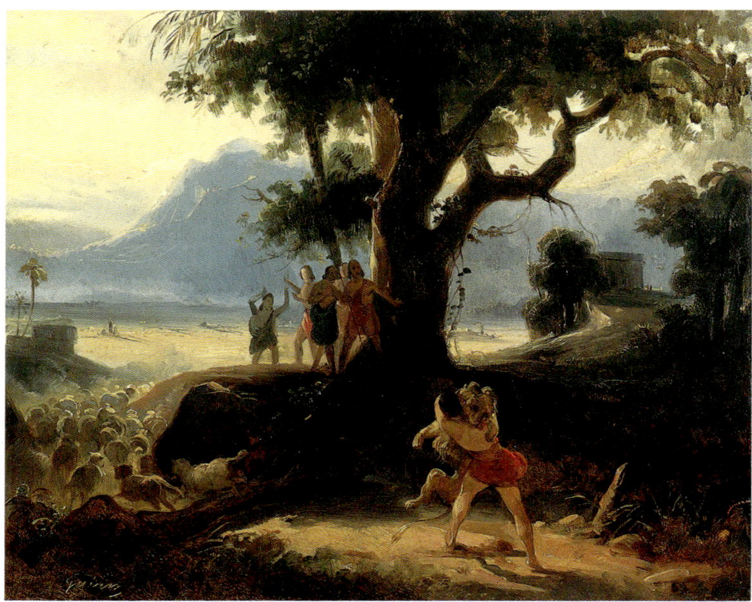

CATALOGUE NO. 85 | EUGÈNE-MODESTE-EDMOND LEPOITEVIN (1806–1870), *Telemachus Crushing the Lion to Death*, 1829. Oil on canvas, 38 × 46 cm.

> But what crowned my fame among the shepherds was that one day a hungry lion came and fell on my flock. He was already beginning a horrible slaughter; I had only my crook in my hand, but I advanced boldly. The lion bristles up his mane, shows me his teeth and his claws, and opens his parched and flaming mouth. His eyes seem very red and fiery; he beats his sides with his long tail: I fell him to the ground. . . . Thrice I threw him down, and thrice he rose again, making all the forest ring with his roarings. At last I strangled him in my arms.[7]

Protean Telemachus, first biblical and now Herculean! The Academicians betrayed Fénelon by suggesting a series of elementary and incoherent details, requiring of the students a desert, some mountains, the little temple of Apollo surrounded by its sacred grove, a few shepherds' huts, and plenty of evening twilight. Lepoitevin was a diligent student and supplied the shepherds with an abundance of sheep—poor panic-stricken beasts, innocent lambs who know that morality will triumph. The tree required in this kind of *concours* does nothing to simplify the geographical confusions. It dominates two tiny but very Egyptian-looking palms, making brilliant use of the slanting golden light. Telemachus and his supernumerary sheep, the graceless outline of struggling man and beast, are symptomatic of the sentimentality in which Homer was doused after Fénelon.

Philocles on Samos

With Philocles we move further and further from Homer, Ulysses, and the Olympian gods. This character is all Fénelon's own. His name means "lover [or friend] of glory." Falling victim to slander, he is forced to accept exile on the island of Samos (no doubt singled out by Fénelon for the fact that Homer is said to have stayed there). There Philocles devotes himself to reading and sculpture. One of his friends, Hegesippus, comes to inform him that he has been reprieved:

> Philocles lived . . . on a mountain a good distance from the city, where a cave served him as a dwelling. . . . Hegesippus goes toward the cave, and finds it open and empty; for Philocles' poverty and simplicity of manners were so great that he had no occasion to shut the door when he went out. A coarse bull-rush mat served him for a bed. . . . As for sculpture, he applied himself to it only for the sake of exercise, to avoid idleness, and to earn his livelihood without being obliged to anyone.
>
> Hegesippus, as he entered the cave, admired the statues which Philocles had begun.[8]

Fénelon then describes the most beautiful work of this amateur sculptor, "a Minerva encouraging the arts; her countenance was soft and noble; her stature tall and easy, and her attitude so lively, that one would have thought she was going to walk. Hegesippus, having viewed the statues with pleasure, went out of the grotto, and beheld at a distance, under a large tree, Philocles reading on the grass."[9]

The reader will recognize elements of the legends of Philoctetes and of Pygmalion, the mythical Greek sculptor who carved a statue so perfect that she came to life, descending from her pedestal to marry her creator. Looking at Louis-Hector Leroux's sketch, the spectator recognizes the much-lauded statue of Minerva, the man lying reading on the grass, and the concealed entrance to a cave. Hegesippus and the book-loving hermit in the foreground, however, are reduced to the merest shadows of statues. In the character and name of Philocles we find something of Philoctetes, who was similarly exiled to an island, although he was wounded more in the flesh than the mind. There is perhaps a reminiscence of the passion of Saint Jerome about him, and the ambition of Prospero. In his solitary retreat Philoctetes does nothing but lament, whereas the exemplary Philocles reads and carves works of art. Fénelon's island, however, knows nothing of the conflicts found in Shakespeare's *Tempest.* Under the overwhelming sun, the somnolent men are absorbed into the shadow of their hermitages, wholly at one with the tranquil nature that surrounds them. During the nineteenth century, Homeric images in painting are often marked by extreme violence. As if in compensation, Fénelon's prose infused the École's sketches—in particular the landscape sketches—with its own excessive suavity.

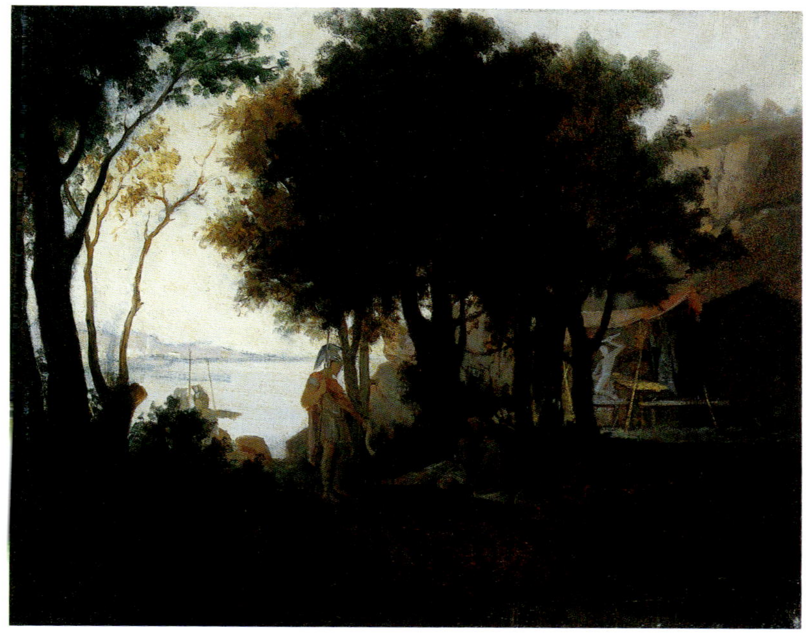

CATALOGUE NO. 86 | LOUIS-HECTOR LEROUX (1829–1900), *Philocles on Samos*, 1857. Oil on canvas, 38 × 46 cm.

Telemachus and Mentor

It is difficult nowadays to arrive at a proper appreciation of the Telemachy (the first four books of the *Odyssey*), without considering it through the filter of Fénelon's prose. Did Homer, in these books, give in too much to didactic allegory? In the figures of Mentes and Mentor, Athena breathes upon the young mind of Telemachus the wisdom that arrives at adulthood like "a seabird rising through the sky." The ancient commentators were quick to forget that Ulysses' son is learning to give rather than take orders.[10] He is reproached for the authoritarian tone he takes with his mother and nurse. What is a "good pupil"? Docility ends the moment the disciple understands that education makes one leave adolescence for the adult world of free thought. Homer locates this moment in the first book of the *Odyssey*, when Telemachus decides to leave the island of his childhood. By contrast, only in the last chapter of *Telemachus* does Fénelon reveal that the figure of Mentor has concealed the goddess Minerva. At this point the owl-goddess takes flight and authorizes her protégé to stretch his own wings. Homer's Telemachus oscillates between an obedient adolescent and a new Ulysses, depending upon Mentor's guise, as he variously embodies imposed wisdom or the wisdom acquired, formed, matured, and assimilated.

Fénelon's Minerva lacks substance. Throughout the narrative, Mentor-Minerva undergoes every earthly tribulation. Exiled among humans, the goddess experiences the full range of human suffering. In the fourth book of *Telemachus*, Mentor is sold (like Joseph) to "one Hasaël, who sought a Greek slave to teach him the manners of Greece."[11] Following his master Hasaël, the slave Mentor by chance meets his pupil Telemachus in

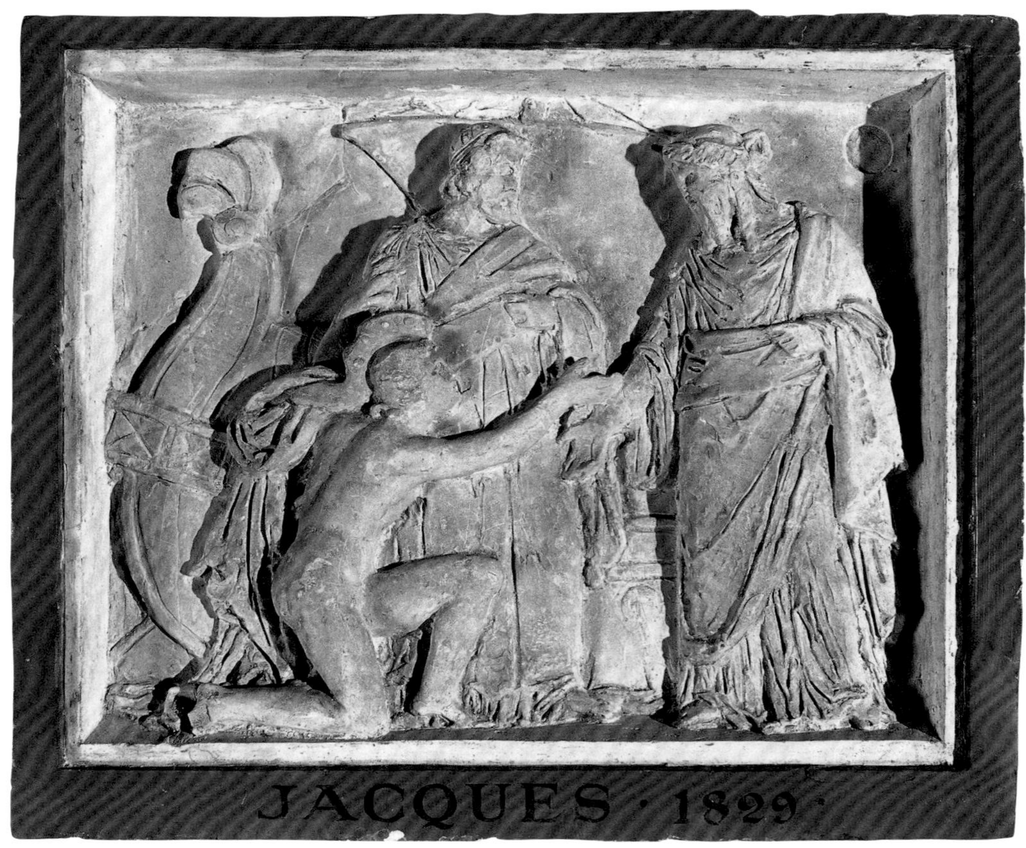

FIGURE 55 | THÉODORE-JOSEPH-NAPOLÉON JACQUES (1804–1876), *Telemachus Finds Mentor the Slave of Hasaël*, 1829. Plaster, 40.3 × 46.5 cm. Sculpture Sketch *concours*.

Cyprus. In Greek mythology it is not unheard of for a god to be condemned to slavery, but when reduced to that state, the gods show nothing of Christ's resignation during his Passion, but behave more mischievously than ever toward man and god alike.

Fénelon colors his ancient themes with Christian religiosity. Pseudo-Mentor/Pseudo-Minerva humbly accepts his new servile state. Like the good disciple that he is, Telemachus kneels before the biblically named Hasaël:

> I prostrated myself before him, and he was surprised to see a stranger in this posture. What would you have, said he? Life, replied I; for I cannot live, unless you permit me to accompany your slave Mentor. I am the son of the great Ulysses, . . . I have sought my father in every sea, accompanied by this man, who was another father to me. Fortune, to fill up the measure of my woes, tore him from me, and made him your slave; suffer me to be so too.
>
> Hasaël, viewing me with a benign and humane aspect, stretched forth his hand and raised me up. . . . "Follow me, thou son of Ulysses, I will be your father till you have found him who gave you life. Though I were not moved with your father's glory, with his calamities not yours, yet would my friendship for Mentor engage me to take care of you. I purchased him indeed as a slave, but I keep him as my faithful friend: the money he cost me has gained me the dearest and most valuable friend I have in the world. In him I have found wisdom; to him I owe whatever I may have of love of virtue. From this moment, he is free, you shall be so too; I ask nothing of either of you but your hearts."[12]

These three characters, among them the son of Ulysses and the goddess Athena, are all servants of Christianity. Homer's studies of slaves show a poignant recognition of their distress: women captives resign their will to their destiny and their master, but never their hearts. They continue to resent their status as slaves and concubines. They weep for their new condition. Grateful to merciful masters, they esteem them only as they are esteemed. None of them perceives slavery as a school of virtue.

We should keep in mind the nobility of Homer's enslaved and defeated protagonists when we read Fénelon. They offer a criterion by which to judge the sketch model by Théodore-Joseph-Napoléon Jacques showing the tripartite meeting, quoted earlier (fig. 55). Compare, for example, this genuflection with that of Priam trembling at the feet of Achilles. Telemachus adores the master to whom he enslaves himself. We can make out—behind the three characters—the sail and prow of the ship that brought Telemachus to Cyprus and which will transport the three men—now brothers—toward a new world of happiness and benevolence. In Fénelon, fable effaces the violence that governs human relations, whereas Homer's narrative never falsifies the brutality of social relations. No doubt Homer and Fénelon have in common a sincere love of their fellow human beings. Thirty centuries after they were conceived, however, Homer's characters still have the weight of truth and emotion, while those of Fénelon vanish into the hypocritical abstraction of a universe in which the strong refuse to abuse their power and the weak take pleasure in their own abasement.

The reassuring images of the ancient world recreated by Fénelon strip from the descendants of the Homeric heroes their density, volume, and vigor. In the late eighteenth century, the violence of history tempted interpreters of the ancient world toward the opposite extreme. In the nineteenth century, the image of the ancient world, as painted by the École's students, was often one of complacent brutality. In search of a calmer and more serene world, the Academicians occasionally turned to the good M. Fénelon.

NOTES

1 François de Salignac de la Mothe-Fénelon, *The Adventures of Telemachus, the Son of Ulysses*, by the Archbishop of Cambray; revised by M. des Maiseaux (1764), 38–39.
2 Noémi Hepp, *Homère en France au XVIIe siècle* (Paris, 1968), 619.
3 Charles Baudelaire, refrain of "L'Invitation au voyage," in *Les Fleurs du Mal* (Paris, 1857).
4 Fénelon, *The Adventures of Telemachus*, 62.
5 Ibid., 61–62.
6 Ibid., 62–63.
7 Ibid., 63.
8 Ibid., 266.
9 Ibid., 266–67.
10 See Félix Buffière, *Les Mythes d'Homère et la pensée grecque* (Paris, 1956), 287.
11 Fénelon, *The Adventures of Telemachus*, 99.
12 Ibid., 100–101.

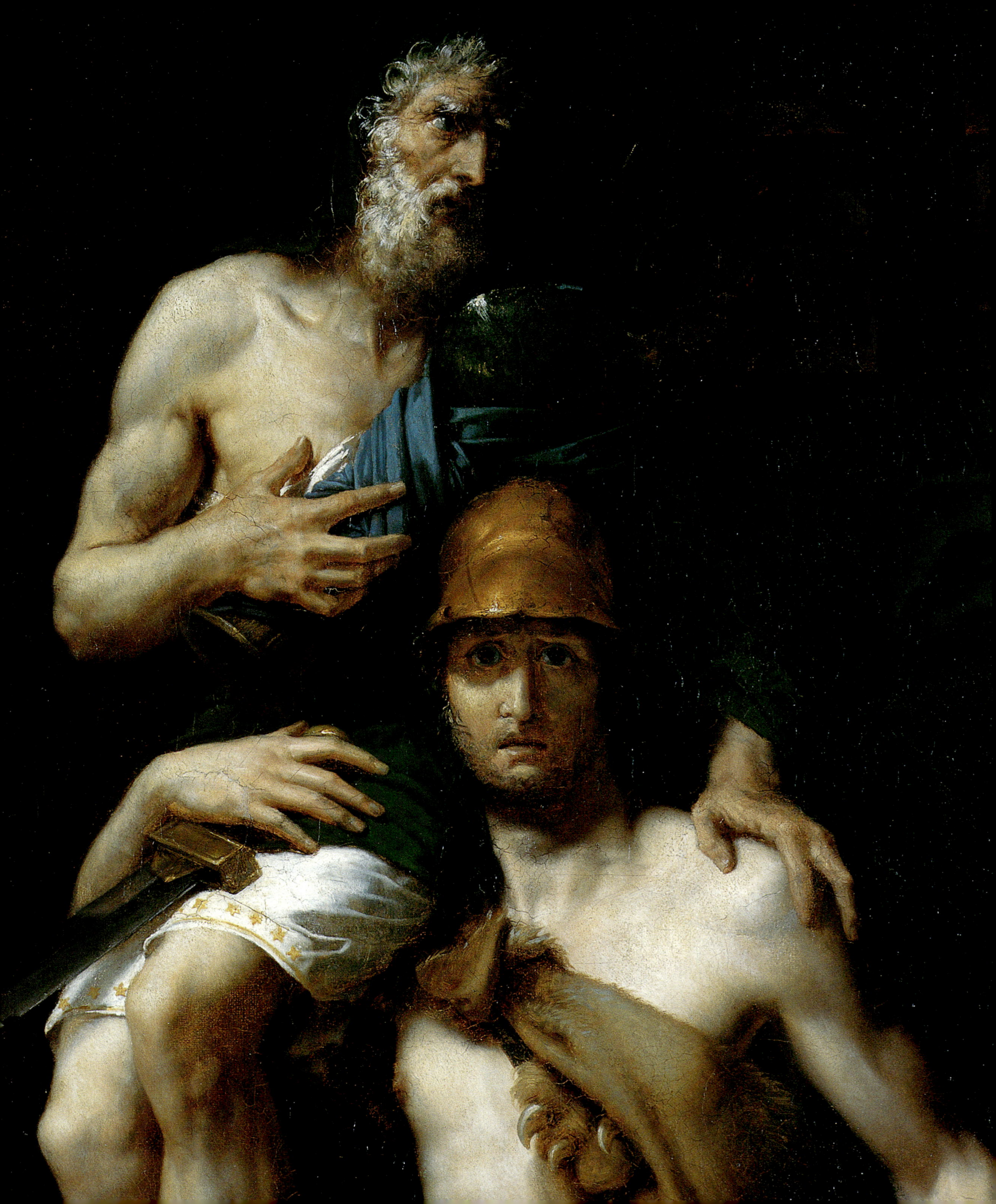

THE *AENEID* | From Homer to Virgil

Virgil (Publius Vergilius Maro) was born in 70 B.C. and died in 19 B.C. In the *Aeneid* he gave to the adventures of the Trojan Aeneas a poetic form independent of the Homeric narrative, spending the last ten years of his life composing the poem, which he never finished. He probably undertook it at the request of Augustus, the first Roman emperor. It is, in any case, certain that he gave his epic a propagandistic tone that is at the opposite pole from the spirit of Homer, his chief inspiration throughout the *Aeneid.* Homer's heroes are not justified in their actions by the interests of the cities they are supposed to govern. Their motivation is their share of plunder, their pleasures, and their captive women. When they are reduced to invoking the interests of their people, the enterprise is usually a murky one.

The *Aeneid* came in the wake of numerous continuations of the Homeric epic, a point to which I shall return. Greek poets, both scholarly and tragic, revived Homer's characters for purposes of ideological and philosophical debate, or in fantastic and novelistic narratives. The Trojan War may never have occurred outside the imagination of bards, but Herodotus and Thucydides made it the genesis of Greek history. Now Virgil sought to make it the fount of Roman national history. The idea and motif were, as ever, supplied by Homer, who was careful to provide even sketchy characters with an individual destiny. He had spared Aeneas, one of the Trojan princes, who was saved by the gods and destined to rule over Asia (*Il.* 20.306–8). Virgil lived at a point when the Roman Empire resembled a heroic legend: Alexander the Great (356–323 B.C.) had wished to be a new Achilles, to reign simultaneously over Europe and Asia, and now Rome was fulfilling his dream. True, Aeneas goes west rather than toward Asia. His very distant descendant Augustus, however, took the opposite road—passing through Greece to conquer the Egyptian Cleopatra and overthrow Anthony's eastern empire—the political reality could, at the cost of a few sophisms, be adapted to the Homeric prediction.

Virgil's triumphant patriotism contradicts Homer's skeptical view of history: the Augustan period was not well suited to indolent or mendacious heroes, to exploits of fake heroism, or to sympathy for the suffering of the weak. Neither poet is a cold, rigorous historian. Homer shows little concern for the details of things or events, describing arms only in order to portray the men who forged or wore them. His vision and similes refer to men with occupations, men immersed in the customs and activities of daily life. Not so Virgil, who shows no interest in the humble, the weak, or the defeated. Moreover, his political circumstances made Greece and the Orient the designated enemies of Roman ambition. Virgil therefore reports everything that Homer omits, in particular the taking of Troy. Scarcely mentioned in Homer, its most violent episodes

DETAIL OF CATALOGUE NO. 88

are recounted in full in the *Aeneid.* Here Laocoön and the Trojan horse initiate their literary careers, not as Ulysses' braggart fantasies but as mythical military exploits testifying to the war crimes of the Greeks. Here, too, begins the view of history as a narrative of the exploits of the great.

The *Aeneid*

The plan of the *Aeneid* pays homage to Homer by following the structure of the *Iliad* and the *Odyssey* in reverse order. In the following summary I shall confine myself to the events represented in works belonging to the École. The first six books follow Aeneas as he leaves behind him the ashes of Troy and travels the Mediterranean in search of a new kingdom. The Greeks have invaded Troy by night; Hector appears to Aeneas in a dream and orders him to abandon the city. In his flight, the Trojan hero carries his father, Anchises, on his shoulders and leads his son, Iulus, who was to give his name to the *gens Iulia* (the family of Caius *Julius* Caesar). He survives various storms sent to hinder him by Iolus, god of the winds. This second *Odyssey* takes him to Carthage, where he recounts the fall of Troy to the Phoenician queen Dido, founder of her own city. The queen gives herself to Aeneas but is abandoned and dies of despair—a political Calypso unable to keep her lover. Aeneas next descends to the Underworld. Where Ulysses had discovered nothingness and eternal death, Aeneas discovers the future, which strongly resembles the present of Virgil and Augustus. The second half of the *Aeneid* unfolds like an optimistic *Iliad.* Upon his arrival in the country of the Latins, Aeneas receives from King Latinus his daughter, Lavinia, in marriage (his first wife having perished in Troy). Lavinia, however, had been promised to Turnus, king of the Rutuli. The resulting war produces its own heroes, of whom the most touching are the Trojans Nisus and Euryalus and two allies of the Rutuli, the Etruscan father and son Mezentius and Lausus. On either side, men sacrifice themselves for the good of the nation without a second thought. Virgil's pantheon is not that of Homer; neither their own quarrels nor human intelligence and insolence can make his gods seem ridiculous. Thus Aeneas is cured of a battle wound by his mother, the goddess Aphrodite, who receives such unflattering treatment in Homer. Thanks to her—in contrast to the fates awaiting such Homeric beneficiaries of divine patronage as Achilles and Paris—the road leading Aeneas from military victory to apotheosis is direct and unswerving.

With the changing times, epic has also changed in tone. Battle is now courteously joined not for the sexual favors of captive women but for the hand of a princess, who is recommended less for her beauty than her dowry—the promise of kingdoms extending the length and breadth of the "Roman sea," the Mediterranean. We should remember that Paris rejected the sovereignty of all Asia to possess the most beautiful woman in the world; that Ulysses left Sparta behind for Ithaca, that rock in the ocean; and that the Greeks took Troy not in order to possess it but to raze it to the ground. In Virgil the spirit of serious conquest and respect for authority are insinuated into the Trojan War, just as Fénelon later introduced the spirit of obedience. "The greatness of Aeneas lies in political history, the greatness of Ulysses in the literary and philosophic tradition," says a historian of Ulysses.[1] Literature was betrayed by one of its greatest practitioners, and for centuries, readers found it difficult to read Homer except through the political prism of Virgil. Thus, for military reasons having little to do with literature, the perfectly judged verses of Virgil and his "polite" characters were for several centuries considered more amiable than the language and spirit of Homer. The artists were even more grateful for the heroically active Aeneas, who runs, flees, fights, and hectors as much as Ulysses, but who never stops, never lies, and never betrays anyone except some women.

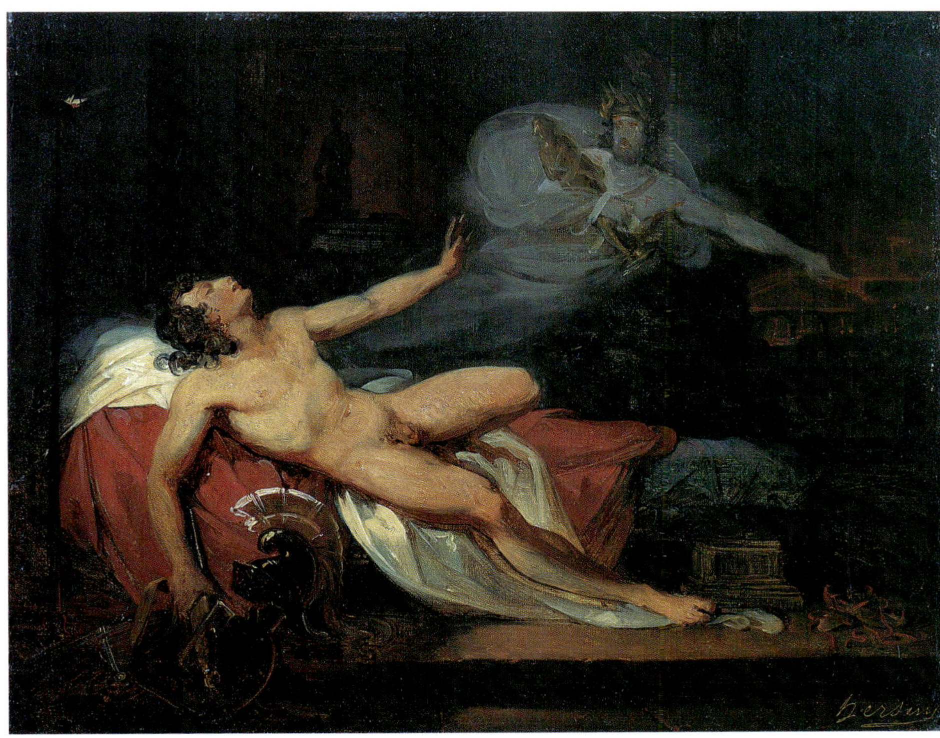

CATALOGUE NO. 87 | HENRI-FRÉDÉRIC SCHOPIN (OR CHOPIN) (1804–1890), *Hector Appears to Aeneas During the Capture of Troy*, 1829. Oil on tracing paper mounted on canvas, 32.5 × 40.5 cm.

The Shade of Hector

In an oil sketch of 1829 by Henri-Frédéric Schopin (cat. no. 87), the shade of the vanquished Hector—with mortal wounds, carrying the statue of the Trojan Vesta, itself drowned in shadows—warns Aeneas that the Trojan era is past:

> "Ah, goddess-born, take flight!" he cries, "and snatch
> yourself out of these flames. The enemy
> has gained the walls; Troy falls from her high peak.
> Our home, our Priam—these have had their due:
> could Pergamus [Troy] be saved by any prowess,
> then my hand would have served. But Troy entrusts
> her holy things and household gods to you . . ."
>
> —*AEN*. 2.289–93; M 2.395–401

He wakes Aeneas in the terrible night. Aeneas sleeps with one eye open and in the nude, as Homeric heroes so often do; his sword and helmet are at his bedside. He dreams, and his gesture follows the gaze that we intuit behind the closed eyes, fixed on the apparition of Hector, which therefore seems to spring forth from his own mind and lead his drowsy body on toward his destiny. Now is the time for men of action rather than sulking, lazy, or garrulous heroes. Achilles neither dreams nor acts, whereas Aeneas dreams, awakens, and acts.

Caylus shows a curious fear of this scene, speaking of "the Picture of the shade of Hector which appears to Aeneas in a dream, perhaps too fearful to be painted; for Hector appears in the state to which Achilles had reduced his body after killing him. But since he wakes Aeneas, since the Hero advises him to abandon the city, these facts seem too intimately linked to the *Aeneid* to be neglected; I am bound at least to mention them."[2] The École's students took account of Caylus's hesitations. The horror of the desecrated body disappears in the mysterious darkness of the dream, which harmonizes so well with the imprecision of the oil sketch.

Cherchez la Femme

CREUSA

To the modern reader, the second book of the *Aeneid* can seem cynical or misogynistic. Hector leaves his wife and child with words of love. Aeneas's father, Anchises, at first refuses to leave the captured Troy. Will Aeneas hurl himself into combat and be killed while defending Troy? His wife, Creusa, echoes the prayers of Andromache to Hector:

> "If you go off to die, then take us, too,
> to face all things with you; but if your past
> still lets you put your hope in arms, which now
> you have put on, then first protect this house.
> To whom is young Iülus left, to whom
> your father and myself, once called your wife?"
> —*AEN.* 2.675–78; M 2.914–19

Aeneas does not reply. Homer's Hector refused to hear his wife's pleas, his rough tone revealing as much pity as regret, as much love of life as hatred of war. Hector was severe where Aeneas is merely insensitive.

A sketch by Paul-Célestin-Louis Leboeuf-Nanteuil (1862; cat. no. 89) denounces Creusa's error: this is a woman restraining a man of action. He can only obey the goddess of war, who whispers to him of his duty and fills him with energy. It would be unfair to compare this sketch, with its bluish coloration, to Carpeaux's plaster group (cat. no. 41). The farewells of Andromache, Hector, and Astyanax would sharply contrast with this Aeneas, who is also held back by his wife yet does not doff his plumed helmet, and clasps not his son but his spear. He takes refuge from Creusa's pleas in the shadow of a statue, the goddess of war or symbol of his ancestors. He knows neither humor nor doubt. Homer's heroes happily abandon their wives for a goddess or captive woman but are more reluctant when it comes to doing battle. That is no certificate of fidelity, to be sure, but at least they prefer women to warfare.

Aeneas is so willing to abandon his wife that he in fact forgets her. Leaving the blazing citadel, he at least thinks to save his father, Anchises—whom he must first convince, for the old man will leave his fatherland only if he can take with him his Penates (statuettes of ancestors)—and he thinks to save his son, Iulus. Thus Aeneas carries his father on his shoulders and leads his son by the hand through this cataclysmic scene. It is a valiant filial and paternal exploit and has proved popular with artists since Raphael painted *The Fire in the Borgo* (Vatican Palace), where he first created this curious silhouette summarizing the solidarity of the three ages of man: the adult carries the old man; the old man carries the family's sacred statue; each guides the other and the child follows the group, while everyone forgets the wife and mother. The École has many examples of this scene, from a print after Raphael to a painting by Merry-Joseph Blondel (cat. no. 88). The scene is sometimes called the "Pietas [piety] of Aeneas" and demands a certain seriousness, although artists gradually discovered the strangeness of this group, their ghostly figures lost in the collapse of their world or silhouetted against the glow of dawn.

What should a woman save in a fire? Creusa is carrying nothing, and so her husband, haggard in the cruel night, forgets her completely, later declaring:

> I cannot say if she had halted or
> had wandered off the road or slumped down, weary.
> My eyes have never had her back again.
> I did not look behind for her, astray,
> or think of her . . .
> —*AEN.* 2.739–41; M 2.996–1000

The painting by Merry-Joseph Blondel (cat. no. 88) shows that she did wander off the road. Father-in-law, husband, and son form a perfect triangle in their departure, while Creusa moves off to the left without seeing or looking at them. A useful error: when the time comes, Aeneas is free to marry the heiress of the Latin territories and thus lay the foundations of the Roman Empire. Since he cannot violate the laws of conjugal morality, the first wife must disappear forever

OPPOSITE CATALOGUE NO. 88 | MERRY-JOSEPH BLONDEL (1781–1853), *Aeneas Carrying His Father Anchises*, 1803. Oil on canvas, 144 × 113 cm.

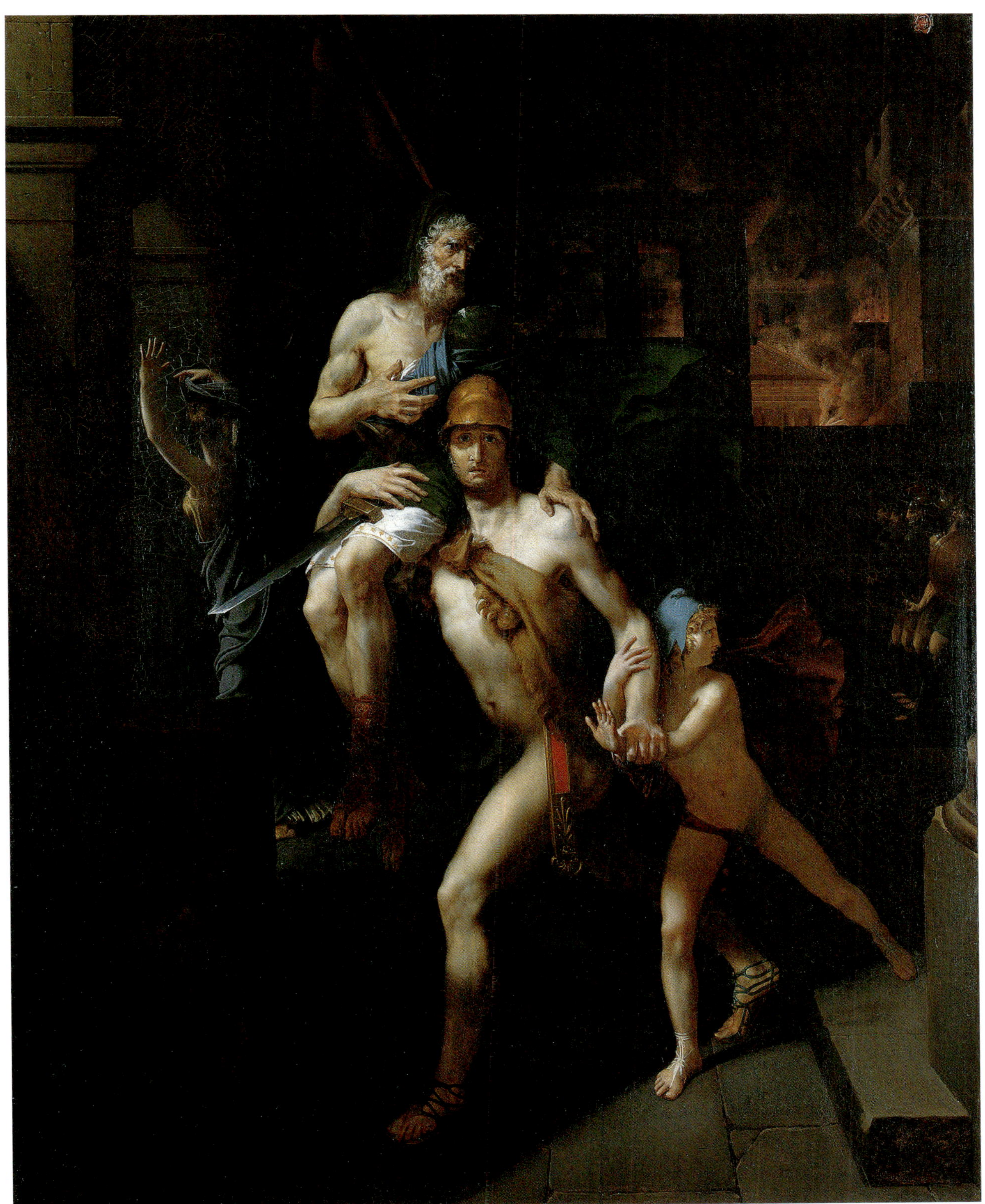

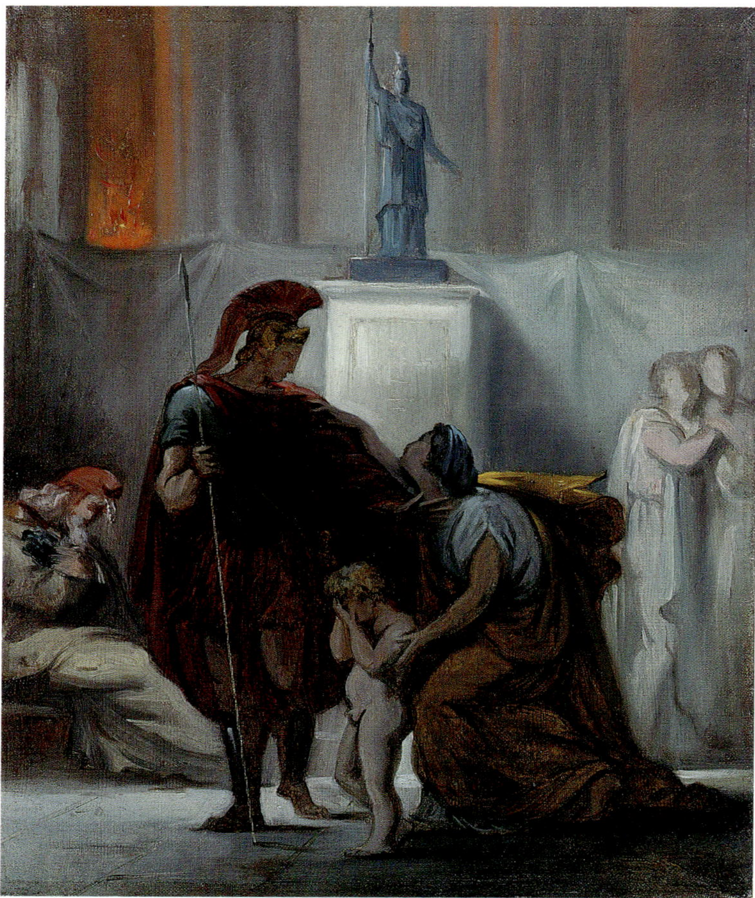

CATALOGUE NO. 89 | PAUL-CÉLESTIN-LOUIS NANTEUIL (called Leboeuf-Nanteuil) (1837–1901), *Creusa Seeks to Retain Aeneas*, 1862. Oil on canvas, 40.5 × 32.5 cm.

into the darkness and flames. Aeneas (or Virgil) claims that her shade returns and congratulates him on her abandonment, anticipating in this wretched self-justification his excuses as he abandons Dido—the feeble explanations of a warrior better able to face the enemy than a woman. The Romans are excellent fighters in wartime but fear womankind. Homer's Greeks incline to chaotic inefficiency in battle but at least stand up to their better halves. They are more likely to be killed by their wives than to kill them, whereas the poor women in Aeneas's life are mostly reduced to suicide.

DIDO

Darkness was not always unfavorable to Aeneas in his adventures with women. A few months and a few oceans later, the steady advance of the *Aeneid* leads Aeneas into the company of Dido, queen of Carthage. How sweet it is to have left his legitimate spouse in the horror of pitch darkness when he meets another woman in the gloom of a convenient cave.

Dido would love to play Calypso to Aeneas's Ulysses for at least a few years. She uses the same stratagem, seducing him in a cave when they seek shelter on a stormy day. In this affair Virgil perceives only one guilty party: the woman.

> . . . she no longer thinks
> of furtive love. For Dido calls it marriage,
> and with this name she covers up her fault.
> —*AEN.* 4.171–72; M 4.226–28

The dark brought on by the storm in Jean-Adrien Guignet's historical landscape (1838; cat. no. 90) is neither romantic nor sensual. Virgil's moralizing has done its work: since the woman gave herself freely, she can be abandoned freely. Aeneas has the best possible excuse: he must go and found Rome. Dido, meanwhile, kills herself.

On at least one occasion the École professors required their students to give more serious thought to Aeneas's ungentlemanly behavior. When, in the sixth book, Aeneas is led by the Sibyl of Cumae, and the precedent of Ulysses, to brave the Underworld, the first person he meets is Dido. The comedy of Calypso and Ulysses is here repeated in a tragic mode. In a celebrated collocation, he recognizes her "per umbras / Obscuram" (shadowy amid the shades) (*Aen.* 6.452–53). Although the medium of the oil sketch might have been designed to render this strikingly Homeric formulation, Henri-Frédéric Schopin made little effort to do so (cat. no. 91). The description might equally befit the shade of Anticleia in the eleventh book of the *Odyssey*, where the intangibility of his beloved mother makes Ulysses doubt his senses and appeals to the loftiest elements of human nature. By contrast, Aeneas's

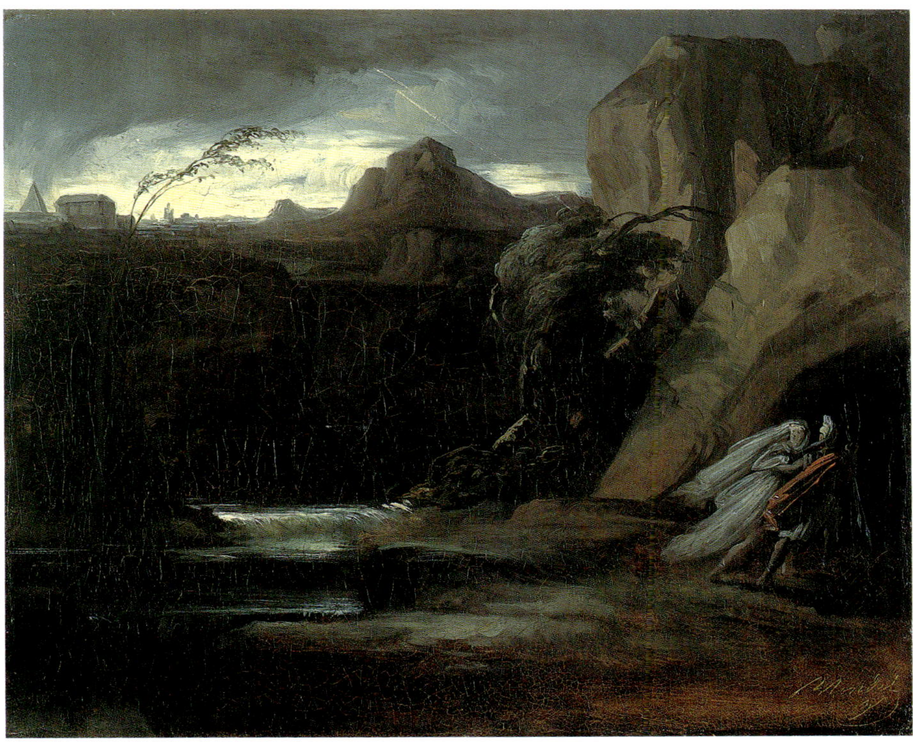

CATALOGUE NO. 90 | JEAN-ADRIEN GUIGNET (1816–1854), *Dido and Aeneas Take Refuge in a Cave During a Storm*, 1838. Oil on canvas, 38 × 46 cm.

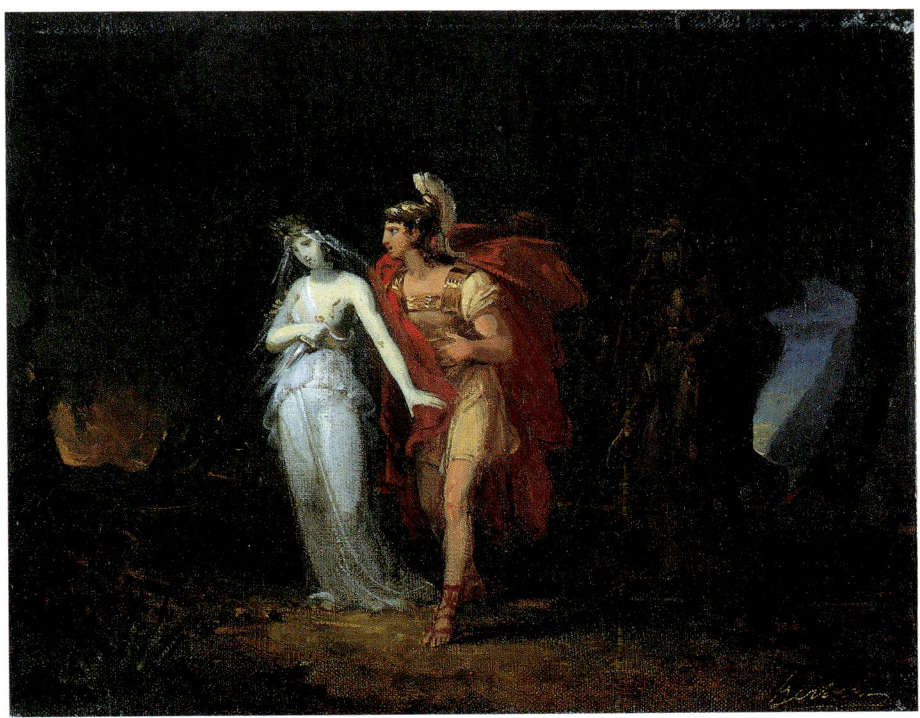

CATALOGUE NO. 91 | HENRI-FRÉDÉRIC SCHOPIN (OR CHOPIN) (1804–1890), *Aeneas in the Underworld*, 1828. Oil on tracing paper mounted on canvas, 32 × 40 cm.

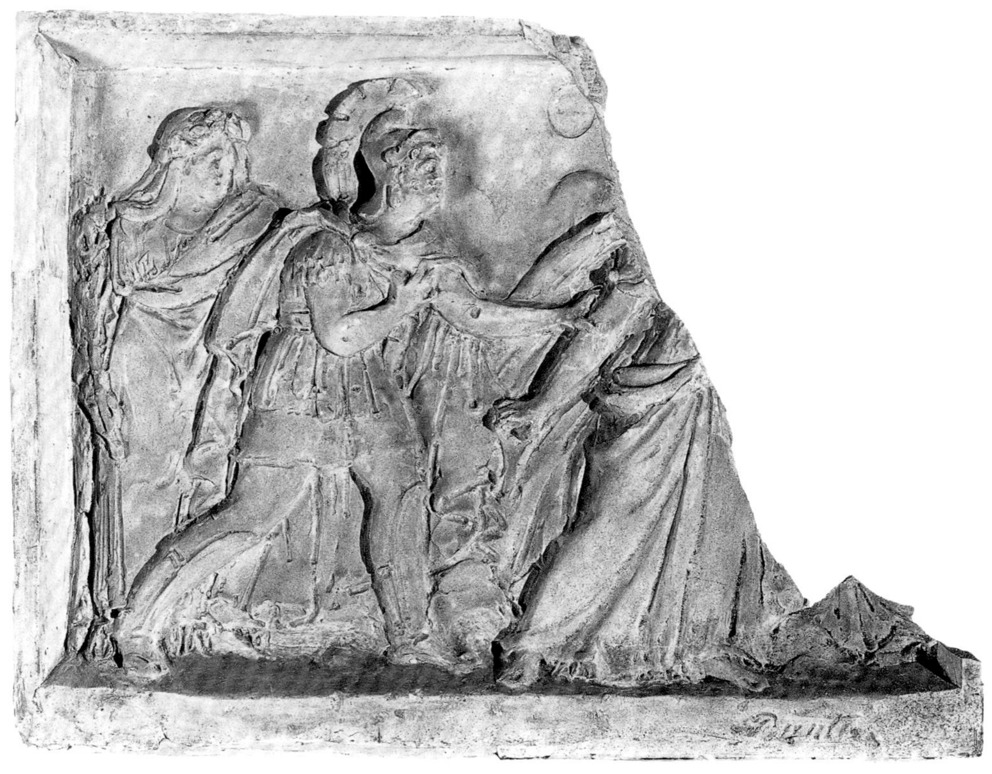

FIGURE 56 | ANTOINE-LAURENT DANTAN, CALLED DANTAN THE ELDER (1798–1878), *Aeneas and the Sibyl in the Underworld Encounter the Shadow of Dido*, 1828. Plaster, 40.5 × 53 cm. Sculpture Sketch *concours*.

justification of his conduct toward Dido is so pitiful that regret for the past is obliterated. At once banal and cowardly, he claims to have deserted his lover on the order of the gods. In Schopin's oil sketch and Dantan's relief sketch (fig. 56) he utters his lamentable excuse. No Greek would have taken it seriously, but Virgil thought it convincing, no doubt because the gods are Roman and are working for the future Rome. In both works the gesture is the same—a hand goes out to the betrayed lover—and the embarrassed pose therefore lacks balance, the one leg excessively rigid and the other too pliant, eloquently bespeaking the cowardice of the inconstant lover. In both works, Dido's outstretched arm—its nudity beautifully lit for our pleasure—disdainfully signals she will not turn toward him. In the sculpture the figure of Dido has retained this contemptuous gesture but lost her face. The clumsy supplication of Aeneas looks all the more wretched and pitiful for the loss. In Schopin's oil sketch, the sibyl stands off amid the shadows, observing the whole sad scene. The École's students took the part of the bereft lover—and we like them the more for it. Their sketches have no caption, so one must borrow the words Daumier placed in *his* Dido's mouth (cat. no. 126): "Dear beloved, you're history."

VENUS

The relations between Aeneas and his mother, Venus, make a striking comparison with the scenes in the *Iliad* in which the tearful Achilles is consoled by his mother, Thetis. Achilles cries like a capricious child, whereas Aeneas never asks his mother for anything; she spontaneously brings him arms and cures his wounds. Between the *Iliad* and the *Aeneid*, divine mothers change less than their sons. O fortunate Romans, whose goddesses neither lie nor kill but rather protect and cure. The Olympians descending to the plain of Troy—even when they intended only to rescue their favorites—acted with their usual omnipotent incompetence and exacerbated the chaos of war. When Aphrodite saves Paris by sweeping him away from his duel with Menelaus, she succeeds only in dishonoring him forever. In her new Roman identity as Venus, mother of Aeneas, Aphrodite no longer commits such blunders. In the eighth book of the *Aeneid,* Aeneas declares that Venus has promised to supply him with new arms (*Aen.* 8.528–31). We have heard no complaints against his old panoply, nor has he asked for anything; yet his mother has decided to offer him arms, as Thetis did to console her son. The aid of Hephaestus (Vulcan) is again solicited. Recounted without a trace of humor, this scene is risible. Venus asks the lame god, her husband, for a present to bestow on her son, who was begotten—amid a host of other lovers—by the mortal Anchises; this is not just any mortal but a Trojan, an enemy to the Greeks, whom Hephaestus has always favored. The methods of persuasion used by Venus are those Hera used to put her own husband to sleep. A mediocre Academy reception piece takes up the story: Samuel Massé's *Arms of Aeneas* (1705). By some misfortune, however, Vulcan's handsome armor does not protect every part of Aeneas, and although he has no "Aeneas's heel," he is hit by a remarkably anonymous arrow that wounds him we know not where. He suffers, withdraws from combat, and places his hopes in his mother's medicine:

> But then Aeneas' pain, unmerited,
> distresses Venus; with a mother's care
> she plucks—from Cretan Ida—dittany,
> a stalk with leaves luxuriant and shaggy
> and purple flower . . .
>
> —AEN. 12.411–14; M 12.556–60

As the academician Jean-Charles-Niçaise Perrin reports in his 1787 reception piece (cat. no. 92), Venus saves her son either by administering the remedy herself or by substituting it for the remedies of the mortal Iapyx. Virgil tells us that although the latter knows his medicinal plants, in desperate cases he has recourse to divine knowledge and intervention. Perrin creates a dialogue between the two healers and adroitly illustrates Iapyx's conclusion:

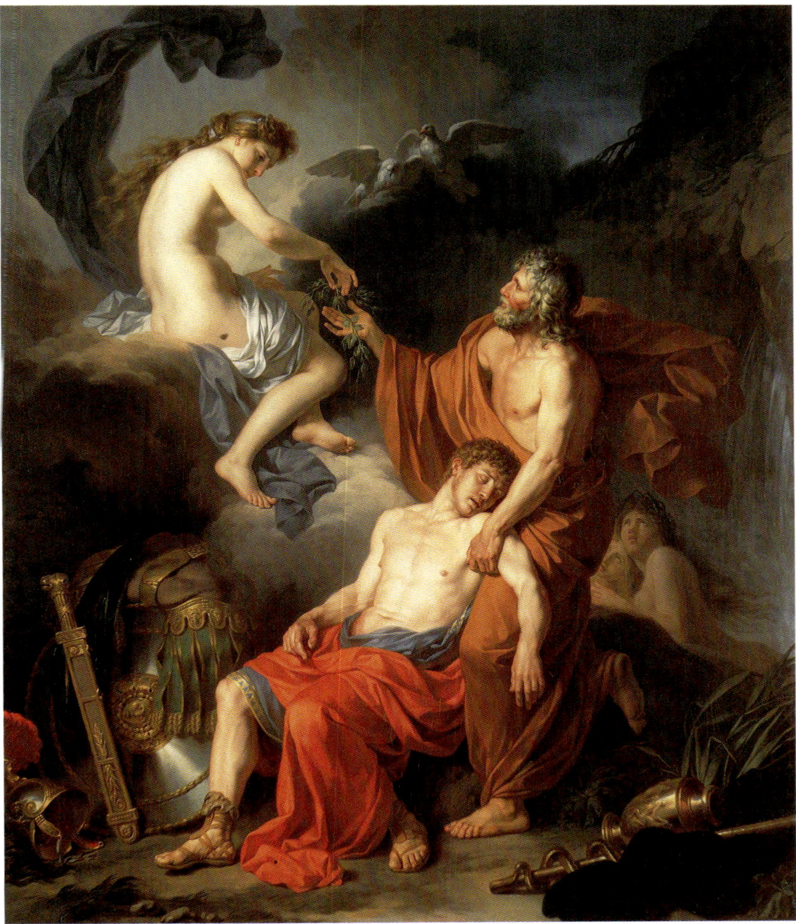

CATALOGUE NO. 92 | JEAN-CHARLES-NIÇAISE PERRIN (1754–1831), *Aeneas Cured of His Wounds,* 1787. Oil on canvas, 197 × 163 cm.

> "This is not the work
> of mortal hands or skillful art; my craft
> has not saved you, Aeneas: here there is
> a greater one—a god—who sends you back
> to greater labors."
>
> —AEN. 12.427–29; M 12.575–79

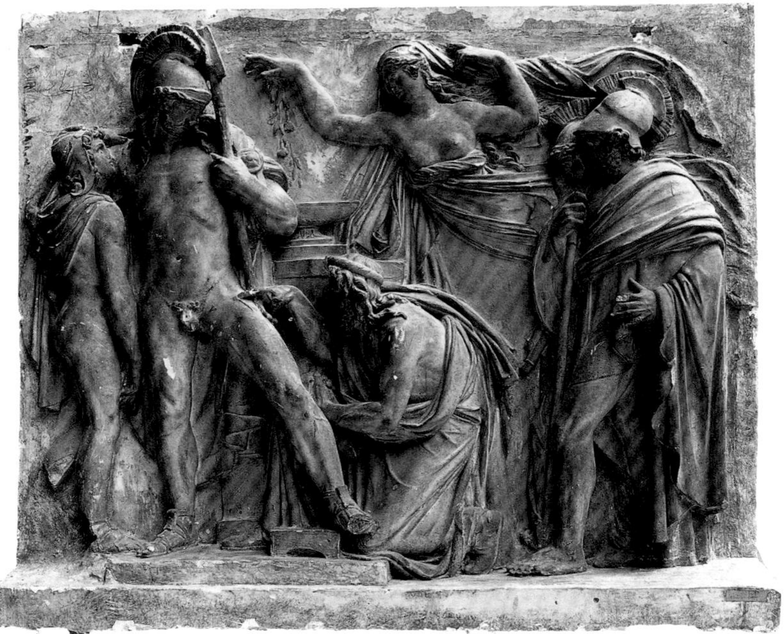

FIGURE 57 | ABEL DIMIER (1794–1864), *The Wounded Aeneas Is Cured by Venus*, 1819. Plaster, 120 × 155 cm. Prix de Rome in Sculpture.

Perrin's composition rises from the wounded man to the healer and then to the nude goddess enthroned amid the clouds and celestial birds. Behind Iapyx, who is thanking the goddess, two water nymphs venerate the fearful evidence of divine omnipotence. In Perrin's painting men and gods mingle in a common sphere, namely, that of virtue (without heroism). Perrin may indeed have represented not the obscure Iapyx but Aesculapius (the Greek Asclepios). This divine physician was struck down by a thunderbolt for his incursion into the privileges of the jealous gods: he could cure even the dead. In 1819 Abel Dimier sculpted the same scene for the relief that won the Grand Prix in sculpture (fig. 57). The wounded hero leans on his son, through whom virtue will be transmitted to the next generation. He rests his faith in the altar of the religion that inspires him, and his hopes in the knowledge of the physician who kneels before him. To one side, the hero's companions also bow their heads in respect. In Virgil's world both gods and princes are venerated.

The Brave and the Foolhardy

With Virgil, the time has come when good and evil are easily distinguished; good defeats evil because force, power, and the gods have allied themselves with moralizing right. During the Italian campaign, two of Aeneas's companions, Nisus and Euryalus, go behind the Rutulian lines as heroic and brutal scouts (*Aen.* 9.449ff.). Their expedition has only slight analogies with that of Ulysses and Diomedes when they set off into the Trojan night to steal the Palladium, if necessary one from the other. O perverse Greeks! O noble simplicity of the Roman soldier! Virgil no doubt wished to introduce in a secondary episode a reference not to Ulysses and Diomedes, those two temple plunderers, but to Achilles and Patroclus, companions in arms.

In the dark forest, Nisus loses sight of Euryalus, who is surprised by an enemy patrol. The vain Euryalus has donned a helmet whose plume catches the moonlight and betrays him. Nisus retraces his steps and kills two Rutuli with his javelins. The furious chieftain Volcens kills his prisoner, and Nisus, mad with grief, hurls himself at the patrol and kills Volcens before he himself dies riddled with wounds. The oil sketch of Henry-Auguste-Calixte-César Serrur (cat. no. 93) and the molded relief of Louis Desprez (fig. 58) were made for the 1820 *concours*. They isolate the heroic couple amid the hostile throng. No longer victims of the gods but martyrs to virtue, the heroes in both sketches fall to the ground, happily aware of having done their duty. (It is understandable that the subject also pleased Anne-Louis Girodet, the artist of virtuous and voluptuous suffering.) The figures are hard to make out in this benighted melee, and the faces of the martyrs tell us nothing about their lives or their truncated hopes. In Homer death in battle is an attack on life and happiness. In Virgil death is the crowning moment in a life

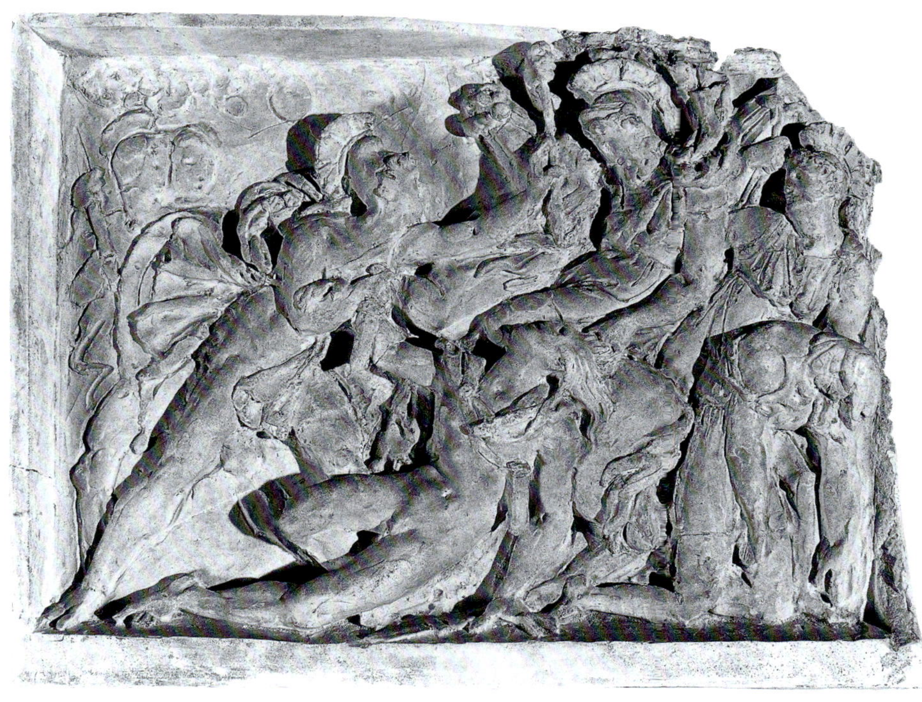

FIGURE 58 | LOUIS DESPREZ (1799–1870), *Nisus and Euryalus*, 1820. Plaster, 41.5 × 49 cm. Sculpture Sketch *concours*.

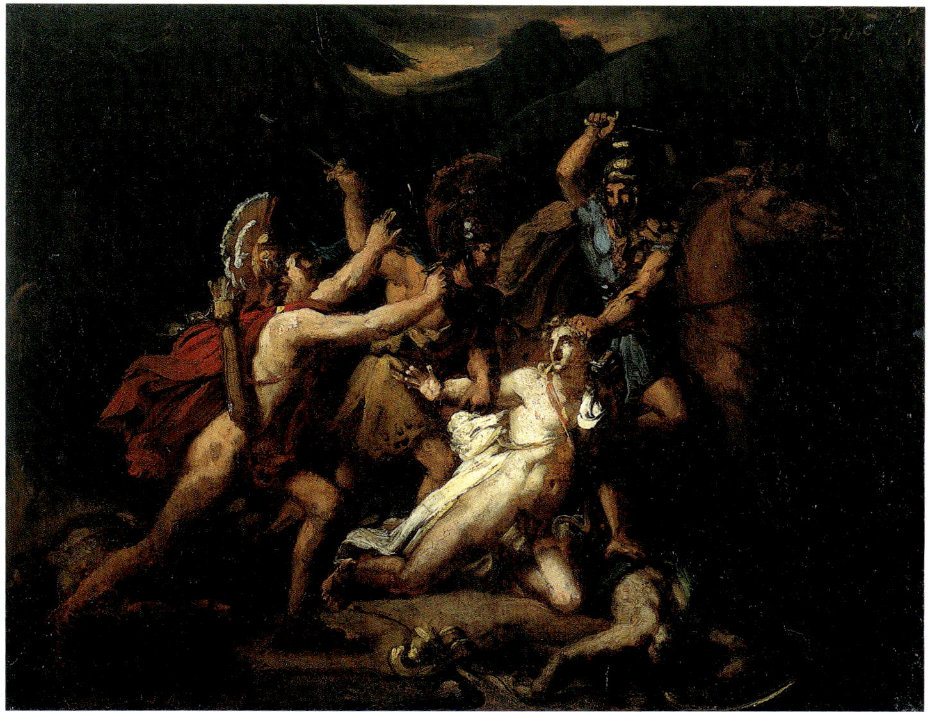

CATALOGUE NO. 93 | HENRY-AUGUSTE-CALIXTE-CÉSAR SERRUR (1794–1865), *Nisus Attempts to Save Euryalus*, 1820. Oil on tracing paper mounted on canvas, 32 × 40.5 cm.

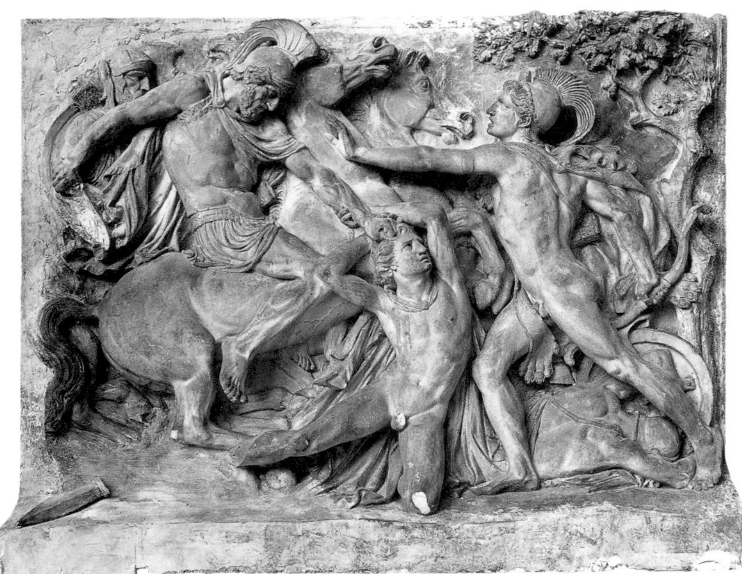

FIGURE 59 | CHARLES-ARTHUR BOURGEOIS (1838–1886), *The Death of Nisus and Euryalus*, 1863. Plaster, 130 × 157 cm. Prix de Rome in Sculpture.

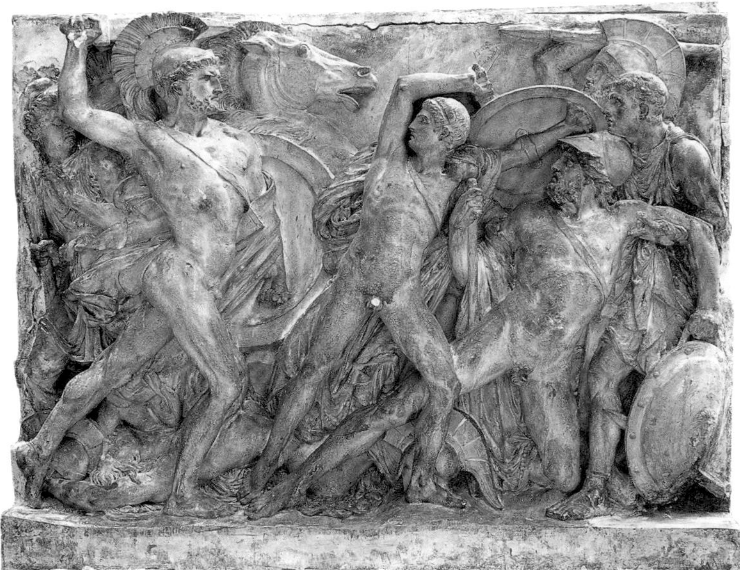

FIGURE 60 | LOUIS-LÉON CUGNOT (1835–1894), *The Wounded Mezentius Is Saved by His Son Lausus's Bravery*, 1859. Plaster, 120 × 150 cm. Prix de Rome in Sculpture.

that poet and painter sacrifice amid somber and glorious backgrounds, amid nudity, rhetorical gestures, and rearing horses. Before Christianity, Virgil had begun to teach humanity that death could be beautiful and the butchery of war heroic. In 1863 Charles-Arthur Bourgeois's Grand Prix–winning sculpture raises the quota of heroic victims of duty; nothing differentiates his self-sacrificing automata from each other (fig. 59).

Virgil the Roman nationalist is a man of order—and not too particular about the orders. It is a fine thing to massacre the enemy; it is admirable to be massacred for the fatherland; and there is nothing more enviable than to face an adversary inspired by similar principles. One book later, after the Rutuli have killed Nisus and Euryalus, it is the turn of their closest allies, the Etruscans, to lose their king, Mezentius, and his son, Lausus. Theirs is a heroic end (*Aen.* 10.791–908) and an ideal subject for a history painter who does not think about or protest against the barbarity of war. This is the moment described by Jean-Alexandre-Joseph Falguière, who won the Prix de Rome in sculpture in 1859 (cat. no. 94) with this subject. (Louis-Léon Cugnot [fig. 60] won the second grand prize.) Aeneas first wounds Mezentius and then kills his son, who interposes; the father survives just long enough to see his son's body and swear vengeance. (His oath was the subject of the 1821 oil sketch *concours* won by Charles-Louis Bazin; cat. no. 95) Falguière's relief is full of conviction. The movements of men and horses all eloquently declare confidence in action. The curves of the bodies are extended and developed in the outstretched arms. Heroes, children, gods, and horses whirl in a dance, and none of them imagine they might die. The heroes have no quarrel with the destiny imposed by the gods or the errors they may themselves commit. Some drops of blood have formed on Mezentius's thigh, but he cares nothing for his wound. Post-Homeric epic does not teach young artists about the ambiguities of truth and virtue, merely the certainty and the invincible force of good. These bodies going to their deaths are bursting with life and happiness. We should

OPPOSITE CATALOGUE NO. 94 | JEAN-ALEXANDRE-JOSEPH FALGUIÈRE (1831–1900), *The Wounded Mezentius Is Saved by the Daring of His Son Lausus*, 1859. Plaster, 127 × 155.5 cm.

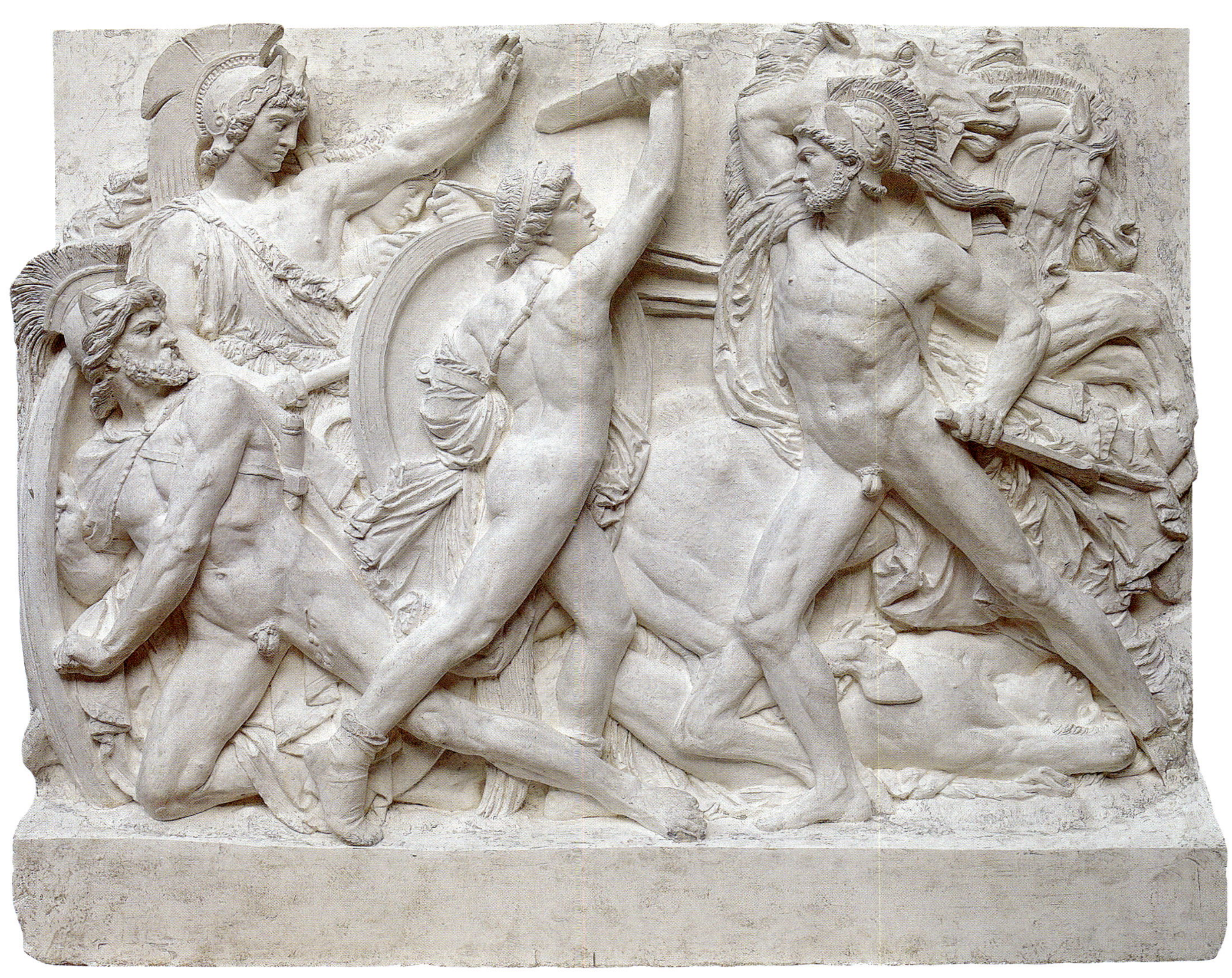

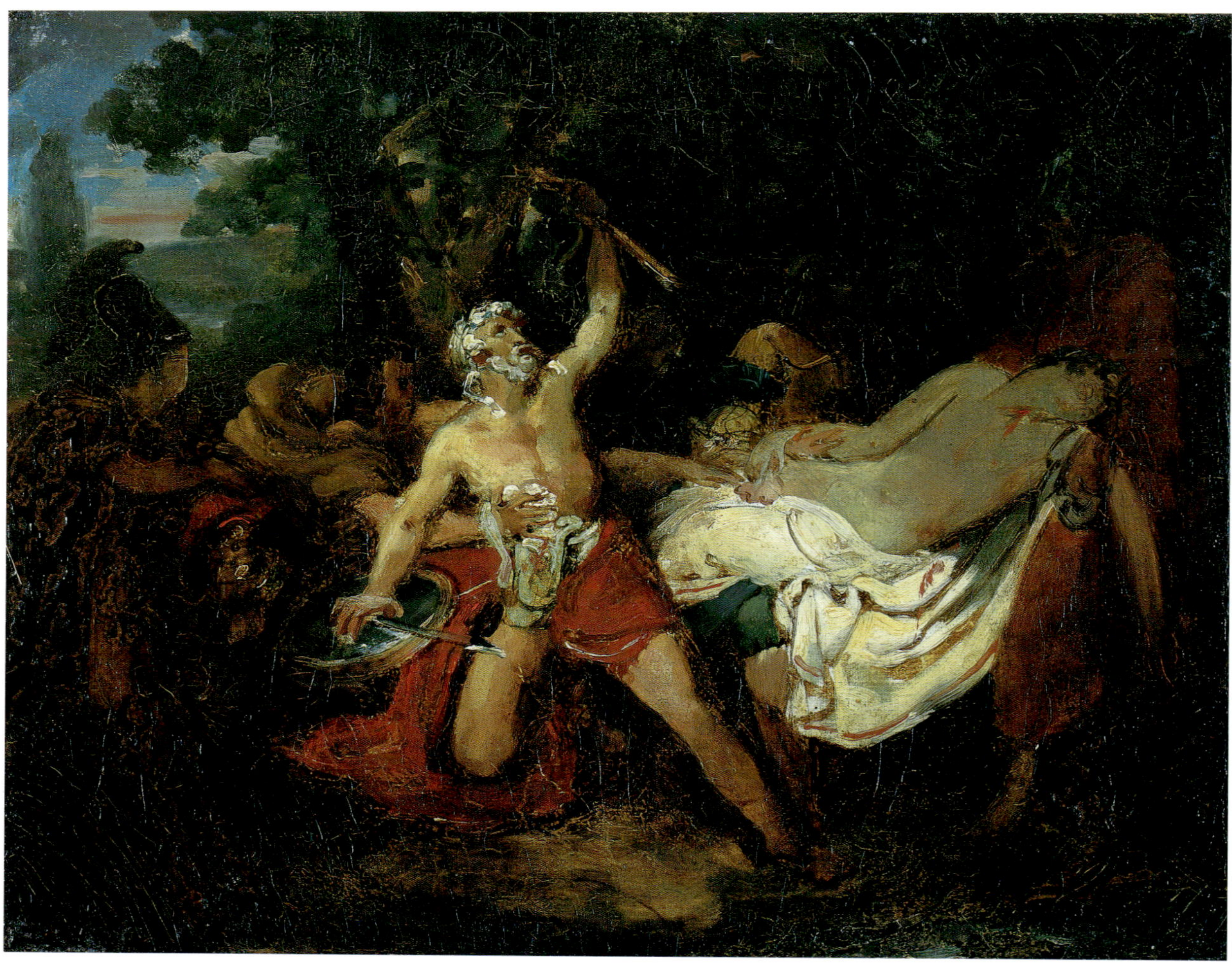

CATALOGUE NO. 95 | CHARLES-LOUIS BAZIN (1802–1859), *The Wounded Mezentius Vows to Avenge His Son Lausus*, 1821. Oil on tracing paper mounted on canvas, 32.5 × 40.5 cm.

remember the horses of Achilles, exasperated by their master's suicidal pride and whinnying their disgust behind the tents as the background to his mourning fury. Falguière's horses like blood and rear up with an ardor equal to that animating their masters.

Falguière's treatment of Virgil is in the poet's warlike spirit, but occasionally a young artist treated Virgilian themes in the pacifist perspective of Homer. The art of the oil sketch has often been considered by scholars to afford a moment of inspired liberty to the young artists of the École who wished to restore to their painting a degree of animation and sensitivity. In the little sketch by Charles-Lous Bazin, the dead son Lausus is Christlike in his burden of grief, and voluptuous as an Adonis. His father, Mezentius, assumes the pose and fury of Laocoön, while the shadowy figures around them attempt to hold up Lausus and restrain the father, who is fated to die at Aeneas's hand. War as depicted in Bazin's sketch does not encourage one to die for the fatherland. The spirit of Virgil has been betrayed and that of Homer is reborn.

Bazin's pain-filled sketch, however, is a happy exception. Virgil narrates his epic without either the skepticism or the irony that make of the Homeric narrative such a constant joy. Transposition into the visual medium paradoxically confers greater vitality on Virgil because he believes in action; especially in the hands of very young artists, action better animates paint and plaster than doubting thoughts and paralyzing emotions. The choice is between the mischief, second thoughts, and concealed motives of Odysseus and the acts of Aeneas, committed with unbounded certainty and sincerity, that is, between the examples of virtue in which Virgil abounds and those of vice, in which Homer is so fertile. Virgil and many another artist following him wanted to assign a sense to everything—to the Latin war and the Trojan War alike—but, like most wars, they had none.

NOTES

1 W. B. Stanford, *The Ulysses Theme: A Study in the Adaptability of a Traditional Hero*, rev. ed. (Oxford, 1963), 137.

2 Comte A.-C.-P de Caylus, *Tableaux tirés de l'Iliade, de l'Odyssée d'Homère et de l'Énéide de Virgile, avec des observations générales sur le costume* (Paris, 1757), 307.

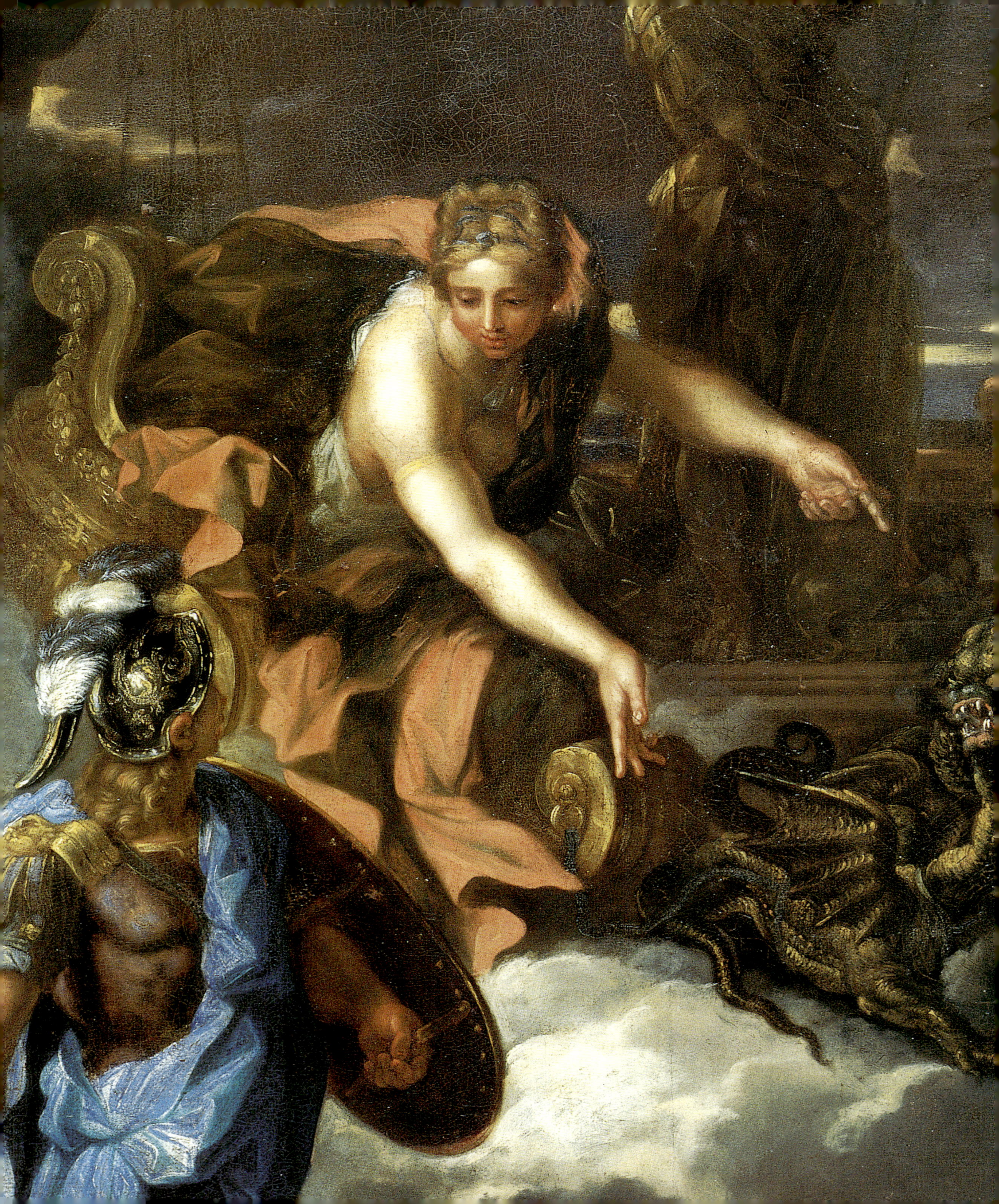

Previous and Parallel Epic Cycles

Homer's genius was situated at the moment when traditional mythology met the nascent skepticism of the Greeks. He therefore built his poems around three destinies, three complex and fully fleshed-out characters: Achilles, Hector, and Ulysses. All Homer's other characters—kings and gods not excepted—seem mere foils to these princes. The tradition offered many other warriors and heroes, however, to whom a poet of similar stature could have imparted the same depth, fragility, and humanity. Aware of the injustice done to these neglected heroes, Lucian and, much later, Fénelon wrote *Dialogues of the Dead*, conversations in the Underworld between heroes of various epochs, often pointing up the contrast between those lucky enough to be immortalized by Homer and those doomed to near-oblivion by their appearance in secondary legends. One can also imagine Homer's regret at having to eliminate so many characters closely related to his own, but too remote from Homer's world (or the world of Troy) by their role in fable, their adventures, or by the compositional necessities of the narrative. Here I will consider a number of those who, born a generation before the combatants of Troy and considered by their successors as masters and models, would have loved to accompany the Greek expeditionary force.

Meleager and the Calydonian Boar Hunt

Fortunately the freedom of poetic composition allows the excluded to return by the back door, in some tableau of an incidental nature that shows Homer was tempted by digressions and flashbacks. These episodes, intelligible even without their context, were easily inserted on the periphery of the Trojan War, creating simple images, dense and tragic, generally observing the unities of time and place. Garrulous raconteurs, with their insistent irrelevance—a standard feature in Homer—are very useful in this respect. The young hide their smiles as the old rattle on. Ingres won his Prix de Rome by depicting the famous embassy to Achilles, one of whose members was Achilles' former tutor Phoenix. He was unable to assuage Achilles' wrath, but, remembering the years when he told his pupil edifying stories, he recounted (in great detail) the admonitory story of Meleager's obduracy (*Il.* 9.543–99).

Three episodes chart the life of Meleager. His first feat was to kill the Calydonian boar, which had been unleashed on his countrymen by Artemis. The swift-footed Atalanta had been of great assistance to him in the chase and he awarded her the boar's head, thereby incurring his mother's curse. His story begins, however, with the anger of Artemis against Oeneus, Meleager's father, the king of Calydon, whom the goddess accuses of not having honored her:

> The rest of the gods had feasted full on oxen, true,
> but the Huntress alone, almighty Zeus's daughter—
> Oeneus gave her nothing. It slipped his mind
> or he failed to care, but what a fatal error!
> How she fumed, Zeus's child who showers arrows,

DETAIL OF CATALOGUE NO. 100

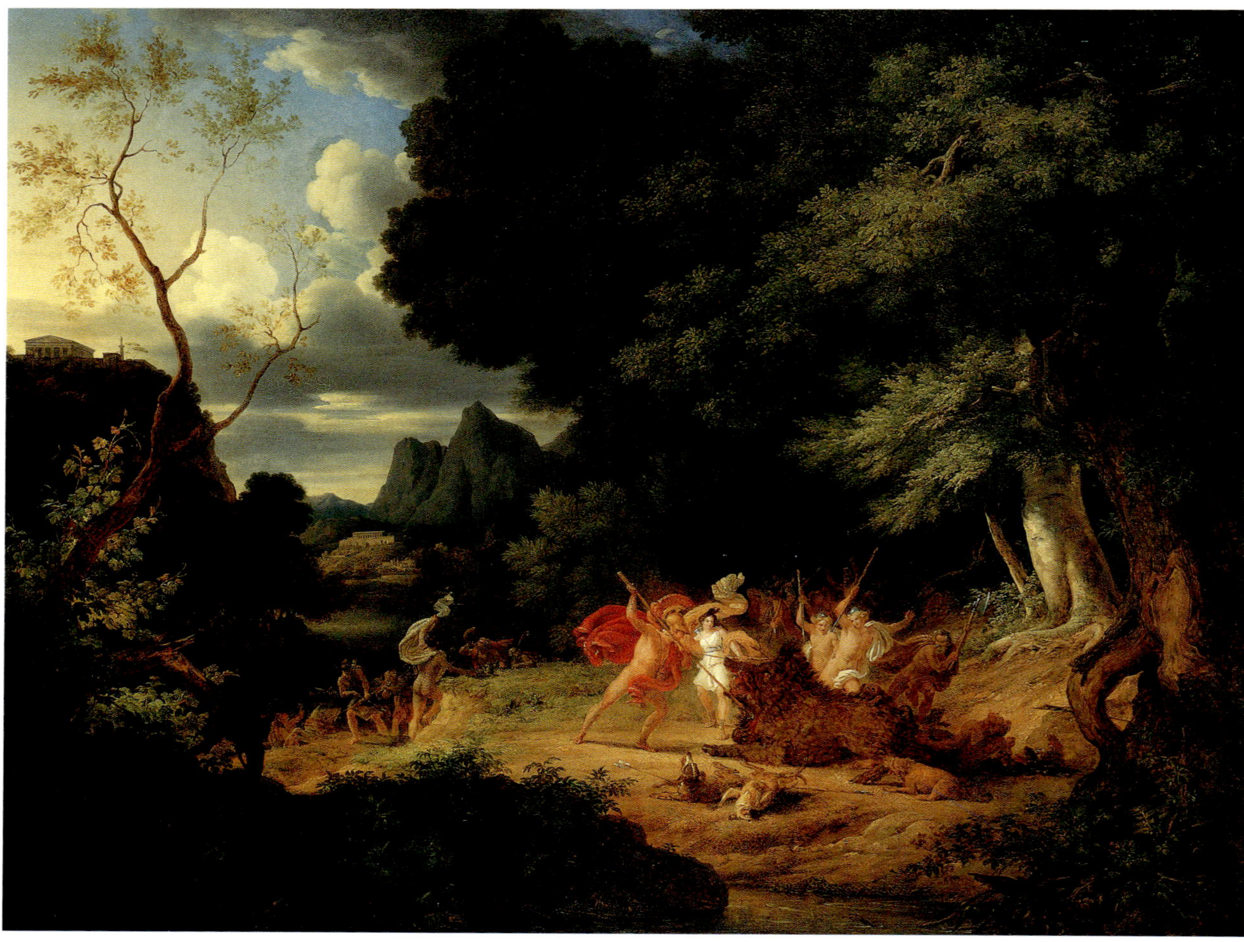

CATALOGUE NO. 96 | ANDRÉ GIROUX (1801–1879), *The Calydonian Boar Hunt*, 1825. Oil on canvas, 114 × 146 cm.

she loosed a bristling wild boar, his tusks gleaming,
crashing his savage, monstrous way through Oeneus' orchard,
ripping up whole trunks from the earth to pitch them headlong,
rows of them, roots and all, appleblossoms and all!
But the son of Oeneus, Meleager, cut him down—
mustering hunters out of a dozen cities,
packs of hounds as well. No slim band of men
could ever finish him off, that rippling killer,
he stacked so many men atop the tear-soaked pyre.
But over his body the goddess raised a terrific din,
a war for the prize, the huge beast's head and shaggy hide—
Curetes locked to the death with brave Aetolians.

—*IL.* 9.543–99; F 9.653–69

In the short story of Meleager, Curetes and Aetolians play the role the Greeks and Trojans might have played if the Trojan War had remained a quarrel between two neighboring villages or, rather, if their village rivalry had not found a Homer. Yet the Curetes and Aetolians get sixty-four verses from Homer, and Europe's attack against Asia receives twenty-four books.

Meleager's pursuit of the Calydonian boar, on the heels of Atalanta, was given its second wind by the founding of the Historical Landscape *concours* in 1817. Here was an ideal subject for the students. In 1825 André Giroux showed the line of hunters encountering the boar as they emerge from a long clearing (cat. no. 96). The background landscape is Italianate in terms of light and profile, but the massed trees of the foreground are so dark that they redirect the gaze toward the small, indistinctly characterized figures spread out in the clearing that leads back to the acropolis. Homer abounds in scenes suitable for historical landscape paintings. The little figures, the town, and the tree—all of them regulation components of the genre—embellish and civilize nature while showing it can be combated and tamed. True, the world of the historical landscape lacks the vitality of the goddesses and untamed natural forces in Homer's tales. The greensward nature painted by the young artists in their Parisian *loges*, remembering the Claude landscapes in the Louvre, seemed to them incompatible with cruelty.

Homer barely mentions (in the penultimate verse cited earlier) Meleager's first outbreak of temper, when he killed his uncles for disputing his right to award the honors of the hunt to Atalanta. This anger worthy of Achilles was set for the Sculpture Sketch *concours* in 1849. No landscape here, not so much as a tree. The winner, one Jean-Baptiste Forgemolle (fig. 61), subsequently disappeared from the history of art. There is an earthy density to his figures, in particular that of Atalanta, exhausted from so much running, frozen in plaster as she recoils from Meleager's unwanted violence. The three combatants, barely roughed out in the clay, demarcate their status and claims with outstretched arms, their arms and legs forming a rough square. Atalanta's hound cowers behind her legs, contemplating the men as they confront each other.

Meleager killed his uncles and thus courted the vengeance of his mother, Althaea (the uncles were on the maternal side). Immured in his anger like Achilles,

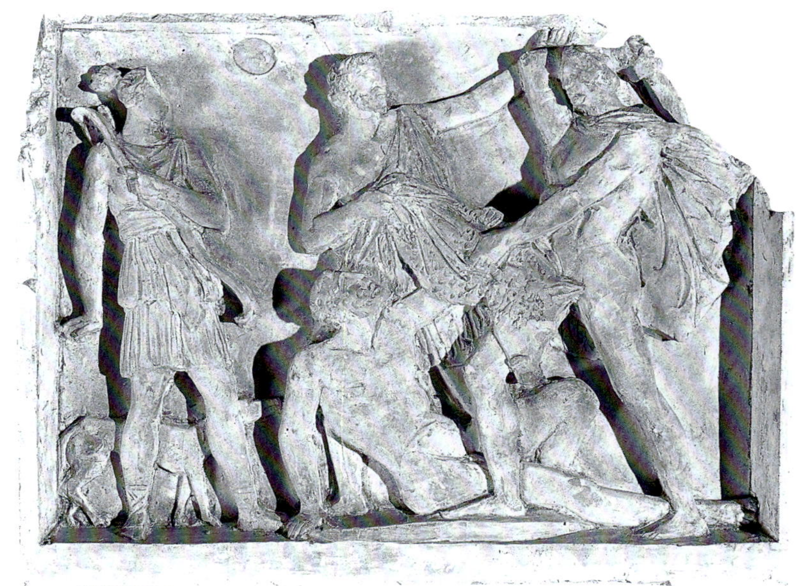

FIGURE 61 | JEAN-BAPTISTE FORGEMOLLE (1824–?), *Meleager Giving in to His Anger*, 1849. Plaster, 30 x 45 cm. Sculpture Sketch *concours*.

he at least continued to enjoy the company of his wife, Cleopatra. The Aetolians, however, now found themselves besieged in their capital of Calydon by the Curetes, their traditional enemies, who were reassured by the continued brooding of their most formidable adversary:

> Now,
> so long as the battle-hungry Meleager fought,
> it was deadly going for the Curetes. No hope
> of holding their ground outside their *own* city walls,
> despite superior numbers. But then, when the wrath
> came sweeping over the man, the same anger that swells
> the chests of others, for all their care and self-control—
> then, heart enraged at his own dear mother Althaea,
> Meleager kept to his bed beside his wedded wife,
> Cleopatra . . . that great beauty. Remember her?
> The daughter of trim-heeled Marpessa, Euenus' child
> . . .
>
> —*IL.* 9.550–60; F 9.669–79

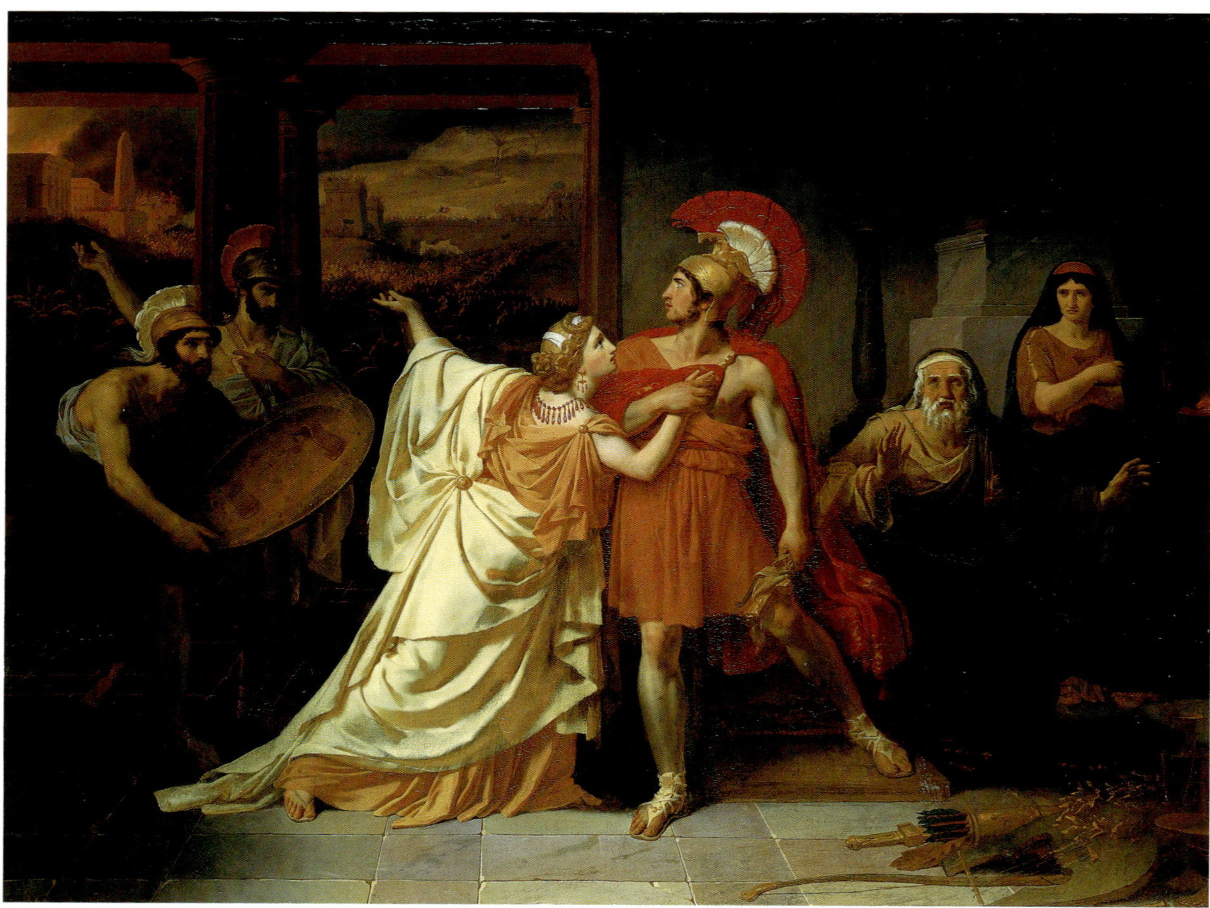

CATALOGUE NO. 97 | ÉMILE SIGNOL (1804–1892), *Meleager Taking Up His Arms*, 1830. Oil on canvas, 115 × 146.5 cm.

The parallel with Achilles is clear in Phoenix's account:

> And over and over the old horseman Oeneus begged him,
> he took a stand at the vaulted chamber's threshold,
> shaking the bolted doors, begging his own son!
> Over and over his brothers and noble mother
> implored him—he refused them all the more—
> and troops of comrades, devoted, dearest friends.
> Not even they could bring his fighting spirit round
> until, at last, rocks were raining down on the chamber,
> Curetes about to mount the towers and torch the great city!
> And then, finally, Meleager's bride, beautiful Cleopatra
> begged him, streaming tears, recounting all the griefs
> that fall to people whose city's seized and plundered—
> the men slaughtered, citadel burned to rubble, enemies
> dragging the children, raping the sashed and lovely women.
> How his spirit leapt when he heard those horrors—
> and buckling his gleaming armor round his body,
> out he rushed to war. And so he saved them all
> from the fatal day, he gave way to his own feelings . . .
>
> —*IL.* 9.550–60; F 9.709–26

In 1830 Émile Signol's painting *Meleager Taking Up His Arms* (cat. no. 97) won the Prix de Rome, but he was clearly uncertain how to depict simultaneously the horror of war, the pleas of Cleopatra, and the relief of the Aetolians. He made the bizarre decision to show a warrior, against the light of the fiery background, already fully armed and about to set out for the front. His comrades form up beside him, staring toward the spectator—that is, into the void. The same theme was set in 1823; Félix-Henry Auvray's sketch (cat. no. 98) is more convincing. Paul Jourdy's 1830 painting of the same subject (fig. 62) did not win the Prix de Rome (perhaps because he did not have time to finish it), but it, too, is an improvement over Signol's work: his Meleager is nude, while members of his panic-stricken family are arranged as if in tiers in the depths of the painting, seen through the column-studded perspective. Meleager's mother, father, and the routed soldiers are distributed about with gestures and poses too clumsy, surely, to persuade the reluctant hero. In Auvray's sketch the naked Meleager sits, as if turned to stone by his certainties, while against him are pitted floods of dark or cold colors that mark the variations of his oscillating moods.

The historian Diodorus Siculus numbered Meleager among the Argonauts, thus identifying him as a man of action. Homer more subtly compares his wrath to that of Achilles in the awkward lesson that the pedagogue Phoenix attempts to give his former ward. In the seventeenth century Rubens and Le Brun illustrated the gallantry of Meleager; the huntsman awarding the spoils to a beautiful stranger without hope of reciprocity in any form was a man for the *précieuses*, as gallant as Hector and as obstinate in his gallantry as Achilles. The academicians of the nineteenth century preferred to see in Meleager a Cincinnatus persuaded to take up his arms for his country. He appears as such in Jourdy's painting, looking more Roman than Greek. But the prize went to Signol's Meleager in his sculptural and theatrical pose.

The Tears of Niobe

Homer often surprises us by inventing a pretext to narrate some legend remote from the Trojan plain. For example, one might have expected a mention of Niobe

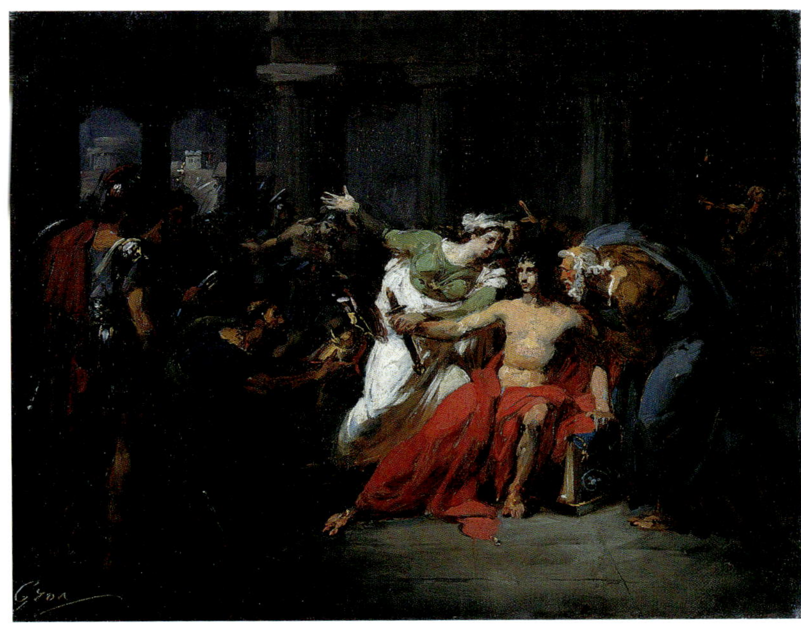

CATALOGUE NO. 98 | FÉLIX-HENRY AUVRAY (1800–1833), *Meleager Taking Up His Arms*, 1823. Oil on tracing paper mounted on canvas, 32.5 × 40.5 cm.

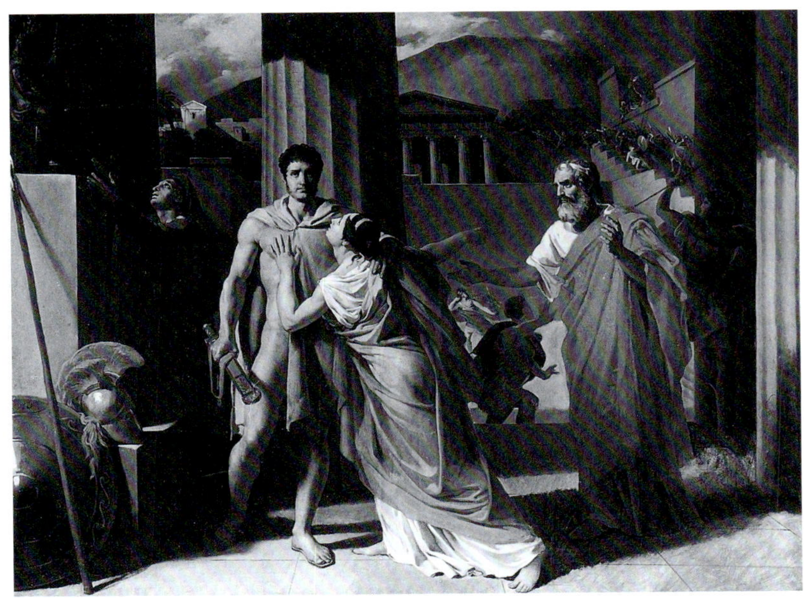

FIGURE 62 | PAUL JOURDY (1805–1856), *Meleager Taking Up Arms at His Wife's Pleading*, 1830. Oil on canvas, 114 × 147 cm.

when Apollo sets about his massacre of the Greeks in the first book of the *Iliad.* Apollo and Artemis were the only children of Leto (Latin: Latona). When Niobe boasted that she was more fortunate in having twelve children than Leto with two, the gods avenged their mother by slaughtering Niobe's entire progeny. It is Achilles (Book 24), however, who invokes the example of Niobe, not to console Priam—who had already lost his favorite son (and who knows how many of his hundred children)—but to convince him to take sustenance:

> Even Niobe with her lustrous hair remembered food,
> though she saw a dozen children killed in her own halls,
> six daughters and six sons in the pride and prime of youth.
> True, lord Apollo killed the sons with his silver bow
> and Artemis showering arrows killed the daughters.
> Both gods were enraged at Niobe. Time and again
> she placed herself on a par with their own mother,
> Leto in her immortal beauty—how she insulted Leto:
> "All you have borne is two, but I have borne so many!"
> So, two as they were, they slaughtered all her children.
> Nine days they lay in their blood, no one to bury them—
> Cronus' son had turned the people into stone . . .
> then on the tenth the gods of heaven interred them.
> And Niobe, gaunt, worn to the bone with weeping,
> turned her thoughts to food. And now, somewhere,
> lost on the crags, on the lonely mountain slopes,
> on Sipylus where, they say, the nymphs who live forever,
> dancing along the Achelous River run to beds of rest—
> there, struck into stone, Niobe still broods
> on the spate of griefs the gods poured out to her.
> —IL. 24.602–17; F 24.708–27

Among the crimes of the gods, the murder of Niobe's children to satisfy the caprice of a vexed or jealous mother is particularly inexcusable. The two archer gods compounded their pettiness with an insult to the human condition, killing the children under their mother's eyes and then refusing them burial. The Greek gods took some time to learn the respect for the dead that marks—so the archaeologists tell us—one of the beginnings of civilization. The barbarity of the gods provokes both disgust and a sentiment of revolt in the face of injustice, a sentiment firmly rooted in the Greek character: a child should not die before its parents and a mother should not have to bury her children. In mourning, surrounded by the unburied corpses of her children, Niobe is indignant, and her anger accuses the gods who offend natural law. The Medici *Niobids* (Galleria degli Uffizi, Florence), and in particular Niobe's vain gesture of protection, will remain forever in the European imagination as an illustration of the suffering of a mother who witnesses the death of those to whom she has given birth, children who should look after her in her old age. The reinterpretations constantly suggested by archaeologists since the sixteenth century—the most brilliantly vivid is surely that of François Perrier—bear witness to the continuing influence of these ancient sculptures.

In 1772 the subject for the Grand Prix in Painting was *The Children of Niobe Killed by Apollo and Diana.* According to a well-established legend, Jacques-Louis David, whose reputation was on the rise, fell victim to a conspiracy of judges and therefore forfeited the Grand Prix, which went instead to Pierre-Charles Jombert (cat. no. 99), while a further prize, held over [*réservé*] from the previous year, went to Anicet-Charles Lemonnier (Musée de Rouen). Strange as it seems, the judges' alleged impropriety may have helped them choose the right work. David made such incompetent use of his colors in painting Niobe that the whole painting (now in a private collection) has darkened badly. As pitifully as she wrings her hands, it is by no means clear that David's *Niobe* was superior even to that of his other fellow contestant, Lemonnier. It cost the judges no great effort, therefore, to refuse him the Grand Prix that they had decided not to give him.

OPPOSITE CATALOGUE NO. 99 | PIERRE-CHARLES JOMBERT (ca. 1748/49–1825?), *The Children of Niobe Killed by Apollo and Diana*, 1772. Oil on canvas, 143 × 112 cm.

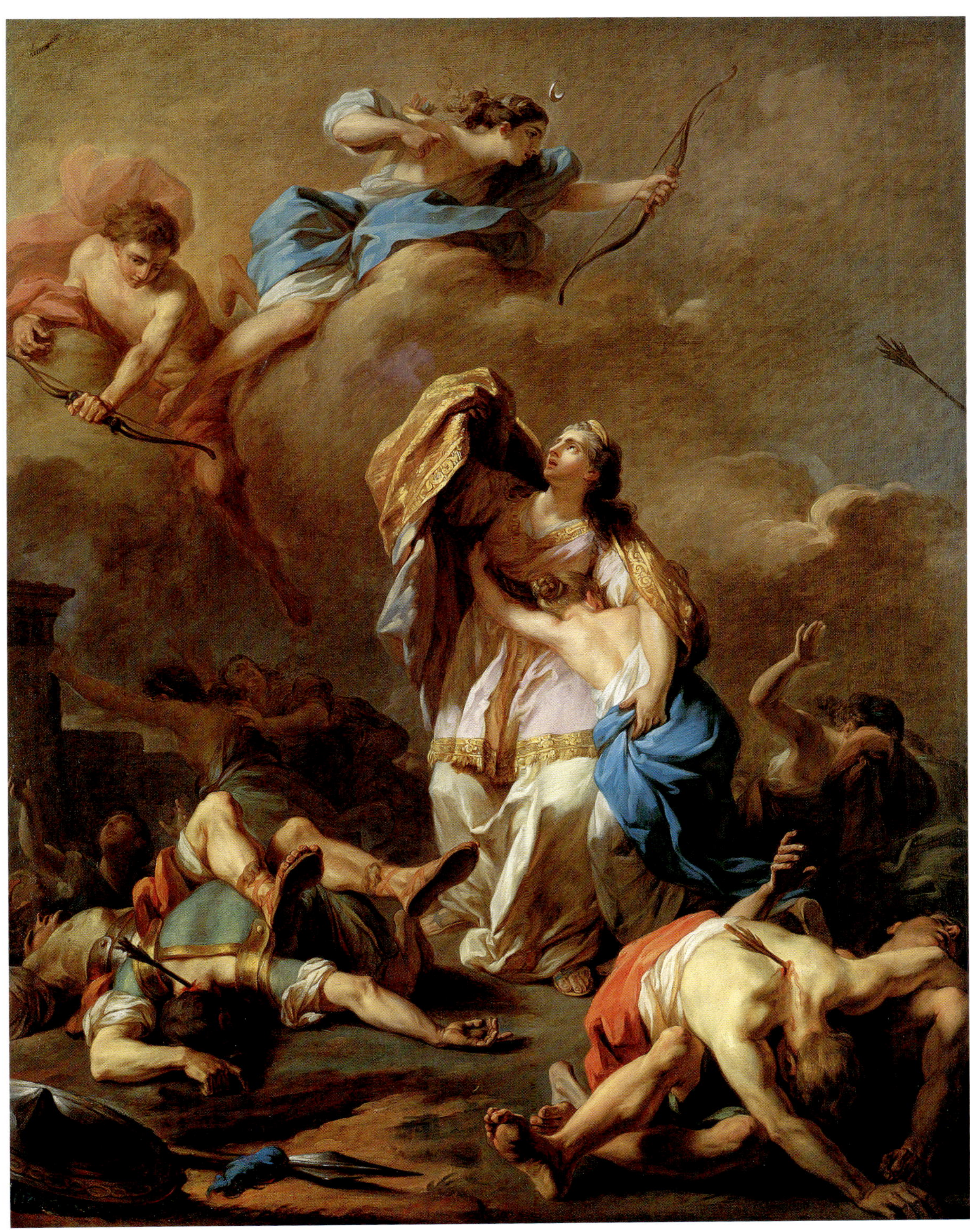

In Jombert's picture Niobe's children lie dead, their faces hidden, but in their mother's white garment and arm raised to the sky we find an elegance and dignity that put to shame the two archers in the sky. Although Jombert has introduced a cloud not mentioned by Homer in this passage, his Niobe gazes at what she supposedly cannot see: the criminal twins seem as if loosely enveloped in a veil of opprobrium. The solidity of Jombert's vision is not unworthy of Delacroix's *Massacre of Chios* and the martyred Greek woman whom the Romantic master posed, two generations later, as a Niobe for modern times.

Jombert and his fellow contestants were doubtless less familiar with Homer's account than Ovid's version of the legend, in which the children slip, one after another, into the arms of death as the eternally proud Niobe duels with the endlessly pitiless gods. In Niobe's raised arms and gaze, Jombert combined the facts of the legend with an intimation that a human who refuses to cower in the face of death is more alive than the allegorical figures seeking to destroy her. Yet these gods whose legs dangle through their concealing vapor avoid the fate of so many *dei ex machina* and do not court ridicule; their intent features, seen through a cover of clouds, contrast with the piles of corpses on the ground and carry within them all the ambiguity of divinity. Although they claim to be allegories, Apollo, god of the Sun, and Artemis, goddess of the Moon, are no more than powerful forces of nature blind to their victims. This is a species of nature that kills more often than it bears fruit. In Homer's terms, epidemics are the "arrows of Apollo."

A refusal of pathos and mawkishness, an affirmation of love and the grandeur of life over the violence of death—this is proclaimed by Niobe and the words of Achilles to Priam: "Niobe . . . worn to the bone with weeping, / turned her thoughts to food." No god has ever merited so noble an observation.

Greek legend, constantly reinventing itself, had its own lesson for the immortals: Niobe's line continued through one of her massacred daughters. A grandson was born to whom was granted the combined lifetimes cut short in his uncles and aunts. This was the horseman Nestor, who in the *Iliad* and the *Odyssey* exemplifies an extended and serene old age, having survived all his younger comrades-at-arms. In the figure of Nestor, Niobe finally triumphs over the children of Leto.

Jason and the Golden Fleece

Jason, Theseus, and Hercules belong to the generation that preceded the Trojan War, to that first race of heroes that Ulysses would have liked to have met (*Od.* 11.631). He himself encounters the three shades in the Underworld, and Homer's narrative touches occasionally on their memory. The pattern of their adventures is not unlike that of the *Odyssey*. Fénelon makes interlocutors of Homer and Achilles in one of his *Dialogues of the Dead*, and rightly observes that there would be no Achilles without Homer. The heroes of Colchis, Athens, and Thebes inspired many other authors—poets lyric and tragic—who recounted or invented their long voyages. None of these, however, had the universal talent of Homer. This is not the place to untangle the many threads by which the careers of the three heroes are interwoven, or even to single out from their epics the episodes that make of them brothers or ancestors of Achilles and Ulysses. The share of human weakness Homer has given his characters is lacking in these heroes. All three are first and foremost monster killers exhibiting their gruesomely bleeding prizes. There is nothing bestial about the poetry of the encounters of Ulysses since his victims are generally of the same species as himself; their defeat, as recounted by the mendacious hero, always involves a satisfying element of derision, fantastic as his inventions may be. There is not much to laugh about with Jason and Hercules.

When Alfred Lanson depicts Jason with the Golden Fleece (fig. 63) and François Lemoine paints Hercules with the pelt of the Nemean lion (cat. no. 101), the

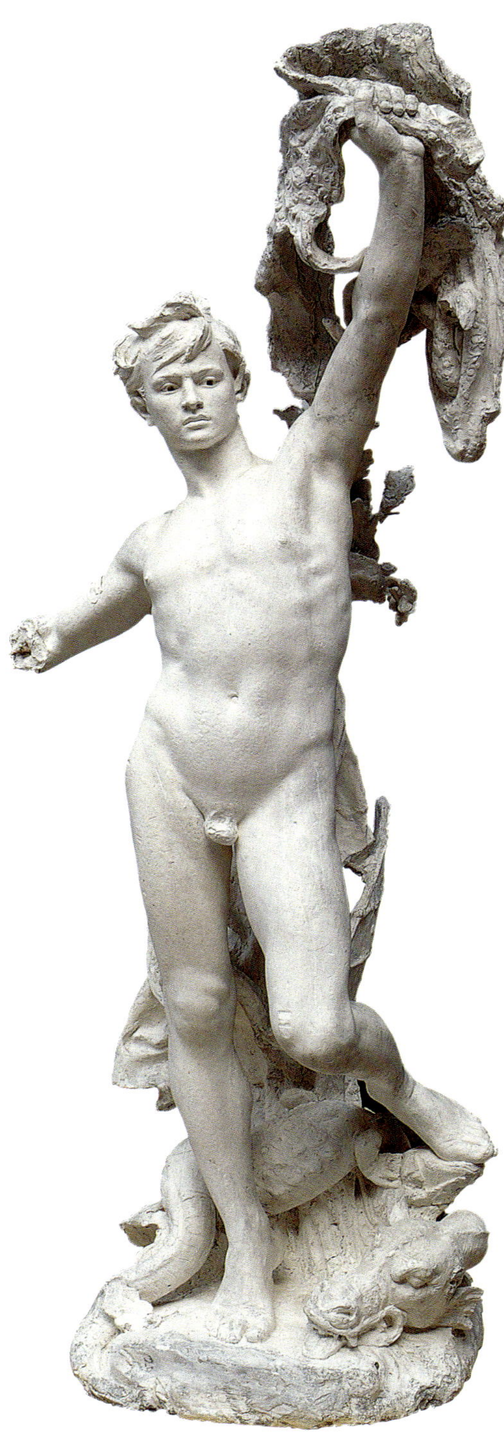

FIGURE 63 | ALFRED-DÉSIRÉ LANSON (1851–1898), *Jason with the Golden Fleece*, 1876. Plaster, 180 × 68 × 60 cm. Prix de Rome in Sculpture.

prizes exhibited by the two heroes take the spectator back before the Trojan War, before the birth of civilization. Their terrifying trophies were passed down from these unimaginative warriors to the Homeric heroes, along with their taste for arms. Philoctetes inherited from Hercules the bow that doomed Troy, and Theseus's mother, Aethtra, helped her son find the sword of Aegeus, his father. This primitive model of the hero is warlike and not averse to bloodshed. The gods who witness his exploits have no need to spur him on to the slaughter.

In 1663 Pierre Monier competed for the Prix de l'Académie with *The Conquest of the Golden Fleece* (cat. no. 100), no doubt making the analogy with the conquests of Louis XIV.[1] (Fortunately the exploits of Jason are more picturesque than those of the Sun King.) The successive episodes run from left to right over the length of the painting, with the story unfolding as in a fresco or *cassone* panel. The essential elements of the fable are present: we see not just the Argonauts' ship but King Aeëtes of Colchis and his daughter, Medea, that dangerous sorceress who betrays her country for the handsome young Jason and who will one day take the most terrible revenge on her former lover, now philandering husband. The taste of adventure on his lips, Jason has fitted out a boat called the *Argo* and summoned all the heroes of his generation to the conquest of the Golden Fleece; they will find it in Colchis, a legendary "pays de Cockaigne" located in the geography of myth somewhere beyond Troy. There fire-breathing bulls protect the Golden Fleece with their iron horns and strike the earth with their brazen hooves. After a long sea voyage, Jason yokes them and forces the team to plough a field. He then finds the Golden Fleece hanging in a tree and retrieves it. His companions, mostly Thessalians like himself, are less civilized than Medea's people. Hercules is the most primitive of all, easily recognizable in Monier's picture by his lion's pelt, although tradition informs us that he had long since deserted the expedition for love of some beardless youth.

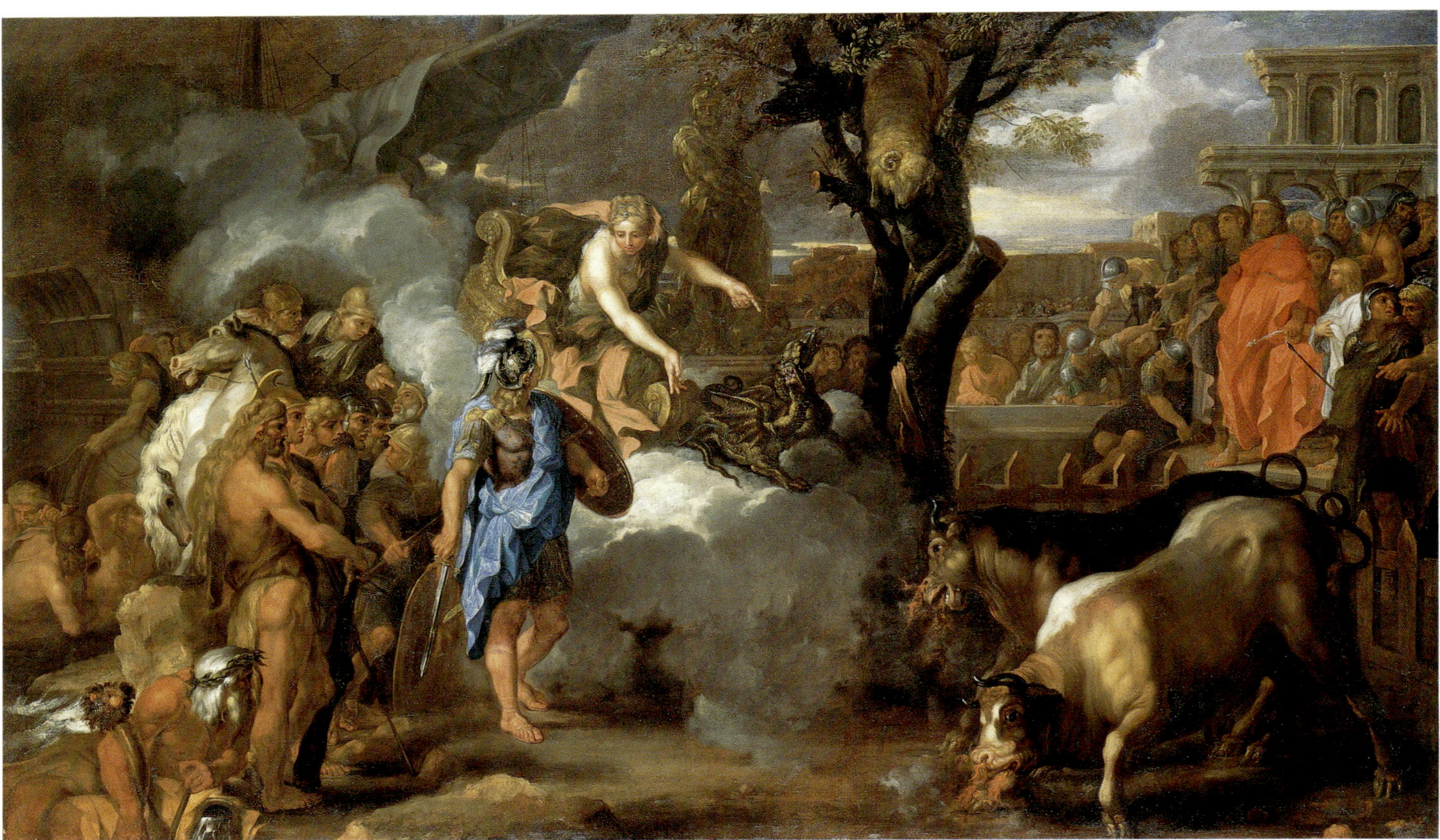

CATALOGUE NO. 100 | PIERRE MONIER (1641–1703), *The Conquest of the Golden Fleece*, 1663. Oil on canvas, 133.7 × 218.5 cm.

The Argonauts represent the Greeks of a pre-Mycenaean age, whereas the Colchidians belong to an orderly Asian monarchy that loves well-regulated spectacles held beneath the powerful architecture of their still unfinished city; they might almost be prototypes of the Trojans. In Monier's work we see Medea behind Jason; the love-struck sorceress hovers like a goddess, drawn through the air by her dragons, and protects her beloved through her charms. To the left, browned by its long sea voyage, the *Argo* sways on the billows of the Black Sea. Jason steps forward, intrepid. To the left, a divinity with the appearance of an old man (probably a river god) looks on with indifference as these brutal events unfold. Finally Ares stands center stage in the form of a statue, dominating the proceedings. It is clear from this distribution of roles that civilization is not on the hero's side—he is a warrior who knows nothing but war—but rather in this rich and erudite Asia from which the Greeks will take gold (the Fleece), science (magic), art, and beauty while bringing plundering violence. This is the story of the Trojan War in a nutshell. Jason was the first Greek to set off for Asia, the first to kidnap a woman, and the first who, by stealing gold, made war merely for profit. He was, in short, a pioneer of the epic mode.

The inspiration for this picture no doubt came from the overly civilized Ovid, whose account of the adventure in the seventh book of the *Metamorphoses* drew on that of Apollonius of Rhodes. Monier therefore showed great intelligence in restoring his hero to the barbarian epoch of Greece. Alfred-Désiré Lanson's *Jason* (fig. 63) won him fame and fortune by combining the melancholy liberty of a Florentine David or Perseus with the dancing posture of a Carpeaux figure. Jason's victim is at his feet and he holds his trophy above his head. His vaguely pensive gaze is tinged with the hesitation of the Homeric hero. The great sculptors of the Renaissance imparted to their ferocious heroes, with their trophies from decapitated foes, the mysterious sadness of conquerors made anxious by their triumph. The École's pupils were sometimes receptive to this heritage. On the face of his Jason, moving toward his destiny, Lanson imprinted a sentiment that must have gripped the students who triumphed in the Prix de Rome: student life is ending; now it is time to become an adult artist.

Hercules

Having fought more battles than all the warriors at Troy combined, Hercules could hardly expect to be more than a supernumerary in the Homeric narrative. Hercules lacks the contradictions that pleased Homer. In art he was the hero of sheer physical strength, although certain artists instilled in him the doubts that make a man of the demigod. Let me begin with the hero.

Hercules (Greek: Heracles) wanders the Mediterranean as Ulysses does, taking on mortals or monsters here and there. But whereas Ulysses happily plunders, the severe Hercules punishes thieves and brigands. According to Virgil (*Aen.* 8.184–279) and Ovid (*Fasti* 1.543–78), Hercules was traveling in primitive Italy when a few of his cattle were stolen by one Cacus—whose cacophonous name is synonymous with the sordid and the ugly—a monster with three fire-breathing heads. Cacus was sufficiently cunning to have the cattle walk backward into the cavern where he kept his ill-gotten gains, hoping to cover his tracks, but the mooing of a cow gave him away. In certain variations of the legend, Cacus has a treacherous sister, called Caca, who helps Hercules find the cavern entrance. Hercules kills Cacus and a Roman cult is founded to celebrate the deed in perpetuity.

Starting in the sixteenth century, the *peintres du roi* and then the academicians saw in Hercules a substitute for their master and protector, his pictorial representative in official works. Fortunately certain compositions restore Hercules' own personality to some degree. In *Hercules Killing Cacus* (1718; cat. no. 101), the work painted by François Lemoine for his reception into the Academy, a few immortals are present, although they can scarcely be said to witness the event. That force of nature Hercules should surely attract the attention of the two naiads luxuriating in the cool surroundings. But, no, the river god who points to the action wins not a single glance for this peasant squabble. Lemoine has removed the marvelous *wonder* (*"le merveilleux"*) from the episode, preferring a ruinous hovel to the cavern in the fable. The demigod is less interesting than the modest witnesses to his exploit. The old woman, the noble animal with its beautiful eyes (Homer's epithet for Hera is *Boopis,* "ox-eyed"), and the russet cruppers of the fleeing bull show greater sensitivity than the two muscular brutes in combat.

Lemoine has moved the action forward from the first generation of heroes to the world of Homeric peasants and serving women. They teach the supposed heroes, such as Ulysses and his father, to plough the land rather than fight for causes in which they do not believe.

The good Hercules was occasionally allowed to demonstrate other talents, more subtle and attractive than his power handling the club or bending the bow. The classicism of courtly academic interpretations,

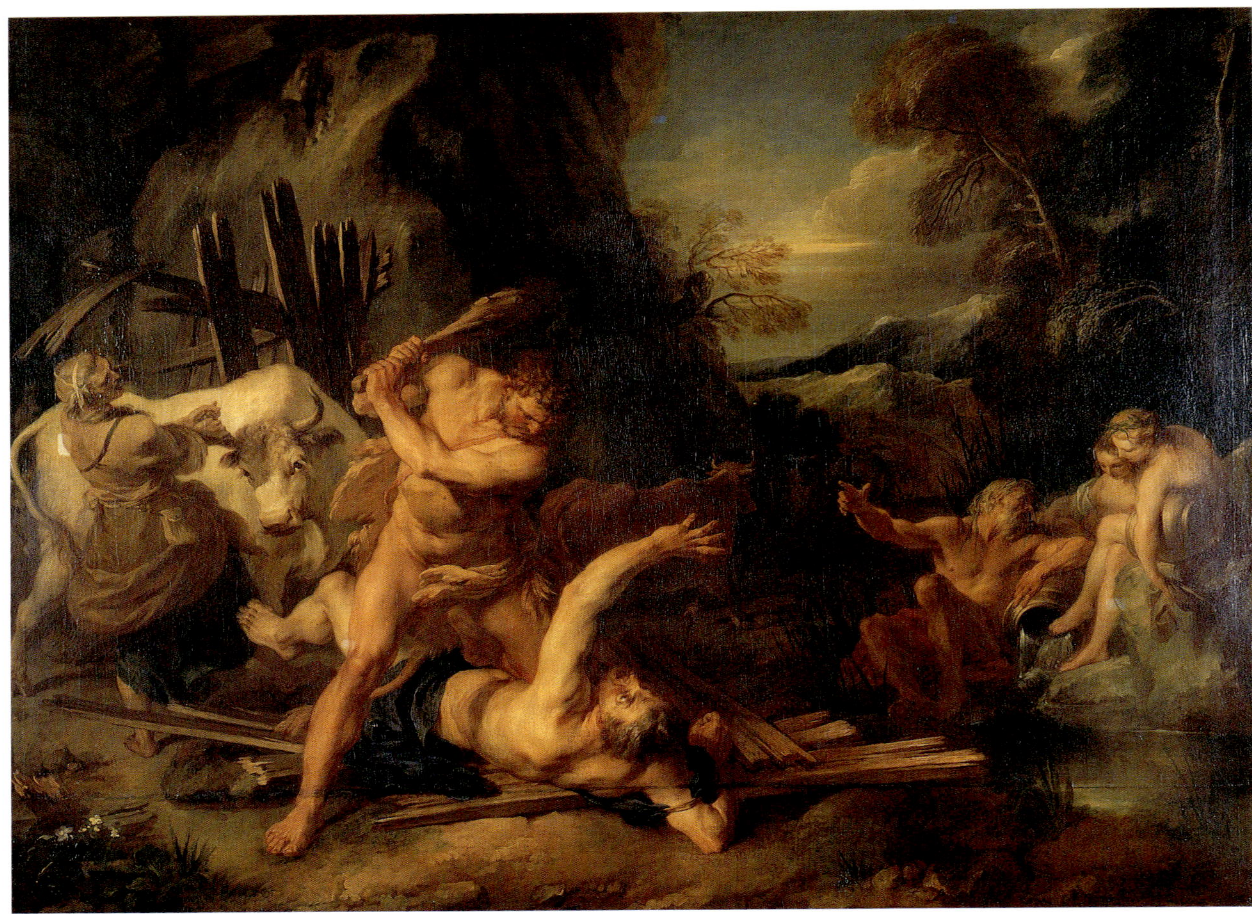

CATALOGUE NO. 101 | FRANÇOIS LEMOINE (1688–1737), *Hercules Killing Cacus*, 1718. Oil on canvas, 131 × 170 cm.

which made Hercules a mere prefiguration of the Sun King, has no part in one sculpture at the École (cat. no. 102). Its swirling movement reminds us that sculpture, like the body, struggles with space: the gaze, leg, and head of this little Hercules seem to radiate his attention in all directions at once, as if he sought to comprehend and dominate the world. His folded arms, however, the near-disgust expressed in his lips, and even the rest he is enjoying on his earthen seat all distance him from his past combats and bring him closer to the characters of Euripides or heroes of Homer. Brian's *Mercury* (cat. no. 13) likewise speaks of the weary eons of immortality. This little terracotta Hercules is tired of his heroic exploits; he may never lift his club again. The sculptures of the École des beaux-arts are not usually subject to the prevailing obsession with attribution, but the very quality of this *Seated Hercules* makes it an exception to that rule. Incomplete as it is, it has been compared to Puget's *Resting Hercules* in the Musée du Louvre. The hero is barely aware of the Nemean pelt on which he sits. His gaze and impulses are focused on a different ordeal; his pose is reminiscent of Hercules hesitating between Vice and Virtue. He may have attempted in the past to sweep the world clean of the monsters that persecute the human race, but the time has come for him to sit and contemplate what he has yet to achieve, and the meaning and usefulness of his actions. He is a long way from academic certainties. Puget may not have been the author of the statuette, but the mind that created this vision of the demigod was obviously as profoundly free and tormented as that of the great sculptor from Toulon himself.

Theseus

Theseus was the son of the Athenian king Aegeus. He slew the Minotaur, sailed with the Argonauts, and fought in the first Trojan War. A great seducer of women and a redoubtable warrior, he knew neither doubt nor anxiety. Like Hercules and Jason, Theseus began in the primitive world of monsters and gods. The habitual ingenuity of legend places him alongside Hercules while still a young child awaiting his destiny. Clad in his emblematic lion's skin, the invincible Hercules visited Troezen, the kingdom of Pittheus, maternal grandfather to Theseus. (Theseus's childhood is seen in Charles-Philippe Larivière's oil sketch for the *concours* of 1822.) As the mythical founder of the Athenian state, Theseus was determined to create a new world founded on order and peace. He therefore straddles the first Trojan War—the prehistoric war—and Homeric times. As cunning as Ulysses, he shares the vigor of Achilles but is less inclined to hesitate. According to Plutarch, his father entrusted the young Theseus to his grandfather in order to protect him from his enemies. Aegeus hid his sword and sandals beneath a stone and confided the location only to Aethra.[2] (She was to reveal the secret only when she judged Theseus strong enough to raise the stone.) Lifting the stone with ease, Theseus took up the arms and entered life and legend.

As in so many Academy reception pieces, a river god and his beloved look on at the scene depicted by

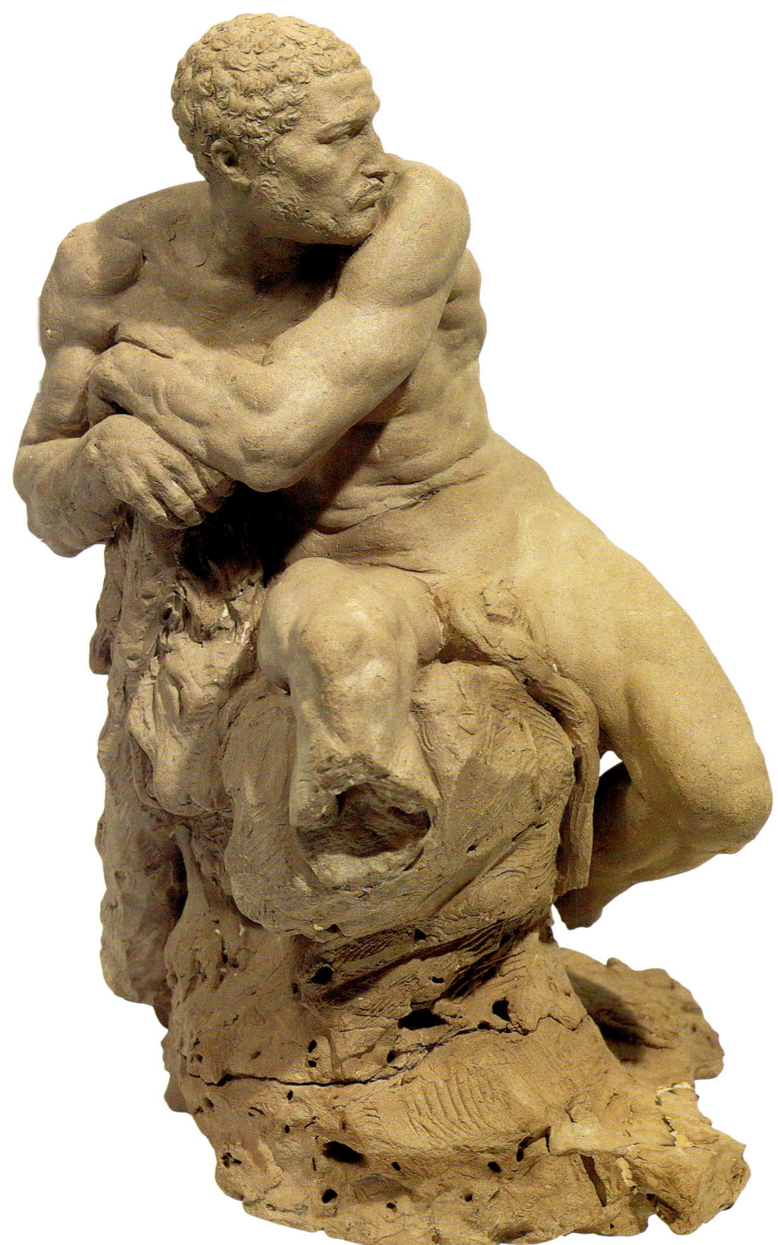

CATALOGUE NO. 102 | ANONYMOUS EIGHTEENTH-CENTURY ARTIST, *Seated Hercules.* Terracotta, 36.8 × 17.5 × 19 cm.

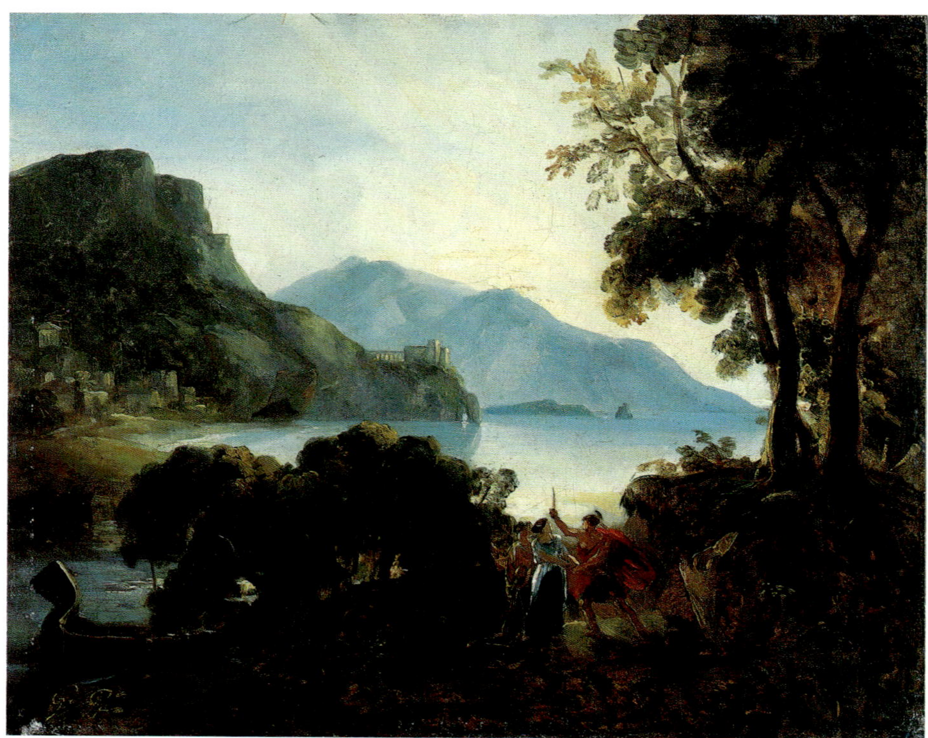

FIGURE 64 | JEAN-BAPTISTE-ADOLPHE GIBERT (1803–1899), *Theseus Finding the Weapons of His Father,* 1825. Oil on canvas, 38 × 46 cm. Oil Sketch *concours.*

Nicolas-Guy Brenet in 1769 (cat. no. 103). Brenet does not show us the founder of Athens, the hero to whom André Gide dedicated a beautiful and optimistic story in his old age. Instead he paints a naïve adolescent discovering his previously concealed origins and the future they promise him. This is a Theseus who asks few questions about the world; he is ready for action now and would have nothing to do with a war where the warriors refuse to fight. In 1825 the École teachers had the felicitous idea of setting this subject in the Historical Landscape *concours.* The rules of the *concours* and the poetic resonance of the narrative attained a miraculous harmony in the winning entry by Jean-Baptiste-Adolphe Gibert (fig. 64). Theseus's raised arm; Aethra's bright tunic; the boat on the shore; the Mediterranean imagined from the candidates' *loges* in the École; the blue light streaming through the trees; the quickly sketched buildings on the successive tiers of mountainside, colored in three hues—everything here is an invitation to set sail for the adult world and nascent civilization.

Plutarch's account continues. A few days later Theseus arrives in Athens, equipped with his father's sword.[3] We see his arrival in Athens in a work painted in 1832 by Hippolyte Flandrin (cat. no. 104), the greatest of Ingres's pupils, at a time when Athens was considered the capital of civilization. Flandrin won the Grand Prix with the best painting to win the prize after that of his master (cat. no. 24). The sorceress Medea has rid herself of Jason and their children and set her sights on the aged Aegeus and his kingdom. Intuiting a rival in the young traveler, she prepares a poison that Aegeus will offer the young traveler. In Flandrin's painting Theseus has drawn his sword to cut a joint of meat. The foreshortened sword threatens the onlooker but saves Theseus, since Aegeus recognizes the token he left to his son, cries out in alarm, and acknowledges the claims of blood over those of his dangerous mistress.

OPPOSITE CATALOGUE NO. 103 | NICOLAS-GUY BRENET (1728–1792), *The Young Theseus Discovers His Father's Arms,* 1769. Oil on canvas, 132 × 145 cm.

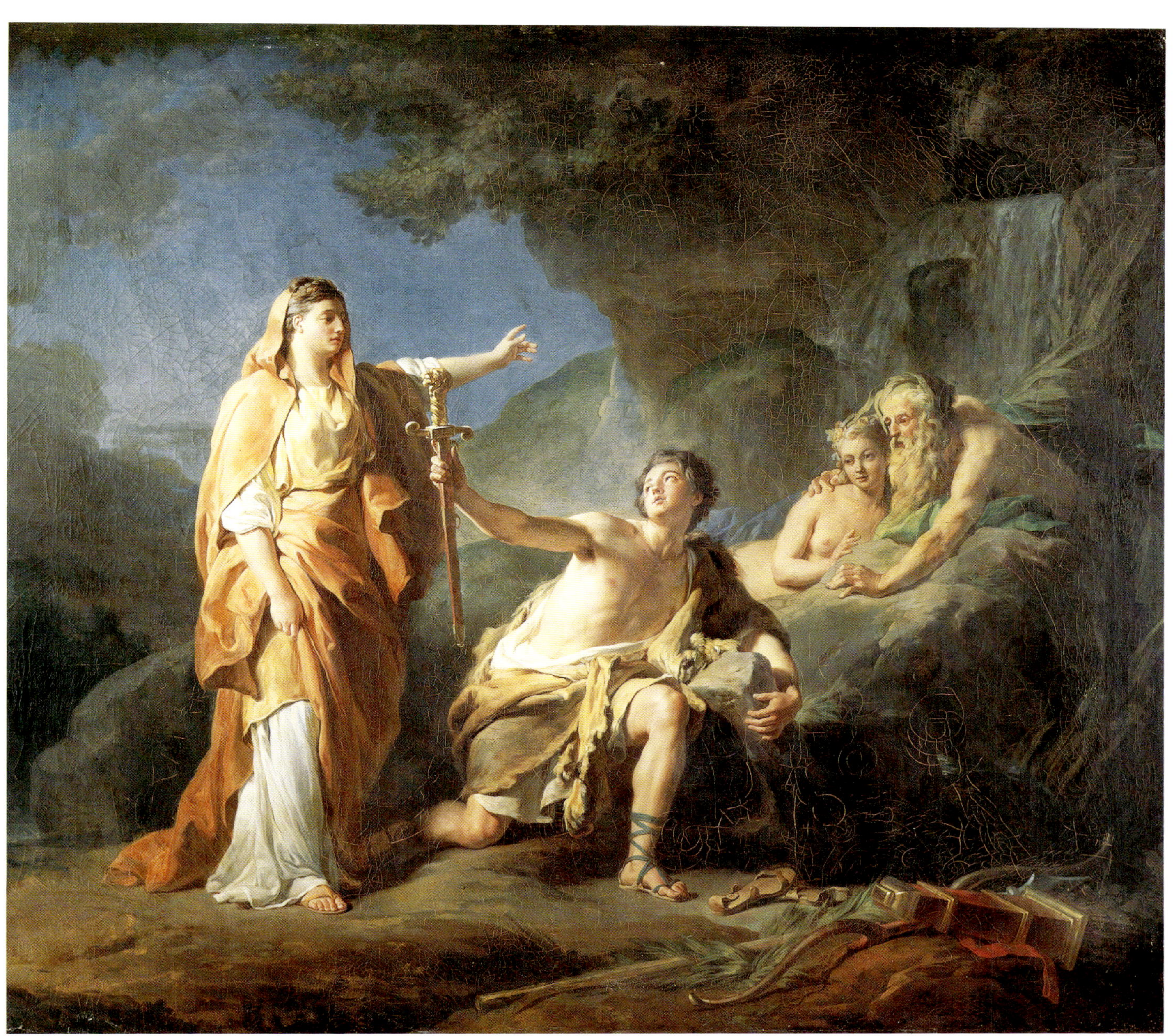

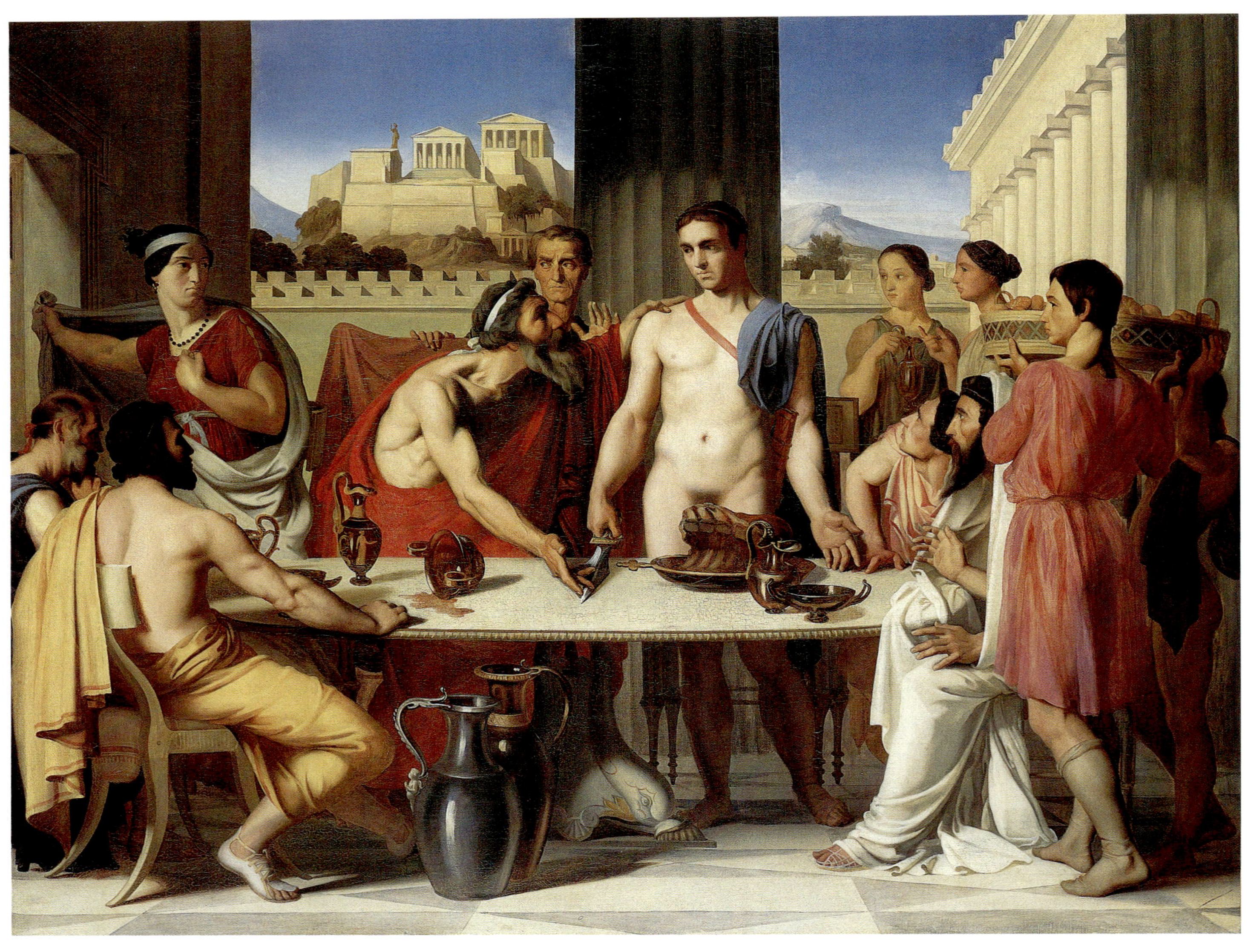

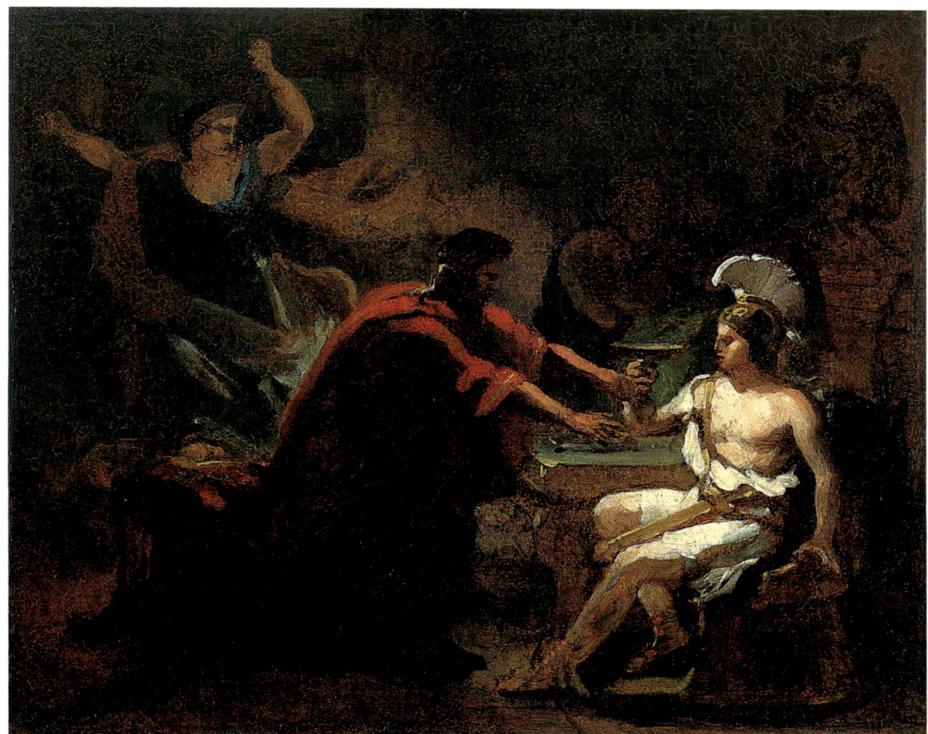

FIGURE 65 | JEAN-ÉTIENNE DUBOIS (1796–1854), *Theseus Recognized by His Father*, 1819. Oil on canvas, 32.5 × 39 cm. Oil Sketch *concours*.

Medea flees his court, and Theseus is acknowledged as prince and as Aegeus's son.

Ingres taught at the École for some time, setting up his studio across the street. Among the pictures presented by his students during this time, that of Hippolyte Flandrin is at once the most faithful to his master's teaching and to the spirit of the ancient text. Plutarch tells us, "When Theseus came to the banquet, he thought it best not to declare beforehand who he was: but in order to give his father a clue, as soon as the meat was served, he drew his sword as if he were about to carve with it, and took care to attract his father's attention. Aegeus at once understood [and] dashed down the cup of poison."[4]

Against the background of a very anachronistic Acropolis and around splendid and dramatic still lifes, the characters assemble for an Athenian Last Supper. Meat replaces bread. The wine fills admirable vessels: a kantharos, now overturned; two oinochoai; and a kylix. Father and son compete for mastery of the situation. There is great pictorial density in the secondary roles. To the left, the sorceress, from a period before urban civilization, takes her abrupt leave. To the right, the servants adopt poses borrowed from Raphael (the basket on the shoulder), looking on with the indifference of the humble at the business of the great. The guests at the table—the Athenian aristocracy—borrow their movements from Leonardo da Vinci; theirs is the revelation not of a new god but of a new political power finally established. Their bodies limn volumes of light and shadow worthy of the architectural details, which themselves prolong the geometry of the table. The vision of Hippolyte Flandrin would never recover the solidity he created in this, the work of a good student.

In 1819 Jean-Étienne Dubois ignored Plutarch's setting and accessories, confining himself to the relations between the characters and their impulsive movements (fig. 65). The son raises the wine cup; the father exclaims, arms outstretched, while Medea contorts her arms in frustrated rage. Flandrin's finished work is

OPPOSITE CATALOGUE NO. 104 | HIPPOLYTE FLANDRIN (1809–1864), *Theseus Recognized by His Father*, 1832. Oil on canvas, 115 × 146 cm.

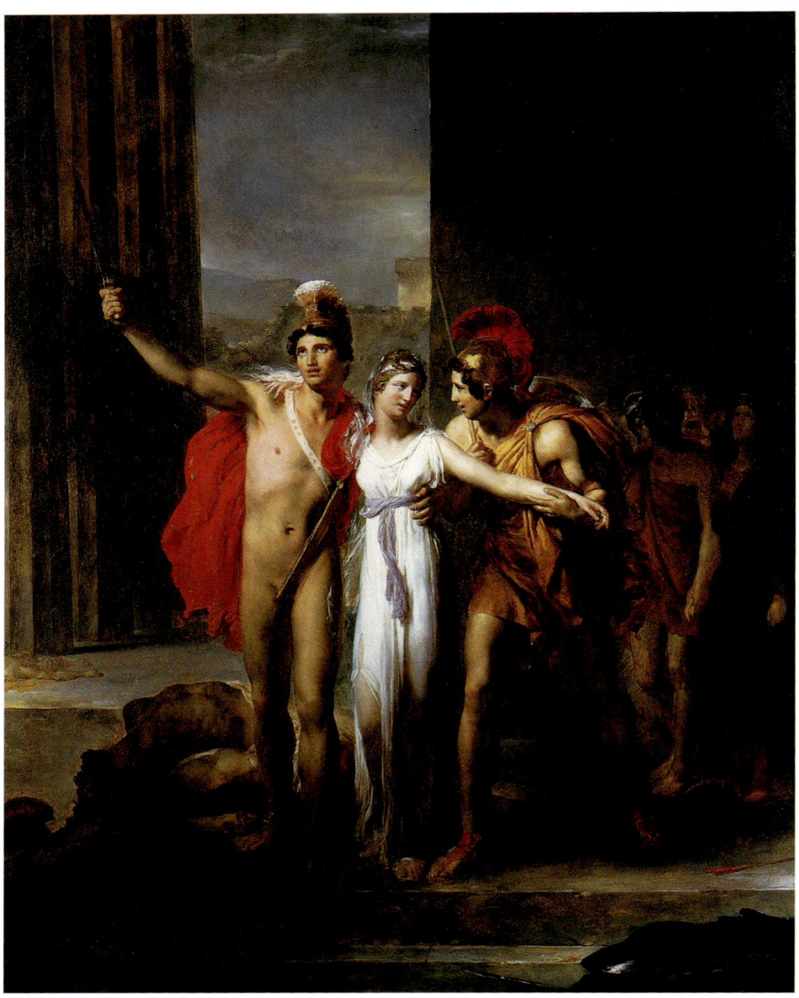

CATALOGUE NO. 105 | LÉON COGNIET (1794–1880), *Castor and Pollux Freeing Helen*, 1817. Oil on canvas, 146 × 113 cm.

infinitely superior to Dubois's sketch. Look at the left arm of Theseus in Dubois's depiction, however; in a succession of curves as elegant as the plume of his helmet, we see the arm widen into a hand clenched in ill-concealed nervousness. In the sketches executed in a matter of hours for the *concours*, the gestures of the characters sometimes transcribe and preserve the tension of the artist, anguished by the passage of minutes.

Theseus was considerably older when he encountered the protagonists of the second Trojan war. Léon Cogniet won the Grand Prix in 1817 (cat. no. 105) with a painting illustrating a further legend known to us from Plutarch.[5] Driven by lust, Theseus kidnapped Helen, still a child, well before Paris. He imprisoned her in the fortress of Aphidnae, in Athenian territory, and placed his mother, Aethra, over her as a guard. The girl promised to be a great beauty, and Theseus had decided to raise and keep her for the pleasure of his later years. He then set forth for the Underworld with the express purpose of carrying off Persephone, and in his absence Helen's brothers Castor and Pollux, as young as she, undertook to set her free. The brilliant success of their expedition restored her to the arms of her mortal father, Tyndareus, and lovers suitable for her age. Castor and Pollux, known as the Dioscuri, established a new king in Athens, who used the support of the aristocracy to overthrow Theseus's government. Between Theseus and the Homeric kings, Greek political thought was maturing as the city of Athens was under construction.

This was an era more in love with life and love than with interminable warfare, and Léon Cogniet portrays it with youthful vigor and talent. True, Helen's brothers trample the corpses of those they have killed. Helen, however, takes evident pleasure in the embrace of her liberators, while the populace behind them is happy to have gained a new king. The thoughtless brawlers now give way to a new generation, which lives in orderly cities amid polite and respectful citizens such as Cogniet discreetly sketches. They adopt customs infused with the new Greek thought. Jason, Hercules, and Theseus were toys in the hands of primitive or barbarian sorceresses. Castor and Pollux (in Cogniet's painting) and, subsequently, Paris, Hector, and Ulysses are mastered by wives, mistresses, and sisters, who are loving, frivolous, coquettish, and human. All of them—Achilles most of all—go into battle reluctantly. By Homeric times humankind has changed, even if the world has not. Humans no longer seek adventure and no longer concern themselves with the divine will. Helen and the Dioscuri are in search of happiness and ignore the corpses they tread underfoot, leaving behind them the darkness of Theseus for the daylight of life.

Prometheus

Some of the great names of mythology are completely absent from Homer. In homage to the father of poetry, his successors often wove a link between those whom he neglected and those who had the good fortune to find a place in his poems. Homer never mentions the exploits of Prometheus, the most blasphemous character in all Greek mythology. Perhaps this Titan, who was born a god but went over to the side of humankind—molding and fostering the human race and illuminating it with fire stolen from Zeus—showed insufficient weaknesses for Homer's taste. At most, Homer evokes Prometheus's torture when speaking of the punishment inflicted on the vicious and obscure giant Tityus:

> . . . two vultures
> hunched on either side of him, digging into his liver,
> beaking deep into the blood-sac, and he with his
> frantic hands
> could never beat them off . . .
> —OD. 11.578–79; F 11.662–65

The modern sensibility instinctively recognizes the noble Prometheus in the tortured giant.

Hesiod first introduced Prometheus in his *Theogony*, but it was Aeschylus who decided to make of the Titan's action a preamble to the wrath of Achilles. When Prometheus stole fire from the gods and bestowed it on mankind, Zeus ordered him to be chained to Mount Caucasus, where an eagle would forever tear at his liver—in Greek physiology the organ of the emotions. Hephaestus (assisted by Might and Violence—in other words, by Tyranny) was charged with the task. Aeschylus confers on the humiliated Prometheus a form of knowledge forbidden even to Zeus himself—that of the future. Indeed, his name means "forethought." Having little trust in the future of either gods or religions, the Greek poets only occasionally endowed a character with the ability to see, but not to influence, the future. Only Prometheus—thanks to his mother, Themis, who represents the Law or Justice that will outlive the gods themselves—knows that the goddess Thetis will give birth to a child stronger than his father. Should Zeus abandon himself to the charms of Thetis, he would bring about his own demise. Gentlemanly tragic hero that he is, Prometheus reveals this to his torturer, thus displaying a generosity like that of Philoctetes to the Achaeans. In a lost tragedy by Aeschylus, the martyred Titan reveals to the king of the gods the threat to his power. Zeus himself does not have the nobility of his prisoner, and he promptly has Thetis raped and impregnated by the mortal Peleus. She who had once been assiduously wooed by Zeus himself is now unable to escape her mortal ravisher—she transforms herself into all kinds of repulsive creatures—and from these monstrous nuptials is born Achilles, the most valiant of all mankind, infinitely stronger than his father, but insignificant when compared to Zeus.

One day, moved perhaps by gratitude—if the gods are capable of this sentiment—Zeus authorizes Hercules to release Prometheus from his eagle. In his *Prometheus* trilogy, Aeschylus thus paints a picture of Zeus as not merely a ridiculous husband but a tyrant on a throne of blood who faces the imminent threat of ignominious overthrow. Represented by artists as different as Johann Heinrich Füssli and Gustave Moreau, the tortured rebel has entered Western literature, assimilated alternately to Satan or Jesus Christ: Rebel Angel or Son of God, Prospero or Caliban.

In 1744 Jean-Charles Frontier painted his Royal Academy reception piece on this theme (cat. no. 106). He was resigned to the injustice of the king of the

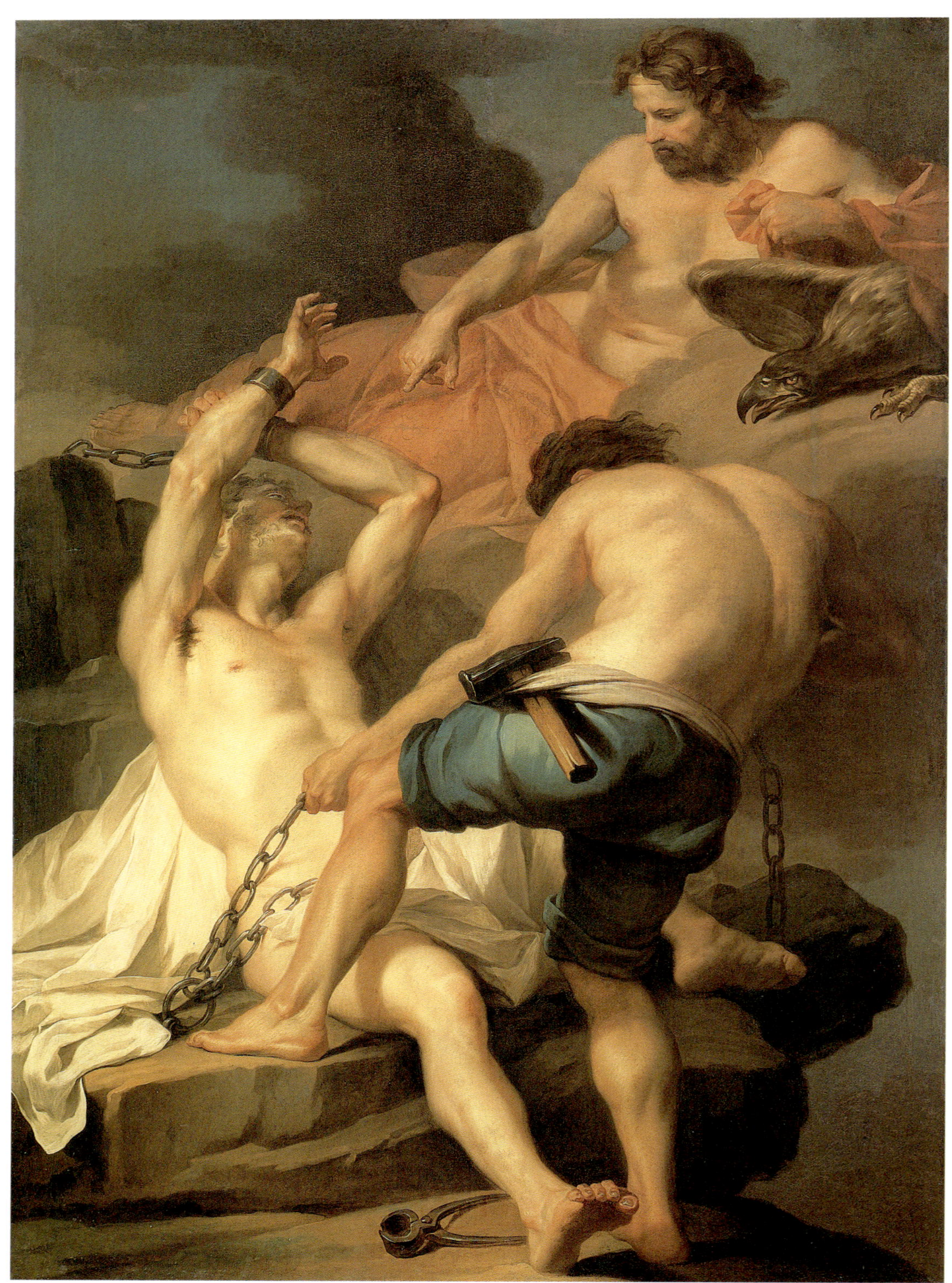

CATALOGUE NO. 106 | JEAN-CHARLES FRONTIER (1701–1763), *Vulcan Enchaining Prometheus*, 1744. Oil on canvas, 201.8 × 145 cm.

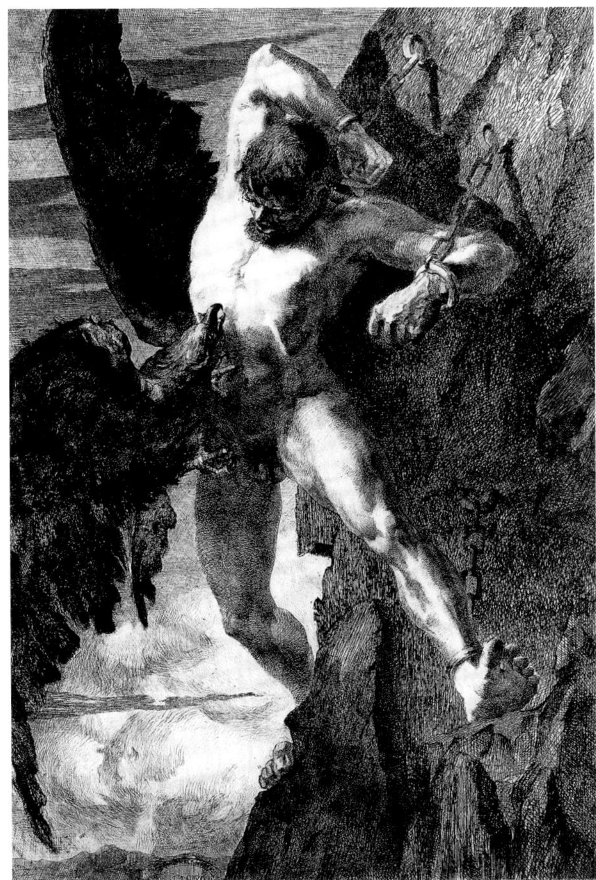

CATALOGUE NO. 107 | RAYMOND-JACQUES BRECHENMACHER (1897–?), *Prometheus*, 1922. Etching and drypoint, 44.2 × 31.7 cm.

gods: Zeus hovers above the scene of a terrible crime for which he himself is wholly responsible, ordering his eagle to devour the liver of Prometheus, who is already being tortured by Hephaestus. The hunchbacked god—muscles distended, his body arched as he stands on Mount Caucasus—recalls the innumerable torturers of Catholic iconography; the chained Prometheus's suffering appears more Christian than classical. In Frontier's painting, Zeus still reigns over the heavenly world, but on earth a martyr is sacrificed for the salvation of humanity. Prometheus, like Christ, is shown with the instruments of his suffering—a hammer and pincers—and will bear stigmata—the torn liver and fettered wrists. He is resigned to his fate. The reader of Aeschylus, Shelley, and Gide is accustomed to a Prometheus quite unlike Christ, a figure who defies all the gods. Artists have often passed over the defiance of Prometheus in favor of powerful and moving anatomical studies. In 1922 Raymond-Jacques Brechenmacher won his Prix de Rome with a print belonging to this same tradition (cat. no. 107). Although spectacular, his composition lacks grandeur. No matter. This is Prometheus, the god who went over to humanity, the immortal who accepted the role of victim, whose revolt put an end to the power of the gods.

NOTES

1 See Jennifer Montagu, "The Painted Enigma and French Seventeenth-Century Art," *Journal of the Warburg and Courtauld Institutes* 31 (1968):326.

2 Plutarch, *Lives: Life of Theseus* 3–6.

3 Ibid., 12.

4 Ibid., 12; quoted in *The Rise and Fall of Athens: Nine Greek Lives*, trans. Ian Scott-Kilvert (London, 1960), 20.

5 Ibid., 31.

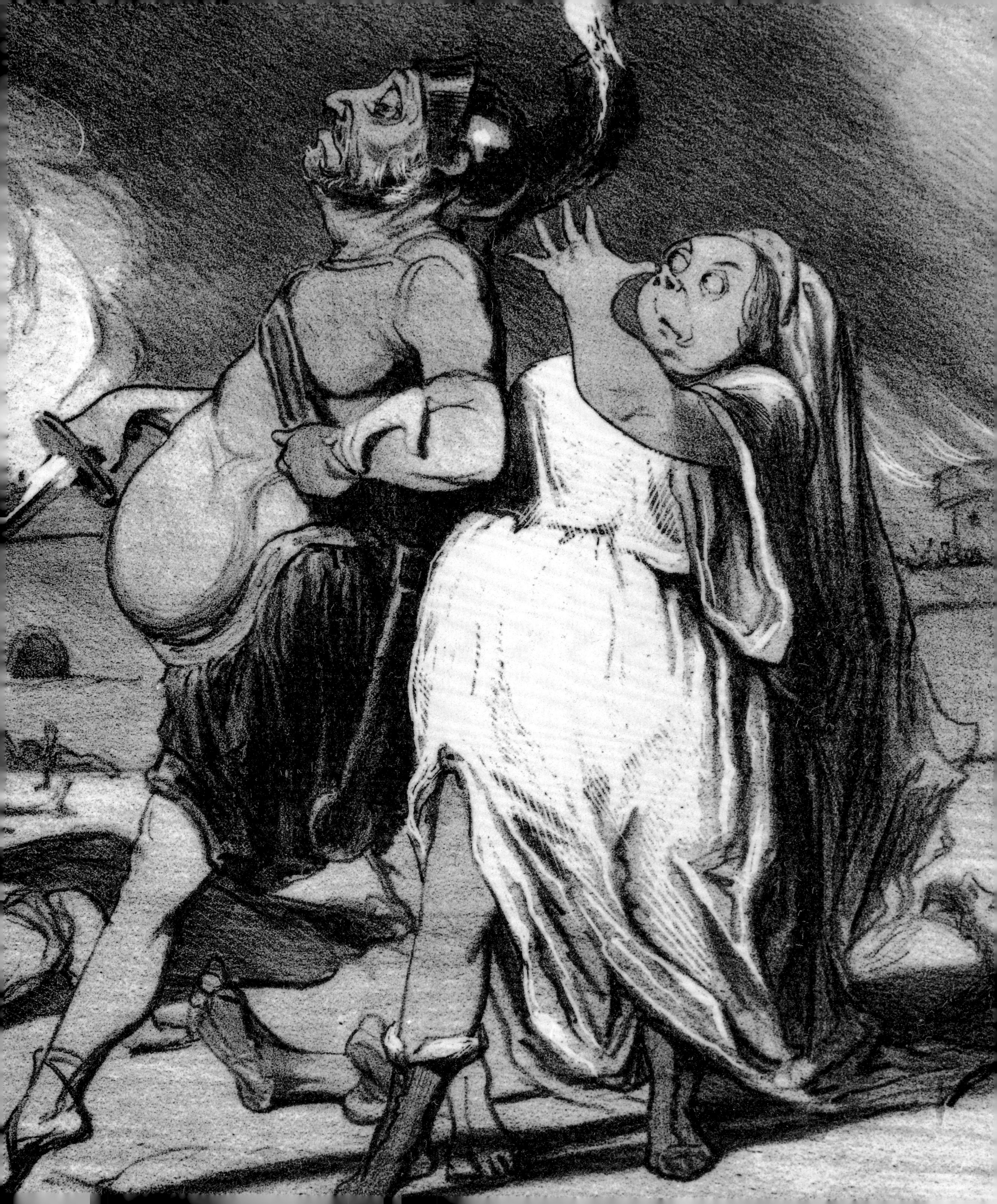

Homer's Laughter

Epic Errors

From the Homeric texts Greece derived the basis of its teaching and its genius. This inspiration was transmitted to Europe along with the educational system it underpinned. In 1933, against a background of mounting perils, Werner Jaeger reminded Europe of all that the Greek ideal of *paideia* (education) had contributed over the previous three thousand years to its civilization now threatened. The Greek system comprised political, social, and moral education taught through literary means. This teaching method included counterexamples—the examples one should *never* follow—although their relation to the model genuinely proposed was complex. True, Homer defends certain human values and no doubt believes in generosity, life, happiness, and peace, but his subject is rapacity, death, tragedy, and war. Moreover, Homer's characters differ from the heroes of most national epics in being far from perfect.

Within the *Iliad*, a story is sometimes told as a counterexample to deter the hero from making the same mistake. Phoenix thus reminds Achilles of the story of Meleager—which Achilles goes on to imitate. This is the first of Homer's lessons: neither men nor gods can resist the lure of error, of the forbidden. Each error is then analyzed by those around the protagonist, sometimes in anger but more often in mirth. Not every epoch has understood the nature of Homer's laughter.

Artists illustrating Homer have not always felt the need for detachment, for what Plato calls "irony," that slight distancing from the inevitable avalanche of stupidity both human and divine. Skeptical humor is a mode of thought little appreciated by the masses and still less by those who govern. In the modern era it was the humanists who most readily adopted Homer's spirit of derision in both literature and the fine arts. The prints and drawings of the École de Fontainebleau, related to the paintings of Primaticcio, show playful heroes on their voyages or in their love affairs, little men mocking monsters or women that attack or reduce them to servitude. From the seventeenth century onward, French readers misunderstood the teachings of Homeric and Post-Homeric Greece, which led to the pessimism of Euripides, himself a master ironist. They long continued to believe that heroes were necessarily serious people, like the statues then in vogue, whose features the Homeric heroes could not help but wear; the smile of the archaic statue had not yet reappeared. The goddesses who accompanied Ulysses in the sixteenth century were elegant, intelligent women—and utterly amoral. Three centuries later they took on the tediously noble attitudes of Joan of Arc. Homer or his spirit took revenge against these posthumous betrayals in his usual fashion, making them objects of derision.

Homer has not always been considered a model of austerity. Indeed, he was first indicted for immorality.

DETAIL OF CATALOGUE NO. 116

In Plato's *Republic*, Socrates denounces Homer's elegant lies and libertine descriptions of the divine. Socrates is in a more humorous vein in the *Phaedrus* (242a) as he walks along the banks of the Ilissos, the river that then flowed through Athens. There he accuses Homer of a much graver crime, namely, that of slandering Helen, for which, says Socrates, he was punished by blindness. The poet Stesichorus, blinded for his indictment of Helen, had recovered his eyesight only by writing a palinode in which he argued Helen had never been to Troy nor ever been unfaithful to Menelaus: beauty cannot be amoral. When Jules-Georges Moteley competed for a Painting Prize in 1888 he placed his *Socrates Conversing with Phaedrus on the Banks of the Ilissos* in the green fields of his childhood home in Normandy. Did Moteley realize that his Socrates was condemning not merely Homer but the academic vision of antiquity? There is certainly something amusing about his Greco-Norman debaters luxuriating in the shade of the damp *bocage*. Plato's verdict on Homer, delivered in *The Republic* and the *Phaedrus*, is a rather contradictory one, but it nevertheless echoes down through the centuries: through his irreverence toward established values and his consummate lies, Homer made vice seem attractive and virtue ridiculous.

Dirty Laughter Is the Preserve of the Gods

But these are peccadilloes. For our carping critics, the chief accusation is that Homer cannot take anything seriously. Théophile Gautier and Marcel Proust defined the Homeric world in terms of laughter: "Laughter it is that distinguishes man from beast and we know from the *Odyssey* of the Grecian bard Homerus that it is the prerogative of the immortal gods, whose eternal leisure is spent in joyous cachinnation till their ribs ache with Olympian mirth."[1]

First we should distinguish Homer's laughter from that of his characters. In one book from the *Iliad* and one from the *Odyssey* we hear the dirty and vulgar laughter of the gods, which was quickly defined as "Homeric." In both cases the butt of divine derision is another immortal. The first book of the *Iliad* ends with the unquenchable laughter of the gods on Olympus. It doesn't take much to keep them amused: too much drink (wine or ambrosia); a man with a limp; or a story of cuckoldry. The celestial designated whipping boy is the good-natured Hephaestus, who remains deeply attached to his mother, Hera, despite the fact that by accidentally dropping him from the height of Olympus she left him with a limp. It is his misfortune he is no fool. Homer knows that no one is as stupid as an intelligent man faced with a beautiful woman. True, Hephaestus obtained from his father, Zeus, the beautiful Aphrodite, who would have cheated on any husband, but when the husband is a hunchbacked artisan, lame and lovelorn, the first suitor she encounters will do. It is Ares, god of war.

Apprised of his misfortune, Hephaestus prepares a trap above the conjugal bed that closes on the lovers:

> Quick, my darling, come, let's go to bed
> and lose ourselves in love! Your husband's away—
> by now he must be off in the wilds of Lemnos,
> consorting with his raucous Sintian friends.
> So he pressed
> and her heart raced with joy to sleep with War
> and off they went to bed and down they lay—
> and down around them came those cunning chains
> of the crafty god of fire, showering down now
> till the couple could not move a limb or lift a finger—
> then they knew at last: there was no way out, not now.
> But now the glorious crippled Smith was drawing near . . .
> He'd turned around, miles short of the Lemnos coast,
> for the Sungod kept *his* watch and told Hephaestus all,
> so back he rushed to his house, his heart consumed with anguish.
> Halting there at the gates, seized with savage rage
> he howled a terrible cry, imploring all the gods,
> "Father Zeus, look here—

the rest of you happy gods who live forever—
here is a sight to make you laugh, revolt you too!
Just because I am crippled, Zeus's daughter Aphrodite
will always spurn me and love that devastating Ares,
just because of his striking looks and racer's legs
while I am a weakling, lame from birth, and who's to
   blame?
Both my parents, who else? If only they'd never bred
   me!
Just look at the two lovers . . . crawled inside my bed,
locked in each other's arms—the sight makes me
   burn!"
   —OD. 8.292–314; F 8.331–56

"The sight of them makes me burn!" he says, and everyone bursts out laughing. All of Olympus rushes to the farce, overjoyed to see the cuckold, the trapped lovers, and the disordered sheets. It is, of course, only the more intelligent gods—Athena the intellectual and Hephaestus the artisan—who deplore reason's inability to compete with the power of beauty and desire. When the bard Demodocos (who has always been taken to be Homer's self-portrait) sings of the love of Mars and Venus, the hedonistic Phaeacians clearly enjoy his song, while the young people perform languorous dances to his music. He thus invented the comic epic, what rhetoricians term "burlesque." "The sight of them makes me burn!"? There they all are in front of the adulterers' bed: Hermes, Apollo, and Poseidon. Allegorical interpretations sought to find in this divine cuckoldry the coupling of Love and Discord, which is indeed the central theme of the *Iliad*—and, on a cursory inspection, that of literature as a whole, or almost all of it. No doubt the gods are amused to find other gods in this crassly human situation? No, the joke is funnier and more masculine: each god would happily take Ares' place in the net if he could but spend a night with Aphrodite:

So the gods would banter
among themselves but lord Apollo goaded Hermes on:
"Tell me, Quicksilver, giver of all good things—
even with those unwieldy shackles wrapped around
   you,
how would you like to bed the golden Aphrodite?"

"Oh, Apollo, if only!" the giant-killer cried.
"Archer, bind me down with triple those endless
   chains!
Let all you gods look on, and all you goddesses too—
How I'd love to bed that golden Aphrodite!"
   —OD. 8.334–42; F 8.376–84

More staid than his nephews, Poseidon alone maintains the dignity of a married man (albeit one who raped his fiancée). He convinces the aggrieved husband to free the lovers and advises the smith to be satisfied with the fate illustrated in Daumier's engraving for *Le Charivari* (cat. no. 110):

When the gods saw Hephaestus had caught 'er
In his chain-mail erotic trap,
They roared their Homeric laughter
—Still roared, alas, without quarter
At every poor cuckolded chap.

Daumier's Mars wears the uniform of the Garde national and crosses his arms in resignation. No need for a bed: like Zeus and Hera, the amorous pair were clearly making love outdoors, at the foot of Olympus, from whence their divine colleagues were enviously observing their pleasure.

Homeric laughter is thus not that of poet or reader but that of the gods themselves. We ourselves laugh at the vulgarity of this band of gods. They delight in a disgraceful story of cuckoldry, all the more so in the fact that the aggrieved husband himself draws back the curtain on it. Dirty laughter is the preserve of the gods. To be honest, however, humans are not averse to it either.

Humor

This is not the only kind of laughter to be heard in Homer. We have also heard discreet laughter and seen men and women smiling together, such as Hector and Andromache over Astyanax flinching at his father's helmet plume. We have often seen Ulysses setting up traps infinitely more imaginative, refined, perverse, and cruel than the chains of Hephaestus. When mocked by the gods, Ulysses subtly makes fools of them—of the Cyclops, Circe (who finds it amusing to transform her visitors into swine), and the Sirens. All these gods learned the meaning of human laughter—and the tricks of the hero with a thousand ruses—the hard way. Polyphemus thinks he is going to eat Mr. Οὖτις, alias Nobody. How can he win a battle with Nobody? Circe can obtain sexual favors from Ulysses only in return for the restoration of his swinish crew.

In place of the gods' dirty laughter, Homer preferred a type of smile synonymous with the highest achievements of Greek art and thought. His ironic distance from his characters is unvarying. It has (to misquote Giraudoux in his *Electra*) "a very beautiful name," this distance, "it's called humor." (It seems fair to misquote Giraudoux, who was himself a master of misquotation.)[2] Homer is a closed book to the humorless. Poets and artists create their own personal forms, and the most obvious Homeric touch is the humor that accompanies intelligence. What could be more absurd than Ulysses and Calypso sniveling with boredom in their shared solitude or this same Ulysses covering himself before Nausicaa with an improvised and not very effective fig leaf (cat. no. 117). These situations not only teach the braggart some modesty but make him more human. When the gods deride a hunchback for being cuckolded, he becomes a little more unhappy, hunchbacked, and cuckolded. Homer's ironic vision, however, enhances the mortals he describes, be it Ulysses or Telemachus, Nestor or Nausicaa. The result is a succession of scenes whose wit has always appealed to artists. We have already seen the modest sketches painted by forgotten artists, describing the old men's endearing weakness for Helen (cat. nos. 37–38), and enjoyed the portrayal by a little-known academician (of no particular genius) of Hera's manipulation of Zeus's blind confidence (cat. no. 21).

Readers of classical times enjoyed these paradoxical scenes. Rereading or rewriting Homer in order to accentuate the more ridiculous traits of his characters has consequently been a commonplace since antiquity, as a student exercise. Such irreverent fidelity to Homer accounts for much of Lucian of Samosata's wit, although he adds a dose of skepticism often characterized as Voltairean. His *True History* plays with Homeric wit, while his *Judgement of the Goddesses* in *The Dialogue of the Gods* shows us Paris greeting the Three Graces in hilarious fashion. It's a striptease: "I wish to see them naked." No objection whatever from the goddesses. What follows is worthy of Giraudoux:

> HERMES: Undress, goddesses. Make your inspection, Paris. I have turned my back.
>
> APHRODITE: Very well, Paris. I shall undress first, so that you may discover that I am not just "white-armed" and vain of "ox-eyes," but that I am equally and uniformly beautiful all over.[3]

Paris takes what he can get from the three beauties, not least an eyeful of their nudity. He hands the palm (the golden apple) to Aphrodite, who promises him many nude women. He bargains so cannily that his reward includes the favors of Helen, Aphrodite, the Graces, and all the allegories of Pleasure (Desire, Love, Lasciviousness, Hymen, and so on).

When artists illustrate Homer, they tend to emphasize the little things: the plume that frightens Astyanax; Argos the dog; the Palladium seized by Diomedes; the branches used by Ulysses to hide his pudenda; or Penelope's loom. These little things suddenly come to seem more meaningful than the hero. They lend themselves more to visual representation than the ironies in which Homer abounds. Hector's plume is first an object of fear and then a plaything at which both parents smile; it speaks Homer's language better than all the battle scenes on the plain of Troy.

In classical times it was assumed that Homer had parodied himself. He was supposed to be the author of the *Batrachomyomachia*, or *Battle of the Frogs and the Mice*, a burlesque epic in which bitter war is waged beneath the impassive gaze of the Olympians. In the unhistorical world of Homer, gods, goddesses, animals, monsters, women, servants, slaves, and objects dance around the putative heroes of his epics, in a ridiculous ballet of derision. The principal theme of the *Odyssey* is that of Ulysses, nude or clad only in his lies, having to face the washerwomen of Phaeacia. A cauldron stands before him; there is a scar on his knee; at his feet a moribund dog covered in fleas; and in his bed a distrustful wife. He cannot help but be modest. Homer did not merely invent epic—and Greek tragedy as well: he destroyed them both in the process. When a sensitive artist sets about painting a superhuman or merely inhuman exploit, the tragic and epic tend to disappear, as an intelligent and skeptical perspective is discovered behind the heroics. Because France in its classical age failed to perceive Homer's humor, his poems were sometimes rewritten as burlesques. Paul Scarron burlesqued Virgil (*Le Virgile travesti*, 1648–53), who deserved it since his is indeed a heroic epic. When Pierre de Chamblain de Marivaux burlesqued Homer (*L'Homère travesti*, 1716), much of the work had already been done for him—by Homer.

Satire and Daumier

Since the fairground poetry of Scarron and Marivaux is absent from this exhibition, the reader must turn back to the burlesque imagery occasionally supplied by Homer himself when, for example, he compares Ulysses to a judge who leaves the court to go to his dinner (*Od.* 12.439–40) and subsequently to a blood pudding on the grill (*Od.* 20.24–28). Ajax the Great is compared to a donkey showered with stones by children but obstinately holding its ground (*Il.* 11.558–65). None of these images has ever been illustrated by a history painter, but they are not so remote from the prints of Daumier. It is often remarked that humor is the weapon of the weak. The powerful are content to see themselves satirized; the reader has already seen that the kings and aristocrats of the eighteenth century liked to have themselves painted as heroic warriors. One example of this shows young lords playing at Achilles in the 1769 Academy Prize (cat. nos. 32–33). They want to see themselves as heroic, but their heroism refers to light opera at best and at worst to blood pudding on the grill. In this respect, no artist is closer to Homer than Honoré Daumier.

Daumier's Version of "Ancient History"

Daumier's series *Ancient History*[4] received the following commentary by an unknown humorist (probably Charles Philipon, founder of *Le Charivari*, where it appeared):

> Alone, constrained by no scientific mission, Daumier wandered the byways of Greece, inspired wherever some memory of the past caught his eye, weeping whenever some touching tradition awaited him. Drawing day and night, he at last rediscovered the primitive Greek sentiment of which we give a first proof in his *Menelaus the Conqueror*. Like any new translation, this chaste and naïve composition will have its detractors. Some will be ignorant enough to criticize in Helen a gesture [thumbing her nose] that has, in our own perverted civilization, acquired a meaning incongruous with chaste remorse. Well, it is full of local color, and Daumier saw the young womenfolk of Hellas make this very same gesture—with extraordinary charm—in the direction of the Bavarian monarch[5]—one more proof of the respectful meaning it has always had in that most poetic of countries.

Rather than praise the martial prowess of Menelaus and the nobility of Daumier's work, *Le Charivari* preferred to inform its intelligent readers—and they were all intelligent—that mythology, the golden age, and Greek and Roman history would each, in turn, receive the Daumier treatment.

The fat Helen thumbing her nose at the Greece of the academic painters was accompanied by magnificent verses, which should be read out loud. They are attributed to invented authors; these private jokes, which I have not attempted to elucidate, no doubt added a little salt to the mockery of bourgeois modernity. Baudelaire, lover of statuary's unwavering line, was particularly sensitive to this act of poetic re-creation on the part of Daumier and Philipon.[6]

Academic Absurdity

Daumier mounted his attack not only against ancient heroes and gods and the taboos surrounding them but principally against those who did not know that the taboos were themselves dead. He was particularly hostile to an artistic tendency that Baudelaire labeled "Neo-Greek":

> Daumier has launched a brutal attack on antiquity, on false antiquity—for none better than he is aware of the great things of antiquity—and has spat upon it; that hot-head Achilles, and that cautious fellow Ulysses, and the sagacious Penelope, and that great booby Telemachus, and the beautiful Helen, bane of Troy, the whole lot of them in fact appear before us under a guise of grotesque ugliness, which recalls those old carcasses of tragic actors taking a pinch of snuff in the wings. In all, a most entertaining piece of irreverence, and one, moreover, that was not without its usefulness. I can see now a friend of mine, a lyric poet and one of the "Pagan School," being highly indignant about it. He called it impious, and spoke of the lovely Helen as others speak of the Virgin Mary. But those of us who have no great respect for the Olympians and for tragedy were naturally inclined to enjoy the joke.[7]

The religion was that of models posing in "classical style" at the École des beaux-arts.

This earnest mentality was all but universal in France during the early nineteenth century. William Makepeace Thackeray's delightful essay "On the Painting of the French School" first appeared in *Fraser's Magazine* in December 1839 in the form of extracts from a letter to Mr. Macgilp of London, accompanied by anecdotes, illustrations, and philosophical considerations. A visit to the École des beaux-arts in 1839 saw him toppling the heroes from their pedestals.

> The subjects are almost all what are called classical. Orestes pursued by every variety of Furies; numbers of little wolf-sucking Romuluses; Hectors and Andromaches in a complication of embraces, and so forth. . . .
>
> What was the consequence, my dear friend? In trying to make themselves into bulls, the frogs make themselves into jackasses, as might be expected. For a hundred and ten years the classical humbug oppressed the nation; and you may see, in this gallery of the Beaux-Arts, seventy years' specimens of the dullness which it engendered.[8]

Endlessly pasting new manifestations of the heroic onto the same characters, in due course the academic artists obliterated their protagonists. Even at the École des beaux-arts during the nineteenth century, it was recognized that the supposed genre of history painting was hardly historical. The muscle-bound heroes, the models with their debauched faces, and the goddesses à la Sarah Bernhardt—this detailed representation of a barbarous world no longer reflected an intelligent notion of the past but rather the prejudices and ignorance of the bourgeoisie, newly enriched by the July Monarchy and the Second Empire. Let us follow in Thackeray's footsteps and analyze two compositions in which the pompous vanity and hollow rhetoric of the *peintres pompiers* are obvious.

Gustave Boulanger's *Ulysses Recognized by Eurycleia* (cat. no. 108) became something of a legend after it won him the Prix de Rome in 1849. The epic is transposed to a salon in the aristocratic neighborhood of the faubourg Saint-Germain. Ulysses has the face of a murderer atop an athlete's physique borrowed from the *Belvedere Torso*: this is a brute combining Daumier's cartoon character Robert Macaire with Honoré de

OPPOSITE CATALOGUE NO. 108 | GUSTAVE BOULANGER (1824–1888), *Ulysses Recognized by Eurycleia*, 1849. Oil on canvas, 147 × 114 cm.

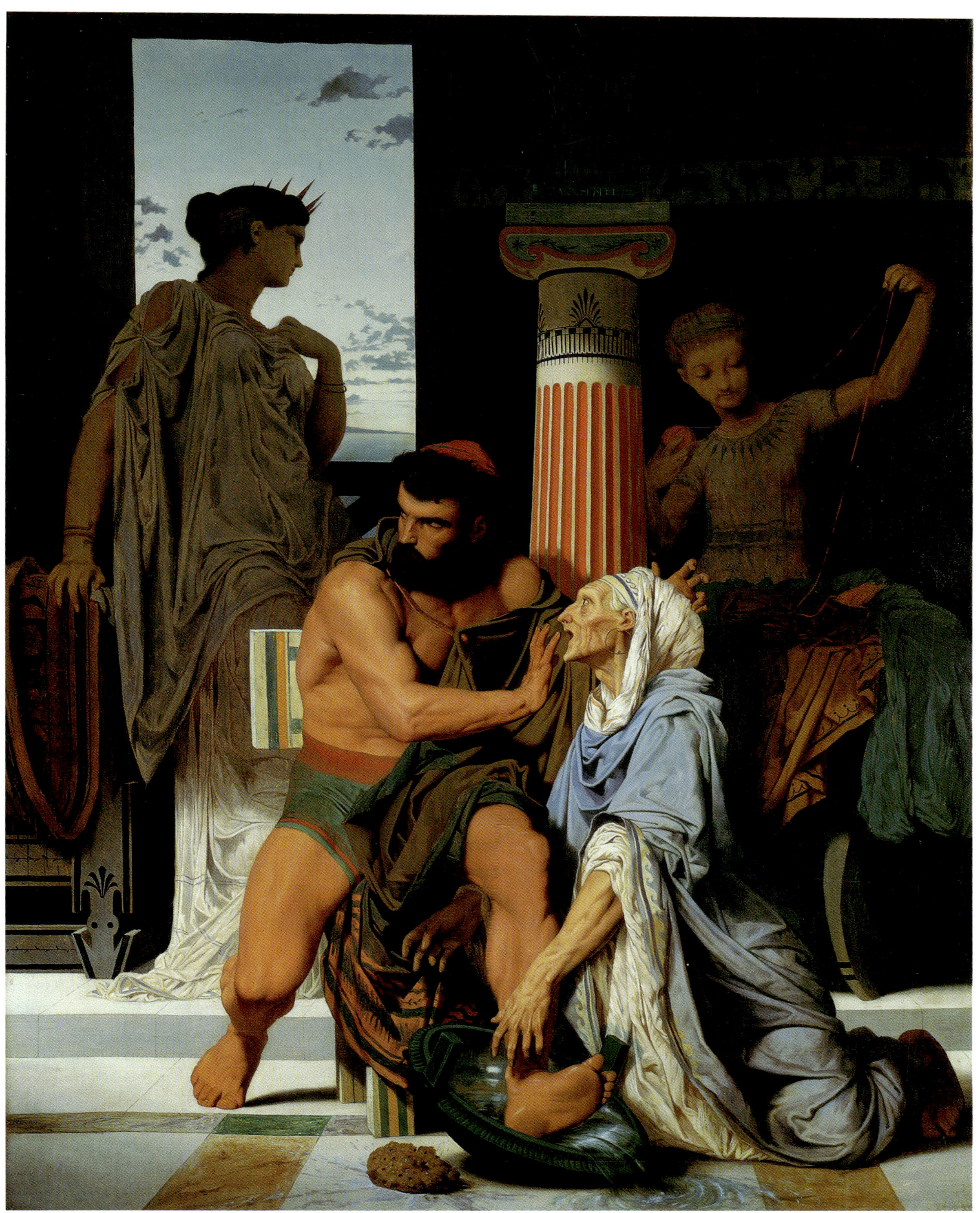

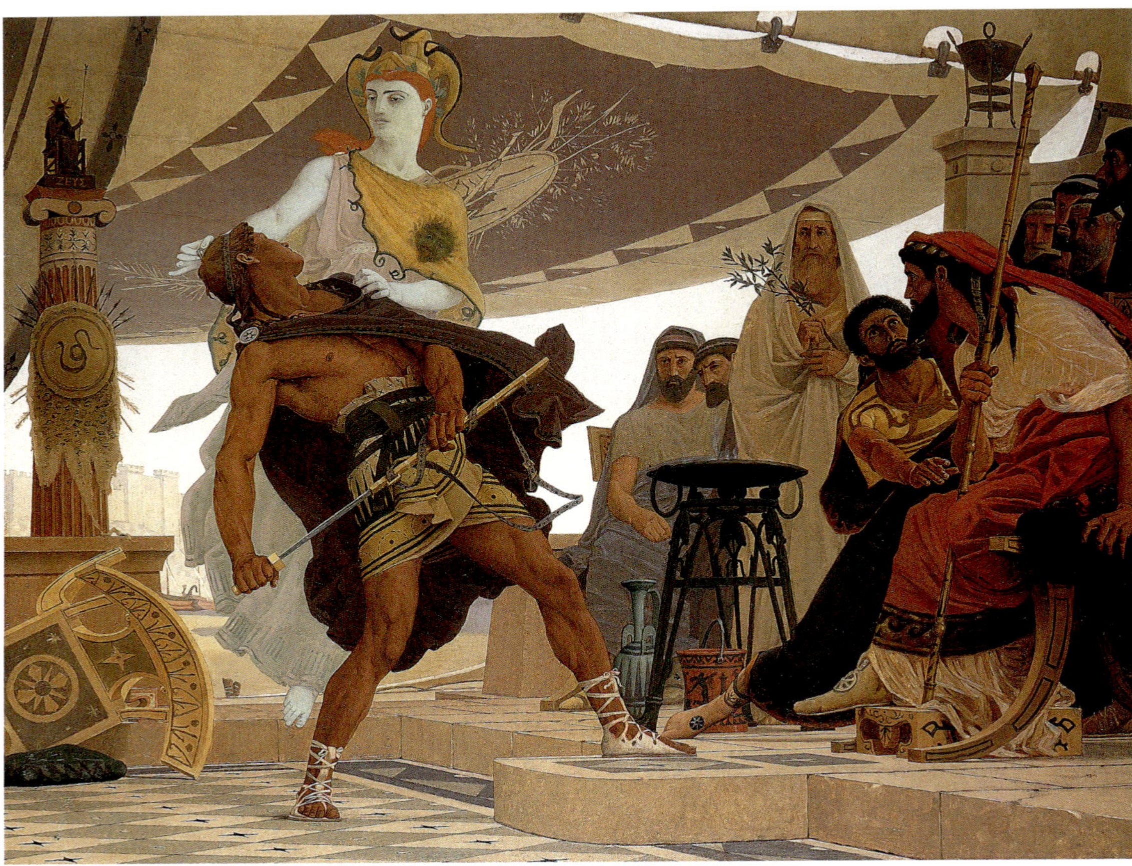

FIGURE 66 | LOUIS-ÉDOUARD-PAUL FOURNIER (1857–1913), *The Wrath of Achilles*, 1881. Oil on canvas, 113 × 145 cm. Prix de Rome in Painting.

Balzac's master criminal Vautrin. Penelope, by contrast, is an interpretation of a Tanagra statuette as a docile doll. The emaciated Eurycleia has the features of a stock procuress from the Romantic stage, while the allegorical statue of Athena simpers in the *contre-jour*. This is a classical setting for the grandiloquent clichés of realism, the world of salons, melodrama, and the ideals and fears of the managerial class. In Homer this is a family scene, hinging on the emotions that unite a man, his wife, and his old wet nurse. In Boulanger's painting, nothing remains but an inadvertent caricature.

Let us now leave the salon for the seaside. Édouard Fournier painted his *Wrath of Achilles* in 1881 (fig. 66). These might be holiday revelers on a Mediterranean beach shielding themselves from the sun in a comfortable tent. Their poses are demonstrative to the point of caricature, and each might be in another world from the others. Achilles falls backward, dragged over by a gigantic Athena. Agamemnon leans forward. Irrelevant details come to the fore: the soldier's espadrilles gleam white in the sun, water is about to be boiled on a tripod for tea, and the arch-priest Calchas wears a vestal's robe. Achilles holds his sword like a violin bow. The geometric decor would be perfect in a bathroom. Three thousand years after Homer, artists of excessive ambition are no less ridiculous than Zeus hoping to dominate Hera, or Agamemnon incapable of commanding his army. Homer's laughter still resounds—louder when it comes at the expense of those who make Homer seem tedious.

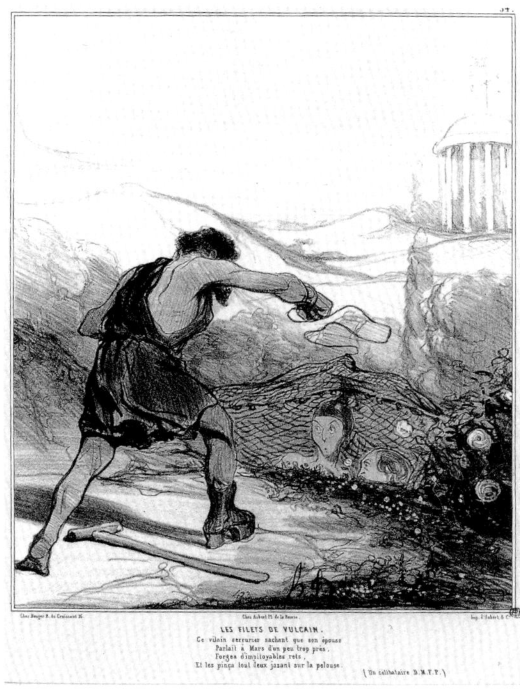

CATALOGUE NO. 109 | HONORÉ DAUMIER (1808–1879), *Vulcan's Net*, from *Ancient History*, 1842, no. 34. Lithograph, 35.2 × 27 cm. Printer: Aubert.

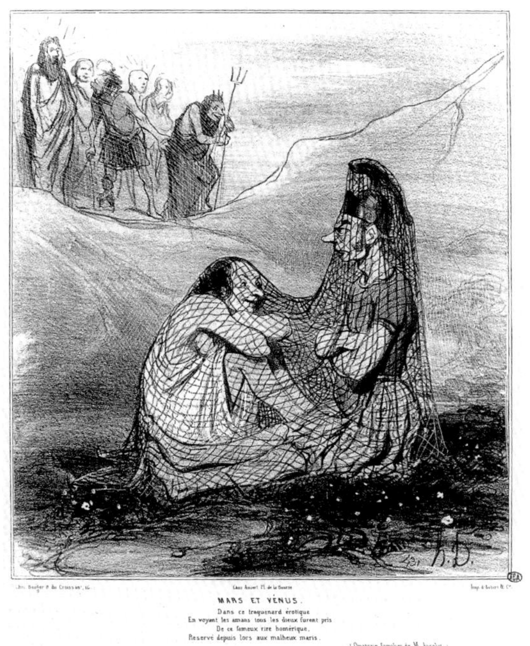

CATALOGUE NO. 110 | HONORÉ DAUMIER (1808–1879), *Mars and Venus*, from *Ancient History*, 1842, no. 38. Lithograph, 34 × 26.2 cm. Printer: Aubert.

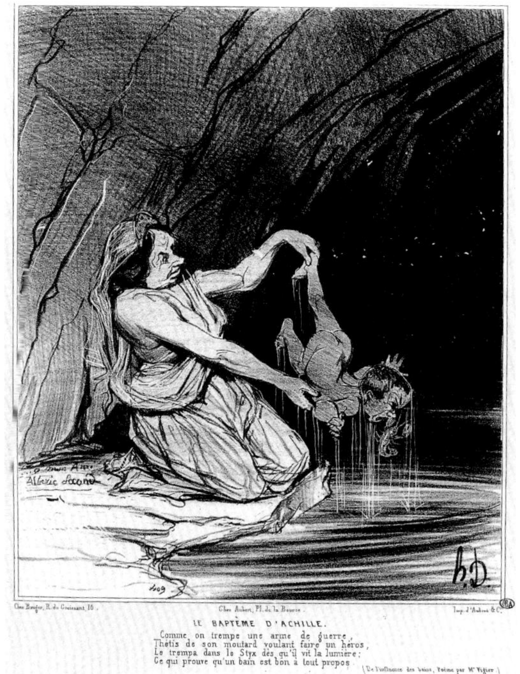

CATALOGUE NO. 111 | HONORÉ DAUMIER (1808–1879), *The Baptism of Achilles*, from *Ancient History*, 1842, no. 22. Lithograph, 34.4 × 26.9 cm. Printer: Aubert.

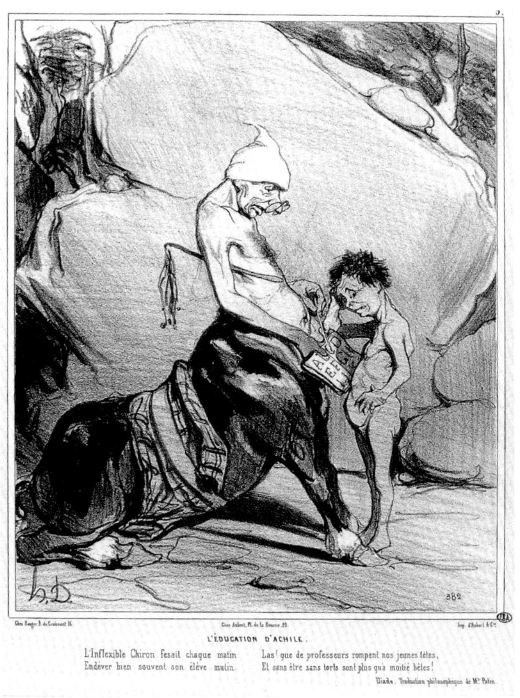

CATALOGUE NO. 112 | HONORÉ DAUMIER (1808–1879), *The Education of Achilles*, from *Ancient History*, 1842, no. 9. Lithograph, 34 × 27 cm. Printer: Aubert.

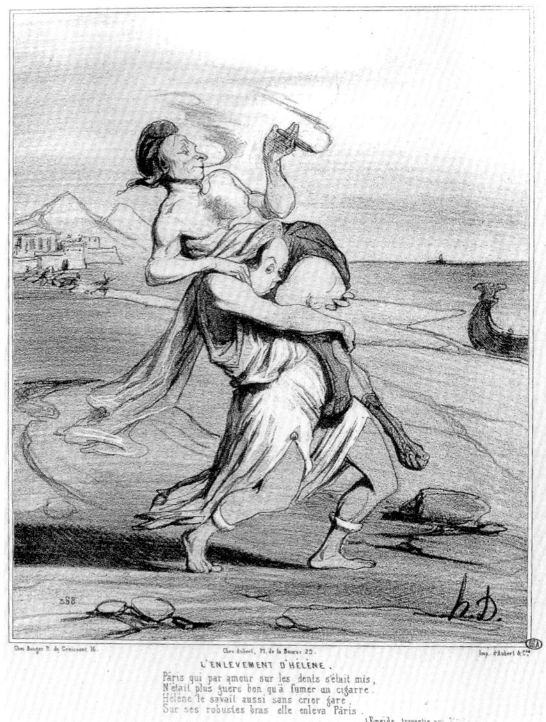

CATALOGUE NO. 113 | HONORÉ DAUMIER (1808–1879), *The Rape of Helen*, from *Ancient History*, 1842, no. 13. Lithograph, 34.4 × 26.9 cm. Printer: Aubert.

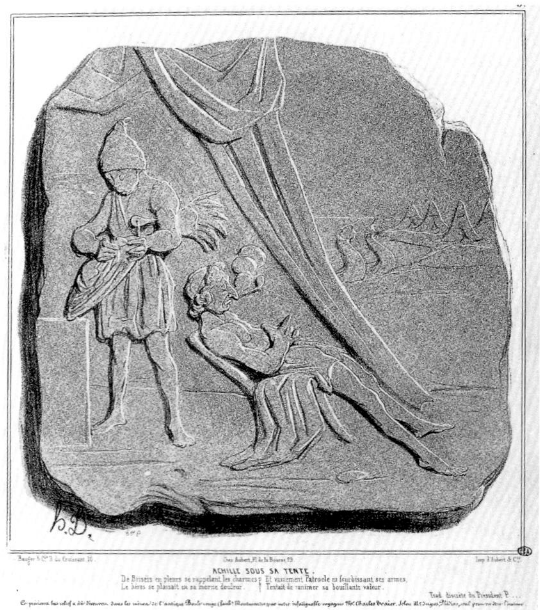

CATALOGUE NO. 115 | HONORÉ DAUMIER (1808–1879), *Achilles in His Tent*, from *Ancient History*, 1842, no. 3. Lithograph, 34.2 × 27.1 cm. Printer: Aubert.

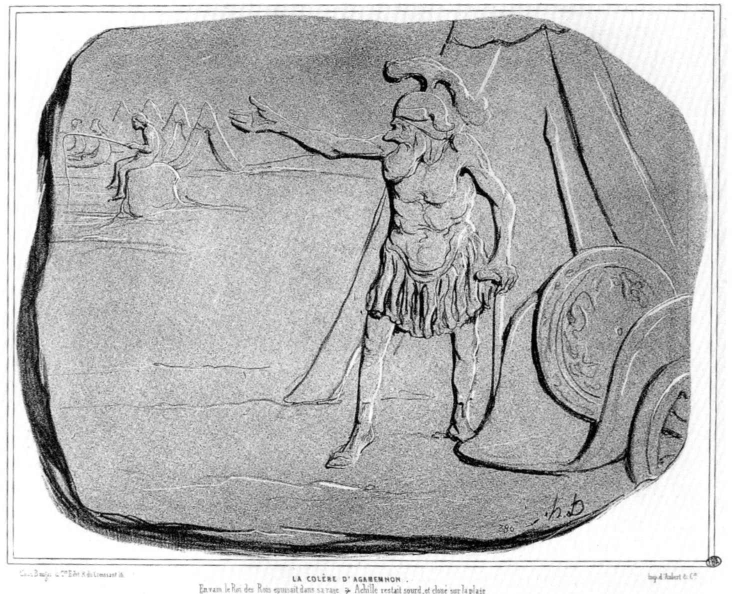

CATALOGUE NO. 114 | HONORÉ DAUMIER (1808–1879), *The Wrath of Agamemnon*, from *Ancient History*, 1842, no. 8. Lithograph, 34.2 × 27 cm. Printer: Aubert.

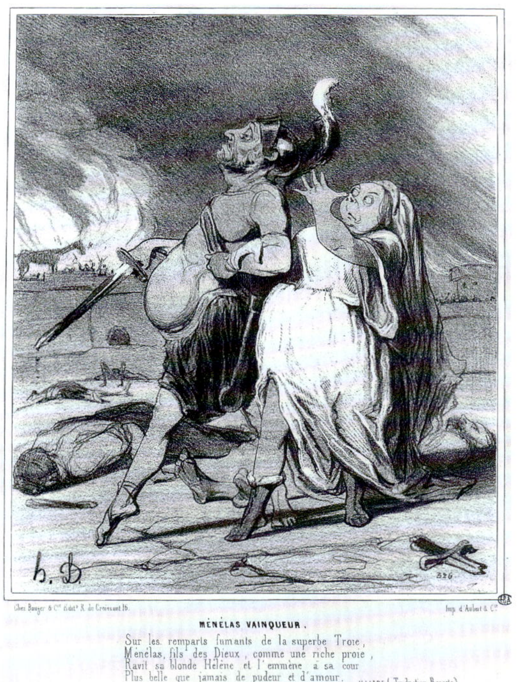

CATALOGUE NO. 116 | HONORÉ DAUMIER (1808–1879), *Menelaus in Victory*, from *Ancient History*, December 1841, no. 1. Lithograph, 34.4 × 26.7 cm. Printer: Aubert.

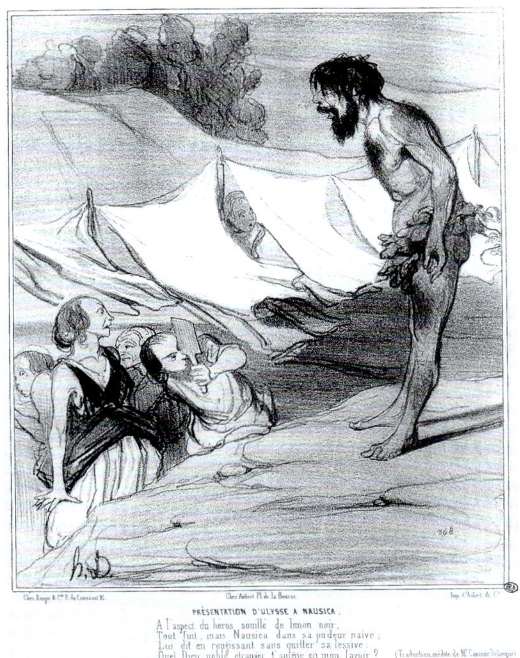

CATALOGUE NO. 117 | HONORÉ DAUMIER (1808–1879), *Ulysses Introduced to Nausicaa*, from *Ancient History*, 1842, no. 4. Lithograph, 34.5 × 26.9 cm. Printer: Aubert.

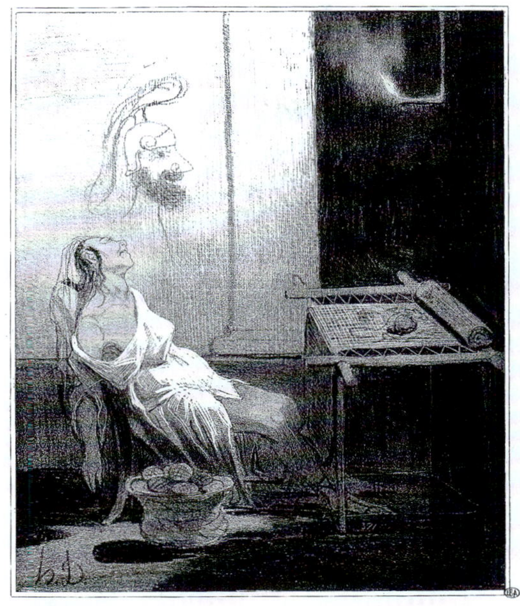

CATALOGUE NO. 118 | HONORÉ DAUMIER (1808–1879), *Penelope's Nights*, from *Ancient History*, 1842, no. 6. Lithograph, 34.4 × 26.9 cm. Printer: Aubert.

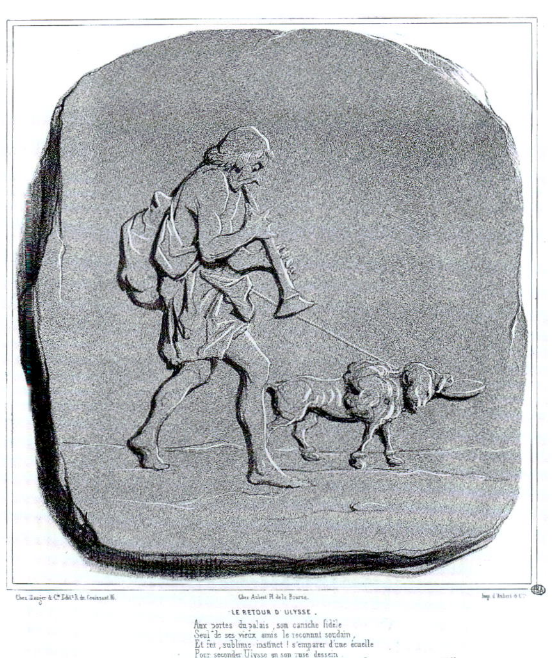

CATALOGUE NO. 119 | HONORÉ DAUMIER (1808–1879), *Ulysses' Return*, from *Ancient History*, 1842, no. 7. Lithograph, 34.2 × 26.9 cm. Printer: Aubert.

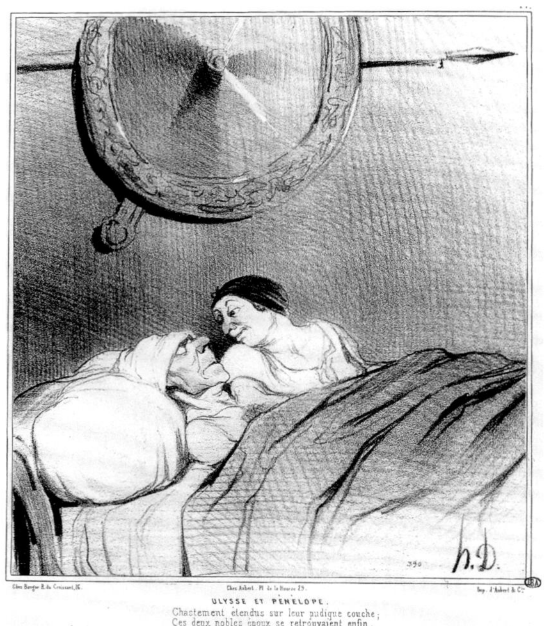

CATALOGUE NO. 120 | HONORÉ DAUMIER (1808–1879), *Ulysses and Penelope*, from *Ancient History*, 1842, no. 14. Lithograph, 34.4 × 26.9 cm. Printer: Aubert.

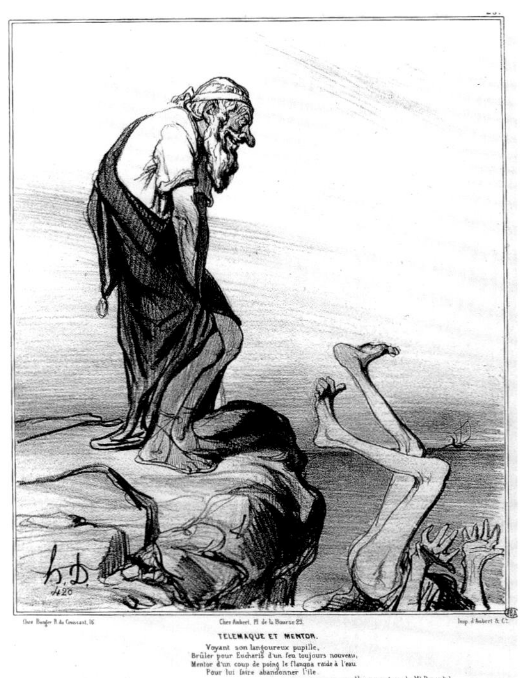

CATALOGUE NO. 122 | HONORÉ DAUMIER (1808–1879), *Telemachus and Mentor*, from *Ancient History*, 1842, no. 29. Lithograph, 35.1 × 26.8 cm. Printer: Aubert.

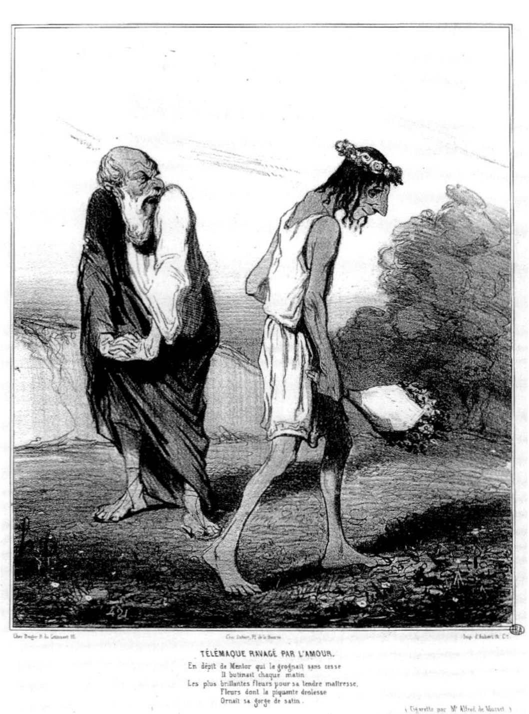

CATALOGUE NO. 121 | HONORÉ DAUMIER (1808–1879), *Telemachus a Prey to Love*, from *Ancient History*, 1842, no. 27. Lithograph, 35 × 27.3 cm. Printer: Aubert.

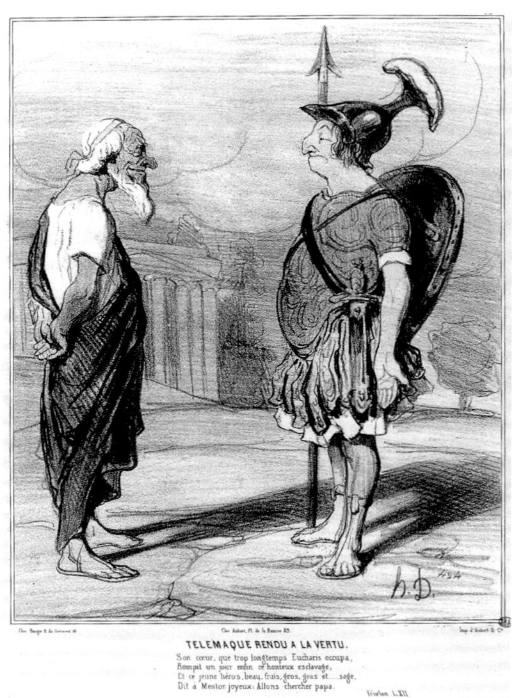

CATALOGUE NO. 123 | HONORÉ DAUMIER (1808–1879), *Telemachus Restored to Virtue*, from *Ancient History*, 1842, no. 32. Lithograph, 35.2 × 27.3 cm. Printer: Aubert.

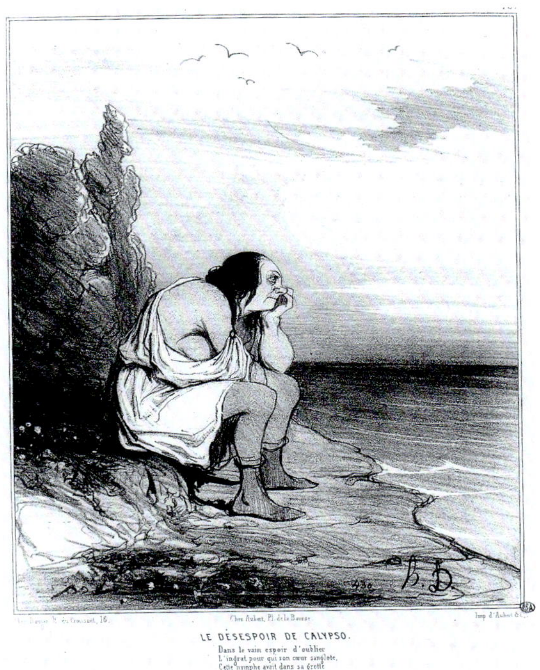

CATALOGUE NO. 124 | HONORÉ DAUMIER (1808–1879), *Calypso's Despair*, from *Ancient History*, 1842, no. 40. Lithograph, 35.2 × 27.2 cm. Printer: Aubert.

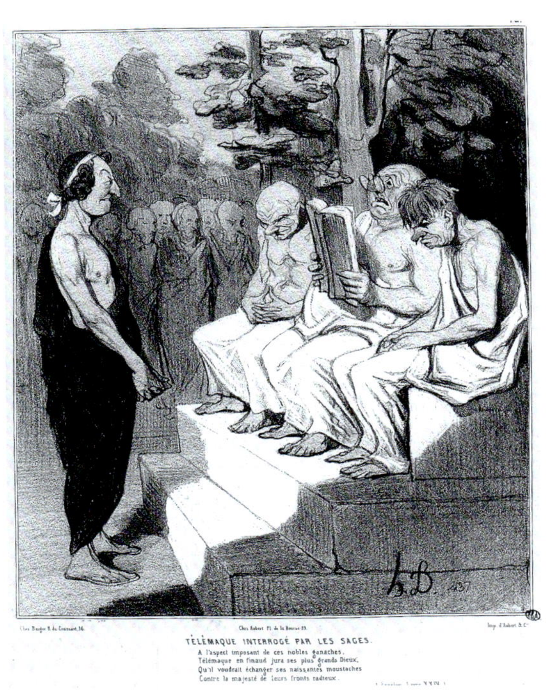

CATALOGUE NO. 125 | HONORÉ DAUMIER (1808–1879), *Telemachus Questioned by the Elders*, from *Ancient History*, 1842, no. 42. Lithograph, 35.5 × 27.2 cm. Printer: Aubert.

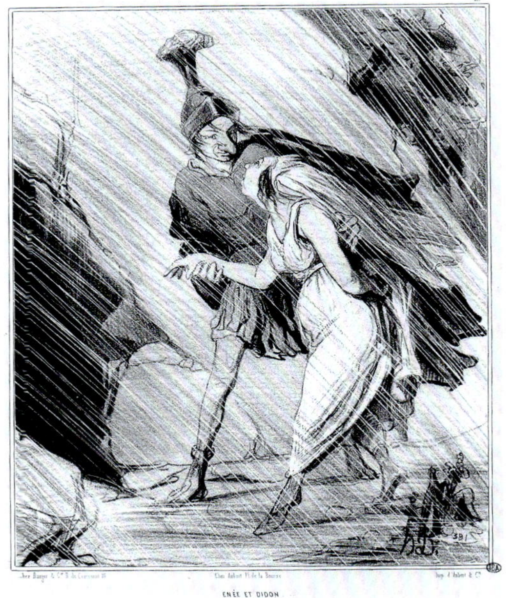

CATALOGUE NO. 126 | HONORÉ DAUMIER (1808–1879), *Dido and Aeneas*, from *Ancient History*, 1842, no. 15. Lithograph, 34.4 × 27 cm. Printer: Aubert.

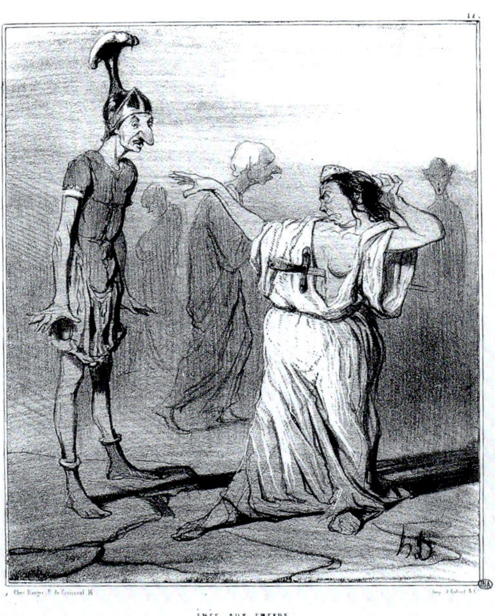

CATALOGUE NO. 127 | HONORÉ DAUMIER (1808–1879), *Aeneas in the Underworld*, from *Ancient History*, 1842, no. 17. Lithograph, 34.3 × 27 cm. Printer: Aubert.

Historical Reconstitution

In this category, one group is outstanding: constant exaggeration of the musculature of Homer's warriors in order to make them more terrifyingly heroic resulted in Greek epic being read as the record of a war fought between cavemen. Regnault (1866; cat. no. 30), Blanchard (1868; fig. 67), and Fournier (1881; fig. 66) consign Achilles and Neoptolemus to prehistory as it was perceived in the late nineteenth century. Their protagonists dress in animal hides and are grimy, disheveled, and bestial. If the beaux-arts style is qualified as *pompier*, it is to this historicizing tendency that the term is best applied. Homer, after all, takes few pains with historical context. It is generally admitted that an imaginary person is the more realistic for being described in his own time rather than in an invented or abstract timescale. Few readers, however, seem to have had this thought even though the poet was clearly mixing the realities of his own time with the resources of legend. What drove these readers to assume the historical reality of a story that Homer himself sets in a prehistoric world? If the Trojan War ever took place, it was during a period about which almost nothing was known until the end of the nineteenth century. When it came to representing Greeks and Trojans, the artists thus adopted one of two simple solutions. One of the finest products of Ingres's teaching, Flandrin's prize-winning painting (cat. no. 104) shows the earliest heroes of Athens inhabiting completely anachronistic buildings like those of the Acropolis, visible in the background. The other solution was to clothe Homer's heroes in animal skins, a uniform that became more or less obligatory at the end of the nineteenth century. The Industrial Revolution thought of totems and other even more primitive objects as pertaining to the Archaic period; they therefore began to spring up in painting.

In Homer's plots there is, of course, a role for costume (rather than fashion): the vine leaves worn by Ulysses before Nausicaa; the women's clothing donned by Achilles at the court of Lycomedes; the taste for elegant helmet plumes and handsome greaves. Humorous as these are, they run counter to received notions of heroic nudity or archaeological primitivism. In his *Romantic Art*, Baudelaire clearly perceived the artistic impasse to which "the Pagan School" led. Each of his observations seems to apply to a Prix de Rome prize-winning painting. Reviewing the Salon of 1859, he speaks of "a school that the kindly Théophile Gautier has termed 'Neo-Greek,' but which I shall, if I may, call 'the finicky school.' In their work erudition serves to disguise lack of imagination. For the most part, this means transposing vulgar everyday life onto a Greek or Roman background."[9] Flaxman and Ingres understood and illustrated the profound modesty of Homer's characters. Yet others failed to see that this modesty is inhabited by a tragic spirituality; they made of Athena an Olympian demimondaine and Ulysses and Achilles Neanderthal warriors. These artistic catastrophes are laughable today, and I present them as a last sign of Homer's laughter.

Homer at the Quat'z'arts

Many École students long continued to believe that nothing was more solemn than old Homer nor more pompous than Greek thought. Yet after Shakespeare and Marivaux and before Giraudoux—indeed, after Homer himself—in 1893 the École's students joined the campaign of derision they themselves had done so much to provoke. Every year at the Bal des Quat'z'arts, they parodied the Molossoi (the companions of Molossos, the son of Neoptolemus and grandson of Achilles) by dressing up and creating fake mythological scenes. They printed invitations full of abominable Greek and Latin puns and sang the following *pompier* song:

> We're told that in history
> Soldiers, Roman and Gaul
> —Cherished sons of Victory—
> Wore helmets all.

OPPOSITE FIGURE 67 | ÉDOUARD-THÉOPHILE BLANCHARD (1844–1879), *The Death of Astyanax*, 1868. Oil on canvas, 145 × 113 cm. Prix de Rome in Painting.

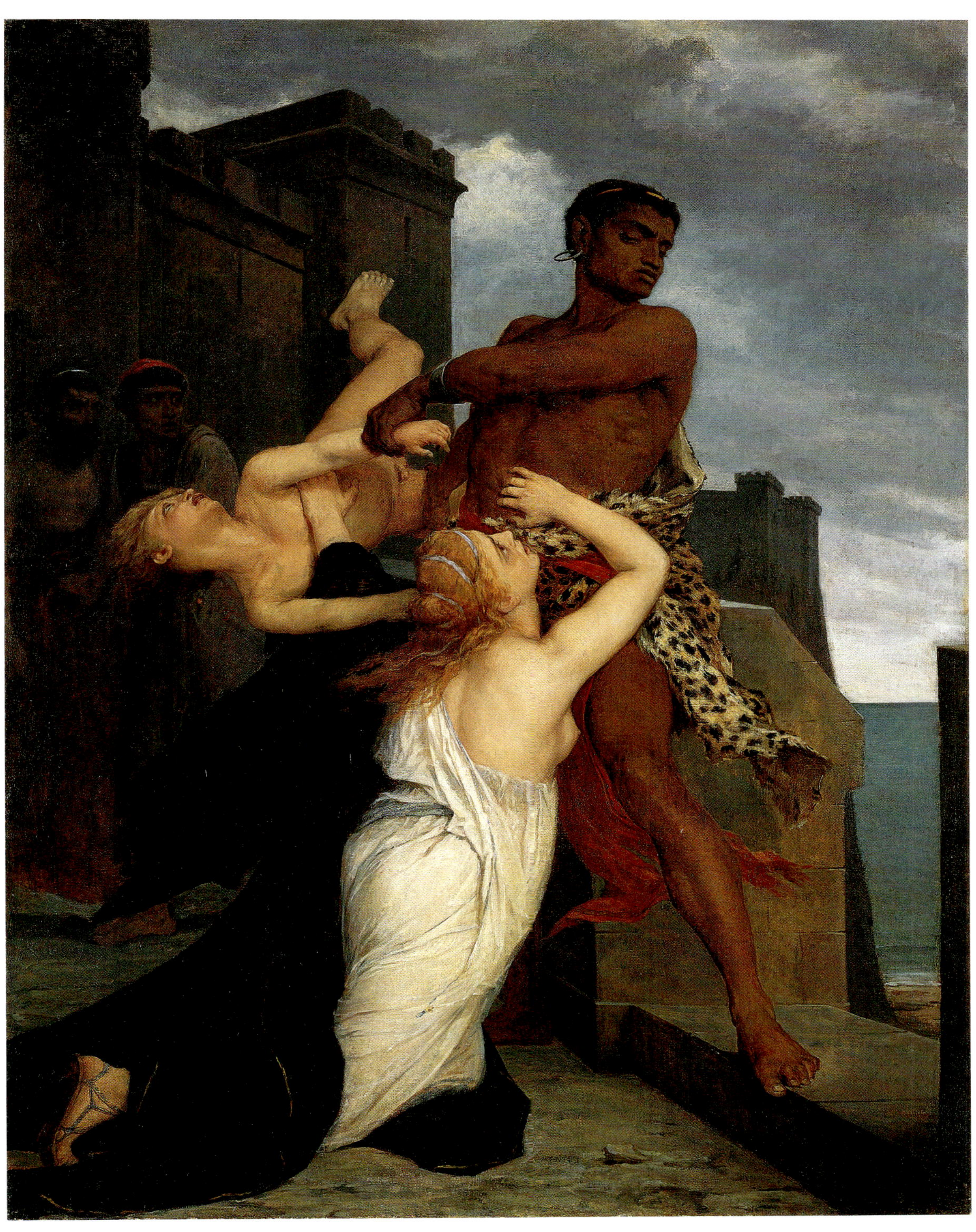

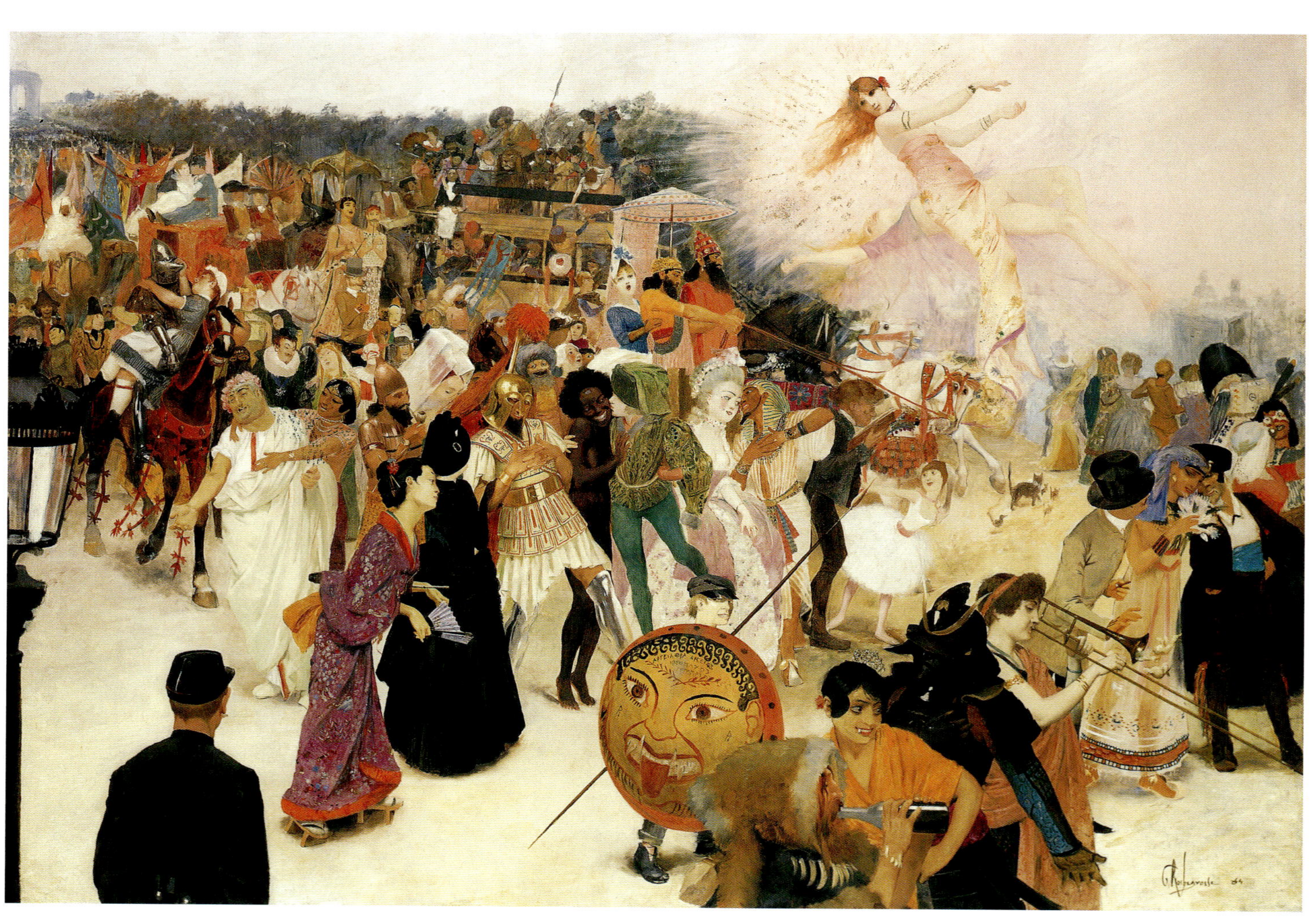

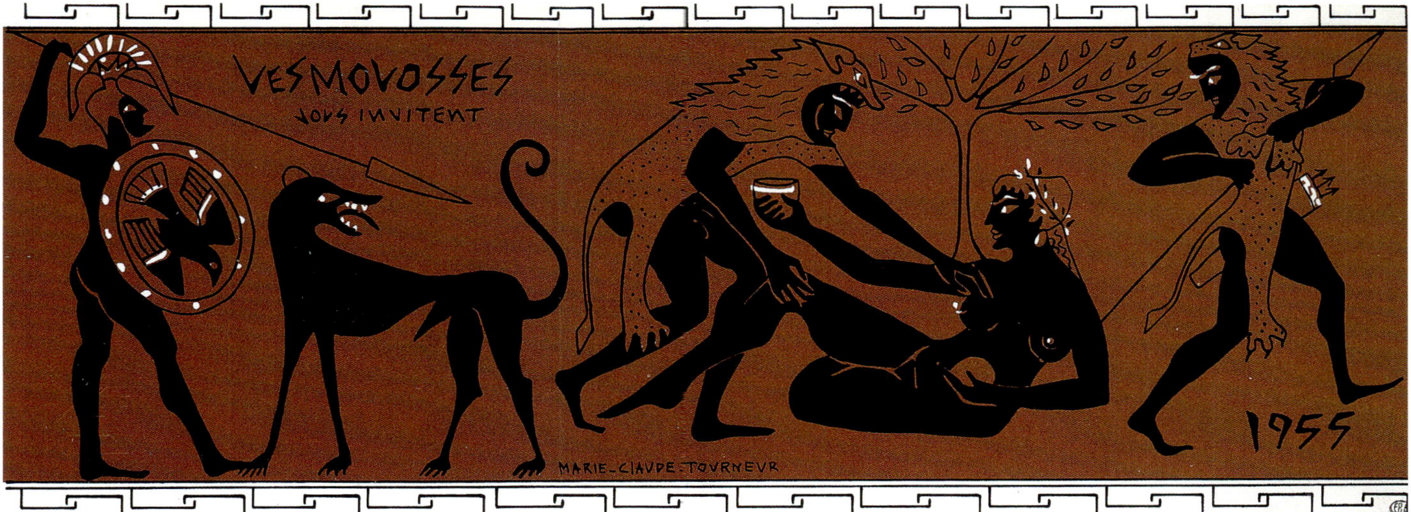

CATALOGUE NO. 129 | ANONYMOUS (CLAUDE-MARIE TOURNEUR?), *Invitation from the Molossoi*, 1955. Lithograph, 14.5 × 13.8 cm.

This tradition military
We consider obligatory
If we sport a helm
It's because, like them,
We're all firemen [*pompiers*].

In 1893 the *pompiers* therefore created the annual Bal des Quat'z'arts. Until 1966 it continued to offer art students and models the chance to parade through the streets of Paris, mimicking ancient poses, garments, and nudity. Beginning in 1900, invitations, programs, posters (cat. nos. 129–30), and, of course, costumes all followed a single—generally ancient—theme. Some of the posters in the collections of the École reproduce Greek vases and Homeric combats, often with a greater sense of the classical world than was elicited by the *concours* in "history and archaeological drawing." For more than sixty years the ancient world was associated with these noisy burlesques, which would begin on a Saturday evening in summer, in rented premises, and spread out into middle-class neighborhoods. The severest critics of the École's teaching—such as the poet and art critic Guillaume Apollinaire—would attend the ball and dance with the students, whom they perceived as victims of an outmoded art. Georges-Antoine Rochegrosse, a former student of the École, learned from the Bal how academicism could parody its own excesses. A sincere lover of antiquity and its artistic resurrection in the Neo-Greek movement, he illustrated José-Maria de Hérédia's *Trophies* and Gustave Flaubert's *Salammbô*. Perhaps he had glimpsed in Petronius's *Satyricon* all that the grotesque could contribute to classical subjects. Rochegrosse's history painting long combined all the picturesque aspects of

OPPOSITE CATALOGUE NO. 128 | GEORGES-ANTOINE ROCHEGROSSE (1859–1938), *Le Bal des Quat'z'arts Descending the Champs-Elysées*, 1904 (?). Oil on canvas, 153 × 215 cm.

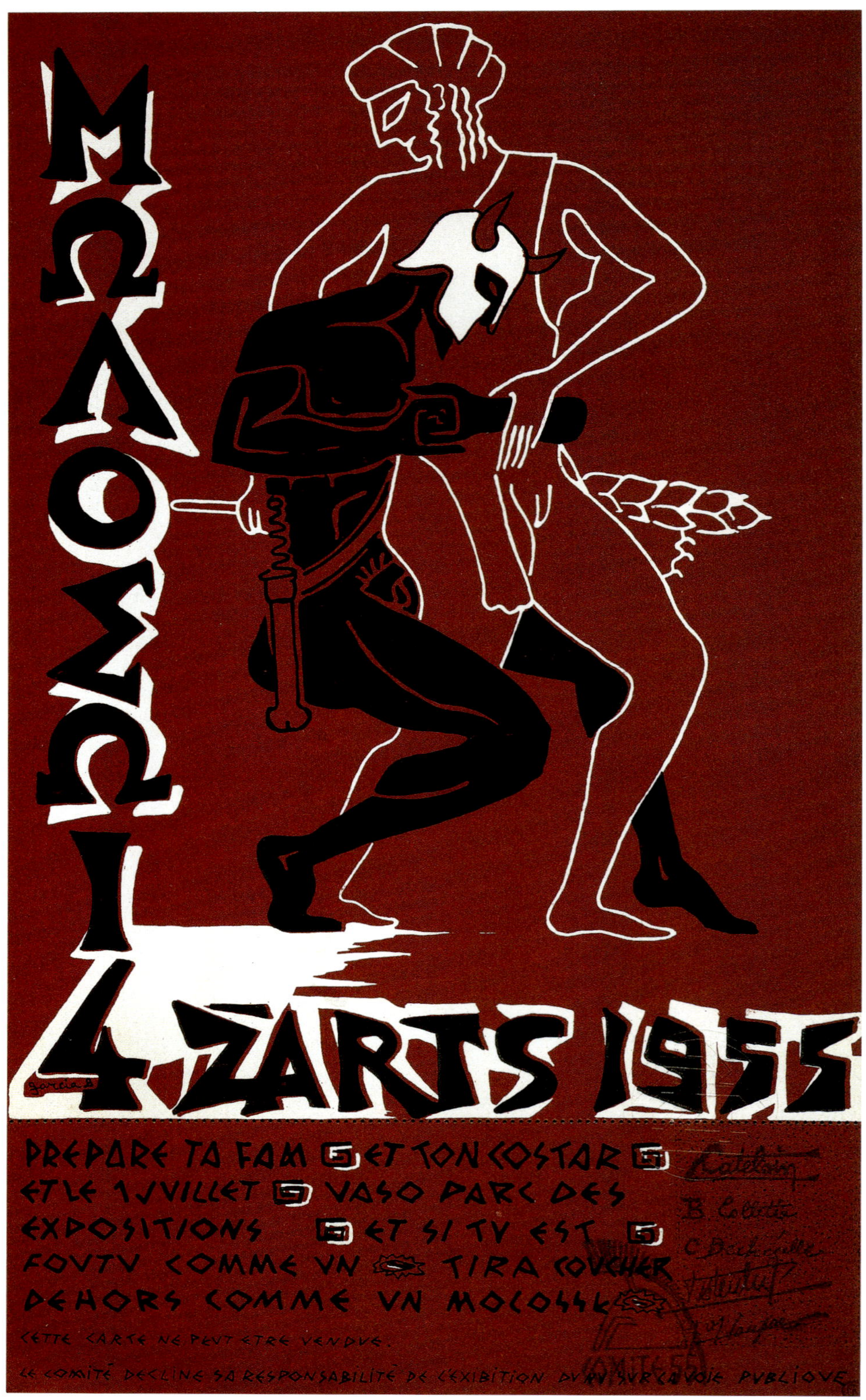

CATALOGUE NO. 130 | ANONYMOUS (several signatures), *The Molossoi*, 1955. Lithograph, 30.4 × 17.8 cm.

the past: the ancient, the sanguinary, and the oriental. His syncretism finds its perfect expression in his depictions of the *Bal des Quat'z'arts* (cat. no. 128), one of which graces the École's collection. The date is difficult to read but may be 1904. It shows a procession of revelers at the foot of the Champs-Élysées wearing costumes from different periods: Greeks with shields or Spartan helmets; a toga-clad Roman emperor; Japanese samurai; Egyptians in floating gowns; Renaissance pages; and Assyrians atop their chariot. Others are more specific: a Lady Godiva; a Henri III; a Marie-Antoinette. A black model plays the *Medici Venus*. A muse figure flies through the air like Athena speeding to the aid of the Greeks, as if to give the scene an Olympian stamp of approval. Rochegrosse no doubt placed side by side details from many successive years of the Bal, creating a procession such as had never been seen, under the patronage of a goddess born not of his imagination but that of his master, Homer.

NOTES

1 Marcel Proust, "Journées de lecture" and author's note, in *Pastiches et mélanges* (Paris, 1914), rpt. in Marcel Proust, *Contre Sainte-Beuve, précédé de Pastiches et Mélanges et suivi d'essais et d'articles*, ed. Pierre Clarac (Paris, 1971), 175. In his ironic note Proust states that the (embellished) quotation is taken from Théophile Gautier's *Le Capitaine Fracasse* (1863). Gautier's picaresque novel is full of Homeric references. In *À la Recherche du temps perdu* Proust's character Bloch likes to parody Leconte de Lisle's Homer translations.

2 A reference to the comment of the Beggar, which closes (act 2, sc. 9) in Giraudoux's play *Electra* (Paris, 1937). The Beggar informs "la femme Narsès" that the phenomenon she is watching has a very beautiful name: "[I]t is called *dawn*" (emphasis added). The French pun is therefore humor / aurore. [Trans.]

3 Lucian of Samosata, *The Judgement of the Goddesses*, trans. A. M. Harmon (London, 1921), 3:397–99.

4 *Ancient History* was published in *Le Charivari*, 1841–43; see Loys Delteil, *Le Peintre-graveur illustré* (Paris, 1926), vol. 22, nos. 925–74.

5 After liberating itself from the Ottomans (1821–29), in 1832 independent Greece chose Otto I of Wittelsbach (son of Ludwig I of Bavaria) as its king.

6 See, e.g., Charles Baudelaire, "Quelques caricaturistes français" (1857), in his *Curiosités esthétiques* (Paris, 1962), 280–81.

7 Charles Baudelaire, "Some French Caricaturists," in *Baudelaire: Selected Writings on Art and Artists*, trans. P. E. Charvet (Cambridge, 1972), 223.

8 William Makepeace Thackeray, "On the French School of Painting," *The Paris Sketch Book*, (London, n.d.), 46.

9 Baudelaire, "Salon de 1859: V. Religion, histoire, fantaisie," in his *Curiosités esthétiques*, 343.

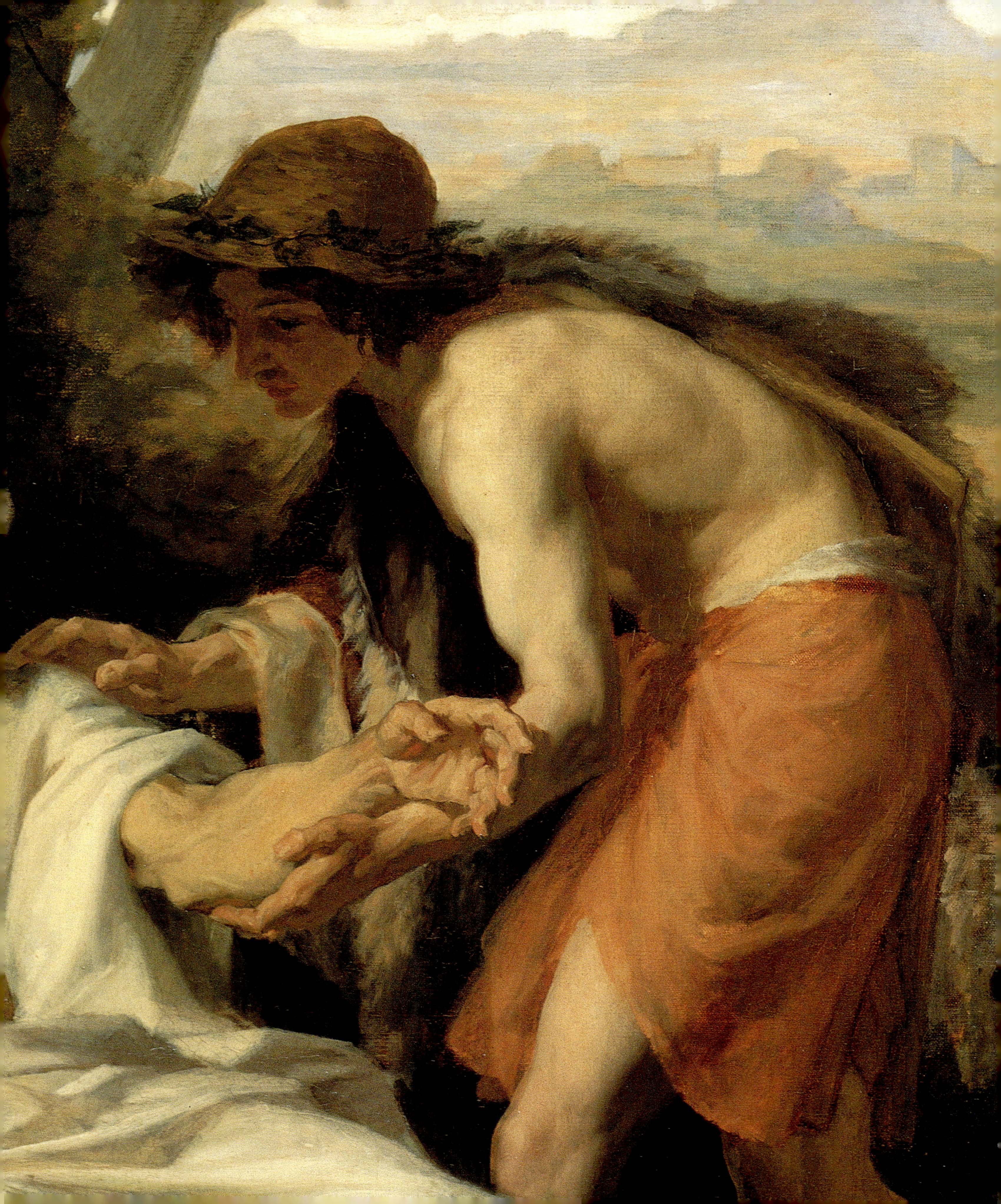

Appendix

Checklist

THE ABBREVIATIONS D (DAHESH MUSEUM OF ART) AND P (PRINCETON UNIVERSITY ART MUSEUM) INDICATE AT WHICH VENUE EACH WORK APPEARED IN THE EXHIBITION. THE KEY TO THE EXHIBITION ABBREVIATIONS USED IN THE CATALOGUE ENTRIES APPEARS AT THE END OF THE CHECKLIST UNDER EXHIBITION CATALOGUES.

THE HISTORICAL BACKGROUND AND THE HOMERIC WORLD

CATALOGUE NO. 1 (D)
Paul Jourdy, 1805–1856
Homer Travels through the Cities of Greece, Singing His Poems
Oil on canvas, 114.1 × 116.5 cm.
Prix de Rome in Painting, 1834 (PRP 77)

EXHIBITIONS: Amiens, 1935: *Prix de Rome*; United States, 1984–85: *The Grand Prix de Rome*, no. 72; Paris, 1986: *Les Concours des Prix de Rome*, no. 87

CATALOGUE NO. 2 (D)
Diogène-Ulysse-Napoléon Maillard, 1840–1926
Homer on the Island of Scyros
Oil on canvas, 113 × 145 cm.
Prix de Rome in Painting, 1864 (PRP 115)

CATALOGUE NO. 3 (P)
Louis-Hector Leroux, 1829–1900
Homer Requesting Hospitality
Oil on canvas, 32.5 × 40.5 cm.
Oil Sketch *concours*, 1855 (Esq p 69)

EXHIBITIONS: Paris, 1889: *Exposition Universelle*; Paris, 1986: *Les Concours d'esquisses peintes*, no. 67, and United States, 1987; Bar-le-Duc, Verdun, 1988: *Louis-Hector Leroux*, no. 3

CATALOGUE NO. 4 (P)
Clément-Amédée Bidot, 1833–?
Homer Requesting Hospitality
Oil on canvas, 32.5 × 40.5 cm.
Oil Sketch *concours*, 1855 (Esq p 70)

EXHIBITION: Paris, 1986: *Les Concours d'esquisses peintes*, no. 68, and United States, 1987

CATALOGUE NO. 5 (D)
Alexandre-Adolphe-Gustave Levasseur, 1808–?
Monument to Homer. Elevation, plan, and section
Watercolor, 32.5 × 26.3 cm.
Prix d'émulation, 1844: Sketches, 1ère classe (Esq 319)

CATALOGUE NO. 6 (P)
Félix Thomas, 1815–1875
Monument to Homer. Elevation, plan, and section
Watercolor, 34.5 × 29.7 cm.
Prix d'émulation, 1844: Sketches, 1ère classe (Esq 318)

CATALOGUE NO. 7 (P)
Eugène-Ferdinand Buttura, 1812–1852
Apollo, Shepherding the Flocks of Admetus, Invents the Lyre
Oil on canvas, 115 × 146 cm.
Prix de Rome in Historical Landscape, 1837 (PRP 81)

EXHIBITIONS: United States, 1984–85: *The Grand Prix de Rome*, no. 112; Paris, 1986: *Les Concours des Prix de Rome*, no. 156; Tokyo, 1996: *Impressionisme*, no. 7; Glasgow, 1997: *Impressionism*, p. 27

CATALOGUE NO. 8 (P)
Charles Garnier, 1825–1898
Temple of Panhellenic Jupiter or Athena, Aegina. Facade, reconstruction, 1852
Watercolor over India ink, 136 (117.5) × 281.5 (264) cm.
Fourth-year dispatch, Prix de Rome in Architecture. (Institut de France donation in 1868)

EXHIBITION: Paris, Houston, Athens, 1982–83: *Paris-Rome-Athènes: Le Voyage en Grèce des architectes français aux XIXe et XXe siècles*, pp. 214ff.

CATALOGUE NO. 9 (D)
Pierre-Amédée-Marcel Béronneau, 1869–1937
The Scene Takes Place on Parnassus
Oil on canvas, 32 × 41 cm.
Oil Sketch *concours*, 1894 (MU 8688)

EXHIBITION: Mexico, 1994–95: *Gustave Moreau*, no. 5

CATALOGUE NO. 10 (D)
Element from an *acroterion* with lion's head, ca. 530 B.C.
Terracotta, 40 × 56 × 36 cm.
(WB 282)

THE GODS

CATALOGUE NO. 11 (D)
Feminine Torso, Roman copy after the *Aphrodite of Cnidus* by Praxiteles, 340 B.C.
Marble, stone base, 103 × 46 × 32 cm.
(MU 7763)

PROVENANCE: Dispatched from the French Academy in Rome, 1841

EXHIBITION: Rome, 1999–2000: *Villa Medici: Il sogno di un cardinale*, no. 23, p. 180

CATALOGUE NO. 12 (D)
Masculine Torso, or Torso of an Athlete (or of Mars). First century B.C., after a Greek original of the fourth century B.C.?
Marble, stone base, 133 × 60 × 37 cm.
(MU 7764)

PROVENANCE: Dispatched from the French Academy in Rome, 1841

EXHIBITION: Rome, 1999–2000: *Villa Medici: Il sogno di un cardinale*, no. 22, p. 178

CATALOGUE NO. 13 (D)
Jean-Louis Brian, 1805–1864
Seated Mercury
Bronze, 93 × 100 cm.
Cast from a plaster model exhibited at the 1864 Salon as no. 2521, by the metal-founder Henri-Léon Thiébault (or Thiébaut)
(MU 4334)

EXHIBITIONS: Paris, 1889: *Exposition universelle*; Paris, 1966: *Hommage à Jean-Louis Brian*, no. 5; Paris, 1980–81: *David d'Angers*

CATALOGUE NO. 14 (P)
François de Troy, 1645–1730
Mercury Overcomes the Vigilance of Argus
Oil on canvas, 148 × 177 cm.
Royal Academy Reception Piece, 1674
(MRA 97); Louvre Inventory: 8206; deposited by the Musée du Louvre with the École des beaux-arts, 1872

EXHIBITIONS: Paris, 1961: *L'Art français au XVIIe siècle . . .*, no. 131; Toulouse-Sceaux, 1997: *François de Troy*, no. 1, p. 109

CATALOGUE NO. 15 (D)
Eugène-Modeste-Edmond Lepoitevin, 1806–1870
Mercury Lulls Argus to Sleep and Kills Him
Oil on canvas, 37.5 × 46 cm.
Historical Landscape Sketch *concours*, 1828 (Esq p ph 7)

EXHIBITION: Paris, 1986: *Les Concours d'esquisses peintes*, and United States, 1987

CATALOGUE NO. 16 (D)
Victor-Francois-Élie Biennoury, 1823–1893
Mercury Lulls Argus to Sleep and Kills Him
Oil on canvas, 32.5 × 40.5 cm.
Historical Landscape Sketch *concours*, 1842 (Esq p 46)

EXHIBITION: Paris, 1986: *Les Concours d'esquisses peintes*, and United States, 1987

CATALOGUE NO. 17 (P)
Nicolas Poussin, 1594–1665
Mercury, Herse, and Aglauros, ca. 1625
Oil on canvas, 53.5 × 77.5 cm.
(MU 69); donation: Gatteaux, 1883

EXHIBITIONS: Paris, 1961: *L'Art français au XVIIe siècle . . .*, no. 126; Paris, 1973: "*La Mort de Germanicus*" *de Poussin au Musée de Minneapolis*, no. 26, p. 20; Rome, 1977–78: *Nicolas Poussin*, no. 6; Paris, 1988: *Claude Mellan*, no. 173, p. 134; Meaux, 1988–89: *De Nicolò dell'Abbate . . .*, no. 57

CATALOGUE NO. 18 (P)
Jean Leblond, 1645–1709
The Titans Crushed by Jupiter's Thunderbolts
Oil on canvas, 146 × 199 cm.
Royal Academy Reception Piece, 1681
(MRA 101); Louvre Inventory: 2623; deposited by the Musée du Louvre with the École des beaux-arts, 1872

CATALOGUE NO. 19 (P)
Charles de La Fosse, 1636–1716
The Rape of Persephone
Oil on canvas, 145 × 181 cm.
Royal Academy Reception Piece, 1673
(MRA 95); Louvre Inventory: 4536; deposited by the Musée du Louvre with the École des beaux-arts, 1872

EXHIBITIONS: Paris, 1961: *L'Art français au XVIIe siècle . . .*, no. 123; Lille, 1968: *Au Temps du Roi Soleil*, no. 20; Okayama-Fukuoka, 1989: *Le Siècle de Louis XIV*, no. 12; Montréal-Rennes-Montpellier, 1993: *Grand Siècle*, no. 104, p. 309; Tours-Toulouse, 2000: *Les Peintres du roi*, no. 7

CATALOGUE NO. 20 (D)
Jean-Charles-Joseph Rémond, 1795–1875
The Rape of Persephone
Oil on canvas, 114 × 146 cm.
Prix de Rome in Historical Landscape, 1821 (PRP 61)

EXHIBITIONS: United States, 1984–85: *The Grand Prix de Rome*, no. 1; Paris, 1986: *Les Concours des Prix de Rome*, no. 152; Tokyo, 1989: *The Prix de Rome*, no. 59

CATALOGUE NO. 21 (P)
Jean-Jacques-François Le Barbier, 1738–1826
Jupiter in the Toils of Sleep
Oil on canvas, 260 × 194 cm.
Royal Academy Reception Piece, 1785
(MRA 128); Louvre Inventory: 2412; deposited by the Musée du Louvre with the École des beaux-arts, 1872

EXHIBITION: Paris, 1785: *Salon*, no. 134

ACHILLES

CATALOGUE NO. 22 (P)
Éloi-Firmin Féron, 1802–1876
Chryses Asks Agamemnon to Return His Daughter
Oil on tracing paper mounted on canvas, 33 × 40.5 cm.
Oil Sketch *concours*, 1822 (Esq p 12)

EXHIBITIONS: Paris, 1889: *Exposition universelle*; Paris, 1986: *Les Concours d'esquisses peintes*, no. 12, and United States, 1987

CATALOGUE NO. 23 (D)
Michel-Martin Drölling, 1786–1851
The Wrath of Achilles
Oil on canvas, 113 × 146 cm.
Prix de Rome in Painting, 1810 (PRP 48)

EXHIBITIONS: Paris, 1913: *David et ses élèves*, no. 88; Malibu, 1982–83; United States, 1984–85: *The Grand Prix de Rome*, no. 47; Paris, 1986: *Les Concours des Prix de Rome*, no. 53; Tokyo, 1989: *The Prix de Rome*, no. 34

CATALOGUE NO. 24 (P)
Jean-Auguste-Dominique Ingres, 1780–1867
Achilles Receives the Ambassadors of Agamemnon
Oil on canvas, 113 × 146 cm.
Prix de Rome in Painting, 1801 (PRP 40)

EXHIBITIONS: Paris, 1867: *Catalogue des tableaux . . .*, no. 53; Rome, 1904: *Exposition rétrospective . . .*; Paris, 1913: *David*, no. 179; Paris, 1934: *David, Ingres, Géricault . . .*, no. 6; Toulouse-Montauban, 1955: *Ingres et ses maîtres . . .*, no. 155 bis; Paris, 1966: Institut de France (soirée du 15 juin 1966); Montauban, 1967: *Ingres et son temps*, no. 8; Paris, 1967: *Évocation de l'Académie de France . . .*, no. 23; Paris, 1967–68: *Ingres . . .*, no. 4; London, 1972: *The Age of the Neoclassicism . . .*, no. 142; Montauban, 1980: *Ingres et sa postérité*; Malibu, 1982–83: Prix de Rome Loan to the Getty Foundation, Malibu; United States, 1984–85: *The Grand Prix de Rome*, no. 39; Paris, 1986: *Les Concours des Prix de Rome*, no. 43; Tokyo, 1989: *The Prix de Rome*; Bologna, 1992–93: *Viaggio a Rossini . . .*, no. 52 [color reprod. p. 99]; Glasgow, 1997: *Impressionism*, p. 27; Mexico City, 1999–2000: *Arte de las Academias . . .*, p. 191; Paris, 2000–2001: *D'après l'Antique*, no. 193; Rome–New York, 2003: *Maestà di Roma . . .*, no. 6; New York, 2003: *French Artists in Rome*, 25

CATALOGUE NO. 25 (P)
Jacques-Ferdinand Humbert, 1842–1934
Eurypylus Wounded
Oil on canvas, 32.5 × 41 cm.
Oil Sketch *concours*, 1863 (Esq p 98)

EXHIBITION: Paris, 1986: *Les Concours d'esquisses peintes*, no. 90, and United States, 1987

CATALOGUE NO. 26 (P)
Jules-Joseph Lefebvre, 1834–1912
Thetis Consoling Achilles
Oil on canvas, 32.5 × 40.5 cm.
Oil Sketch *concours*, 1858 (Esq p 76)

EXHIBITIONS: Paris, 1889: *Exposition Universelle*; Paris, 1986: *Les Concours d'esquisses peintes*, no. 74, and United States, 1987

CATALOGUE NO. 27 (D)
Joseph Brian, 1801–1861
Thetis Brings Achilles the Arms Forged by Vulcan
Plaster, 40 × 47 cm.
Sketch Model *concours*, 1829 (MU 4434)

CATALOGUE NO. 28 (D)
Jean Alaux ("The Roman"), 1786–1864
Briseis Mourning Patroclus
Oil on canvas, 113.1 × 146 cm.
Prix de Rome in Painting, 1815 (PRP 53)

EXHIBITIONS: United States, 1984–85: *The Grand Prix de Rome*, no. 52; Paris, 1986: *Les Concours des Prix de Rome*, no. 60; Tokyo, 1989: *The Prix de Rome*, no. 37

CATALOGUE NO. 29 (P)
Léon Cogniet, 1794–1880
Briseis Mourning Patroclus
Oil on tracing paper mounted to canvas, 29.5 × 37.5 cm.
Sketch for the Grand Prix in Painting, 1815 (MU 11712. Purchased: Étude Habaux, Hôtel Drouot, Paris, 1980)

EXHIBITIONS: Paris, 1986: *Les Concours des Prix de Rome*, no. 61; Orléans, 1990: *Léon Cogniet*, no. 20

CATALOGUE NO. 30 (D)
Henri Regnault, 1843–1871
Thetis Brings Achilles the Arms Forged by Vulcan
Oil on canvas, 113 × 146 cm.
Prix de Rome in Painting, 1866 (PRP 117)

EXHIBITIONS: Rome, 1904: *Exposition rétrospective . . .*; Paris, 1987: *Le Siècle des dictionnaires*, no. 151; Saint-Cloud, 1991–92: *Henri Regnault*, no. 14

CATALOGUE NO. 31 (D)
Constant-Ambroise Roux, 1865–1929
Enflamed with Anger Following the Death of Patroclus, Achilles Dons the Armor Brought by His Mother Thetis
Plaster, 142 × 89 × 89 cm.
Prix de Rome in Sculpture, 1894 (PRS 83)

CATALOGUE NO. 32 (P)
Joseph-Barthélemy Lebouteux, 1742–?
Achilles Places the Body of Hector at the Feet of the Dead Patroclus
Oil on canvas, 111 × 147 cm.
Prix de Peinture de l'Académie royale, 1769 (PRP 16)

EXHIBITION: Le Mans, 1989: *Vertu antique, vertu révolutionnaire*

CATALOGUE NO. 33 (P)
Pierre Lacour, 1745–1814
Achilles Places the Body of Hector at the Feet of the Dead Patroclus
Oil on canvas, 111 × 147 cm.
Prix de Peinture de l'Académie royale, 1769 (PRP 16 bis)

EXHIBITION: Bordeaux, 1989: *Le Port des lumières: La Peinture à Bordeaux, 1750–1800*, no. 57

CATALOGUE NO. 34 (P)
Henri-Frédéric Schopin (or Chopin), 1804–1890
Achilles Pursued by the River God Xanthos
Oil on canvas, 113 × 146 cm.
Prix de Rome in Painting, 1831 (PRP 73)

EXHIBITIONS: United States, 1984–85: *The Grand Prix de Rome*, no. 69; Paris, 1986: *Les Concours des Prix de Rome*, no. 84

CATALOGUE NO. 35 (D)
Jérôme-Martin Langlois, 1779–1836
Priam at the Feet of Achilles
Oil on canvas, 113 × 146 cm.
Prix de Rome in Painting, 1809 (PRP 47)

EXHIBITIONS: Paris, 1913: *David et ses élèves*, no. 195; United States, 1984–85: *The Grand Prix de Rome*; Paris, 1986: *Les Concours des Prix de Rome*, no. 52; Tokyo, 1989: *The Prix de Rome*, no. 33

CATALOGUE NO. 36 (P)
Joseph Wencker, 1848–1919
Priam at the Feet of Achilles
Oil on canvas, 145 × 113 cm.
Prix de Rome in Painting, 1876 (PRP 127)

EXHIBITION: New York–Palm Beach, 2002–3: *Dagnan-Bouveret*, fig. 32

FAR FROM COMBAT: THE GREAT SCENES

CATALOGUE NO. 37 (D)
Louis-Édouard-Paul Fournier, 1857–1913
Helen and the Elders (The Triumph of Helen)
Oil on canvas, 32.5 × 40.5 cm.
Oil Sketch *concours*, 1880 (Esq p 134)

CATALOGUE NO. 38 (D)
Jean-Baptiste Marty, 1857–?
Helen and the Elders
Oil on canvas, 32.5 × 40.5 cm.
Oil Sketch *concours*, 1880 (Esq p 135)

CATALOGUE NO. 39 (P)
Félix-Henry Auvray, 1800–1833
Hector Reproaches Paris
Oil on tracing paper mounted on canvas, 32.5 × 40.5 cm.
Oil Sketch *concours*, 1823 (Esq p 14)
Countersigned *H. Lemot*, upper right.

EXHIBITION: Paris, 1986: *Les Concours d'esquisses peintes*, no. 14, and United States, 1987

CATALOGUE NO. 40 (P)
Antoine-Louis Barye, 1796–1875
Hector Reproaches Paris
Plaster, 33.5 × 45 cm.
Sculpture Sketch *concours*, 1823 (MU 4421)

EXHIBITION: Paris, 1956–57: *Barye*, no. 102

CATALOGUE NO. 41 (D)
Jean-Baptiste Carpeaux, 1827–1875
Hector Holding His Son Astyanax in His Arms
Plaster, 131 × 51 × 48 cm.
Prix de Rome in Sculpture, 1854 (PRS 42)

CATALOGUE NO. 42 (D)
Jacques-Louis David, 1748–1825
Andromache Mourning Hector
Oil on canvas, 275 × 203 cm.
Royal Academy Reception Piece, 1783 (MRA 129 bis)
David-Chassagnolle Legacy, 1893

EXHIBITIONS: Paris: *Salon* of 1783, no. 162; Paris, 1826: *Explication des ouvrages . . .*, no. 39; Rome, 1904: *Exposition retrospective*; Paris, 1913: *David et ses élèves*, no. 18; Paris, 1934: *David, Ingres, Géricault . . .*, no. 3; Paris, 1936: *Gros, ses amis, ses élèves*, no. 203; Paris, 1948: *David*, no. 11; Hamburg-Munich, 1952–53: *Meisterwerke*, no. 12; Munich, 1962: *De David à Cézanne*, no. 70; Paris, 1965: *L'Art français au XVIIIe siècle*, no. 109; Paris, 1973: *La Mort de Germanicus*, no. 94; Paris, 1974–75: *De David à Delacroix . . .*, no. 31, pl. 25, p. 69; Rome, 1981–82: *David e Roma*, no. 32; Cologne-Zurich-Lyon, 1987–88: *Triomphe et mort du héros*, no. 20; Paris, 1989–90: *Jacques-Louis David*, no. 56; Paris, 1992: *Accrochage d'été*

CATALOGUE NO. 43 (P)
François Rude, 1784–1855
Attention Mingled with Fear (Andromache)
Plaster, 66.5 × 39.5 × 31 cm.
Expressive Head *concours*, 1812 (TES 5)

EXHIBITIONS: Paris, 1889: *Exposition universelle*; Paris, 1934: *David, Ingres, Géricault . . .*, no. 199; Dijon, 1955: *François Rude*, no. 7; Paris, 1986: *La Sculpture française au XIXe siècle*, no. 5, p. 46; Paris, 1999: *Duchenne de Boulogne*, p. 250

CATALOGUE NO. 44 (P)
Pierre II Legros, 1666–1719
Combat of Athletes or Gladiators (or *Combat of Hercules and Antaeus*)
Marble, 80 × 50 cm.
Musée des Monuments français (WB 285)

CATALOGUE NO. 45 (D)
Jacques Perrin, 1847–1925
Ulysses Throwing the Discus
Plaster, 36 × 20.5 × 21 cm.
Sculpture Sketch *concours*, 1871, second-place medal (MU 4520)

PHILOCTETES

CATALOGUE NO. 46 (P)
Pierre-François-Grégoire Giraud, 1783–1836
The Wounded Philoctetes on the Island of Lemnos
Plaster, 96 × 37 × 43 cm.
Prix de Rome in Sculpture, 1806 (PRS 3)

CATALOGUE NO. 47 (D)
Alfred-Édouard Lepère, 1827–1904
The Wounded Philoctetes on the Island of Lemnos Surrenders to His Sorrows
Plaster, 103 × 85 × 53 cm.
Prix de Rome in Sculpture, 1852 (PRS 41)

CATALOGUE NO. 48 (P)
Joseph-Marius Ramus, 1805–1886
Anger Mingled with Contempt (Philoctetes Faces Ulysses)
Plaster, 77.5 × 51 × 34 cm.
Expressive Head *concours*, 1829 (TES 14)

EXHIBITIONS: Paris, 1889: *Exposition universelle*; Paris, 1986: *La Sculpture française au XIXe siècle*, no. 6, p. 47; Paris, 1999: *Duchenne de Boulogne*, p. 250.

CATALOGUE NO. 49 (D)
Jean-Jacques (James) Pradier, 1790–1852
Neoptolemus Prevents Philoctetes from Loosing His Arrows Against Ulysses
Plaster (cast, 1901), 128 × 154 × 30 cm.
Prix de Rome in Sculpture, 1813 (MU 10283); donation: Conseil de la Ville de Genève, 1901

CATALOGUE NO. 50 (D)
Gabriel-Jules Thomas, 1824–1905
Philoctetes Leaves for the Siege of Troy
Plaster, 127 × 57 × 62 cm.
Prix de Rome in Sculpture, 1848 (PRS 36)

THE FALL OF TROY

CATALOGUE NO. 51 (P)
Charles-Alphonse-Achille Gumery, 1827–1871
Achilles Wounded in the Heel by Paris
Plaster, 128 × 65 × 60 cm.
Prix de Rome in Sculpture, 1850 (PRS 38)

CATALOGUE NO. 52 (D)
Pierre-Jules Cavelier, 1814–1894
Diomedes Carrying Off the Palladium
Plaster, 119 × 40 × 54 cm.
Prix de Rome in Sculpture, 1842 (PRS 30)

CATALOGUE NO. 53 (P)
Antoine-Jean-Baptiste Thomas (1791–1834)
Oenone Refuses to Aid the Wounded Paris
Oil on canvas, 114 × 146 cm.
Prix de Rome in Painting, 1816 (PRP 54)

EXHIBITIONS: United States, 1984–85: *The Grand Prix de Rome*, no. 53; Paris, 1986: *Les Concours des Prix de Rome*, no. 63; Tokyo, 1989: *The Prix de Rome*, no. 38; Paris, 1991–92: *Géricault*, no. 70

CATALOGUE NO. 54 (D)
Guillaume Duchenne de Boulogne, 1806–1875
Laocoön, Contraction of the Superciliary, 1856–57
Corrected plaster cast (on pedestal), 65.5 × 39.5 × 32.5 cm.
Seal on pedestal: Maison de l'empereur, Musées impériaux (MU 11913); donation: Mme Duchenne de Boulogne in 1876

EXHIBITION: Paris, 1999: *Duchenne de Boulogne*, p. 250

BIBLIOGRAPHY: Guillaume Duchenne de Boulogne, *Méchanisme de la physionomie humaine ou analyse électro-physiologique de l'expression des passions* (Paris, 1876), fig. 71

CATALOGUE NO. 55 (P)
Pierre-Jean David, known as David d'Angers, 1788–1856
Pain (Variation on the "Laocoön")
Plaster, 67.7 × 30.5 × 26 cm.
Expressive Head *concours*, 1811 (TES 4)

EXHIBITIONS: Paris, 1889: *Exposition universelle*; Paris, 1934: *David, Ingres, Géricault . . .*, no. 194; Paris, 1966: *David d'Angers*, no. 5; Paris, 1999: *Duchenne de Boulogne*, p. 250

CATALOGUE NO. 56 (P)
Eugène-Ernest Hillemacher, 1818–1887
Hecuba Discovering the Corpse of Her Son Polydorus
Oil on canvas, 32.5 × 40.5 cm.
Oil Sketch *concours*, 1840 (Esq p 43)

EXHIBITIONS: Paris, 1889: *Exposition universelle*; Paris, 1986: *Les Concours d'esquisses peintes*, no. 44, and United States, 1987

CATALOGUE NO. 57 (D)
Jean-Albert Cresswell, 1864–1936
Hecuba Despairs at the Sight of Her Murdered Son
Oil on canvas, 38.5 × 46 cm.
Oil Sketch *concours*, 1885 (Esq p 159)

CATALOGUE NO. 58 (D)
Emmanuel-Pierre-Louis Croizé, 1859–?
Hecuba Despairs at the Sight of Her Murdered Son
Oil on canvas, 46 × 38.5 cm.
Oil Sketch *concours*, 1885 (Esq p 160)

CATALOGUE NO. 59 (D)
André-Victor-Édouard Devambez, 1867–1943
Hecuba Despairs at the Sight of Her Murdered Son
Oil on canvas, 46 × 38.5 cm.
Oil Sketch *concours*, 1885 (Esq p 161)

CATALOGUE NO. 60 (P)
Jean-Georges Vibert, 1840–1902
The Death of Priam
Oil on canvas, 32.5 × 40.5 cm.
Oil Sketch *concours*, 1861 (Esq p 85)

EXHIBITION: Paris, 1986: *Les Concours d'esquisses peintes*, no. 81, and United States, 1987

CATALOGUE NO. 61 (D)
Jules-Joseph Lefebvre, 1834–1912
The Death of Priam
Oil on canvas, 114 × 146 cm.
Prix de Rome in Painting, 1861 (PRP 111)

EXHIBITIONS: Paris, 1986: *Les Concours des Prix de Rome*, no. 148; Tokyo, 1989: *Les Prix de Rome*, no. 57

CATALOGUE NO. 62 (D)
Victor-Alfred Latapie, 1823–?
The Abduction of Polxyena
Oil on canvas, 33 × 41 cm.
Painted Sketch *concours*, 1846

EXHIBITION: Paris, 1986: *Les Concours d'esquisses peintes*, no. 55, and United States, 1987

CATALOGUE NO. 63 (D)
Jules-Casimir Wielhorsky, 1875–?
Menelaus Forces Andromache to Quit the Sanctuary
Oil on canvas, 38 × 46.5 cm.
Oil Sketch *concours*, 1896 (Esq p 218)

CATALOGUE NO. 64 (D)
Jules-Félix Coutan, 1848–1939
Ajax, Defying the Gods, Is Struck by Lightning
Plaster, 128 × 67 × 67 cm.
Prix de Rome in Sculpture, 1872 (PRS 61)

THE *ORESTEIA*

CATALOGUE NO. 65 (P)
Henry-Auguste-Calixte-César Serrur, 1794–1865
Orestes and Pylades Desire Helen's Destruction
Oil on tracing paper mounted on canvas, 32.5 × 40.5 cm.
Oil Sketch *concours*, 1820 (Esq p. 8)

EXHIBITION: Paris, 1986: *Les Concours d'esquisses peintes*, no. 8, and United States, 1987

CATALOGUE NO. 66 (D)
Henri Naudé, 1859–?
Orestes Seeks Refuge at the Statue of Apollo
Wax, diam. 50 cm.
Prix de Rome for Engraving on Medallions and Semiprecious Stones, 1884 (PRGM 27)

CATALOGUE NO. 67 (D)
Raymond Barthélemy, 1833–1902
Orestes Seeks Refuge at the Altar of Minerva
Plaster, 132 × 107 × 52 cm.
Prix de Rome in Sculpture, 1860 (PRS 49)

THE VOYAGES OF ULYSSES

CATALOGUE NO. 68 (D)
Jean-François Auburtin, 1866–1930
The Departure of Ulysses and Penelope for Ithaca
Oil on canvas, 36.5 × 43 cm.
Oil Sketch *concours*, Prix Fortin d'Ivry, 1892 (Esq p 200)

CATALOGUE NO. 69 (P)
Théophile Caudron, 1805–1848
Ulysses Feigns Madness
Plaster, 35 × 47 cm.
Sculpture Sketch *concours*, 1830 (MU 4436)

CATALOGUE NO. 70 (P)
Jean-Nicolas-Alphonse Isambert, 1818–?
The Departure of Ulysses
Oil on canvas, 32 × 40.5 cm.
Oil Sketch *concours*, 1846 (Esq p 53)

EXHIBITION: Paris, 1986: *Les Concours d'esquisses peintes*, no. 54, and United States, 1987

CATALOGUE NO. 71 (D)
Gustave-Auguste Corlin, 1875–1924
Ulysses and the Shade of His Mother
Oil on canvas, 46 × 38.5 cm.
Oil Sketch *concours*, Prix Fortin d'Ivry, 1901 (Esq p 236)

CATALOGUE NO. 72 (P)
Paul Flandrin, 1811–1902
Ulysses and Nausicaa
Oil on canvas, 38.5 × 46 cm.
Historical Landscape Oil Sketch *concours*, 1832 (Esq p ph 12)

EXHIBITIONS: Paris-Lyon, 1984–85: *Hippolyte, Auguste et Paul Flandrin . . .*, no. 160; Paris, 1986: *Les Concours d'esquisses peintes*, no. 103, and United States, 1987

CATALOGUE NO. 73 (D)
Théodore-François-Alexis Ledieu, 1806–?
Ulysses and Nausicaa
Oil on canvas, 37.5 × 45.5 cm.
Historical Landscape Oil Sketch *concours*, 1832 (Esq p ph 13)

EXHIBITION: Paris, 1986: *Les Concours d'esquisses peintes*, no. 104, and United States, 1987

CATALOGUE NO. 74 (P)
Romain-Étienne-Gabriel Prieur, 1806–1879
Ulysses and Nausicaa
Oil on canvas, 114 × 146 cm.
Prix de Rome in Historical Landscape, 1833 (PRP 76)

EXHIBITIONS: United States, 1984–85: *The Grand Prix de Rome*, no. 111; Paris, 1986: *Les Concours des Prix de Rome*, no. 155; Tokyo, 1989: *The Prix de Rome*, no. 60

CATALOGUE NO. 75 (D)
Achille Benouville, 1815–1891
Ulysses and Nausicaa
Oil on canvas, 114 × 146 cm.
Prix de Rome in Historical Landscape, 1845 (PRP 92)

EXHIBITIONS: Paris, 1934: *David, Ingres, Géricault . . .*, no. 1; United States, 1984–85: *The Grand Prix de Rome*, no. 114; Paris, 1986: *Les Concours des Prix de Rome*, no. 160; Tokyo, 1989: *The Prix de Rome*, no. 61

CATALOGUE NO. 76 (D)
Louis-Augustin Baralis, 1862–?
Ulysses in the Palace of Alcinous
Plaster, 79 × 61 cm.
Sculpture Sketch Prize ("Prix Lemaire"), 1888 (MU 7875)

ULYSSES IN ITHACA

CATALOGUE NO. 77 (D)
Henri-Lucien Doucet, 1856–1895
The Recognition of Ulysses and Telemachus
Oil on canvas, 145 × 113 cm.
Prix de Rome in Painting, 1880 (PRP 131)

EXHIBITION: Rome, 1904: *Exposition rétrospective . . .*

CATALOGUE NO. 78 (D)
Étienne-Jules Ramey, 1796–1852
Ulysses Recognized by His Dog
Plaster, 109 × 44 × 39 cm.
Prix de Rome in Sculpture, 1815 (PRS 5)

CATALOGUE NO. 79A (P)
Pierre-Amédée Durand (1789–1873)
Ulysses Recognized by His Dog, 1810
Plaster, 113 × 69 cm.
Prix de Rome in Engraving on Metal and Semiprecious Stone, 1810 (PRGM 3)

CATALOGUE NO. 79B (P)
After Pierre-Amédée Durand (1789–1873)
Ulysses Recognized by His Dog
Modern steel casting, diam. 8 cm.

CATALOGUE NO. 80 (P)
Clément Belle, 1722–1806
Ulysses Recognized by His Wet Nurse Eurycleia
Oil on canvas, 195 × 256 cm.
Academy Reception Piece, 1761 (MRA 121); Louvre Inventory: 2495; deposited by the Musée du Louvre with the École des beaux-arts

CATALOGUE NO. 81 (P)
Émile Signol, 1804–1892
Ulysses Recognized by Eurycleia
Oil on tracing paper mounted on canvas, 32 × 41 cm.
Oil Sketch *concours*, 1826 (Esq p 20)

EXHIBITION: Paris, 1986: *Les Concours d'esquisses peintes*, no. 20, and United States, 1987.

CATALOGUE NO. 82 (D)
Louis-Vincent-Léon Pallière, 1787–1820
Ulysses and Telemachus Massacre Penelope's Suitors
Oil on canvas, 110 × 140 cm.
Prix de Rome in Painting, 1812 (PRP 50)

EXHIBITIONS: United States, 1984–85: *The Grand Prix de Rome*, no. 49; Paris, 1986: *Les Concours des Prix de Rome*, no. 55

CATALOGUE NO. 83 (D)
Henri-Achille Zo, 1873–1933
Ulysses and Laertes
Oil on canvas, 32.5 × 40.5 cm.
Oil Sketch *concours*, 1896 (Esq p 216)

THE ADVENTURES OF TELEMACHUS

CATALOGUE NO. 84 (P)
Félix-Auguste Clément, 1826–1888
Calypso Invites Telemachus and Mentor to Rest in a Cave
Oil on canvas, 46 × 38 cm.
Historical Landscape Oil Sketch *concours*, 1851 (Esq p ph 29); deposited with the Musée de Valence in July 1993

EXHIBITION: Paris, 1986: *Les Concours d'esquisses peintes*, no. 120, and United States, 1987.

CATALOGUE NO. 85 (P)
Eugène-Modeste-Edmond Lepoitevin, 1806–1870
Telemachus Crushing the Lion to Death
Oil on canvas, 38 × 46 cm.
Historical Landscape Oil Sketch *concours*, 1829 (Esq p ph 8)

EXHIBITION: Paris, 1986: *Les Concours d'esquisses peintes*, no. 98, and United States, 1987

CATALOGUE NO. 86 (P)
Louis-Hector Leroux, 1829–1900
Philocles on Samos
Oil on canvas, 38 × 46 cm.
Historical Landscape Oil Sketch *concours*, 1857 (Esq p ph 37)

EXHIBITION: Paris, 1986: *Les Concours d'esquisses peintes*, no. 128, and United States, 1987; Bar-le-Duc, Verdun, 1988: *Louis-Hector Leroux*, no. 8

THE *AENEID*: FROM HOMER TO VIRGIL

CATALOGUE NO. 87 (P)
Henri-Frédéric Schopin (or Chopin), 1804–1890
Hector Appears to Aeneas During the Capture of Troy
Oil on tracing paper mounted on canvas, 32.5 × 40.5 cm.
Oil Sketch *concours*, 1829 (Esq p 25).
Countersigned lower right: *Hersent*

EXHIBITION: Paris, 1986: *Les Concours d'esquisses peintes*, no. 25, and United States, 1987

CATALOGUE NO. 88 (D)
Merry-Joseph Blondel, 1781–1853
Aeneas Carrying His Father Anchises
Oil on canvas, 144 × 113 cm.
Prix de Rome in Painting, 1803 (PRP 42); bought and donated to the school by Adolphe Thiers, minister, in 1834

EXHIBITIONS: United States, 1984–85: *The Grand Prix de Rome*, no. 41; Paris, 1986: *Les Concours des Prix de Rome*, no. 45; Tokyo, 1989: *The Prix de Rome*, no. 29

CATALOGUE NO. 89 (D)
Paul-Célestin-Louis Nanteuil (called Leboeuf-Nanteuil), 1837–1901
Creusa Seeks to Retain Aeneas
Oil on canvas, 40.5 × 32.5 cm.
Oil Sketch *concours*, 1862 (Esq p 92)

EXHIBITION: Paris, 1986: *Les Concours d'esquisses peintes*, no. 86, and United States, 1987

CATALOGUE NO. 90 (P)
Jean-Adrien Guignet, 1816–1854
Dido and Aeneas Take Refuge in a Cave During a Storm
Oil on canvas, 38 × 46 cm.
Historical Landscape Oil Sketch *concours*, 1838 (Esq p ph 20)

EXHIBITION: Paris, 1986: *Les Concours d'esquisses peintes*, no. 111, and United States, 1987

CATALOGUE NO. 91 (P)
Henri-Frédéric Schopin (or Chopin), 1804–1890
Aeneas in the Underworld
Oil on tracing paper mounted on canvas, 32 × 40 cm.
Oil Sketch *concours*, 1828 (Esq p 23).
Countersigned lower right: *Hersent*

EXHIBITION: Paris, 1986: *Les Concours d'esquisses peintes*, no. 23, and United States, 1987

CATALOGUE NO. 92 (P)
Jean-Charles-Nicaise Perrin, 1754–1831
Aeneas Cured of His Wounds
Oil on canvas, 197 × 163 cm.
Academy Reception Piece, 1787 (MRA 129); Louvre Inventory: 7168; deposited by the Musée du Louvre with the École des beaux-arts, 1872

EXHIBITIONS: Paris, 1787: *Salon*, no. 166; Washington, D.C., 1976: *The Eye of Thomas Jefferson*, no. 262; Montargis, 1989: *Un peintre sous la Révolution*, no. 25; Tours-Toulouse, 2000: *Les Peintres du roi*, no. 56

CATALOGUE NO. 93 (P)
Henry-Auguste-Calixte-César Serrur, 1794–1865
Nisus Attempts to Save Euryalus
Oil on tracing paper mounted on canvas, 32 × 40.5 cm.
Oil Sketch *concours*, 1820 (Esq p 9).
Countersigned upper right: *Gros Pr.*

EXHIBITION: Paris, 1986: *Les Concours d'esquisses peintes*, no. 9, and United States, 1987

CATALOGUE NO. 94 (D)
Jean-Alexandre-Joseph Falguière, 1831–1900
The Wounded Mezentius Is Saved by the Daring of His Son Lausus
Plaster, 127 × 155.5 cm.
Prix de Rome in Sculpture, 1859 (PRS 47)

CATALOGUE NO. 95 (D)
Charles-Louis Bazin, 1802–1859
The Wounded Mezentius Vows to Avenge His Son Lausus
Oil on tracing paper mounted on canvas, 32.5 × 40.5 cm.
Oil Sketch *concours*, Oct. 1821 (Esq p 11)

EXHIBITION: Paris, 1986: *Les Concours d'esquisses peintes*, no. 11, and United States, 1987

PREVIOUS AND PARALLEL EPIC CYCLES

CATALOGUE NO. 96 (D)
André Giroux, 1801–1879
The Calydonian Boar Hunt
Oil on canvas, 114 × 146 cm.
Prix de Rome in Historical Landscape, 1825 (PRP 66)

EXHIBITIONS: United States, 1984–85: *The Grand Prix de Rome*, no. 109; Paris, 1986: *Les Concours des Prix de Rome*, no. 153; Paris, 1997–98: *Histoire de la forêt*, pp. 140 and 153.

CATALOGUE NO. 97 (P)
Émile Signol, 1804–1892
Meleager Taking Up His Arms
Oil on canvas, 115 × 146.5 cm.
Prix de Rome in Painting, 1830 (PRP 72)

EXHIBITIONS: United States, 1984–85: *The Grand Prix de Rome*, no. 68; Paris, 1986: *Les Concours des Prix de Rome*, no. 83; Tokyo, 1989: *The Prix de Rome*, no. 42

CATALOGUE NO. 98 (P)
Félix-Henry Auvray, 1800–1833
Meleager Taking Up His Arms
Oil on tracing paper mounted on canvas, 32.5 × 40.5 cm.
Oil Sketch *concours*, 1823 (Esq p 15). Countersigned, lower left: *Gros*

EXHIBITION: Paris, 1986: *Les Concours d'esquisses peintes*, no. 15, and United States, 1987

CATALOGUE NO. 99 (P)
Pierre-Charles Jombert, ca. 1748/49–1825?
The Children of Niobe Killed by Apollo and Diana
Oil on canvas, 143 × 112 cm.
Prix de Peinture de l'Académie royale, 1772 (PRP 17)

HISTORICAL NOTE: This work was formerly attributed to Anicet-Charles-Gabriel Lemonnier (1773–1824). Lemonnier's reception piece, with which this painting was long identified, hangs in the Musée des Beaux-Arts in Rouen.

CATALOGUE NO. 100 (P)
Pierre Monier, 1641–1703
The Conquest of the Golden Fleece
Oil on canvas, 133.7 × 2:8.5 cm.
Prix de Peinture de l'Académie royale, 1663 (MU 2606)

HISTORICAL NOTE: This painting was formerly attributed to Thomas Blanchet (1614 [1617?]–1689). The prize-winning Monier painting and Blanchet's reception piece—*Cadmus After the Dragon's Defeat*—were long confused. Blanchet's painting is in the Musee de Semur-en-Auxois.

EXHIBITION: Manderen, Moselle, château de Malbrouck, 1998: *La Toison d'or*, no. 34, p. 169

CATALOGUE NO. 101 (P)
François Lemoine, 1688–1737
Hercules Killing Cacus
Oil on canvas, 131 × 170 cm.
Royal Academy Reception Piece, 1718 (MRA 111); Louvre Inventory 6714; deposited by the Musée du Louvre with the École de beaux-arts, 1872

EXHIBITIONS: Paris, 1965: *L'Art français au XVIIIe siècle*, no. 115; Tours-Toulouse, 2000: *Les Peintres du roi*, no. 25

CATALOGUE NO. 102 (F)
Anonymous eighteenth-century artist
Seated Hercules
Terracotta, 36.8 × 17.5 × 19 cm.
His de la Salle Donation to the École des beaux arts, 1884 (MU 1248)

EXHIBITIONS: Paris, 1933: *L'Art français des XVIIe et XVIIIe siècles . . .*, no. 203; Paris, 1934: *Les Artistes français en Italie . . .*, no. 781; Paris, 1937: *Chefs-d'oeuvre de l'art français*, no. 1072; Paris, 1947–48: *Beautés de la Provence*, no. 244; Paris, 1961: *L'Art français au XVIIe siècle . . .*, no. 133; Marseilles, 1994–95: *Pierre Puget*, no. 30

CATALOGUE NO. 103 (P)
Nicolas-Guy Brenet, 1728–1792
The Young Theseus Discovers His Father's Arms
Oil on canvas, 132 × 145 cm.
Royal Academy Reception Piece, 1769 (MRA 125); Louvre inventory 2851; deposited by the Musée du Louvre with the École des beaux-arts, 1872

EXHIBITIONS: Paris, 1769: *Salon*, no. 122; Paris, 1965: *L'Art français au XVIIIe siècle*, no. 107; Paris, 1984–85: *Diderot et l'art . . .*, no. 38; Lyon, 1998–99: *La Fascination de l'antique . . .*

CATALOGUE NO. 104 (D)
Hippolyte Flandrin, 1809–1864
Theseus Recognized by His Father
Oil on canvas, 115 × 146 cm.
Prix de Rome in Painting, 1832 (PRP 74)

EXHIBITIONS: Paris, 1865: *Exposition des oeuvres d'Hippolyte Flandrin . . .*, no. 2; Rome, 1904: *Exposition rétrospective . . .*; Paris-Lyon, 1984–85: *Hippolyte, Auguste et Paul Flandrin . . .*, no. 3; Paris, 1986: *Les Concours des Prix de Rome*, no. 85; Tokyo, 1989: *The Prix de Rome*, no. 43; Tokyo, 1996: *Naissance de l'Impressionisme*, no. 1, p. 33; Glasgow, 1997: *Impressionism*; Montauban-Besançon, 1999–2000: *Les Élèves d'Ingres*

CATALOGUE NO. 105 (D)
Léon Cogniet, 1794–1880
Castor and Pollux Freeing Helen
Oil on canvas, 146 × 113 cm.
Prix de Rome in Painting, 1817 (PRP 55)

EXHIBITIONS: United States, 1984–85: *The Grand Prix de Rome*, no. 54; Paris, 1986: *Les Concours des Prix de Rome*, no. 64; Tokyo, 1989: *The Prix de Rome*, no. 39; Orléans, 1990: *Léon Cogniet . . .* , no. 22; Manderen, Moselle, château de Malbrouck, 1998: *La Toison d'or*, no. 11, p. 154; Stendal, 1999–2000: *Wiedergeburt griechischer Götter und Helden . . .*

CATALOGUE NO. 106 (P)
Jean-Charles Frontier, 1701–1763
Vulcan Enchaining Prometheus
Oil on canvas, 201.8 × 145 cm.
Royal Academy Reception Piece, 1744 (MRA 117); Louvre Inventory 4641; deposited by the Musée du Louvre with the École des Beaux-Arts, 1872

CATALOGUE NO. 107 (D)
Raymond-Jacques Brechenmacher, 1897–?
Prometheus
Etching and drypoint, 44.2 × 31.7 cm.
Prix de Rome in Engraving, 1922 (PRG 99)

HOMER'S LAUGHTER

CATALOGUE NO. 108 (D)
Gustave Boulanger, 1824–1888
Ulysses Recognized by Eurycleia
Oil on canvas, 147 × 114 cm.
Prix de Rome in Painting, 1849 (PRP 94)

EXHIBITIONS: Rome, 1904: *Exposition rétrospective . . .* ; United States, 1984–85: *The Grand Prix de Rome*, no. 86; Paris, 1986: *Les Concours des Prix de Rome*, no. 112; Tokyo, 1989: *The Prix de Rome*, no. 50; Nantes-Paris-Plaisance, 1995–96: *Les Années romantiques*, no. 20, pl. 175

CATALOGUE NO. 109 (D)
Honoré Daumier, 1808–1879
Vulcan's Net, from *Ancient History*, 1842, no. 34
Lithograph, 32.5 × 27 cm. Printer: Aubert
Purchased by the École des beaux-arts, 2001 (PC 79905–34)

The villainous locksmith, all too aware
That Mars of his wife had too large a share,
Cast his pitiless toils o'er the sinful pair
And netted them chatting in their grassy lair.

—A CELIBATE D.M.F.P.

CATALOGUE NO. 110 (D)
Honoré Daumier, 1808–1879
Mars and Venus, from *Ancient History*, 1842, no. 38
Lithograph, 34 × 26.2 cm. Printer: Aubert
Wasset Legacy, 1896 (Est 4828, PC 79905–38)

When the gods saw Hephaestus had caught 'er
In his chain-mail erotic trap,
They roared their Homeric laughter
—Still roared, alas, without quarter
At every poor cuckolded chap.

—QUATRAIN WELL KNOWN TO M. ANCELOT

CATALOGUE NO. 111 (D)
Honoré Daumier, 1808–1879
The Baptism of Achilles, from *Ancient History*, 1842, no. 22
Lithograph, 34.4 × 26.9 cm. Printer: Aubert
Purchased by the École des beaux-arts, 2001 (PC 79905–22)

One tempers the steel of an arm.
Thetis wanted to temper her bairn.
So she dipped the sweet babe in the Styx.
He did have a temper. The blessing was mixed.

—ON THE INFLUENCE OF BATHING, POEM BY M. VIGIER

CATALOGUE NO. 112 (D)
Honoré Daumier, 1808–1879
The Education of Achilles, from *Ancient History*, 1842, no. 9
Lithograph, 34 × 27 cm. Printer: Aubert
Purchased by the École des beaux-arts, 2001 (PC 79905–9)

Chiron was strict; he drove Achilles wild
(Not that Achilles' temper was mild).
Though we ourselves were not taught by centaurs,
How beastly they were—and how stupid!—our mentors.

—*ILIAD*. PHILOSOPHICAL TRANSLATION BY M. PATIN

CATALOGUE NO. 113 (D)
Honoré Daumier, 1808–1879
The Rape of Helen, from *Ancient History*, 1842, no. 13
Lithograph, 34.4 × 26.9 cm. Printer: Aubert
Purchased by the École des beaux-arts, 2001 (PC 79905–13)

Paris was all worn out by desire
Fit for nothing but smoking cigars
Helen perceived it, and did not inquire
But just carried him off in her arms.

—*AENEID*, TRAVESTIED BY M. PATIN

CATALOGUE NO. 114 (D)
Honoré Daumier, 1808–1879
The Wrath of Agamemnon, from *Ancient History*, 1842, no. 8
Lithograph, 34.2 × 27 cm. Printer: Aubert
Acquired by the École des beaux-arts, 2001 (PC 79905–8)

In vain Agamemnon had unleashed in dudgeon
All kinds of improper speech
Achilles heedless sat on the beach
Wailing for Briseis and fishing for gudgeon.

CATALOGUE NO. 115 (D)
Honoré Daumier, 1808–1879
Achilles in His Tent, from *Ancient History*, 1842, no. 3
Lithograph, 34.2 × 27.1 cm. Printer: Aubert
Purchased by the École des beaux-arts, 2001 (PC 79905–3)

"This wonderful low relief was discovered in the ruins of the former Boule Rouge (faubourg Montmartre) by the indefatigable traveler Mr. Texier. According to Mr. Ingres, only Phidias could have made it."

Tearful, Achilles remembered the charms
Of Briseis and gave himself up to despair.
Patroclus polished and polished his arms
But could not refurbish his martial flair.

—DISCREET TRANSLATION BY PRESIDENT P.

CATALOGUE NO. 116 (D)

Honoré Daumier, 1808–1879
Menelaus in Victory, from *Ancient History*, December 1841, no. 1
Lithograph, 34.4 × 26.7 cm. Printer: Aubert
Purchased by the École des beaux-arts, 2001 (PC 79905–1)

On the smoking ramparts of the conquered city,
The god-like Menelaus at last took pity,
Ravished blonde Helen and dragged her back to Sparta:
To virtue Queen Helen was ever a martyr.

—*ILIAD*, THE BARESTE TRANSLATION

CATALOGUE NO. 117 (D)

Honoré Daumier, 1808–1879
Ulysses Introduced to Nausicaa, from *Ancient History*, 1842, no. 4
Lithograph, 34.5 × 26.9 cm. Printer: Aubert
Purchased by the École des beaux-arts, 2001 (PC 79905–4)

Seeing our hero all muddy and sordid,
Others fled. Only Nausicaa applauded.
She looks up from her soaping to say:
"Noble stranger, what brings you this way?"

—UNPUBLISHED TRANSLATION BY M. CASIMIR DELAVIGNE

CATALOGUE NO. 118 (D)

Honoré Daumier, 1808–1879
Penelope's Nights, from *Ancient History*, 1842, no. 6
Lithograph, 34.4 × 26.9 cm. Printer: Aubert
Purchased by the École des beaux-arts, 2001 (PC 79905–6)

Her husband's profile like an *objet d'art*
To her uxorious dreams shone like a star
Her brain and finger must both have been deft
To make such ingenious use of her weft.

—INDISCREET TRANSLATION BY M. VILLEMAIN

CATALOGUE NO. 119 (D)

Honoré Daumier, 1808–1879
Ulysses' Return, from *Ancient History*, 1842, no. 7
Lithograph, 34.2 × 26.9 cm. Printer: Aubert
Purchased by the École des beaux-arts, 2001 (PC 79905–7)

At the doors of the palace the faithful hound
Greeted his master with a sudden bound.
Sure his master's plan would prove a winner,
The hero's mutt aspires to *his* dog's dinner.

—*ODYSSEY*. LIGHT POEMS BY M. VATOUT

CATALOGUE NO. 120 (D)

Honoré Daumier, 1808–1879
Ulysses and Penelope, from *Ancient History*, 1842, no. 14
Lithograph, 34.4 × 26.9 cm. Printer: Aubert
Purchased by the École des beaux-arts, 2001 (PC 79905–14)

Chastely stretched out on the marital bed,
The noble pair are at last reunited.
Alas, his long absence no passion's ignited;
He snores, while she kisses the sleepyhead.

—HUMOROUS WORKS BY M. VATOUT

CATALOGUE NO. 121 (D)

Honoré Daumier, 1808–1879
Telemachus a Prey to Love, from *Ancient History*, 1842, no. 27.
Lithograph, 35 × 27.3 cm. Printer: Aubert
Purchased by the École des beaux-arts, 2001 (PC 79905–27)

The sun rose in the west;
In Mentor's despite,
He plundered for his mistress
the brightest and the best;
His cares she did requite;
And with his blooms the sorceress
Adorned her satin breast.

—CIGARETTE BY M. ALFRED DE MUSSET

CATALOGUE NO. 122 (D)

Honoré Daumier, 1808–1879
Telemachus and Mentor, from *Ancient History*, 1842, no. 29
Lithograph, 35.1 × 26. 8 cm. Printer: Aubert
Purchased by the École des beaux-arts, 2001 (PC 79905–29)

Mentor sees his languid ward
With love of Eucharis aflame,
Deems his ward is much to blame,
So chucks him in the sea.
They leave Calypso's seaboard:
His ward of love swims free!

—SOLITARY QUATRAIN BY M. DUPONCHEL

CATALOGUE NO. 123 (D)

Honoré Daumier, 1808–1879
Telemachus Restored to Virtue, from *Ancient History*, 1842, no. 32

Lithograph, 35.2 × 27.3 cm. Printer: Aubert
Purchased by the École des beaux-arts, 2001 (PC 79905–32)

His heart, too long to Eucharis a prey
O'erthrew his amorous servitude one day.
Then this young sprightly hero, wise but sad,
His joyful Mentor asked: "Let's look for Dad?"

—FÉNELON, BK. XII

CATALOGUE NO. 124 (D)
Honoré Daumier, 1808–1879
Calypso's Despair, from *Ancient History,* 1842, no. 40.
Lithograph, 35.2 × 27.2 cm. Printer: Aubert
Purchased by the École des beaux-arts, 2001 (PC 79909–40)

In vain she hopes she might forget
Th' ungrateful man she didn't get,
If she could have a change of scene . . .
Re-papering her grot in green?

—FÉNELON, VARIANT OF BK. XI

CATALOGUE NO. 125 (D)
Honoré Daumier, 1808–1879
Telemachus Questioned by the Elders, from *Ancient History,* 1842, no. 42.
Lithograph, 35.5 × 27.2 cm. Printer: Aubert
Purchased by the École des beaux-arts, 2001 (PC 79905–42)

Telemachus was really struck by these old fellers
And swore that he'd give up his bum-fluff whiskers
If only he could have the sun reverberate
So brightly from his own well-furnished pate.

—FÉNELON, BK. 24

CATALOGUE NO. 126 (D)
Honoré Daumier, 1808–1879
Dido and Aeneas, from *Ancient History,* 1842, no. 15
Lithograph, 34.4 × 27 cm. Printer: Aubert
Purchased by the École des beaux-arts, 2001 (PC 79905–15)

The skies were obscured by a tactful mist
And neither had a waterproof to hand.
Solution? In a grot—surely it was planned?—
She her Aeneas and he his Dido kissed.

—*AENEID,* CORRECTED BY M. VILLEMAIN

CATALOGUE NO. 127 (D)
Honoré Daumier, 1808–1879
Aeneas in the Underworld, from *Ancient History,* 1842, no. 17
Lithograph, 34.3 × 27 cm. Printer: Aubert
Purchased by the École des beaux-arts, 2001 (PC 79905–17)

O horrid! He sees the woman he adores
A dagger in her heart and garments gory.
Her charming gesture modesty ensures,
She sweetly says: "My dear, you're history."

—*AENEID,* TRANSLATED BY M. TROGNON

CATALOGUE NO. 128 (D)
Georges-Antoine Rochegrosse, 1859–1938
Le Bal des Quat'z'arts Descending the Champs-Elysées
Oil on canvas, 153 × 215 cm. (signed lower right: *Rochegrosse 04* [?])
Purchased by the École des beaux-arts, 1978 (MU 11706)

EXHIBITION: Paris, 1987: *La Carrière de l'architecte au XIX*[e] *siècle*, no. 57

CATALOGUE NO. 129 (D)
Anonymous (Claude-Marie Tourneur?), 1955
Invitation from the Molossoi
Lithograph, 14.5 × 38 cm
(PC 78826–5)

CATALOGUE NO. 130 (D)
Anonymous (several signatures), 1955
The Molossoi
Lithograph, 30.4 × 17.8 cm.
ΜΩΛΟΣΣΩΙ 4ZARTS 1955 [incorrect Greek spelling]

ON THE DETACHABLE COUPON: BRING YER APPETITE AND ZOOT . . . AND ON 1 JULY SEEYER AT THE PARC DES EXPOSITIONS. IF YOU'RE [FUCKED/]BUILT LIKE A [obscene drawing] Y'CN SLEEP OUT LIKE A MOLOSSOS
This invitation may not be sold. The committee cannot accept responsibility for the exhibition of the nude on a public highway.

EXHIBITION CATALOGUES

PARIS, Salon de 1755.

PARIS, Salon de 1769.

PARIS, Salon de 1783.

PARIS, Salon de 1787.

PARIS, 1800. Musée des Monuments français, Alexandre Lenoir, *Notice historique . . . du dépôt,* 5ème édition. Paris: an VIII (1800).

PARIS, 1826: *Explication des ouvrages de peinture exposés au profit des Grecs.* Paris: Galerie Lebrun, 1826.

PARIS, 1865: *Exposition des œuvres d'Hippolyte Flandrin à l'Ecole Impériale des Beaux-Arts.* Paris: Comité de l'association des artistes . . . , 1865.

PARIS, 1867: *Catalogue des tableaux, études peintes, dessins et croquis de J.-A.-D. Ingres . . . exposés dans les galeries du palais de l'École impériale des Beaux-Arts,* no. 53. 2 vols. Paris: École des beaux-arts, 1867.

Paris, 1889: Paris, *Exposition Universelle*, 1889.

Rome, 1904: *Exposition rétrospective à l'occasion de la visite de Monsieur le Président de la République*. Rome: Société romaine des beaux-arts, 1904.

Paris, 1913: *David et ses élèves*. Paris: Palais des beaux-arts, 1913.

Paris, 1933: *Art français des XVIIe et XVIIIe siècles: Exposition de dessins de maîtres, livres, pièces d'archives et sculptures faisant partie des collections de l'École*. Paris: École des beaux-arts, 1933.

Paris, 1934: *David, Ingres, Géricault et leur temps*. Exhibition of paintings, drawings, lithographs, and sculptures forming part of the collection of the École. Paris: École des beaux-arts, 1934.

Paris, 1934: *Les Artistes français en Italie de Poussin à Renoir*. Paris: Musée des arts décoratifs, 1934.

Paris, 1935: *Exposition des concours de Rome de 1934 et 1834 (sauf la sculpture) à l'occasion de l'exposition annuelle des travaux d'élèves*. Amiens: École des beaux-arts, 1935.

Paris, 1936: *Gros: ses amis, ses élèves*. Paris: Petit Palais, 1936.

Paris, 1937: *Chefs-d'œuvre de l'art français*. Paris: Palais national des arts, 1937.

Paris, 1947–48: *Beautés de la Provence*. Paris: Galerie Charpentier, 1947–48.

Paris, 1948: *David: exposition en l'honneur du deuxième centenaire de sa naissance*. Paris: Orangerie des Tuileries, 1948.

Hamburg-Munich, 1952–53: *Meisterwerke der französischen Malerei von Poussin bis Ingres*. Hamburg: Kunsthalle; Munich: Alte Pinakothek, 1952–53.

Toulouse-Montauban, 1955: *Ingres et ses maîtres, de Roques à David*. Toulouse: Musée des Augustins; Montauban, Musée Ingres, 1955.

Dijon, 1955: *François Rude, 1784–1855*. Dijon: Musée des beaux-arts, 1955.

Paris, 1956–57: *Barye: sculptures, peintures et aquarelles des collections publiques françaises*. Paris: Musée du Louvre, 1956–57.

Paris, 1961: *L'Art français au XVIIe siècle: exposition de dessins, tableaux, sculptures, gravures et documents d'archives conservés dans les collections de l'École*. Paris: École des beaux-arts, 1961.

Munich, 1964: *De David à Cézanne*, Munich: Pinakothek, 1964.

Paris, 1965: *L'Art français au XVIIIe siècle*. Paris: École des beaux-arts, 1965.

Paris, 1966 (1): *David d'Angers, 1788–1856*. Paris: Hôtel de la Monnaie, 1966.

Paris, 1966 (2): *Hommage à Jean-Louis Brian*. Paris: Institut de France, Académie des beaux-arts, 1966.

Paris, 1966 (3): Institut de France (evening of June 15, 1966).

Paris, 1967: *Évocation de l'Académie de France à Rome à l'occasion de son troisième centenaire*. Paris: Institut de France, 1967.

Montauban, 1967: *Ingres et son temps*, no. 8. Montauban: Musée Ingres, 1967.

Paris, 1967–68: *Ingres*. Paris: Petit Palais, 1967–68.

Lille, 1968: *Au temps du Roi Soleil: les peintres de Louis XIV, 1660–1715*. Lille: Palais des beaux-arts, 1968.

London, 1972: *The Age of Neoclassicism*. London: Royal Academy of Arts and Victoria and Albert Museum, 1972.

Paris, 1972–73: *L'École de Fontainebleau*. Paris: Grand Palais, 1972–73.

Paris, 1973: *"La Mort de Germanicus" de Poussin du Musée de Minneapolis*. Paris: Musée du Louvre, 1973.

Paris, 1974–75: *De David à Delacroix: la peinture française de 1774 à 1830*. Paris: Grand Palais, 1974–75.

Washington, D.C., 1976: *The Eye of Thomas Jefferson*. Washington, D.C., 1976.

Rome, 1977–78: *Nicolas Poussin, 1594–1665*. Rome: Académie de France, 1977–78.

Antibes, 1977: *Les Cinquante derniers premiers Grands Prix de Rome chez Picasso*. Antibes: Musée Picasso, 1977.

Montauban, 1980: *Ingres et sa postérité*. Montauban: Musée Ingres, 1980.

Los Angeles, 1980: *The Romantics to Rodin*. Los Angeles County Museum of Art, 1980.

Paris, 1980–81: *David d'Angers, maître d'Hébert*. Paris: Musée Hébert, 1980–81.

TOKYO-OSAKA, 1981: *Ingres*. Tokyo: National Museum of Western Art; Osaka: National Museum of Art, 1981.

ROME, 1981–82: *David e Roma*. Rome: Académie de France, 1981–82.

MALIBU, 1982–83: Prix de Rome loaned to the Getty Foundation at Malibu, Calif., from December 1982 to December 1983 (no catalogue).

PARIS-ATHENS-HOUSTON, 1982–83: *Paris-Rome-Athènes: le voyage en Grèce des architectes français aux XIXe et XXe siècles*. Paris: École des beaux-arts; Athens: École française d'Athènes; Houston, Tex.: Museum of Fine Arts, 1982–83.

PARIS, 1983–84: *Hommage à Raphaël: Raphaël et l'art français*. Paris: Galeries nationales du Grand Palais, 1983–84.

PARIS, 1984–85: *Diderot et l'art de Boucher à David: les Salons, 1759–1781*. Paris: Hôtel de la Monnaie, 1984–85.

PARIS-LYON, 1984–85: *Hippolyte, Auguste et Paul Flandrin: une fraternité picturale au XIXe siècle*. Paris: Musée du Luxembourg; Lyon, Musée des beaux-arts, 1984–85.

UNITED STATES, 1984–85: *The Grand Prix de Rome, 1797–1863*. National Academy of Design, New York, January–March 1984; The Virginia Museum of Fine Arts, Richmond, April–May 1984; Indianapolis Museum of Art, Indianapolis, Ind., July–August 1984; The Walters Art Gallery, Baltimore, Md., September–October 1984; Phoenix Art Museum, Phoenix, Ariz., November 1984–January 1985; The Society of the Four Arts, Palm Beach, Fla., February–March 1985; San Antonio Museum of Art, San Antonio, Tex., April–June 1985; New Orleans Museum of Art, New Orléans, La., July–September 1985.

NEMOURS, 1985: *Fontainebleau et l'estampe en France au XVIe siècle: iconographie et contradictions*. Nemours: Château-musée de Nemours, 1985.

PARIS, 1986 (1): Philippe Grunchec, *Les Concours d'esquisses peintes, 1816–1863*. 2 vols. Paris: École des beaux-arts, 1986.

PARIS, 1986 (2): *La Sculpture française au XIXe siècle*. Paris: Galeries nationales du Grand Palais, 1986.

PARIS, 1986 (3): *Les Concours des Prix de Rome, 1797–1863*. 2 vols. (vol. 1, 1986; vol. 2, 1989). Paris: École nationale supérieure des beaux-arts, 1986.

PARIS, 1987 (1): *La Carrière de l'architecte au XIXe siècle*. Paris: Musée d'Orsay, 1987.

PARIS, 1987 (2): *Le Siècle des dictionnaires*. Paris: Musée d'Orsay, 1987.

UNITED STATES, 1987: National Academy of Design, New York; Elvehjem Museum, Madison, Wis.; Denver Art Museum, Denver, Colo.; Lowe Art Museum, Coral Gables, Fla., 1987.

COLOGNE-ZURICH-LYON, 1987–88: *Triomphe et mort du Héros: la peinture d'histoire de Rubens à Manet*. Cologne: Wallraf-Richartz Museum; Zurich: Kunsthaus; Lyon: Musée des beaux-arts, 1987–88.

PARIS, 1988: *L'Oeil d'or: Claude Mellan, 1598–1688*. Paris: Bibliothèque nationale, 1988.

VERDUN–BAR-LE-DUC, 1988: *Louis-Hector Leroux*. Verdun and Bar-le-Duc, 1988.

MEAUX, 1988–89: *De Nicolò dell'Abbate à Nicolas Poussin: aux sources du classicisme, 1550–1650*. Meaux: Musée Bossuet, 1988–89.

LE MANS, 1989: *Vertu antique, vertu révolutionnaire*. Le Mans: Musée du Tessé, 1989.

MONTARGIS, 1989: *Un peintre sous la Révolution: Jean Charles-Nicaise Perrin (1754–1831)*. Montargis: Musée Girodet, 1989.

OKAYAMA-FUKUOKA, 1989: *Le Siècle de Louis XIV: la peinture française de Poussin à Watteau*. Okayama: Prefectural Museum; Fukuoka: Municipal Museum, 1989.

TOKYO, 1989: *The Prix de Rome in Painting*. Tokyo: Shoto Museum of Art, 1989.

PARIS-VERSAILLES, 1989–90: *David, 1748– 1825*. Paris: Musée du Louvre; Versailles: Musée national du Château, 1989–90.

ORLÉANS, 1990: *Léon Cogniet (1794–1880)*. Orléans: Musée des beaux-arts, 1990.

SAINT-CLOUD, 1991–92: *Henri Regnault (1843–1871)*. Saint-Cloud: Musée municipal, 1991–92.

PARIS, 1991–92: *Géricault*. Paris: Galeries nationales du Grand Palais, 1991–92.

PARIS–PHILADELPHIA–FORT WORTH, 1991–92: *Les Amours des dieux: la peinture mythologique de Watteau à David*. Paris:

Grand Palais; Philadelphia, Pa.: Philadelphia Museum of Art, 1992; Fort Worth, Tex.: Kimbell Art Museum, 1992.

PARIS, 1992: *Accrochage d'été des collections permanentes de l'École nationale supérieure des beaux-arts.* Paris: École des beaux-arts, 1992.

BOLOGNA, 1992–93: *Viaggio a Rossini.* Bologna: Museo Civico Archeologico, 1992–93.

MONTREAL-RENNES-MONTPELLIER, 1993: *Le Grand Siècle: la peinture française du XVIIe siècle dans les collections publiques françaises.* Montreal: Musée des beaux-arts; Rennes: Musée des beaux-arts; Montpellier: Musée Fabre, 1993.

MARSEILLE, 1994–95: *Pierre Puget: peintre, sculpteur, architecte (1620–1694).* Marseille: Centre de la Vieille Charité, Musée des beaux-arts, 1994–95.

MEXICO, 1994–95: *Gustave Moreau y su legada.* Mexico: Centro cultural arte contemporaneo, 1994–95.

NANTES-PARIS-PIACENZA, 1995–96: *Les Années romantiques, 1815–1850.* Nantes: Musée des beaux-arts; Paris: Galeries nationales du Grand Palais; Piacenza: Palazzo Gotico, 1995–96.

TOKYO, 1996: *Birth of Impressionism.* Tokyo: Tobu Museum, 1996.

GLASGOW, 1997: *The Birth of Impressionism, from Constable to Monet.* Glasgow: Glasgow Museums, 1997.

PARIS, 1997: *Prud'hon ou le rêve du bonheur.* Paris: Galeries nationales du Grand Palais, 1997.

TOULOUSE-SCEAUX, 1997: *François de Troy (1645–1730): dessins et peintures.* Toulouse: Musée Paul-Dupuy; Sceaux: Musée d'Ile de France, 1997.

PARIS, 1997–98: *Histoire de la forêt: la forêt française du XIIe au XXe siècle.* Paris: Centre historique des Archives nationales, Musée de l'Histoire de France, 1997–98.

MANDEREN, 1998: *La Toison d'or: un mythe européen.* Manderen: Château de Malbrouck, September 5–December 13, 1998.

CONDÉ-SUR-NOIREAU, 1998–99: *Autour de Georges Moteley (1865–1923).* Condé-sur-Noireau: Mairie, 1998–99.

LYON, 1998–99: *La Fascination de l'antique, 1700–1770: Rome découverte, Rome inventée.* Lyon: Musée de la civilisation gallo-romaine, 1998–99.

PARIS, 1999: *Duchenne de Boulogne, 1806–1875.* Paris: École des beaux-arts, 1999.

MEXICO, 1999–2000: *Arte de las academias: Francia y Mexico, siglos XVII–XIX.* Mexico: Antiguo Colegio de San Ildefonso (Museum), 1999–2000.

MONTAUBAN-BESANCON, 1999–2000: *Les Élèves d'Ingres.* Montauban: Musée Ingres, 1999; Besançon: Musée des beaux-arts et d'archéologie, 2000.

ROME, 1999–2000: *Villa Medici: Il sogno di un cardinale: collezioni e artisti di Ferdinando de' Medici.* Rome: Accademia di Francia a Roma, 1999–2000.

STENDAL, 1999–2000: *Wiedergeburt Griechischer Götter und Helden: Homer in der Kunst der Goethezeit.* Mainz: Verlag Philipp von Zabern, 1999.

TOURS-TOULOUSE, 2000: *Les Peintres du roi, 1648–1793.* Tours: Musée des beaux-arts, March 18–June 18, 2000; Toulouse: Musée des Augustins, June 30–October 2, 2000.

PARIS, 2000–2001: *D'après l'Antique.* Paris: Musée du Louvre, 2000–2001.

NEW YORK–PALM BEACH, 2002–3: *Against the Modern: Dagnan-Bouveret and the Transformation of the Academic Tradition.* New York: Dahesh Museum of Art at the National Academy of Design, September 10–December 7, 2002; Palm Beach, Fla.: Society of the Four Arts, January 3–February 9, 2003.

ROME–NEW YORK, 2003: *Maestà di Roma. D'Ingres à Degas: les artistes français à Rome.* Rome: Villa Médicis, March 7–June 29, 2003; New York: Dahesh Museum of Art, September 3–November 2, 2003.

NEW YORK, 2003: *French Artists in Rome: Ingres to Degas, 1803–1873.* New York: Dahesh Museum of Art, September 3–November 2, 2003.

Glossary of Works, Places, Events, and Persons, Real and Imaginary

Achaeans (or Dardanians) | Long established on the Greek peninsula, the Achaeans were conquered around 1200 B.C. by the Dorians (who were also Greek). Homer uses the term to refer to the Greeks as a whole.

Achilles | Son of Peleus, king of Phthia (in Thessaly), and Thetis. See "Achilles."

Acroterion | Element of Greek architecture serving as a pedestal for a statue at the apex or lower corners of a pediment; can also refer to the combination of pedestal and sculpture.

Aegina (or Agina) | Island located off the coast of Athens. On the pediment of the temple of Aphaia in Aegina were sculptures of the heroes of the first and second Trojan Wars (500–480 B.C.). These were "restored" by the Danish sculptor Thorvaldsen, only to be returned to their earlier state following the Second World War. They can be seen in the Glyptothek in Munich.

Aegisthus | Lover of Clytemnestra, who was the wife of Aegisthus's cousin Agamemnon. Having killed the returning Agamemnon, he was eventually killed by Orestes, the latter's son.

Aeneas | Trojan warrior, son of Aphrodite and Anchises. Homer announces that he will survive the fall of Troy. Founder of Rome in Virgil's *Aeneid*. See "The *Aeneid*."

Aeneid | Virgil's epic poem describing the adventures of Aeneas.

Aeschylus | [Gk. *Aischulos*; Latin name Aeschylus] (525/24–456 B.C.): Earliest of the Athenian tragedians, most notably author of the *Oresteia* trilogy (*Agamemnon, The Libation Bearers* [or *The Choephori*], *The Eumenides*). His *Prometheus Enchained* combines Homeric material with the myth recounted by Hesiod, creating a character who lives on in European thought as the Titan who fought for human liberty against the arbitrary rule of the gods.

Aethra | Mother of Theseus. See also Theseus.

Aetolia | Region of central Greece, north of the Gulf of Corinth. See also Calydon.

Agamemnon | Leader of the Greek coalition and king of Argos. Maladroit, he provokes the anger of Achilles and the hatred of his wife, Clytemnestra, who kills him upon his return from Troy.

Ajax | Son of Telamon, called the Greater Ajax. He is considered the best Greek warrior following the death of Achilles. When Ulysses obtains this title by means of trickery, Ajax, mad with rage, kills himself.

Ajax | Son of Oileus, called the Lesser Ajax. He was king of the Locrians. He rapes Cassandra in the temple of Athena during the sack of Troy. Athena asks Poseidon to wreck Ajax's ships upon his return to Greece. He dies hurling his defiance at the gods.

Alcinous (or Alkinoos) | King of Phaeacia (an island near Ithaca) and father of Nausicaa. He receives the wandering Odysseus at his court and secures his passage to Ithaca.

Alexander | See Paris

Alexander the Great | (356–323 B.C.): King of Macedonia. He was raised by his tutor Aristotle to revere Homer and Achilles. His Asian conquests were interpreted as a new *Iliad.*

Anchises | Trojan prince; father of Aeneas by Aphrodite. Saved by his son during the fall of Troy, he accompanied him on his wanderings.

Andromache | Daughter of Eetion, wife of Hector, and mother of Astyanax. Her life after the fall of Troy is recounted by Virgil and Euripides. Neoptolemus took Andromache to Epirus, where his wife, Hermione, attempted to kill her. Andromache subsequently married Helenus, Hector's only surviving brother, and lived happily ever after.

Anticleia | Wife of Laertes and mother of Odysseus. Her shade greets Odysseus in the Underworld.

Antinous (or Antinoos) | Best known of the suitors who seek to marry Penelope. See also Suitors.

Aphrodite | [also called Cypris or the Cytherean; Latin name Venus]: Mother of Aeneas. Goddess of love and desire, whose name is sometimes synonymous with desire. Judged more beautiful than Athena or Hera by Paris, whom she protects, she is portrayed in the *Odyssey* as wife of Hephaestus and mistress of Ares (Mars).

Apollo | [or Phoebus; Gk. *Phoibos*; Latin name Phebus]: Son of Zeus and Leto. God of the sun; archer; and god of music. With his sister, Artemis, he slaughtered Niobe's children as punishment for her boasting. He opposes the Greeks at Troy because Agamemnon has threatened Chryses, his priest. The sanctuary of the Pythia, priestess of Apollo at Delphi, appears in Aeschylus's *Oresteia* but not in the Homeric poems.

Apollodorus | (of Athens; first half of second century B.C.): Grammarian; author of the *Bibliotheca*, the first attempt to bring history to bear on mythology.

Apollonius of Rhodes | (third–second century B.C.): Greek poet. He described the adventures of Jason in his *Argonautica*.

Apotropaic | [sayings] The means by which mortals seek to avoid the jealousy of the gods. The worst outcome is presented as inevitable, tempting the gods to intervene out of vanity and render fate less implacable. The implied pessimism of this discourse also takes into account the fact that the gods are jealous of humans who appear happier than themselves and tend to eradicate such happiness.

Apuleius | (second century A.D.): Latin writer and author of the *Metamorphoses*, better known as *The Golden Ass*. This work contains the story of Psyche, whose eroticism has a Neoplatonic significance.

Aragon, Louis | (b. Neuilly-sur-Seine, 1897; d. Paris, 1982): French writer and political activist. In 1922, Aragon rewrote Fénelon's *Adventures of Telemachus*. See also Fénelon, François de Salignac de la Mothe-Fénelon.

Ares | [Greek for "war"; Latin name Mars]: Son of Zeus and Hera. He is the god of war, often appearing on the battlefield in order to set off some further episode of mass bloodshed. Lover of Aphrodite, he was surprised in bed with her by her husband, Hephaestus.

Arete | [Greek for "virtue"]: Niece and wife of Alcinous; mother of Nausicaa.

Argians (or Danaans) | Inhabitants of Argos and, by extension, Greeks in general.

Argo | Name of Jason's ship. His companions are thus called the Argonauts.

Argos | City where Agamemnon was king. Also the name of Odysseus's dog, which dies after recognizing him.

Argus | [Gk. *Argos*]: Hundred-eyed monster, depicted as either a man or a peacock, that was slain by Hermes.

Arnold, Matthew | (b. Laleham, 1822; d. Liverpool, 1888): English poet and teacher who published *On Translating Homer* in 1861.

Artemis | [Latin name Diana]: Daughter of Zeus and Leto and sister of Apollo. She is the goddess of hunting, responsible for sudden deaths. Artemis and Apollo together slaughtered the children of Niobe as punishment for the latter's boasting.

Ascanius | [Latin name Iulus]: Son of Aeneas (in the *Aeneid*). Under his Latin name he is said to be at the origin of the Iulian clan, the family of Julius Caesar and his adopted son Octavian (Augustus).

Astyanax (or Scamander) | Son of Hector and Andromache. After the fall of Troy, he was thrown from the battlements by order of Neoptolemus.

Atalanta | Young huntress who declared that she would marry the man who could outrun her in a race and put to death those who failed. Hippomenes (or Meleager) threw down golden apples as he ran and won when she stopped to collect them. She helped Meleager kill the great Calydonian boar.

Athena | [or Pallas; Latin name Minerva] Daughter of Zeus. Virgin: goddess of intelligence. Having been judged by Paris inferior in beauty to Aphrodite, she hates the Trojans. Untiring warrior in the *Iliad*, she is the ironic accomplice of Odysseus and counselor to Telemachus in the *Odyssey*. See also Mentes and Mentor.

Athenians | The Athenians are rarely mentioned in the *Iliad*, perhaps because Homer excluded Theseus, the great Athenian hero, from the war of Troy.

Atrides | Sons of Atreus, in particular Agamemnon and Menelaus. The Atrides were afflicted with a series of murders and vendettas that ended with the generation of Orestes and Electra.

Aulis | Located on the west coast of the Aegean, in Boeotia, it was the point where the Greek fleet assembled before sailing for Troy. There Agamemnon sacrificed his daughter Iphigenia to secure favorable winds.

Automedon | Thessalian warrior; friend to Achilles.

Bal des Quat'z'arts | [Quatre Arts, with false liaison: *Quatres Arts*] Annual ball organized by the students of the four arts (painting, sculpture, architecture, engraving) from 1893 to 1966. Posters and invitations frequently featured classical themes. Students and models dressed in Greek style or went naked as statues.

Batrachomyomachia | ["battle of the frogs and mice"] Burlesque of the Homeric poems, probably composed between the sixth and fourth centuries BC; the animal epic was long attributed by the ancient world to Homer himself.

Bellay, Joachim du | (b. Le Liré, Anjou, 1522; d. Paris, 1560): French poet, member of the Pléiade, author of *Regrets* (1557) and *The Antiquities of Rome* (1558). He frequently evokes Homer, particularly in the *Regrets*.

Berlioz, Hector | (b. La Côte-Saint-André, 1803; d. Paris, 1869): The greatest French Romantic composer—with a Homeric first name—he composed his opera *The Trojans* between 1856 and 1858. Inspired by Virgil and Euripides, the five-act opera is divided into two parts in its definitive version. Cassandra and then Dido refuse to accept the tragedy that awaits humanity.

Boccaccio, Giovanni | (Certaldo, 1313–1375): Italian writer best known as the author of the *Decameron*. He also wrote a narrative poem entitled *Il Filostrato* (1337–39) based on the story of Troilus and Cressida.

Briseis | Captive of Achilles, whom Agamemnon seized to replace Chryseis when the latter was handed back to her father, Chryses, thus involuntarily provoking the wrath of Achilles. Following the death of Patroclus, she was returned to Achilles. See "Achilles."

Butler, Samuel | (b. Bingham, 1835; d. London, 1902): English writer and author of *Erewhon*, he wrote two works on the authorship of the Homeric poems—*On the Trapanese Origin of the Odyssey* (1893) and *The Authoress of the Odyssey . . .* (1897)—in which he argued that the *Odyssey* was written by a Sicilian Nausicaa.

Caca | Sister of Cacus, she helped Hercules find the oxen stolen by her brother.

Cacus | Italian brigand who tried to steal oxen from Hercules and died in the attempt. The fable is recorded by Virgil and Propertius.

Calchas | Greek soothsayer during the Trojan War.

Calderón de la Barca, Pedro | (Madrid, 1600–1681): Spanish Golden Age dramatist who twice treated the relationship of Odysseus and Circe, first in *The Greatest Enchantment: Love* (*El mayor encanto amor*, 1635) and then in the *auto sacramental* (a sacred play celebrating the presence of God in the Eucharist) entitled *The Enchantments of Guilt* (*Los encantos de la culpa*, 1649).

Calydon | Town in Aetolia (north of Corinth) saved by its king, Meleager, from complete destruction.

Carthage | City founded by Phoenicians from Tyre. In the *Aeneid*, the queen of Carthage is Dido.

Cassandra | Daughter of Priam and Hecuba. Having tricked Apollo into bestowing the gift of clairvoyance, she was punished by the disbelief with which her prophecies were greeted, notably those concerning the wooden horse. Captive and mistress of Agamemnon, she was murdered with him by Clytemnestra, his wife.

Cassas, Louis-François | (b. Azay-le-Ferron, 1756; d. Versailles, 1827): French architect; pupil of Jean-Jacques Lagrenée. He traveled to Syria with the French diplomat and scholar Choiseul-Gouffier, completing his *Picturesque Voyage in Syria, Phoenicia, Palestine, and Lower Egypt* in 1797. In 1837 the École des beaux-arts received his magnificent collection of architectural models.

Castor | See Dioscuri.

Caylus, Anne-Claude-Philippe de Tubières, comte de | (Paris, 1692–1765): French scholar and antiquarian. He searched for the ruins of Troy and published a *Collection of Egyptian, Etruscan, Greek, Roman and Gallic Antiquities* (1752–67). By 1757 he was de facto dictator at the Académie royale, to which he dedicated *Pictures Taken from the "Iliad" and "Odyssey" of Homer and the "Aeneid" of Virgil, with general remarks about costumes*, followed in 1758 by his *Story of Hercules the Theban, Drawn from Various Authors, to which Is Adjoined a Description of the Pictures It Might Supply*. His influence was opposed by Diderot and Lessing.

Cerberus | Three-headed dog guarding the entrance to the Underworld. Various heroes escaped its clutches and entered the Underworld. Hercules stifled it, while Orpheus and Theseus lulled it to sleep.

Ceres | See Demeter.

Chapman, George | (b. Hitchin, Hertfordshire, ca. 1559; d. London, 1634): English poet and dramatist. He translated the *Iliad* in 1611 and the *Odyssey* in 1614–15.

Charis, Charites | In the *Iliad* she is the loving wife of Hephaestus, but in the *Odyssey* Hephaestus is married to the adulterous Aphrodite. See also Graces.

Charybdis | See Scylla.

Chaucer, Geoffrey | (London, b. ca. 1340–45; d. 1400): English poet and author of the *Canterbury Tales.* He wrote a *Troilus and Criseyde* (1382–86?) of remarkable psychological finesse.

Chénier, André | (b. Constantinople, 1762; d. Paris, 1794): French poet; victim of the Revolution. One of the poems in his *Bucoliques* (1819), "The Blind Bard" ["L'Aveugle"], popularized the myth of Homer as a wandering bard.

Chios | [mod. Gk. *Khios*]: Island in the Aegean where Homer is supposed to have founded a school.

Chiron | Centaur (half-man, half-horse), he was tutor to Achilles, teaching him music and gymnastics.

Choiseul-Gouffier, Marie-Gabriel-Florent-Auguste de | (b. Paris, 1752; d. Aix-la-Chapelle, 1817): French diplomat and scholar, ambassador to Constantinople (1784–92). In 1782 he published his *Picturesque Voyage in Greece.* A portion of his cast collection, confiscated in 1792, was inherited by the École des beaux-arts.

Chryseis | Daughter of Chryses. Agamemnon is forced by Apollo to restore the captive Chryseis to her father. Agamemnon then demands that Achilles hand over Briseis in Chryseis's stead, provoking the wrath of Achilles. Medieval and later accounts inspired by Homer award a more important role to Chryseis, who is renamed Cressida. See also Chryses; Shakespeare, William.

Chryses | Priest of Apollo. The god forces Agamemnon to return Chryseis (whom he wanted to make his captive mistress) to her father.

Circe | Immortal sorceress, forced by Odysseus to restore to human form those of his companions whom she had transformed into pigs. She takes Odysseus as her lover and directs him to the Underworld. Telegonus, her son by Odysseus, will one day reach Ithaca and kill his father.

Cithara | See Lyre.

Claudel, Paul | (b. Villeneuve-sur-Fère, 1868; d. Paris, 1955): French poet and dramatist. In 1914 Claudel wrote *Two Summer Poems*, one of which is a lyrical farce entitled *Protée*, which describes the return of Helen after the fall of Troy.

Cleopatra | Wife of Meleager, she convinces him to take up arms and defend their city of Calydon, which is about to be destroyed by the Curetes.

Clytemnestra | Daughter of Zeus and Tyndareus's wife Leda, Clytemnestra is wife of Agamemnon and sister of Helen. She and her lover Aegisthus kill Agamemnon upon his return from Troy. Orestes, her son by Agamemnon, later kills her to avenge the death of his father.

Cressida | See Chryseis; Shakespeare, William.

Cronus | [Gk. *Kronos*; Latin name Saturnus; English Saturn]: A Titan overthrown by Zeus, his son.

Cupid | See Eros.

Curetes | Enemies of the Aetolians who took advantage of Meleager's anger to lay siege to Calydon.

Cyclades | Archipelago located in the southern Aegean Sea.

Cyclops | [Greek for "round-eyed"]: In the *Odyssey* a group of one-eyed, anthropophagous shepherds. After Homer, the Cyclops are presented as workers in the forge of Hephaestus, the divine smithy to the gods. See also Polyphemus.

Cyme | [Latin name Cumes]: A town in Ionian Asia where Homer is said to have stayed.

Cypris | See Aphrodite.

Cythera | An island on the southern tip of the Peloponnese, where a famous cult honoring Aphrodite flourished. See also Aphrodite.

Dacier, Anne Lefebvre | [Madame Dacier] (b. Preuilly, 1647; d. Paris, 1720): French philologist. Her translations of the *Iliad* (1699) and the *Odyssey* (1708), although respectful, were stylistically insipid. The Quarrel of the Ancients and Moderns (starting in 1687) continued in the Quarrel of Homer (1711–17), which was triggered by the publication of Madame Dacier's translation.

Danaans | See Argians.

Dante Alighieri | (b. Florence, 1265; d. Ravenna, 1321): Italian (Tuscan) poet and author of the *Divine Comedy*, of which the first part, the *Inferno*, offered a new vision of the character of Odysseus.

Dardanians | See Achaeans.

Dares Phrygius | Apocryphal ally of the Trojans in the Trojan War. He is said to have written (in Greek) the *De Excidio Troiae Historia* (History of the Destruction of Troy). This text appeared in Latin in the sixth century A.D., probably following a slightly earlier Greek work. It presents the Trojan Wars from the Trojan point of view (with limited divine intervention) and forms the basis of the medieval versions of the story of Troy. See also Dictys Cretensis.

Deidamia | Daughter of Lycomedes, she bore a son (Neoptolemus) to Achilles.

Demeter | [Latin name Ceres] Goddess of the earth and of harvests, she was the mother of Persephone.

Diana | See Artemis.

Dictys Cretensis | Apocryphal Greek warrior supposed to have fought in the Trojan War. He is presumed to have written (in Greek) the *Ephemeris belli Troiani* (Chronicle of the Trojan War), a text that appeared in Latin around the fourth century A.D., probably following a slightly earlier Greek work. This work presents the Trojan War from the Greek perspective (with limited divine intervention). Together with Dares' *History of the Destruction of Troy*, it underpins the medieval versions of the history of Troy. See also Dares Phrygius.

Diderot, Denis | (b. Langres, 1713; d. Paris, 1784): French *philosophe* and man of letters. Diderot had a passionate interest in the Homeric poems. He refers to them constantly in his *Salons*, which constitute the most brilliant art criticism written in eighteenth-century France.

Dido | Queen of Carthage. She came from Tyre, in Phoenicia, to found the city of Carthage. Her lover, Aeneas, abandoned her there, following which she committed suicide.

Diodorus Siculus | (first century B.C.): Greek historian. His *Bibliotheca Historica* inserts the legendary cycles into universal history.

Diomedes | Son of Tydeus. One of the most valiant of Greek warriors, he attacked the gods—successfully. Having stolen the Palladium, he prevented Odysseus from stealing it and robbing him of the credit for this feat. See also Palladium.

Dioscuri | ["sons of Zeus"] Collective name given to Castor and Pollux, sons of Zeus and Leda (the wife of Tyndareus). Brothers of Helen and Clytemnestra, they liberated Helen when she was abducted by Theseus.

Discord | [Gk. *Eris*]: Allegorical goddess. Enraged at not having been invited to the marriage of Peleus and Thetis, she threw the Apple of Discord, on which was written "To the most beautiful," in front of three rival goddesses (Athena, Hera, and Aphrodite). See Judgment of Paris.

Doris | Daughter of Oceanus, wife of Nereus, and mother of the Nereids.

Dryden, John | (b. Aldwinkle All Saints, Northamptonshire, 1631; d. London 1700): English poet who published a translation of the first book of the *Iliad* in his *Fables, Ancient and Modern* (1700).

Earth Shaker | See Poseidon.

Ekphrasis | [Greek for "description"]: The description of real or imaginary works of art constituted a genre in ancient literature. Artists of modern times have attempted to reconstruct lost masterpieces of Greek art on the basis of such descriptions.

Electra | Daughter of Agamemnon and Clytemnestra and elder sister of Orestes. She encouraged him to avenge their father's death. Electra does not appear in the Homeric cycle.

Elpenor | One of Odysseus's companions. In no way remarkable, he died a foolish death. His shade importunes Odysseus in the Underworld. He has thus become the paradigm of the individual who lives through epic events unawares. Jean Giraudoux's witty eponymous tale (1920) is based on this character.

Epeus | [Gk. *Epeios*]: Epeus built the Trojan Horse. He is one of the few artists whose name appears in the Homeric poems.

Erinyes | See Eumenides.

Eris | See Discord.

Eros | [Lat. *Cupido*, or Cupid] God of desire and love, son of Aphrodite (and Hermes or Ares). Eros does not appear in Homer. He plays a role in many allegories and philosophical theories, which distinguish three Erotes, corresponding to the three Graces and three aspirations of the Soul (Psyche, whose lover is Eros).

Etruscans | A people of mysterious origins and Hellenistic civilization, established in Italy before the Latins and Romans, who long dominated them and then disappeared. Virgil made the Etruscans the enemies of Aeneas and his Trojans.

Eumenides | [Greek for "kindly ones"]: Euphemistic term for Erinyes [Latin name Furies], who pursue Orestes but must bow to the judgment of Athena and Apollo.

Eupithes | An eminent citizen of Ithaca in the *Odyssey*; father of Antinous, the main suitor for Penelope's hand. Seeking revenge for his son, he provokes an uprising and is killed by Odysseus.

Euripides | (ca. 485–ca. 406 B.C.): Athenian tragic poet, author of several plays on Homeric subjects, all of them profoundly pessimistic and irreligious.

Euryalus | One of Aeneas's companions in the *Aeneid*. Together with his comrade Nisus, he dies heroically during the war against the Rutuli. See also Nisus.

Eurypylus | A Thessalian warrior in the *Iliad* who is wounded by Paris and cured by Patroclus. See also Paris; Patroclus.

Fauré, Gabriel | (b. Pamiers, 1845; d. Paris, 1924): French composer who came late to opera with his *Penelope* (1913).

Fénelon, François de Salignac de la Mothe- | (b. Fénelon, Périgord, 1651; d. Cambrai, 1715): Author, archbishop of Cambrai, tutor (1689–94) to the duc de Bourgogne, grandson of Louis XIV and heir to the throne. His *Adventures of Telemachus* was published in 1699. This moralizing adaptation of the *Odyssey* and the *Aeneid* was more widely read in the eighteenth century than the Homeric poems. See "The Advenures of Telemachus."

France, Anatole | (b. Paris, 1844; d. Saint-Cyr-sur-Loire, 1924): French author born in one of the buildings of the present-day École des beaux-arts. He published several stories inspired by Homer in *Clio* ("The Singer of Cymes," 1895 and 1899), and a commentary on Odysseus's visit to the Underworld in *Pierre Nozière* (1899).

Franciade | See Lemaire des Belges, Jean; Ronsard, Pierre de.

Francus | Supposed son of Hector. Invented by French poets in order to prove a Trojan origin for France.

Ganymede | Beautiful young boy abducted by Zeus to become his lover and cupbearer.

Gargara | One of the summits of Mount Ida in the Troad.

Giants | See Gigantomachy.

Gide, André | (Paris, 1869–1951): French novelist and man of letters. In 1899 Gide published *Philoctetes*, a drama based on Sophocles' tragedy of the same name.

Gigantomachy | War between the Giants and the Olympians. The Giants were serpent-tailed monsters who preceded the Olympian gods and revolted against their power. These wars are often confused with the Olympians' war against the Titans. See also Titans.

Giono, Jean | (Manosque, Basses-Alpes, 1895–1970): French regionalist writer whose short novel *Birth of the Odyssey* (1930) envisions Odysseus as a braggart overtaken by his own inventions and sees Homeric Greece as a world of lies.

Giraudoux, Jean | (b. Bellac, 1882; d. Paris, 1944): French novelist and playwright. Author of the plays *The Trojan War Shall Not Take Place* (1935) and *Electra* (1937), which share a subtle mixture of tragedy and humor. See also Elpenor.

Glaucus | Shepherd of Chios said to have given shelter to the blind poet Homer and led him to his master.

Goethe, Johann Wolfgang von | (b. Frankfurt am Main, 1849; d. Weimar, 1832): German poet, playwright, and novelist. In his play *Faust*, Helen embodies the ideal of beauty. Goethe dreamed of rewriting the *Iliad* in German (the *Achilleis*) and of transforming the story of Nausicaa into a tragedy. Although neither project was ever completed, some of the most beautiful verses in the German language resulted.

Graces | [Gk. *Charites*, pl. of *Charis*]: In Homer they are simply the three daughters of Zeus. In modern iconology they are sometimes assimilated with the three goddesses of the Judgment of Paris.

Graves, Robert von Ranke | (b. Wimbledon, 1895; d. Majorca, 1985): English poet and scholar. He produced popular translations of classical narratives, including Apuleius's *Golden Ass* (1950) and *The Anger of Achilles: Homer's "Iliad"* (1957).

Greek Anthology | See *Palatine Anthology*.

Greeks | See Hellenes.

Hades | [Latin name Pluto, from the Gk. *ploutos*, "rich"]: Zeus's brother, Hades is king of the Underworld. He abducts Persephone. In Homer his name refers to death or the world of the dead.

Halévy, Ludovic | See Offenbach, Jacques.

Hamlet | Eponymous hero of Shakespeare's tragedy who borrows many aspects of his character from Achilles and Orestes, to whom he is often compared. See also Laertes.

Hasaël | Invented character in Fénelon's *Adventures of Telemachus*, a Syrian to whom Mentor is sold as a slave. His name is derived from the biblical Asahel (2 Sam. 2:18). See also Fénelon, François de Salignac de la Mothe-.

Hebe | Daughter of Zeus and Hera and wife of Hercules following his apotheosis. She serves the nectar of the gods.

Hector | Son of Priam and Hecuba, husband of Andromache, and father of the doomed Astyanax. The best and most humane of the Trojan warriors, he kills Patroclus and is killed by Achilles. His role in the legend is much enhanced by Homer, and he was long considered the main figure in the Trojan War, especially in the Middle Ages.

Hecuba | [Latin version of Gk. *Hecabe*] Wife of Priam and mother of many children whose successive deaths she witnesses. She is one of Euripides' greatest tragic heroines.

Hegesippus | Character invented by Fénelon in *The Adventures of Telemachus*; the envoy of Diomedes.

Helen | Daughter of Zeus (in the form of a swan) and Leda, the wife of Tyndareus. She was renowned for her beauty and was courted by all the Greeks. She married Menelaus but eloped with Paris, thus causing the Trojan War. The poets invented many excuses to justify her behavior.

Helenus | Sole son of Priam to survive the fall of Troy. A seer and rejected suitor for Helen's hand following the death of Paris, he goes over to the Greeks and reveals to them that Troy can only be taken with the help of Hercules' bow. He later marries Andromache.

Hellenes | Thessalian people whose name, by extension, is applied to all the Greeks. The word "Greek" [Gk. *Graikos*] does not appear in Homer, being the name of a small group of people from the island of Euboea. The Greeks referred to themselves as Hellenes.

Hephaestus | [Latin name *Vulcanus*; or Vulcan]: Lame son of Zeus and Hera, whose limp makes the gods laugh. A skilled blacksmith who fashions the arms of Achilles. He traps his wife Aphrodite *in flagrante* with Ares. Rather than punish them, the gods laugh at the cuckolded husband.

Hera | [Latin name Juno] Sister and wife of Zeus. Paris having failed to award her the apple, she hates the Trojans. Homer and legend recount her fury at Zeus's philandering. She uses her charms to obtain from Zeus what she dares not ask for openly. See also Judgment of Paris.

Heraclitus | (the Rhetor; first century B.C. or A.D.): Greek philosopher. Author of *Quaestiones Homericae*, which interprets Homer's poems in terms of cosmic or moral allegory.

Hercules | [Gk. *Heracles*] Homer recounts his birth. The son of Zeus and Alcmene, he is known principally for his twelve labors. His legend is connected with the history of Ilium (Troy), which he destroyed in the first Trojan War. Following his suicide, he is both a shade (whom Ulysses meets in the Underworld) and a god (who marries Hebe and lives on Olympus).

Hermes | [Gk. *Argeiphontes*, killer of Argos; Latin name Mercury] Son of Zeus. He steals the cattle of Apollo but makes friends with the Sun God by teaching him the use of the lyre. He is ordered by Zeus to kill Argus, the many-eyed monster. He conducts souls to the Underworld (*Psychopompos*, "one who escorts souls").

Hermione | Daughter of Menelaus and Helen. In Euripides' play *Orestes* Hermione is taken hostage by Orestes following the murder of Agamemnon. She then marries Neoptolemus and attempts to kill his captive mistress Andromache. She finally marries Orestes.

Herodotus | (Halicarnassus, fifth century B.C.): The father of history. In his *Enquiry*, as he describes his *Histories*, Herodotus states that Helen was not the sole cause of the Trojan War. An anonymous life of Homer, the *De genere vitaque Homeri libellus*, by Pseudo-Herodotus (second or third century A.D.), was long attributed to Herodotus.

Hesiod | (eighth century B.C.): A poet of Boeotia (the region around Thebes, west of Athens). His *Theogony* includes many references to Homeric characters. Hesiod possesses a religious faith in the forces of nature that is quite alien to Homer.

Hesione | Daughter of Laomedon and sister of Priam. Hercules saved her from the sea monster to which she was to be sacrificed but, cheated of his reward by her father, he destroyed Troy. See also Trojan War.

Hexameter | All the Homeric poems are in dactylic hexameters (six feet, divided into two parts), which was not originally a Greek meter. Homer was fairly free in adapting it. Hesiod also wrote in this meter, as did the authors of the *Hymns* consequently known as *Homeric*. The Latin poets (notably Virgil in the *Aeneid*) adopted the same meter, which was by then considered the epic meter. Certain modern authors (notably Goethe) have attempted to import it into modern languages.

Hobbes, Thomas | (b. Malmesbury, Wiltshire, 1588; d. Hardwick, Devonshire, 1679): Great English philosopher. Late in his life he published translations of the *Odyssey* and the *Iliad* (1674–75).

Homer | (eighth–seventh centuries B.C.?): Author to whom the *Iliad* and the *Odyssey* are attributed. The texts of these were determined in an official transcription by Pisistratus in the sixth century B.C. Legends concerning Homer's life arose in antiquity. Since the seventeenth century, the question has been raised as to how many poets are concealed under this name. Today textual critics believe that the Homeric poems are the work of an oral tradition refined by the technique, knowledge, and memory of several rhapsodes. Since every reading of Homer mirrors its epoch, this verdict is unlikely to prove definitive.

Homeric Hymns | Composed after the poems of Homer in the same dactylic hexameter as the *Iliad* and *Odyssey*, the *Homeric Hymns* are dedicated to divinities, most of whom have a place in the world of Homer. Although the general tone is more religious, something of Homer's satirical bite is occasionally retained.

Icarius | Father of Penelope. He would have liked her to remain in Sparta with her Ithacan husband Odysseus. See also Penelope.

Ida | Phrygian mountain from which the gods look down on the Trojan War. There Paris shepherded his flocks before the war. (This place should not be confused with Mount Ida in Crete, where the infant Zeus was nourished by the goat Amalthea.)

Idomeneus | King of Crete and ally of the Greeks. In non-Homeric legend he vows to sacrifice the first thing he sees upon his return in exchange for a safe homecoming. This turns out to be his own son.

Iliad | Composed in Greek, the poem of Ilium, that is, Troy. The first Homeric poem recounts a single episode—the wrath of Achilles—which has no decisive influence on the outcome of the interminable siege of the Asian city.

Ilium | See Troy.

Ino | A Nereid. Goddess of spindrift.

Ionia | The Hellenized regions of Anatolia, where the Ionian dialect of Greek was spoken. Homer uses the term "Ionians" to refer to the inhabitants of Attica (the region around Athens). For the inhabitants of Anatolia and Asia, the term later came to designate the Greeks as a whole, which it still does today. Modern Greek is essentially derived from the Ionian dialect, of which Attic (the language of the Athenians) was a particular form.

Ios | A small island in the Cycladic archipelago, where certain ancient historians believed Homer died.

Iphigenia | [Latin name Iphianissa] Daughter of Agamemnon and Clytemnestra. She is sacrificed by her father on the beach at Aulis in exchange for favorable winds for the Greek fleet to set sail for Troy.

Irus | Drunken beggar beaten by the disguised Odysseus in his palace at Ithaca.

Ithaca | Island in the Adriatic Sea ruled by Odysseus.

Iulus | See Ascanius.

Jaccottet, Philippe | (b. Moudon, Switzerland, 1925): Major poet and translator into French of Musil, Hölderlin, and (in 1982) the *Odyssey*.

Jason | A hero whose journey aboard the *Argonaut* prefigures the Greek expedition and, above all, the wanderings of Odysseus. See "Previous and Parallel Epic Cycles."

Joyce, James | (b. Dublin, 1882; d. Zurich, 1941): Irish writer. His novel *Ulysses* (1922) is the most ambitious and significant literary adaptation ever made of one of the Homeric poems.

Judgment of Paris | The goddesses Athena, Hera, and Aphrodite send Hermes to ask the shepherd Paris to decide which of them is the most beautiful and thus the rightful owner of the Apple of Discord.

Jupiter | See Zeus.

Kazantzakis, Nikos | (b. Heraklion, 1885; d. Freiburg-im-Briesgau, 1957): Great Greek poet and novelist. He published an *Odyssey* (in Greek *Odysseus*) in verse in 1938. It is an ambitious sequel to the adventures of Odysseus.

Ker and Keres | Divinities of death; death itself. See also Moirai.

Laconia | Region of the southern Pelopponese.

Lacadaemon | See Sparta.

Laertes | Odysseus's father in the *Odyssey*. He renounces his royal status before the Trojan War and becomes a peasant. Shakespeare gave his name to Ophelia's brother in *Hamlet*.

La Motte, Antoine Houdar de | (Paris, 1672–1731): French poet and playwright, whose reputation is owed to his controversial translation of the *Iliad* (1714), which was intended to improve Homer by rendering him suitable to the taste of the age. See also Quarrel of Homer.

Laocoön (or Laocoon) | Trojan priest of Apollo. He provoked the god's anger by engaging in intercourse with his wife in front of the consecrated statue. He alone among the Trojans perceived the danger of the wooden horse, but Apollo sent sea serpents to kill him and his sons when he argued for its destruction. This was taken as a sign that he was wrong. Although Homer alludes to the warnings of Laocoön, the legend is best known from the *Aeneid.* See also Lessing, Gotthold Ephraim.

Laomedon | King of Troy and father of Priam. He asks for Hercules' aid but refuses him the promised reward. The result is the first Trojan War, leading to the death of all of Laomedon's children except for Priam and Hesione.

Lares | See Penates.

Latinus | The aboriginal king of Italy in the *Aeneid*, after whom the Latins are named. He gives his daughter Lavinia in marriage to Aeneas, and they found the Roman race.

Latona | See Leto.

Lausus | Son of Mezentius. See also Mezentius.

Lavinia | See Latinus.

Leconte de Lisle, Charles-Marie-René | (b. Saint-Paul, Réunion, 1818; d. Louveciennes, 1894): Poet of the Parnassian school. He hoped to restore to French the language and style of the Homeric poems that he translated (*Iliad*, 1867; *Odyssey, Homeric Hymns, Batrachomyomachia*, 1868), in particular by accurately transcribing names and historical terms.

Leda | Wife of Tyndareus and mother of Clytemnestra, Helen, and Castor and Pollux. She was seduced by Zeus, who appeared to her in the form of a swan.

Lemaire des Belges, Jean | (Bavai, 1473–ca. 1515–25): Poet and author. In his *Illustrations of Gaul and Singularities of Troy* (1509–12) he attempted to impose a national French reading of the Trojan War, based on a non-Homeric protagonist invented for this purpose, namely, Francus, purported son of Hector and mythical founder of France. See also Francus.

Lemnos | Island in the Aegean Sea, opposite Troy, on which the wounded Philoctetes is marooned. It is inhabited by the Sinties.

Lessing, Gotthold Ephraim | (b. Kamens, Saxony, 1729; d. Brunswick, 1781): German critic and playwright. His treatise *Laocoön* (1766) repeatedly refers to Homer and the works of art inspired by him. It distinguishes the aesthetics of poetry from those of painting. All modern art criticism derives from this treatise.

Leto | [Latin name Latona] Mother by Zeus of Apollo and Artemis. She demands the death of Niobe's children.

Little Iliad | One of a cycle of epics composed after the Homeric poems (seventh century B.C.; attributed to Lesches of Mytilene) recounting episodes excluded by Homer. This is a lost work known to us from ancient summaries.

Locris | Homeland of Ajax, son of Oileus.

Longinus (Pseudo-) | Since its *editio princeps* (1544) the treatise *On the Sublime* has been attributed to the Neoplatonic rhetorician-teacher Dionysius Longinus. In fact, the historical Longinus, minister to Queen Zenobia of Palmyra, was called Cassius Longinus. The author of this treatise (who probably lived in the first century A.D.) remains unknown, but he exercised an enormous influence in Western literary criticism by affirming the originality of thought of the artist.

Lucian of Samosata | (ca. A.D. 120–ca. 180): Greek satirist in whose many dialogues the heroes and gods of Homer are given humorous and satirical voices.

Lycomedes | King of Scyros. When the recruiters for the Trojan War arrived, Achilles dressed up as a girl and was concealed among the daughters of Lycomedes. Ulysses having introduced some arms among the presents for the girls, Achilles revealed himself by seizing them. Achilles left Deidamia, one of the daughters, pregnant with a son, alternately named Neoptolemus or Pyrrhus. See also Neoptolemus.

Lyre | An instrument that Homer also refers to as a *cithara* or *phorminx.* His verses were meant to be sung to the accompaniment of the lyre, which was therefore considered the symbolic instrument of the poet.

Machaon | Doctor to the Greek army at Troy.

Marivaux, Pierre Carlet de Chamblain de | (Paris, 1688–1763): Great French playwright and novelist. In 1716 he published a parody of Homer entitled *Homer Travestied or the Iliad Burlesqued.*

Marpessa | Mother of Cleopatra and mother-in-law to Meleager.

Mars | See Ares.

Meilhac, Henri | See Offenbach, Jacques.

Meleager | See "Previous and Parallel Epic Cycles."

Menelaus | King of Sparta and brother of Agamemnon. He wins the hand of Helen but loses her to Paris. After the fall of Troy he agrees to return to married life with her and lives happily.

Menoetius | Father of Patroclus.

Mentes and Mentor | Athena takes on the features of two different mortals in the *Odyssey*. Mentor is an Ithacan friend of Odysseus. Mentes (according to Athena) is king of the Taphians. In Fénelon's *Adventures of Telemachus* Mentor/Athena is one of the two main characters.

Mercury | See Hermes.

Mezentius | In the *Aeneid* he is the king of the Etruscans and ally of the Rutuli against the Trojans. Father of Lausus, who dies at the same time as he.

Minerva | See Athena.

Moirai | [Latin name Parcae] Divinities of fate and death. See also Ker and Keres.

Molossians | Inhabitants of Epirus, a region in southwest continental Greece. They take their name from Molossos, the son of Pyrrhus and Andromache.

Monteverdi, Claudio | (b. Cremona, 1567; d. Venice, 1643): One of the three extant operas of this Venetian composer, *Il ritorno d'Ulisse in patria* (1640) is surely the least performed. This "drama in music" (with a libretto by Giacomo Badoaro) offers a Renaissance reading of books 13–21 of the *Odyssey*.

Muses | Daughters of Zeus. They are the source of inspiration of poets. In the Homeric poems they inhabit Olympus and not Parnassus.

Mycenae | City of the Argolis, subordinate to Argos. This was the principal historical center of Greece during the Bronze Age (fourteenth–twelfth centuries B.C.), several centuries before the composition of the Homeric poems. It is no longer thought that Homer really embodies memories of the Mycenaean civilization.

Nausicaa | Daughter of Alcinous, the king of the Phaeacians. She discovers the naked, shipwrecked Odysseus and dreams of marrying him. Since classical times, some critics have seen in Nausicaa (surely the subtlest of Homer's creations) the true author of the *Odyssey*. See also Butler, Samuel.

Nekuia | Name given to Odysseus's visit to the Underworld (*Odyssey*, book 11). The *Aeneid* also has its *Nekuia* (book 6).

Neleid | See Nestor.

Neoptolemus | [Latin name Pyrrhus: "the red-haired"] Son of Achilles and Deidamia. Following the death of his father, he distinguishes himself by convincing Philoctetes to rejoin the Greek army and by killing the aged Priam. Although married to Hermione, he loved his captive mistress Andromache, a situation portrayed by Euripides and Racine.

Neptune | See Poseidon.

Nereus, Nereids | The maritime god Nereus is father to fifty sea nymphs, the Nereids, of whom the most famous are Thetis and Amphitrite.

Nestor | Son of Neleus (thus his name Neleid) and king of Pylos. The oldest Greek warrior, he lavishes extensive advice on the younger warriors. Achilles ignores him (*Iliad*), while Telemachus obeys him implicitly (*Odyssey*).

Niobe | Mortal mother of seven sons and seven daughters, who compared herself favorably with Leto, mother of two, and brought down her hatred. The children of Leto, Apollo and Artemis, then slaughtered Niobe's entire offspring.

Nisus | Companion of Aeneas. He is killed, together with his comrade Euryalus, in the war against the Rutuli. See also Euryalus.

Nostos | Greek word meaning "return," or the desire to return (hence the word nostalgia, "pain of the desire to return"). This is Odysseus's state in the *Odyssey*. The *Nostoi* is a lost cycle of epic poems recounting the return of the Greek warriors from Troy.

Nymph | Female divinity personifying an aspect of nature.

Oceanus | A Titan. Husband of his sister, Tethys. He is represented as the circular river surrounding the flat circle of the Earth.

Odysseus | [Latin name Ulixes, thus Ulysses] King of Ithaca. Major protagonist in the *Iliad* and hero of the *Odyssey*. See "The Voyages of Ulysses" and "Ulysses in Ithaca."

Odyssey | [Gk. *Odusseia*, "story of Odysseus"] Second and last of the Homeric poems.

Oedipus | King of Thebes. He killed his father and married his mother. His name appears in Homer, but there are no links between the two cycles of legends.

Oenone | Nymph loved by Paris before the Judgment episode. Resentful that he abandoned her for Helen, when she alone is able to cure him, she refuses to do so. Struck with remorse, she kills herself on his dead body.

Offenbach, Jacques | (b. Cologne, 1819; d. Paris, 1880): Composer laureate of France's Second Empire (1852–70), he set the heroes of the Trojan War to music in *La Belle Hélène* (1864). He imparted to the music a gaiety it shared with the libretto by Henri Meilhac and Ludovic Halévy and the performance of its star singer, Hortense Schneider.

Ogygia | The island on which Calypso detained Odysseus for seven years.

Oileus | Father of the Lesser Ajax.

Olympians | The gods who inhabit Olympus.

Olympus | The residence of the gods. It is a mountain in Thessaly or the sky itself.

Oresteia | The story of Orestes, partly evoked in the *Odyssey* and subsequently taken up in Greek tragedy, notably in Aeschylus's trilogy of the same name. See also Aeschylus; Euripides; Sophocles.

Orestes | Son of Agamemnon and Clytemnestra. He avenged his father by killing his mother and was rescued from the ensuing madness by Apollo and Athena.

Ovid | (43 B.C.–A.D. 17–19): Latin poet. Author of the *Metamorphoses*. Books 11–15 of this poem are full of stories about Homeric warriors and gods; some of them inspired more artists than the versions of Homer himself. In his *Heroides* Ovid imagined love letters purportedly written by famous heroines to their lovers or spouses, including Helen to Paris, Dido to Aeneas, and Penelope to Odysseus.

Palatine Anthology | [also known as the *Greek Anthology*] A manuscript of Greek epigrams in the Palatine Library at Heidelberg. It provides an overview of Greek poetry from the earliest anonymous verses to the seventh century A.D.

Palladium | Statue of Pallas stolen from Troy by Odysseus and Diomedes.

Pallas | See Athena.

Parcae | See Moirai.

Paris (also called Alexander) | Son of Priam. He was exposed at birth because it was prophesied he would bring about the destruction of Troy. He judges Aphrodite more beautiful than Hera or Athena. Aphrodite rewards him with her protection and with the most beautiful mortal, Helen. Hector reproaches his lack of enthusiasm for battle. He kills Achilles with an arrow and is in turn killed by an arrow shot by the archer Philoctetes. Oenone, his former lover, refuses to save him. See also Oenone.

Parnassus | Mountain in Phocis, famous as the residence of the Muses. Odysseus is hurt there during a hunt.

Patroclus | Son of Monoetius and inseparable friend of Achilles. Donning the latter's armor, he is killed by Hector. The songs of the *Iliad* devoted to him are called the Patroclide.

Pausanias | (second century A.D.): Greek traveler and author. His *Description of Greece* (*Periegesis*) contains reliable analyses of artistic works no longer extant.

Peleus | Father of Achilles. It was prophesied that the son of the goddess Thetis would be greater than his father. Zeus desired her, but, deterred by the prophecy, ordered the mortal Peleus to rape and marry Thetis. The son of this marriage was Achilles.

Peloponnesus | The large southern peninsula of Greece.

Penates | Domestic divinities of the Etruscans and Romans, like the Lares; they are represented by statuettes.

Penelope | Daughter of Icarius, cousin of Helen, and wife of Odysseus. During Odysseus's long absence, she refuses to choose among the suitors who besiege her with offers of marriage. She finally agrees to choose one when she has finished weaving a shroud, which she nightly undoes, but her ruse is discovered by a serving woman. She greets her returning husband with suspicion.

Phaeacians | People inhabiting an island in the Adriatic (near Ithaca) generally identified as Corfu.

Persephone (or Proserpine) | See Demeter; Hades.

Phemius | Ithacan bard who sings for Penelope's suitors but is spared by Odysseus upon his return.

Philocles | [Greek for "lover (or friend) of glory"] Invented character in Fénelon's *Adventures of Telemachus.*

Philoctetes | Friend of Hercules, who bequeathes him his bow. Wounded, he is marooned by the Greeks on the island of Lemnos. He must subsequently be persuaded to rejoin the expedition since Troy cannot be taken without his bow. Subject of Sophocles' eponymous tragedy. See also Gide, André; Lemnos.

Phoebus | See Apollo.

Phoenicians | Asian navigators. Phoenicia was located in present-day Lebanon, its principal town being Tyre. Phoenician colonists led by Dido founded Carthage.

Phoenix | Aged warrior, formerly Achilles' tutor. He forms part of the embassy sent to persuade Achilles to reenter the combat.

Phrygia, Phrygians | This region and its inhabitants designate the Troas (or Troad) and the Trojans.

Phthia | Achilles' homeland in Thessaly.

Pirithous | Devoted friend of Theseus, with whom he abducted Helen.

Plato | (428–347 B.C.): Greek philosopher. In his *Republic* and *Phaedrus* Socrates condemns the immorality of Homer.

Pléiade, la | Named after the seven stars comprising the Pleiades, this group of poets (the most famous of whom is Joachim du Bellay) was centered around the sixteenth-century French Renaissance poet Pierre de Ronsard. See also Bellay, Joachim du; Ronsard, Pierre de.

Plutarch | (ca. A.D. 44–after 120): Greek historian and moralist. He often includes mythological elements in his *Lives.* A work called the *Life and Poetry of Homer* (by Pseudo-Plutarch) was falsely attributed to him.

Pluto | See Hades.

Polites | Son of Priam. He is killed at the same time as his father by Neoptolemus.

Pollux | See Dioscuri.

Polydorus | Son of Priam and Hecuba, he is killed by Polymnestor, the king of the Chersonesus, to whom he had been entrusted. His body is thrown into the sea and discovered by Hecuba, his mother.

Polymnestor | King of the Chersonesus who kills Polydorus, son of Priam and Hecuba. The latter avenges her son by blinding the assassin and killing his children.

Polyphemus | A one-eyed Cyclops who herds sheep on a remote island. He imprisons Odysseus and eats some of his companions. Odysseus blinds him and escapes.

Polyxena | One of the daughters of Priam and Hecuba. She is sacrificed by Neoptolemus on the tomb of Achilles, his father. She is not mentioned in Homer.

Pontonous | Herald of Alcinous. See also Alcinous.

Poseidon | [Greek for "Earth Shaker"; Latin name Neptune] Brother of Zeus. God of the sea. He supports the Greeks against the Trojans.

Pound, Ezra | (b. Hailey, Idaho, 1885; d. Venice, 1972): American poet. He wished to follow in the footsteps of Homer and Ovid with his *Cantos* (1919–59). The first of these is inspired by the episode of Circe and the *Nekuia.*

Priam | King of Troy. Husband of Hecuba. Spared by Hercules during the first Trojan War, he sees his sons killed one by one (only Helenus survives). In the *Iliad* his political role is passed over, but the scenes in which he appears are among the finest in Homer. According to the legend recorded by Virgil, he is killed by Neoptolemus.

Prometheus | Titan who stole the secret of fire for humanity. As punishment, Zeus chains him to Mount Caucasus, where an eagle forever tears at his liver. For post-Homeric developments of this myth, see also Aeschylus.

Propertius | (b. ca. 50 B.C.): Latin elegiac poet. One of his poems recounts the story of Hercules and Cacus.

Proteus | A sea god depicted as a grumpy old man who can change his shape at will.

Pseudo-Herodotus | See Herodotus.

Pseudo-Plutarch | See Plutarch.

Psychopomp | See Hermes.

Pylades | Cousin and friend of Orestes. He helped him avenge his father and married Orestes' sister Electra.

Pyrrhus | See Neoptolemus.

Quarrel of Homer | [*Querelle d'Homère*] A controversy that erupted in eighteenth-century French intellectual life (1711–17) around the translations of Madame Dacier and Houdar de La Motte. The Ancients considered the classical poems beyond comparison, while the Moderns believed in the progress of art. The debate effectively pitted those who could not read Homer against those who could not understand him. See "Reading Homer in France."

Racine, Jean | (b. La Ferté-Milon, Aisne, 1639; d. Paris, 1699): French seventeenth-century playwright. Two of his tragedies evoke the Trojan War: *Andromache* (1667) and *Iphigenia in Aulis* (1674). Written in 1662, Racine's *Remarks on the Odyssey* offer a very perceptive view of Homer's characters.

Rhapsode (or Bard) | Professional reciter of poetry—occasionally of his own composition.

Ronsard, Pierre de | (b. Couture, 1524; d. Saint-Cosme-lez-Tours, 1585): French Renaissance poet. A member of the Pléiade, he devoted many pieces to Homeric characters, notably Helen and Cassandra. In 1572 he published a *Franciade*, in which, following Lemaire des Belges, the French are said to be the descendants of a Trojan hero named Francus, purported son of Hector.

Rutuli | An Italian people, ruled by Turnus, who fight to repel the Trojans of Aeneas.

Sainte-Maure, Benoît de (or Sainte-More) | (twelfth century): Author of a poem, written in French verse, called *The Story of Troy* [*Le Roman de Troie*] (ca. 1160), which was widely read and translated in Europe.

Samos | Island in the Aegean, one of the Southern Sporades.

Satyrs (or Sileni) | Male nature gods that are half-animal, half-human.

Scamander | See Xanthus.

Scarron, Paul | (Paris, 1610–60): French poet and novelist. He wrote *Virgil Travestied* (1648–53), a verse burlesque of Virgil's *Aeneid*.

Scaean Gates | The gates of Troy near which one of the most celebrated scenes of the *Iliad* (bk. 3) is set.

Schliemann, Heinrich | (b. Neubukow, Mecklemburg-Schwerin, 1822; d. Naples, 1890): German archaeologist. He identified the site of Troy on the hill of Hissarlik, in Turkey. He also excavated the sites of Mycenae, Tiryns, and Ithaca.

Scylla and Charybdis | Immortal female monsters. They devour ships sailing between Italy and Sicily. Odysseus twice escapes their clutches.

Scyros | Island in the center of the Aegean Sea on which Achilles hides when recruitment for the Trojan expedition is taking place. Later accounts have the blind Homer visiting the island.

Shakespeare, William | (Stratford-on-Avon, 1564–1616): English poet and playwright. The tragedy of *Troilus and Cressida* (1601–2) presents a humorous treatment of certain themes from the *Iliad*, notably the wrath of Achilles. See also Hamlet.

Shelley, Percy Bysshe | (b. Horsham, Sussex, 1792; d. Viareggio, 1822): English Romantic poet. He translated seven of the *Homeric Hymns* in the period 1817–20.

Shield of Achilles | At the request of Thetis, Hephaestus forges new arms for Achilles. The representation of the shield upon which the divine smithy presents his conception of civilization became a bravura challenge for all artists from antiquity onward.

Sileni | See Satyrs.

Sinon | Greek spy (in the *Aeneid*) who persuades the Trojans to admit the wooden horse into their citadel. He is not mentioned in Homer.

Sinties | Inhabitants of Lemnos.

Sirens | Half-women, half-birds whose magical song lured sailors into their clutches.

Socrates | See Plato.

Sophocles | (ca. 496–406 B.C.): Athenian tragic poet. Author of tragedies on Homeric themes, including *Philoctetes*, *Electra*, and *Ajax*.

Sparta (Lacadaemon) | City ruled by King Menelaus.

Statius, Publius Papinius | (Naples, ca. A.D. 45–ca. 100): Latin poet. Author of the *Thebaid*. He attempted to compose an epic of the entire life of Achilles, the *Achilleid*, which remained unfinished.

Stesichorus | (seventh–sixth century B.C.): Greek lyric poet said to have been blinded for composing a poem critical of Helen and to have written a "Palinode for Helen" denying that she had ever been to Troy, whereupon he regained his sight. Homer was not so lucky.

Styx | River of the Underworld. Mortals immersed in its magical waters became invulnerable.

Suitors | Given the length of Odysseus's absence, the young aristocrats of Ithaca sue for Penelope's hand in marriage, hoping thereby to rule over the island. They are slaughtered by the returning Odysseus and conducted to the Underworld by Hermes in his role as Psychopomp.

Syros | Island in the Cycladic archipelago.

Telamon | King of Salamis and father of the Greater Ajax. In the first Trojan War he heroically entered the citadel before Hercules. He also took part in the expedition of the Argonauts.

Telemachus | Son of Odysseus. The books of the *Odyssey* recounting his voyage are called the *Telemachy*. (See "The Adventures of Telemachus.") See also Fénelon, François de Salignac de la Mothe-.

Termosiris | [name derived from the Egyptian god Osiris] Identified in *The Adventures of Telemachus* as an Egyptian priest, and no doubt a transposition of Proteus.

Tethys | Sister and wife of Oceanus. She is the goddess of the sea.

Themis | Personification of Justice. According to Aeschylus, she was the mother of Prometheus.

Theogony | Poem by Hesiod that affirms the divine ordering of the world and of nature. See also Hesiod.

Theseus | Son of Aegeus and Aethra. Athenian hero of many legends. He abducts Helen before the start of the Trojan War.

Thessaly | Region of northern Greece near Mount Olympus.

Thetis | A Nereid, mother of Achilles. She is first pursued by Zeus, who subsequently orders the mortal Peleus to rape her (Themis having predicted that her son would be greater than his father). Discord (Eris) is not invited to Thetis's wedding and avenges herself by throwing down among the goddesses Athena, Hera, and Aphrodite the Apple of Discord, on which is inscribed "To the most beautiful." Achilles is born to Thetis and the Trojan War is born of the Apple of Discord.

Tlepolemus | One of the sons of Hercules. He takes part in the Trojan War on the Greek side and is killed by Sarpedon. His presence allows Homer to evoke Tlepolemus's father and the first Trojan War.

Thorvaldsen, Bertel | (Copenhagen, 1770–1844): Great Neoclassical sculptor from Denmark. He attempted to revive the Greek spirit in his sculptures of Greek subjects. In 1816 he was asked to restore the statues from the temple of Aphaia in Aegina. The statues were restored to their pre-Thorvaldsen state after the Second World War.

Thucydides | (ca. 460–400 B.C.): Greek historian. In *The Peloponnesian War* this most lucid of Greek historians considers the Trojan War as an early event in the eastward extension of Greek power.

Tiresias | Blind seer. He is the only shade that Odysseus meets in the Underworld who has retained a sense of the passing of time.

Titans | Sons of Uranus, who reigned over the gods before Zeus. The monstrous Titans are thrown down into Tartarus (a region of the Underworld) by the Olympian deities. The Giants are often confused with the Titans. See also Gigantomachy.

Tritons | Male sea gods who are half-man, half-fish. They form part of Poseidon's cortege.

Troas (or Troad) | Plain of Troy.

Troilus and Cressida | See Shakespeare, William.

Trojan Wars (first and second) | According to legend, there were two Trojan Wars. Homer recounts the second in the *Iliad*. The first, a human generation earlier, pitted Hercules against Priam's father.

Troy (or Ilium) | The war between Trojans and Greeks forms the historical background—and even the foreground—of Homer's poems. It seems probable (but cannot be proven) that such a war took place several centuries before Homer narrated it, perhaps in the very late Bronze Age (ca. 1200 B.C.), a period of Greek colonial expansion in the Mediterranean. Oral tradition and collective memory have, in that case, preserved and embellished the memory of its main events.

Turnus | King of the Rutuli. As recounted in the *Aeneid*, Turnus has been promised the hand of Lavinia. When she is betrothed to Aeneas, Turnus declares war on the Trojans.

Tychius | Name of the cobbler who stitched together Ajax's shield. Pseudo-Herodotus claims that Homer uses this name in the *Iliad* in gratitude to a saddler who had given him hospitality.

Tyndareus | Mortal father of Helen, Clytemnestra, and Castor and Pollux; brother of Icarius. He made all of Helen's suitors promise to come to the aid of her chosen husband should the latter ever lose his wife to another man.

Ulysses | See Odysseus.

Venus | See Aphrodite.

Virgil | (70–19 B.C.): Roman poet. See "The *Aeneid.*"

Vulcan | See Hephaestus.

Walcott, Derek | (b. Castries, St. Lucia, 1930): Caribbean poet. He won the Nobel Prize in 1992, two years after the publication of his epic *Omeros.*

Xanthus (or Scamander) | River god presiding over the river that flows through the plain of Troy. He rises up against the slaughter perpetrated by Achilles. Eighteenth-century travelers thought they could identify the Homeric river among those still flowing in Troas. Scamander is also the second name of Astyanax, the son of Hector and Andromache.

Xanthus | One of Achilles' horses, who roundly tells him that he, too, will suffer the fate of Hector.

Zeus | [Latin name Jupiter, or *Jupater. Ju* derives from the same Indo-European roots as *Zeus*: *dyau*, "light of the sky"] Son of the Titan Cronus. Zeus is king of the gods and master of lightning and the thunderbolt. He overcame the assault by the Titans, the preceding generation of gods. His power is theoretically absolute, but he knows it is limited by Destiny. The *Iliad* portrays him as a victim of the trickery of goddesses, in particular his wife Hera. See also Thetis.

Zeuxis | (ca. 425–397 B.C.): Greek painter. He painted a legendary *Helen at Her Toilet* for the temple of Hera in Crotona.

Index of Artists

NOTE: PAGES CONTAINING ILLUSTRATIONS ARE INDICATED BY *ITALICS.*